Hoover Institution Publications

The Writing of History in the Soviet Union

The Writing of History in the Soviet Union

by

Anatole G. Mazour

Hoover Institution Press

Stanford University · Stanford, California

947. 007
M 47 w

MN

Hoover Institution Publications 87
Standard Book Number 8179-1871-X
Library of Congress Card Number 76-99084
Printed in the United States of America
Copyright © 1971 by the Board of Trustees of the Leland Stanford
Junior University

To George V. Vernadsky
Teacher and Scholar

Contents

Preface

Russian historiography suffers as much from the enthusiasm of its admirers as from the attacks of its severest critics — the Kremlinologists. Both camps came to amass evidence to prove their theses. The praise from inside of the party-liners, the adulation of the orthodox Marxists and other Soviet schools of philosophy is a matter of fact and is to be expected. In fact, it is from this closed circuit that the historical field has been enriched, by way of extensive source publications and monographic studies. There is, however, another side to the coin: this parochial praise in most cases stripped historical writing of originality. An artificial home-bred patriotism led to ignorance and distortion of world conditions.

From outside came equally debatable interpretations of Soviet historiography that have rendered little aid in any effort to dispel the dim atmosphere in which legends, accusations, and misinformation circulated freely and abundantly. For a short period a fashionable version of "continuity in Russian history" made its appearance. Non-Soviet writers gleefully detected, or thought they did, a "continuity" throughout history with regard to Russian imperialism, expansionism, colonialism, or authoritarianism. There re-emerged the thread-worn "scratch a Russian find a Tartar" belief and the half-Asian theory which was conveniently woven into historical writings. To top it all, ideological superstructures blocked further rational judgment. In theory, each "school" condemned partiality and advocated objectivity; in fact, each rendered lip service to Clio while exerting every effort to prove that its prejudicial views were correct and scientifically supported.

The path of Soviet historiography is neither a straight nor a smooth one. From the start, Soviet historians have sought an entirely new version of Russian history. Students of the pre-Soviet period were labelled as bourgeois tools, as falsificators and pseudo-objectivists who distorted the past and failed to comprehend the law of history (*zakonomernost'*). Yet Soviet historiography too has been subject to interpretations and views it regarded as unacceptable. The changes insisted upon were often accompanied by convulsions and "purges" which left victims strewn along the wayside. Such phenomena as the cult of Stalin, as the difficulty of applying Marxian canons to Russian history, as the lack of trained students of history, as the injection of Soviet chauvinism into history since the 1930's, as the difficulty of attaining unanimous agreement on the nature of Marxian teachings, delivered devastating havoc to the historical profession at frequent intervals. To make things worse, the sharp twists and turns in the party line added further confusion and even gave risks to those who expressed their views in print.

Ever since the Communist Party came to power the student of history has had to be on guard against "bourgeois objectivity," and aware of the quick shifts within the official line. By the time the Soviet regime was to celebrate its fiftieth anniversary there was a considerable accumulation of conflicting theories, criss-cross party lines, and ideological taboos to contend with.

The Stalin regime itself contributed irreparable damage to historical science. Stalin's political omnipotence carried with it an academic dictum that made objective historical research impossible, as Stalin wrote history himself or censored works written by others. One would seriously err to assume that Stalinism represented a mere vulgar materialistic philosophy of history. Along with the narrow dogmatism of Stalinism and economism can be discerned an element of idealism as an interpretation of history. It is not certain whether Stalin had a firm philosophy of history; his methodology of primary sources was crude, to say the least; his writings and edited works show appalling falsifications or sheer inventions to suit his fancy, to prove his political views. Stalinism cannot be dismissed as a mere paranoid fancy either; historical interpretation was simply a reflection of an established tyranny forced upon writers. Consensus by terror became the rule in all fields, including the writing of history.

Has methodology in historical inquiry changed since Stalin's death? On the surface there are signs of revolt against former distortions of factual evidence. There is an insistence upon "respect for facts, without which history as a science is unthinkable." Yet, weighty recommendations such as this one, by B. N. Ponomarev, a member of the Academy of Sciences, have failed to alter certain basic principles. One seldom finds in Soviet history even of more recent date a multi-causational interpretation of the past; economic development is cited as the single force. Objectivity is not to be frowned upon, but only so long as the facts support the preconceived patterns of events, which naturally arouses some disturbing thoughts about the health of historical science.[1]

Another member of the Soviet Academy of Sciences, E. M. Zhukov, at the annual meeting of the Historical Section, similarly urged historians to arm themselves with factual, documentary, and source materials related to their respective fields. "The analysis of these materials," he stated, "must be deep, critical, include definite generalizations and conclusions." A scholar cannot, he maintained further, pass by certain events, or ignore documentary evidence or facts arbitrarily. A true historical study must be objective; a conclusion bold and free from any indirect influence. Such, he declared, is the law of scientific advancement.

Shortly after the death of Stalin *Pravda* published an article (July 1, 1953) in which it glorified "the people-creators" of history and attacked the cult of heroes and "eminent personalities," which it said was a characteristic theory of bourgeois philosophy that led straight to fascism.

[1]See the official line as expounded by the party mouthpiece B. N. Ponomarev, "Zadachi istoricheskoi nauki i podgotovki nauchnopedagogicheskikh kadrov v oblasti istorii." *Voprosy istorii,* No. 1 (1963), 3-35.

The article in *Pravda* occupied nearly a full page and constituted essentials of an address delivered at Moscow State University by F. Konstantinov, editor of the journal *Voprosy filosofii* and one of the Communist Party's leading theoreticians.

Kings, statesmen, or great captains do not make history. The people make history, and the kings, captains, and leaders merely personify the forces residing in economic and social relationships.

"Revolutions do not occur if economic and political conditions have not ripened," said *Pravda*, "if in the people there has not originated the consciousness of the overthrowing of an outworn system."

Sympathetically analyzing the situation, one is willing to concede that ritualistic Marxist obeisances to Marx, Engels, or Lenin as the source of eternal historical wisdom are the price the Soviet historian has to pay if he is to publish the result of his research. These curtsies may be overlooked if they are not forced into the interpretation to the exclusion of historical evidence. But it is a deeply offensive thing when the historian is denied the right to act as a dispassionate reporter, and it becomes downright intolerable when he must become an ideological champion, using history in the service of party goals. Today, the new party litany demands criticism of the cult of Stalin, citing Lenin's advice to utilize all the evidence and not resort to selected citations out of context. But the unpleasant fact is that the goal of all research remains the same—to prove a preconceived pattern of history.[2]

That historical literature since 1956 abounds with anti-Stalinist comments is an undeniable fact. Many historians are delighted with the opportunity to denounce "quotism" *(tsitatnichestvo)*, or to condemn stock formulas chosen to prove a preconceived thesis. However, attacking Stalin for his "cult of the individual" is one matter, but to question the Marxist law of history *(zakonomernost')* is an entirely different matter. Condemning party diversionism, which is acceptable, is not to be confused with wandering off onto the path of "bourgeois pseudo-objectivism," for the latter course might lead one to question the inevitable triumph of communism. Rarely does one come across any work based on the assumption that "sociological laws are incapable of interpreting historical events"; this would imply the use of "deviationist" evidence.[3]

One encouraging sign is that there is a revived emphasis upon the study of "concrete facts," upon "realities" in history, rather than upon exercises

[2]See A. Ia. Gurevich, "Obshchii zakon i konkretnaia zakonomernost' v istorii." *Voprosy istorii*, No. 8 (1965), 14-30.

[3]A good illustration is the case of Professor Boris E. Shtein. In September 1952 the Presidium of the Soviet Academy of Sciences called to account I. M. Maiskii, one time Soviet Ambassador to London, for his responsibility in connection with the publication of an unsatisfactory book concerning "bourgeois falsification of history." Professor Shtein's book was sharply criticized previously by the Communist journal *Bolshevik*. The journal found that while Shtein was exposing the falsification of history by bourgeois sources, he had, himself, committed a series of errors, not the

in sociological schematism. Is Soviet historiography nursed on Marxism, then, still capable of teaching historical truth? Some flickering signs may be so interpreted, but only time will show whether they are genuine promises or false hopes.

Soviet historians have suffered attack not only for their "bourgeois views," or for their ignorance of "Marxist-Leninist science," but also for their failure to prove the inexorable triumph of communism. To help rectify this failure, it was decided in 1946 to establish a Commission on the History of Historiography, headed by the ubiquitous historian M. V. Nechkina, to function within the Institute of History of the Academy of Sciences. Under party guidance all historical research, coordination as well as interpretation, was to follow a line defined by leading party members.

Establishing central directives was one thing, but their actual application to history was a totally different matter. To begin with there was the ever-present problem of periodization, a problem of special importance to the field of general history. The different methods of periodization suggested all had to meet one test—they all had to prove that Marxist–Leninist laws of history were operative. A correct periodization must demonstrate the social and economic forces which invariably led to the triumph of socialism, the establishment of a classless society and a communist order.

How then was history to be periodized to this purpose? Ever since the 1920's this has been a crucial issue. On this account much bad blood has run between spokesmen of the party and individual non-conformist scholars, or between spokesmen of the party and individual writers who deviate from the designated line. Among the latter particularly were representatives from the different national republics: the Ukraine, Georgia, Kazakhstan, and White Russia.

The centralists, as they were labelled, charged that the so-called federalists were imbued with bourgeois patriotism, and unable to take into account the "laws of historical development" as taught by Marx and later by Lenin. Communist leaders insist that any historian who honestly follows the "laws" of history is bound to be "scientifically objective." The failure to convince scholars of this dogmatic belief, not to mention the seasonal vicissitudes within the party line, explains the endless debates on periodization, on the nature of feudalism, on the date of arrival of capitalism in Russia, and on

least important of which was to allege that the United States had attempted to avert the outbreak of the Second World War. Professor Shtein was accused of displaying "objectivity" and an apologetic attitude with respect to various important historic problems.

The Academy of Sciences' President accepted the full justice of criticism of the magazine *Bolshevik* and ruled that the Institute of History committed a serious mistake in approving the publication of Professor Shtein's book. The President placed the blame for this mistake on I. M. Maiskii, presently member of the academy and senior scientific collaborator of the institute. It was declared that Maiskii had approved Professor Shtein's book in a careless fashion, without analytical discussion of the work at the institute council. The Presidium also administered a serious rebuke to the responsible director, V. V. Biriukovich, for the publication of the book.

the character of agrarian socialism. It has become almost a tradition with Soviet historians to exhaust themselves in theory. Since the party does not tolerate the idea that "every man be his own historian," the field of history is periodically turned into an open battleground.

The surprising thing is to discover how much has actually been accomplished during the fifty years of Soviet rule. Much chaff there is, undoubtedly, but there is also some high-quality grain buried under the mountainous Marxian superstructure imposed upon by the party. For this accomplishment alone, if for no other, Soviet historiography merits careful attention.

Finally, a note about the book presented here. Shortly after completing a revision of my *Modern Russian Historiography* (Van Nostrand, 1956) I came to realize the need for a similar study focused on a much more limited period, since 1917. This was nearly twelve years ago, and in the intervening years I amassed such quantities of notes that my archival skill was flattered but my ability to bring it all into some reasonable synthesized form was seriously challenged. When at last I gathered sufficient courage to terminate my collecting and face the true task of putting the assembled mass of records into book form I soon realized that its complete utilization would require at least three volumes. This would have rewarded the author's toil, but would surely have taxed the patience of the reader, not to mention the financial courage of the publisher. Thus it became necessary to confine the narrative to a concentrated account rather than to indulge in detailed description of voluminous works. Or, to put it in other words, a task began that might be called "the agony of selection."

Deciding what was to be retained and what left out, what to be discussed extensively, and what to be cited with aphoristic brevity, if at all, proved a most exasperating task. Extreme brevity could easily turn an historiography into a mere bibliography. In general, the rule I used was that only authors who have made substantial contributions to historical science were included. This, I readily admit, leaves much arbitrary discretion to an author, and the only justification he can present is that his effort was as genuine and objective as humanly possible. A disturbing discovery made during the writing process was that nearly all Soviet historians are "faceless"; that is, they offer scant personal biographical data, a factor which tends to make historiography somewhat lifeless. How different it was in dealing with the lively pre-revolutionary historians!

A standard system of transliteration from Russian into English is still a pious desire; thus far no single system is completely satisfactory. After considerable consultation and thought the phonetic transliteration cited below has been adopted for use in this volume. In only a few cases has there been a departure from the established rule, and that was in cases where the rule might be in conflict with the universally accepted spelling, such as, for instance, in the case of Herzen or Trotsky instead of Hertsen or Trotskii. The apostrophe to indicate a soft sign was in most cases omitted to simplify further transliteration and particularly to aid readers who are less familiar with the Russian language.

The following transliteration has been adopted:

Е,	е	....	E, e
Ж,	ж	....	Zh, zh
И,	и	....	I, i
У,	у	....	U, u
Х,	х	....	Kh, kh
Ц,	ц	....	Ts, ts
Ч,	ч	....	Ch, ch
Щ,	щ	....	Shch, shch
	ы	....	y
Э,	э	....	E, e
Ю,	ю	....	Iu, iu
Я,	я	....	Ia, ia

One additional note. I wish to take the opportunity to thank the Hoover Institution, its Editorial Board, and its library staff for making it possible to have this study appear in print. To Mrs. Marina P. Tinkoff-Utechin I am most indebted, for her daily readiness to extend her cooperation in locating necessary information, whether in the Hoover Library or anywhere else in the country. And with this appreciative note I conclude more than twelve years of toil.

A. G. M.

*   *   *   *   *   *   *

EDITOR'S NOTE

The format of the footnotes followed throughout this book adheres to the author's original style—a blend of footnotes and bibliographic entries—and has not been basically altered by the editor.

CHAPTER I

The Formative Years

> *"Whoever in writing*
> *modern history shall*
> *follow truth too near the*
> *heels, it may haply strike*
> *his teeth."*
> Sir Walter Raleigh

A. GENERAL SURVEY

In 1967, observing the fiftieth anniversary of the Revolution, the Soviet government included the science of history in its record of impressive achievements. The accolade reflected the close attention accorded history under the Soviet regime, on the theory that without history there can be no understanding of the material development which determines the basic nature of human society. Time and again Soviet historiographers have stressed the importance of studying the past, of understanding the nature of the continuous struggle for the emancipation of the toiling masses, of the relentless drive toward communist goals. The philosophy of history and party ideology are inseparable; any effort to dissociate the two is regarded as a grave ideological error and leads to serious consequences.

Upon coming to power in October, 1917, the Soviet government had the advantage of a rich legacy in the field of historical science. To be sure, the legacy did not suit the Marxist pattern of history, but no effort was spared to fit it into a Procrustean bed and to prove that any non-Marxist interpretation is nothing but "falsification of history." This was bound to turn the study of history into a battle against the old guard, against revisionists and diversionists and all other manner of renegades or heretics within the ranks of fellow travellers or even among full-fledged members of the party.

Shortly after the Communists assumed political power, a handful of old Bolshevik historians founded several centers of historical studies. Among these early leaders were some prominent party historians, M. N. Pokrovskii, N. N. Baturin, M. S. Olminskii, N. M. Liadov. With the exception of Pokrovskii these were men known better for their loyalty to the party than to the field of history. For this reason these men were bound to meet strong opposition from the members of the old school. The latter, ideologically alien, were in many cases discriminated against, persecuted, barred from either teaching or writing, and badly dispersed. At the same time the new Marxist historical craft was hardly in existence.

From the early 1920's on, Pokrovskii felt, as did other Marxian writers, that if history were to be rewritten to suit the proper ideological interpretation a newly trained generation of scholars must enter the historical field. To this

1

end a Socialist Academy of Social Sciences was founded in June, 1918. (This was renamed the Communist Academy in 1924.) Simultaneously, under the chairmanship of Pokrovskii, the Institute of Red Professorship was organized, where students were to be trained in various fields of history and the related sciences while being indoctrinated in the art of Marxian historiography.

The new institutions included such seasoned Marxists, Russian as well as foreign, as Franz Mehring, Sen Katayama, Clara Zetkin, Karl Kautsky, Karl Liebknecht, Rosa Luxemburg, and Friedrich W. Adler. Along with the training of a new generation of Marxist historians these groups initiated an intensive effort to seek out and publish new original source materials. Many archival collections, formerly unavailable to research, were now opened to students who were urged to utilize the newly opened depositories. The materials were helpful in correcting earlier accounts, in expanding fields of interests, and in some cases such as diplomatic history, in opening entirely new opportunities. Among these were the papers from the Foreign Office Archives, papers of the royal family, and documents related to the outbreak of the First World War.

In November, 1919, the Academy set up several sections for the study of the following subjects: the history of socialism, the history of the Russian revolutionary movement, and the history of the labor movement. Other fields of study were added subsequently, such as foreign affairs, Soviet law, art and literature. M. N. Pokrovskii was head of the Russian revolutionary movement study, V. P. Volgin in charge of the history of socialism, F. Ia. Kon of the Second International, V. P. Miliutin of economic history, S. A. Lozovskii of labor, F. A. Rotshtein of foreign affairs and the First World War, and V. M. Fritché of the field of literature and art. Later some of these sections joined the recently founded Institute of Karl Marx and Friedrich Engels.

The scheme of research assigned to these sections was thus: the section assigned to study the Russian revolutionary movement was requested to analyze mainly the sources on the period preceding the revolution of 1917. Periodical publications and newspaper files were to be completed wherever such a need would occur as were the works of socialist writers of the nineteenth century. Bibliographical data were to be scrupulously gathered and various guides to books and periodical literature published. There was also a request for the publication of all works of such leading figures of the past century as A. I. Herzen and V. G. Belinskii.

The section on economics was assigned three fields: (1) Russian economy in the world economic system; (2) developments in world economy; and (3) the general theory and methodology of economic problems. The first field was broken up into the following subtopics: prewar economy, the influence of the war and the February Revolution on the national economy, the economic state of affairs on the eve of the October Revolution, the national economy under the dictatorship of the proletariat.

The section devoted to labor problems was charged with the following tasks: (1) to gather literature in that field; (2) to systematize and classify all sources; (3) to compile statistical data for the study in any field of labor problems.

As is obvious, the emphasis was upon recent Russian history. It stressed economic development, social changes, revolutionary movements, foreign affairs, imperialism, and the background of the First World War. Laudable as this program was, its progress was often hindered by one factor—scarcity of qualified historians. It took several years before constructive compilatory work could begin. There was a shortage of bibliographical guides, and while archival material was now available in an ever-increasing amount, the new sources called for a systematized method of publication and utilization. During these first few years the gathering of sources, itemization, and compilatory processes went on simultaneously, and often unsystematically. In many cases published sources lacked essential commentaries or proper indexes. It was not until 1924 that some notable progress began to be made.

For the sake of convenience we may divide the half century of Soviet historical development into several periods. The years from 1917 to approximately the middle of the 1930's may be considered the first one; it can be truly described as the Pokrovskii period. From the October Revolution until his death in 1932 Pokrovskii dominated the scene without noticeable challenge. Throughout this period an extraordinary effort was exerted in order to form a Marxian school of history, and at the same time to bring to light as many new documentary materials as possible, centralize the archival sources, and open these for historical research. Four achievements stand out particularly: the founding of the Socialist Academy in 1918; the founding of Sverdlovsk University; the organization of the *Istpart* (see p. 10); and the founding in 1921 of the Institute of Red Professorship.

Soviet historians generally believe that by the 1920's Lenin had already succeeded in formulating with relative finality the basic periodization of history. It was Lenin, they assert, who defined with scientific accuracy the origins of Russian society, its evolutionary process and ultimate form. It was he who analyzed and defined social changes, class formations, and the forthcoming role of the toiling class in the developments of the twentieth century.

According to Soviet writers, historical science in Russia prior to 1917 was completely dominated by bourgeois intellectualism. In this term they included a wide range of views, extending from the indigenous Slavophilic-patriotic elements of the right, through the liberal-positivist interpretation of the middle-of-the-road liberals, to the socialist idealists of the left.[1]

The October Revolution caught these bourgeois historians in a complete state of disarray.[2] Some of them, along with other intellectuals, migrated to western Europe; others simply "sat on the shores and waited for more favorable weather"; while still others, the "islanders," fortified themselves to combat the alien, hostile force. Lacking unity, fighting singly, boycotting, they were doomed from the start. Slowly and with considerable reluctance, mem-

[1]As an illustration see O. L. Veinshtein, "Ustanovlenie sovetskoi istoricheskoi nauki." *Voprosy istorii*, No. 7 (1966), 32-47.

[2]R. Iu. Vipper, *Krizis istoricheskoi nauki*. (Kazan, 1921).

bers of this group began to shift their stand from open hostility to neutrality. In 1922, at the Eleventh Congress of the Communist Party, Lenin urged the party to refrain from repressive measures against scholars, even when hostile to the Soviet regime, and to follow a policy of cautious persuasion. This explains in part the surprising and even open attacks on the Soviet system in several liberal publications during the early few years of the new regime. Centers of intellectual opposition were not entirely suppressed until almost 1923.

Among the freely existing opposition may be mentioned such an organization as the Free Philosophical Society, founded in 1919 at the University of Petrograd. This society had its own publication, *Mysl'*, which, under the protective claim of neutrality, expressed its view with a fair degree of freedom. In Moscow a similar philosophical association was led by eminent scholars such as N. A. Berdiaev or M. Gershenzon. This group initiated its periodical, *Mysl' i slovo*, while at the University of Moscow was the Psychological Society, which took a somewhat similar critical stand against the philosophy of communism and the Soviet State.

During the first few years of the New Economic Policy (NEP) there appeared a large number of private publications. In 1922 there were approximately one hundred publishing houses in the country, most of them in Moscow. Though censored, these managed to publish many anti-Marxian treatises. The reason for such laxity was the rule that only open appeal to counterrevolution and violent overthrow of the political system would justify suppression; inimical views in the form of philosophical discussion were considered tolerable. Utilizing this liberal policy, men like N. O. Lossky, V. V. Savich, E. L. Radlov, N. A. Berdiaev, and S. L. Frank could frankly air their views publicly. Professor L. P. Karsavin even managed to publish a theological treatise in which he presented his Augustinian interpretation of history.

In 1923 a group of "incorrigibles," who led an isolated intellectual life, were allowed to leave the country and join the Russian émigrés in western Europe. These included R. Iu. Vipper, N. O. Lossky, N. A. Berdiaev, and F. A. Stepun. Their departure thinned the ranks of critics and seriously reduced critical publications. The intellectual opposition was gradually led to complete ineffectiveness. Pokrovskii, the tireless critic of these "islanders sniping from their ivory towers," systematically campaigned against them. The campaign increased in intensity after the end of the Civil War and foreign intervention; it was relaxed temporarily during the NEP period, but by the end of the 1920's was renewed with greater vigor. By 1930 Pokrovskii was able to announce that the Communist Party was ready to launch an offensive long overdue, to eradicate once and for all the alien ideologies and silence bourgeois historians.[3]

There were several reasons for the end of the truce. One was that the government was no longer preoccupied with the military campaigns of the Civil War and the conflict with Poland. Another, probably even more weighty reason, was that the appalling shortage of properly trained historians was

[3]*Vestnik Kommunisticheskoi akademii*, Nos. 4-5 (1932), 36.

ending. The period required to train a new generation of students steeped in Marxian philosophy, and to win at least partial cooperation from members of the old guard, was reaching an end; the new generation was completing its education and reducing the dependence upon the old intelligentsia. The Soviet government was no longer willing to allow its opponents to participate in educational activities.

Through heroic efforts by such institutions as the Socialist Academy of Social Sciences (later the Communist Academy) and the Institute of Red Professorship, the decade of the 1930's saw the first cadres of Marxist historians take up their tasks and contribute to Soviet historiography.

Who was qualified to enter these newly established institutions? In 1921 there were no more than 105 students enrolled in the Institute of Red Professorship. These came from among party members and intellectuals or were selected from among instructors of the various communist educational institutions.[4] By 1928 the Institute of Red Professorship, including its allied branches, had 483 registered students, while four years later there were over 1,000. The departments in the Institute included history, economics, philosophy, and law. Among the outstanding teachers were M. N. Pokrovskii, V. P. Volgin, N. M. Lukin, A. M. Deborin, M. A. Reisner, A. N. Savin, E. A. Kosminskii, E. S. Varga, A. V. Lunacharskii, V. I. Nevskii, E. M. Iaroslavskii. Of the graduate students who were to play a prominent part in history in later years were such members as I. I. Mints, N. L. Rubinshtein, A. L. Sidorov, B. N. Ponomarev, A. M. Pankratova, M. V. Nechkina. Students who chose the field of history generally emphasized modern and recent European and Russian history.[5] Ancient, medieval, and early modern history were less popular and were taught in many cases by senior professors who were likely to be non-party members. A shortage of scholars in these fields compelled the administration to employ non-Marxists, and these particular departments were sometimes referred to as the "reactionary nests." Nonetheless, as urgently advised by Lenin himself, the attitude toward these scholars was courteous.

Among the various institutions devoted to history should be included the Institute of History of Material Culture of the Academy of Sciences (IIMK) which in 1937 was renamed as the State Academy of History of Material Culture (GAIMK). Founded by a special decree, signed by Lenin in April, 1919, it replaced the former Archeological Commission. The Institute of History functioned until 1937 under the chairmanship of the eminent scholar N. Ia. Marr. In these years, it had one cardinal goal—to rewrite history by giving it a materialistic interpretation acceptable to Marxists.

By 1930, the Institute had expanded from a limited archeological organization to a much broader one: it included sections devoted to the study of ancient and medieval history. Each section in turn was subdivided into smaller units dealing with Oriental, Occidental, Byzantine, and Russian history.

[4]"Instituty krasnoi professury." *Sovetskaia istoricheskaia entsiklopediia*, VI, 110.

[5]A good summary of the early preparation in the social sciences may be found in M. N. Pokrovskii, *Obshchestvennye nauki za 10 let.* (Moscow, 1928).

The Institute was responsible for the organization of annual archeological expeditions. The department of archeology was devoted to such fields as the Paleolithic, Neolithic, Bronze, and Classical Ages; some sections centered their attention on Scythian-Sarmatian, Caucasian, Central Asian, Slavic, or Russian archeological studies. The cumulative serial publications of these sections are extensive and their importance is universally recognized. Roughly these are divided under the following headings: (1) Materials and Investigations in Archeology of the USSR; (2) Soviet Archeology; (3) Reports on Field Works. The Institute has its own extensive library and is authorized to instruct and grant degrees in the appropriate fields.

In 1921 the faculty of social sciences of Moscow University organized an Institute of History headed by the prominent Russian medievalist, D. M. Petrushevskii. Though not a party member Petrushevskii commanded respect as a scholar and distinguished author of several important publications. Former professor of the Universities of Warsaw, St. Petersburg, and Moscow, he resigned his position in Moscow in 1911 as a protest against the policy of the Ministry of Education and did not return to the lecture platform until 1917. His special field was English medieval history, and his generally recognized study is the revolt led by Wat Tyler in the fourteenth century. Originally published at the turn of the century, the two-volume book appeared in four editions, the last one in 1937. As a moderate liberal, Petrushevskii was often under attack from the communists who sought his dismissal; among his severest critics was Pokrovskii himself. The absence of scholars of his caliber in his field caused the authorities to retain him on the faculty, although criticism continued throughout the entire period of Petrushevskii's teaching career.

In 1929 pressures became too strong and Pokrovskii declared that he came to recognize that all pre-revolutionary methods of historical research were unacceptable and that even the institution Petrushevskii headed had outlived its original purpose.[6] As a result the Institute of History was transferred to the Communist Academy where it came under more effective Marxian surveillance.

The Socialist Academy, founded in 1918, was an entirely educational institution where lectures in the various social sciences were delivered. Research was limited to problems of socialism and a few subjects of history.

On April 17, 1924, the Socialist Academy was renamed the Communist Academy and in November, 1926, by a newly granted charter, it was officially recognized as an institute for research in natural and social sciences. In December, 1929, a branch of the Communist Academy was opened in Leningrad (LOKA). The latter included the following fields of study: history, literature, philosophy, art, linguistics, jurisprudence, world and national politics, and agriculture. The Communist Academy included about one hundred active members, not counting corresponding members. Beginning in 1922 it published a periodical, *Vestnik Sotsialisticheskoi akademii;* after 1924

[6]*Istorik-marksist,* No. 14 (1929), 5. See also *Vestnik Kommunisticheskoi akademii,* Nos. 4-5 (1932), 50-57.

the publication appeared under the title of *Vestnik Kommunisticheskoi akademii*, which lasted until 1935. On February 8, 1936, the Soviet government closed the Communist Academy, and all the members, affiliates, and the research staff joined the Academy of Sciences of the USSR. The most notable change to observe here was that the ranks of the venerable body of academicians were now to be joined by leading party members, among them V. P. Volgin, A. I. Tiumenev, and N. M. Lukin, to mention only a few. From the ranks of Pokrovskii's seminars and the various academies emerged such Soviet historians as M. V. Nechkina, A. S. Ierusalimskii, S. D. Skazkin, and N. M. Druzhinin. These younger students, with the cooperation of their senior colleagues, enriched historical science by a fusion of old and new talents. Their cooperative effort resulted in the publication of many valuable sources, such as those pertaining to the one hundred and fiftieth anniversary of the Pugachev rebellion, the hundredth anniversary of the Decembrist revolt, or the twentieth anniversary of the Revolution of 1905.

In 1925, a Society of Marxist Historians was formed within the Academy. The aim of the Society was to bring together students of history for presentation of papers followed by discussions, organize special meetings on such occasions as jubilees, and last though by no means least, constantly to be on guard against the "vulgarization of history." Originally the Society started with 29 active and 11 contributing members, but membership rapidly expanded and by 1929 it reached nearly 400. In 1926 the Society initiated its own periodical, *Istorik-marksist*, "dedicated to every phase of historical science." This journal was soon followed by several others, such as *Borba klassov* or *Istoriia proletariata SSSR*. On December 28, 1928, the First All-Union Conference of Marxist Historians was held, at which bourgeois historians received their share of criticism. But the fiercest fire was aimed at those who tried to smuggle anti-Marxian, Russian chauvinistic, and local nationalistic ideas into Soviet historiography.

The conference set up plans for an improved administration of archives and for the utilization of the already amassed materials. It dealt with projects that provided for the preparation of a publication of the *Great Soviet Encyclopedia*. The gathered members warned against narrow specialization; they cautioned against superficialities in the philosophy of materialism and in methodology of history, and against objectivity in science. They also urged careful delineation between bourgeois and communist interpretations of history. Those who supported the resolutions and party clichés could hardly have envisioned the changes that were soon to follow with the departure of Pokrovskii from the scene and with the firm establishment of the Stalin cult.

B. M. N. POKROVSKII

During this earliest Soviet period, in which every effort was bent on rewriting and reinterpreting history in Marxian terms, M. N. Pokrovskii emerges as the dominating figure. Born in Moscow on August 17, 1868, Pokrovskii was the son of a civil servant. His student years were profoundly influenced by two of his eminent teachers, P. G. Vinogradov and V. O. Kliuchevskii,

7

whose concern with economic history influenced Pokrovskii to a degree that he abandoned much of his early idealism and turned to the study of economics. Pokrovskii took fire in the courses of Vinogradov and Kliuchevskii in order to set a conflagration of his own.

In 1899, Pokrovskii contributed eight articles to a four-volume *Reader in Medieval History* compiled by P. G. Vinogradov. One of these articles was entitled "A Description of Economic Conditions in the *Russian Pravda*." Simultaneously, while studying Marxian philosophy, Pokrovskii began his teaching career in a private girls' school.

In the fall of 1902 the District Office of Education abruptly barred Pokrovskii from teaching. He devoted himself entirely to writing, mainly articles in political magazines. In these he revealed that basically his views of history were similar to those advocated by bourgeois idealists. Two years later Pokrovskii joined a Moscow group that published a magazine called *Pravda,* the mouthpiece of the so-called Legal Marxists, among whom were several Bolshevik members. In one of these articles Pokrovskii criticized Kliuchevskii for his bourgeois idealism in interpreting political history. As a contributor to *Pravda* Pokrovskii came to associate with several prominent Marxists such as A. A. Bogdanov (Malinovskii), a strong believer in empirical philosophy. For several years Pokrovskii came under the influence of the Legal Marxists, a fact frequently called to his attention by his critics later in his career.

From the end of 1905 until the First World War Pokrovskii turned once more to the writing of history. Between 1907 and 1910 he contributed several chapters to a nine-volume history of Russia. In the seventh edition of the *Granat History*, as this publication is called, no less than thirty chapters were written by Pokrovskii. During these years he resided first in Finland and later in western Europe. While in Finland he already began to work on his four-volume *Russkaia istoriia s drevneishikh vremen,* published between 1910 and 1914 (Moscow). This was followed by his *Ocherk istorii russkoi kultury* in two parts (5th ed., Petrograd, 1923).

A good portion of Pokrovskii's contribution to nineteenth-century Russian history deals with foreign affairs. His novel approach was his endeavor to show that tsarist foreign policy was determined by domestic conditions and formulated by the ruling social classes. Soviet critics later considered these articles fallacious, schematic, and lacking a true analytical grasp of the conditions that determined Russian foreign policies. In a later edition of his writings Pokrovskii himself agreed with his critics. He admitted that his presentation of nineteenth-century Russian foreign policy overemphasized the ideological attitude of the ruling Russian class and underestimated the national economic interests. Another weakness Marxist critics detected in Pokrovskii's interpretation was his overestimating the importance of the role of trade and trade capital in Russian history.

One must not, however, discard lightly Pokrovskii's *Russian History from the Earliest Times,* for at the time it was written it represented a pioneering attempt at a systematic narrative of the past from a Marxist viewpoint. Pokrovskii's *Ocherk istorii russkoi kultury* was mainly a critical challenge of P.N. Miliukov's well-known study originally published in 1896 under a similar title.[7] Pokrovskii questioned Miliukov's methodology and tried to prove that only a materialistic interpretation could reveal the true development of Russia's cultural history. Miliukov endeavored to emphasize the natural growth of population and the military and financial policies of the state as vital contributory factors in the formation of Russian class society. To Pokrovskii economic developments were of primary importance; the means of production was the determining factor in the formation of classes. He also analyzed the established political system, which, as a Marxist, he associated with the system of production. From the latter, according to Pokrovskii, evolved all state institutions as well as the entire legal system. It was particularly this thesis that his critics continued to regard as revealing his "schematism" and fallacious "legal Marxism," and that prevented him from mastering a true Marxist interpretation of Russian history.

Like so many other party members Pokrovskii believed that the Russian Revolution would serve as the signal to similar developments throughout western Europe. It was mainly for this reason that Pokrovskii regarded events in his own country of "local nature"; the final victory he envisioned in continental dimensions. Nor did he show serious concern with the possibility that the revolution might fail. This perhaps, at least in part, explains his deviations from the party line. Thus Pokrovskii joined Bukharin's "left wing Communists" who vehemently opposed surrender to Germany at Brest-Litovsk. As a delegate to Brest-Litovsk during the negotiations Pokrovskii disagreed with the party on the idea of a temporary respite as advocated by Lenin, though he later publicly admitted that he was wrong.

Though he was engaged in a wide variety of activities Pokrovskii's absorbing interest was history. After the Revolution in 1917 he keenly felt that new tools for teaching history and properly trained teachers were both vitally needed. He urged that prizes be awarded for superior history textbooks and that the quality of teaching be improved, but the shortage of historians meant that neither of these goals could be easily attained. During the maiden years of the Revolution the textbooks of such historians of the "old bourgeois school" as Platonov, Liubavskii, or Presniakov remained in use for the simple reason that no others were to be found. Likewise, the "old guard" professors remained at their posts, though they dutifully paid homage to Marx, Marxism, or to the "Glorious October Revolution." In 1920, to meet the urgent need, Pokrovskii himself wrote *Russkaia istoriia v samom szhatom ocherke,* which covered the period until the middle of the nineteenth century, as a model of the type of textbook required. The book consisted largely of lectures he delivered in 1906-1907, as well as those he read at Sverdlovsk University in 1919. Later Pokrovskii himself said that it turned out to be a "short history" because there was no time in those days "to twaddle" (*rastabaryvat'*). One had, he explained, to pack the largest number of facts in the shortest form since most of the readers at the time might have to depart momentarily for the front. To enable them to link the past with the present, to see the histor-

---

[7]P. N. Miliukov, *Ocherki po istorii russkoi kultury.* Parts I-III (St. Petersburg, 1896-1903). Part I (6th ed., 1909).

9

ical significance of the struggle in which they were engaged and for which they might pay with their lives, Pokrovskii presented his textbook.

The *Short History of Russia*, with some minor amendments, was approved by no other than Lenin himself. He congratulated Pokrovskii on his accomplishment, but added the following amendment:

To make a textbook (and this it must become), it must be supplemented with a chronological index. This is, roughly, what I am suggesting: first column, chronology; second column, bourgeois view (briefly); third column, your view, Marxian, indicating the pages of your book. The student must know both your book and the index so that there be no skimming, so that they should retain the facts, and so that they should learn to compare the old science and the new.[8]

Pokrovskii himself was not entirely pleased with his accomplishment. He regarded the new edition of his textbook as a temporary solution of a problem that required an immediate answer. His book aimed at a total departure from the style of history which consisted of a tale of the tsars and their deeds. "Instead of puppets in crowns and in purple the author took the real tsar—Tsar-Capital, autocratically ruling Russia from Ivan IV to Nicholas the Last," he declared.

At the end of the Civil War Pokrovskii undertook an unbelievable number of tasks. In May, 1919, he was appointed Deputy Commissar of Education. Shortly after, he became head of the Education Division of Higher Learning. He was named chairman of the State Council on Education in charge of university reforms. This implied many duties, since the Council incorporated the administration of such diverse agencies as the State Board of Education, the Central Archives, and the Central Museum. In 1920, Pokrovskii was made a member of the Commission on the History of the October Revolution and the Russian Communist Party, known better by its abbreviated name of *Istpart*.[9] A year later Pokrovskii became head of the "Academic Center" at the Commissariat of Education.

Pokrovskii also served as chairman of the Presidium of the Socialist (since 1924 Communist) Academy; he was Chancellor of the Institute of Red Professorship formed in 1921; he was chairman of the Society of Marxist Historians formed in 1925, and editor of both *Krasnyi arkhiv* and *Istorik-marksist.* As member of the Communist Party Pokrovskii was charged with numerous and often time-consuming tasks. In 1922, for instance, he served as public prosecutor at the trial of a group of right-wing Social Revolutionary Party members. In 1928 he headed a delegation of Soviet historians to the International Historical Congress at Oslo. In 1929 the Communist Academy set up a History Institute with Pokrovskii as director. During the same year he was named member of the Academy of Sciences and assigned the direction of

[8]M. N. Pokrovskii, *Russkaia istoriia v samom szhatom ocherke.* (Moscow, 1920). See Preface.

[9]*Istpart* was the commission charged with the gathering and the study of materials pertaining to the history of the October Revolution and the history of the Russian Communist Party. In 1928 *Istpart* merged with the Lenin Institute. Then, in 1931, the Lenin Institute merged with the Marx-Engels Institute to form the Marx-Engels-Lenin Institute.

the Archeographic Commission.

Despite these burdensome assignments Pokrovskii managed to publish his own writings extensively. In 1923 the third part of his *Short History* appeared, as an essay entitled "The Class Struggle in Russian Historical Literature," covering the early part of the twentieth century. Three years later, *Istoriia revoliutsionnogo dvizheniia v otdelnykh ocherkakh* (Moscow, 1926) was published. In 1925 he published an essay on Marxism and the peculiarities of historical development of Russia, and in 1927 there appeared under his name a collection of articles generally entitled *Dekabristy*. The following year saw another collection of articles in similar book form under the title of *Imperialistic War*. These articles were written at various intervals during 1916-1927. In 1929, a third volume of his collected articles, covering the period between 1917 and 1927, was entitled *The October Revolution*. Simultaneously he edited large numbers of documents, including a series on the Decembrists, another on the 1905 Revolution, and a third containing sources related to the year 1917.

Pokrovskii had freely expressed his philosophy of history orally and in print. "History," he wrote on one occasion, "is the most political of all the sciences. History is politics of the past, without which one is unable to practice politics of the present."[10] Elsewhere he noted: "All these Chicherins, Kavelins, Kliuchevskiis, Chuprovs, Petrazhitskiis—all of them directly reflected a definite class struggle that was carried on throughout the nineteenth century in Russia and . . . history, written by these gentlemen, represents nothing else but politics projected into the past."[11]

Scientific historiography can be construed as scientific history only when based on the principle of class struggle, believed Pokrovskii. The historian, he insisted, must exert all his energy to one purpose—to see that history is used as an ideological weapon. The themes over which he labors, as well as the conclusions he derives, must be subordinated to party interests. In this Pokrovskii saw no conflict whatever, for to him objectivity and party principles were identical, indivisible.

According to Pokrovskii, Marxist-Leninist principles of party membership are not and cannot be in conflict with objective "law-governed phenomena" (*zakonomernost'*); only in bourgeois interpretations of history do these come into conflict with objectivism. According to both Lenin and Pokrovskii, the objectivist, as he explains the need of facts, is prone to go astray with facts. The materialist reveals the nature of class contradictions in a manner that inevitably leads to clearer understanding of the true nature of historical processes.

Under Pokrovskii's guidance a legion of young historians was trained in the Marxian philosophy of history. These men subsequently wrote many universally recognized standard works; among them are such distinguished Soviet historians as M. V. Nechkina, S. M. Dubrovskii, I. I. Mints,

[10]M. N. Pokrovskii, *Istoricheskaia nauka i borba klassov.* 2nd ed. (Moscow, 1933), 360.

[11]*Vestnik Kommunisticheskoi akademii,* Vol. XXVI (2), (1928), 5-6.

11

A. V. Shestakov, A. I. Gukovskii, and many others.[12] In later years some of
them rode the high crest of Stalinism to join in condemning their formerly
revered teacher. Some of them lived long enough to regret it, as in the case of
E. A. Lutskii and S. M. Dubrovskii, and publicly recanted; others died in time
not to be troubled by guilty consciences, as in the case of A. M. Pankratova,
while the rest preferred to cover whatever remorse they may have felt by
convenient silence.

Pokrovskii's critics found numerous ideological sins with which to charge
him. In the last part of his *Short History of Russia*, Pokrovskii was accused
of assigning an exaggerated role in the 1905 disturbance to the kulak elements.
In various articles and prefaces where he interpreted the origin of imperialism
in Russia prior to 1914, Pokrovskii minimized the aggressive character of
German imperialism and thus lessened German responsibility for the outbreak
of the war in 1914. In regarding the February Revolution of 1917 as the
beginning of the proletarian revolution, Pokrovskii introduced an interpretation entirely contrary to party view.

Pokrovskii confronted these errors with valor, and endeavored publicly to
correct his mistakes. In 1927 he admitted that he overestimated the influence
of trade capital upon Russian development. Answering his critic, Rakhmetov,
Pokrovskii pleaded that all his life he had opposed the theory that denied the
importance of trade capital in internal and external economic development in
Russia. In the midst of heated debates, Pokrovskii explained, it was only
natural to err in being carried away by his own argument. Then, with rare
magnanimity, he counselled his students to correct in their writings this error
or any others they might detect in his published works.

In 1928, on the occasion of his sixtieth birthday and his becoming a member of the Academy of Sciences, Pokrovskii was publicly hailed as the cory-
phaeus of historical science. Much of the flattery showered upon him at this
time was regretted only a few years later, after his death. Yet even during the
1920's, some party members had not forgiven or forgotten his political vacillations, and labelled him a Trotskyist engaged in "Trotskyite prose writing."[13]
Pokrovskii's multiple activities must have taxed his health too heavily, and

[12]M. V. Nechkina, *Obshchestvo soedinennykh Slavian.* (Moscow, 1927). E. M. Iaroslavskii, *Dekabrskoe vosstanie.* (Moscow, 1925). P. Gorin, *Ocherki po istorii Sovetov
rabochikh deputatov v 1905 g.* (Moscow, 1925; 2nd ed., Moscow, 1930). A. V.
Shestakov, *Krestianskaia revoliutsiia 1905-1907 gg.* (Moscow, 1926). S. M.
Dubrovskii, *Stolypinskaia reforma. Kapitalizatsiia selskogo khoziaistva v XX veke.*
(Moscow, 1925; 2nd ed., Moscow, 1930). A. M. Pankratova, *Fabzavkomy Rossii v
borbe za sotsialisticheskuiu fabriku.* (Moscow, 1923). A. M. Pankratova, *Fabzavkomy
i profsoiuzy v revoliutsii 1917 g.* (Moscow, 1927). A. I. Gukovskii, *Frantsuzskaia
interventsiia na iuge Rossii.* (Moscow, 1929). I. I. Mints, *Angliiskaia interventsiia
na Severe.* (Moscow, 1931).

[13]The following articles appeared in a special issue of *Istorik-marksist* in honor of
Pokrovskii's sixtieth birthday: A. V. Shestakov, "M. N. Pokrovskii—istorik-marksist."
D. Kin, "M. N. Pokrovskii kak istorik Oktiabrskoi revoliutsii." P. Gorin, "M. N. Pokrovskii kak istorik pervoi russkoi revoliutsii." N. Rubinshtein, "M. N. Pokrovskii—
istorik vneshnei politiki." *Istorik-marksist,* No. 9 (1928), 3-78. V. Miliutin, "M. N.

he finally broke down completely. During the summer of 1931 he was forced to go to the hospital where he spent the remainder of his life. Bedridden, he still continued to edit documents related to the outbreak of the war in 1914. Replying to one of his colleagues who reminded him of their former cooperation he wrote: "Your letter stirred within me so many memories about the years 1906-1907, when I, no longer young, though still a young member of the party, looked ahead. Now there is nothing ahead of me except the crematorium. But on the way to that institution I still hope to nip once more at the honorable imperialists while editing documents related to their war." Shortly before his death one of his former students who paid him a visit observed: "It was strange to see a man with such a lively mind in such disharmony with a dying body." He died of cancer on April 10, 1932.[14]

Pokrovskii died in good time to escape the fury that followed during the middle 1930's. Only a few years after his death his own former students turned against him with bitter attacks. Pokrovskii was more fortunate than, for instance, his contemporary, V. I. Nevskii, Director of the Lenin Public Library, editor of *Krasnaia letopis,* frequent contributor to various magazines, and author of several works, who died in 1937 as one of the early victims of the political purges.[15] The story of Pokrovskii's posthumous fortunes reflects, as did his life, the whole story of an era in Soviet historical science.

Looking back, we can trace three periods in the life of Pokrovskii. The first one was between his graduation from the university in 1891 and the Revolution of 1905, years he himself characterized as the "period of democratic illusions and economic materialism."[16] It was the time of his being a

Pokrovskii (K 60-letiiu so dnia rozhdeniia)," and A. Lunacharskii, "K iubileiu M. N. Pokrovskogo," in *Vestnik Kommunisticheskoi akademii,* Book XXIX (5), (1028), 3-8; 9-12. *Na boevom postu marksizma.* (Moscow, 1929). N. Rubinshtein, "M. N. Pokrovskii—istorik Rossii." *Pod znamenem marksizma,* Nos. 10-11 (1924), 189-209. M. N. Pokrovskii, "Neskolko zamechanii na statiu t. Rubinshteina." *Pod znamenem marksizma,* Nos. 10-11 (1924), 210-212. A. Shestakov, "Proletarskii istorik M. N. Pokrovskii." *Izvestiia,* October 25, 1928. E. Krivosheina, "Voinstvuiushchii istorik-bolshevik." *Izvestiia,* October 25, 1928. B. Freidlin, "M. N. Pokrovskii kak istorik rabochego dvizheniia." *Istoriia proletariata SSSR,* No. 10 (1932), 3-16. V. Nevskii, "M. N. Pokrovskii—istorik Oktiabria." *Istoriia proletariata SSSR,* No. 12 (1932), 3-20.

[14] P. O. Gorin, *M. N. Pokrovskii—bolshevik-istorik.* (Moscow, n.d.), 92.

[15] V. I. Nevskii (Krivobokov), *Ocherki po istorii RKP(b).* Vol. I. (Moscow, 1925). *Predshestvenniki nashei partii (Severnyi soiuz russkikh rabochikh).* (Moscow, 1930). *Iuzhnorusskii soiuz v g. Nikolaeve 1897 g,* ([Moscow] 1922). *Rabochee dvizhenie v ianvarskie dni 1905 g.* (Moscow, 1930). *Sovety i vooruzhennoe vosstanie v 1905 g.* (Moscow, n.d.). "Karl Marks i russkoe revoliutsionne dvizhenie." *Istoriia proletariata SSSR,* Nos. 1-2 (1933). "K voprosu o rabochem dvizhenii v 70-e gody." *Istorik-marksist,* No. 4 (1927), 125-178. See also No. 15 (1930), 86-103. An autobiographic sketch of Nevskii is to be found in *Entsiklopedicheskii slovar "Granat,"* Vol. XLI, Part II, 74-80.

[16] M. N. Pokrovskii, "Po povodu stati tov. Rubinshteina." *Pod znamenem marksizma,* Nos. 10-11 (1924), 210.

13

"bourgeois-democrat." The second period was between 1905 and 1917, when he became an active member of the Bolshevik Party, a recognized scholar and Marxist historian. Finally, the third period was from the October Revolution until the end of his life. This is the time when he became the founder of Soviet historiography, editor of the Marxist historical review and of numerous other publications, and champion in the struggle against the pre-revolutionary school of historians.

In his great, early work *History of Russia from the Earliest Times,* Pokrovskii had endeavored to present in terms of Marxian dialectics the entire course of Russian history, from the early period of eastern Slavdom to the twentieth century. Pokrovskii traced social developments, the process of class formation and recurrent class struggles, utilizing a vast amount of source material.

No historian prior to Pokrovskii had undertaken the task of a Marxian presentation of Russian history through such length and breadth. The work represents an extraordinary effort to weave a broad plausible synthesis of Russia's past. It was no fragmentation of history into artificially created "eras," "epochs," or "periods," but an endeavor to narrate an all-embracing account of Russian history as he saw it. His opponents, and he had many of them, criticized Pokrovskii's interpretation, pointing out a legion of fallacies, yet there was no denying his significant contribution to historical science. His challenging interpretations of such subjects as the revolutionary movement or the underlying social formations from which class antagonism evolved are presented with a degree of freshness, originality, and vigor which most readers recognize. It is this approach that distinguishes Pokrovskii from previous writers, including V. O. Kliuchevskii and P. G. Vinogradov, his teachers and early mentors.

Pokrovskii was fortunate to come into the historical profession at a time when an imposing accumulation of source materials had already been published by earlier scholars. What was needed was not so much the "pick and shovel" toil as the discerning eye to see some meaningful pattern in this data. Whatever the defects pointed out later by his critics, Pokrovskii moved a long way ahead with the initial need for a systematized Marxian historical presentation of Russian history.

A central point in much of this criticism was the charge of "legal Marxism," a heresy that implies the application of materialistic without dialectical interpretation of history. And although, as was shown, Pokrovskii himself admitted it, and he stressed the fact now not mentioned, that it lasted only during the 1890's, critics kept insisting that it had a lasting effect upon his writings.[17]

It became fashionable after the middle of the 1930's, even among Pokrovskii's former students and admirers, to stress his fallacious philosophy of history. He was blamed for substituting abstract sociological schematism for chronological sequential narrative. His entire party record came in for a reex-

[17]M. N. Pokrovskii, *Istoricheskaia nauka i borba klassov.* 2nd ed. (Moscow, 1933), 268.

14

amination, in the attempt to trace the source of his ideological fallacies in the literary and political activities of his early life.

Though Pokrovskii joined the Bolshevik Party in 1905, he never toed the party line faithfully; he cooperated with many refractory members such as A.A. Bogdanov or L.D. Trotsky before 1917. And although he opposed Trotsky and criticized his historical concepts during the 1920's, some members of the party continued to remind him of his past deviations. Even after Pokrovskii joined the party his frequent tendencies to side with critics of Lenin were noted. Though he later endeavored to dissociate himself from these critics, the charge was made that basically he never freed himself of his bourgeois evolutionary theories, as distinct from the genuine revolutionary historical materialism.[18]

A few months before his death, Pokrovskii accused some of his colleagues of "academism"—insisting upon subjective treatment of history and refusing to be active political participants—calling them "misguided members of the profession detached from reality." Soviet historians took Pokrovskii severely to task for this during the 1930's and 1940's. They also criticized his sociological schematism and his abstract generalities, and during the rise of home-spun Soviet patriotism they suddenly uncovered Pokrovskii's disregard of national interest in his writings, condeming his view that "history is politics of the past." Critics now detected his former political waverings, his party deviations and disloyalties. Not until the early 1960's was Pokrovskii re-examined and treated with circumspection. The line of argument now was that though Pokrovskii frequently deviated from Marxism, he must still be considered an historian who earnestly tried to find a genuine Marxist conception in the field of Russian history. A recent writer, A. I. Gukovskii, aptly described Pokrovskii as a "rebel in a liberal camp."[19]

According to Pokrovskii, development of Russian society passed through five stages: primitive communism, feudalism, handicraft economy, trade capitalism, industrial capitalism. Later, in his *Outline of the History of Russian Culture*, Pokrovskii limited the stages to only three: primitive collectivism, handicraft economy, and capitalistic economy, while the last stage he subdivided into two, trade and industrial capitalism. This differed from the official Marxist concept that never recognized handicraft economy and trade capitalism as distinct formations in Russian history.[20]

Nationalism as a serious factor in history had always been underestimated by Pokrovskii; nor did he take seriously the theory of Russian distinctiveness as a key to historical interpretation. He vigorously continued to reject the view that Russia was innately different in not having passed through such

[18] M. N. Pokrovskii, *Ekonomicheskii materializm.* (Petrograd, 1920), 4. See also M. N. Pokrovskii, *"Ekonomisty," predtechi menshevikov. Ekonomizm i rabochee dvizhenie v Rossii na poroge XX veka.* (Moscow, 1923).

[19] *Voprosy istorii*, No. 8 (1968), 122.

[20] M. N. Pokrovskii, *Ocherk istorii russkoi kultury.* Part I, 2nd ed. (Moscow, 1917), 36-37.

Western experiences as medieval feudalism, the Renaissance, or the Reformation. According to Pokrovskii, feudalism was determined by any one of the following characteristics or by all of them operating simultaneously: (1) domination by a landowning nobility, (2) a close relationship between landownership and political power, (3) an established hierarchy within the landowning class, with a vassalage system that forms the familiar feudal pyramid.[21]

Pokrovskii agreed with N. P. Pavlov-Silvanskii regarding the essence of a feudal society as an amalgamation of private and state law. Like so many of his contemporaries Pokrovskii too tended to overemphasize the political and juridical significance in the feudal structure. He too considered certain characteristics such as fragmented political authority as a general sign of feudalism. Agreeing with Pavlov-Silvanskii, Pokrovskii maintained that since up to the sixteenth century there was no true state law system in Russia, there could be no Russian state in a modern sense. "Feudalism," wrote Pokrovskii, "is better known as an economic system than as a legal system." His interpretation of feudalism as a "stateless society" came to be regarded by Soviet historians as perhaps the most vulnerable of all his theories.[22]

Much of Pokrovskii's writing is undeniably schematic. Such are, as an illustration, his chapters that deal with trade capitalism or where he discusses the influence of grain prices on socio-political movements in Russia. The fundamental force in history, as Pokrovskii saw it, was the irresistible, the irrepressible, ever-present material need; the role of the individual or any other cultural determinant he relegated to the backstage of history. There is a certain mechanical interpretation in his view of historical events that borders on vulgarization and schematism, as has been rightly pointed out by his opponents.

Nevertheless it should not be forgotten that Pokrovskii was a pioneer in his endeavor to construct a generalized Marxist history of Russia. Some of his interpretations were his own, and probably never occurred to Karl Marx—for example, his phases of handicraft economy or trade capitalism in the economic development of Russia. His theory of primitive communism and feudalism, though still vulnerable, seems more plausible. Whatever phase of history Pokrovskii had dealt with, had to fit into his scheme where class struggle and economic development were determining factors in the growth of the Russian state and Russian society. He held on tenaciously to the view that only through the empirical method can one find the right interpretation of the past. Despite many of Pokrovskii's glaring weaknesses, as one writer aptly summarized, "No future student of Russian history will be able to dispense with his work or find complete satisfaction in them."[23]

[21] M. N. Pokrovskii, *Russkaia istoriia s drevneishikh vremen.* 6th ed. (Moscow, 1924), Vol. I, 28.

[22] A brief survey of Pokrovskii's "oversimplification of history" may be found in *Sovetskaia istoriografiia klassovoi borby i revoliutsionnogo dvizheniia v Rossii.* (Leningrad, 1967), Part I, 5-17.

[23] M. N. Pokrovskii, *Russia from the Earliest Times to the Rise of Capitalism.* (New York, 1931). See Preface by J. D. Clarkson.

Two years after his death in 1932, Pokrovskii's works were still widely in use, particularly his *Short History of Russia,* which appeared in five post-humous editions. His other works, the general history of Russia as well as his *Outline of the History of Russian Culture,* were popularly accepted. A special editorial committee was set up by the Communist Academy, headed by A. S. Bubnov, to publish all of Pokrovskii's works posthumously.[24]

This period of tolerance ended in 1934. The bitter struggle and raging disputes over the enforcement of the five-year plans, the threat of Nazi Germany, and the wave of deliberately cultivated Soviet patriotism as a reaction to the Nazi anti-Soviet campaign, all these brought Soviet historical writing face to face with problems that demanded an entirely different approach to national history. Pokrovskii's interpretation of the national struggle for emancipation, particularly against foreign intrusions, was no more acceptable; indeed, it came to be considered dangerous. The Central Committee of the party adopted a resolution condemning Pokrovskii's version of Russian history, and simultaneously the Soviet government issued a statement that "among some of our historians there spread erroneous historical views characteristic of the so-called 'historical school' of M. N. Pokrovskii."

In considering the "errors" of Pokrovskii it must be borne in mind that the campaign against him was carried out against the background of the "cult of the individual," during which a whole group of historians were blacklisted or fell under the long dark shadow of Stalinism. Among these were such prominent men as N. M. Lukin, S. A. Piontkovskii, and P. O. Gorin. The charges levelled against them were serious.

On January 12, 1939, *Pravda* published an article by Emelian Iaroslavskii entitled "Anti-Marxist Distortions and Vulgarization of the So-called 'School' of M. N. Pokrovskii," in which all his writings were severely censured. Instead of the recently adopted project to publish all of Pokrovskii's works, the Institute of History of the Academy of Sciences issued a collection of articles under the title of *Against the Historical Concept of M. N. Pokrovskii.* A year later followed another issue under the title of *Against the Anti-Marxist Conception of M. N. Pokrovskii.*[25] Here Pokrovskii was accused of anti-Leninism, bourgeois methodology, and distortion of the history of the Civil War. The war years added another note; Pokrovskii was now castigated for misrepresenting nationalism, for his Great Russian bias, for underestimating healthy aspects of patriotism, for overestimating German culture, for failing to interpret the

[24]M. N. Pokrovskii, *Istoricheskaia nauka i borba klassov. Istoriograficheskie ocherki, kriticheskie stati i zametki.* (Moscow, 1933). 2 parts. M. N. Pokrovskii, *Russkaia istoriia s drevneishikh vremen.* Vols. I-IV. (Moscow, 1933-34). M. N. Pokrovskii, *Imperialisticheskaia voina.* (Moscow, 1934).

[25]*Protiv istoricheskoi kontseptsii M. N. Pokrovskogo. Sbornik statei.* (Moscow, 1939), Part I. *Protiv antimarksistskoi kontseptsii M. N. Pokrovskogo. Sbornik statei.* (Moscow, 1940), Part II. Cf. *Istoriia i istoriki. Istoriografiia istorii SSSR. Sbornik statei.* (Moscow, 1965). See also E. A. Lutskii, "Izvrashchenie M. N. Pokrovskim istorii ino-strannoi voennoi interventsii i grazhdanskoi voiny v SSSR (1918-1920 gg.)." *Protiv antimarksistskoi kontseptsii M. N. Pokrovskogo.* (Moscow, 1940), Part II.

17

genuine meaning of Russian imperialism, which was far less evil than British or French imperialism, and thereby "morally disarming the Russian people."[26]

An article in the *Great Soviet Encyclopedia* (Vol. 33) on Pokrovskii states that his activity played a "rather positive part in the struggle with bourgeois historiography, though it simultaneously delivered considerable harm to the development of Soviet historical writing and the training of Marxist-historians."

It became fashionable to label Pokrovskii's works as "schematic sociology" and "mechanical economism" rather than history. A joint decree of the Council of People's Commissars of the USSR and the Central Committee of the All-Union Communist Party of May 16, 1934, condemned all former abstract, formal history textbooks as well as the teaching methods employed to date. Henceforth, it was ordered, history must be taught in chronological sequence and students must memorize important dates and significant events. The historian E. Tarlé, an old critic of Pokrovskii, returned from banishment to Moscow.

The decree of May 16, signed by V. Molotov and J. Stalin, not only placed the official stamp of disapproval on Pokrovskii, but ordered new textbooks for the schools. The order called for five textbooks; (1) a history of the ancient world, (2) a history of the Middle Ages, (3) a modern history, (4) a history of the USSR, and (5) a modern history of dependent and colonial countries. A number of men were designated to begin immediately on the new history textbooks, and the training of qualified specialists in each of the fields was begun.

One of the charges levelled was that though Pokrovskii was a true economic determinist, he based his interpretations on historical materialism *as he saw it*. He believed, the critics maintained, that objective universal laws mold historical developments. Phenomena such as patriotism, chauvinism, racism, imperialism, colonialism, all have a tendency to emerge anywhere in one form or another, but are particularly symbolic of a decaying capitalistic order. Pokrovskii assumed, critics further pointed out, that the laws of historical development can lead to the discovery by methodology of dialectical materialism; that these laws are inevitable, immutable and universal.

In this sense it can be said that Pokrovskii was a "universalist" who hated any form associated with the decaying bourgeois-capitalist order. To Pokrovskii all forms of colonialism, whether English in India, French in Indochina, Italian in Tripoli, Belgian in the Congo, or Russian in Persia, were equally abhorrent. But by the middle of the 1930's this point of view encountered the strong head winds of Stalinism, with its home-spun Soviet patriotism, to which Pokrovskii's "cosmopolitanism" was not palatable. A campaign had already been launched to purge historical science of all "deviationism." The First All-Union Conference of Marxist Historians approved the decision to consolidate forces and drive out any remnants of the old philosophies of history. The campaign was for nothing less than "total Marxism" against "pluralism," "creeping empiricism," "selecticism," "Trotskyism," or any other deviationism.

[26]N. L. Rubinshtein, *Russkaia istoriografiia.* (Moscow, 1941). See particularly Ch. 34 on Pokrovskii and Ch. 36 on Stalin. See also *Dvadtsat piat let istoricheskoi nauki v SSSR.* (Moscow, 1942).

One of the serious reasons for Pokrovskii's vulnerability is the fact he was never a consistent adherent to dialectical materialism, and therefore critics were always able to select parts of his writings that appeared most open to attack. For a long while, for instance, Pokrovskii followed the line of economic materialism, a philosophy that, according to his critics, was rejected from the very start. Economic materialism, they maintained, had a tendency to vulgarize and emasculate historical processes, and deny the role of progressive ideas in history. In some of his early writings Pokrovskii said that the "world is a combination of our imagination."[27] This, his critics claimed, was a typical idealistic theory borrowed from A. A. Bogdanov; it led to the false and condemned philosophy of empirio-criticism, or the belief of Ernst Mach, the Austrian philosopher who contended that all empirical statements can be in the end reduced to sensations. In his *Empirio-Criticism,* Lenin took Mach to task with all the vigor for which he was noted. Furthermore, argued his critics, Pokrovskii did not recognize that there were laws of nature, independent of our consciousness. This was bound to lead Pokrovskii to a chain of fatal errors: it would result in the acceptance of E. Mach, to an agreement with the views of Herbert Spencer and with the economism of A. A. Bogdanov, and lead directly in the end to Trotskyism.

Other critics discovered that Pokrovskii at one time belonged to the so-called *Otzovists* (Recallers) group in 1908. This was a faction of the Bolshevik Party which demanded the recall of all Social-Democratic deputies from the Third Duma, and termination of all legal opposition to or cooperation with the monarchical regime. Lenin himself opposed this group on the grounds that all legal and illegal means should be employed to combat the regime.

Criticism was heaped upon criticism: Pokrovskii's theory that history is politics projected into the past tended, it was asserted, to distort historical perspectives. It permitted such interpretations as that Pugachev's bands were the early Red Guard units of the eighteenth century; that Chernyshevskii was a Menshevik; or that Tkachev was the "first Russian Marxist," which places history on its head. It was only logical, the same critics asserted, that Pokrovskii denied any Kievan period in the history of the Russian state. To talk about a unified Russian state during the Kievan period, Pokrovskii stated, is a clear misunderstanding.[28] Nor did Pokrovskii believe that there existed social classes during the Kievan period of the tenth and eleventh centuries. To Pokrovskii the conversion of Kievan Russia to Christianity was not to be associated with a beginning of Western influence, but represented a far less profound change, since everything remained as before, animism ruling as usual.[29]

Kievan Russia revolved around a sociological scheme which Pokrovskii named "trade capital." Whether it was the wars during the Kievan period, or

[27]M. N. Pokrovskii, *Istoricheskaia nauka i borba klassov. Istoriograficheskie ocherki, kriticheskie stati i zametki.* (Moscow, 1933), 18. See Z. D. Ermakova, "Bibliografiia rabot M. N. Pokrovskogo." *Istorik-marksist,* Nos. 1-2 (1932), 216-248.

[28]M. N. Pokrovskii, *Russkaia istoriia s drevneishikh vremen.* (Moscow, 1920), Vol. I, 170.

[29]M. N. Pokrovskii, *Russkaia istoriia v samom szhatom vide.* (Moscow, 1929), 36.

the struggle between the Oprichnina and the Boyars, or the uprising led by
E. I. Pugachev when Cossack trade capital warred against Moscow trade capital, it was all the same. The Decembrist revolt, the emancipation of the serfs, the Russo-Japanese war, the World War, all these represented some form of struggle between two forms of capitalism—trade versus industrial capitalism, according to a theory that Pokrovskii held tenaciously until 1931. Even peasant uprisings were motivated by the force of trade capital. Razin's rebellion in 1670 was indirectly tied with the development of trade capitalism.[30]

He regarded the Russo-Japanese war as a trade-capital adventure and not, as Lenin saw, a sign of "military-feudal imperialism."[31] Pokrovskii presents the entire Far Eastern development as two forms of capitalism slugging it out at the court in St. Petersburg, one faction headed by Count Witte, who hoped to gain the upper hand by peaceful means, and the other, the violent form of trade capitalism, which employed every means to establish economic domination. As to Russia's foreign policy, Pokrovskii maintained, until 1906 it could not be regarded as imperialistic; it was only after the Russo-Japanese war that the country assumed the posture of aggressive imperialism. As Pokrovskii himself admitted, until 1924 he sat between two chairs, one, the concept of Hilferding, the other of Lenin; hence his fallacious and inconsistent thinking.

Repeating Bogdanov's theory, Pokrovskii believed that tsarist autocracy was not a legacy of the old feudal order, but the creation of trade capitalism derived from the preceding stage of capitalist economy. Pokrovskii also considered the kulak element as the "single politically accepted and most democratic element." Hence his Menshevist-Trotskyite tendency to underestimate the impact of the peasant bourgeois-democratic participation in the revolution.

Another of Pokrovskii's errors, his critics say, was his ascribing war guilt of 1914 to Russia. In 1915 he presented a paper in Paris which, with a few minor alterations, he published in 1919. In the original paper Pokrovskii started to prove that Germany not only had no aspirations toward territorial annexations, but tried to prevent annexationist aims of her more belligerent ally Austria-Hungary.[32] Germany went to war, according to Pokrovskii, because she feared an attack upon herself. He did not believe that France had any annexationist ambitions either, and he denied serious conflict between Germany and Great Britain. The main culprit was the Russian landlord class that enticed the French rentier and the English conservative elements to attack Germany. This interpretation suited German nationalists perfectly.

The February Revolution Pokrovskii came to interpret as the "workers' revolution," and not as the Bolsheviks commonly regarded it, the bourgeois-democratic stage. Whereas Lenin viewed the events of February as the preliminary step to socialist revolution, Pokrovskii disagreed. He believed Russia

[30]M. N. Pokrovskii, *Russkaia istoriia v samom szhatom vide.* (Moscow, 1929), 80.

[31]*1905 god. Sbornik,* Vol. I, 606.

[32]M. N. Pokrovskii, *Imperialisticheskaia voina. Sbornik statei, 1915-1927 gg.* (Moscow, 1928). See the article entitled "Vinovniki voiny."

to be unready for a socialist revolution, and that the events of February would be followed by an evolutionary process and not a violent development. On one occasion he insisted that the Russian revolution was bound either to move on to a universal stage or to fall altogether—Europe would not let it stand as a challenge to its social and economic order.

All these false theories were brought to the fore by Pokrovskii's opponents, who explained them all by the fact that he never was anything but a bourgeois trained historian. The impact of Kliuchevskii and Vinogradov on him, in addition to his being a former adherent of the "Legal Marxists," left impressions too deep to be erased. To be sure, argued his opponents, he wrote prodigiously; he was the founder and leader of several vital educational institutions, and he trained many pupils who gained distinction; he headed many organizations of national importance, issued textbooks, and directed educational policies. But ideologically he was vulnerable, and his party record was that of a deviationist.

Not until the early 1960's did Soviet historians begin to reevaluate Pokrovskii and acknowledge that he deserved an honorable mention in history. It must never be forgotten, argued those who belatedly came to his defense, that it was Pokrovskii who managed to train a whole school of militant Marxist historians. This achievement had to be acknowledged—dourly—by even some of his severest critics.

It deserves mention, finally, that Pokrovskii and many of his followers were personally men of impressive erudition. That they engaged in true historical research and valued the importance of primary sources is best testified by the volume of documentary materials published under his guidance. This same statement could not be applied to the epigones who turned against him to toe the Stalin line. Pokrovskii was cosmopolitan, he carried all his life the stamp of nineteenth-century cultural tradition; the critics who followed him were dwarfs in comparision, noted for their insularity and intellectual parochialism, chauvinistic, and ready to trade safety for honor.

Pokrovskii's stature is even more impressive when one compares his achievements with those of the barren 1930's and 1940's. The stifling intellectual climate of this period, in which revising history to suit political needs became a standard practice, is sufficient to place Pokrovskii in a more favorable light. After his departure from the scene methodology of primary sources and the philosophy of history became obsolete, and gave way to the distortion of facts or their sheer invention to create the Stalin legend. This is best illustrated by the *Short History of the All-Union Communist Party (Bolsheviks)*, edited by none other than Stalin himself.

Everyone had to be a propagandist first and a historian second. A travesty of truth came to pass for history. To many historians research lost validity or importance, the main purpose being to prove a chosen conclusion even in the face of incontrovertible evidence. Finally, the Presidium of the Academy of Sciences, History Section, decided "to take radical measures to improve the preparation of manuscripts and their passing for publication by the Institute of History."

To assure conformity a procedure for approval of pubication of manuscripts was adopted that worked somewhat as follows. A manuscript was submitted first to examination by the History Section of the Institute of History. If it was passed the manuscript was sent next to a "responsible editor." If the editor approved, it was moved to the Scientific Council, which in turn passed it on to the Academy's Editorial and Publishing Bureau. The Bureau consulted further experts in the field and then forwarded it to the Academy's Publishing House. Upon publication it was sent out to reviewers of different magazines; and if misfortune befell the author and the book was adversely criticized, it might be withdrawn from circulation and all those involved in passing it, including the author, might then regret their action. This procedure is still in effect.

The historian who still managed to retain his integrity found himself at the mercy of a jingoistic Soviet mediocrity that ruled supreme. Writing history in a true sense became a politically precarious occupation, and since true heroes are seldom in a majority most historians hastily learned by sheer physical instinct which synthesis was good for their health and which was not—how to pay tribute to Caesar and how to respect Clio. History indeed became, as Vladimir Dedijer aptly described it, "an atheistic theology."

A partial return to sanity followed the Twentieth Congress of the Communist Party at which the "cult of the individual" was denounced. Soviet historians cautiously began to revise their views of Pokrovskii as the Marxist historian and teacher.[33] During the early 1960's a new campaign was initiated by S. M. Dubrovskii, during which he urged a reevaluation of Pokrovskii's writings and an end to the distortion of his views.[34] Finally, during the Twenty-second Congress, the party once more took up for a reexamination the role Pokrovoskii had played in Soviet historiography. This time the verdict was even more temperate; it reads in part: "In his [Pokrovskii's] scientific as in his political activities, there were not a few errors. That is true and, of course, that is to be considered. But it is well known that he defended Marx-

---

[33]M. E. Naidenov, "Velikaia Oktiabrskaia sotsialisticheskaia revoliutsiia v sovetskoi istoriografii." *Voprosy istorii*, No. 10 (1957), 171. V. G. Rusliakova, "Borba s falsifikatsiei i vulgarizatsiei istorii Velikoi Oktiabrskoi sotsialisticheskoi revoliutsii (1917-1937 gg.)." *Sbornik statei po istorii rabochego klassa i sovetskoi istoriografii.* (Moscow, 1958), 249-250. V. F. Inkin and A. G. Chernykh, "O pervom etape razvitiia sovetskoi istoricheskoi nauki." *Istoriia SSSR*, No. 5 (1960), 75-81. M. E. Naidenov, "Problemy periodizatsii sovetskoi istoricheskoi nauki." *Istoriia SSSR*, No. 1 (1961), 81-96. See also article on Pokrovskii by A. S. Roslova, in *Istoriografiia istorii SSSR s drevneishikh vremen do Velikoi Oktiabrskoi sotsialisticheskoi revoliutsii.* (Moscow, 1961), Ch. 29.

[34]S. I. Dubrovskii, "Akademik M. N. Pokrovskii i ego rol v razvitii sovetskoi istoricheskoi nauki." *Voprosy istorii*, No. 3 (1962), 3-40. O. Sokolov, "Ob istoricheskikh vzgliadakh M. N. Pokrovskogo." *Voprosy istorii*, No. 8 (1963), 30-41. A. L. Shapiro, *Russkaia istoriografiia v period imperializma. Kurs lektsii.* (Leningrad, 1962). M. V. Nechkina, "O periodizatsii istorii sovetskoi istoricheskoi nauki." *Istoriia SSSR*, No. 1 (1960), 83-85. E. A. Lutskii, "Osnovnye printsipy periodizatsii razvitiia sovetskoi istoricheskoi nauki." *Istoriia SSSR*, No. 2 (1961), 110-112. M. V. Nechkina, Iu. A. Poliakov, and L. V. Cherepnin, "Nekotorye voprosy istorii sovetskoi istoricheskoi nauki." *Kommunist*, No. 9 (1961), 61-63.

ism and contributed much to the development in the field of history." The Congress reassigned Pokrovskii to a more honored place in the ranks of Soviet historians.[35]

[35] *XXII sezd Kommunisticheskoi partii Sovetskogo Soiuza. Stenograficheskii otchet.* Vol. II, 185. See also: M. A. Suslov, "XXII sezd KPSS i zadachi kafedr obshchestvennykh nauk." *Kommunist,* No. 3 (1962), 21. A. L. Shapiro, *Russkaia istoriografiia v period imperializma. Kurs lektsii.* (Leningrad, 1962), 189-208. S. M. Dubrovskii, "Akademik M. N. Pokrovskii i ego rol v razvitii sovetskoi istoricheskoi nauki." *Voprosy istorii,* No. 3 (1962), 3-30, 31-40. "Zadachi istoricheskoi nauki v svete reshenii iiunskogo plenuma TsK KPSS." *Voprosy istorii,* No. 8 (1963). *Kommunist,* No. 4 (1962).

CHAPTER II

Historiography and Publication
of Sources

A. HISTORIOGRAPHY. THE RUBINSHTEIN CASE

Historiography has received ample attention during the Soviet period. Aside from the work of many individual writers there has been a collective effort to present a full account of accomplishments in historical literature during the first fifty years of Soviet rule, such as the recent four-volume publication of the Historical Section of the Academy of Sciences.[1] Though the comprehensive historiography is an impressive undertaking and of considerable value, it suffers from one vulnerable feature particularly—it is so vast in its endeavor to cover the field that it resembles a bibliography more closely than a historiography. Moreover, not all chapters are of equal scholarly quality, since this is a collective work and the legion of contributors vary widely in talent and qualifications. It was published after the death of Stalin, but the cult of the individual still seems to hover over it; some of the chapters still reflect the old platitudes and retain a stifling air of   ·
restraint.

In 1962-1963 a two-volume guide was published by the Chief Administration of Personal Archival Collections of the State Archives of the USSR. The publication appeared in a limited edition and the two volumes became a bibliographical rarity almost from the day of their issue. An equally indispensable guide to publications in the field of history and related disciplines is the projected three-volume set under the direction of I. P. Doronin. This is a project worked on by the Main Library of the Social Sciences of the Academy of Sciences.[2]

[1]*Ocherki istorii istoricheskoi nauki v SSSR.* (Moscow, 1955-1956). 4 vols. (A fifth volume is in preparation.) See also bibliographies of recent date which excellently complement these volumes: *Istoriia istoricheskoi nauki v SSSR. Dooktiabrskii period. Bibliografiia.* (Moscow, 1965). Another: *Istoriia SSSR. Annotirovannyi perechen russkikh bibliografii, izdannykh do 1965 g.* 2nd ed. (Moscow, 1966). Reviews of the 4-volume historiography may be found in the following periodicals: *Voprosy istorii,* No. 12 (1955), 188-194; No. 7 (1956), 116-125; 125-127; No. 3 (1962), 130-137; No. 6 (1966), 157-159. *Kommunist,* No. 6 (1956), 109-114. *Istoricheskaia nauka na Urale za 50 let, 1917-1967. Materialy 3-ei nauchnoi sessii vuzov Uralskogo ekonomicheskogo raiona (istoricheskie nauki).* Issue I. *Istoriia SSSR.* (Sverdlovsk, 1967). For other historiographies see under individual constituent republics such as Ukraine, Kazakhstan, etc.

[2]*Lichnye arkhivnye fondy v gosudarstvennykh khranilishchakh SSSR. Ukazatel.* (Moscow, 1962-1963). 2 vols. (See review in *Voprosy istorii,* No. 6 [1964], 144-146.) *Istoriia SSSR. Ukazatel sovetskoi literatury, 1917-1952. Istoriia SSSR s drevneishikh vremen do vstupleniia Rossii v period kapitalizma.* (Moscow, 1956-). Vol. I-.

In addition, there are valuable writings to be found in periodical publications.[3]
Other important collective works include the volume that deals with the limited period between the Twentieth and Twenty-second Communist Party Congresses, and the collection of essays under the general title *Istoriia i istoriki* (*History and Historians*). The former volume covers the period between February, 1956, and October, 1961, while the latter volume covers three main topics: (1) Lenin and historical science, (2) fundamental problems in Soviet historiography, such as serfdom, revolutionary movements, economic development, and foreign relations, and (3) individual historians and their works, such as M. N. Pokrovskii, V. O. Kliuchevskii, B. N. Chicherin, and V. I. Nevskii.[4]

There are a goodly number of monographs by individual authors who contributed considerably to Soviet historiography. One of these is by P.A. Lavrov, who has written on the subject of the pre-1914 labor movement in the Ukraine. Another is a most informative essay on Ukrainian historiography of the Soviet period by V. A. Diadichenko, F. E. Los', and V. G. Sarbei.[5] A graphic survey by V. A. Fedorov covers historiography in the field of agrarian unrest during the last decades of serfdom.[6] Finally, there is the comprehensive work by N. L. Rubinshtein, a unique case in Soviet historiography that deserves to be discussed in detail because of the light it sheds

[3]To mention only a few: D. S. Likhachev, "O letopisnom periode russkoi istoriografii." *Voprosy istorii*, No. 9 (1948), 21-40. V. V. Mavrodin, "Sovetskaia istoricheskaia literatura o krestianskikh voinakh v Rossii XVII- XVIII vekov." *Voprosy istorii*, No. 5 (1961), 24-47. V. V. Mavrodin, "Sovetskaia istoriografiia sotsialno-ekonomicheskogo stroia Kievskoi Rusi." *Istoriia SSSR*, No. 1 (1962), 52-73. M. N. Tikhomirov, "Nachalo russkoi istoriografii." *Voprosy istorii*, No. 5 (1960). A. M. Sakharov, "Problema obrazovaniia Russkogo tsentralizovannogo gosudarstva v sovetskoi istoriografii." *Voprosy istorii*, No. 9 (1961), 70-88. A. A. Zimin and A. A. Preobrazhenskii, "Izuchenie v sovetskoi istoricheskoi nauke klassovoi borby perioda feodalizma v Rossii (do nachala XIX veka)." *Voprosy istorii*, No. 12 (1957), 135-160.

[4]*Sovetskaia istoricheskaia nauka ot XX k XXII sezdu KPSS. Istoriia SSSR. Sbornik statei.* (Moscow, 1962). *Istoriia i istoriki. Istoriografiia istorii SSSR. Sbornik statei.* (Moscow, 1965).

[5]P. A. Lavrov, *Ukrainskaia sovetskaia istoriografiia o rabochem dvizhenii na Ukraine v 1912-1914 gg.* (Moscow, 1962). V. A. Diadichenko, F. E. Los', and V. G. Sarbei, "Razvitie istoricheskoi nauki na Ukraine (1917-1963 gg.)." *Voprosy istorii*, No. 1 (1964), 3-26.

[6]V. A. Fedorov, "Istoriografiia krestianskogo dvizheniia v Rossii perioda razlozheniia krepostnichestva." *Voprosy istorii*, No. 2 (1966), 148-156. See also *Nekotorye problemy istorii sovetskogo obshchestva (istoriografiia).* (Moscow, 1964). *Ocherki po istorii istoriografii sovetskogo obshchestva.* (Moscow, 1965). "Vazhnye problemy istoriografii sovetskogo obshchestva." *Voprosy istorii*, No. 4 (1966), 130-133. S. S. Khesin, "Nekotorye voprosy istoriografii pervykh let sovetskoi vlasti." *Istoriia SSSR*, No. 3 (1961), 103-115.

on the conditions in which students of history work and publish.[7] Shortly after its publication the book was condemned, banned, and never reappeared. Not many copies survived after the bank was placed on this extensive monograph, covering the field from the earliest chronicles to the present day. A few libraries abroad own these copies and are usually kept under lock and key. The work of Rubinshtein remains the single volume that is indispensable to the student of Russian historiography. The tale of Rubinshtein's experience illustrates virtually every sensitive point in Russian historiography; it could be entitled "The Adventures of a History Book."

Rubinshtein's *Russian Historiography* appeared late in 1941 and because of the war it escaped close attention. Then, in 1948, the magazine *Voprosy istorii* initiated a discussion of the book. The announcement of the editor reads that "recognizing fully the urgent need of N. L. Rubinshtein's book, the editorial staff invites historians, scientific institutions and faculty members to participate in this discussion."[8] The invitation came as a result of a short notice by a certain I. Mordvishin in the monthly publication, concerning a discussion of Rubinshtein's *Historiography* held by the history department at the Ivanov Institute of Education. According to the writer, Rubinshtein had committed a grave error in stating that Marxism was a direct continuation of bourgeois science. He cited Rubinshtein as saying, while he discusses the development of historical science during the second half of the nineteenth century: "The best that bourgeois science created at the beginning of the nineteenth century now came in the development of Marxism. The dialectical materialism of Marx and Engels was a creative summary of a developed philosophical thought resting on a new historical basis." (See p. 347 in Rubinshtein.) The error, writes Mordvishin, lay in a failure to comprehend the true nature of Marxism, which led Rubinshtein to a point where he had to say a kind word about aristocratic and bourgeois historians. Mordvishin also found Rubinshtein in error when he assumed that Russian historical science lagged behind western historiography until almost recent times, and that Russian writers merely repeated what had already been said in the West. Thus, according to Rubinshtein, M. T. Kachenovskii copied Niebuhr and Schlözer; S. M. Soloviev merely repeated G. W. F. Hegel, Henry T. Buckle, or Karl Ritter, etc.

Another critic, M. I. Zelenskii, accused Rubinshtein of similar misconceptions; of overestimating such mediocre German historians as G. S. Bayer, G. F. Müller, or A. L. Schlözer. According to Zelenskii, Rubinshtein regarded

[7]N. L. Rubinshtein, *Russkaia istoriografiia.* (Moscow, 1941). I. Mordvishin, "Obsuzhdenie knigi Prof. N. L. Rubinshteina." *Voprosy istorii,* No. 1 (1948), 154. A. Votinov, "Obsuzhdenie knigi N. L. Rubinshteina 'Russkaia istoriografiia'." *Voprosy istorii,* No. 6 (1948), 126-135. N. L. Rubinshtein, "Osnovnye problemy postroeniia russkoi istoriografii XVIII veka." *Voprosy istorii,* No. 2 (1948), 89-93. See obituary notice in *Istoriia SSSR,* No. 3 (1963), 239-241.

[8]*Voprosy istorii,* No. 1 (1948), 154.

these as the most eminent representatives of historical science in Russia in the eighteenth century. Rubinshtein was equally wrong, the same critic asserts, when he discussed the complex development of N. G. Chernyshevskii or N. A. Dobroliubov as revolutionary philosophers, since they were far ahead of either Hegel or Feuerbach. Nor was Rubinshtein right when he assumed that different historical schools arise not necessarily from antagonistic ideologies, but come to coexist peacefully, so to speak.

More critics jumped on the bandwagon to attack Rubinshtein over the thread-worn Normanist theory, which emphasizes the role of the Vikings in the formation of the Russian state. This, argued the later critics, only proved that Rubinshtein had accepted a pseudo-scientific and harmful theory; it showed that he lacked faith in Russia, in her national, spiritual, and political maturity. This charge touched on a tender spot, particularly in view of recent excesses with Aryanism.[9] The sum total, the resolution read, was that Rubinshtein's *Historiography* was badly in need of a basic revision before it could be used in any school as a text. But the matter did not rest there.

Voprosy istorii now pursued the debate and launched into a full-scale analysis of this "pernicious work" in all earnest. Rubinshtein himself, sensing the oncoming storm, was ready to go to Canossa: he published a generally apologetic essay, reviewing the "Basic Problems in Organization of Russian Historiography," deflecting attention from himself with laudatory comments about A. A. Zhdanov's militant views and criticisms of another book on the history of western European philosophy by G. F. Aleksandrov.[10] As a safety device it proved of little value. Then he tried to explain timidly that his intention was not to prove the dominating influence of western historiography upon Russia, but the reciprocal impact of each upon the other. It was all of no avail.

Heavier cannon were soon moved into action when M. N. Tikhomirov appeared on the scene with a critical essay; Tikhomirov was no small fry from the Ivanov Institution of Education, but one of the eminent members of the Academy of Sciences.[11] He started with high compliments to Rubinshtein for presenting for the first time a historiography of such general and extensive scope. Though somewhat too bulky, with its 659 pages, says Tikhomirov, the work of Rubinshtein represents nonetheless a useful aid to

[9] V. V. Mavrodin, *Borba s normanizmom v russkoi istoricheskoi nauke.* (Leningrad, 1942).

[10] A. A. Zhdanov, *Vystuplenie na diskussii po knige G. F. Aleksandrova 'Istoriia zapadno-evropeiskoi filosofii' 24 iiunia 1947 g.* (Moscow, 1951).

[11] I. Mordvishin, "Obsuzhdenie knigi truda N. L. Rubinshteina." *Voprosy istorii,* No. 1 (1948), 154. N. L. Rubinshtein, "Osnovnye problemy postroenii russkoi istoriografii." *Voprosy istorii,* No. 2 (1948), 88-93. M. N. Tikhomirov, "Russkaia istoriografiia XVIII veka." *Voprosy istorii,* No. 2 (1948), 93-99.

historical science. Because the book appeared in 1941 amidst war conditions, Tikhomirov added, it escaped immediate attention of reviewers. The flattery ended here and the real attack started.

The time had now come, stated Tikhomirov, when Rubinshtein's *Historiography* must be examined more carefully, since the work includes not only statements and interpretations of debatable nature, but some which are simply incorrect. Tikhomirov limited his analytical review to the section on the eighteenth century. In this review he began by questioning the treatment of this period as such, convenient as it might be, through the scheme of examining individual historians rather than stressing, so to speak, the *Zeitgeist* in which they had lived and had written. Following that he came to the most vulnerable point, and the one where he intended to concentrate his attack—the Normanist theory.

It must be admitted that Tikhomirov, in criticizing Rubinshtein, displayed more poise than his fellows, less ideological fire, and more matter-of-fact argument, and therefore was the more convincing. He castigated the author not for raising the problem of Normanism and the subject of the origin of the Russian state, but for failing to include a description of the background against which the subject was to become a most heatedly debated issue. Rubinshtein erred particularly, argued Tikhomirov, where he dealt with Bayer's sojourn in Russia and his encounter with Lomonosov. Rubinshtein regards Bayer as an eminent scholar, perhaps the only one of his time in Russia. But, pray, says Tikhomirov, what did he produce? He had written something on the Scythians, something on Scandinavian sagas, but mostly on the role of the Normans delivering the blessings of Western civilization to the barbarous Russian tribes. Was this thesis, queries Tikhomirov, the result of profound research? Did he derive his observations from convincing evidence? Or was he swayed by the "barbarous" German elements at the court of Empress Anne, who was surrounded by the German clique headed by Bühren? Who knows?

In a strong nationalistic vein Tikhomirov then reminded Rubinshtein that the "prominent linguist," as he called Bayer, who knew Greek, Sanskrit, and Chinese, never deigned to learn Russian despite the fact that he studied Russian history. Why? asked Tikhomirov. Because, he answered himself, Bayer was a dull, uncultivated, militant German, devoid of any true interest in science. "Russian historiography of the eighteenth century was formed by Russians and for Russians," stated Tikhomirov. The Germans were mere technicians of science and as such they contributed their share where they were best and no more. This is, concludes Tikhomirov, where Rubinshtein went wrong. Eighteenth-century historiography was not dominated by Bayer or Schlözer, as one gathers from Rubinshtein's account, but by men like Tatishchev, Lomonosov, Shcherbatov, and later Karamzin.

Tikhomirov's attack was only the opening gun. There followed a five-day session, March 15-20, 1948, at an All-Union Conference of Heads of University Departments and Pedagogical Institutes, whose central theme was Rubinshtein's *Russian Historiography*. To this conference were invited also members of the Academy of Sciences and others associated with the field of Russian history. A parade of critics followed one another to the rostrum to list the sins committed by Rubinshtein. Some of these critics found that Rubinshtein's main failure was the bourgeois-idealistic views which he applied in his interpretation of Russian historiography. Some found faults in his failure to emphasize the original and independent historical thought Russian historians have demonstrated, and instead, stressing the methodology and philosophical background borrowed from western Europe. There were others who attacked Rubinshtein for portraying each historian as writing in some kind of an abstract environment; others added that he dealt with historians who give the impression that they lived in an environment of perfect harmony, free of conflicting views or interests. The result, these people complained, is a mere "portrait gallery" of historians, one linked to the other in some kind of an endless chain, elaborating a thesis that is merely a step further than that of his predecessor—"a true chain development." For this reason, as one critic concluded, Rubinshtein became a captive of a Miliukov, a Soloviev, or of a Bestuzhev-Riumin. For the same reason the work is politically colorless and carries only a "toothless criticism of the Normanist theory."[12]

The Rubinshtein case has been chosen as a typical one, so as to illustrate the climate in which the historians were then working. The cult of the individual was rapidly reaching its peak; formalism, cosmopolitanism, and the cultivation of a Soviet jingoism dominated intellectual life. One is therefore not surprised to find Rubinshtein chided for his failure to pay adequate tribute to such "coryphaei in Marxist historical science as V. I. Lenin and J. V. Stalin," while alloting so much space to bourgeois historians. This, one critic pointed out, might produce an "erroneous impression of the contribution Lenin and Stalin had made in the development of historical science." The same critic, A. M. Mal'kov, demanded that Lenin and Stalin should have preceded in importance such historians as Miliukov, Pavlov-Silvanskii, Struve, and Rozhkov.

Mordvishin criticized Rubinshtein for failing to show, as A. A. Zhdanov had clearly stated, "that Marxism was the greatest revolution in science"; for in failing to stress that, the author had committed the gravest error. Other sins pointed out were "academic objectivism," political sterility, and other terms borrowed from the harangue by Zhdanov, whose speech must have been the most fateful one in setting off the entire episode. Zhdanov himself accused Rubinshtein of "looking for an opportunity to say a good word about every historian"; and the more noble or bourgeois that historian proved to be, and particularly if he happened to be of foreign extraction, the more incense was burned by Rubinshtein while describing him. It was for this reason, Zhdanov concluded, that so much lavish praise was given to

[12]It was only in 1966 that R. A. Kireeva dared to include Rubinshtein's *Historiography* as one of the "most important works of Soviet scholars." See R. A. Kireeva, *V. O. Kliuchevskii kak istorik russkoi istoricheskoi nauki.* (Moscow, 1966).

29

such mediocrities as G. S. Bayer, G. F. Müller, or A. L. Schlözer. Characteristically, Professor O. L. Veinshtein, who originally praised Rubinshtein, now hastened to climb the bandwagon of critics and humbly confess how wrong he was when he wrote his original review.[13] Rubinshtein in the end promised to rewrite his work, taking into account the points that had been ticked off during the session as wrong. He never did, for he died in January, 1963.[14]

There is a conspicuous void for almost a decade from the time the *Historiography* of Rubinshtein was banned. This was partly due to the disruption of the war years, but mainly due to severe censorship during the later 1940's, as symbolized by the notorious and virulent attack by A. A. Zhdanov upon all writers. Not until the middle of the 1950's can we begin to trace signs of a revived interest and fruitful effort in the field of historiography. Aside from the four-volume study already mentioned there emerged several works concentrated on special periods and subjects related to historical writings, of which only some may be cited.[15]

[13]*Istoricheskii zhurnal*, No. 10 (1942), 119-122, carries the original review of O. L. Veinshtein. Cf.. *Voprosy istorii*, No. 6 (1948), 130-131, where he retreats from the original views.

[14]There is a rare obituary notice describing the plight of Rubinshtein in *Istoriia SSSR*, No. 3 (1963), 239-241.

[15]V. I. Astakhov, *Kurs lektsii po russkoi istoriografii (do kontsa XIX v.).* (Kharkov, 1965). V. I. Astakhov, *Kurs lektsii po russkoi istoriografii (Epokha promyshlennogo kapitalizma).* Part II. (Kharkov, 1962). S. V. Bakhrushin, "Istoriografiia Sibiri." *Sibirskaia sovetskaia entsiklopediia,* Vol. II (1931), 377-380. L. G. Beskrovnyi, *Ocherki po istochnikovedeniiu voennoi istorii Rossii.* (Moscow, 1957). L. G. Beskrovnyi, *Ocherki voennoi istoriografii.* (Moscow, 1962). L. V. Cherepnin, *Kurs russkoi istoriografii (do serediny XIX v.).* (Kharkov, 1960). L. V. Cherepnin, *Russkaia istoriografiia do XIX v. Kurs lektsii.* (Moscow, 1957). M. N. Chernomorskii, *Istorikovedenie istorii SSSR, XIX-XX vv.(Sovetskii period).* (Moscow, 1966). *Istoriia i istoriki. Istoriografiia istorii SSSR.. Sbornik statei.* (Moscow, 1965). *Istoriografiia istorii SSSR s drevneishikh vremen do Velikoi Oktiabrskoi sotsialisticheskoi revoliutsii.* V. E. Illeritskii and I. A. Kudriavtsev, eds. (Moscow, 1961). *Istoriografiia Sibiri (XVIII vek).* (Kemerovo, 1963). *Istoriografiia sotsialisticheskogo i kommunisticheskogo stroitelstva v SSSR. Sbornik statei.* (Moscow, 1963). A. I. Koblents, *Andrei Ivanovich Bogdanov, 1692-1766. Iz proshlogo russkoi istoricheskoi nauki i knigovedeniia.* (Moscow, 1966). V. N. Kotov, *Istoriografiia istorii SSSR (1917-1934 gg.).* (Kiev, 1966). S. I. Krandievskii, *Ocherki po istoriografii ekonomicheskoi istorii (XVII-XIX vv.).* (Kharkov, 1964). *Maloissledovannye istochniki po istorii SSSR, XIX-XX vv. (Istochnikovedcheskii analiz).* (Moscow, 1964). M. I. Marchenko, *Ukrainska istoriografiia s davnikh chasiv do seredini XIX st.* (Kiev, 1959). V. G. Mirzoev, *Prisoedinenie i osvoenie Sibiri v istoricheskoi literature XVII veka.* (Moscow, 1960). S. F. Naida and V. P. Naumov, *Sovetskaia istoriografiia grazhdanskoi voiny i inostrannoi interventsii v SSSR.* (Moscow, 1966). *Obzor istochnikov istorii KPSS (kurs lektsii).* (Moscow, Izd-vo Moskovskogo universiteta, 1961). (This work was withdrawn from circulation in the USSR shortly after its appearance. There are a few copies in the United States, one of which is in the Hoover Library.) *Ocherki po*

Aside from historiographies some Soviet scholars began to reappraise the so-called "bourgeois" historians of the pre-revolutionary period. The disdain with which these men were originally treated yielded to a more practical acknowledgement of service they rendered to historical science. As one writer, L. Ivanov, declares while reviewing the reissued works of Platonov: "We recognize the accumulated mass of factual information but sweep aside his interpretations."[16] Not only were the writings of the old guard recognized, but many of their works were republished, and the rich legacy they had left came to be utilized once again.[17]

According to one Soviet historian the writings of Soloviev and Kliuchevskii represent the "greatest achievement in bourgeois historiography of the second half of the nineteenth and early twentieth century." Accordingly, the complete works of Kliuchevskii were reissued. The sixth volume includes lectures on Russian historiography published for the first time.[18]

istoriografii sovetskogo obshchestva. Sbornik statei. M. E. Naidenov, S. F. Naida, and L. M. Papin, eds. (Moscow, 1967). S. L. Peshtich, *Russkaia istoriografiia XVIII v.* (Leningrad, 1960). V. I. Picheta,*Vvedenie v russkuiu istoriiu. (Istochniki i istoriografiia).* (Moscow, 1922). A. L. Shapiro,"Filosofskie voprosy v kurse russkoi istoriografii perioda imperializma." *Voprosy istoriografii.* (Voronezh, University of Voronezh, History Faculty, 1960). A. L. Shapiro, *Russkaia istoriografiia v period imperializma. Kurs lektsii.* (Leningrad, 1962). O. I. Shvedova, *Istoriki SSSR. Ukazatel pechatnykh trudov.* (Moscow, 1941). (This guide lists some 2,000 titles published by 800 historians during the XVIII-XIX centuries.) V. I. Strelskii, *Istochnikovedenie istorii SSSR: Period imperializma—konets XIX v.—1917 g.* (Moscow, 1962). V. I. Strelskii, *Osnovnye printsipy nauchnoi kritiki istochnikov po istorii SSSR.* (Kiev, 1961). M. N. Tikhomirov, "Nachalo russkoi istoriografii." *Voprosy istorii,* No. 5 (1960), 41-56. K. B. Vinogradov, *Burzhuaznaia istoriografiia pervoi mirovoi voiny i mezhdunarodnye otnosheniia 1914-1917 gg.* (Moscow, 1962). I. L. Sherman, *Sovetskaia istoriografiia grazhdanskoi voiny v SSSR (1920-1931).* (Kharkov, 1964).

[16]*Istorik-marksist,* No. 4 (1938), 156.

[17]As an example of the republished old works, there stands out the extensive history of S. M. Soloviev, *Istoriia Rossii* (Moscow, 1959-1966), 29 vols. In the Preface written by L. V. Cherepnin the author states: "To the Soviet reader the methodology of Soloviev is of course alien. . . . Nonetheless, to this day his work preserves its scholarly significance thanks to its rich historical material, interesting, valuable and lively observations on a number of past problems of our native land." See also A. M. Zhelekhvostseva, "Bibliograficheskaia spravka o S. M. Solovieve." *Istorik-marksist,* No. 3 (1940), 114-126.

[18]V. O. Kliuchevskii, *Kurs russkoi istorii.* (Moscow, 1937). 5 vols. Reviewed by V. Lebedev in *Istorik-marksist,* No. 4 (68), (1938), 143-145. *Sochineniia.* (Moscow, 1956-1959). 8 vols. Each volume is accompanied by valuable commentaries by A. A. Zimin, M. N. Tikhomirov, and others. Reviews of this edition appeared in *Voprosy istorii,* No. 8 (1958), 154-159, and in *Istoriia SSSR,* No. 2 (1957), 206-207. A reappraisal of Kliuchevskii by a Soviet historian is presented by Zimin. See A. A. Zimin, "Formirovanie istoricheskikh vzgliadov V. O. Kliuchevskogo v 60-e gody XIX v." *Istoricheskie zapiski,* No. 69 (1961), 178-196. V. O. Kliuchevskii, *Pisma,*

The emphasis on contributions made by pre-revolutionary historians proceeded from articles where they were first introduced to Soviet readers to publication of their works. Thus, reviewing A. E. Presniakov's two-volume *Lectures on Russian History*, Iu. V. Gautier highly praised the author while L. V. Cherepnin referred to Presniakov "as one of the most eminent Russian historians of the period of imperialism." He urged Soviet readers to consult Presnaikov's writings, in which they would find a mass of factual information and gather valuable observations despite the author's idealistic bourgeois interpretation of history.[19]

Other "idealists" and "bourgeois" historians came in for a reappraisal and reinterpretation. Such was, for instance, the case of V. I. Semevskii, in whom Soviet critics belatedly came to recognize one of the most outstanding historians of the Russian peasantry "despite the idealist-populist methodology" he used, for "the enormous factual material in his writings will long retain its significance for research students."[20]

A. A. Shakhmatov was another historian whose eminence and erudition came in for recognition by Soviet scholars. This distinguished linguist, archeographer and expert on the Russian chronicles regained his fully deserved recognition in Soviet historiography in 1952, when V. T. Pashuto published an article in *Voprosy istorii* in which he paid high tribute to Shakhmatov. Such praise had not been seen in print since 1922, when a special *In Memoriam* volume was published two years after the death of Shakhmatov. Written at the height of the "cult of the individual," when the "genius work of Stalin" and the "wise directives of the party" had to be incorporated while analyzing Shakhmatov's achievements, it is surprising that it appeared in print at all. Amidst the hosannas to the chief of state and censure of every "deviationist," this genuine tribute to A. A. Shakhmatov was most salutary.[21]

The reappearance of some of the distinguished historical works of pre-revolutionary years has been gratifying. To trace only a few of these, in some chronological order, we may mention two of the earliest reissues, those of 1918: M. M. Bogoslovskii's *Byt i nravy russkogo dvorianstva v pervoi polovine XVIII veka*, published in 1918; and M. K. Liubavskii's *Lektsii po drevnei istorii do kontsa XVI veka*, first published in 1915 and reprinted in 1918. In 1923 reappeared Iu. I. Gessen's *Istoriia Evreev v Rossii*, originally published in 1914. The well known study of N. P. Pavlov-

dnevniki, aforizmy i mysli ob istorii. (Moscow, 1968). See also A. I. Iakovlev. "V. O. Kliuchevskii (1841-1911)." *Zapiski Nauchno-issledovatelskogo instituta,* No. 6. (Saransk, 1946). M. V. Nechkina, "Istoriia izuchenii V. O. Kliuchevskogo." *Istoricheskie zapiski,* No. 84 (1969), 247-248.

[19]*Istorik-marksist,* No. 4 (1938), 145-148. See also L. V. Cherepnin, "Ob istoricheskikh vzgliadakh A.E. Presniakova." *Istoricheskie zapiski,* No. 33 (1950), 203-231.

[20]S. I. Volkov, "V. I. Semevskii (K nauchnoi biografii)." *Istoriia SSSR,* No. 5 (1959), 113-122.

[21]V. T. Pashuto, "A. A. Shakhmatov—burzhuaznyi istochnikoved." *Voprosy istorii,* No. 2 (1952), 47-73.

Silvanskii, *Feodalizm v drevnei Rusi*, originally published in 1907, reappeared in a new edition prefaced by M. N. Pokrovskii in 1924. Two outstanding monographs, one by Iu. V. Gautier, *Zamoskovnyi krai v XVII veke*, and the other by M. A. Diakonov, *Ocherki obshchestvennogo i gosudarstvennogo stroia drevnei Rusi*, originally published in 1906 and 1908 respectively, were republished in 1937. During the same year appeared the outstanding work of S. F. Platonov, *Ocherki po istorii smuty v Moskovskom gosudarstve XVI-XVII vv.*, printed first in 1899. The monograph was favorably reviewed in *Istorik-marksist*.[22] Another reissue of an old work was that of E. I. Zaozerskii, *Tsar Aleksei Mikhailovich v svoem khoziaistve*, dated originally to 1917, while in 1934 the republication of the well-known monograph of M. I. Tugan-Baranovskii, *Russkaia fabrika v proshlom i nastoiashchem. Istoricheskoe razvitie russkoi fabriki v XIX veke*, took place. The earliest edition of Tugan-Baranovskii's book goes as far back as 1898. Last, though surely not least, should be mentioned the republication in 1937 of V. O. Kliuchevskii's five-volume *Kurs russkoi istorii*, while the 1950's saw a reissue of his complete works, *Sochineniia* (Moscow, 1956-1959), in eight volumes.

B. PUBLICATION OF SOURCES AND THE
ARCHEOGRAPHIC COMMISSION

Increased research in Russian history, particularly in the earliest period where there is usually less ideological interference, necessitated not only improvement in methodology, but in search and use of original source materials. This resulted in a wider interest in allied fields of history, in such disciplines as paleography, numismatics, heraldry, historical geography, and, last though far from least, archeology. *Istochnikovedenie*, or the discipline dedicated to the study of historical resources, became a widely recognized field, and led to a wider search for new materials and a reevaluation of old ones.

A legion of scholars have surveyed various national archives and national and local museums, and examined most of the historical records found in these depositories. As a result of this careful survey V. N. Shumilov has published a description of the materials they examined in the State Central Archives. An equally valuable publication is the one that surveys all manuscripts kept in the Moscow Lenin Library, edited by I. M. Kudriavtsev.[23] The library of the Academy of Sciences has its own collection of manuscripts, chronicles, genealogical records and other source materials of vital importance to early Russian history. A second and much enlarged edition cataloguing these appeared in 1959, edited by A. I. Andreev. Under his able

[22] *Istorik-marksist*, No. 4 (1938), 153-156.

[23] V. N. Shumilov, comp., *Obzor dokumentalnykh materialov Tsentralnogo arkhiva drevnikh aktov po istorii SSSR perioda feodalizma XI-XV vv.* M. N. Tikhomirov, ed. (Moscow, 1954). I. M. Kudriavtsev, ed., *Muzeinoe sobranie rukopisei Gosudarstvennoi biblioteki SSSR imeni V. I. Lenina.* (Moscow, 1961-). Vol. I-.

33

editorship a most accommodating guide has been published, describing the Archives of the Leningrad division of the Institute of History.[24] Other guides worth mentioning are one by V. V. Lukianov, which describes the nature of the manuscripts kept in the Iaroslavl Museum and Archives, and the guide by V. I. Malyshev.[25]

In February, 1956, the Soviet Council of Ministers adopted a series of regulations for the preservation and utilization of national archival materials. Shortly after, the Academy of Sciences formed the Archeographic Commission headed by M. N. Tikhomirov. The Commission included some of the most prominent Soviet scholars drawn from all over the country. Its noble predecessor was the organization of the same name, which was set up in 1834 and, except for some organizational changes, functioned until 1948.[26] The Commission newly formed in 1956 differed from the preceding one in several aspects: it has improved the coordination of publication of sources, set up standards for transcriptions of names and places, and definition of archaic terms. The present Commission has founded two journals, one of general nature, *Istoricheskii arkhiv*, and the other, devoted to the publication of vital sources, headed *Materialy po istorii SSSR*. The Archeographic Commission also publishes an annual volume, *Arkheograficheskii ezhegodnik*, which includes summaries of works accomplished in the field of history during the preceding year. The Chief Archival Administration of the Council of Ministers since 1957 has published an Information Bulletin, which was renamed *Voprosy arkhivovedeniia* in 1961. This is a journal which systematically discusses the entire field of archeology, and examines current problems or outlines forthcoming projects.

The Archeographic Commission has improved the cooperation between the central organization and the peripheral museums and archival institutions. It has increased the efficiency of expeditions in search of new sources, and has organized regular meetings at which papers are delivered and discussed. Finally, the Commission in 1956 named a special committee in charge of restoration, conservation, and filming of historical documents.

[24]A. I. Andreev, ed., *Opisanie rukopisnogo otdela biblioteki Akademii nauk SSSR.* (Moscow, 1959-). Vol. 1-. *Arkhiv Akademii nauk SSSR. Obozrenie arkhivnykh materialov.* Vols. I-II, IV-V. (Moscow, 1933-1963). These volumes contain descriptions of collections of individual members of the Academy in the field of history, as well as of the institutions that carry on research in related fields.

[25]V. V. Lukianov, "Kratkoe opisanie rukopisei Iaroslavskogo kraevedcheskogo muzeia." *Kraevedcheskie zapiski*, Issue III (1958). (Iaroslavl, 1958). V. I. Malyshev, *Ust-Tsilemskie rukopisnye sborniki XVI-XX vv.* (Syktyvkar, 1960). A. I. Andreev, ed., *Putevoditel po Arkhivu Leningradskogo otdeleniia Instituta istorii.* (Moscow, 1958). *Opisanie kollektsii rukopisei Gosudarstvennogo arkhiva Iaroslavskoi oblasti XIV-XX vekov.* (Iaroslavl, 1957).

[26]On the history of the origin of the Archeographic Commission see Anatole G. Mazour, *Modern Russian Historiography.* (Princeton, N.J., 1958), 55-57 and *passim*.

The *Yearbook* has already proved of considerable value to scholars, having incorporated such historical records as those gathered by B. B. Kafengauz on the customs duty records of the eighteenth century (*Tamozhennye knigi*), records pertaining to the socio-economic history of eighteenth- and nineteenth-century Russia gathered by V. K. Iatsunskii, immunity charters of the sixteenth century found by S. M. Kashtanov, and the latest interpretation of the early Russian Code of Laws (*Russkaia Pravda*) by S. N. Valk.[27] Much of the published materials incorporates government-granted charters issued on various occasions, official acts and decrees of the twelfth to sixteenth centuries, and all kinds of legal acts pertaining to the formation of a central national government.[28]

A particularly notable achievement is the completion of a study and publication of the Chronicles which was begun in the middle of the nineteenth century, and finally finished in 1949. The success of this laborious task was due in no small degree to the formation of a group of highly qualified expert scholars at the Institute of History at the Academy of Sciences, headed by the eminent historian M. N. Tikhomirov. The Chronicles are accompanied by explanatory notations and textual commentaries.[29] In the course of this work, many newly uncovered Chronicles were published, such as the Piskarevskii Chronicle, found by O. A. Iakovleva and edited by M. N. Tikhomirov. An explanatory description of the Chronicles and their historical utilization is presented in the finest scholarly tradition by two experts, A. N. Nasonov and A. A. Zimin. Their books contain a comparative study of the published Chronicles, an analytical examination of each Chronicle, and citations of a general nature, serving as information to students of earlier periods in Russian history.[30]

[27] See Iu. O. Bem, "O rabote Arkheograficheskoi komissii Otdeleniia istoricheskikh nauk AN SSSR." *Voprosy istorii*, No. 9, (1961), 125-130. A. Ts. Merzon, "Ustiuzhskie tamozhennye knigi XVII v." *Problemy istochnikovedeniia*, VI, (1958), 67-129. K. V. Bazilevich, "Tamozhennye knigi kak istochnik ekonomicheskoi istorii Rossii." *Problemy istochnikovedeniia*, I, (1933). K. V. Bazilevich, "K voprosu ob izuchenii tamozhennykh knig XVII v." *Problemy istochnikovedeniia*, II, (1936). A. Ts. Merzon, *Tamozhennye knigi XVII v.* (Moscow, 1957).

[28] Among these stand out such publications as *Akty sotsialno-ekonomicheskoi istorii severo-vostochnoi Rusi kontsa XIV-XVI vekov.* (Moscow, 1958). 2 vols. *Akty feodalnogo zemlevladeniia i khoziaistva XIV-XVI vekov.* (Moscow, 1956-1961). 3 parts. L. V. Cherepnin, ed., *Pamiatniki russkogo prava.* (Moscow, 1956). 4 parts. L. V. Cherepnin, *Russkie feodalnye arkhivy XIV-XV vekov.* (Moscow, 1948-1951). 2 parts.

[29] D. S. Likhachev, *Russkie letopisi i ikh kulturno-istoricheskoe znachenie.* (Moscow, 1947). M. D. Priselkov, *Istoriia russkogo letopisaniia.* (Leningrad, 1940). *Polnoe sobranie russkikh letopisei.* (Moscow, 1841-1949). 25 vols.

[30] M. N. Tikhomirov, "Piskarevskii letopisets kak istoricheskii istochnik o sobytiiakh XVI—nachala XVII v." *Istoriia SSSR*, No. 3 (1957), 112-122. A. N. Nasonov,

The record of achievement of the Archeographic Commission is impressive. Under its direct or indirect guidance, during the short period since its establishment in 1956, several hundred volumes of documents of different kinds have been issued, most of which deal with social history. For understandable reasons it has had to include writings of prominent party leaders such as M. V. Frunze, M. I. Kalinin, or P. I. Stuchka, not to mention Lenin's writings, stenographic reports of party congresses, and similar materials.

A number of publications deal with foreign relations, with China, France, and Czechoslovakia. A six-volume work is dedicated to the problem of proletarian solidarity on a global scale. Newly published sources cover the Civil War and the intervention. Among these are original materials that deal with the problem of food supply of urban communities during the critical

"Letopisnye pamiatniki khranilishch Moskvy (novye materialy)." *Problemy istochnikovedeniia*, Vol. IV (1955), 243-285. See also "Materialy i issledovaniia po istorii russkogo letopisaniia." *Problemy istochnikovedeniia*, Vol. VI (1958), 235-274. A more general survey is presented by A. A. Zimin, *Russkie letopisi i khronografy kontsa XV-XVI vv.* (Moscow, 1960). The extensive works of M. D. Priselkov have convincingly shown the close relationship between philology and source studies (*istochnikovedenie*), particularly in early Russian history. The writings of Priselkov have not only proven his scholarship, but represent an outstanding achievement in both philology and history. M. N. Tikhomirov, ed. *Polnoe sobranie russkikh letopisei. Vologodsko-Permskaia letopis. Iosaifovskaia letopis.* (Moscow, 1954). A. N. Nasonov, "O neizdannoi rukopisi A. A. Shakhmatova: Obozrenie letopisnykh svodov." *Problemy istochnikovedeniia*, Vol. II (1936), 279-298. A. N. Nasonov, "Materialy i issledovaniia po istorii russkogo letopisaniia." *Problemy istochnikovedeniia*, Vol. VI (1958), 235-274. A. N. Nasonov, "Nachalnye etapy Kievskogo letopisaniia v sviazi s razvitiem drevnerusskogo gosudarstva." *Problemy istochnikovedeniia*, Vol. VII (1959), 416-462. A. N. Nasonov, "Ob otnoshenii letopisaniia Pereiaslavlia-Russkogo k Kievskomu (XI v.)." *Problemy istochnikovedeniia*, Vol. VIII (1959), 466-494. A. N. Nasonov, "Moskovskii svod 1479 goda i ego iuzhnorusskii istochnik." *Problemy istochnikovedeniia*, Vol. IX (1967), 350-385. A. N. Nasonov, "Maloissledovannye voprosy Rostovo-Suzdalskogo letopisaniia XII veka." *Problemy istochnikovedeniia*, Vol. X (1962), 349-392. A. N. Nasonov, "Lavrentievskaia letopis i Vladimirskoe velikokniazheskoe letopisanie pervoi poloviny XIII v." *Problemy istochnikovedeniia*, Vol. XI (1963), 429-480. A. A. Zimin, *Russkie letopisi i khronografy kontsa XV-XVI v.* (Moscow, 1960). S. N. Azbelev, *Novgorodskie letopisi XVII v.* (Novgorod, 1960). N. I. Il'in, *Letopisnaia statia 6523 i ee istochnik.* (Moscow, 1957). For further information consult the publication *Problemy istochnikovedeniia.* On the general history of the Russian Chronicles see D. S. Likhachev, *Russkie letopisi i ikh kulturno-itoricheskoe znachenie.* (Moscow, 1947). See also V. P. Liubimov, "Ob izdanii 'Russkoi Pravdy'." *Problemy istochnikovedeniia*, Vol. II (1936), 299-314. V. I. Buganov, "Russkoe letopisanie v sovetskoi istoriografii." *Voprosy istorii*, No. 12 (1966), 144-155. M. N. Tikhomirov, "Nachalo russkoi istoriografii." *Voprosy istorii*, No. 5 (1960), 41-56. In 1966 L. M. Marasinova published a most recently discovered collection of Pskov charters of the XIV-XV centuries. These include fifteen newly uncovered charters accompanied by commentaries and helpful notes of archeographic, geographic, and linguistic nature. See L. M. Marasinova, *Novye pskovskie gramoty XIV-XV vekov.* A. M. Sakharov, ed. (Moscow, 1966). See review in *Istoriia SSSR*, No. 4 (1967), 153-155.

. .

Civil War years, with the early stages of nationalization of industry, the organization of socialist production, and the forcible collection of provisions throughout the countryside.[31]

The amount of material proved so huge that it became necessary to adopt a specific classification scheme. It was decided to divide the bulk of the gathered materials roughly into four categories: sources exclusively for research, sources of academic character, popular writings, material of pedagogical nature. The first two were to be used predominantly by historians while the others were designed for the general reading public and for educational institutions.

A great deal of effort has also been made during the Soviet period in collecting literary writings of earlier centuries. These have been published and accompanied with commentaries by eminent scholars. Such, for illustration, is the publication by A. A. Zimin of the sixteenth-century writings of Ivan S. Peresvetov and his contemporaries. This volume constitutes an excellent source for the study of social and cultural conditions of the time in Russia; in 1549, Peresvetov wrote a lengthy treatise in which he urged social and military reforms, censuring the Boyars, particularly those elements who opposed social changes and defended their obsolete privileges.[32]

[31] *Sovetsko-kitaiskie otnosheniia, 1917-1957 gg. Sbornik dokumentov.* (Moscow, 1959). *Sovetsko-frantsuzskie otnosheniia vo vremia Velikoi Otechestvennoi voiny, 1941-1945 gg. Dokumenty i materialy.* (Moscow, 1959). *Sovetsko-chekhoslovatskie otnosheniia vo vremia Velikoi Otechestvennoi voiny 1941-1945 gg. Dokumenty i materialy.* (Moscow, 1960). *Boevoe sodruzhestvo trudiashchikhsia zarubezhnykh stran s narodami Sovetskoi Rossii (1917-1922 gg.).* (Moscow, 1957). *Mezhdunarodnaia proletarskaia solidarnost trudiashchikhsia v borbe s nastupleniem fashizma (1928-1932).* (Moscow, 1960). *Mezhdunarodnaia solidarnost trudiashchikhsia v borbe s nastupleniem reaktsii v voennoi opasnostiu (1925-1927).* (Moscow, 1959). *Iz istorii grazhdanskoi voiny SSSR (mai 1918—mart 1919).* (Moscow, 1960-). Vol. I-. *Boevye podvigi chastei Krasnoi Armii (1918-1922 gg.).* (Moscow, 1957). *Natsionalizatsiia promyshlennosti i organizatsiia sotsialisticheskogo proizvodstva v Petrograde (1917-1920 gg.).* (Leningrad, 1958-1960). 2 vols. *Rabochii kontrol i natsionalizatsiia promyshlennosti na Ukraine (mart 1917—mart 1921 g.). Sbornik dokumentov i materialov.* (Kiev, 1957). *Natsionalizatsiia promyshlennosti na Urale (oktiabr 1917—iiul 1918 g.). Sbornik dokumentov.* (Sverdlovsk, 1958).

[32] I. S. Peresvetov, *Sochineniia.* D. S. Likhachev, ed.; text prepared by A. A. Zimin. (Moscow, 1956). A. A. Zimin, *I. S. Peresvetov i ego sovremenniki. Ocherki po istorii obshchestvennoi mysli serediny XVI veka.* (Moscow, 1958). See also I. U. Budovnits, *Russkaia publitsistika XVI v.* (Moscow, 1947). I. I. Polosin, "O chelobitnykh Peresvetova." *Uchenye zapiski Moskovskogo gosudarstvennogo universiteta. Kafedra istorii SSSR.* Vol. XXXV. A. L. Sakketti, "Politicheskaia programma I. S. Peresvetova." *Vestnik Moskovskogo universiteta. Seriia obshchestvennykh nauk.* No. 1, (1951). G. N. Moiseeva, *Vaalamskaia beseda—pamiatnik russkoi publitsistiki serediny XVI veka.* (Moscow, 1958). *Povesti o zhizni Mikhaila Klopskogo.* Introduction and preparation of text by L. A. Dmitrieva. (Moscow, n.d.). (Klopskii was a fifteenth-century abbot of a Novgorodian monastery.) N. A. Kazakova, *Vassian Patrikeev i ego sochineniia.* (Moscow, 1960).

Another recent publication concerns Iosif (Sanin) Volotskii (1439-1515), Abbot of Volokolamsk monastery, often referred to as the "nursery of bishops." Abbot Iosif Volotskii was one of the militant leaders who campaigned against the Novgorodian heretics known as the Judaizers, and advocated absolute monarchical government. Of his forty "Messages" the most noteworthy one is entitled "The Enlightener." Iosif Volotskii was the most determined opponent of Nilus of Sorsk, the head of the heretical center in the upper Trans-Volga region. Religious issues that were vital for their time were at stake, such as the recognition of holy relics, of icons, of the church hierarchy and of monasticism. Some of the heretics denied the divinity of Jesus or refused to recognize the Holy Trinity.[33]

Istochnikovedenie or the science of study of historical resources became a widely recognized discipline. Aside from the publication of the periodical, *Problemy istochnikovedeniia,* scholars like M. N. Tikhomirov, S. A. Nikitin, and S. N. Valk have devoted special studies to this field. Although the two volumes published by Tikhomirov and Nikitin have been subjected to severe criticism by V. Shvarev, they still serve as helpful guides to documentary literature in the field of Russian history. Tikhomirov published a revised and much expanded volume some years later, but some of the bibliographical references in the new edition had been abridged.[34]

Another volume in the same field is by S. N. Valk. The author surveys Soviet documentary publications of Russian history from the earliest times to 1941. The chapters deal with materials covering the periods as follows: from earliest times to 1800; the nineteenth century; the twentieth century; the Soviet period. Although Valk's work has also been subjected to criticism, as were the two volumes of Tikhomirov and Nikitin (and what writings have not been subjected to criticism in Soviet historical literature!), still one will find much valuable reference material here.[35]

The publication of the numerous records has been done with extreme care and the commentaries in each case are of high scholarly quality. The

[33]*Poslaniia Iosifa Volokolamskogo.* A. A. Zimin and Ia. S. Lurie, eds. (Moscow, 1959). See also N. A. Kazakova and Ia. S. Lurie, *Antifeodalnye ereticheskie dvizheniia na Rusi XIV nachala XVI veka.* (Moscow, 1955).

[34]*Istochnikovedenie istorii SSSR. Kurs istochnikovedeniia istorii SSSR.* (Moscow, 1940). 2 vols. Vol. I by M. N. Tikhomirov lists sources from earliest times to the end of the XVIII century; Vol. II by S. A. Nikitin lists sources from the XVIII century to the 1890's. Each chapter includes lists of the most important historical documents published before and after 1917 and are accompanied by informative commentaries. A critical review of the two volumes by V. Shvarev may be found in *Voprosy istorii,* No. 12 (1951), 200-202. See also M. N. Tikhomirov, *Istochnikovedenie istorii SSSR.* Issue I. *S drevneishego vremeni do kontsa XVIII veka.* (Moscow, 1962). L. G. Beskrovnyi, *Ocherki po istochnikovedeniiu voennoi istorii Rossii.* (Moscow, 1957). This work begins from the earliest times and ends with the first decade of the XX century; it includes a survey of sources, chronicles, folklore, cartography, memoirs, and military records.

[35]S. N. Valk, *Sovetskaia arkheografiia.* (Moscow, 1948).

new editions are noted for their successful synchronization of all archeographic, paleographic, and orthographic differences. This enables both students of history and of linguistics to utilize the source materials more profitably. The technique of publication of sources has been developed to such a high degree that students of allied disciplines have been called upon to cooperate in the preparation of materials for publication. The formation of a coordinating center has proved of utmost benefit.

Much as has been gathered and published on Russian and Soviet foreign affairs, including an extensive world diplomatic history, much more is still left to be done. This has been acknowledged on many occasions by Soviet historians themselves. To advance this field in Soviet historiography it became necessary to publish more documentary sources in order to enable writers to handle broader themes or deal with subjects not yet written on. It was also necessary, as has been recognized by Soviet historians, to find a more general agreement on periodization. The American historian, Peter Gay, might rightly believe that "to all but the professional historians periodization is a mystery or a bore. Debates over just what stretch of time to subsume under a single name, or just what name to apply, appear as verbal games empty of serious content." But to Soviet historians to whom this has been a subject of frequent discussion the issue is critical. They have never been able to reach common consent as to the best method of periodization, although there has been an acceptable plan for handling the period between 1917 and 1920. There were and still are sharp differences of opinion, for instance, on the period of 1920-1940.[36]

Some suggested periodization of recent Soviet diplomatic history has met a more general approval. This suggestion is somewhat as follows: the years 1921-1925 can be considered as the period of establishment of normal diplomatic relations with the outside world; the period of peaceful coexistence is from 1925 to 1930; this is followed by the period of futile efforts at disarmament, by cultural and scientific relations with "bourgeois nations," and by establishment of friendly relations with the so-called "underdeveloped" and colonial countries. There is a greater consent on periodization in international affairs than in the field of domestic affairs. In part, perhaps, it is because of an increased demand for special monographic works on Soviet relations with individual countries, such as with the United States, Great Britain, Latin American states, China, Japan, or with the peoples of Africa.[37]

[36]See *Mezhdunarodnaia zhizn*, Nos. 2, 5, 7, 8 (1958).

[37]K. A. Krutikov, "Iz istorii sovetsko-kitaiskikh nauchnykh i kulturnykh sviazei." *Istoriia SSSR*, No. 4 (1959), 3-20. M. S. Kuzmin, "Iz istorii sovetsko-frantsuzskikh kulturnykh sviazei." *Istoriia SSSR*, No. 3 (1960), 140-143. V. A. Shishkin, "Iz istorii chekhoslovatsko-sovetskikh kulturnykh sviazei, 1918-1925 gg." *Vestnik istorii mirovoi kultury*, No. 6 (1960). A. M. Sakharov and G. M. Prokhorov, *Druzheskaia pomoshch i vzaimovygodnoe sotrudnichestvo (ekonomicheskie sviazi SSSR s promyshlenno-slaborazvytymi stranami Vostoka).* (Moscow, 1959). M. S. Getmanets, *Ekonomicheskoe sotrudnichestvo s slaborazvytymi stranami.* (Kiev, 1957). R. G.

The seventeenth and eighteen centuries occupy a special place in Russian history. Several significant events took place during this period: three most virulent nation-wide peasant revolts led by S. T. Razin, I. I. Bolotnikov, and E. I. Pugachev left deep imprints upon later events; the institution of serfdom crystallized sufficiently to assume its final form; and lastly, the monarchical regime consolidated itself to become the absolutist regime of Russia. Here we will refer only to the main sources that pertain to some of these critical events.

In the first place considerable progress has been made in the gathering of general written records that are related to the seventeenth and eighteenth centuries. These have been of enormous historical value. Such were the special collection of sources that appeared under various titles, some of which have already been referred to, *Materialy po istorii SSSR, Arkheografichskii ezhegodnik, XVIII vek,* or periodicals like *Problemy istochnikovedeniia* and *Istoricheskii arkhiv.* There are equally important publications of a more general nature, such as the series of documents entitled *Pamiatniki russkogo prava.* The fifth and sixth issues of this publication are of special interest since they deal entirely with the seventeenth and eighteenth centuries. The fifth issue includes a variety of sources such as government acts concerning land tenure, and acts of the Zemskii Sobor or National Assembly, particularly covering the fateful sessions of the years 1613, 1636, 1642, and 1651. The same publication also includes different official decrees while the sixth issue cites the complete text of the Code of Laws adopted in 1649, the *Sobornoe Ulozhenie.* Both of these issues are accompanied by most helpful scholarly commentaries.[38]

Other documents related to the period, compiled by M. T. Beliavskii, deal largely with the second half of the eighteenth century. This collection includes government manifestoes, decrees, and charters. Still another volume of historical value is the tenth volume of the *Pisma i bumagi Petra Velikogo.* Here not only official documents, but commentaries accompanying the volume, are of special importance to the student specializing in this period.[39]

Iskandarov, *K voprosu o pomoshchi slaborazvitym stranam.* (Moscow, 1960). *Sovetsko-arabskie druzhestvennye otnosheniia.* A. F. Sultanov, ed. (Moscow, 1961). L. A. Fitupi and V. D. Shchetinin, *Problemy ekonomicheskoi pomoshchi slaborazvitym stranam.* (Moscow, 1961). M. A. Kocharian, *Druzhba i sotrudnichestvo SSSR i Indii.* (Moscow, 1959). G. N. Oleinichenko, *Sovetsko-indiiskie otnosheniia (1954-1956).* (Moscow, 1958). M. A. Kocharian, *Sovetsko-indiiskie otnosheniia (1947-1958 gg.).* (Moscow, 1959). On Soviet relations with Latin American countries see: *Latinskaia Amerika v proshlom i nastoiashchem. Sbornik statei.* (Moscow, 1960).

[38]*Pamiatniki russkogo prava.* Issue V. *Pamiatniki prava perioda soslovno-predstavitelnoi monarkhii. Pervaia polovina XVII v.* L. V. Cherepnin, ed. (Moscow, 1959). Issue VI. *Sobornoe Ulozhenie tsaria Alekseia Mikhailovicha 1649 g.* K. A. Sofronenko, ed. (Moscow, 1957).

[39]*Dvorianskaia imperiia XVIII v. (Osnovnye zakonodatelnye Akty).* (Moscow, 1960). *Pisma i bumagi imperatora Petra Velikogo.* A. P. Glagoleva and E. P. Podiapolskaia, comps., B. B. Kafengauz, ed. (Moscow, 1956).

Source materials concerning a number of national minorities are now available to the historian. Thus several individual and collective works have emerged dealing with such subjects as early relations of Russia with Kabarda, Dagestan, Adygeia, Udmurtia, or Bashkiria. Equally important are the documentary publications dealing with Georgia or Buriatia. Many of these documents have never before appeared in print nor been utilized in original form. These offer excellent source material in the field of history of imperial expansion and relations with the national and racial minorities within the Russian state. The sources on Bashkiria are of special significance in the field of social and economic development.[40]

The institute of History of Belorussia has published a series of documents of the period of feudalism. Another documentary collection concerns the relations between the landowning administrative organs and the peasantry. This collection sheds much light on agrarian conditions in western Russia during the fifteenth and sixteenth centuries.[41] On the other hand, several Soviet publications have dealt with the eastern aboriginal population of Siberia. Thus, in 1960, a series of documents was initiated under the editorship of G. N. Rumiantsev on the history of Buriatia. Equally significant is the recent publication of the Iakutsk archival records, which include rare sources, chronicles official records of all kinds, private papers, and other materials. In particular, there are materials on agrarian developments, land claims, and other problems of the eighteenth century, compiled by G. P. Basharin. A search for all available documentary evidence is being carried on in Bokhara, by O. D. Chekhovich, since much remains to be accomplished here as in the adjacent areas. Finally, there is the economically important area of Nizhnii-Novgorod in the seventeenth century, dealt with in a recently published collection of sources edited by S. I. Arkhangelskii.[42]

[40]*Sbornik statei po istorii Kabardy.* Issues I-II. (Nalchik, 1951). *Kabardino-russkie otnosheniia v XVI-XVIII vv.* T. Kh. Kumykov, E. N. Kusheva, and N. A. Smirnov, eds. (Moscow, 1957). *Russko-dagestanskie otnosheniia XVII-pervoi chetverti XVIII v.* R. G. Marshaev, comp. (Makhach-Kala, 1958). *Russko-adygeiskie torgovye sviazi 1793-1860 gg.* (Maikop, 1957). *Istoricheskie dokumenty Imeritinskogo tsarstva i Guriiskogo i Odishskogo kniazhestva 1466-1770 gg.* Sh. V. Burdzhanadze, comp. (Tbilisi, 1958). *Dokumenty po istorii Udmurtii XV-XVII vekov.* A. A. Aleksandrov, V. E. Gusev, and P. M. Filimonova, eds. (Izhevsk, 1958). *Materialy po istorii Bashkirskoi ASSR.* B. D. Grekov, ed. (Moscow, 1936-1939). 3 parts. A. N. Usmanov, *Prisoedinenie Bashkirii k Moskovskomu gosudarstvu.* (Ufa, 1949). N. V. Ustiugov, "Bashkirskoe vosstanie 1662-1664 gg." *Istoricheskie zapiski,* No. 24 (1947), 30-110. N. V. Ustiugov, *Bashkirskoe vosstanie 1737-1739.* (Moscow, 1950).

[41]*Tiazhby Litovskikh krestian i zhitelei mestechek s upravleniiami imenii.* (Volnius, 1959).

[42]*Sbornik dokumentov po istorii Buriatii XVII v.* G. N. Rumiantsev and S. B. Okun, comps., G. N. Rumiantsev, ed. (Ulan-Ude, 1960). *Istoriia Iakutosoi ASSR.* (Moscow, 1955-1957). 2 vols. G. P. Basharin, *Istoriia agrarnykh otnoshenii v Iakutii*

C. REGIONAL HISTORY

The search for source materials in regional history reflects an intensified interest in that field following the Revolution. The field of socio-economic history of the constituent or autonomous republics stands out prominently. Thus, in the Ukrainian Republic, a legion of historians have turned their attention to the seventeenth century, during which the struggle for national survival was at its bitterest stage. For singling out this high–tension crisis in national history, the writers have found themselves accused of "bourgeois nationalism."

Many historians like A. I. Baranovich, P. K. Fedorenko, V. I. Legkii, K. I. Stetsiuk, and V. A. Diadichenko have enriched the historical literature of eastern Europe. Their writings deal usually with the subject of Ukrainian-Russian unification, with the common struggle against any form of feudalism, be it Russian, Polish, or Ukrainian. Some writers, notably, V. A. Golobutskii, concentrated their attention upon the Ukrainian Cossacks.[43]

A large number of monographs and articles on regional agrarian history have expanded Ukrainian and White Russian historical literature, and as a by-product contributed greatly to the seventeenth- and eighteenth-century periods of Polish history. A variety of subjects related to feudalism and the opposition against it, problems of hereditary and tenant claims, various forms of rents, peasant conditions, religious, economic, and social strife, all combined to keep the Ukraine in continuous ferment and are extensively dealt with in recent Soviet historiography.[44]

In other regional areas formerly neglected or barely explored, Chuvashia, Iakutia, Moldavia, the Caucasus, for instance, research in history has also expanded impressively. Feudal relationships, land ownership, and conditions of the peasantry have come under intensive research. The recurrent theme

(60-e gody XVIII—seredina XIX vv.). (Moscow, 1956). O. D. Chekhovich, "Bukharskaia letopis XVIII veka 'Ubaidullo-noma'." *Problemy istochnikovedeniia,* Vol. VIII, (1959), 191-227. S. I. Arkhangelskii, ed., *Nizhnii-Novgorod v XVII veke. Sbornik dokumentov.* N. I. Privalov, comp. (Gorky, 1961).

[43] A. I. Baranovich, *Ukraina nakanune Osvoboditelnoi voiny serediny XVII v.* (Moscow, 1959). P. K. Fedorenko, *Rudni Livoberezhnoi Ukrainy v XVII-XVIII vv.* (Moscow, 1960). V. I. Legkii, *Krestianstvo Ukrainy v nachalnyi period Osvoboditelnoi voiny 1648-1654 gg.* (Leningrad, 1959). K. I. Stetsiuk, *Narodni rukhy na Livoberezhnii i Slobids' kii Ukraini v 50-70kh rokakh XVII st.* (Kiev, 1960). V. A. Diadichenko, *Narisi suspilno-politichnogo ustroiu Livoberezhnoi Ukrainy kintsia XVII—pochatku XVIII st.* (Kiev, 1957). V· A. Golobutskii, *Zaporozhskoe kazachestvo.* (Kiev, 1957). V. A. Golobutskii, *Chernomorskoe kazachestvo,* (Kiev, 1960).

[44] D. L. Pokhilevich, *Krestiane Belorussii i Litvy v XVI-XVIII vv.* (Lvov, 1957). E. P. Shlossberg, "K voprosu ob izmenenii feodalnoi renty v Belorussii XVII-XVIII vv. (po dannym inventarei feodalnykh vladenii)." *Ezhegodnik za 1958 god,* pp. 61-104. Iu. M. Grossman, "Razvitie otrabotochnoi renty v gosudarstvennykh imeniiakh Russkogo otrabotochnogo voevodstva vo vtoroi polovine XVI—pervoi polovine XVII v." *Ezhegodnik za 1959 god,* pp. 94-100.

is the feudal peculiarities among nomadic peoples such as the Bashkirs or Kazakhs. A special session on pre-revolutionary history was held in 1954 in Tashkent, the proceedings of which were published a year later. Here the central theme was the patriarchal and feudal period in Central Asia and Kazakhstan.[45] A number of monographs on Kazakhstan dealt with such subjects as early relations with Russia, economic and political conditions, or social and economic developments in Bashkiria. A notable contribution was made by B. O. Dolgikh on racial and tribal composition of the native Siberian population in the seventeenth century.[46]

D. SOURCES ON EARLY SOCIO-ECONOMIC HISTORY

Socio-economic history has been enriched by several recently published documentary collections, one of which deals with general monastic land-holding practices, another of which describes more specifically the land tenure of the well-known Volokolamsk monastery, and a third which cites the records of the Office of the Moscow Metropolitan.[47] The subject is

[45]V. D. Dimitriev, *Chuvashia v XVIII v.* (Ioshkar-Ola, 1959). I. V. Kuznetsov, *Krestiane Chuvashii.* (Cheboksary, 1959). G. P. Basharin, *Zemelnye otnosheniia u iakutov v XVII-XVIII vv.* (Moscow, 1958). P. V. Sovetov, "Uslovnoe zemlevladenie v Moldavii XVI-XVIII vv. i ego otlichie ot drugikh stran Vostochnoi Evropy." *Ezhegodnik za 1958 god*, pp. 128-140. P. V. Sovetov, "Zakonodatelnaia politika po zemelnym pravonarusheniiam v Moldvaii (do serediny XVII v.)." *Ezhegodnik za 1959 god*, pp. 112-123. F. A. Grekul, "O 'reforme' 1749 goda v Moldavii." *Istoriia SSSR*, No. 1 (1961), 71-80. On the Tashkent session in 1954 see *Materialy nauchnoi sessii, posviashchennoi istorii Srednei Azii i Kazakhstana v dooktiabrskii period.* (Tashkent, 1955). *Istoriia Chuvashskoi ASSR.* Vol. I, *S drevneishikh vremen do Velikoi Oktiabrskoi sotsialisticheskoi revoliutsii.* Vol. II, *Ot Velikoi Oktiabrskoi revoliutsii do nashikh dnei.* (Cheboksary, 1966-1967).

[46]S. Z. Zimanov, *Obshchestvennyi stroi kazakhov v pervoi polovine XIX v.* (Alma-Ata, 1958). S. Z. Zimanov, *Politicheskii stroi Kazakhstana v kontse XVIII i pervoi polovine XIX v.* (Alma-Ata, 1960). N. G. Apollova, *Ekonomicheskie i politicheskie sviazi Kazakhstana s Rossiei v XVIII—nachale XIX v.* (Moscow, 1960). N. F. Demidova, "Sotsialno-ekonomicheskie otnosheniia Bashkirii v pervoi chetverti XVIII v." *Materialy nauchnoi sessii, posviashchennoi 400-letiiu Bashkirii k Russkomu gosudarstvu.* (Ufa, 1958), 23-67. B. O. Dolgikh, *Rodo-plemennoi sostav narodov Sibiri v XVII v.* (Moscow, 1959). See also *Narody Sibiri.* M. G. Levin and L. P. Potapov, eds. (Moscow, Academy of Sciences, 1956); translated into English (Chicago, University of Chicago Press, 1964).

[47]See *Sbornik statei k 70-letiiu A. A. Novoselskogo. Voprosy sotsialno-ekonomicheskoi istorii i istochnikovedeniia perioda feodalizma v Rossii.* (Moscow, 1961). Of special interest are the studies of I. A. Golubtsov and A. A. Zimin. See also *Zapiski otdela rukopisei Gosudarstvennoi biblioteki im. V. I. Lenina.* Issues XVIII and XXIV include the studies of S. M. Kashtanov and L. I. Ivin. Of the other documentary collections related to socio-economic history see the following: *Akty feodalnogo zemlevladeniia i khoziaistva XIV-XVI vekov.* Part II, A. A. Simin, comp., is of special interest. (Moscow, 1956). Part III, L. V. Cherepnin, comp. (Moscow, 1961). Of similar interest

43

pursued further by S. M. Kashtanov, who systematically investigated the various sixteenth-century charters, the nature of immunities these provided, the degree of independence they granted to feudal tenants or any other privileges they might have included. Having done this, Kashtanov then compiled a chronological list of charters granted between 1504 and 1584.[48] With the aid of other related documentary evidence Kashtanov successfully traced the legal and financial policies of the period and reached the conclusion that the immunities granted were conditional and implied payment of feudal fees. Large feudal grants often gave the landlord legal and administrative freedom, and a right to collect customs duties, without interference from the central authorities. Kashtanov analyzed 1,139 charters, citing places and dates of publication of those formerly published, and giving precise information about others, as to location of the originals and the contents of each. The cited charters cover a period of eighty years, 1504-1584.[49]

With the aid of the above-cited sources scholars have been able to present a much clearer account of the conditions prevailing among the peasantry, particularly those who lived on monastic property. Of these writers, A. G. Mankov managed not only to compile original documentary evidence but, on the basis of the amassed evidence, to write an excellent account of prevailing conditions among the peasantry throughout the sixteenth century.[50]

and importance is *Akty sotsialno-ekonomicheskoi istorii Severo-Vostochnoi Rusi* I. A. Golubtsov, comp., L. V. Cherepnin, ed. (Moscow, 1958).

[48] See S. M. Kashtanov, "K voprosu o klassifikatsii i sostavlenie zagolovkov zhalovannykh gramot." *Istoricheskii arkhiv*, No. 3 (1956), 211-217.

[49] See S. M. Kashtanov, "Immunitetnye gramoty 1534-1538 gg. kak istochnik po istorii vnutrennei politiki perioda regentstva Eleny Glinskoi." *Problemy istochnikovedeniia*, Vol. VIII (1959), 372-420. S. M. Kashtanov, "Khronologicheskii perechen immunitetnykh gramot XVI veka." *Arkheograficheskii ezhegodnik za 1957 god.* (Moscow, 1958), 302-376. *Ibid.*, for 1960 (Moscow, 1962), 129-200. S. M. Kashtanov, "Feodalnyi immunitet v gody boyarskogo pravleniia (1538-1548 gg.)." *Istoricheskie zapiski*, No. 66 (1960), 239-268. S. M. Kashtanov, "K probleme proiskhozhdeniia feodalnogo immuniteta." *Nauchnye doklady vysshei shkoly. Istoricheskie nauki*, No. 4 (1959). S. M. Kashtanov, "K voprosu o klassifikatsii i sostavlenii zagolovkov zhalovannykh gramot." *Istoricheskii arkhiv*, No. 3 (1956), 211-217. Some of the charters appeared in *Akty feodalnogo zemlevladeniia i khoziaistva.* Part I, L. V. Cherepnin, comp. (Moscow, 1951). See also *Akty sotsialno-ekonomicheskoi istorii Severo-Vostochnoi Rusi. Akty Troitse-Sergieva monastyria kontsa XIV—nachala XVI vv.* Vol. I. S. B. Veselovskii, comp. (Moscow, 1952).

[50] A. G. Mankov, "Opisanie prikhodnykh i raskhodnykh knig monastyrei Russkogo gosudarstva XVI v. [1531-1600]." In A. G. Mankov, *Tseny i ikh dvizhenie v Russkom gosudarstve XVI veke.* (Moscow, 1951), 246-269. A. G. Mankov, "Khoziaistvennye knigi monastyrskikh votchin XVI veka kak istochnik po istorii krestian." *Problemy istochnikovedeniia*, Vol. IV (1955), 286-306. *Materialy po istorii krestian v Russkom gosudarstve XVI v. Sbornik dokumentov.* A. G. Mankov, comp. and ed. (Leningrad, 1955).

E. SOURCES ON CENTRAL AND LOCAL ADMINISTRATION

During the few decades of Soviet rule, scholars have uncovered an impressive amount of entirely new source material on the history of the development of both central and local administration in Russia. One of the most original discoveries in the field was made by A. A. Zimin, who found a collection of legal documents that pertains to the causes of widespread revolts and government means of their suppression during the middle of the sixteenth century. Included in the recent discoveries were many new local charters (*gubnye gramoty*), formerly not even suspected to be in existence.[51]

An inventory of the court archives for the year 1570 and of archival materials of the Department of Foreign Affairs for 1614 revealed much that historians were unable to find elsewhere since most of the records were totally lost or destroyed during frequently occurring fires.[52]

Careful research was carried out during the 1950's by V. I. Buganov on the *Razriadnye knigi* (Books of Ranks), where government decrees, and military, civil, and court appointments were carefully recorded. This was a laborious task of examining more than two hundred books, carefully scrutinizing each, analyzing date of issuance, solving many editorial difficulties, and making extensive comparisons with related documents elsewhere. Cumulatively the arduous labor rendered much valuable data that pertains to military history, internal and external conditions, and the development of state institutions during the sixteenth century.[53]

[51]A. A. Zimin, *Gubnye gramoty XVI veka iz Muzeinogo sobraniia. Zapiski otdela rukopisei gosudarstvennoi biblioteki Leningrada.* Issue XVIII. (Moscow, 1956). "Ustavnaia kniga Razboinoi izby," in *Pamiatniki russkogo prava perioda ukrepleniia Russkogo tsentralizovannogo gosudarstva XV-XVII vv.* L. V. Cherepnin, ed. (Moscow, 1956). N. E. Nosov, "Gubnoi nakaz Novgorodskoi zemle 1559 g." *Istoricheskii arkhiv*, No. 4 (1959), 212-217.

[52]*Opisi Tsarskogo arkhiva XVI v. i arkhiva Posolskogo prikaza 1614 g.* S. O. Shmidt, ed. (Moscow, 1960). See also S. O. Shmidt, "K istorii sostavleniia opisei Tsarskogo arkhiva XVI veka." *Arkheograficheskii ezhegodnik za 1958 god.* (Moscow, 1959).

[53]V. I. Buganov, "Obzor spiskov razriadnykh knig poslednei chetverti XV—nachala XVII v." *Problemy istochnikovedeniia,* Vol. VI (1958), 153-158. V. I. Buganov, "Sokrashchennaia redaktsiia razriadnykh knig 1550-1636 gg." *Problemy istochnikovedeniia,* Vol. IX (1961), 270-279.

CHAPTER III

Early Russian History

A. ARCHEOLOGY IN AID OF HISTORY

The field of early Russian history, quite understandably, was woefully neglected during the early period following the Revolution. From the start there was an overpowering interest in more recent events, and in addition, a study of earlier history required more specially trained men, with linguistic equipment, including Greek and Latin, not to mention some of the western languages. Such qualifications among young students of this time were rare indeed. It was only after the vogue for current history had subsided in the 1930's and more properly trained students began to emerge that an interest in early history was revived.

Perhaps the earliest sign of departure from current history was demonstrated by an increased interest in medieval Russian, mainly feudal, history. There was an effort at a reevaluation of the entire period of medieval history in the light of a Marxist philosophy. In dealing with earlier periods Marxist historians were bound to come into serious conflict with "bourgeois historians" over a number of subjects. Clashing views came about over such matters as the origin of a class society in Russia, which in turn raised the larger question of whether western yardsticks could be applied to early Slavic society. There were the inescapable questions of the origin of the Kievan state, of the nature of early feudalism, of the status of the peasantry and the nature of social unrest in Kievan society.

Having rejected the old "bourgeois school," the new Soviet generation was compelled to start from scratch. They extracted from pre-revolutionary writings the items that suited them best and challenged the rest. Most of the Soviet students were compelled to turn once more to the original sources, and especially to recently uncovered materials; for this reason we find an increased interest in archeology. It was commonly admitted that the precise nature of early Russian society might always be subject to debate, but, it was argued hopefully, with the constant growth of factual material a broader knowledge might be gained. The increased amount of hard evidence was largely due to improved and expanded archeological excavations, to better techniques of comparative anthropology, and to advances in other social sciences. Various seminars were organized on subjects related to the early Kievan state, to the formation of a feudal society, to the status of the peasantry, or to the origin of social classes.

Thus it happened that the branch of science that could be utilized by historians and supported by state aid, archeology, came to make considerable advance. What is even more important, there was little interference from party officialdom either in writing or in the interpretation of discoveries by students of archeology. This is best attested by the large number

46

of young archeologists who enthusiastically joined various expeditions and returned with impressive data from many parts of the Soviet Union.[1] Among the legion who stand out prominently are B. A. Rybakov, T. S. Passek, S. B. Kiselev, and B. B. Piotrovskii.

New archeological discoveries were made in Novgorod under the direction of A. V. Artsikhovskii. For some three decades he was in charge of the Novgorod archeological expedition and served as editor of the Soviet publication *Arkheologiia* as well as of *Vestnik Moskovskogo universiteta. Seriia istorii.* His expeditions uncovered charters that greatly enriched historical information concerning the cultural heritage of early Slavdom in eastern Europe. Many new sources were discovered in the fields of folklore, *byliny, skazaniia,* and folksongs. The excavations in Novgorod have uncovered a wealth of birchbark documents dating from the eleventh to the fifteenth century. These represent the greatest archeological discovery, not to mention some 3,000 samples of medieval cloth, probably the largest such collection uncovered anywhere. Collectively these constituted vital source material for the study of the general cultural history of the Slavic communities, and prepared the way for the publication of literary writings of the feudal Russian period issued by the Department of Early Russian Literature of the Pushkin Museum. Finally, mention should be made of the impressive achievements of the Central Asian or Khorezm Archeological-Ethnographic Expedition that resulted in the publication between 1945 and 1953 of three volumes under the editorship of S. P. Tolstov.[2]

Other important contributions have come from B. A. Rybakov, who specialized in ancient peoples who inhabited the territory of the USSR, and did some significant research in Slavonic and Russian archeology,[3] and Tatiana S. Passek, who is the expert on the Neolithic and Bronze Ages in the USSR. In 1934 she directed excavations in Tripole where cultural monuments of Moldavian and Ukrainian early civilization were uncovered.[4]

[1] See, for instance, *Materialy i issledovaniia po arkheologii SSSR. Institut materialnoi kultury.* By 1967 the Institute had published 148 volumes of archeological reports. See also *Materialy po istorii Sibiri: Drevniaia Sibir. Sibirskii arkheologicheskii sbornik.* (1966). Also, *Trudy Khorezmskoi arkheologo-etnograficheskoi ekspeditsii.* S. P. Tolstov, ed. (Moscow, 1952-1958). 3 vols.

[2] A. V. Artsikhovskii, *Kurgany viatichei.* (Moscow, 1930). *Drevne-russkie miniatiury kak istoricheskii istochnik.* (Moscow, 1944). *Vvedenie v arkheologiiu.* (Moscow, 1947). *Raskopki na Slavne v Novgorode.* (Moscow, 1949). *Raskopki v Novgorode v 1952 g.* (Moscow, 1953). *Novye otkrytiia v Novgorode.* (Moscow, 1955). *Osnovy arkheologii.* (Moscow, 1955). A. V. Artsikhovskii and M. N. Tikhomirov, *Novgorodskie gramoty na bereste.* (Moscow, 1953-1962). 5 vols. P. I. Zasurtsev, *Novgorod, otkrytyi arkheologami.* (Moscow, 1967). *Trudy Khorezmskoi arkheologo-etnograficheskoi ekspeditsii.* S. P. Tolstov, ed. (Moscow, 1952-1958). 3 vols. L. V. Cherepnin, *Novgorodskie berestyanye gramtoy kak istoricheskii istochnik.* (Moscow, 1969).

[3] B. A. Rybakov, *Remeslo drevnei Rusi.* (Moscow, 1948). *Drevnosti Chernigova.* (Moscow, 1949). *Istoriia kultury drevnei Rusi.* (Moscow, 1948-1951). 2 vols. *Skazaniia, byliny i letopisi drevnei Rusi.* (Moscow, 1963).

[4] Tatiana S. Passek, *Tripolskaia kultura.* (Moscow, 1939). *Periodizatsiia tripolskikh poselenii.* (Moscow, 1949). *Ramnezemledelcheskie plemena Podnestrovia.* (Moscow, 1961).

A number of monographic studies have appeared under the editorial supervision of the Pushkin Museum. The above-mentioned writing along with others of scholars like A. A. Zimin, who contributed to the history of the formation of the state, benefited immeasurably from the archeological research.[5] Others, like Ia. S. Lurie or A. I. Klibanov, who wrote about the earliest humanist movements and religious heresies in Russia, are equally indebted to some of the research students in archeology.

Gradually the number of trained scholars increased and from among these emerged some eminent students of history who made considerable and lasting contributions. S. V. Iushkov, B. A. Rybakov, P. N. Tretiakov, and L. V. Cherepnin are only a few.[6] Subsidiary contributions, such as works on the genesis of capitalism in Russia or the development of light industry, followed these earlier studies. Among these were the monographic works and articles by students like B. B. Kafengauz, P. G. Liubomirov, and E. I. Zaozerskaia.[7]

As one examines the various Marxist-oriented studies in the field of Russian feudalism, what general conclusion or impression can be drawn? First, the consensus is that feudalism as a socio-economic formation is a result

[5]A. A. Zimin, *O slozhenii Prikaznoi sistemy na Rusi.* (Moscow, 1954). *K istorii voennykh reform 50kh godov XVI veka.* (Moscow, 1956). *Gubnye gramoty XVI v. iz Muzeinogo sobraniia.* (Moscow, 1956). (*Gubnye gramoty* were charters issued during the years when Ivan IV was a minor and the Boyars ruled the state. These were issued to authorize local governments to prosecute and punish various criminals [*likhie liudi*].) See V. O. Kliuchevskii, *History of Russia,* Vol. II.

[6]S. V. Iushkov, *Feodalnye otnosheniia i Kievskaia Rus.* (Moscow, 1924). *Ocherki po istorii feodalizma v Kievskoi Rusi.* (Moscow, 1939). *Obshchestvenno-politicheskii stroi i pravo Kievskogo gosudarstva.* (Moscow, 1949). For a complete list of Iushkov's publications see *Serafim Vladimirovich Iushkov. K 60-letiiu so dnia rozhdeniia i 35-letiiu nauchno-pedagogicheskoi i obshchestvennoi deiatelnosti. Bibliograficheskii ukazatel trudov.* (Moscow, Vsesoiuznyi institut iuridicheskikh nauk Ministerstva iustitsii SSSR, 1948). P. N. Tretiakov, *Kostromskie kurgany.* (Moscow, 1931). *Podsechnoe zemledelie v Vostochnoi Evrope* (Assartage in Eastern Europe). (Moscow, 1932). *Severnye vostochnoslavianskie plemena.* (Moscow, 1941; 2nd ed., 1953). *Srednevekovye zamchishcha Smolenshchiny* (Medieval fortresses of the Smolensk region). (Moscow, 1962). L. V. Cherepnin, *Materialy dlia bibliografii po istorii mordovskogo naroda.* (Saransk, 1941). "Izuchenie v SSSR problem otechestvennoi istorii perioda feodalizma." *Voprosy istorii,* No. 1 (1962), 34-66. *Issledovanie o "Russkoi Pravde." Proiskhozhdenie tekstov.* (Moscow, 1941). *Obrazovanie Russkogo tsentralizovannogo gosudarstva v XIV-XV vekakh. Ocherki sotsialno-ekonomicheskoi i politicheskoi istorii Rusi.* (Moscow, 1960). See *Voprosy istorii,* No. 9 (1961), 70-88, an article by A. M. Sakharov which complements Cherepnin's study. See also L. V. Cherepnin, *Russkie feodalnye arkhivy XIV-XV vekov.* (Moscow, 1948).

[7]B. B. Kafengauz. A complete list of his works is cited in *Absoliutizm v Rossii XVII-XVIII vv. Sbornik statei k semidesiatiletiiu so dnia rozhdeniia i sorokaletiiu nauchno—pedagogicheskoi deiatelnosti B. B. Kafengauza.* N. M. Druzhinin, ed. (Moscow, Akademiia nauk SSSR, Institut istorii, 1964), 508-518. *Severnaia voina i nishtadskii mir (1700-1721 gg.).* (Moscow, 1944). "Problemy istorii Rossii XVII-XVIII vv. v trudakh

of a "lawful" (*zakonomernyi*) stage of a fairly universal nature. Contrary to bourgeois interpretations, the Soviet view is that feudalism reflects a social relationship which rests on a basis of class principles.[8]

When the field of Soviet medieval history fell into neglect during the first decade or so of the Soviet regime, there were two reasons. One was the comparatively small number of trained men and the other the Soviet attitude toward what they call the "distance theory," namely, that it is not at all necessary to be removed from events in order to write history. Armed with Marxian dialectics they contended they could deal with recent history as successfully as with earlier periods. And for this reason, if for no others, the student of history was urged to "get nearer to contemporary events and demonstrate a bold and creative interest in the field." But practice had proven that such "bold and creative interest" was politically much more risky than medieval history or archeology.

If there was a lack of trained historians in these areas, there was no lack of discussion. During the late 1920's there were frequent debates about various phases of early Russian history. Some dealt with the formation of feudalism or the genesis of centralized national government in Russia, while others discussed the problem of periodization in history, a recurrent subject that has never been satisfactorily settled; some took up the growth of trade during the late medieval period, the question of primary accumulation of capital, or the origins of Russian capitalism.[9] The debates were often noted for their acrimonious attacks, for dogmatic preconception of "lawful" developments in history, and later for their injection of "the cult of the individual" into discussions. Combined, these left historians at a dead center without ever establishing any specific, generally accepted methodology. At the end of the proceedings it left the historian enervated, in a state of confusion, and, what was most sad, invisibly barred from becoming his own historian.

And still, despite these frequent, almost paralyzing obstacles, a constantly rising interest in early Russian history could be detected. If few outstanding works were published, at least the discussions kept alive the

sovetskikh uchenykh," in *Sovetskaia istoricheskaia nauka ot XX k XXII sezdu KPSS. Istoriia SSSR. Sbornik statei.* (Moscow, 1962), 137-186. "Voprosy istoriografii epokhi Petra Velikogo v osveshchenii sovetskoi istoricheskoi nauki," in *Piotr Velikii, Sbornik statei.* A. I. Andreev, ed. (Moscow, 1947), 334-389. *Istoriia khoziaistva Demidovykh v XVIII-XIX vv. Opyt issledovaniia po istorii uralskoi metallurgii.* Vol. I. (Moscow, 1949). *I. T. Pososhkov; zhizn i deiatelnost.* 2nd ed. (Moscow, 1951). P. G. Liubomirov, *Ocherki po istorii russkoi promyshlennosti XVII, XVIII i nachalo XIX veka.* (Moscow, 1947). *Ocherk istorii nizhegorodskogo opolcheniia 1611-1613 gg.* (Moscow, 1939). E. I. Zaozerskaia, *Razvitie legkoi promyshlennosti v Moskve v pervoi chetverti XVIII veka.* (Moscow, 1953). *Rabochaia sila i klassovaia borba na tekstilnykh manufakturakh v 20-60 gg. XVIII v.* (Moscow, 1960). *Manufaktura pri Petre I.* (Moscow, 1947).

[8]See, for example, L. V. Cherepnin, *Russkie feodalnye arkhivy.* (Moscow, 1948), 5.

[9]F. Ia. Polianskii, *Pervonachalnoe nakoplenie kapitala v Rossii.* (Moscow, 1958).

interest in the field. A paradoxical situation seemed to have formed in which, amidst paralyzing ideological futility, healthy scholarship came to emerge. Then, in addition to the problems already mentioned, the assignment of paying proper respect to the "cult of the individual" in history was added. It was in the light of this principle that figures like Ivan IV or Peter I were to be represented. Not until the middle of the 1950's was the historian relieved from the Stalinist burden that rested upon him.

One of the subjects frequently debated and frequently subjected to withering criticism was the genesis of feudalism in eastern Europe. The debates usually centered around the effort to find some kind of chronological framework into which one might fit the early period of Russian history. The subject was handled with unusual skill and a fair degree of success by B. A. Rybakov, in *Ocherki po istorii russkoi derevni X-XIII vv.* (Moscow, 1956), aided mainly by his recently conducted archeological excavations. Enjoying the advantage of richer source material, Rybakov and others were able to produce a more convincing account and interpretation of the development of Russian feudalism.

Rybakov plausibly argues that the turning point in the early period of the Slavic tribes was the first century of our era. By the fourth century the basis for ancient tribal forms virtually vanished. Hereafter, definite signs of a formation of a feudal order, particularly in the Dnieper region, become increasingly clear. Adjacent to the steppes and forest zones there is detected a symptomatic decline of tribal relationship which, as elsewhere, yielded to feudal forms. The family basis shows a decline, and larger social units absorbing the family commence to appear on the stage of communal life. The family was held together by economic ties, but subsidiary to large social groupings in charge of functions the family was incapable of coping with. Adding to the Chronicles, and the archeological, ethnographic, and philological evidence that supports his thesis, Rybakov now carries the interpretation further, discussing the early form of the commune or *mir* which came to prevail among the eastern Slavs.[10]

Archeological research has uncovered that the gradual shift from collective to individual production and from collective to individual property ownership brought social inequality. This is particularly borne out by the character of the articles and the increased number of coins found during excavations. There is further evidence of increased foreign trade during the seventh and eighth centuries, judging by the presence of coins and other evidence of foreign tradesmen.

Rybakov also studied the genesis of the state among eastern Slavs. Basing his conclusions on a variety of theories cautiously derived from his field work, he came to accept the view that the core of earliest Russian statehood must have been sometime during the sixth century in the area of the Ros, a tributary of the Dnieper. Other tribes followed fairly similar patterns of

[10]See *Ocherki istorii SSSR*, Vol. II. On the crisis of the institution of slavery and the genesis of feudalism see particularly pp. 831-833 and 877-878; on the institution of the *mir* see pp. 837-841 and 850-852.

settlement by joining neighboring communities. Eventually this gave rise to a large federated community which became the basis of the early Slavic state, Kievan Rus.[11]

Soviet scholars readily admit that there are still a goodly number of questions concerning the formation of the Kievan feudal society that need to be clarified. But they also believe that the basic principles are well established, that it is only a matter of studying minor details before the entire subject is thoroughly explored. The general scheme which indicates the transformation of the early Slavic peoples from the primitive communal condition to a class society, followed by a feudal and then capitalistic order, has been accepted as an established fact. What remains to be done is further study of the economic factors which led to such a transformation. This must include methods of production and acquisition of means of production. Having reached that conclusion, Soviet scholars now believe that they have totally undermined the entire Normanist theory. The Norman interpretation, which holds that the earliest Russian state was established at Kiev under Norse leadership, is nothing but a bourgeois philosophy of history to serve imperialistic ends, they say. The Russian state, they assert, had already been formed long before anyone had ever heard of the Vikings.

These conclusions are comforting to Marxist historians since they fit neatly into their own philosophy. To substantiate this, Soviet historians have utilized the latest archeological discoveries, which they believe cannot be lightly dismissed. A few recent works based on the latest discoveries serve as illustration. These reveal the favorable agricultural conditions that already prevailed in Kiev, Novgorod, and elsewhere prior to the formation of the state. In this pre-feudal system, advanced agricultural implements to suit the type of soil to be tilled were widely employed, and they continued to be used during the feudal era for some time.[12]

Of all the studies on early Kievan Russia, or as Soviet historians prefer to call the field, medieval Russian history, the period of the seventh to the tenth centuries was perhaps the most explored, while the following centuries received less attention. Of the various studies, the ones by L. V. Cherepnin deserve particular attention.[13] In studying the *smerds,* commonly regarded as the

[11]See *Istoriia SSSR.* Vol. I, *Pervobytno-ovshchinnyi rabovladelcheskii stroi. Period feodalizma.* (Moscow, 1956), 12-40. Chapters 1 and 2 were written by B. A. Rybakov.

[12]V. V. Sedov, *Selskie poseleniia tsentralnykh raionov Smolenskoi zemli.* (Moscow, 1960). Note particularly pp. 73-75. V. P. Levasheva, *Selskoe khoziaistvo. Ocherki po istorii russkoi derevni X-XIII vv.* In *Trudy Gosudarstvennogo istoricheskogo muzeia.* Issue 32. (Moscow, 1956). V. I. Dovzhenok, "Ob urovne razvitiia zemledeliia v Kievskoi Rusi." *Istoriia SSSR,* No. 5 (1960), 59-74. A. V. Kirianov, "Istoriia zemledeliia novgorodskoi zemli X-XV vv." *Materialy i issledovaniia po arkheologii SSSR,* No. 65 (1959).

[13]L. V. Cherepnin, "Izuchenie v SSSR problem otechestvennoi istorii perioda feodalizma." *Voprosy istorii,* No. 1 (1966), 34-66. L. V. Cherepnin, *Obrazovanie Russkogo tsentralizovannogo gosudarstva v XIV-XV vekakh. Ocherki sotsialno-*

51

land-owning free peasants, Cherepnin notices that in the course of time there is less reference to that class and eventually it is hardly noted. This, in his view, confirms the belief that feudalism gradually established itself and succeeded in altering the status of the *smerd* class entirely. The argument of Cherepnin is that the *smerds*, dwelling in communities, were most likely tied by degrees to the feudal estates. From this he deduced further that the decline of the *smerd* class confirms the opinion that sometime during the twelfth or thirteenth century the state yielded entirely to landlord feudalism.

Another historian, I. I. Smirnov, expanded Cherepnin's thesis a step further. Smirnov believes that by the twelfth and thirteenth centuries the *votchina* or patrimonial estate, which was as a rule held on service tenure, had also undergone substantial changes in its structure. Whereas prior to the twelfth century, Smirnov says, the *votchina* represented a feudal economy based on the *cheliad* or household servants, the new social formation became the *verv*, the commune, or *mir*, including serf household labor. Thus, observes Smirnov, the old social organization absorbed the *verv* as well as the *smerd*, making them all dependents of the feudal prince.[14] Smirnov considers these as the first signs of feudal development, the *votchina* becoming a well-established seigniory. This assertion has not been accepted unanimously by other Soviet scholars, who maintain that though Smirnov's thesis is well construed, the subject requires further research and additional evidence before it can be entirely accepted. Critics also contend that Smirnov's deduction is not based on a wide geographical range. The political and economic dependence of the commune upon the *votchina* came later, and not throughout the entire country, and therefore some doubts linger as to whether Smirnov's thesis is nationally valid. Furthermore, if the theory is correct it inadvertently confirms the small role the *votchina* played in the economic and social life of Kievan Russia during the preceding centuries. This, then, destroys all accepted theories about the nature of Kievan society and the Kievan state.

Smirnov has also made a study of the status of the *kholop* class, or domestic serfs, in Kievan Russia during the eleventh and thirteenth centuries. The author examined minutely the laws that concerned the *kholops* during the eleventh century. These frequently refer to the "free men" who own *kholops*.[15] As one examines the laws of the next two centuries, Smirnov points out, the importance of the *kholop* rises, since not only the princely domains, but the boyar *votchina*, and the estates owned by the church, all

ekonomicheskoi i politicheskoi istorii Rusi. (Moscow, 1960). L. V. Cherepnin, "Iz istorii formirovaniia klassa feodalno-zavisimogo krestianstva na Rusi." *Istoricheskie zapiski,* No. 56 (1956), 235-264.

[14] I. I. Smirnov, "Problema 'smerdov' v Prostrannoi Pravde." *Istoricheskie zapiski,* No. 64 (1959), 225-302.

[15] I. I. Smirnov, "K probleme kholopstva v Prostrannoi Pravde. Kholop i feodalnaia votchina." *Istoricheskie zapiski,* No. 68 (1961), 238-270.

claim the *kholop* as property. The difference between the *smerd* and the *kholop* becomes less discernible and by the twelfth century the latter became an integral part of the socio-economic system of feudal Kievan society. The study leaves several problems unanswered. For instance, what precisely did the *kholop* represent in the preceding century? Similarly, it could be queried, what precisely was the change that took place during the following two centuries? And while pursuing the subject further it might be asked, what was the nature of the socio-economic relationship during the period discussed by the author? Professor Smirnov either fails to consider these questions or has not yet sufficiently verified some pertinent aspects of the problem.

We find an increased interest in the development of towns in early Russian history. In 1956 there appeared a new and enlarged edition of M. N. Tikhomirov's study of early Russian towns.[16] His contention is that during the feudal period the towns served not only as centers of trade and commerce, but became part of a feudal order that prevailed for some time. His conclusion is that the appearance of towns marked the beginning of a division of labor in early Russian society during the feudal period.[17]

An extensive study of trade, commerce, and social conditions in early Russian feudal towns was done by M. K. Karger.[18] A closely related study by B. A. Rybakov explores trade in early Kievan Russia by way of extensive archeological work. Since Rybakov's study centered mainly around the area of Liubach, and the final results have not yet been made public, it remains to be seen whether it will add new evidence. M. F. Luchniskii and V. L. Ianin deal with the weight and currency systems of early Russia, both of which became, according to these writers, well established during the tenth century. According to Ianin, Kievan money and weight systems were highly developed, which attests to the advanced economic conditions the state had already reached during the eleventh century.

Archeology rendered considerable aid to the study of early Kievan history. Along with the written records such as charters, inventories, and codes of laws, other forms of evidence such as artifacts and inscriptions casting light on linguistic peculiarities came into scholars' hands. These, along with other available records, came to the aid of the historian to recreate a clearer picture of conditions during the tenth to the fourteenth centuries. A considerable group of scholars who utilized the historical and archeological sources recreated descriptions of the peasantry, the agricultural economy, type of agricultural produce, form of implements, and general social conditions. To mention only a few, these include

[16]M. N. Tikhomirov, *Drevnerusskie goroda.* 2nd ed. enlarged and revised. (Moscow, 1956).

[17]M. N. Tikhomirov, *Drevnerusskie goroda.* See also *Srednevekovaia Moskva XIV-XV vekakh.* (Moscow, 1946; 2nd ed., 1956).

[18]*Drevnii Kiev.* (Moscow, 1959-1961). 2 vols. *Istoriia Kieva.* (Kiev, Ukrainian Academy of Sciences, 1963-1964). 2 vols.

works by A. D. Gorskii, N. A. Gorskaia, I. U. Budovnits, and G. E. Kochin. A. D. Gorskii has written an admirable account of the economic conditions of the northeastern peasantry of the fourteenth and fifteenth centuries. N. A. Gorskaia dealt with a subject related to agricultural conditions—implements used by the peasantry during the second half of the sixteenth century. I. U. Budovnits made a special study of socio-political thought in early Russia, while G. E. Kochin's research was mostly in the field of agricultural development during the thirteenth century.[19]

Most of the studies of the early period of agricultural economy are limited in scope both territorially and chronologically. For example, the works of Gorskii concentrate largely in the area of the northwest; N. A. Gorskaia chose to study only central regions. Others, such as K. N. Koptev, centered attention mainly upon Pskov and Novgorod. Only G. E. Kochin pioneered a more general approach to agriculture throughout Russia. This study covers standards of soil tilling, types of soil in various localities, and kinds of tools employed in the different areas. Kochin has studied the means of colonization used by the state, and also the widely applied three-field system in northwestern Russia during the early half of the fifteenth century, as shown by charters and other records of the time.

The overall impression one gathers from the original sources, and there are not too many, as well as from the works of various scholars, is that methods of agriculture remained primitive and unaltered for a long period. Even the political crises which recurred from time to time hardly affected agricultural progress or accelerated the tempo of advancement, as is so well shown by the study of A. D. Gorskii.

B.   B. D. GREKOV (1882-1953)

Recently opened archival depositories have offered the historian the rare opportunity to start afresh, either with a reinterpretation of an existing subject or initiation of an entirely new one. Successful efforts have been made in both directions, as illustrated by the distinguished scholar B. D. Grekov (1882-1953), whose work on the rural economy of early Kievan society represents a significant contribution to historical science.

Grekov's studies began with his research on contracts of landless Novgorod peasants *(Novgorodskie bobylskie poriadnye),* published in 1912 as his M.A.

---

[19] A. D. Gorskii, *Ocherki ekonomicheskogo polozheniia krestian severo-vostochnoi Rusi XIV-XV vv.* (Moscow, 1960). N. A. Gorskaia, "Zemledelcheskie orudiia v tsentralnoi chasti Russkogo gosudarstva vtoroi poloviny XVI—nachala XVII v." *Materialy po istorii selskogo khoziaistva i krestianstva SSSR.* Vol. III. (Moscow, 1959). I. U. Budovnits, *Obshchestvenno-politicheskaia mysl' drevnei Rusi (XI-XIV vv.).* (Moscow, 1960). G. E. Kochin, "Razvitie zemledeliia na Rusi s kontsa XIII po konets XV v." *Voprosy ekonomiki i klassovykh otnoshenii v Russkom gosudarstve XII-XVII vekov. Pamiatniki istorii Kievskogo gosudarstva IX-XII vv. Sbornik dokumentov.* G. E. Kochin, comp.; preface by B. D. Grekov. (Leningrad, 1936).

54

dissertation. Two years later he published studies on the household of the Novgorod St. Sophia, its organization and internal relations within the patrimonial estate *(Novgorodskii dom Sv. Sofii. Opyt izucheniia organizatsii i vnutrennikh otnoshenii krupnoi tserkovnoi votchiny).* In 1926-1927 there appeared a more thorough investigation of the economic history of the Novgorod St. Sophia household *(Ocherki po istorii khoziaistva Novgorodskogo Sofiiskogo doma XVI-XVII vv.)* Here Grekov already cast aside the juridical interpretation of feudalism prevailing at the time and came to emphasize the socio-economic aspects of feudalism. He centered his study on the St. Sophia household and estate, minutely scrutinizing data related to the peasants, to the serfs, the landless peasantry, and other social groups; defining each, describing the status, the economic place, and the legal rights each was entitled to, if any, he cumulatively produced the most thorough account of Novgorodian society in this period.

Eventually B. D. Grekov turned his attention to early Russian history and the eastern Slavs. In 1929 he published his first general work on the history of Kievan Rus under the title *Povest vremennykh let o pokhode Vladimira na Korsun.* This was followed by his reexamination of feudal relations in Kievan society, *Feodalnye otnosheniia v Kievskom gosudarstve.* An entirely new, revised and considerably enlarged edition under the title of *Kievskaia Rus* was published in 1949. This capital work is based on written records, as well as archeological, linguistic, and ethnographic documents. Grekov examined every phase of life in Kievan Russia—economic, social, political, and cultural.

As a result of this extensive research Grekov came to refute the often mentioned theory that slavery in Kievan society was the cause of its decline and eventual dismemberment. Grekov minimizes the extent of slavery and argues that the eastern Slavs passed from communal to feudal society, by-passing slavery altogether. He shows further that the economic basis of Kievan Rus was a highly developed agricultural system, and not hunting or trapping as believed by others, thereby also demolishing the view of a backward economic state among the eastern Slavs, often referred to as a part of the Normanist theory. By the ninth century, Grekov asserts, Kiev was already noted as a well-organized state.[20] Simultaneously he challenged the point of view of M. S. Hrushevskii, who regarded Kievan Russia as exclusively a Ukrainian state. Grekov's thesis is that Kievan Rus never was an exclusively Ukrainian state, but a common cradle of Russian, Ukrainian, and White Russian culture. In his *Kultura Kievskoi Rusi,* published in 1944, Grekov cites additional evidence of the high cultural level Kievan Russia had reached, the international role it had played, and the generally advanced stage it achieved.

Grekov also studied the western and southern branches of Slavdom and their legal system *(Pravda).* As a result of his research in this field he published in 1948 a monograph entitled *Vinodolskii statut ob obshchestvennom*

[20]B. D. Grekov, *Kievskaia Rus.* 2nd ed. (Moscow, 1949). B. D. Grekov, *Borba Rusi za sozdanie svoego gosudarstva.* (Moscow, 1945).

i politicheskom stroe Vinodola, followed three years later by a sequential volume, *Politsa. Opyt izucheniia obshchestvennykh otnoshenii v Politse XV-XVII vv.* Shortly before his death in 1953, Grekov completed his last work, *Polskaia Pravda.*

Above all else, Grekov's interest was focused on the peasantry. In 1926, he completed his monographic study, *Iuriev den i zapovednye gody,* and four years later his research on the origins of serfdom in Russia, *Proiskhozhdenie krepostnogo prava v Rossii.* Cumulatively Grekov's works present a full picture of the peasantry from the ninth to the seventeenth century, culminated by a general survey he published in 1940, *Glavneishie etapy v istorii krepostnogo prava v Rossii,* in which he traces the significant stages in the development of the institution of serfdom.

Grekov's imposing works should not obscure several of his outstanding short articles such as "Monastyrskie detenyshi" or "Krestiane novoporiad-chiki," published in 1945 and 1946, respectively. Shortly before his death his much enlarged major work appeared in a two-volume edition, *Krestiane na Rusi s drevneishikh vremen do XVII v.* This work culminates a lifetime effort, and serves either to reinforce or to refute many of the former theories on the origin of serfdom in Russia by scholars like M. A. Diakonov or V. O. Kliuchevskii, who based their theories on rent-contract and indebtedness, respectively. With trenchant analytical skill, Grekov presents the picture on a much wider canvas, analyzing the peasantry of all eastern Europe, including Lithuania and Poland.

Grekov reveals an amazingly broad grasp and understanding of historical problems. He edited a series of documentary collections on the development of feudal factories, on the legal system, and on Central Asian history. He demonstrated a keen interest in historiography and was the author of several essays in which he analyzed the historical views of V. I. Lenin, M. N. Pokrovskii, V. G. Vasilevskii, and S. A. Zhebelev. He was also author of several textbooks, notably *Istoriia SSSR. Istoriia kultury drevnei Rusi.*[21]

Not even Grekov could avoid becoming involved in the threadbare arguments with the Normanists. He believed that the influence of the Scandinavians was negligible in the establishment of the early Kievan state. Grekov refuted the argument of the Normanists that Kievan economic life was based predominantly upon trade centered largely in towns. His argument was that the economy of early Kievan society was primarily agrarian in nature, and that the peasantry played a paramount role, forming the basis of Kievan economic growth while trade was only a subsidiary factor. It was because of the predominance of agriculture that Kievan society experienced the transformation into a feudalistic one. His contention was impressively backed by much newly published archival material.

[21]The most important works of B. D. Grekov are available only in a four-volume edition of collected works, *Izbrannye trudy.* (Moscow, 1957-1960). See also: B. D. Grekov, *Materialy k bibliografii uchenykh SSSR. Seriia istorii.* 2nd ed. (Moscow, 1947). V. I. Shunkov, "Grekov, B. D. Tvorcheskii put." *Sbornik: Akademiku B. D. Grekovu ko dniu 70-letiia.* (Moscow, 1952).

In analyzing Kievan society, Soviet historians came to question another former belief, that the peasantry was originally free, and that only at the end of the sixteenth century had they lost their freedom with the establishment of the institution of serfdom. In recent years this view has come to be radically revised, leading to the firm conviction that peasant freedom had in fact been curbed long before the assumed dates. The various obligations imposed upon the peasantry at a much earlier date had already represented a serious encroachment upon the peasant's economic independence, his political freedom, and his legal status.

Soviet historians also came to question the entire theory that serfdom originated from the special problems facing the state. Serfdom resulted, according to the Soviet view, mainly from the aspiring ambitions of the pampered upper classes, whose interests the state most carefully took to heart. The protective, sheltering policy of the state led to the institutionalized form of peasant-landlord relationship, which by the turn of the seventeenth century had assumed an established form within Russian society.

C. RISE OF A CENTRALIZED STATE

The decline of Kievan Russia, which led to the eventual shift northward of the national center, has been widely discussed by Soviet historians, notably by B. A. Rybakov, V. T. Pashuto, and L. V. Cherepnin, among many others.[22] According to Rybakov, Kievan Russia's decline is explained by the inherent weaknesses of the peculiar territorial and political bonds that held the eastern Slavs together from the earliest times. V. T. Pashuto, on the other hand, endeavors to show that feudalism in Kievan and later Russian society was based on the principle of a vassalage system similar to the one known in western Europe, and which had similar effects upon society. Basically this thesis is not too different from the views held by Soloviev and later by Kliuchevskii, who placed all responsibility on the "vagrant" princes with their retinues and the chaotic people's assemblies. Pashuto devotes much of this discussion to the political history and weak form of government of early Kievan Russia; he examines further the socio-economic forces that favored the formation and later the dismemberment of the state. Social conditions are discussed at considerable length in an essay which incorporates a description of the views of the "bourgeois historians."

During the second half of the 1950's, L. V. Cherepnin gathered much new factual material related to the genesis of political centralization in Russia. His emphasis is particularly upon the social and economic factors which he regards as being of utmost importance in formation of the centralized state. After he traces minutely the process of political unification dur-

---

[22]B. A. Rybakov, "Spornye voprosy obrazovaniia Kievskoi Rusi." *Voprosy istorii,* No. 9 (1960), 18-26. V. T. Pashuto, *Geroicheskaia borba russkogo naroda za nezavisimost (XIII vek).* (Moscow, 1956). See also *Ocherki istorii SSSR, XII-XIII vv.* (Moscow, 1961). L. V. Cherepnin, *Obrazovanie Russkogo tsentralizovannogo gosudarstva v XIV-XV vekakh. Ocherki sotsialno-ekonomicheskoi Rusi.* (Moscow, 1960).

ing the fourteenth and fifteenth centuries, and examines the developments which are peculiarly Russian, Cherepnin discusses the formation of centralized government organs amidst feudal conditions. Following the Soviet pattern, he endeavors to show that feudalism in Russia developed precisely within the same general circumstances as elsewhere, but he then carries the thesis further than any of the preceding authors. Analyzing the economic relations between town and countryside, as well as among the principalities, Cherepnin concludes that economic development with its property differentiation and conflicting class interests was bound to result in a more centralized form of government.

Cherepnin devotes much of his study to agrarian conditions during the fourteenth and fifteenth centuries, which he analyzes especially from the vantage point of the consolidation and expansion of the state. He includes such subjects as the expansion of the feudal system throughout the territory populated by the eastern Slavs, the fragmentation of the feudal system, and the rise of the institution of serfdom. Along with these he analyzes the growth of land ownership, and the stabilization of a feudal hierarchy which would be inclined to support political consolidation as long as a firmer hand promised effective protection to its vested interests. The author then traces the growth of class struggle both in the towns and throughout the countryside.

I. I. Smirnov, who traces the breakdown of economic particularism and gradual growth of the national state, also examines the close relationship between Russian economic and political development and the consolidation of serfdom.[23]

There have been two studies of Novgorod in the fifteenth and sixteenth centuries: one by V. N. Bernadskii, who stresses largely the political events during the 1470's which led to the annexation of the Novgorodian lands to Moscow, including the vast area generally referred to as Ugria. The other is by A. P. Pronshtein who analyzes mainly socio-economic conditions during the last period of Novgorodian independence. The annexation act was the culmination of fifteenth-century Muscovite expansion.[24]

How did Moscow succeed in taking over Novgorod as well as its extensive territorial possessions in the northeast? According to Bernadskii, the "transition from the feudal order, or more likely, from the feudal disorder, to an autocratic regime" was made possible by an advanced productive capacity accompanied by a sharper division of labor in Moscow. Bernadskii

[23]I. I. Smirnov, *Ocherki politicheskoi istorii Russkogo gosudarstva 30-50 godov XVII veka.* (Moscow, 1958).

[24]V. N. Bernadskii, *Novgorod i Novgorodskaia zemlia v XV veke.* (Leningrad, 1954). See also V. N. Bernadskii, "Politika Ivana III v Novgorode," *Uchenye zapiski Leningradskogo gosudarstvennogo pedagogicheskogo instituta,* Vol. LXI (Leningrad, 1941). A. P. Pronshtein, *Velikii Novgorod v XVI veke. Ocherk sotsialno-ekonomicheskoi i politicheskoi istorii russkogo naroda.* (Kharkov, 1957). Cf. K. V. Bazilevich, *Vneshniaia politika Russkogo tsentralizovanogo gosudarstva.* (Moscow, 1952).

shows the growth of productivity in the fourteenth and fifteenth centuries was due mainly to exploitation of the valuable resources of the northeastern territory (Ugria); it was further aided by the central regions of Novgorod, largely due to the growth of a money-commodity economy and a proportionate expansion of markets. On the other hand, Bernadskii contends, the Novgorodian state was undermined by a rising struggle between townsmen and peasantry which weakened the state to a degree where it could no more withstand the pressure from Moscow.

Among the historians who undertook a reinterpretation of the conditions and causes that brought about the formation of the unified Russian state by the end of the fifteenth century the view of A. M. Sakharov stands out. His basic thesis is his denial of all analogies of centralization in Russia with those of western European states.[25] Sakharov maintains that the Russian and the western European monarchies had entirely different socioeconomic backgrounds. Centralization in western countries assumed the form of absolute monarchies during the late feudal period; their socioeconomic basis was the growth of cities and the rise of the middle class. During the fifteenth century, Sakharov believes, centralized states also appeared in several eastern European countries, but here the pure feudal monarchies emerged mainly for reasons of security and border defense. The basis of the Russian centralized state, Sakharov maintains, was the expansion of feudal landownership and growth of the peasantry's dependency upon the feudal system.

A good deal of study has been carried out in the field of comparative development of centralized authority in England and France on one hand and Russia on the other. Thus E. V. Gutnova wrote on the origin of the English Parliament while N. A. Sidorova did research on the rise of early urban culture in France, and both writers have given attention to comparisons between these countries and Russia.[26] In both England and France the early centralized state came not as an absolute monarchical regime, but as a monarchy with an estate-representative institution. They were purely feudal states, supported primarily by a class-society, a domineering, feudal, landholding class. Centralization was further supported by many townsmen whose interests were mainly in trade beyond their localities.

Both in England and France, as elsewhere in western Europe, centralization was closely associated with the rise of cities and expansion of markets which advanced by degrees from a local to a national level. Thus the city, with its surge for market expansion, produced the early townspeople (Soviet writers prefer to call them bourgeois) as binding elements. In the frag-

[25] A. M. Sakharov, "Problema obrazovaniia Russkogo tsentralizovannogo gosudarstva v sovetskoi istoriografii." *Voprosy istorii*, No. 9 (1961), 70-88. See also his article, "Obrazovanie Russkogo tsentralizovannogo gosudarstva." *Prepodavanie istorii v shkole*, No. 4 (1961).

[26] E. V. Gutnova, *Vozniknovenie angliiskogo parlamenta.* (Moscow, 1960). N. A. Sidorova, *Ocherki po istorii rannei gorodskoi kultury Frantsii.* (Moscow, 1953).

mented medieval feudal society this class became instrumental in the process of national formation. For a period of time feudal and bourgeois societies, so to speak, coexisted. But it was only natural to expect that in due course the cooperation would become difficult, for the interests of the two groups were often contradictory. The bourgeois elements would support centralized authority or the monarchy in self–defense against the feudal aristocracy. In short, the rise of the state under centralized authority was the result of the growth of the middle class or bourgeois element in the towns and the decline of the landlord feudal class in the countryside, both contributing to the rise of the absolute monarchy.

Discussions and differences in interpretation such as those between A. M. Sakharov and many of his colleagues were based largely on the comparisons of different stages in the development of the centralized monarchy. The weakness of the arguments on both sides lies mainly in the fact that both focus their attention on the absolute monarchy rather than on administrative authority. Sakharov, for instance, endeavored to show that the transformation of the monarchy with its class–representative institutions into an absolute monarchy in western Europe was similar to the developments in Russia. But there was also a great difference in that socio-economic developments brought about the course of events in the first case, whereas in Russia, on the other hand, it was mainly considerations of geographic conditions and frontier security that forced absolute monarchy to the foreground.

Soviet scholars have spent much effort and time debating about the beginning of the centralized state in Russia. A. M. Sakharov declares that secular as well as ecclesiastical elements were important in the process of unification. M. N. Pokrovskii maintained his old thesis that trade capital played a decisive part in the unification and centralization of the State, though shortly before his death he seemed to have backed down from this view. Pokrovskii had long contended that there were two periods: the "medieval feudal" state, which was at about the turn of the sixteenth century, and the "bureaucratic monarchy," which represented the transitional stage during the seventeenth century. Both came about in consequence of the development of trade capital, Pokrovskii believed. External factors he either ignored or was unaware of.

During the 1930's, disciples of M. N. Pokrovskii saw the fallacy of this theory and began to search for new interpretations. Two historians in particular dealt with this problem, S. V. Bakhrushin and K. V. Bazilevich. These men began to search for a better answer in studies comparing the rise of centralized states in western Europe and in Russia. Both Bakhrushin and Bazilevich began with the fact that during the seventeenth century there was already a well-formed national market in Russia, which was instrumental in unifying the country economically and eventually politically. Bazilevich also states that in the fifteenth century a money economy was already well established, in which the towns played a leading part and which the nobility seemed to have supported for one reason or another. The consequence of this development was described by Bazilevich as a feudal monarchy resting upon the nobility. At this point the thesis was left at rest.

Later A. M. Sakharov took up the argument, expanding the same thesis along somewhat different lines. Economic centralization, says Sakharov, did not yet mean political centralization of a feudal society. To regard seventeenth-century Russia as an entirely centralized monarchy would be erroneous.[27] According to Sakharov, what actually was witnessed was a development which can be justly regarded as the beginning of capitalism. This led historians to consider socio-economic factors in Russian political unification. S. V. Iushkov, L. V. Cherepnin, and V. T. Pashuto came to stress class struggle as the main factor in the formation of a centralized system. Pashuto as well as Cherepnin believed that a bourgeois class served to reduce national disunity and that the development of a home market was a logical result. To prove this point, intensified research commenced in Russian social, political, and economic development of the fourteenth through the sixteenth centuries.

In 1960, L. V. Cherepnin published a monograph on the formation of the Russian centralized state.[28] In this work Cherepnin endeavored to show that the formation of a unified state could first be detected in the sphere of agricultural development. This thesis Cherepnin bases on extensive documentary evidence, showing that serfdom appeared not only as a consequence, but as a condition, of political unification, largely because of effective backing of landowners against peasant labor. Cherepnin discusses the part trade, the towns, and commodity circulation played in advancing unification of the state. Economic ties were already observed during the fourteenth and fifteenth centuries, while commercial ties were of lesser consequence at this time. It was only from the seventeenth century on that trade became a decisive factor, when the merchants in the feudal society formed their own class. During the fourteenth and fifteenth centuries the dominant role in domestic trade was still played by the feudal nobility.

Cherepnin's thesis that there existed an alliance of common interests between the Grand Prince and the townsmen has been seriously questioned by several historians. This was perhaps true in exceptional cases, such as in Novgorod or Pskov during this period, but not as a rule throughout the country. There are further questions over the assertion that a certain relationship developed between feudal and town elements which served to advance political unification. A more convincing point was Cherepnin's suggestion of class friction during the same period, though this idea calls for further research and needs additional evidence. A comparison of centralization in eastern and western European countries leaves out vital differences. For example, there is no mention of the Mongolian impact upon Russia, which surely must have had some hampering effect.

[27]A. M. Sakharov, "Problema obrazovaniia Russkogo tsentralizovannogo gosudarstva v Sovetskoi istoriografii." *Voprosy istorii,* No. 9 (1961), 70-88.

[28]L. V. Cherepnin, *Obrazovanie Russkogo tsentralizovannogo gosudarstva v XIV-XV vekakh.* (Moscow, 1960).

Some historians begin the subject of centralization at a later date—the sixteenth century. To set precise dates on such a subject is well-nigh impossible and historians fully recognize this; there is no full agreement even on the stages the country had passed through before attaining a centralized government. Each writer chooses his own chronological pattern.

One example concerns the origin of the term itself, the "Russian state." M. N. Tikhomirov believes, after much research, that the term can already be found in fifteenth-century records. In the following century the terms "Russian land" and "Russia" are used intermittently, meaning the country that embraced all the component parts. Tikhomirov concludes that centralization within Russia must have already been attained during the second half of the fourteenth century, or possibly the fifteenth. Therefore, he says the term "Russian state" must have been established about the fifteenth century while "Russia" was more a "dialectological peculiarity" that one came across a century before in the northeast.[29]

In his study of sixteenth-century Russia, M. N. Tikhomirov adds that during the period under consideration, the country had already gained sufficient political unity that foreign aggression, though devastating, came nowhere near conquering the emerging colossus. Russia already sprawled from the western borders to the Urals and beyond and kept reaching out almost to the shores of the Black Sea.[30]

L. V. Cherepnin dates the formation of the Russian state to the end of the thirteenth century; by the beginning of the fourteenth, he says, the term is already in use in official documents. The formation of territorial unity, and of political and administrative machinery within Russia, continued throughout the sixteenth century.[31] Cherepnin therefore divides his study into six main chapters corresponding to his view of the formation of the state. He begins with an account of fragmented Russia as it existed at the beginning of the fourteenth century; following this he discusses the prerequisites of political unification such as trade, growth of towns, and agriculture and its relation to expanded markets. The fourth and fifth chapters deal with the rise of Moscow as the center of the struggle for independence against the Mongols, and for national expansion against Novgorod, Tver, and the background of unrest among the peasantry. Finally, the last chapter deals with consolidation of Moscow's hegemony by incorporation of such autonomous domains as Novgorod and the principalities of Tver, Rostov, Iaroslav, and others.

V. V. Mavrodin, on the other hand, treats the subject somewhat differently, perhaps partly because of the cult atmosphere in which he wrote

[29]M. N. Tikhomirov, "O proiskhozhdenii nazvaniia 'Rossiia'." *Voprosy istorii,* No. 11 (1953), 93-96.

[30]M. N. Tikhomirov, *Rossiia v XVII stoletii.* (Moscow, 1962).

[31]L. V. Cherepnin, *Obrazovanie Russkogo tsentralizovannogo gosudarstva v XIV-XV vekakh. Ocherki sotsialno-ekonomicheskoi i politicheskoi istorii Rusi.* (Moscow, 1960).

his study. His thesis is somewhat like this: the entire process was mainly the work of three sovereigns, Ivan III, Basil III, and Ivan IV. The prerequisite was sufficient national security to withstand aggression from without, and to bring about social and economic consolidation within. This implied control over the peasantry, and economic power over the latter granted to families like the Odoevskiis, the Shuiskiis, or the Vorotynskiis. The culmination was achieved by Ivan IV, the sovereign with "a strong will and character" supported by a "progressive army of the Oprichnina."[32]

I. I. Smirnov considers the Russian centralized state to have come about somewhere between the end of the fifteenth century and beginning of the seventeenth. This development, Smirnov says, implied the gradual disappearance of old forms of authority and administration that characterized decentralized feudalism, and the rise of new institutions of centralized national authority. The change was accompanied by a complex class rivalry between feudal lords and peasants, between social groupings in towns and cities, and within the ruling class itself. In the end, Smirnov considers centralization completed by the first quarter of the seventeenth century, while Cherepnin considers that it happened during the preceding century. A. A. Zimin, on the other hand, regards Smirnov's dates as questionable, though he admits that centralization might have continued during the reign of Ivan IV.[33]

On general chronological patterns Smirnov and Cherepnin seem to agree, such as placing the beginning of the decline of feudalism and the genesis of the Russian state at the end of the fifteenth century and throughout the sixteenth. According to Cherepnin the decline of the various principalities and their absorption within the Muscovite state was slow; it extended into the second half of the sixteenth century. It marked the termination of the political and economic independence of the feudal classes and their respective princes, with their deep-seated adherence to their vanishing particularism and privileges. The same process called for the setting up of central and local administrations bound by uniform judicial procedure, by a unified military system, and loyal to centralized authority. What was more, it also implied the creation of a loyal aristocracy, a uniformity of obligation and privileges, a unified system of taxation. In short, it necessitated a complete liquidation of one social order and the establishment of a new one.

Many students of history, such as V. S. Shulgin, N. E. Nosov, S. M. Kashtanov, I. I. Smirnov, or A. A. Zimin, have endeavored to account for other and equally significant changes that took place during the same pe-

[32]V. V. Mavrodin, *Obrazovanie edinogo Russkogo gosudarstva.* (Moscow, 1951).

L. V. Cherepnin, *Obrazovanie Russkogo tsentralizovannogo gosudarstva v XIV-XV vekakh. Ocherki sotsialno-ekonomicheskoi i politicheskoi istorii Rusi.* (Moscow, 1960).

[33]I. I. Smirnov, *Ocherki politicheskoi istorii Russkogo gosudarstva 30-50kh godov XVI veka.* (Moscow, 1958). Cf. A. A. Zimin, *Reformy Ivana Groznogo. Ocherki sotsialno-ekonomicheskoi i politicheskoi istorii Rossii serediny XVI v.* (Moscow, 1960).

riod. They found that some of these changes were by no means evolutionary or peaceful, but were accompanied by social disruption and political violence. As the old order receded into the background, the feudal class fought to retain whatever privileges it could, a phenomenon seen particularly during the years of Ivan IV's minority. The Shuiiskiis, descendants of Rurik and the Belskiis, descendants of the Lithuanian prince Gedimin, fought frequently and tried tenaciously to hold to the privilege and power that kept slipping from under them.

If this struggle at court undermined centralized government, it simultaneously bled the struggling parties white. The rivalry within the ranks of the Boyars not only prevented the formation of a united front in defense of their common interests, but at the same time alienated the upper social classes from the local and less privileged social groups which sought to establish or extend their own privileges. Undoubtedly Ivan IV, after he ascended the throne, was greatly assisted by these internecine struggles and utilized them masterfully—even brutally—to his own end. These events are dealt with graphically by Zimin, Tikhomirov, and Smirnov, who worked on this period especially.

Casting aside the Marxist clichés Soviet historians frequently employ, they bring out succinctly the fact that the lack of unity within the upper ranks of the aristocracy doomed its political aspirations. What is important to note is that this loss of power extended its damaging effect to the entire social structure. The sanguinary feuds that developed, temporarily subsiding and then erupting again, kept engulfing other social groups. Some of the participants were determined to defend hereditary privileges, even at the risk of political suicide, rather than yield to centralized authority. Only a handful of them were able to read the writing on the wall and come to terms with history. In the end, the others paid dearly for their unyielding position. In all fairness, it must be said that it seems doubtful whether the statesmen themselves clearly visualized the end results of the social upheaval they encouraged.[34]

If the actors on the stage of history were at times unaware of the true nature of the drama, were there observers who were able to interpret it intelligently? Some historians believe so. S. O. Shmidt, for instance, re-examined the National Assemblies that were summoned during the middle of the sixteenth century, and he came to think that there was a pervading sentiment of despondency in the atmosphere. The theory, though interesting, is not entirely convincing. Much remains obscure mainly because there is a conspicuous lack of evidence, particularly concerning unrest throughout the countryside or the aspirations of the various groups. It is obvious that one of the compelling reasons for summoning the National or the Church Assembly was the rise of social unrest; the demand for reforms on one hand

[34]S. O. Shmidt, "Pravitelstvennaia deiatelnost A. F. Adasheva." *Uchenye zapiski Moskovskogo gosudarstvennogo universiteta*, Issue 167. (Moscow, 1954).

and fear of possible consequences on the other, according to Soviet writers, were the reasons for seeking aid from the National Assemblies.[35]

Soviet historians hold the view that the reforms promulgated between 1530 and 1550 were really initiated in the provinces, and the government was forced to act in accordance with them. In addition, it is believed, local unrest was often aroused either by military policies or by creeping serfdom.[36] Another writer, A. K. Leontiev, explored minutely the basic reforms of the first half of the sixteenth century. In the end he tried to show that the changes undertaken were all bent toward one end—further consolidation of centralized administration, in order to stabilize the feudal order, and effectively control the peasantry that had been recently attached to the soil. There is a general view that in this particular field much of the documentary evidence is yet to be explored, and therefore conclusions cannot be accepted with any degree of finality.[37]

In the field of the political history of feudal Russia the accomplishments are modest as compared, for instance, with the history of peasant revolts. In part this lag is explained by the fact that the opportunities for historians to utilize new materials were less favorable than in other fields. To some extent it was also due to Soviet political conditions: the "cult of the individual" presented circumstances that were scarcely conducive to the writing of political history; it called for the prudent scholar to exercise caution and ideological tact, or best of all, to avoid it altogether.

During the "cult of the individual," historiography was completely dominated by the adulation of monarchs such as Ivan IV or Peter I, and military men like A. V. Suvorov or M. I. Kutuzov. The situation lasted until the Twentieth Congress of the Communist Party in February, 1956, and immediately thereafter, in May, 1956, the academician S. M. Dubrovskii delivered a paper before the Institute of History in which he took to task some of the works that had dealt with Ivan IV. Dubrovskii did for the historians what Khrushchev did for the party—he brought an end to the excessive idealization and adulation of Ivan IV, the tendency to overestimate beyond all proportions the political role of that tsar. Previously, even scholars of considerable prominence, such as R. Iu. Vipper, S. V. Bakhrushin, or I. I. Smirnov, had surrendered to adulatory praise of Ivan IV as the genius states-

---

[35]S. O. Shmidt, "Sobory serediny XVI veka." *Istoriia SSSR*, No. 4, (1960), 66-92. A. M. Samsonov, *Antifeodalnye narodnye dvizheniia v Rossii i tserkov.* (Moscow, 1955). See also A. A. Zimin and A. A. Preobrazhenskii, "Izuchenie v sovetskoi nauke klassovoi borby perioda feodalizma v Rossii (do nachala XIX v.)." *Voprosy istorii*, No. 12 (1957), 135-159. See particularly pp. 140-142.

[36]S. M. Kashtanov, "K probleme mestnogo upravleniia v Rossii pervoi poloviny XVI veka." *Istoriia SSSR*, No. 6 (1959), 134-148. N. E. Nosov, *Ocherki po istorii mestnogo upravleniia v Russkom gosudarstve pervoi poloviny XVI veka.* (Moscow, 1957).

[37]A. K. Leontiev, *Obrazovanie prikaznoi sistemy upravleniia v Russkom gosudarstve. Iz istorii sozdaniia tsentralizovannogo apparata v kontse XV-pervoi polovine XVI v.* (Moscow, 1961).

man and as the sovereign battling against all sorts of odds, implying, of course, a comparison with the infallible leadership of Stalin.38

This worship of heroes in history spread like an epidemic from monographic studies to articles and textbooks, infiltrating and demoralizing scholarship and adding to the distortion of history. As one author stated: "After the conference [of the XX Party Congress] medievalists radically reinterpreted their research in the political history of Russia. In the works issued during the second half of the 1950's stands out the first explanation of the objective laws of historical process."39 What euphemism!

How the cult, as Khrushchev stated, "became at a certain specific stage the source of a whole series of exceedingly serious and grave perversions of party principles, of party democracy, or revolutionary legality," is yet to be recorded in history. It is premature to deal with such a grave and vital subject, particularly in view of the fact that the indictment as presented by Khrushchev before the Twentieth Congress still remains, at least officially, a secret document unavailable to the Soviet citizen.

38S. M. Dubrovskii, "Protiv idealizatsii deiatelnosti Ivana IV." *Voprosy istorii*, No. 8 (1956), 121-129.

39*Sovetskaia istoricheskaia nauka ot XX k XXII sezdu KPSS. Istoriia SSSR. Sbornik statei.* (Moscow, 1962), 65-66.

CHAPTER IV

Russia During and After the Reign of Ivan IV

A. IVAN IV AND THE OPRICHNINA

In 1947, when the Academy of Sciences published a two-volume jubilee edition, marking the thirtieth anniversary of the Revolution, S. V. Bakhrushin contributed an essay under the title "Ivan the Terrible in Light of the Latest Research." His main theme was expressed by the concluding lines: "Thus, in light of the new research, Ivan the Terrible appears as a majestic and powerful figure, as one of the greatest statesmen in Russian history." Another article, by I. U. Budovnits, similarly elevates Ivan IV to a high pedestal in history. The writings referred to sum up a situation that had been building up since the 1920's and was rapidly reaching its culmination. Historical writings on sixteenth-century Russia have dealt largely with political and feudal developments. From the late 1920's through the 1940's, most of the writers seemed to have accepted the view that the centralized monarchy in Russia, formed during the sixteenth century, represented a progressive political stage, while the Tsar honorably fulfilled a dual purpose: he promoted the economic and cultural life of the state at the same time that he successfully provided for national defense.

Throughout the Stalin period, historical writings that dealt with sixteenth-century Russia, as historians later admitted somewhat diffidently, followed a "subjective tendency in evaluating historical events."[1] The role of the individual sovereign was both magnified and glorified. Thus Ivan III and Ivan IV, for illustration, were presented as model leaders responsible for the centralization of the Russian state, the perfect embodiment of positive political achievement and statesmanship. The people and the state became synonymous, objects ruled by a wise sovereign or at least a just one; the occupant of the throne became the fountain of social justice, defender of the people against the class selfishness and unjustifiable privileges.

Three studies of the period are most illustrative in this connection, and might be cited at some length. One is by R. Iu. Vipper, another by S. V. Bakhrushin, and a third by I. I. Smirnov. Though all three deal generally with the second half of the sixteenth century, their primary theme is the "wise rule" and the personality of Ivan IV.[2] Vipper himself wrote: "The

---

[1]*Sovetskaia istoricheskaia nauka ot XX k XXII sezdu KPSS.* (Moscow, 1962), 92.

[2]R. Iu. Vipper, *Ivan Groznyi.* (Moscow, 1944). (Originally published in 1922, the 1944 edition glorifies Ivan I even more. There is an English translation of *Ivan Groznyi* published by the Foreign Languages Publishing House [Moscow, 1947].) S. V. Bakhrushin, *Ivan Groznyi.* (Moscow, 1942). This is incorporated in Bakhrushin's collected works, Vol. II (Moscow, 1954), 256-328. I. I. Smirnov, *Ivan Groznyi.* (Leningrad, 1944).

influence of what we call one's philosophy upon the student of research is so strong, that in literary sources, in historical evidence, he seems to read and see what he wishes to read and see, and selects and evaluates those things which coincide with his own tastes in the direction of his own interests." In precisely this spirit, Vipper wrote, describing the ruinous Livonian war during the reign of Ivan IV: "What, then, saved the Moscow military monarchy from the impending catastrophe, why did a revolution not follow on the heels of the war?" And he answers himself, that it was only because of the "political sagacity, the organized institutions and skill of the dynasty, that it was able to rise above all the classes that held the country in subordination and maintain order," saving the Muscovite state.

The correspondence between Ivan IV and Kurbskii, says the historian, reveals the former as a character who was "clever, talented, full of seething energy, and irascible." Moreover, he says, the Oprichnina, the monarch's ferocious private police force, should not be depicted as a "gesture of horror and despair, which conformed to the high-strung character of Ivan IV," but as "primarily a great military-administrative reform, called forth by the growing difficulties of the great war for access to the Baltic Sea and for the opening of intercourse with western Europe." Though Ivan IV was not a gifted military leader, he possessed "technical talent in engineering and a wide and practical outlook on questions of military organization." All in all, says Vipper, Ivan IV distinguished himself "as a first-class talent in diplomacy, and was entirely in his element when it came to international affairs."

Bakhrushin shows greater restraint in his high valuation, but presents Ivan IV as the "People's Tsar," whose "reforms assured order within the country and defense against external enemies." These reforms were met with the "enthusiastic support of the Russian people. The nobility, the peasant masses and townsmen only gained from the enforcement of state centralization." Joining the chorus of praise, I. I. Smirnov presents Ivan IV as a great statesman and national champion, quoting Vipper and Bakhrushin to support his thesis. Another writer, I. U. Budovnits, in a lengthy essay presents Ivan IV along similar lines, as a great national benefactor.[3]

This historical interpretation of Ivan IV met with total approval and delight on the part of Stalin. In 1947, Stalin received the well-known film producer and director S. M. Eisenshtein and N. K. Cherkasov, the actor who played the lead in Eisenshtein's "Ivan the Terrible." Stalin agreed that Ivan IV was a great and wise ruler, that the Oprichnina "played a progressive role," and that the notorious Maliuta Skuratov, head of the organization, was a valorous military leader who heroically lost his life in the Livonian war. The chief error of Ivan IV, according to Stalin, was that he failed to liquidate the five remaining great feudal families; when they managed to sur-

[3]I. U. Budovnits, "Ivan Groznyi v russkoi istoricheskoi literature." *Istoricheskie zapiski*, No. 21 (1947), 271-330.

vive, it left the fight unfinished. Had he completed this, there would not
have been any Time of Trouble.[4]
   The character of Ivan IV has always been and still continues to be a debatable subject among historians. Debates were largely encouraged by the
scantiness of historical documents bearing on his personality. It should be
borne in mind that the Time of Trouble and the great fire of 1626 had
destroyed the archives of Moscow to such an extent that only incidental
odds and ends were left available to the historian.
   In summary, it can be said that the general theme during this period was
somewhat as follows: Ivan IV was undeniably cruel, but that characteristic
was common to most sovereigns of his time. Moreover, cruelty could be
justified by the same reasoning Lenin had used with respect to Peter I: that
one has to combat barbarism with barbaric means. This interpretation was
current at a time when there were few Marxist historians about, as in the
1920's, when Vipper was writing. Members of the old school, the surviving
non-Marxists who remained in Russia, were either silent or were the ones
who "managed to adapt themselves" and discovered "aboriginal Bolshevism"
in the character of such sovereigns as Ivan IV, who fought the Boyars instead
of the bourgeoisie, or Peter I, who led a desperate campaign against an obsolete structure of state and society comparable with the current fight against
decaying capitalism.
   As time went on and the cult of Stalin entrenched itself, this interpretation came to suit the cultists most advantageously. The idealized role of
Ivan IV, the virtues seen in the Oprichnina, "the desperadoes and cut-throats
who formed the guard," as one history book colorfully described it, all led
to the unavoidable deduction that history seems to repeat itself: the wise
leadership of Stalin could only be understood in the light of the proven wisdom of Ivan IV or Peter I.[5]
   Shortly after the death of Stalin, and particularly following the celebrated
denunciation by N. S. Khrushchev, a reappraisal of Ivan IV began. The
first important discussion took place in May, 1956, when scholars from Moscow and Leningrad met to hear a paper delivered by S. M. Dubrovskii
under the title of "The Cult of the Individual and Some Works on Problems
of History. An Analysis of Ivan IV and Others."[6] The paper aroused an

[4]N. K. Cherkasov, Zapiski sovetskogo aktera. (Moscow, 1953). Cited by S. M. Dubrovskii in Voprosy istorii, No. 8 (1956), 121-129.

[5]Two bibliographical compilations of works on sixteenth-century Russian history
may be recommended. One is Bibliografiia sovetskikh russkikh rabot po literature
XI-XVII vv. za 1917-1957 gg. N. F. Droblenkova, comp., V. P. Adrianova-Peretts,
ed. (Moscow, 1961). Another is Ocherki istorii SSSR. Period feodalizma, konets
XV—nachalo XVII v. A. N. Nasonov, L. V. Cherepnin, and A. A. Zimin, eds.
(Moscow, 1955).

[6]S. M. Dubrovskii, "Protiv idealizatsii deiatelnosti Ivana IV." Voprosy istorii, No. 8
(1956), 121-129. Also M. D. Kurmacheva, "Ob otsenke deiatelnosti Ivana Groznogo."
Voprosy istorii, No. 9 (1956), 195-203.

animated discussion during which there appeared to be general agreement that R. Iu. Vipper, S. V. Bakhrushin, I. I. Smirnov, and I. U. Budnovnits had all demonstrated a tendency to idealize the reign of Ivan IV and the notorious Oprichnina. They had, it was agreed, minimized the feudal character of the centralized state and the institution of serfdom. S. M. Dubrovskii bluntly stated that the Stalinist interpretation of Ivan IV was not only false, but harmful politically, for it distorted the course of events during the sixteenth century.

The severe verdict by Dubrovskii was reflected in the general temper of the discussions. In his zeal to condemn the cult of Stalin, Dubrovskii most likely overemphasized the negative aspects of the rule of Ivan IV. He even went so far as to question the validity of writings attributed to the monarch. V. N. Sheviakov, in an equally negative vein, presented a revised view of the Oprichnina.[7] There was a feeling at this meeting that a more dispassionate jury would have to reexamine the issues in order to present a truly objective historical verdict. The "cult of the individual" would have to be dissociated from the basic principles involved in interpreting the sixteenth century. To isolate the compelling cause for the transformation that took place during these years implied a careful, detached scrutiny of the reactivated foreign policy and the social changes that characterized Russia at the time. Only such an approach would lead to a true comprehension of the mass movement and the virulent social revolution that soon followed the reign of Ivan IV, known in history as the Time of Troubles.

A special footnote concerning the Oprichnina: at no time had this institution been studied more intensively than during the middle of the present century. The version current while Stalin was in power came up for a total reappraisal soon after his death. If previously it had been a "progressive military force," it later came to be a tyrannical system which tended to undermine "the productive capacity of the country," and gradually led the nation to the crisis Russia came to face by the end of the sixteenth and early seventeenth centuries.[8]

With the aid of newly uncovered materials, a number of scholars came to publish noteworthy studies in which the negative aspects of the Oprichnina were no longer glossed over. Perhaps the first encouraging sign was the publication of S. B. Veselovskii's eminent work, which had been banned during Stalin's lifetime. Others on the same subject were soon to follow.[9]

---

[7] V. N. Sheviakov, "K voprosu ob oprichnine Ivana IV." *Voprosy istorii,* No. 9 (1956), 71-77.

[8] *Ibid.*

[9] *Ibid.* See also V. B. Korbin, "Sostav oprichnogo dvora Ivana Groznogo." In *Arkheograficheskii ezhegodnik, 1959.* (Moscow, 1960). A. A. Zimin, *Reformy Ivana Groznogo.* (Moscow, 1960). R. G. Skrynnikov, "Oprichnaia zemelnaia reforma Groznogo." *Istoricheskie zapiski,* No. 70 (1961), 223-250. S. M. Kashtanov, "K izucheniiu oprichniny Ivana Groznogo." *Istoriia SSSR,* No. 2 (1963), 96-117. S. B. Veselovskii, *Issledovaniia po istorii oprichniny.* (Moscow, 1963). See an

If the Oprichnina was instrumental in terminating feudal land disbursement of the princely and boyar landholdings, it weakened simultaneously whatever claim to representative government there was. The Zemskii Sobor, active as it was during the 1540's and 1550's, showed signs of decline throughout the second half of that century. Some Soviet writers also called attention to the fact that the foreign policy of Ivan IV was weakened rather than strengthened by the creation of the Oprichnina. The drain, both political and economic, caused by the Oprichnina, and the effects of the tyranny it exercised were bound to affect negatively the war effort in Livonia. Recent Soviet historiography seriously came to question former assertions that Boyar dominance was largely destroyed by the Oprichnina. It was the tyranny it established that created the political explosive which was in the end to destroy the Boyar class.

Scholarly objective writing did occasionally manage to appear, even though it displayed extreme prudence. Thus, P. A. Sadikov wrote a commendable piece of work on the Oprichnina, covering its origin, administration, land grants, its relation to the church, and other paramount problems relative to that institution. The author not only based his work on records formerly unknown or never before utilized, but incorporated an appendix that adds value to his study as a documentary source book.[10]

Another historian, A. A. Zimin, had scrupulously studied the central administration of the Oprichnina. His conclusion, essentially, was that the group was instrumental in consolidating the feudal elements in the government by leaving routine administrative functions and judicial power to the Boyar Duma. The old theory that the Oprichnina had much to do with inciting class warfare has lately been seriously discredited.[11]

Some of Ivan IV's policies during the last years of his reign present bewildering inconsistencies. For instance, instead of pursuing his policy of centralization, he suddenly reverted to a feudal practice in delegating power to the converted Tartar, Sai Bulat of Kasimov, in 1574, after renaming him Simeon Bekbulatovich. Ivan IV conferred upon Simeon the title of "Grand Prince of All Russia." Bekbulatovich administered the country for some two years, and then was exiled to Tver. Here he was named governor of a prov-

earlier study of the subject by the same author, "Uchrezhdenie oprichnogo dvora v 1565 g. i otmena ego v 1572 g." *Voprosy istorii*, No. 1 (1946), 86-104.

[10]P. A. Sadikov, *Ocherki po istorii oprichniny.* (Moscow, 1950).

[11]V. B. Kobrin, *Sotsialnyi sostav oprichnogo dvora.* (A doctoral dissertation). (Moscow, 1961). See also S. S. Pechuro,"Zemskie sluzhilye liudi v gody oprichniny (K postanovke voprosa)." *Trudy MGIAI* [Moskovskii gosudarstvennyi istoriko-arkhivnyi institut], Vol. XVI (Moscow, 1961). A. A. Zimin, "Preobrazovaniia gosudarstvennogo apparata v gody oprichniny." *Nauchnye doklady vysshei shkoly. Istoricheskie nauki*, No. 4 (1961).

ince for a short period and endowed quite generously with land. Such episodes remain puzzling to historians.[12]

There is a general feeling among historians that Russian political history of the 1560's and 1570's is still in need of much research. Since the 1960's the complaint has been heard that the Oprichnina has been given undeserved credit for the consolidation of the national state. The latest research has convincingly shown that the reforms which advanced political centralization had more to do with the consolidation of autocracy than with the Oprichnina.[13]

Centralization advanced during the early 1550's, marked by extension of the national authority at the expense of local government, by consolidation of the military bureaucracy, and by reorganization of the military and financial administrations. These changes were bound to lead to a firmer establishment of absolutism. Though the ruler still presumably cooperated with the Boyar Duma, the newly rising tenure nobility was gaining the upper hand while the Duma was slowly retreating. This was best demonstrated by the increasing tendency of the Tsar to seek counsel from his personally chosen favorites, while the Duma and the Third Estate were increasingly ignored.[14]

The Zemskii Sobor was a subject of extensive research in historical literature before 1917. After the Revolution it temporarily declined in interest, mainly due to concentration of attention in other fields, until in the 1950's there was a revival of attention. In 1958, M. N. Tikhomirov once more raised the question of the role the Zemskii Sobor had played in its checkered history. L. V. Cherepnin soon joined the field of study, as did S. O. Shmidt, who concentrated particularly on the middle period of the sixteenth century.[15]

In his large monographic work, already referred to, I. I. Smirnov reexamined many questions related to the Boyar rule of the 1530's and 1540's. In the end Smirnov suggests an original interpretation of Ivan IV's reforms

[12]V. I. Koretskii, "Zemskii Sobor 1575 g. i postanovlenie Simeona Bekbulatovicha 'velikim kniazem vseia Rusi'." *Istoricheskii arkhiv*, No. 2 (1959), 148-156.
S. O. Shmidt, comp. "Neizdannye dokumenty XVI veka." *Istoricheskii arkhiv*, No. 4 (1916), 149-158. S. M. Kashtanov, "O vnutrennei politike Ivana Groznogo v period 'velikogo knizheniia' Simeona Bekbulatovicha." *Trudy MGIAI* [Moskovskii gosudarstvennyi istoriko-arkhivnyi institut], Vol. XVI (1961).

[13]L. V. Cherepnin, "Osnovnye etapy razvitiia feodalizma v Rossii." *Desiatyi mezhdunarodnyi kongress istorikov v Rime* [September, 1955]. *Doklady sovetskoi delegatsii.* (Moscow, 1956).

[14]G. B. Galperin, "K voprosu o forme pravleniia Russkogo gosudarstva XV-pervoi poloviny XVI v.," and I. B. Zilberman, "Printsip suvereniteta vlasti vl russkoi politicheskoi literature XVI v.," both essays in *Uchenye zapiski Leningradskogo gosudarstvennogo universiteta*, No. 255 (Leningrad, 1958).

[15]M. N. Tikhomirov, "Soslovno-predstavitelnye uchrezhdeniia (Zemskie Sobory) v Rossii XVI v." *Voprosy istorii*, No. 5 (1958), 3-22. L. Tcherepnine, "Le rôle des Semski Sobory en Russie lors de la guerre des paysans au début du XVII siècle." A reprint. (1960). S. O. Shmidt, "Sobory serediny XVI v." *Istoriia SSSR*, No. 4 (1960), 66-92.

during the second half of his reign.[16] He deals with the multilateral nature of the political struggle during the same period: the antagonism between the peasantry and lower townsmen on one hand and the feudal aristocratic class on the other, and the gradual involvement of the other social elements in the conflict.

Smirnov shows that it was the tenant-holding elements that were largely instrumental in bringing about political centralization. He reexamines the oft-mentioned role of the Boyar Council and the crucial political part it played in the middle of the sixteenth century, and concludes that the Concil, though enjoying political eminence, was by no means the only institution of importance. To quote Smirnov: "The development of the centralized state finds its main and decisive expression not in the altered place or in the importance of the Boyar Council, but first of all in the growth and development of the bureaucratic apparatus, in the increased prestige of the departments [prikazy] and their scribes [diaki]"

Smirnov stresses another symptomatic development of political significance in the sixteenth century: the men who "were not members of the Boyar Council or who occupied relatively modest positions became prominently active in consolidation of the autocracy and centralization of the administration."[17] Smirnov shows further the anomalous position in which the Boyar Council found itself. On the one hand the Council presumably served as the highest political organ of a state rapidly moving toward a centralized system of government, while on the other, the very same Council remained the stronghold of precisely those princely and Boyar elements that were inimical to any effort at centralization. Small wonder the Tsar had to rely increasingly upon his "Intimate Council" during the 1550's. This council, Smirnov believes, included mostly representatives of political circles that opposed the oligarchical Boyar rule prior to Ivan IV's formal ascension to the throne. It was for this reason, if for no other, that they supported a strong monarchy. In view of this situation, Smirnov explains the reforms of the 1530's as precautionary measures against the excessive influence the Boyars might enjoy and abuse.

The striking feature of Soviet historiography—the emphasis on class interests as the primary motivating force throughout the ages—is apparent in the writings that deal with the fifteenth and sixteenth centuries. Detail of interpretation concerning such subjects as the reforms of this period, the character of the state, or the social unrest of the times may vary so long as the basic principles that characterize the centuries are commonly accepted. For example, debates have been going on among historians as to what particular groups within the ruling class played the primary part in the reforms of the middle 1550's, and why. I. I. Smirnov and A. A. Zimin carried on a discus-

[16]I. I. Smirnov, *Ocherki politicheskoi istorii Russkogo gosudarstva 30-50kh godov XVI veka.* (Moscow, 1958).

[17]I. I. Smirnov, *Ocherki politicheskoi istorii Russkogo gosudarstva 30-50kh godov XVI veka,* p. 193.

73

sion for some time as to the precise role the various social elements played in the legislature during this time. As a result, Zimin published a monograph in which he severely took Smirnov to task.[18]

Zimin holds the view that two periods stand out in the history of the "Intimate Council" of Ivan IV: one at about 1549, when, under the influence of Aleksei F. Adashev, national policy was noted for its moderation; the second period was later, when the government adopted a policy that favored the tenant landlords (dvorianstvo) at the expense of the older feudal hereditary aristocracy.[19] This policy brought about intensified class antagonism within the ranks of the upper classes and sharpened rivalry for political influence. The policies of the second period mark an effort on the part of the government to restrain the excessive land claims of the hereditary aristocracy and curb their former privileges.

On the other hand, Smirnov and his followers stress the unifying rather than the divisive aims of the landed aristocracy and their continuous encroachment upon the peasantry and the townsmen, particularly the lower social elements. The differences of opinion between Zimin and Smirnov and their corresponding followers seem not so much about centralization as over the methods of exploitation of the free and semi-free groups in Russia. The question of centralization entered as a side issue and is considered of secondary importance. It was only in the face of mass uprisings that the feudal hereditary class and recently created tenant landlord group cast aside their "liberalism," patched up their differences, and closed ranks in order to meet the challenge.[20]

A great deal of research has been carried out in the history of administrative development. A. K. Leontiev has made a careful study of the various ministries (prikazy) and their administrative agencies, while others have explored the development of the military system during the same period; foreign policy remains the least investigated field.[21]

[18] A. A. Zimin, Reformy Ivana Groznogo. (Moscow, 1960). A. A. Zimin, "K istorii voennykh reform 50kh godov XVI v." Istoricheskie zapiski, No. 55 (1956), 314-359; A. A. Zimin, "O sostave dvortsovykh uchrezhdenii Russkogo gosudarstva kontsa XV i XVI v." Istoricheskie zapiski, No. 63 (1958), 180-205; A. A. Zimin, " 'Prigovor' 1555-56 g. i likvidatsiia sistemy kormlenii v Russkom gosudarstve." Istoriia SSSR, No. 1 (1958), 178-182.

[19] On the subject of Adashev's role in the government and policy see S. O. Shmidt, "Pravitelstvennaia deiatelnost A. F. Adasheva." Uchenye zapiski MGU, Kafedra istorii SSSR, No. 167. (Moscow, 1954).

[20] N. E. Nosov, Ocherki po istorii mestnogo upravleniia Russkogo gosudarstva pervoi poloviny XVI veka. (Moscow, 1957). Also as additional information on the subject see the essay by S. M. Kashtanov, "K probleme mestnogo upravleniia v Rossii pervoi poloviny XVI veka." Istoriia SSSR, No. 6 (1959), 134-148.

[21] A. K. Leontiev, Obrazovanie prikaznoi sistemy upravleniia v Russkom gosudarstve. Iz istorii sozdaniia tsentralizovannogo gosudarstvennogo apparata v kontse XV--pervoi poloviny XVI v. (Moscow, 1961). A. V. Chernov, Vooruzhennye sily Russkogo gosudarstva v XV-XVII vv. (Moscow, 1954). V. I. Buganov, " 'Gosudarev razriad' 1556 g. i reformy 50kh godov XVI v." Istoriia SSSR, No. 5 (1957), 220-231.

While most students of history concentrated their attention on the reorganization of the central administration, others were investigating local administrative changes. In an outstanding monograph, N. E. Nosov reported on his minute investigation of the early formation of town and city administrative organs.[22] Anyone who studies sixteenth-century administrative reforms recognizes the work of Nosov as an indispensable one. His work is complemented by an equally outstanding study by S. M. Kashtanov.[23]

Soviet historiography of the period has lately been enriched from another direction by a series of biographies of leading individuals who shaped decisive national policies.[24] There have also been some outstanding monographic studies that resulted from extensive research into the status of the land nobility, the changes in the immunities granted by the centralized authorities during the first half of the sixteenth century, and the immunity charters themselves as a source of historical study.[25]

In summary, it can be said that sixteenth-century reforms and the impact of Ivan IV have been widely studied in Soviet historiography. Among the leading students of this period, as was noted, is I. I. Smirnov, whose interest in the personality of Ivan IV led to a more detailed study of the reforms of his time. With equal interest, A. A. Zimin examined the important legislation of the time. His research resulted in a whole series of articles which were later combined into a more general study and monograph. Other aspects of the mid-sixteenth century were treated equally well by other scholars.[26] Students of this period have been noted not only for their use of archival

[22]N. E. Nosov, *Ocherki po istorii mestnogo upravleniia Russkogo gosudarstva pervoi poloviny XVI veka.* (Moscow, 1957). See also his article "Gubnoi nakaz Novgorodskoi zemle 1559 g." *Istoricheskii arkhiv,* No. 4 (1959), 212-217.

[23]S. M. Kashtanov, "K probleme mestnogo upravleniia v pervoi polovine XVI veka." *Istoriia SSSR,* No. 6 (1959), 134-148. S. M. Kashtanov, "Ogranichenie feodalnogo immuniteta pravitelstvom Russkogo tsentralizovannogo gosudarstva v pervoi treti XVI veka." *Trudy MGIAI* [Moskovskii gosudarstvennyi istoriko-arkhivnyi institut], Vol. II (Moscow, 1958).

[24]D. N. Al'shits, "Krestotselovanie zapisi Vladimira Andreevicha Staritskogo i nedoshedshee zaveshchanie Ivana Groznogo." *Istoriia SSSR,* No. 4 (1959), 147-155. S. O. Shmidt, "Pravitelstvennaia deiatelnost A. F. Adasheva." *Uchenye zapiski Moskovskogo gosudarstvennogo universiteta,* No. 167 (Moscow, 1954). Biographical sketches of Ivan IV are given by A. A. Zimin in his *Reformy Ivana Groznogo* and by I. I. Smirnov in his *Ocherki politicheskoi istorii Russkogo gosudarstva 30-50kh godov XVI veka.*

[25]S. M. Kashtanov, "Feodalnyi immunitet v gody boiarskogo pravleniia (1538-1548 gg.)." *Istoricheskie zapiski,* No. 66 (1960), 239-268. A. N. Nasonov, "Ob otnoshenii letopisaniia Pereiaslavlia-Russkogo k Kievskomu (XII vek)." *Problemy istochnikovedeniia,* No. 8 (1959), 466-494.

[26]Here is a brief bibliographical list selected at random on the subject concerned. I. I. Smirnov, *Ocherki politicheskoi istorii Russkogo gosudarstva 30-50kh godov XVI veka.* (Moscow, 1958). A. A. Zimin, *Reformy Ivana Groznogo. Ocherki sotsialno-ekonomicheskoi i politicheskoi istorii Rossii serediny XVI v.* (Moscow,

materials, but for combining these with the analytical studies of the early twentieth century, so that their works are often polemical in nature. In defense of their views they employ newly uncovered archival materials and documentary evidence used formerly, and now add a new interpretation of the material. The field of sixteenth-century Russian history is far from dormant as far as reinterpretation is concerned.[27]

One of the subjects Soviet historians debated frequently during the 1950's was: In whose interests, in fact, were the various mid-sixteenth-century reforms put into effect? I. I. Smirnov maintained that they favored mainly the nobility. The reforms were designed and rammed through by that group, and put into effect for their exclusive interests. S. V. Bakhrushin and others argued that because of war conditions (Kazan, Astrakhan), and because they were a result of collective efforts, the reforms in essence had had to be of a compromise nature. The latter view seems to be the prevailing one among Soviet historians. The reasoning seems plausible.[28] The reforms show that basically they were aimed at levelling the privileges of both the Boyars and the tenant landlords. The Boyars were not entirely stripped of their privileges and had to agree to an extension of those granted to other

1960). A. A. Zimin, "O slozhenii prikaznoi sistemy na Rusi." In *Doklady i soobshcheniia Instituta istorii Akademii nauk SSSR*, No. 3 (Moscow, 1954). A. A. Zimin, "K istorii voennykh reform 50kh godov XVI v." *Istoricheskie zapiski*, Vol. 55 (1956), 344-359. A. A. Zimin, " 'Prigovor' 1555-56 g. i likvidatsiia sistemy kormlenii v Russkom gosudarstve." *Istoriia SSSR*, No. 1 (1958), 178-182. A. A. Zimin, "K izucheniiu tamozhennoi reformy serediny XVI veka." *Istoricheskii arkhiv*, No. 6 (1961), 129-133. Iu. A. Tikhonov, "Tamozhennaia politika Russkogo gosudarstva v seredine XVI do 60kh godov XVII v." *Istoricheskie zapiski*, No. 53 (1955), 258-90. A. V. Chernov, *Vooruzhennye sily Russkogo gosudarstva v XV-XVII vv.* (Moscow, 1954). A. V. Chernov, "O klassifikatsii tsentralnykh pravitelstvennykh uchrezhdenii XVI-XVII vv." *Istoricheskii arkhiv*, No. 1 (1958), 195-201. V. I. Buganov, " 'Gosudarev razriad' 1556 g. i reformy 50kh godov XVI v." *Istoriia SSSR*, No. 5 (1957), 220-231. A. G. Poliak, *Kommentarii k izdaniiu 'Pamiatniki russkogo prava'.* No. 4 (Moscow, 1956). V. Volynskii, "Nazrevshie voprosy v izuchenii istorii razvitiia prikaznogo upravleniia na Rusi." In *Sbornik studencheskikh rabot Sredneaziatskogo gosudarstvennogo universiteta im. V. I. Lenina.* No. 4 (Tashkent, 1956). S. O. Shmidt, "Tsarskii arkhiv serediny XVI v. i arkhivy pravitelstvennykh uchrezhdenii (Opyt izucheniia opisi Tsarskogo arkhiva)." *Trudy MGIAI* [Moskovskii gosudarstvennyi istoriko-arkhivnyi institut], Vol. V (Moscow, 1957). S. O. Shmidt, "K istorii Tsarskogo arkhiva serediny XVI v." *Trudy MGIAI*, Vol. XI (Moscow, 1958).

[27]The work of N. E. Nosov may be cited as an illustration of the polemical nature of current Soviet writings. He has challenged the long-accepted view of feuds between the Boyars and the nobility of later date in the capital. See N. E. Nosov, "Boyarskaia kniga 1556. (Iz istorii proiskhozhdeniia chetvertchikov)." *Voprosy ekonomiki i klassovykh otnoshenii v Russkom gosudarstve XII-XVII vekov. Sbornik.*

[28]S. O. Shmidt, "Predposylki i pervye gody 'Kazanskoi voiny' (1545-1549)." *Trudy MGIAI* [Moskovskii gosudarstvennyi istoriko-arkhivnyi institut], Vol. VI (Moscow, 1954).

social groups. This helped to improve the economy and consólidate political conditions by way of increased social contentment. When order was established by way of extension of privileges to the high and lesser nobility, not only the state, but the church as well was bound to enjoy the benefits of social stability, and enabled to enhance the status of the Metropolitan. Some of the historians cited above also took the view that the reforms proved instrumental in attaining a sort of church-state alliance against the people and promoted further centralization of the state. This view is somewhat in doubt. Secular and ecclesiastical cooperation probably came about largely as a by-product of a wider distribution of privileges rather than a deliberately envisioned scheme of alliance.

The question of the political role played by the Zemskii Sobor in Russian history has been a subject of lively discussions. In 1958, a lengthy article by the eminent Soviet scholar M. N. Tikhomirov appeared in the leading historical journal, *Voprosy istorii.*[29] The article awakened an interest in the subject and reopened discussions among Soviet historians. One of the main questions widely debated was the nature of the class structure of the Zemskii Sobor: To what degree had it reflected the consolidated state and to what extent did it represent Russian society of the time?

The subject was pursued by L. V. Cherepnin, A. A. Zimin, V. I. Koretskii, and several others. Cherepnin dealt extensively with the role of the Zemskii Sobor during the peasant revolts in the early part of the seventeenth century. A. A. Zimin published the gathered acts of the assembly of 1612-1613, while V. I. Koretskii analyzed the proceedings of the session summoned in 1575.[30]

The question as to why the Zemskii Sobor did not develop into a Western type of parliamentary body has been approached by many writers. The undeniable fact is that whereas in western European countries, monarchies "with their class representative assemblies," as Soviet historians describe them, eventually became parliamentary governments, in Russia the opposite developed: the Zemskii Sobor vanished entirely from the political scene and the monarchy assumed absolute power. The question that arises is: What were the distinctive characteristics of the Zemskii Sobor that were not shared by similar institutions in other countries? Why was Russian centralization bound to take the road of absolutism instead of developing a parliamentary system? Much remains to be explored and classified before an acceptable interpretation is presented. A comparative study of all available evidence con-

[29] M. N. Tikhomirov, "Soslovno-predstavitelnye uchrezhdeniia (Zemski Sobory) v Rossii XVI v." *Voprosy istorii,* No. 5 (1958), 3-22. See also S. B. Veselovskii, "Sinodik opalnykh tsaria Ivana, kak istoricheskii istochnik." *Problemy istochnikovedeniia,* No. 3 (1940). A. A. Zimin, "Sostav boyarskoi dumy v XV i XVI vv." *Arkheograficheskii ezhegodnik za 1957 god.* (Moscow, 1958). Vol. I, 55-63.

[30] L. V. Cherepnin published his study in *Etudes présentées à la Commission Internationale pour l'histoire des Assemblées d'Etats,* Vol. XXIII (1960). A. A. Zimin's work appeared in *Zapiski otdela rukopisei Gosudarstvennoi biblioteki im. Lenina,* No. 18 (1957). I. V. Koretskii's views are to be found in *Istoricheskii arkhiv,* No. 2 (1959).

cerning development of monarchical and parliamentary systems in Russia and western Europe during the sixteenth century is still being awaited.

B. FEUDAL SOCIETY

Russian historiography, both before 1917 and after, has devoted much attention to defining the nature of feudalism in Russia and the ways in which it resembles or differs from the institution of feudalism in the West. Some scholars focused their attention on the juridical, and others on the economic, aspects of the peasantry; some of them were concerned with the origins of serfdom, which to Soviet scholars is usually synonymous with feudalism. L. V. Cherepnin has published a careful analytical study of the different peasant categories in relation to their juridical or economic status; for example, the *smerd* or former land-owning peasant; the *izgoi*—a member of society who did not fit into any social group and who might be the illiterate son of a priest, or a bankrupted merchant, or a former *kholop* (household servant) who won his freedom; the *zakup*—the peasant who received an advance payment and became dependent upon the landlord benefactor; the *serebrennik*—the peasant who found himself transferred for financial compensation to another landlord; the *starozbil*—the peasant who was able to trace his ancestry far back within the location he resided and paid his dues either to the state or the landlord. Having defined these categories, Cherepnin suggested that the frequent early references to these categories and their gradual disappearance from the records serve as evidence of the different phases in the development of feudal Russian society.[31]

Another historian, V. I. Koretskii, uncovered new legal data which he ably reconstructed to show that legislation of the end of the sixteenth and beginning of the seventeenth century indicates a step-by-step attachment of the peasants to the land, and correspondingly, an official recognition of the institution of serfdom. V. M. Paneiakh devoted his attention to the status of the *kholops*, basing a good deal of his study on the Ukaz issued in 1601. He particularly bases his thesis on the application of the Ukaz in the following years, as it related to the attachment of the peasants to the land.[32] These and other writers have clarified many details concerning the complex system of obligatory service that developed during this time. The precise amount of feudal dues, rent, and other financial obligations paid during this

[31]L. V. Cherepnin, "Atkovyi material kak istochnik po istorii russkogo krestianstva XV veka (iz istorii proizvoditelnykh sil i proizvodstvennykh otnoshenii)." *Problemy istochnikovedeniia,*No. 4 (1955), 307-349. B. D. Grekov, *Izbrannye trudy.* Vol. II. (Moscow, 1959).

[32]V. M. Paneiakh, "K voprosu o tak nazyvaemykh derevenskikh sluzhilykh kabalakh Spaso-Prilutskogo monastyria." *Problemy istochnikovedeniia,* No. 5 (1956), 210-230. V. M. Paneiakh, "K voprosu ob ukaze 1601 goda." *Problemy istochnikovedeniia,* No. 9 (1961), 262-269. V. I. Koretskii, "Iz istorii zakreposhcheniia krestian v Rossii v kontse XVI–nachala XVII v. (K probleme 'zapovednykh let' i otmeny Iureva dnia)." *Istoriia SSSR,* No. 1 (1957), 161-191.

period is less clearly shown. Many details concerning the form of feudal payments—whether in money, in kind, or in labor—during the fifteenth and sixteenth centuries also require further clarification.

In his first-rate work on the peasantry in early Russian history, B. D. Grekov points out the changes that took place during these centuries. The changes that were witnessed, Grekov observes, were identical or very similar to those that took place in western Europe. Grekov's study has been accepted as definitive by Soviet historians, though monographic studies concerning what Marxists call "the period of the reorganization of agricultural economy along capitalistic lines within the frame of feudalism" are still in process. Equally important research is still to be carried out on such subjects as the gradual engagement of feudal lords in trade and commerce, and the impact it had upon the entire social and economic system.

Barshchina (corvée) was not yet a stabilized practice during the sixteenth century, when it appears to have changed from rendering obligatory service in the field to payments in kind or money. In some localities corvée was by *obrok* or money payments. The subject, though of vital interest, is complicated by a scarcity of sources that might elucidate some of the more pertinent questions. There is hope that archeology might help find the answers in the form of uncovered artifacts. Thus far, the information needed has been extremely limited.[33]

Much research has been done in the development of private land ownership. In their works on the development of the Russian centralized state, S. V. Bakhrushin, K. V. Bazilevich, and particularly L. V. Cherepnin dealt at great length with the gradual change in the status of the princely and boyar patrimonial estates *(votchinas)*, the political consolidation of the state, and its impact upon claims to ownership of these estates.[34] For some inexplicable reason, most historians have had a far greater interest in landownership among the upper classes than among the peasantry. The impact of the centralized state upon peasant tenure still remains a mystery. There is, for instance, still much confusion as to the shift of ownership of certain lands from the peasantry to the state; there is no clear explanation as to how the peasants lost their claims to the land, or by what means this transfer was carried out. While some believe that the so-called "black land" had always belonged to the state, as A. D. Gorskii reasonably argues, for example, and that a feudal system seldom permits peasant landownership, others remain unconvinced. Writers like D. P. Makovskii or P. I. Liashchenko contend that methods of sale, exchange, grant, or other forms of land acquisition favored private ownership. It should also be noted that whatever interpretation is held, few students of the period imply that the development of the feudal system had been decisive in land tenure.

---

[33] B. D. Grekov, "Glavneishie etapy istorii russkoi feodalnoi votchiny." *Izbrannye trudy*, Vol. III (Moscow, 1960), 203-222.

[34] L. V. Cherepnin, *Obrazovanie Russkogo tsentralizovannogo gosudarstva v XIV-XV vekakh. Ocherki sotsialno-ekonomicheskoi i politicheskoi istorii Rossii.* (Moscow, 1960).

In 1957 M. N. Tikhomirov published his study on medieval Moscow. Two years later A. M. Sakharov's work on northeastern towns of Russia appeared. These two excellent studies were followed by L. V. Cherepnin's book on the formation of the centralized state in Russia and V. N. Bernadskii's outstanding monograph on Novgorod.[35] Cumulatively these works indicate impressive progress in the field of feudal studies in Soviet historiography; in addition, they complement each other in one important respect—they prove the similarity in basic development of medieval towns and cities in eastern and western Europe.

Certain differences in interpretation do stand out among historians. For instance, A. M. Sakharov, in his monograph on northeastern Russian cities says that feudalism often acted as a factor retarding the growth of urban communities; he also believes that other writers have exaggerated the economic and political role of northeastern Russian towns and cities during the fourteenth and fifteenth centuries. The rising number of Russian towns during this period, emphasized by others, does not seem to impress Sakharov. He discusses this especially in a chapter which he contributed to a general history of the USSR.[36]

Sakharov minimizes the importance of towns because, he believes, the towns of this period represented nothing but centers of exchange of locally produced commodities. He challenges the interpretation of M. N. Tikhomirov and of B. A. Rybakov, and minimizes the important of the town meetings *(veche)* or the guild organizations which some writers emphasize strongly. The invasion of the Mongols and the rise of the centralized Grand Duchy of Moscow caused the guilds to be handled quite differently from those of western Europe, and in no way encouraged their growth in any comparable manner. The Grand Duke of Moscow forced all the towns and cities into submission and destroyed whatever municipal autonomy there was. Sakharov is therefore skeptical about the existence of either a third estate or an "urban revolutionary element" mentioned by others.[37]

Sakharov's views were challenged head-on by L. V. Cherepnin, who argued that Sakharov neglected the socio-economic development of the Russian towns and cities of this period and the role they played in the political life of

[35]M. N. Tikhomirov, *Srednevekovaia Moskva XIV-XV vekakh.* (Moscow, 1946; 2nd ed., 1956). A. M. Sakharov, *Goroda Severo-Vostochnoi Rusi, XIV-XV vekov.* (Moscow, 1959). See also Sakharov's article, "Problema obrazovaniia tsentralizovannogo gosudarstva v sovetskoi istoriografii." *Voprosy istorii,* No. 9 (1961), 70-88. (Note summary in English, pp. 219-221.) L. V. Cherepnin, *Obrazovanie Russkogo tsentralizovannogo gosudarstva v XIV-XV vekakh.* (Moscow, 1960). V. N. Bernadskii, *Novgorod i Novgorodskaia zemlia v XV v.* (Moscow, 1961).

[36]*Ocherki istorii SSSR. Period feodalizma XIV-XIX vv.* (Moscow, 1953). Also in *Istoriia SSSR s drevneishikh vremen do 1861,* Vol. I (Moscow, 1956), Chaps. 7-8.

[37]A. M. Sakharov, *Goroda Severo-Vostochnoi Rusi XIV-XV vekov.* (Moscow, 1959), 129, 138.

the country. Cherepnin argued that Russian medieval towns and cities played a paramount part in the formation of the centralized state.[38]

For reasons that are not too clear, the study of medieval urban communities remains scanty. With the exception of a few works such as that of A. P. Pronshtein, the subject is far from being adequately explored. Pronshtein's study includes much valuable original material and presents some challenging conclusions. The one serious fallacy of his thesis is that he bases it upon Novgorod, which was a unique case, completely unlike other cities, so that the role it played can hardly be applicable to any of the other cities.[39] Even after Novgorod was incorporated into the Muscovite state, that city retained many of its unique characteristics. A collection of essays was published in 1966 which successfully pulled together the different studies into an overall picture of national development, while reflecting the peculiarities of the local communities. The volume is a notable contribution to Soviet historiography, filling in some serious gaps in the field.[40]

As one examines the level of development of commodity-financial relations and the market during the feudal period in Russia, one notes two seemingly contradictory tendencies in the literature. Some authors tend to magnify, others to minimize, the role the urban communities played in the feudal economy of Russia during the fourteenth and fifteenth centuries. A. M. Sakharov takes as an illustration the history of the towns of northeastern Russia of this period.[41] He shows the absence of firm economic ties among them; production, he points out further, was weak and inadequate and for these very reasons could hardly have stimulated trade. It was not until the seventeenth century, Sakharov argues, when the early elements of capitalism began to emerge, that it is at all reasonable to speak of the economic life of the country. Sakharov adds that only in the foreign sphere could trade have been considered a factor of vital importance.

Out of this and other discussions emerged the protracted debates among Soviet historians on the so-called ascending and descending issue. There were as many interpretations as there were writers on the exact placement in time of the descending line of feudalism and the ascending line of capitalism. To cite a single illustration, V. A. Golobutskii contended that the introduction of hired labor and the appearance of a commodity-money economy at a time when feudal conditions still existed can be regarded as the initial steps

[38]L. V. Cherepnin, *Obrazovanie Russkogo tsentralizovannogo gosudarstva v XIV-XV vekakh.* (Moscow, 1960). See particularly pp. 129, 444, 451-452.

[39]A. P. Pronshtein, *Velikii Novgorod v XVI veke. Ocherk sotsialno-ekonomicheskoi i politicheskoi istorii russkogo goroda.* (Kharkov, 1957).

[40]*Goroda feodalnoi Rossii. Sbornik statei pamiati N. V. Ustiugova.* (Moscow, 1966). *Istoriia SSSR*, No. 3 (1967), 156-161.

[41]A. M. Sakharov, *Goroda Severo-Vostochnoi Rusi XIV-XV vekov.* (Moscow, 1959), 151.

toward capitalistic development.[42] Therefore, Golobutskii states, we are already able to detect, during the fifteenth century, the descending line of the feudal phase and an ascending bourgeois influence in Russia. But what about the consolidation of the later institution of serfdom? Golobutskii's ingenious explanation is that serfdom only served as evidence of the beginning of a decline of feudalism; it only proved that serfdom was a desperate effort on the part of the old feudal class to find means of adapting itself in the midst of changing economic conditions and retaining its feudal way of life.

The "descending" and "ascending" theories were pursued at length. M. V. Nechkina challenged Golobutskii's entire interpretation during a symposium on agrarian history of eastern Europe as well as in historical writings.[43] D. P. Makovskii also challenged Golobutskii in his analytical study of the development of commodity-money relations in Russian agrarian history of the sixteenth century.[44] Makovskii contends that free-labor employment had been practiced long before capitalism, even in feudal conditions. Eventually, free labor deteriorated into a semi-slave situation or a system of outright exploitation. Makovskii argues further that the establishment of centralized authority must have had positive as well as negative effects upon the economic development of Russia. Russian capitalism, he believes, neither initiated serfdom nor caused its doom. Makovskii equally rejected the idea that capitalism suffered from the wars and the intervention of Poland and Sweden as some maintain. He insisted that there was neither adequate nor convincing evidence to support this view. His opponents believe that Makovskii exaggerates the importance of the commodity-money relationship or the free-labor employment system as it existed in the sixteenth century in rural communities. To identify this as a capitalistic system, they say, is totally erroneous.

There are few outstanding works that fully embrace the economic and social developments of sixteenth-century Russia. Vital problems in the field have been touched upon by M. V. Nechkina,[45] stimulating challenges have been presented, and the subjects have generally given rise to various views,

[42]V. A. Golobutskii, "O nachale 'niskhodiashchei' stadii feodalnoi formatsii." *Voprosy istorii*, No. 9 (1959), 123-137. K. V. Sivkov, "Vazhnyi etap v perekhode ot feodalnogo k burzhuaznomu zemlevladeniiu v Rossii." *Voprosy istorii*, No. 3 (1958), 24-43.

[43]I. V. Kuznetsov, "O 'voskhodiashchei' i 'niskhodiashchei' stadiiakh feodalizma v Rossii." *Voprosy istorii*, No. 11 (1959), 79-92. The most adequate presentation of the subject may be found in the *Ezhegodnik po agrarnoi istorii Vostochnoi Evropy, 1959* (Moscow, 1961). V. A. Golobutskii, "O nachale 'niskhodiashchei' stadii feodalnoi formatsii." *Voprosy istorii*, No. 9 (1959), 123-137.

[44]D. P. Makovskii, *Razvitie tovarno-denezhnykh otnoshenii v selskom khoziaistve Russkogo gosudarstva XVI veke.* (Smolensk, 1960).

[45]M. V. Nechkina, "O 'voskhodiashchei' i 'niskhodiashchei' stadiiakh feodalnoi formatsii. (K postanovke voprosa)." *Voprosy istorii*, No. 7 (1958), 86-108.

challenges, interpretations, and animated rebuttals. Accounts of these exchanges have often been cited in various periodicals, mostly in *Voprosy istorii*. There has been much heat in the exchange of views with little light being shed, but the discussions accomplished one thing at least—they steered historians to associated fields of study where attention was much needed.

A. I. Kopanev, for example, investigated sixteenth-century demography.[46] Having employed a vast body of research, he pointed out population shifts that took place within Russia during the sixteenth century. He included in the analysis also the territories recently annexed by Moscow, illustrating the role these played in economic life during the second half of the sixteenth century, and described the serious population decline in the northwestern and central regions. Another writer, G. A. Pobedimova, investigated demographic problems of the same period in the northwestern regions of Moscow, near the Volokolamsk monastery. V. K. Iatsunskii made a similar study of population distribution from the second quarter of the eighteenth century until the early twentieth century.[47] There is not yet a definitive work in this field.

Agrarian history has naturally come to be regarded as a central theme among students of this early period. One of the major questions has been: By what means did serfdom entrench itself locally and nationally so as to become eventually a national institution? There has been general agreement among recent writers that the spread of serfdom did not advance with equal speed throughout the country. Within the Moscow principality it came earlier and moved faster, while in the northern areas serfdom penetrated more slowly and was recognized much later.[48]

V. I. Koretskii revealed much supporting evidence concerning the process of peasant attachment to the soil during the end of the sixteenth and seventeenth centuries. He utilized largely the archival records that deal with peasants who escaped and were forcibly returned to lawful claimants. On the basis of the evidence, the author was able to reconstruct the judicial picture as it existed at the time, particularly the legal innovations introduced as a result of the legislative acts of 1580-1581. The culminating point in this process, the author came to believe, was the ukaz of 1592-1593, banning further departure of peasants from the land they held at the time the law went into effect. Koretskii then developed the theme further, showing step by step how serfdom came to apply to other social groups such as the *kholops*. Koretskii's study is of great assistance to students of the seventeenth century,

[46]A. I. Kopanev, "Naselenie Russkogo gosudarstva v XVI veke." *Istoricheskie zapiski*, No. 64 (1959), 233-254.

[47]G. A. Pobedimova, "K voprosu o stabilnosti naseleniia votchiny XVI v. (Na primere Iosifo-Volokolamskogo monastyria)." *Voprosy ekonomiki i klassovykh otnoshenii v Russkom gosudarstve XII-XVII vv. Sbornik*. V. K. Iatsunkii, "Izmeneniia v razmeshchenii naseleniia Evropeiskoi Rossii v 1724-1916 gg." *Istoriia SSSR*, No. 1 (1959), 192-224.

[48]S. M. Kashtanov, "K probleme mestnogo upravleniia v Rossii pervoi poloviny XVI v." *Istoriia SSSR*, No. 6 (1959), 134-148.

for he traces effectively the deep roots of peasant discontent and the causes underlying the violent resentment that was eventually to become nationwide.[49] Along the frontiers, however, the discontented elements formed a united and effective resistance movement. The rebellious masses not only arose against centralized authority, but they insisted upon autonomous privileges and firmly rejected serfdom in any shape or form. Some even envisioned the formation of a "peasant state" headed by an "acceptable tsar." The rebellion led by I. Bolotnikov at the opening of the seventeenth century was to become the true prelude to the forcible assertion of the Cossacks' autonomous rights, even though the rebels were defeated on this occasion.[50]

The various studies in agrarian development of the sixteenth and early seventeenth centuries raised several vital issues among Soviet historians. To what extent, for instance, did all the economic, social, and legal changes that were witnessed during this period affect the course of later events? Did these mark progress or regression? Were they steps toward a feudal reaction or signs of slowly encroaching capitalistic developments? How did serfdom, which established itself in the early seventeenth century, compare with the feudal order of western Europe?[51] Some writers believed that the agrarian economy of the middle sixteenth century was hardly a factor to favor capitalistic development. Others seriously questioned whether the prevailing economic conditions in Russia during the sixteenth century were in any way comparable to conditions in western Europe. Whatever the answer to these queries, they stimulated an inquisitive spirit among many students of history.[52]

[49]V. I. Koretskii, "Iz istorii zakreposhcheniia krestian v Rossii v kontse XVI–nachale XVII v." *Istoriia SSSR*, No. 1 (1957), 161-191.

[50]*Ezhegodnik po agrarnoi istorii Vostochnoi Evropy, 1958.* Issue I (Tallin, 1959). Issue II (Moscow, 1961).

[51]S. D. Skazkin, "Osnovnye problemy tak nazyvaemogo 'vtorogo izdaniia krepostinchestva' v Srednei i Vostochnoi Evrope." *Voprosy istorii*, No. 2 (1958), 96-119. See also the arguments Skazkin presented to a symposium on agrarian history cited in *Ezhegodnik po agrarnoi istorii Vostochnoi Evropy, 1958*, p. 141.

[52]D. P. Makovskii, *Razvitie tovarno-denezhnykh otnoshenii v selskom khoziaistve Russkogo gosudarstva v XVI veke.* (Smolensk, 1960). S. G. Strumilin, "K voprosu o genezise kapitalizma v Rossii." *Voprosy istorii*, No. 9 (1961), 56-69. V. A. Golobutskii, "O nachale 'niskhodiashchei' stadii feodalnoi formatsii." *Voprosy istorii*, No. 9 (1959), 123-137. S. G. Strumilin, "O vnutrennem rynke Rossii XVI-XVII vv." *Istoriia SSSR* (1959), 75-87. A. L. Sidorov, "Nekotorye problemy razvitiia rossiiskogo kapitalizma v sovetskoi istoricheskoi nauke." *Problemy istorii*, No. 12 (1961), 26-62. A. A. Preobrazhenskii and Iu. A. Tikhonov, "Itogi izucheniia nachalnogo etapa skladyvaniia vserossiiskogo rynka (XVII v.)." *Voprosy istorii*, No. 4 (1961), 80-109. *Sbornik statei. Voprosy genezisa kapitalizma v Rossii.* (Leningrad, 1960). M. V. Nechkina, "O 'voskhodiashchei' i 'niskhodiashchei' stadiiakh feodalnoi formatsii." *Voprosy istorii*, No. 7 (1958), 86-108.

Much less research has been done in the history of individual principalities and early towns in Russia; only a few cities, such as Novgorod, Pskov, and Moscow, have been dealt with. Novgorod has been of particular interest; agriculture could not become a dominant economic factor here, because of poor soil conditions. For this reason, trade and commerce came to play a far more significant part here than elsewhere. Transit fees constituted an important source of revenue in addition to profitable commerce. Geographic location was turned to advantage since its remoteness saved Novgorod from eastern as well as southern invasions.

A. P. Pronshtein has recently contributed an outstanding study of Novgorod, while the Academy of Sciences has published a six-volume joint work on the history of Moscow. This still leaves a widely unexplored field: the history of numerous other cities that either rivaled Moscow for control or struggled to retain their independent status. Subjects such as the formation of social classes in towns and cities, economic development, and other aspects of urban community life have been equally neglected.[53] Some cities seem to reveal centrifugal tendencies in being gradually absorbed within the centralized Muscovite state. Such was the case of Pskov or Novgorod. A. P. Pronshtein, for instance, believes that the incorporation of Novgorod by Moscow was followed by a revival of economic prosperity, despite its loss of political freedom. By the middle of the sixteenth century Novgorod witnessed its highest degree of economic prosperity.[54] However, Pronshtein seems to underestimate the economic impact that the campaign of Ivan IV against Novgorod, in 1570, must have had. In this regard, a study by G. S. Rabinovich is an excellent complementary work to the one by Pronshtein.[55]

A few students of the sixteenth century have addressed themselves specifically to cultural history and social thought. A. I. Klibanov deals with the reformation movement in Russia and the attempts exerted by some groups or individuals to free religious thought from the grip of dogmatism; the same movement also favored the extension of liberalized education to more people. The development of social thought is extensively dealt with by A. A. Zimin

[53]The approximate number of cities and their characteristics are lucidly described by A. A. Zimin in "Sostav russkikh gorodov XVI v." *Istoricheskie zapiski*, No. 52 (1955), 336-347.

[54]A. P. Pronshtein, *Velikii Novgorod v XVI veke. Ocherk sotsialno-ekonomicheskoi i politicheskoi istorii russkogo goroda.* (Kharkov, 1957). M. N. Tikhomirov, *Pskovskoe vosstanie 1650 g.* (Moscow, 1935). M. N. Tikhomirov, "Novgorodskoe vosstanie 1650 g." *Istoricheskie zapiski*, No. 7 (1945). M. N. Tikhomirov, *Drevneishie goroda.* (Moscow, 1946). M. N. Tikhomirov, *Krestianskie i gorodskie vosstaniia na Rusi XI-XIII vv.* (Moscow, 1955). N. N. Maslennikova, *Prisoedinenie Pskova k Russkomu gosudarstvu.* (Moscow, 1955).

[55]A. P. Rabinovich, "Novgorodskie remesla XVI v." In *Uchenye zapiski Leningradskogo pedagogicheskogo instituta im. A. I. Gertsena.* Vol. XXXIX (Leningrad, 1941). B. D. Grekov, *Ocherki po istorii khoziaistva Novgorodskogo Sofiiskogo Doma XV-XVII vv. Izbrannye trudy,*Vol. III (Moscow, 1940), 40-191.

in the course of a book on the career of I. S. Peresvetov, the sixteenth-century thinker, military theoretician, and author of several projects of liberal reforms which he presented to Ivan IV. The author's sources cast much light upon the social and political ideas that prevailed during the middle of the sixteenth century, and particularly the political developments and religious conditions of the time. Mention must also be made of a study by G. N. Moiseeva which devoted special attention to the position of the nobility during the same period.[56]

C. FOREIGN AFFAIRS

During the first two decades following the Revolution, with the exception of documentary publications of recent diplomatic history, very little had been written about earlier periods of foreign affairs. There was a conspicuous scarcity of monographic studies on the subject, or even articles in historical journals. The main interest centered on twentieth-century diplomacy, and particularly on foreign policy related to the First World War. There was also an overemphasis upon diplomatic relations with western European nations and, to a lesser degree, relations with Near Eastern, Middle Eastern, and Far Eastern countries. Documentary sources gathered hastily from the Foreign Office archives stressed mostly secret negotiations, treaties, "imperialistic plottings," or processes of extracting "unequal treaties" in Asia.[57]

As the years passed, attention began to shift to other fields and periods of diplomatic history. There was a keener interest in Russian foreign policy since the sixteenth century—e.g., the successful eastward expansion resulting from the downfall of the khanates of Kazan and extending beyond the Urals, and the less successful expansive efforts in the west, which turned on the struggle for an outlet to the Baltic Sea. Foreign affairs of this early period were closely related to domestic policies, having to do with political and administrative centralization. The incorporation of enormous territories in the east intensified the need for further administrative centralization, and marked the early stages in the formation of the multi-racial, multi-lingual Russian state.

[56]A. I. Klibanov, *Reformatsionnye dvizheniia v Rossii v XIV–pervoi polovine XVI v.* (Moscow, 1960). A. A. Zimin, *I. S. Peresvetov i ego sovremenniki. Ocherki po istorii russkoi obshchestvenno-politicheskoi mysli serediny XVI v.* (Moscow, 1958). (See a review of this work in the *Slavonic and East European Review*, No. 89 [London, 1959].) I. U. Budovnits, *Russkaia publitsistika XVI v.* (Moscow, 1947). I. I. Polosin, "O chelobitnykh Peresvetova." *Uchenye zapiski Moskovskogo gosudarstvennogo pedagogicheskogo instituta im. V. I. Lenina.* Vol. XXXV. *Kafedra istorii.* Issue 2 (Moscow, 1946). G. N. Moiseeva, *Valaamskaia beseda—pamiatnik russkoi publitsistiki serediny XVI veka.* (Moscow, 1958).

[57]Foreign affairs during the reign of Ivan IV are dealt with, though briefly, by S. V. Bakhrushin, "Ivan Groznyi v svete noveishikh issledovanii." *Nauchnye trudy*, Vol. II (Moscow, 1954), 353-361.

Political centralization was further encouraged by the rising threat of the Ottoman Empire. Thus, if the danger of Asian invasions diminished from about the middle of the sixteenth century on, threats from the south increased. In his brief laudatory characterization of Ivan IV, I. I. Smirnov presents a lucidly drawn account of Moscow's effort to master the situation by consolidation in the east and a defensive policy in the south, and the impact of both undertakings upon domestic policy. This phase of foreign policy is still far from being entirely explored, and demands further investigation in depth instead of casual reference in general or related writings.[58]

For some time, the reason for the absence of extensive studies in this field was the scarcity of sources. Most of the diplomatic documents related to this period, including the archives of the khanates of Kazan and Astrakhan, were no longer in existence. But things change, and since the 1930's a number of historians have extended their interests. Source materials on Russian relations with the Ottoman Empire, Persia, the Crimean khanate, the Nogai Tartars, the Central Asian peoples, the northern Caucasus, Bashkiria, and Siberia have been published at an accelerating rate. In light of recently published materials it has become increasingly evident what impact foreign policy had upon Russian internal affairs throughout the sixteenth century and those following.[59]

[58]I. I. Smirnov, *Ivan Groznyi. (Leningrad, 1944).*

[59]The following is a selected list of references of recent works in the field discussed above: E. P. Alekseeva, *Ocherki po ekonomike i kulture narodov Cherkessii v XVI-XVII vv.* (Cherkessk, 1957). S. V. Bakhrushin, *Ocherki po istorii kolonizatsii Sibiri v XVI i XVII vv. Nauchnye trudy,* Vol. III (Moscow, 1955). S. V. Bakhrushin, *Ocherki po istorii Krasnoiarskogo uezda v XVII v. Nauchnye trudy,* Vol. IV (Moscow, 1959). Z. I. Boiarshinova, *Naselenie Zapadnoi Sibiri do nachala russkoi kolonizatsii.* (Tomsk, 1960). G. D. Burdei, "Vzaimootnosheniia Rossii s Turtsiei i Krymom v period borby za Povolzhie v 40-50kh godakh XVI v." *Uchenye zapiski Saratovskogo gosudarstvennogo universiteta im. N. G. Chernyshevskogo.* Vol. XVII (1956). I. P. Emelianov, *Ocherki po istorii Udmurtskoi ASSR.* (Izhevsk, 1958). A. V. Fadeev, *Rossiia i vostochnyi krizis 20kh godov XIX veka.* (Moscow, 1958). Kh. G. Gimadi, "Ob istoricheskom znachenii prisoedineniia Tatarii k Russkomu gosudarstvu." *Izvestiia Kazanskogo filiala Akademii nauk SSSR* (1955). *Seriia gumanitarnykh nauk.* Issue I. *440-letie prisoedineniia Bashkirii k Russkomu gosudarstvu.* (Ufa, 1960). P. T. Iakovleva, *Pervyi russko-kitaiskii dogovor 1689 g.* (Moscow, 1958). *Istoriia Tatarskoi ASSR.* (Kazan, 1955). M. Iu. Iudashev, "Nekotorye dokumentalnye dannye o sviaziakh Srednei Azii s Rossiei (XVI-XVII vv.)." *Izvestiia Akademii nauk Uzbekskoi SSSR. Seriia obshchestvennykh nauk,* No. 4 (Tashkent, 1958). M. S. Kapitsa, *Sovetsko-kitaiskie otnosheniia.* (Moscow, 1958). T. Kh. Kumykov, "K voprosu o prisoedinenii Kabardy k Rossii." *Sbornik po istorii Kabardy.* Kabardinskii nauchno-issledovatelskii institut pri Sovete ministrov Kabardinskoi ASSR, comp. Issue V. (Nalchik, 1956). Sh. A. Meskhia and Ia. Z. Tsintsadze, *Iz istorii russko-gruzinskikh vzaimootnoshenii X-XVII vv.* (Tbilisi, 1958). *Mezhdunarodnye sviazi Rossii do XVIII v.* (Moscow, 1961). M. V. Levchenko, *Ocherki po istorii russko-vizantiiskikh otnoshenii.* (Moscow, 1956). *Ocherki Kabardy s drevneishikh vremen do nashikh dnei.* (Moscow, 1957). *Ocherki po istorii Bashkirskoi ASSR.* (Ufa, 1957). B. A. Romanov, *Ocherki diplomaticheskoi istorii*

Late in the reign of Ivan IV the Baltic situation became an issue of utmost importance, both at home and abroad. The outbreak of the war in Livonia, according to Ia. Ia. Zutis, caused widespread revolts among the peasantry against the German landlords who had dominated rural communities for centuries. Kh. Kh. Kruus studied the diplomatic implications of the Livonian war as seen in western European historical literature. Strategic aspects of the war are ably handled by I. P. Shaskolskii, while G. A. Novitskii and L. A. Derbov address themselves to Russo-Swedish and Russo-Polish relations respectively. Military history, describing particularly the role played by artillery in the Livonian war, is handled by L. N. Kuzheleva. P. V. Snesarevskii has reexamined the mission of Antonio Possevino and the role played by the Vatican during the second half of the sixteenth century.[60]

Excellent studies of Anglo-Russian relations in the second half of the sixteenth century have been written by N. Nakashidze and by N. F. Prochetov, who emphasizes the two decades of the 1580's and 1590's. Ia. S. Lurie and E. M. Shakhmaliev have each written on the same events in brief articles. Similarly, a monographic study by G. Jordaniia of Franco-Russian relations during the late sixteenth and early seventeenth centuries represents a careful investigation in a related field. A more general survey of Russia's position in the European state system from the fifteenth through the eighteenth centuries is soundly interpreted by B. F. Porshnev.[61]

russko-iaponskoi voiny 1895-1907 gg. (Moscow, 1955). V. I. Sergeev, "K voprosu o pokhode v Sibir druzhiny Ermaka." *Voprosy istorii,* No. 1 (1959), 117-129. S. O. Shmidt, "Predposylki i pervye gody 'Kazanskoi voiny' (1545-1549)." *Trudy MGIAI* [Moskovskii gosudarstvennyi istoriko-arkhivnyi institut], Vol. VI (Moscow, 1954). M. N. Tikhomirov, "Prisoedinenie Chuvashii k Rossii." *Materialy k istorii Chuvashskoi ASSR.* Issue I. (Cheboksary, 1958). A. N. Usmanov, *Prisoedinenie Bashkirii Russkomu gosudarstvu.* (Ufa, 1960).

[60]Ia. Ia. Zutis, "K voprosu o Livonskoi politike Ivana IV." *Izvestiia Akademii Nauk SSSR. Seriia istorii i filosofii,* Vol. IX, No. 2 (1952). Kh. Kh. Kruus, " 'Baltiiskii vopros' v zarubezhnoi istoricheskoi literature." *Voprosy istorii,* No. 6 (1959), 108-119. V. D. Koroliuk, *Livonskaia voina.* (Moscow, 1954). I. P. Shaskolskii, "Russko-livonskie peregovory 1554 g. i voprosy o livonskoi dani." *Sbornik Mezhdunarodnye sviazi Rossii do XVII v.* (Moscow, 1961). G. A. Novitskii, "Russkoshvedskie otnosheniia v seredine XVI veka i voina 1554-1557 gg." *Vestnik Moskovskogo universiteta. Seriia istorii i filosofii,* No. 2 (1956). G. A. Novitskii, "Novye dannye o russkom feodalnom zemlevladenii v period Livonskoi voiny (1558-1582)." *Voprosy istorii,* No. 4 (1956), 134-138. L. A. Derbov, "Borba Russkogo gosudarstva za Pribaltiku i Belorussiiu v 60kh godakh XVI veka." *Uchenye zapiski Saratovskogo gosudarstvennogo universiteta im. N. G. Chernyshevskogo,* Vol. XXXIX (Saratov, 1954). P. V. Snesarevskii, "Missiia Possevino v Rossii. Proiski Vatikana v Rossii vo vtoroi polovine XVI veka." *Uchenye zapiski Kaliningradskogo gosudarstvennogo pedagogicheskogo instituta.* Issue I (1955). L. N. Kuzheleva, "O boevom ispolzovanii artillerii v vazhneishikh srzheniiakh Livonskoi voiny 1558-1583 gg." *Sbornik issledovanii i materialov Artilleriiskogo istoricheskogo muzeia.* Issue III (Leningrad, 1958).

[61]N. I. Nakashidze, *Russko-angliiskie otnosheniia vo vtoroi polovine XVI v.* (Tbilisi, 1955). N. F. Prochetov, *Anglo-russkie otnosheniia v kontse XVI v. (80-90e gody).*

There are several large publications dealing with seventeenth-century Russian foreign relations. Among these are one on Russo-Indian relations, another volume on Russo-Mongolian, and a third one on Russo-Swedish relations. All three of these include rare and recently discovered materials found in various archival depositories.[62] In addition, the publications of recent date, it might be mentioned, show remarkable improvement in the cataloguing of the archival materials as well as an increase in the quantity included, which extends to manuscripts, official records, and various other primary sources. Recently founded museums that dwell largely upon relations of Russia with many of the countries mentioned must not be overlooked. For reasons of space limitation we are able to concern ourselves only with published material here.

The long-neglected history of foreign relations and of the racial and national components of the Soviet Union has come to life in recent years, largely due to further documentary publications. How the multi-racial, multi-lingual state was formed, and the nature of the relations between that state and its neighbors in the east and in the west have been subjects of increased interest. For various reasons, such as political inadvisability or linguistic difficulties, the subjects have not always been pursued with consistent zeal. Still, the constant accumulation of materials has led students to undertake and expand research, with impressive results.[63]

(Gorky, 1955). Ia. S. Lurie, "Russko-angliiskie otnosheniia i mezhdunarodnaia politika vtoroi poloviny XVI veka. (K postanovke voprosa)." *Sbornik. Mezhdunarodnye sviazi Rossii do XVII veka.* E. M. Shakhmaliev, "Ob anglo-russkikh torgovykh protivorechiiakh na Perednem Vostoke vtoroi poloviny XVI veka." *Uchenye zapiski Azerbaidzhanskogo gosudarstvennogo universiteta im. S. M. Kirova.* No. 5 (1958). G. Jordaniia, *Ocherki po istorii franko-russkikh otnoshenii kontsa XVI i pervoi poloviny XVII vv.* (Tbilisi, 1959). 2 vols. B. F. Porshnev, "K voprosu o meste Rossii v sisteme evropeiskikh gosudarstv v XV-XVIII vv." *Uchenye zapiski Akademii obshchestvennykh nauk.* Issue II (Moscow, 1948).

[62]*Russko-indiiskie otnosheniia v XVII v.* K. A. Antonova, N. M. Goldberg, and T. D. Lavrentsova, eds. (Moscow, 1958). *Russko-mongolskie otnosheniia 1607-1636 gg.* I. Ia. Zlatkin and N. V. Ustiugov, eds. (Moscow, 1959). *Russko-shvedskie ekonomicheskie otnosheniia v XVII v.* M. P. Viatkin and I. N. Firsov, eds. (Moscow, 1960).

[63]N. B. Baykova, "K voprosu o russko-indiiskikh torgovykh otnosheniiakh v XVI-XVII vv." *Trudy Instituta vostokovedeniia Akademii nauk. Uzbekistan SSR.* Series IV. (Tashkent, 1956). A. N. Usmanov, *400-letie prisoedineniia Bashkirii k Russkomu gosudarstvu.* (Ufa, 1958). A. N. Usmanov, *Prisoedinenie Bashkirii k Russkomu gosudarstvu.* (Ufa, 1960). V. I. Savchenko, *Istoricheskie sviazi latyshskogo i russkogo narodov.* (Riga, 1959). B. Ia. Ramm, *Papstvo i Rus v X-XV vekakh.* (Moscow, 1959). L. A. Derbov, *Borba Russkogo gosudarstva za Pribaltiku i Belorussiiu v 60kh godakh XVI v.* University of Saratov Publications, Historical Series, No. 47 (1956). G. A. Novitskii, *Russko-shvedskie otnosheniia v seredine XVI v. i voina 1554-1557 gg.* Moscow State University Series of History and Philosophy, Vol. II (Moscow, 1956). G. A. Novitskii, "Voprosy torgovli v russko-shvedskikh otnosheniiakh XVI v." *Skandinavskii sbornik,* Issue II (Tallin, 1957). A. L. Khoroshkevich, "Torgovlia inostrannymi tkaniami v Novgorode XIV-XV vv." *Isto-*

The field of seventeenth-century foreign relations of Russia has been enriched recently by such publications as V. I. Buganov's research on problems
of national defense in the south during that period. Another contribution is
by Z. I. Roginskii, who deals with Anglo-Russian relations during the 1640's,
while I. V. Galaktionov has gathered documentary evidence on the signing of
the Russo-Polish truce of Andrusovo in 1667. G. M. Lifshits has published
source materials accompanied by commentaries on the Azov campaign of
1696.[64]

Recent research in Far Eastern diplomatic history brought about a reissue
of the Peking archival documents. The text of the Treaty of Nerchinsk,
accompanied by up-dated commentaries, was published by P. E. Skachkov
and V. S. Miasnikov. The work includes records related to the mission of
F. A. Golovin. The third part of the *Journal* of Vice Admiral Ia. S. Barsh,
recently published, renders a complete account of conditions in the Russian
navy during the middle of the eighteenth century. In 1957, a collection of
sources on the first diplomatic mission of Russia to Japan, in 1792-1794,
appeared in the *Istoricheskii arkhiv*.[65]

All this adds substantially to Soviet historiography. Soviet historians have
repeatedly urged the proper authorities, on various occasions, to initiate a

richeskie zapiski, No. 63 (1958), 206-243. A. L. Khoroshkevich, "Iz istorii ganzei-
skoi torgovli (Vvoz v Novgorod blagorodnykh metallov v XIV-XV vv.)." *Srednie
veka*, Issue XX (1961). A. L. Khoroshkevich, *Torgovlia Velikogo Novgoroda s Pri-
baltikoi i zapadnoi Evropy v XIV-XV vekakh.* (Moscow, 1963). A. N. Kitushin,
"Rannie russko-vengerskie sviazi (IX-XV vv.)." *Uchenye zapiski Azerbaidzhanskogo
gos. universiteta* (Baku), No. 6 (1956). M. A. Pavlushkova, "Russko-vengerskie
otnosheniia do nachala XIII v." *Istoriia SSSR*, No. 6 (1959), 149-155. M. M.
Gromyko, "Russko-niderlandskaia torgovlia na Murmanskom beregu v XVI v."
Srednie veka, No. 17 (1960). For an excellent collection of source materials on
XVIII-XIX century Franco-Russian relations and cultural impact see *Literaturnoe
nasledstvo*, Vols. 29-30 (1938), 31-32 (1937), 33-34 (1939).

[64]V. I. Buganov, "Zasechnaia kniga 1638 g." *Zapiski otdela rukopisei GBL* (Moscow,
1960), 181-253. Z. I. Roginskii, *London 1645-1646 godov. Novye istochniki
o poezdke gontsa Gerasima Semionovicha Dokhturova v Angliiu.* (Iaroslavl, 1960).
I. V. Galaktionov, "K istorii Andrusovskogo peremiriia 1667 g." *Istoricheskii arkhiv*,
No. 6 (1959), 82-90. G. M. Lifshits, comp., "Iz istorii Azovskogo pokhoda 1696 g."
Istoricheskii arkhiv, No. 2 (1959), 157-163.

[65]I. F. Kurdiukov, comp., "Iz istorii russko-kitaiskikh otnoshenii (1695-1720 gg.)."
Istoricheskii arkhiv, No. 3 (1957), 174-184. N. F. Demidova and V. S. Miasnikov,
"O datirovke gramot imperatorov kitaiskoi dinastii tsariu Mikhailu Feodorovichu."
Problemy istochnikovedeniia, No. 1 (1960), 164-167. *Russko-kitaiskie otnosheniia
1689-1916 gg. Ofitsialnye dokumenty.* P. E. Skachkov and V. S. Miasnikov,
comps. (Moscow, 1958). P. T. Iakovleva, *Pervyi russko-kitaiskii dogovor 1689
goda.* (Moscow, 1958). (This study cites the text of the credentials, "veritelnaia i
proezzhaia gramoty," of F. A. Golovin.) V. I. Pishvanova, " 'Journal' vitse-admirala
Ia. S. Barsha, [Part 3] 1741-1755." *Trudy Gosudarstvennoi biblioteki [GPB]* im.
M. E. Saltykova-Shchedrina, Vol. I (14) (Leningrad, 1957), 7-117. A. A. Preobrazhenskii, "Pervoe russkoe posolstvo v Iaponiiu." *Istoricheskii arkhiv*, No. 4 (1961),
113-148.

more systematic publication of all diplomatic documents on the seventeenth and eighteenth centuries. To date, the materials published are still quite fragmentary and poorly coordinated.[66] An effort has been made by various students of history to utilize fragmentary and often casually uncovered materials—in some cases quite successfully. Some students originally published the results of their research in periodicals, and later included them in their monographic studies. I. V. Galaktionov has published his findings in his monograph on the Russo-Polish truce of Andrusovo of 1667; Z. I. Roginskii has studied Anglo-Russian relations during the time of Cromwell; N. A. Mokhov has dealt with Russo-Moldavian relations during the second quarter of the seventeenth century; while G. A. Nekrasov has written a unique work on Russo-Swedish relations and their effect upon the policies of other European nations during 1721-1726. Interest was maintained in Russian policies in Asia, as evidenced by two monographs: one by N. P. Shastina, on Russo-Mongolian relations during the seventeenth century, and the other by P. T. Iakovleva, a monographic work on the Sino-Russian treaty of Nerchinsk, concluded in 1689.[67]

The publication of *The Letters and Papers of Peter I*, initiated in 1887, continued for many years. The ninth volume appeared in 1951, containing a wealth of material on both diplomatic and military history during his reign.[68] These nine volumes include a considerable portion of the sources related to the struggle for the Baltic coast, Russo-Swedish and Russo-Turkish relations, the war in the south, and the capture of Azov. The published papers seem to indicate that there is little likelihood of finding much new and startling material on the Northern War which ended with the Treaty of Nystad in 1721. In his volume on the Northern War, E. V. Tarlé incorporated excellent vignettes of Peter I, Charles XII, and Mazeppa, as military leaders, as statesmen, and as national and continental figures. Tarlé's presentation of the

[66]See, for illustration, such fragmentary data as the following: E. P. Podiapolskaia, "Shifrovannaia perepiska v Rossii v pervoi chetverti XVIII veka." *Problemy istochnikovedeniia*, No. 8 (1959), 314-342. T. N. Kopreeva, "Neizvestnaia zapiska A. L. Ordyn-Nashchokina o russko-polskikh otnosheniiakh vtoroi poloviny XVII v." *Problemy istochnikovedeniia*, No. 9 (1961), 195-220. A. A. Novoselskii, "Raznovidnosti krymskikh stateinykh spiskov XVII v. i priemy ikh sostavleniia." *Problemy istochnikovedeniia*, No. 9 (1961), 182-194. T. K. Krylova, "Stateinye spiski russkikh diplomatov (1700-1714 gg.)." *Problemy istochnikovedeniia*, No. 9 (1961), 163-181.

[67]I. V. Galaktionov, *Iz istorii russko-polskogo sblizheniia v 50-60kh godakh XVII v. (Andrusovkoe peremirie).* (Saratov, 1960). Z. I. Roginskii, "Iz istorii anglo-russkikh otnoshenii v period protektorata Kromvelia." *Novaia i noveishaia istoriia*, No. 5 (1958), 71-78. N. A. Mokhov, "Politicheskie sviazi Rossii i Moldavii vo vtoroi chetverti XVIII v." *O rumyno-russkikh i rumyno-sovetskikh sviaziakh.* (Moscow, 1960), 113-132. G. A. Nekrasov, *Russko-shvedskie otnosheniia i politika velikikh derzhav v 1721-1726 gg.* (Moscow, 1964). N. P. Shastina, *Russko-mongolskie posolskie otnosheniia XVII v.* (Moscow, 1958). P. T. Iakovleva, *Pervyi russko-kitaiskii dogovor 1689 g.* (Moscow, 1958).

[68]*Pisma i bumagi Petra Velikogo.* (Moscow, 1887-1951). 9 vols.

protracted war is brilliant and shows how that conflict, in the end, completely changed the balance of power in northern Europe.[69]

Foreign policy during the reign of Peter I is a subject that has attracted many Soviet students of history. Aside from the excellent collection of materials on Peter I compiled and interpreted by M. M. Bogoslovskii (though never completed), S. A. Feigina and L. A. Nikiforov have each contributed important studies on the Aaland and Nystad settlements that terminated the Northern War with Sweden. Both works are based on recently gathered archival sources. The journey of Peter I to Paris in 1717 and the Treaty of Amsterdam concluded between France and Russia served as a diplomatic prelude to the Aaland Congress. It was in response to pressure from England, as Nikiforov revealed, that Sweden terminated the earlier negotiations.[70] In part, the previous negotiations with France proved vital in Russia's presentation of a well-elaborated plan that incorporated the conditions of a peace settlement with Sweden. At the renewed negotiations at Nystad, Russia succeeded in winning favorable terms, and thus, for the first time, brought the eastern European Empire into the ranks of the great European powers.

The period following the death of Peter I has been of lesser concern as far as foreign relations are concerned. There is a lucid account of Russian foreign policy during the eighteenth century in the scholarly series of *Outlines of the USSR*, but this is of a very general nature.[71] Further monographic studies in the field of foreign relations of the period following Peter I would be most desirable.

There are two articles on the subject which should be mentioned. One is by A. M. Stanislavskaia, on Russia and Greece at the end of the eighteenth and the beginning of the nineteenth century; the other, by G. A. Arsh, concerns Russo-Albanian relations during 1787-1791. The former analyzes Russia's policy in the Ionion Islands and the role the Russian government played in the history of Greek national liberation. The latter discusses the efforts of Ali Pasha to establish closer collaboration with Russia; it is based on sources found recently or not utilized before. Both articles correct former misrepresentation of Russia's part in the Balkans in the eighteenth century.[72]

[69]E. V. Tarlé, *Sochineniia.* (Moscow, 1957-1962). 12 vols.

[70]M. M. Bogoslovskii, *Piotr I. Materialy dlia biografii.* (Moscow, 1940-1948). 5 vols. S. A. Feigina, *Alandskii kongress. Vneshniaia politika Rossii v kontse severnoi voiny.* (Moscow, 1959). L. A. Nikiforov, *Vneshniaia politika Rossii v poslednie gody severnoi voiny. Nishtadskii mir.* (Moscow, 1959).

[71]*Ocherki istorii SSSR. Period feodalizma Rossii v pervoi chetverti XVIII v. Preobrazovaniia Petra I.* (Moscow, Academy of Sciences, 1954). *Rossiia vo vtoroi chetverti XVIII v.* (Moscow, 1957). *Rossiia vo vtoroi polovine XVIII v.* (Moscow, 1956).

[72]A. M. Stanislavskaia, "Rossiia i Gretsiia v kontse XVIII v." *Istoriia SSSR*, No. 1 (1960), 59-76. G. A. Arsh, "Russko-albanskie sviazi v period russko-turetskoi voiny 1787-1791 gg." *Istoricheskie zapiski*, No. 63 (1958), 159-268.

Tarlé's complete works incorporate all his monographic studies that pertain to the second half of the eighteenth century.[73] To the writings already cited should be added the work of E. Ia. Fainberg on Russo-Japanese relations between 1697 and 1875, and the article by R. V. Makarova on Russia's Far Eastern policy at the end of the eighteenth century.[74]

[73] E. V. Tarlé, *Sochineniia.* (Moscow, 1957-1962). 12 vols.

[74] E. Ia. Fainberg, *Russko-iaponskie otnosheniia 1697-1875 gg.* (Moscow, 1960). R. V. Makarova, "Iz istorii dalnevostochnoi politiki Rossii vo vtoroi polovine XVIII veka." *Trudy MGIAI* [Moskovskii gosudarstvennyi istoriko-arkhivnyi institut], Vol. XIV (Moscow, 1960), 322-348.

CHAPTER V

Russian History, XVII–XVIII Centuries

A. GENERAL CONDITIONS

Soviet historical literature has placed strong emphasis upon national economic developments and class struggle as the determining factors in history. This practice holds good in studies of seventeenth- and eighteenth-century Russia. In addition to such general studies as the essay of B. F. Porshnev concerning socio-political conditions in Russia during the early 1730's,[1] such diverse fields as military history, church history, and cultural history all display a clear socio-economic orientation.

Several writers have published their research on Russian custom houses, their history, their abolition and replacement by national tariff policies during 1724-1731. This development was to have special economic impact upon general conditions of Siberia in particular. M. Ia. Volkov investigated the tariff reforms of 1753-1757 which, according to the author, not only proved of great economic advantage to the nobility, but revealed also the growth of a national market in Russia, and an increase in bourgeois influence.[2]

The development of the state and the national administration during the seventeenth and eighteenth centuries has received relatively little attention in Soviet historiography. One of the notable monographs in the field is by K. A. Sofronenko, discussing the changing status of the Ukraine in the Russian Empire; another, by N. P. Eroshkin, surveys seventeenth- and eighteenth-century state institutions. Two monographs by A. V. Chernov on state institutions and legislative materials of the eighteenth century are particularly informative.[3]

[1] B. F. Porshnev, "Sotsialno-politicheskaia obstanovka v Rossii vo vremia Smolenskoi voiny." *Istoriia SSSR*, No. 5 (1957), 112-140.

[2] V. A. Aleksandrov and E. V. Chistiakova, "K tamozhennoi politike v Sibiri v period skladyvaniia vserossiiskogo rynka (vtoraia polovina XVII v.)." *Voprosy istorii*, No. 2 (1959), 132-143. A. N. Kopylov, "Tamozhennaia politika v Sibiri v XVII v." *Russkoe gosudarstvo v XVII v.* (Moscow, 1961), 330-370. R. I. Kozintseva, "Ot tamozhennogo tarifa 1724 g. k tarifu 1731 g." *Voprosy genezisa kapitalizma v Rossii.* (Leningrad, 1960), 182-216. M. Ia. Volkov, "Otmena vnutrennikh tamozhen v Rossii," *Istoriia SSSR*, No. 2 (1957), 78-95. M. Ia. Volkov, "Iz istorii borby za ukrainskii rynok vo vtoroi chetverti XVIII veka." *Vestnik Moskovskogo universiteta*, Seriia IX, *Istoriia*, No. 1 (1961).

[3] K. A. Sofronenko, *Malorossiiskii prikaz Russkogo gosudarstva vtoroi poloviny XVII v. i nachala XVIII v.* (Moscow, 1960). N. P. Eroshkin, *Ocherki istorii gosudarstvennykh uchrezhdenii do-revoliutsionnoi Rossii.* (Moscow, 1960). A. V. Chernov, "K istorii Pomestnogo prikaza." *Trudy MGIAI* [Moskovskii gosudarstvennyi istoriko-arkhivnyi institut], Vol. IX (Moscow, 1957), 194-250. A. V. Chernov, *Gosudarstvennye uchrezhdeniia Rossii v XVII veke (Zakonodatelnye materialy. Spravochnoe posobie).* (Moscow, 1960).

Many historians of the seventeenth and eighteenth centuries focused their attention on the Zemskii Sobor, which came into political prominence during that time, playing a most active part in state affairs, and then declining as suddenly as it had risen to prominence. Economic and financial developments claimed the attention of A. A. Zimin, M. N. Tikhomirov, and A. I. Kozachenko, who brought to light the acts of the Zemskii Sobor sessions of 1612-1613, of 1650, and of 1653, respectively. L. V. Cherepnin also made a most original comparative study of the legislation attaching peasants to the soil in Moldavia and in Russia during the middle of the seventeenth century.[4]

A collection of documents compiled by I. A. Golubtsov explains the tax reforms that were promulgated during 1679-1681. Closely related is another study, by I. G. Spasskii, on the financial reforms of the mid-seventeenth century. The two works present a fairly adequate account of the financial state of affairs of Russia in this century.[5]

During his research on tax reforms, I. A. Golubtsov came across the correspondence between Tsar Alexis and the Ukrainian Hetman Bogdan Khmelnitskii, a document never used by historians before. Another historian, A. N. Maltsev, uncovered records that shed additional light on peasant conditions in the Ukraine and in Belorussia during the middle of the seventeenth century. M. T. Beliavskii published an extensive collection of newly found sources pertaining to the peasant question during the early period of the reign of Catherine II.[6]

A good many documentary publications concerning this period deal with aspects of commerce and trade, and this includes metallurgical and mining development, particularly salt mining. S. I. Sakovich has compiled vital

[4]M. N. Tikhomirov, "Dokumenty zemskogo sobora 1650 g." *Istoricheskii arkhiv,* No. 4 (1958), 141-156; No. 5, 129-146; No. 6, 139-154. A. I. Kozachenko, "K istorii zemskogo sobora 1653 g." *Istoricheskii arkhiv,* No. 4 (1957), 223-227. L. V. Cherepnin, " 'Sobornoe Ulozhenie' 1649 goda i 'Pravila' Vasile Lupu 1646 goda, kak istochniki po istorii zakreposhcheniia krestian v Rossii i v Moldavii." *O rumyno-russkikh i rumyno-sovetskikh sviaziakh.* (Moscow, 1960), 55-70.

[5]I. A. Golubtsov, "K istorii podatnoi reformy 1679-1681 gg." *Istoricheskii arkhiv,* No. 5 (1959), 155-167. I. G. Spasskii, "Denezhnoe khoziaistvo Russkogo gosudarstva v seredine XVII v. i reformy 1654-1663 gg." *Arkheograficheskii ezhegodnik za 1959 god.* (Moscow, 1960), 103-156. See also K. V. Sivkov, "Istochniki po istorii selskogo khoziaistva Rossii vo vtoroi polovine XVIII veka." *Problemy istochnikovedeniia,* No. 8 (1959), 144-190.

[6]I. A. Golubstov, "Dve neizdannye gramoty iz perepiski tsaria Alekseia Mikhailovicha s getmanom Khmelnitskim 1656 g." *Slavianskii arkhiv.* (Moscow, 1956), 76-87. A. N. Maltsev, "Novye dokumenty po istorii sotsialnykh otnoshenii na Ukraine v seredine XVII v."*Arkheograficheskii ezhegodnik za 1958 god.* (Moscow, 1960), 331-334. A. N. Maltsev, "K istorii krestianskogo dvizheniia i politiki tsarskogo pravitelstva v Belorussii v seredine XVII v." *Istoricheskii arkhiv,* No. 2 (1958), 215-219. M. T. Beliavskii, "Novye dokumenty ob obsuzhdenii krestianskogo voprosa v 1766-1768 gg." *Arkheograficheskii ezhegodnik za 1958 god.* (Moscow, 1960), 387-430.

records on retail trade in Moscow, all based on custom house reports of the end of the seventeenth century. These and others have added illuminating details to the economic history of Moscow. A second publication of equal importance, compiled by V. G. Geiman, deals with the salt market, including salt mining, an important branch of the economy during the seventeenth century.[7]

Many of the recently uncovered sources add much valuable information on conditions in the manufacturing enterprises. E. I. Zaozerskaia made an extensive study of commercial enterprises within the jurisdiction of the Department of Commerce and Office of Manufacturing Industry (*Kommertskollegiia* and *Manufaktur-kontora*), while P. K. Fedorenko made a similar study of conditions in the east Ukrainian metallurgical industry.[8] Materials published by S. M. Troitskii describe the national budget and the general state of financial affairs at the middle of the eighteenth century. A recently discovered diary of I. P. Annenkov, a Russian landlord, adds further fascinating information on conditions in a Russian manor during the same period.[9] Finally, we should mention the collection of documents related to the Russian-American Company, published by the staffs of the Krasnoiarsk regional state archives and the Pedagogical Institute. The recently found documents deal with the activities of the Company and the operations of Russian tradesmen at the end of the eighteenth century in the northern Pacific region. These supplement the earlier works of S. B. Okun on the Russian-American Company and the Russian settlements in America.[10]

[7]S. I. Sakovich, comp., *Iz istorii torgovli i promyshlennosti Rossii kontsa XVII v.* (Moscow, 1956). V. G. Geiman, "Materialy po istorii russkoi solianoi promyshlennosti pervoi chetverti XVII v." *Trudy Gosudarstvennoi publichnoi biblioteki im. M. E. Saltykova-Shchedrina,* Vol. V (8) (Leningrad, 1958), 71-104. *Goroda feodalnoi Rossii.* (Moscow, 1966).

[8]E. I. Zaozerskaia, "Vedomost o sostoianii promyshlennykh predpriiatii, nakhodivshikhsia v vedenii Kommerts-kollegii i Manufaktur-kontory." *Materialy po istorii SSSR.* Vol. V, *Dokumenty po istorii XVIII v.* (Moscow, 1957). P. K. Fedorenko, "Materialy po istorii metallurgii Levoberezhnoi Ukrainy v XVII-XVIII vv." *Materialy po istorii SSSR.* Vol. V, *Dokumenty po istorii XVIII v.,* pp. 115-204. This publication includes an account of two rare prosperous communities, their wealth deriving largely from enterprising engagement of local peasants in flourishing trade and commerce. The account casts many sidelights on several aspects of trade and commerce of the time. See A. M. Razgon, "Opisanie promyshlenno-torgovykh sel Ivanova i Vasilevskogo, sostavlennoe krestianami-zemskimi votchinnykh pravlenii." *Materialy po istorii SSSR.* Vol. V, *Dokumenty po istorii XVIII v.,* pp. 283-463.

[9]S. M. Troitskii, "Iz istorii finansov v Rossii v seredine XVIII v." *Istoricheskii arkhiv,* No. 2, (1957), 122-135. F. I. Lappo and V. I. Samsonov, "Dnevnik kurskogo pomeshchika I. P. Annenkova." *Materialy po istorii SSSR,* I, 659-823.

[10]*K istorii Rossiisko-amerikanskoi kompanii. Sbornik dokumentalnykh materialov.* (Krasnoiarsk, 1957). S. B. Okun, *Rossiisko-amerikanskaia kompaniia.* B. D. Grekov, ed. and preface. (Moscow, 1939). S. B. Okun, "Polozhenie promyslovykh rabochikh v russkikh poseleniiakh v Amerike." *Uchenye zapiski. Seriia istoricheskikh*

The burgeoning field of demography has provided useful data bearing on general economic conditions of the country. The work of A. G. Rashin is of special value, dealing with the effect of serfdom upon population mobility during the centuries under discussion.[11]

Demographers have recently made fair estimates of the size of the serf population during the first quarter of the eighteenth century. Studies in related fields indicate that the census figures serve as one of the most valuable and accurate historical sources on population movement in the country, as well as economic conditions.[12]

A well-balanced study has been made by V. K. Iatsunskii on the distribution of Russian population between 1724 and 1916, outlining the rapid growth of settlers in the south and the Volga region and the slower increase in other areas. These trends, the author explains, were caused by economic conditions, by the scarcity of land for cultivation, and by other considerations.[13] There are in preparation other studies of the various census data compiled since the reign of Peter I. These will provide much needed information that might solve many unanswered questions connected with agrarian history and the peasantry during the seventeenth and eighteenth centuries. Along with these investigations, studies will have to be undertaken of other closely related subjects, such as the conditions of the nobility and of the gentry, the level of labor production, the national income and budget, the annual crop production, prices, and a multitude of other subjects. Combined, these will add much to a fuller study of Russian history, particularly agricultural history of the past two centuries or so.

Soviet demography has only lately begun to advance, encouraged perhaps by analytical investigations of data rendered by the recent census. Several writers in the field, such as A. G. Rashin, V. M. Kabuzan, and V. K. Iatsunskii, have done remarkably well in demographic research.[14] Material on

nauk, No. 48, Issue 5 (Leningrad, 1939), 157-170. See also *Russkie otkrytiia v Tikhom Okeane i Severnoi Amerike v 18-19 vv. Sbornik materialov*. A. I. Andreev, ed. (Leningrad, 1944).

[11] A. G. Rashin, *Naselenie Rossii za sto let (1811-1913 gg.). Statisticheskie ocherki*. (Moscow, 1956).

[12] "Tabel pervoi revizii narodonaseleniia Rossii (1718-1727 gg.)." *Istoricheskii arkhiv*, No. 3 (1959), 126-165. V. M. Kabuzan, "Materialy revizii kak istoricheskii istochnik." *Trudy MGIAI* [Moskovskii gosudarstvennyi istoriko-arkhivnyi institut], Vol. X (Moscow, 1957), 387-390. V. M. Kabuzan, "Materialy revizii kak istochnik po istorii naseleniia Rossii XVIII–pervoi poloviny XIX v." *Istoriia SSSR*, No. 5 (1959), 128-140.

[13] V. K. Iatsunskii, "Izmeneniia v razmeshchenii naseleniia Evropeiskoi Rossii." *Istoriia SSSR*, No. 1 (1957), 192-224.

[14] A. G. Rashin has published several important articles in *Istoricheskie zapiski*. See, for instance, "Dinamika chislennosti i protsessy formirovaniia gorodskogo naseleniia Rossii v XIX-XX v.," No. 34 (1950), 32-81; "Gramotnost i narodnoe obrazovanie v Rossii v XIX v.," No. 37; "O chislennosti i territorialnom razmeshchenii rabochikh Rossii v period kapitalizma," No. 46.

the trends of general population growth (or decline) throughout the country, growth of urban population, reduction of illiteracy, and occupational data has all been gathered by Rashin. Further study of Soviet urbanization has been made by P. G. Ryndziunskii, who deals mainly with the first half of the past century and shows the consolidation of a city population in the midst of the decaying feudal order. Ryndziunskii also discusses the impeding influence which the feudal order had upon the process of urbanization as well as upon the socio-economic development of Russian cities. He concludes that prior to 1861 cities in Russia grew in one of two ways: in a slow and legitimized manner, or by an intensive thrust brought about by the anti-feudal atmosphere and popular movements. Ryndziunskii also shows that the growth patterns of cities in Russia and in western Europe, during the decline of feudalism and rise of capitalism, were basically alike.[15]

The development of Russian military power during the seventeenth century has likewise been treated in Soviet historiography from a broad point of view. Traditionally, military history usually included only such subjects as mobilization, military equipment, and provisioning the troops; it often dealt with the army's political influence or the role it played in palace revolutions throughout the eighteenth century. The older histories often devoted much space to the service the army rendered to the nobility, aiding the latter to assert effectively its privileged position in society. Recently the field has been broadened by including many other military, political, economic, or social aspects of the history of Russia's armed forces. L. G. Beskrovnyi, for example, deals with the subject as an inseparable part of the imperial socio-economic system.[16]

In 1959, in connection with the 150th anniversary of the battle of Poltava, the Soviet Academy of Sciences, in collaboration with the Ukrainian

[15]A. G. Rashin, *Naselenie Rossii za sto let (1811-1913 gg.). Statisticheskie ocherki.* (Moscow, 1956). V. K. Iatsunskii, "Izmeneniia v razmeshchenii naseleniia Evropeiskoi Rossii v 1724-1916 gg." *Istoriia SSSR*, No. 1 (1957), 192-224. V. M. Kabuzan, "Materialy revizii kak istochnik po istorii naseleniia Rossii XVIII–pervoi poloviny XIX v. (1718-1858)." *Istoriia SSSR*, No. 5 (1959), 128-140. P. G. Ryndziunskii, *Gorodskoe grazhdanstvo doreformennoi Rossii.* (Moscow, 1958). P. G. Ryndziunskii, "Gorodskoe naselenie." *Ocherki ekonomicheskoi istorii Rossii pervoi poloviny XIX veka.* (Moscow, 1959). G. M. Maksimov, "Dvizhenie i sostav naseleniia SSSR." *Istoriia SSSR*, No. 1 (1961), 28-48. L. B. Genkin, "Knigi po istorii gorodov SSSR." *Istoriia SSSR*, No. 5 (1959), 148-156. L. S. Gaponenko and V. M. Kabuzan, "Materialy selskokhoziaistvennykh perepisei 1916-1917 gg. kak istochnik dlia opredeleniia chislennosti naseleniia Rossii nakanune Oktiabrskoi revoliutsii." *Istoriia SSSR*, No. 6 (1961), 97-115.

[16]L. G. Beskrovnyi, *Ocherki po istochnikovedeniiu voennoi istorii Rossii.* (Moscow, 1957). L. G. Beskrovnyi, *Russkaia armiia i flot v XVIII v.* (Moscow, 1958). L. G. Beskrovnyi, ed., *Russkaia voennaia periodicheskaia pechat: 1702-1916, Bibliograficheskii ukazatel.* Z. P. Levasheva and K. V. Sinitsyna, comps. (Moscow, 1959). L. G. Beskrovnyi, *Ocherki voennoi istoriografii Rossii.* (Moscow, 1962). T. K. Krylova, "Poltavskaia pobeda i russkaia diplomatiia." *Piotr Velikii. Sbornik statei.* A. I. Andreev, ed. (Moscow, 1947).

Academy, published a collection of essays covering different aspects of the event. The collection of articles, based on many original and primary sources, deals mainly with military science and foreign affairs during the reign of Peter the Great. Another collection of essays appeared under the title *Poltava Victory*. This one deals with foreign relations and Russia's position in Continental affairs, as well as with the nature of the struggle with Sweden.[17]

Popular movements of the seventeenth and eighteenth centuries, generally referred to in Soviet historiography as "anti-feudal opinion" in Russian society, have engrossed many historians. These movements affected many phases of the economic, political, and social life of the time. By publishing the works and letters of Father Avvakum, the leading Archpriest schismatic and martyr, for example, historians contributed to the study of seventeenth-century social and religious development.[18] Several other studies have contributed to related fields. One is an analysis of the cultural ties between Sweden and Russia, by L. V. Cherepnin. Another, a study of the little-known seventeenth-century Russian historian A. I. Lyzlov, was written by E. V. Chistiakova. A third is the keen analytical study by S. N. Azbelev of the seventeenth-century Novgorodian Chronicles. Though Azbelev discusses mainly the textual contents, he also has much to say about the literary style and the broad interpretative connotations of the Chronicles. Finally, newly found materials on Iurii Krizhanich and his work have been published by L. M. Mordukhovich.[19]

[17]*Poltava*. [Essays by B. B. Kafengauz, T. K. Krylova, E. P. Podiapolskaia, and others.] (Moscow, 1959). *Poltavskaia pobeda.* (Moscow, 1959). V. E. Shutoi, *Borba narodnykh mass protiv nashestviia armii Karla XII, 1700-1709.* (Moscow, 1958). V. E. Shutoi, "O pismakh naseleniia Ukrainy russkomu pravitelstvu v sviazi s izmenoi Mazepy (1708)." *Istoriia SSSR,* No. 3 (1961), 163-170. *Voprosy istorii,* No. 6 (1961), 201-208.

[18]*Zhitie protopopa Avvakuma, im samim napisannoe, i drugie ego sochineniia.* N. K. Gudzii, ed., foreword by V. E. Gusev. (Moscow, 1960). N. M. Nikolskii, *Sibirskaia ssylka Avvakuma. Uchenye zapiski Instituta istorii RANION,* Vol. II (Moscow, 1927). V. I. Malyshev, "Dva neizvestnykh pisma protopopa Avvakuma." *Trudy ODRL* [Otdel drevnerusskoi literatury], Vol. XIV (Moscow, 1958), 413-420. V. I. Malyshev, "Bibliografiia sochinenii protopopa Avvakuma i literatury o nem 1917-1953 godov." *Trudy ODRL* [Otdel drevnerusskoi literatury], Vol. X (Moscow, 1954), 435-446.

[19]L. V. Cherepnin, "Novye materialy o diake Ivane Timofeeve–avtore 'Vremennika'." *Istoricheskii arkhiv,* No. 4 (1960), 162-177. L. V. Cherepnin, "Materialy po istorii russkoi kultury i russko-shvedskikh kulturnykh sviazei XVII v. v arkhivakh Shvetsii." *Trudy ODRL* [Otdel drevnerusskoi literatury], Vol. XVII (Moscow, 1961), 454-470. E. V. Chistiakova, "Russkii istorik A. I. Lyzlov i ego kniga 'Skifskaia istoriia'." *Vestnik istorii mirovoi kultury,* No. 1 (25), (1961), 117-127. S. L. Peshtich, "Sinopsis kak istoricheskoe proizvedenie." *Trudy ODRL* [Otdel drevnerusskoi literatury], Vol. XV (Moscow, 1958), 284-300. S. N. Azbelev, *Novgorodskie letopisi XVII veka.* (Novgorod, 1960). L. M. Mordukhovich, "Iz rukopisnogo nasledstva Iu. Krizhanicha." *Istoricheskii arkhiv,* No. 1 (1958), 154-189.

A series of original source materials have been published, dealing with people and events prominent in eighteenth-century Russian history. The memoirs of A. Bolotov concern such figures as M. V. Lomonosov and A. N. Radishchev. Essays on some of these men appeared in a journal called *XVIII Vek. Sbornik,* published by the Institute of Russian Literature of the Academy of Sciences. One of the new publications concerns the case of a group of Russian students who became involved in student unrest at Leipzig, in 1767, and were brought to trial in that city. Among the defendants were F. V. Ushakov and A. N. Radishchev, the harbinger of the later Decembrists.[20]

Another study of high quality, by two authors, N. V. Ustiugov and N. S. Chaev, concerns the Russian Church in the seventeenth century. This, however, is a mere introduction to a field of study which sadly lacks supplementary research, especially on such subjects as the secularization of ecclesiastical property during the eighteenth century and its effects upon political and religious development in the nation.[21]

The subject of Church history, to the surprise of no one, has long been in abeyance in Soviet historiography. Interest in the field was rare and casual, and whatever was written was extremely tendentious. Rarely was there a serious effort to discuss the subject in any scholarly manner. The pre-revolutionary study on the history of the Russian Church, by N. M. Nikolskii, was published in 1930, but it was not until the late 1950's that some historians began to acknowledge this regrettable gap in Soviet historiography.[22] "We are convinced," writes one historian, "that it is impossible to produce a thorough history of Russia without adequate attention to the history of the Russian Orthodox Church, that former economic, political, and ideological power which for centuries had dominated Russian and other peoples of our land and was responsible for political, cultural, and at times economic development."[23]

During the 1960's scholars began to devote more serious attention to Church history, and a number of works of notable historical value appeared. Several distinguished scholars have contributed to the field, notably A. M.

[20] A. Bolotov, *Zhizn i prikliucheniia.* (Moscow, 1931). 3 vols. "Volneniia russkikh studentov v Leipzige v 1767 godu (sledstvennoe delo A. N. Radishcheva, F. V. Ushakova i drugikh russkikh studentov v sude Leiptsigskogo universiteta)." Preface and commentaries by A. I. Startsev, tr. B. A. Schlichter. *Zapiski otdela rukopisei GBL.* Vol. XVIII (Moscow, 1956), 230-327.

[21] N. V. Ustiugov and N. S. Chaev, "Russkaia tserkov v XVII veke." *Russkoe gosudarstvo v XVII v.* (Moscow, 1961), 295-329.

[22] Originally N. M. Nikolskii contributed two chapters to the *History of Russia* (Granat edition): "Religioznoe dvizhenie," IV, 43-68, and "Raskol i sektanstvo vo vtoroi polovine XIX veka," V, 228-272. See *Istoriia Rossii v XIX veke.* (Moscow, 1907-1910). N. M. Nikolskii, *Istoriia russkoi tserkvi.* (Moscow, 1930).

[23] G. N. Golikov, "K izucheniiu istorii russkoi tserkvi." *Voprosy istorii,* No. 6 (1968), 167-182.

Borisov, I. U. Budovnits, N. A. Kazakova, Ia. S. Lurie, V. I. Koretskii, and A. I. Klibanov.[24] In addition, the Moscow patriarchate has presented its own version of the history of the Russian Church, its organization, status, and activities.[25] Finally, in 1967, there appeared a collective work under the editorship of N. A. Smirnov, with selections contributed by such eminent Soviet scholars as E. F. Grekulov, A. A. Zimin, V. I. Koretskii, A. M. Sakharov, and others.[26] The appearance of this volume was greeted in Soviet historiography as a "remarkable event." It represents a rare effort to interpret the complex subject of the history of the Church in Russia in a truly synthesized, lucid form, without vulgar bias or "atheistic hysteria."

B. REGIONAL HISTORY: SIBERIA, CENTRAL ASIA, THE UKRAINE, THE CAUCASUS

A second revised and enlarged edition of A. I. Andreev's extensive study of seventeenth-century Siberian source materials appeared in 1960. This became an indispensable work to anyone concerned with the earlier period of Siberian history. A second volume, covering the eighteenth century, is to follow and promises to be of equal importance. M. O. Kosven has written on V. N. Tatishchev and his administrative activities in western Siberia, as well as on the "Great Northern Expedition of 1733-1743." Several other relevant works referred to below are in the field of Siberian cartography. Finally,

[24]A. M. Borisov, "Tserkov i vosstanie pod rukovodstvom S. Razina." *Voprosy istorii,* No. 8, (1965), 74-83. I. U. Budovnits, *Monastyri na Rusi i borba s nimi krestian v XIV-XVI vv.* (Moscow, 1966). S. S. Dmitriev, "Pravoslavnaia tserkov i gosudarstvo v poreformennoi Rossii." *Istoriia SSSR,* No. 4 (1966), 20-54. A. V. Fadeev, "Razmyshleniia ob istorii kultury." *Voprosy istorii,* No. 1 (1964), 27-43. N. Gantaev, *Tserkov i feodalizm na Rusi.* (Moscow, 1960). N. A. Kazakova and Ia. S. Lurie, *Antifeodalnye ereticheskie dvizheniia v XIV-XVI vv.* (Moscow, 1955). A. I. Klibanov, *Reformatsionnye dvizheniia v Rossii v XIV—pervoi polovine XVI v.* (Moscow, 1960). V. I. Koretskii, "Borba krestian s monastyriami v Rossii XVI—nachala XVII v." *Voprosy istorii, religii i ateizma,* Vol. VI (Moscow, 1958). A. P. Novoseltsev et al., *Drevnerusskoe gosudarstvo i ego mezhdunarodnoe znachenie.* (Moscow, 1965). A. M. Sakharov, "Tserkov i obrazovanie Russkogo tsentralizovannogo gosudarstva." *Voprosy istorii,* No. 1 (1966), 49-65. M. N. Tikhomirov, "Monastyrvotchinnik XVI veka." *Istoricheskie zapiski,* No. 3 (1938), 130-160. M. N. Tikhomirov, *Russkaia kultura X-XVIII vv.* (Moscow, 1968). N. A. Smirnov, ed., *Tserkov v istorii Rossii (IX v.—1917 g.). Kriticheskie orcherki.* (Moscow, 1967). S. B. Veselovskii, "Monastyrskoe zemlevladenie v Moskovskoi Rusi vo vtoroi polovine XVI v." *Istoricheskie zapiski,* No. 10 (1941), 95-117.

[25]*Russkaia pvavoslavnaia tserkov. Ustroistvo, polozhenie, deiatelnost.* (Izdanie Moskovskoi patriarkhii, 1958).

[26]N. A. Smirnov, ed., *Tserkov v istorii Rossii (IX v.—1917 g.). Kriticheskie ocherki.* (Moscow, 1967).

should be mentioned the helpful historiography covering the period 1917-1945, and published in 1968.[27]

In 1969 there appeared a five-volume history of Siberia, under the editorship of A. P. Okladnikov. The first volume covers the early period; the second deals with the period from the annexation of Siberia by Moscow to the 1850's; the third takes up the years 1855-1917; the fourth considers the period between 1917 and 1937; and the final volume covers the years 1937-1945. These five volumes constitute an outstanding contribution to a subject that has long been neglected.[28] Siberia comprises about fifty-six per cent of the entire territory of the Soviet Union, and accounts for more than three-fourths of its natural resources, including some ninety per cent of its coal, sixty per cent of its hydroelectric power, and seventy per cent of its rich oil deposits and rare metals.

The history of the Ukraine, of the Caucasus, and of Central Asia has recently been expanded and enriched by the publication of new source

[27]A. I. Andreev, "Trudy G.-F. Millera." G. -F. Miller, *Istoriia Sibiri.* (Moscow, 1937), Vol. I, 57-144. A. I. Andreev, "Perepiska V. N. Tatishcheva za 1746-1750 gg." *Istoricheskii arkhiv*, No. 6 (1951), 245-314. A. I. Andreev, *Ocherki po istochnikovedeniiu Sibiri.* Issue I. *XVII vek.* (Moscow, 1960). A. I. Andreev, "Izuchenie Iakutii XVII v." *Uchenye zapiski Instituta iazykovedeniia, literatury i istorii Iakutskogo filiala Akademii nauk SSSR.* Issue IV (1956), 3-32. M. O. Kosven, "Iz istorii russkoi istoricheskoi nauki XVIII veka. Nauchno-organizatsionnaia deiatelnost V. N. Tatishcheva." *Istoriia SSSR*, No. 3 (1961), 160-166. M. O. Kosven, "Etnograficheskie rezultaty Velikoi severnoi ekspeditsii 1733-1743 gg." *Trudy Instituta etnografii im. Miklukho-Maklaia*, Vol. LXIV (Moscow, 1961), 167-212. Iu. A. Limonov, " 'Rospis' pervogo obshchego chertezha Sibiri (opyt datirovki)." *Problemy istochnikovedeniia*, No. 8 (1959), 343-360. M. I. Navrot, "Okladnaia kniga Sibiri 1697 g." *Problemy istochnikovedeniia*, No. 5 (1956), 184-209. N. A. Dvoretskaia, "Arkheograficheskii obzor spiskov povestei o pokhode Ermaka." *Trudy ODRL [Otdel drevnerusskoi literatury]*, Vol. XIII (Moscow, 1957). N. A. Dvoretskaia, "Ofitsialnaia i folklornaia otsenka pokhoda Ermaka v Sibir." *Trudy ODRL*, Vol. XIV (Moscow, 1958). A. I. Andreev, "Chertezhi i karty Rossii XVII veka, naidennye v poslednie gody." *Voprosy ekonomiki i klassovykh otnoshenii v Russkom gosudarstve XII-XVII vv.* (Leningrad, 1960), 80-90. A. I. Andreev, "Pervye issledovateli Aleutskikh ostrovov." *Istoricheskie zapiski*, No. 68 (1961), 290-306. A. A. Zimin, "Russkie geograficheskie spravochniki XVII v." *Zapiski otdela rukopisei GBL [Gosudarstvennoi biblioteki Leningrada]*, Issue XXI (Moscow, 1959), 220-231. A. A. Uranosov, "K istorii sostavleniia knigi Bolshomu chertezhu." *Voprosy istorii estestvoznaniia i tekhniki*, Issue I (Moscow, 1957), 188-190. P. A. Potapov, *Ocherki po istorii altaitsev.* (Moscow, 1953). *Istoriografiia Sovetskoi Sibiri, 1917-1945 gg.* (Novosibirsk, 1968).

[28]*Istoriia Sibiri s drevneishikh vremen do nashikh dnei.* (Leningrad, 1968-69). 5 vols. See also *Voprosy istorii Sibiri.* (Irkutsk, Irkutskii gosudarstvennyi pedagogicheskii institut, 1967). See particularly I, 3-147. It is perhaps of interest to note that in reviewing this publication one critic points out the failure to include the role sectarianism played in the history of Siberia. See *Istoriia Sibiri*, No. 1 (1969) 155-158.

material as well as general historical studies. Contributions to Caucasian history include those of G. O. Gregorian and A. G. Ioannisian on Armenia, the four-volume collective work on the history of Azerbaidzhan, and the economic history of the same area by A. S. Sumbatzade. Of equal importance in Caucasian history are the publications of N. A. Smirnov, Z. V. Anchabadze, S. K. Bushuev, and many others.[29]

In view of the recent jubilee marking the 300 years of unification of the Ukraine and Russia, extensive studies have been carried out on the various periods of Ukrainian history. The Ukrainian Academy of Sciences

[29]See cited bibliography footnote No. 59 in Chapter IV. The following may be added: ARMENIA: G. O. Gregorian, *Iz istorii armianskoi peredovoi obshchestvennoi mysli (Vtoraia polovina XVIII v.).* (Erevan, 1957). A. G. Ioannisian, *Ocherki istorii armianskoi osvoboditelnoi mysli.* (Erevan, 1957-1959). 2 vols. AZERBAIDZHAN: P. A. Azizbekova, *V. I. Lenin i sotsialisticheskie preobrazovaniia v Azerbaidzhane, 1920-1923 gg.* (Moscow, 1962). S. Belenkii, *Revoliutsiia 1917 g. v Azerbaidzhane (khronika sobytii).* (Baku, 1927). A. N. Guliev and V. D. Mochalov, eds., *Prisoedinenie Azerbaidzhana k Rossii i ego progressivnye posledstviia v oblasti ekonomiki i kultury (XIX—nachalo XX vv.).* (Baku, 1955). I. A. Guseinov, ed., *Istoriia Azerbaidzhana.* (Baku, 1958-1963). 3 vols. in 4. M. Iskenderov, *Iz istorii borby kommunisticheskoi partii Azerbaidzhana za pobedu sovetskoi vlasti.* (Baku, 1958). T. Kocharli, *Velikii podvig; borba Kommunisticheskoi partii za sotsialisticheskuiu industrializatsiiu Azerbaidzhana, 1926-1932 gg.* (Baku, 1965). A. S. Mil'man, *Politicheskii stroi Azerbaidzhana v XIX-nachale XX vekov; administrativnyi apparat i sud, formy i metody kolonialnogo upravleniia.* (Baku, 1966). A. P. Novoseltsev, "Iz istorii klassovoi borby v Azerbaidzhane i Vostochnoi Armenii XVII-XVIII vv." *Istoricheskie zapiski,* No. 67 (1960), 234-255. F. S. Shabanov, *Razvitie sovetskoi gosudarstvennosti v Azerbaidzhane.* (Moscow, 1959). A. S. Sumbatzade, *Promyshlennost Azerbaidzhana v XIX v.* (Baku, 1964). E. A. Takarzhevskii, *Iz istorii inostrannoi interventsii i grazhdanskoi voiny v Azerbaidzhane.* (Baku, 1927). CAUCASUS: *Muridism na Kavkaze.* (Moscow, 1963). I. F. Muzhev, *Ocherki istorii revoliutsionnogo dvizheniia na Severnom Kavkaze v 1905-1907 gg.* (Nalchik, 1957). *Narodnoe khoziaistvo Grusinskoi SSR.* (Moscow, 1957). A. Ia. Pantsakhava, *K voprosu o razvitii agrarnykh otnoshenii v doreformennoi Vostochnoi Gruzii.* (Moscow, 1957). N. A. Smirnov, *Istoriia Kabardy s drevneishikh vremen do nashikh dnei.* (Moscow, 1957). N. A. Smirnov, *Politika Rossii na Kavkaze v XVI-XIX vv.* (Moscow, 1958). Z. V. Anchabadze, *Ocherki ekonomicheskoi istorii Gruzii pervoi poloviny XIX veka.* (Tbilisi, 1966). S. K. Bushuev, *Iz istorii vneshne-politicheskikh otnoshenii v period prisoedineniia Kavkaza k Rossii (20-70e gody XIX veka).* (Moscow, 1955). A. V. Fadeev, *Ocherki ekonomicheskogo razvitiia stepnogo Predkavkazia v doreformennyi period.* (Moscow, 1957). A. V. Fadeev, *Ocherki istorii balkarskogo naroda.* (Nalchik, 1961). V. M. Bukalova, "Antifeodalnaia borba kabardinskikh krestian vo vtoroi polovine XVIII v." *Voprosy istorii,* No. 6 (1961), 75-84. *Istoriia Kabardino-Balkarskoi ASSR.* (Nalchik, 1967). 2 vols. A. S. Kabanov, *Nalchik—stolitsa Sovetskoi Kabardy. Kratkii istoriko-ekonomicheskii ocherk.* (Nalchik, 1950). E. I. Krupnov, *Kratkii ocherk arkheologii Kabardinskoi ASSR.* (Nalchik, 1946). *Narodnoe khoziaistvo Kabardino—Balkarskoi ASSR; statisticheskii sbornik.* (Nalchik, 1964). *Sbornik statei po istorii Kabardy.* (Nalchik, 1951). 2 issues. *Kabardino-russkie otnosheniia v 16-18 vv. Dokumenty i materialy.* (Moscow, 1957). 2 vols.

published an eight-volume history of the Ukrainian people; M. I. Marchenko and S. O. Iakovlev published an informative Ukrainian historiography; M. N. Leshchenko issued his study on the revolution of 1905 in the Ukraine; I. O. Gurzhii completed his research on serfdom in the nineteenth century in the Ukraine; and many other excellent works have appeared.[30]

Historical writings relevant to such constituent or autonomous republics as Urmutia, Bashkiria, Kirgizia, Uzbekistan, Iakutia, and Kazakhstan have been quantitatively impressive; of their qualitative value, there is some doubt. A vast literature has been produced since 1917. Aside from general historical accounts, there have been archeological reports, as in the case of the impressive accomplishments of the Khorezm expedition, and studies of the feudal period, modern imperialism, and the incorporation of the component republics into the Soviet Union. Without exception, Soviet historians interpret the incorporation of these peoples into the former Russian Empire and later into the Soviet Union, not as an act of colonization, but as a policy of "friendly cooperation that existed between the Russian and other peoples, despite the imperialistic aspirations of the former ruling class or of the tsarist regime."

Much of the writing produced during the Stalin period has to be taken with a pinch of salt, particularly that relating to the modern period. Much of it can be dispensed with without much loss to historical science; some should be read with tongue in cheek, as the authors themselves must have written it. Of more enduring value are the works that deal with the early

[30]*UKRAINE.* G. D. Bakulev, *Razvitie ugolnoi promyshlennosti Donetskogo basseina.* (Moscow, 1955). *Bolsheviki Ukrainy v period mezhdu pervoi i vtoroi burzhuazno-demokraticheskimi revoliutsiiami v Rossii, iiun 1907 g.—fevral 1917 g.; sbornik dokumentov i materialov.* (Kiev, 1960). P. I. Denisenko, ed., *Listovki bolshevikov Ukrainy perioda pervoi russkoi revoliutsii, 1905-1907 gg.* (Kiev, 1955). B. D. Grekov, *Kievskaia Rus.* (Moscow, 1949). I. O. Gurzhii, *Rozklad feodalno-kripostnits'koi sistemy v silskomu gospodarstvi Ukrainy pershoi poloviny XIX st.* (Kiev, 1954). S. O. Iakovlev, *Ukrainska radianska arkheografiia.* [Historiography]. (Kiev, 1965). *Istorichni dzherela ta ikh vykorystannia.* (Kiev, 1966). O. K. Kosymenko, *Istoriia Ukrainskoi SSR.* (Kiev, 1965). M. N. Leshchenko, *Selianskii rukh na Ukraine pershoi rossiiskoi revoliutsii.* (Kiev, 1956). F. Los', *Formirovanie rabochego klassa na Ukraine i ego revoliutsionnaia borba v kontse XIX—nachala XX stoletiia.* (Kiev, 1955). F. E. Los', ed., *Revoliutsiia 1905-07 gg. na Ukraine; sbornik dokumentov i materialov.* (Kiev, 1958). 2 vols. F. E. Los', *Ukraina v roku stolypinskoi reaktsii.* (Kiev, 1944). M. I. Marchenko, *Ukrainska istoriografiia, z davnikh chasiv do serediny XIX st.* (Kiev, 1959). A. A. Nesterenko, *Ocherki istorii promyshlennosti i polozhenii proletariata Ukrainy v kontse XIX i nachale XX v.* (Moscow, 1954). V. T. Pashuto, *Ocherki po istorii Galitsko-Volynskoi Rusi.* (Moscow, 1950). P. Shmorgun, *Rady robotnichikh deputativ na Ukraini v 1905 r.* (Kiev, 1955). O. V. Sluts'kyi, *Radianske i kulturne budivnitstvo na Ukraini v pershi roki borot'by za sotsialistichnu industrializatsiiu krainu, 1926-1929 rr.* (Kiev, 1957). *Sorok rokiv Radianskoi Ukrainy. Dokumenty i materialy pro sviatkuvannia 40-richchia Ukrainskoi Radianskoi Sotsialistichnoi Respubliki.* (Kiev, 1959). P. P. Gudzenko et al., eds., *Vossoedineniia Ukrainy s Rossiei; dokumenty i materialy.* (Moscow, 1954). 3 vols. *Z istorii*

104

history of these peoples. The list below is an attempt to cite selected writings that merit the attention of students of history.[31]

ekonomichnoi dumki na Ukraini. (Kiev, 1959). *Z istorii pervishnogo nagromazhennia kapitalu na Ukraine; chumatskii promysel i iogo rol' u sotsialno-ekonomichnomu rozvitku Ukrainy XVIII-pershoi poloviny XIX st.* (Kiev, 1964). *Z istorii Ukrainskoi RSR.* (Kiev, 1957-1963). 8 vols.

[31]*ARMENIA:* A. S. Ambarian, *Razvitie kapitalisticheskikh otnoshenii v armianskoi derevne.* (Erevan, 1959). S. G. Areshian, *Armianskaia pechat' i tsarskaia tsenzura.* (Erevan, 1957). A. O. Marukhian, E. M. Murzaev, and S. N. Riazantsev, eds., *Armianskaia SSR.* (Moscow, 1955). M. A. Adonts, *Ekonomicheskoe razvitie vostochnoi Armenii v XIX veke.* (Erevan, 1957). P. T. Arutiunian, *Osvoboditelnoe dvizhenie armianskogo naroda v pervoi chetverti XVIII veka.* (Moscow, 1964). G. M. Bartikian, *Istochniki izucheniia pavlikianskogo dvizheniia.* (Erevan, 1961). A. Z. Begiian, *Obrazovanie i upravlenie suverennogo Sovetskogo Armianskogo gosudarstva.* (Erevan, 1962). B. A. Borian, *Armeniia, mezhdunarodnaia diplomatiia i SSSR.* (Moscow, 1928-1929). 2 vols. A. M. Esaian, *Mul'kadarskoe pravo v Armenii; ocherki po istorii krupnogo zemlevladeniia v dorevoliutsionnoi Armenii v XVIII-XX vv.* (Erevan, 1948). G. A. Gapantsian, *Khaiasa—kolybel armian. Etnogenez armian i ikh nachalnaia istoriia.* (Erevan, 1947). Z. T. Gregorian, *Prisoedinenie Vostochnoi Armenii k Rossii v nachale XIX veka.* (Moscow, 1959). *Istoriia armianskogo naroda.* (Erevan, 1951-). Vol. I- . Ia. A. Manandian, *O torgovle i gorodakh Armenii v sviazi s mirovoi torgovlei drevnikh vremen.* (Erevan, 1930; 2nd ed., 1954). A. O. Marukhian, ed., *Vosstanovlenie narodnogo khoziaistva Armianskoi SSR; materialy i dokumenty.* (Erevan, 1958). G. G. Mikaelian, *Istoriia Kilikiiskogo armianskogo gosudarstva.* (Erevan, 1952). V. Rshtuni and K. Stepanian, *Krestianskoe dvizhenie v Armenii v XIX v.* (Erevan, 1948). M. G. Nersisian, ed., *Genotsid armian v Osmanskoi imperii; sbornik dokumentov i materialov.* (Erevan, 1966). M. G. Nersisian, *Iz istorii russko-armianskikh otnoshenii.* (Erevan, 1956-1961). 2 vols. O. E. Tumanian, *Razvitie ekonomiki Armenii s nachala XIX veka do ustanovleniia Sovetskoi vlasti.* 2nd ed. (Erevan, 1954).

BASHKIRIA: B. K. Iuldashev, *Obrazovanie Bashkirskoi ASSR; istoricheskii ocherk.* (Ufa, 1958). N. V. Ustiugov and R. G. Kuzeev, eds., *Materialy nauchnoi sessii posviashchennoi 400-letiiu gosudarstva.* [Bashkiria]. (Ufa, 1958). *Narodnoe khoziaistvo Bashkirskoi ASSR; statisticheskii sbornik [1917-1967].* (Ufa, 1967). B. K. Iuldashev, ed., *Obrazovanie Bashkirskoi Avtonomnoi Sovetskoi Sotsialisticheskoi Respubliki. Sbornik dokumentov i materialov.* (Ufa, 1959). R. M. Raimov, *Obrazovanie Bashkirskoi Avtonomnoi Sovetskoi Sotsialisticheskoi Respubliki.* (Moscow, 1952). K. I. Takhaev, *Prirodnye usloviia i resursy Bashkirskoi ASSR; ekonomiko-geograficheskaia kharakteristika.* (Ufa, 1959). A. N. Usmanov, *Prisoedinenie Bashkirii k Russkomu gosudarstvu.* (Ufa, 1960). N. V. Ustiugov, "O kharaktere bashkirskikh vosstanii XVII—pervoi poloviny XVIII v." *Materialy nauchnoi sessii, posviashchennoi 400-letiiu prisoedineniia Bashkirii k Russkomu gosudarstvu.* (Moscow, 1960), 86-126.

IAKUTIA: G. P. Basharin, *Istoriia agrarnykh otnoshenii v Iakutii (60e gody XVIII— seredina XIX vekov).* (Moscow, 1956). L. V. Pustovalov, ed., *Bibliografiia Iakutskoi ASSR, 1931-1935.* (Moscow, 1958-). Vol. I- . *Borba za ustanovlenie i uprochenie sovetskoi vlasti v Iakutii; sbornik dokumentov i materialov.* (Irkutsk, 1957-1962). 2 vols. G. P. Basharin, ed., *Iakutskii arkhiv; sbornik statei i dokumentov.* (Iakutsk, 1962-1966). 3 vols. *Istoriia Iakutskoi ASSR.* (Moscow, 1955-1965). 3 vols.

C. AGRARIAN HISTORY

In recent years, socio-economic history has been enriched by expanded documentary evidence, which has led, among other things, to a reappraisal

F. G. Safronov, ed., *Iz istorii Iakutii XVII-XVIII vekov; sbornik statei.* (Iakutsk, 1965). G. G. Kolesov, *Sovetskaia Iakutiia.* (Moscow, 1937). Ia. P. Alkor and B. D. Grekov, eds. *Kolonialnaia politika Moskovskogo gosudarstva v Iakutii XVII v.; sborni dokumentov.* (Leningrad, 1936). M. A. Krotov, *Rodnaia Iakutiia.* 2nd ed. (Iakutsk, 1957). V. V. Mitiushkin, *Sotsialisticheskaia Iakutiia.* (Iakutsk, 1960). *Prirodnye usloviia i narodnoe khoziaistov Iakutskoi ASSR.* (Iakutsk, 1965). V. F. Vasiutin, ed. *Problemy razvitiia promyshlennosti i transporta Iakutskoi ASSR.* (Moscow, 1958). S. A. Tokarev, *Ocherk istorii iakutskogo naroda.* (Moscow, 1940).

KAZAKHSTAN: K. Beisembiev, *Ideino-politicheskie techeniia v Kazakhstane kontsa XIX nachala XX veka.* (Alma-Ata, 1961). K. Beisembiev, *Iz istorii obshchestvennoi mysli Kazakhstana vtoroi poloviny XIX veka.* (Alma-Ata, 1957). E. B. Bekmakhanov, *Prisoedinenie Kazakhstana k Rossii.* (Alma-Ata, 1957). *Istoriia Kazakhskoi SSR.* (Alma-Ata, 1957-1959). 2 vols. A. K. Kanapin, *Kulturnoe stroitelstvo v Kazakhstane.* (Alma-Ata, 1964). E. A. Masanov, *Ocherk istorii etnograficheskogo izucheniia kazakhskogo naroda v SSSR.* (Alma-Ata, 1966). G. V. Nechitailo, *Organizatsionno-massovaia rabota gorodskikh sovetov Kazakhstana.* (Alma-Ata, 1957). S. A. Neishtadt, *Sotsialisticheskoe preobrazovanie ekonomiki Kazakhskoi SSR v 1917-1937 godakh (ot dokapitalisticheskikh otnoshenii k sotsializmu, minuia kapitalizm).* (Alma-Ata, 1957). S. B. Nurmukhamedov, *Ocherki istorii sotsialisticheskogo stroitelstva v Kazakhstane, 1933-1940 gg.* (Alma-Ata, 1966). *O zakonomernostiakh perekhoda narodov ranee otstalykh stran k sotsializmu (na primere kazakhskogo naroda).* (Alma-Ata, 1961). *Obrazovanie Kazakhskoi ASSR.* (Alma-Ata, 1957). *Obshchestvenno-ekonomicheskii stroi kazakhov v XVIII-XIX vekakh.* (Alma-Ata, 1959). G. Sapargaliev, *Karatelnaia politika tsarizma v Kazakhstane 1905-1917 gg.* (Alma-Ata, 1966). *Sovetskoe gosudarstvo v borbe za razvitie sotsialisticheskoi kultury v Kazakhstane.* (Alma-Ata, 1957).

KIRGIZIA: V. V. Bartold, *Kirgizy. (Istoricheskii ocherk).* (Frunze, 1943). *Dvadtsat-piat let Kirgizskoi SSR. [Sbornik statei].* (Frunze, 1951). B. Dzhamgerchinov, *Ocherki politicheskoi istorii Kirgizii XIX veka.* (Frunze, 1966). B. Dzhamgerchinov, *Prisoedinenie Kirgizii k Rossii.* (Moscow, 1959). *Istoriia Kirgizii.* (Frunze, 1963). 2 vols. *Narodnoe khoziaistvo kirgizskoi SSR.* (Frunze, 1957). S. N. Riazantsev, *Kirgiziia.* 2nd ed. (Moscow, 1951). T. R. Ryskulov, *Kirgizstan.* (Moscow, 1935). V. P. Sherstobitov, *Ocherk istorii nauki v sovetskom Kirgizstane, 1918-1960 gg.* (Frunze, 1961).

TADZHIKSTAN: B. G. Gafurov and N. Prokhorov, *Padenie Bulkharskogo emirata. K 20-letiiu sovetskoi revoliutsii v Bukhare (1920-1940).* (Stalinabad, 1940). M. Irkaev, *Ocherk istorii Sovetskogo Tadzhikstana (1917-1957 gg.).* (Stalinabad, 1957). N. A. Islamov, *Tadzhikskaia SSR; kratkii istoriko-ekonomicheskii ocherk.* (Moscow, 1958). B. G. Gafurov and B. A. Litvinskii, eds. *Istoriia Tadzhikskogo naroda s drevneishikh vremen.* (Moscow, 1963-1965). 3 vols. in 5. Z. Sh. Radzhabov, ed., *Iz istorii kulturnogo stroitelstva v Tadzhikstane v 1924-1941 gg.* (Dushanbe, 1966). 2 vols. P. Luknitskii, *Tadzhikstan.* (Moscow, 1951). I. K. Narzikulov, ed., *Tadzhikskaia SSR; ekonomiko-geograficheskaia kharakteristika.* (Moscow, 1956).

TURKESTAN: Iu. N. Aleskerov, *Interventsiia i grazhdanskaia voina v Srednei Azii.* (Tashkent, 1959). Ia. M. Dosumov, *Ocherki istorii Kara-Kalpakskoi ASSR, 1917-1927 gg.* (Tashkent, 1960). R. A. Narullin, *Sovety Turkestanskoi ASSR v period*

of former views on the agricultural economy of earlier Russian history. Despite all recent research, however, there remains a serious gap in the field

inostrannoi interventsii i grazhdanskoi voiny. (Tashkent, 1965). A. V. Piaskovskii, *Revoliutsiia v Srednei Azii i Kazakhstane.* (Tashkent, 1962). A. V. Piaskovskii et al., eds. *Vosstanie 1916 goda v Srednei Azii i Kazakhstane; sbornik dokumentov.* (Moscow, 1956). M. N. Tikhomirov, *Prisoedinenie [oazisa] Merva k Rossii.* (Moscow, 1960). K. Tursunov, *Vosstanie 1916 goda v Srednei Azii i Kazakhstane.* (Tashkent, 1962).

TURKMENIA: I. S. Braginskii, S. Burdzhalov, and V. A. Romodin, "K voprosu o znachenii prisoedineniia Srednei Azii k Rossii." *Voprosy istorii,* No. 8 (1953), 21-40. A. Karyev, V. G. Moshkova, A. N. Nasonov, and A. Iu. Iakubovskii. *Ocherki iz istorii turkmenskogo naroda VIII-XIX vv.* (Ashkhabad, 1954). D. S. Kiselev, *Razvitie sovetskoi gosudarstvennosti v Turkmenistane.* (Ashkhabad, 1963). *Materialy po istorii turkmen i Turkmenii.* (Moscow, 1938-39). 2 vols. V. G. Mel'kumov, ed., *Obrazovanie Turkmenskoi SSR i sozdanie Kompartii Turkmenistana, 1924-1925 gg.; sbornik dokumentov.* (Ashkhabad, 1966). *Narodnoe khoziaistvo Turkmenskoi SSR; statisticheskii sbornik.* (Ashkhabad, 1957). A. V. Piaskovskii, *Turkmenistan v period pervoi russkoi revoliutsii 1905-1907 gg.* (Ashkhabad, 1955). *Revoliutsiia v natsionalnykh raionakh Rossii. Sbornik statei.* (Moscow, 1949). P. G. Skosyrev, *Turkmenistan.* (Moscow, 1955). S. P. Tolstov, *Drevnii Khorezm. Opyt istoriko-arkheologicheskogo issledovaniia.* (Moscow, 1948). *Turkmeniia.* (Leningrad, Academy of Sciences, 1929).

UDMURTIA: I. P. Emelianov, ed., *Ocherki istorii Udmurtskoi ASSR.* (Izhevsk, 1958). 2 vols. I. P. Emelianov, ed., *Oktiabrskaia sotsialisticheskaia revoliutsiia v Udmurtii; sbornik dokumentov i materialov (1917-1918 gg.).* (Izhevsk, 1957). I. P. Emelianov, ed., *Udmurtiia v period inostrannoi interventsii i grazhdanskoi voiny; sbornik dokumentov.* (Izhevsk, 1960-1963). 2 vols. *Narodnoe khoziaistvo Udmurtskoi ASSR; statisticheskii sbornik.* (Izhevsk, 1957). S. A. Tokarev, *Krestianskie kartofelnye bunty.* (Kirov, 1939).

UZBEKISTAN: R. Kh. Abdushukurov, *Oktiabrskaia revoliutsiia, rassvet Uzbekskoi sotsialisticheskoi natsii i sblizhenie ee s natsiiami SSSR.* (Tashkent, 1962). R. Kh. Aminov, ed., *Istoriia rabochego klassa Uzbekistana.* (Tashkent, 1964-1966). 3 vols. R. Kh. Aminov, ed., *Ocherki istorii Uzbekskoi SSR, 1956-1965 gg.* (Tashkent, 1966). M. P. Avsharova, ed., *Uzbekistan, 1956 g.; bibliograficheskii ukazatel literatury.* (Tashkent, 1960). V. V. Bartold, *Istoriia Turkestana.* (Tashkent, 1922). K. N. Bedrintsev, ed., *Ekonomicheskoe raionirovanie Uzbekistana.* (Tashkent, 1966). *Bibliografiia izdanii Akademii [nauk Uzbekskoi SSR]; sistematicheskii ukazatel knig i statei.* (Tashkent, 1958-1963). 2 vols. O. B. Dzhamalov, ed., *Problemy razvitiia ekonomiki Uzbekistana.* (Tashkent, 1963). O. B. Dzhamalov, *Razvitie dvukh form sotsialisticheskoi sobstvennosti i problemy ikh sblizheniia.* (Tashkent, 1965). V. I. Efimov, ed., *Materialy po istorii narodnoi Uzbekskoi SSR.* (Samarkand, 1963). Kh. Sh. Inoiatov, ed., *Istoriia grazhdanskoi voiny v Uzbekistane.* (Tashkent, Akademiia nauk Uzbekskoi SSR, 1964-). Vol. 1- . T. N. Kary-Niiazov, *Ocherki istorii kultury Sovetskogo Uzbekistana.* (Moscow, 1955). N. L. Korzhenevskii, *Sredniaia Aziia.* (Tashkent, 1941). M. Musaev, *Uzbekskaia SSR; kratkii istoriko-ekonomicheskii ocherk. Narodnoe khoziaistvo Uzbekskoi SSR za 50 let; sbornik statisticheskikh materialov.* (Tashkent, 1967). V. Ia. Nepomnin, *Istoricheskii opyt stroitelstva sotsializma v Uzbekistane, 1917-1937.* (Tashkent, 1960). V. A. Shishkin, ed., *Istoriia materialnoi kultury Uzbekistana.* (Tashkent, Akademiia nauk Uzbekskoi SSR, 1959-1966). 7 vols. I. N. Togoev, *Razvitie*

of agricultural history. This is explained at least partly by the methodological weakness in the organization of materials relative to the field.[32] Experience has proven on several occasions that classification of source materials and the cross-referencing, indexing, and arrangement of glossaries are of vital importance. Only fragments of these indispensable records have been systematically published. The same could be said about the cadasters of the various administrative offices charged with the recording of "attached peasants."[33]

ekonomiki i kultury Sovetskogo Uzbekistana. (Tashkent, 1957). M. F. Tokarev, *Voprosy ekonomiki otraslei narodnogo khoziaistva Uzbekistana; sbornik statei.* (Tashkent, 1966). S. P. Tolstov et al., eds. *Istoriia Uzbekskoi SSR.* (Tashkent, 1955-1956). 2 vols. in 3. K. Tursunov, *Obrazovanie Uzbekskoi Sovetskoi Sotsialisticheskoi Respubliki.* (Tashkent, 1957). S. P. Tolstov, "Rabota khorezmskoi arkheologo-etnograficheskoi ekspeditsii 1951-1954 godov." *Voprosy istorii*, No. 3 (1955), 173-180. *Uzbekistan. Ekonomiko-geograficheskaia kharakteristika.* (Tashkent, 1950). *Uzbekskaia SSR. Ekonomiko-geograficheskie ocherki.* (Tashkent, 1963). M. G. Vakhabov, *Formirovanie Uzbekskoi sotsialisticheskoi natsii.* (Tashkent, 1961). (See also footnote No. 60, Ch. IV.)

WHITE RUSSIA (BELORUSSIA): Russko-belorusskie sviazi; sbornik dokumentov, 1570-1667. (Minsk, 1963). K. V. Kiselev, ed., *Belorusskaia SSR v mezhdunarodnykh otnosheniiakh; mezhdunarodnye dogovory, konventsii i soglasheniia BSSR s inostrannymi gosudarstvami, 1944-1959.* (Minsk, 1960). *Belorusskaia Sovetskaia Sotsialisticheskaia Respublika.* (Minsk, 1927). K. V. Kiselev, ed., *Belorusskaia SSR na mezhdunarodnoi arene.* (Moscow, 1964). V. A. Poluian, *Revoliutsionnoe i natsionalno-osvoboditelnoe dvizhenie v Zapadnoi Belorussii v 1920-1939 gg.* (Minsk, 1962). *Rabochii klass BSSR v poslevoennye gody, 1945-1950.* (Moscow, 1962). A. I. Azarov, E. P. Lukianov, and V. N. Zhigalov, eds., *Revoliutsionnoe dvizhenie v Belorussii 1905-1907 gg.; dokumenty i materialy.* (Minsk, 1955). V. A. Krutalevich, ed., *Revoliutsionnye komitety BSSR (noiabr 1918—iiul 1920 g.). Sbornik dokumentov i materialov.* (Minsk, 1961). T. S. Gorbunov et al., eds., *Velikaia Oktiabrskaia sotsialisticheskaia revoliutsiia v Belorussii; dokumenty i materialy.* (Minsk, 1957). 2 vols. *Vosstanie v Litve i Belorussii 1863-1864 gg.* (Moscow, 1965).

[32]V. K. Iatsunskii., "K voprosu o sobranii i publikatsiiakh materialov po istorii tsen v Rossii." *Problemy istochnikovedeniia*, No. 4 (1955), 350-357. V. K. Iatsunskii, "O vyiavlenii i publikatsii istochnikov po sotsialno-ekonomicheskoi istorii Rossii XVII-XIX vv." *Arkheograficheskii ezhegodnik za 1957 god.* (Moscow, 1958), 169-186. K. V. Sivkov, "Istochniki po istorii selskogo khoziaistva Rossii vo vtoroi polovine XVIII v." *Problemy istochnikovedeniia*, No. 8 (1959), 144-190. B. G. Litvak, "O nekotorykh priemakh publikatsii istochnikov statisticheskogo kharaktera." *Istoricheskii arkhiv*, No. 2 (1957), 155-166.

[33]A. I. Iakovlev, ed., *Tamozhennye knigi Moskovskogo gosudarstva XVII veka.* (Moscow, 1950-1951). 3 vols. A. Ts. Merzon, *Tamozhennye knigi XVII v.* (Moscow, 1957). A. Ts. Merzon, "Ustiuzhskie tamozhennye knigi XVII v." *Problemy istochnikovedeniia*, No. 6 (1958), 67-129. B. B. Kafengauz, "Tamozhennye knigi XVIII veka." *Arkheograficheskii ezhegodnik za 1957 god.* (Moscow, 1958), 127-137. G. D. Kapustina, "Zapisnye knigi Moskovskoi krepostnoi kontory kak istoricheskii istochnik (pervaia chetvert' XVIII veka)." *Problemy istochnikovedeniia*, No. 7 (1959), 216-273.

Historical research on the peasantry has produced some impressive writings, such as those of B. D. Grekov, S. B. Veselovskii, and L. V. Cherepnin. For some inexplicable reason the situation of the peasants in the seventeenth and eighteenth centuries has received less attention than that during the two centuries following, though the entire period of time is covered in well-known collaborative works by Soviet scholars. This research has also led to the publication of newly found archival materials, and a reinterpretation of Russian agrarian history of this period.[34]

One of the main reasons for the advance in agrarian history was the existence of a specially formed commission, headed first by the late B. D. Grekov and then by N. M. Druzhinin, for the purpose of research in agriculture and the peasantry. This commission, in cooperation with the Soviet Academy of Agricultural Sciences, annually holds a symposium on agrarian history and compiles materials of historical importance. Papers delivered at the annual meetings, some of which are later expanded and published, present collectively an impressive effort in the field of agrarian history.

The series "Materials on the History of Agriculture of the USSR" is devoted to various phases of agricultural economy, including such topics as the history of wheat since neolithic times and the history of cultivation of the potato, of barley, cotton, tea, and other products. There are volumes on single themes, such as the culture of oats, buckwheat, corn, or sugar beets, or the technology of agriculture. The series has included extensive studies of veterinary sciences and animal husbandry in widely scattered parts of the world.[35]

A number of monographs have been published by V. I. Shunkov, V. N. Sherstoboev, and other experts on agriculture in Siberia.[36] Shunkov convincingly shows that by the end of the seventeenth century the acreage of cultivated land in the east was already adequate to support the population of Siberia without imports from western Russia. There have been other valuable monographs by S. V. Bakhrushin and F. G. Safronov, as well as scholarly articles by various authors on such subjects as the peasant popula-

[34]A. A. Novoselskii and N. V. Ustiugov, eds., *Ocherki istorii SSSR. Period feodalizma, XVII v.* (Moscow, 1955). B. B. Kafengauz and N. I. Pavlenko, eds., *Ocherki istorii SSSR. Pervaia chetvert' XVIII v.* (Moscow, 1954). A. I. Baranovich et al., eds. *Ocherki istorii SSSR. Vtoraia chetvert XVIII v.* (Moscow, 1957). A. I. Baranovich, B. B. Kafengauz, P. K. Alefirenko et al., eds. *Ocherki istorii SSSR. Vtoraia polovina XVIII v.* (Moscow, 1956).

[35]*Materialy po istorii zemledeliia SSSR. Sbornik II.* (Moscow, 1956). Vols. III-IV. (Moscow, 1960). See also *Istoriia Krestianstva Ukrainskoi SSR.* Institut istorii Akademii Nauk Uk. SSR. (Kiev, 1967).

[36]V. I. Shunkov, *Ocherki po istorii zemledeliia Sibiri (XVIII vek).* (Moscow, 1956). V. I. Shunkov, "Iz istorii zemledeliia Buriatii." *Trudy Buriatskogo kompleksnogo nauchno-issledovatelskogo instituta,* Issue I (Ulan-Ude, 1959), 65-70. V. N. Sherstoboev, *Ilimskaia pashnia.* Vol. II (Irkutsk, 1957).

tion, colonization of various portions of Siberia in the seventeenth century, and grain cultivation in western Siberia.[37]

Similar studies in agriculture centered on southeastern and southern Russia; E. I. Druzhinina wrote on the population of New Russia (Novorossiia), the Kuban area, and the Crimea after the Russo-Turkish wars of the second half of the eighteenth century.[38] Others have made similar studies of the Volga and Don areas.

A subject frequently discussed among Soviet historians was the nature of class struggle within rural and town communities. M. N. Tikhomirov, A. A. Zimin, I. I. Smirnov, L. V. Cherepnin, and many others have written on the subject.[39] As the field broadened it came to embrace additional subjects, political conflicts of national importance, clashes of feudal and anti-feudal interests that were bound to have an impact upon the social and economic system of the peasantry, social antagonisms of various kinds, and town and country rivalry. Some studies centered exclusively upon regional developments, such as the monograph of L. V. Cherepnin, stressing the socio-political struggle in the Principality of Pskov during the last quarter of the fif-

[37]S. V. Bakhrushin, *Nauchnye trudy*. (Moscow, 1959). Vol. IV, 5-172, deals with the region of Krasnoiarsk. F. G. Safronov, *Krestianskaia kolonizatsiia basseinov Leny i Ilima v XVII v.* (Iakutsk, 1956). O. I. Kashik, "Iz istorii zaseleniia Irkutskogo uezda v XVII—nachale XVIII v." *Uchenye zapiski Irkutskogo gosudarstvennogo pedagogicheskogo instituta,* Issue XVI (1958), 227-273. A. N. Kopylov, "Yeniseiskii zemledelcheskii raion v seredine XVII v.i ego znachenie dlia snabzheniia Vostochnoi Sibiri khlebom." *Trudy MGIAI* [Moskovskii gosudarstvennyi istoriko-arkhivnyi institut], Vol. X (Moscow, 1957), 115-134. A. A. Preobrazhenskii, *Ocherki kolonizatsii Zapadnogo Urala v XVII—nachale XVIII veka.* (Moscow, 1956). N. V. Ustiugov, "Iz istorii russkoi krestianskoi kolonizatsii Iuzhnogo Zauralia v XVIII v." *Ezhegodnik po agrarnoi istorii Vostochnoi Evropy za 1958 g.* (Tallin, 1959).

[38]E. I. Druzhinina, *Severnoe Prichernomorie v 1775-1800 gg.* (Moscow, 1959).

[39]A. A. Zimin and A. A. Preobrazhenskii, "Izuchenie v sovetskoi istoricheskoi nauke klassovoi borby perioda feodalizma v Rossii (do nachala XIX veka.)." *Voprosy istorii,* No. 12 (1957), 135-160. A. A. Zimin, *Reformy Ivana Groznogo. Ocherki sotsialno-ekonomicheskoi istorii serediny XVI v.* (Moscow, 1960). (See particularly Ch. VI.) A. A. Zimin, *Oprichnina Ivana Groznogo.* (Moscow, 1964). A. A. Zimin, "Zemskii Sobor 1566 g." *Istoricheskie zapiski,* No. 71 (1962), 196-235. A. A. Zimin,"Osnovnye etapy i formy klassovoi borby v Rossii kontsa XV-XVI veka." *Voprosy istorii,* No. 3 (1965), 38-52. I. I. Smirnov, *Vosstanie Bolotnikova, 1606-1607.* (Moscow, 1951). I. I. Smirnov, *Ocherki politicheskoi istorii Russkogo gosudarstva 30-50kh godov XVI veka.* (Moscow, 1958). L. V. Cherepnin, *Obrazovanie Russkogo tsentralizovannogo gosudarstva v XIV-XV vekakh. Ocherki sotsialno-ekonomicheskoi i politicheskoi istorii Rusi.* (Moscow, 1960). L. V. Cherepnin, "Klassovaia borba v 1682 g. na iuge Moskovskogo gosudarstva." *Istoricheskie zapiski,* Vol. IV (1938), 41-75.

teenth century, or his study of the mass uprisings in Moscow in 1382 and in 1445.[40]

D. PEASANT REVOLTS AND SOCIAL CHANGES

The subject of peasant revolts in the history of Russia has been a favorite topic of discussion for many years, but it came to a climax in 1958, when a symposium was initiated in the historical journal *Voprosy istorii,* which lasted for no less than three years. The main theme was the nature of the peasant revolts during the early seventeenth century, their aims and their impact upon the country at large. The discussions were concentrated on the background to the uprisings and the forces that impelled the peasants to revolt. The view of A. A. Zimin, generally accepted among historians, though seriously challenged by I. I. Smirnov, was that an actual revolt, such as the one led by Bolotnikov in 1606-1608, was only the culmination of a long period of social and political discontent. For this reason, he urged

[40]M. N. Tikhomirov, *Krestianskie i gorodskie vosstaniia na Rusi XI-XIII vv.* (Moscow, 1955). A general survey of Russian towns of the XV-XVII centuries may be found in the study by M. N. Tikhomirov, "Spisok russkikh gorodov dalnikh i blizhnikh." *Istoricheskie zapiski,* No. 40 (1952), 214-260. Two excellent bibliographical studies in the same field can be recommended: one by A. A. Zimin, and A. A. Preobrazhenskii, "Izuchenie v Sovetskoi istoricheskoi nauke klassovoi borby perioda feodalizma v Rossii (do nachala XIX veka)." *Voprosy istorii,* No. 12 (1957), 135-160; the other is by V. V. Mavrodin,"Sovetskaia istoricheskaia literatura o krestianskikh voinakh v Rossii XVII-XVIII vekov." *Voprosy istorii,* No. 5 (1961), 24-47. V. V. Mavrodin, I. Z. Kadson, N. I. Sergeeva, and T. P. Rzhanikova, "Ob osobennostiakh krestianskikh voin v Rossii." *Voprosy istorii,* No. 2 (1956), 69-79. R. V. Ovchinnikov, "Nekotorye voprosy krestianskoi voiny nachala XVII veka v Rossii." *Voprosy istorii,* No. 7, (1959), 69-83. See also V. N. Bernadskii, "Klassovaia borba v russkom gorode v tretei chetverti XVIII veka." *Uchenye zapiski Leningradskogo pedagogicheskogo instituta,* Vol. 131 (1957). S. Piontkovskii, "Istoriografiia krestianskikh voin v Rossii." *Istorik-marksist,* No. 6(34), (1933), 80-119. A more recently published collection of documentary sources on Russian towns of the XVI-XVII centuries was by G. Anpilogov, *Novye dokumenty o Rossii kontsa XVI—nachala XVII v.* (Moscow, 1967). (See particularly Part III on the history of Elets and Voronezh.) V. I. Koretskii, "Iz istorii krestianskoi voiny v Rossii nachala XVII veka." *Voprosy istorii,* No. 3 (1959), 118-137.

Much new material on the Bolotnikov rebellion (1606-1608) has been uncovered by Soviet historians since the 1940's. Of the recent writings based on the latest sources may be cited the fóllowing: A. A. Zimin, "K istorii vosstaniia Bolotnikova." *Istoricheskie zapiski,* No. 24 (1947), 353-385. V. I. Koretskii, "K istorii vosstaniia I. I. Bolotnikova." *Istoricheskii arkhiv,* No. 2 (1956), 126-145. V. I. Koretskii, "Novoe o Bolotnikove." *Sovetskie arkhivy,* No. 4 (1967). V. I. Koretskii, "Letopisets s novymi izvestiiami o vosstanii Bolotnikova." *Istoriia SSSR,* No. 4 (1968), 120-130. M. N. Tikhomirov, "Novyi istochnik po istorii vosstaniia Bolotnikova." *Istoricheskii arkhiv,* No. 6 (1951), 81-130. G. N. Bibikov, "Novye dannye o vosstanii Bolotnikova." *Istoricheskii arkhiv,* No. 1 (1936), 5-24.

scholars to scrutinize not only the events of the revolt itself, but the accumulated ferment which gradually led to the outburst.[41]

With a few dissenting opinions, such as that of V. I. Koretskii, the three-year discussion represented an effort to reappraise the sources available and works written to that date. Since no new sources were mentioned or known to the discussants, one faction argued, not without plausible reason, that a final reevaluation of the subject matter would be untimely and ill advised. The symposium ended without any definite answers to numerous pertinent queries on the various aspects of the main theme, the general character of the peasant revolts in the history of Russia. It might be added that the research of Koretskii alone succeeded in bringing to light some new materials that added more information, though nothing basically different, on the reasons for peasant discontent.[42]

Even the organ of the Marxist historians, *Voprosy istorii,* which sponsored the symposium, was forced to admit in summarizing the three years of discussions that there was a need for new sources and better elucidation of a confusing terminology employed by many writers. There was chronological confusion throughout these discussions; there was forceful assertion and equally strong challenge of the thesis that the peasant uprisings of the sixteenth and seventeenth centuries in Russia delivered a decisive blow to feudalism. Critics rightly asked how decisive this blow to feudalism could have been if the feudal order, as the Marxists define it, lasted for more than two centuries after the peasant revolts. A. A. Zimin asserted that the peasant war checked the introduction of serfdom at least for a half a century. This contention too was subjected to debate: his adversaries contended that some laws which virtually legalized serfdom went into effect by the end of the

[41]A. A. Zimin, "Nekotorye voprosy istorii krestianskoi voiny v Rossii v nachale XVII veka." *Voprosy istorii,* No. 3 (1958), 97-113. V. V. Mavrodin, "Osnovnye problemy krestianskoi voiny v Rossii 1773-1775 godov." *Voprosy istorii,* No. 8 (1964), 60-76. V. V. Mavrodin, "Sovetskaia istoricheskaia literatura o krestianskikh voinakh v Rossii XVII-XVIII vekov." *Voprosy istorii,* No. 5 (1961), 24-47. I. I. Smirnov, "O nekotorykh voprosakh istorii borby klassov v Russkom gosudarstve nachala XVII veka." *Voprosy istorii,* No. 12 (1958), 116-131. I. M. Skliar, "O nachalnom etape pervoi krestianskoi voiny v Rossii." *Voprosy istorii,* No. 6 (1960), 90-101. L. V. Cherepnin, "Osnovnye etapy razvitiia feodalnoi sobstvennosti na Rusi (do XVII veka)." *Voprosy istorii,* No. 4 (1953), 38-63.

[42]See the recently uncovered documents related to the revolt of Bolotnikov published and accompanied by comments of V. I. Koretskii, "K istorii vosstaniia Bolotnikova." *Istoricheskii arkhiv,* No. 2 (1956), 126-145. Also V. I. Koretskii, "Iz krestianskoi voiny v Rossii nachala XVI veka." *Voprosy istorii,* No. 3 (1959), 118-137. Equally important are Koretskii's newly uncovered sources on the struggle of the peasants against monastic landholdings in sixteenth-century Russia. See *Voprosy istorii religii i ateizma,* Vol. VI (1958), and Vol. VI (1959), where the question of famine and the role of the church is discussed. Also, see A. G. Maikov and A. I. Kopanev, *Vosstanie Bolotnikova.* (Moscow, 1959). A more general account and useful information may be found in I. I. Smirnov, *Vosstanie Bolotnikova (1606-1607).* (Moscow, 1951).

sixteenth century, that is, before the outbreak of the peasant war. The struggle for control over what one writer graphically described as "the callused peasant hands" was virtually determined by 1600, they declared, after which it was only a matter of consolidation and enforcement of such control. I. S. Shepelev devoted himself to a different aspect of the same subject—peasant revolts and their relation to the struggle against foreign oppression.[43]

The discussion left much debris to be cleared away when the symposium ended. Lucidity was required in carelessly employed terminology such as "civil strife," "peasant war," "class struggle in feudal periods," and the like. It was rightly asserted that until there was a commonly agreed upon definition of such terms all discussions would be futile.

Some participants in the symposium, V. V. Mavrodin, for instance, raised such pertinent questions as: Why did the first peasant war break out at the beginning of the seventeenth century and not at another date? Or, What was the relation of the war to the socio-economic development of the time? These queries never received any satisfactory answers.[44]

Nevertheless, documentary evidence and publication in the field of peasant discontent and widespread violence during the seventeenth and eighteenth centuries has produced a great volume of worthwhile material. In 1933, M. N. Tikhomirov completed a critical survey of Russian and foreign source materials, including official acts and private and official correspondence related to such events as the uprising of Stenka Razin.[45] Since 1956, particularly, there has appeared in print much material related to peasant uprisings during 1670-1671 and 1773-1775. A notable contribution was the two-volume publication by E. A. Shvetsova on the Stenka Razin rebellion, including several hundred documents.[46] Skillfully arranged, the collection offers rewarding material to the student of history. It covers the course of the rebellion until January, 1671, incorporating many documents that have never been published before and deal mainly with the impact of the revolt upon regions that did not actually take active part in the uprising against the feudal order.

M. N. Tikhomirov has published materials on the Streletskii revolt in 1682, and there are also published materials that cover the uprisings of 1648 and 1662 in Moscow. Some collections deal with judicial investigations of social unrest among the townsmen, while documentary evidence gathered by A. P. Gudzinskaia deals with the revolt of peasants attached to

[43]I. S. Shepelev, *Osvoboditelnaia i klassovaia borba v Russkom gosudarstve v 1608-1610 gg.* (Piatigorsk, 1957).

[44]"O krestianskoi voine v Russkom gosudarstve v nachale XVII v." *Voprosy istorii,* No. 5 (1961), 102-120.

[45]"Istochniki po istorii razinshchiny." *Problemy istochnikovedeniia,* No. 1 (1933), 50-69.

[46]E. A. Shvetsova, comp. *Krestianskaia voina pod predvoditelstvom S. T. Razina.* (Moscow, 1954-1957). 2 vols.

factories. Combined, these represent an imposing amount of primary source materials which the historian of seventeenth- and eighteenth-century social developments should not overlook.[47]

The revolt of the Cossacks and peasants in 1707-1709 in the Don region, under the leadership of K. Bulavin, has been regarded rather casually in the past. Recently this tendency was corrected by E. P. Podiapolskaia, who compiled a collection of newly found documents. This collection reveals a fuller picture of social conditions in southern and central Russia and discloses for the first time the names of Bulavin's assistants. The most valuable aspect of the collection is the manifestoes and appeals of the rebels to the population at large. These help clarify the underlying causes of the unrest, the original goals of the rebellion, and the eventual outburst of violent action.[48]

Equally interesting are the materials discovered by N. V. Ustiugov concerning the struggle conducted by the serfs attached to factories, and by A. A. Preobrazhenskii concerning the peasantry of the Urals. Other centers of discontent in the towns and countryside of central Russia are dealt with by A. V. Muraviev, V. I. Lebedev, and others. The general impression left by these works is that widespread unrest and outright violence had been witnessed throughout most of the reign of Peter I. This situation was the

[47]M. N. Tikhomirov, "Zapiski prikaznykh liudei XVII v." *Trudy Otdela drevnerusskoi literatury,* Vol. XII (Moscow, 1956), 442-457. V. I. Buganov, "Opisanie moskovskogo vosstaniia 1648 g. v Arkhivskom sbornike." *Istoricheskii arkhiv,* No. 4 (1957), 227-230. V. I. Koretskii, "Izvestie o nepovinovenii krestian v votchine Antonievo-Siiskogo monastyria vo vtoroi polovine XVI v." *Istoricheskii arkhiv,* No. 4 (1957), 231-233. V. I. Buganov, "Novye istochniki o moskovskom vosstanii 1662 g." *Problemy istochnikovedeniia,* No. 7 (1959), 348-356. V. I. Buganov, "Sledstvie o moskovskom vosstanii 1662 g." *Istoricheskie zapiski,* No. 65 (1959), 278-302. V. I. Buganov, "K voprosu o moskovskom vosstanii 1662 g." *Voprosy istorii,* No. 5 (1959), 160-175. V. I. Buganov, "O sotsialnom sostave uchastnikov moskovskogo vosstaniia 1662 g." *Istoricheskie zapiski,* No. 66 (1960), 312-317. V. I. Buganov, "Zapiski sovremennika o moskovskikh vosstaniiakh 1648 i 1662 gg." *Arkheograficheskii ezhegodnik za 1958 god.* (Moscow, 1960), 99-114. V. I. Buganov, "Dokumenty iz sledstvennogo dela o vosstanii 1662 g." *Istoricheskii arkhiv,* No. 1 (1961), 146-153. V. A. Kuchkin, "Imena uchastnikov vosstaniia v perepisnoi knige Bronnoi slobody." *Istoricheskii arkhiv,* No. 1 (1961), 144-145. E. V. Chistiakova, "Sostav sledstvennykh del o gorodskikh vosstaniiakh na Iuge Rossii v seredine XVII veka." *Arkheograficheskii ezhegodnik za 1958 god.* (Moscow, 1960). 90-97. E. V. Chistiakova, "Prigovornye zapisi XVII veka." *Voprosy istorii,* No. 3 (1956), 136-137. A. P. Gudzinskaia, "Volneniia pripisnykh krestian Vyshegorodskoi volosti vo vtoroi polovine XVII v." *Istoricheskii arkhiv,* No. 2 (1960), 145-158.

[48]E. P. Podiapolskaia, "Novye materialy o vosstanii na Donu i v Tsentralnoi Rossii v 1707-1709 gg." *Materialy po istorii SSSR,* Vol. V, 503-564. E. P. Podiapolskaia, "Novoe o vosstanii K. Bulavina." *Istoricheskii arkhiv,* No. 6 (1960), 119-142. K. M. Bibikova, "Bibliograficheskii ukazatel literatury i dokumentov po istorii Bulavinskogo vosstaniia." *Krestianskie i natsionalnye dvizheniia nakanune obrazovania Rossiiskoi imperii. Bulavinskoe vosstanie (1707-1708 gg.).* Trudy Istoriko-arkheograficheskogo instituta. Akademiia nauk SSSR. Vol. XIII (Moscow, 1935), 495-510.

product of social and economic conditions, caused by the reforms which few understood and many found alien because of their religious convictions or because of the immediate hardships the reforms imposed in the form of taxes or military service.

The study of the peasant movement between 1730 and 1760, by Pelageia K. Alefirenko, shows in great detail the means employed by the peasants to manifest their opposition: mass disobedience to both officials and landlords, petitions and appeals for relief to the government, defection, or outright rebellion. Alefirenko lists some thirty-five uprisings during this time in central Russia alone.

E. I. Zaozerskaia discusses similar unrest in the textile and other industries, unrest which took the form of work stoppage, protests, and escape by peasants from plants and shops to which they had been attached.[49]

Soviet historiography devotes much attention to the two revolts led by S. Razin in the seventeenth century and E. Pugachev in the eighteenth century. Studies of the Razin rebellion have included special studies of the non-Russian population, mainly the Chuvash, as participants in the violent outburst that swept the country during the 1670's. The most extensive study of this episode has been carried out by I. V. Stepanov. Others, such as T. I. Smirnova, have dealt with the role played by the escaped serfs in the revolt. The period generally is considered under the main heading of "Peasant Anti-Feudal Revolts."[50]

[49]N. V. Ustiugov, "Iz istorii borby chernososhnykh krestian protiv pripiski k promyshlennym predpriiatiiam." *Iz istorii rabochego klassa i revoliutsionnogo dvizheniia.* (Moscow, 1958), 73-80. A. A. Preobrazhenskii, "Klassovaia borba uralskikh krestian i masterovykh liudei v nachale XVIII v." *Istoricheskie zapiski,* No. 58 (1956), 246-272. V. I. Lebedev, "Neizvestnye volneniia pri Petre I (1722-1724 gg.)." *Istoriia SSSR,* No. 1 (1961), 159-162. A. V. Muraviev, "Iz materialov po istorii klassovoi borby v russkom gorode nachala XVIII veka." In *Arkheograficheskii ezhegodnik za 1959 god,* pp. 157-163. P. K. Alefirenko, *Krestianskoe dvizhenie i krestianskii vopros v 30-50kh godakh XVIII v.* (Moscow, 1958). E. I. Zaozerskaia, *Rabochaia sila i klassovaia borba na tekstilnykh manufakturakh Rossii v 20-60kh godakh XVIII v.* (Moscow, 1960).

[50]I. V. Stepanov, "Krestianskaia voina pod predvoditelstvom Stepana Razina v Srednem Povolzhie." *Uchenye zapiski Leningradskogo gosudarstvennogo universiteta,* No. 205 (1956), 125-166. I. V. Stepanov, "Sotsialno-politicheskaia obstanovka na Donu nakanune krestianskoi voiny pod predvoditelstvom S. T. Razina." *Uchenye zapiski LGU,* No. 270 (1959), 34-59. E. V. Chistiakova, "Astrakhan v period vosstaniia Stepana Razina." *Istoriia SSSR,* No. 5 (1957), 188-202. I. P. Pan'kov, "Novye materialy o krestianskoi voine pod predvoditelstvom Stepana Razina." *Uchenye zapiski Chardzhousskogo gosudarstvennogo instituta,* Issue 1 (1956), 51-65. N. R. Romanov, "Borba krestian protiv feodalno-krepostnicheskogo gneta. Uchastie chuvashskogo naroda v krestianskoi voine pod predvoditelstvom S. T. Razina." *Materialy po istorii Chuvashskoi ASSR,* Issue I (Cheboksary, 1958), 189-207. T. I. Smirnova, "Pobegi krestian nakanune vystupleniia S. Razina." *Voprosy istorii,* No. 6 (1956), 129-131. I. I. Smirnov, *Krestianskie voiny v Rossii XVII-XVIII vv.* (Moscow, 1966).

Other local revolts were studied by P. A. Kolesnikov, who centered his attention upon the Vologodsk region, and by V. A. Aleksandrov and Z. Ia. Boiarshinova, who investigated unrest in eastern Siberia. N. V. Ustiugov and G. N. Obraztsov have investigated conditions of the peasantry residing on monastic estates, showing the sharp contradictions that had arisen between the peasants and the privileged landowners over numerous issues.[51]

Despite the extensive research done by Soviet scholars in recent years, various aspects of the history of social unrest, particularly during the second half of the seventeenth century, are still left to be explored. The essay of A. G. Mankov only confirms the amount of work still remaining to be accomplished.[52]

A long-neglected subject in the history of social and religious discontent of seventeenth- and eighteenth-century Russia is the impact which must have been produced by the schism. There are, however, two essays by L. E. Ankundinova that stand out particularly, offering an original interpretation and a utilization of new source material. One of them deals with the social composition of the ranks of Old Believers, the other with the socio-political views of the early schismatics.[53]

A. V. Chernov, N. B. Golikova, and M. D. Rabinovich utilized recently discovered sources to describe the Astrakhan uprising in 1707-1708, involving the rebellious *streltsy* troops and the general trials of all those affiliated with the movement during the reign of Peter I. These writers have definitely disproved the old contention that the Astrakhan rebellion was caused mainly by the former *streltsy* units that were banished to Astrakhan. The rebellion

[51]P. A. Kolesnikov, *Iz istorii klassovoi borby vologodskikh krestian v XVII veke.* (Vologda, 1957). P. A. Kolesnikov, "Vosstanie v Tot'me i v Totemskom uezde XVII v." *Russkoe gosudarstvo v XVII veke.* (Moscow, 1961), 272-283. Z. Ia. Boiarshinova, "Volneniia v Tomske v XVII veke." *Voprosy istorii,* No. 6 (1956), 109-115. V. A. Aleksandrov, "Narodnye vosstaniia v Vostochnoi Sibiri vo vtoroi polovine XVII veka." *Istoricheskie zapiski,* No. 59 (1957), 255-309. Iu. E. Puretskii, "Sotsialnye otnosheniia v Ustiuge Velikom i Ustiuzhskom uezde v 20-40kh godakh XVII v. po materialam dozora 1639 g." *Trudy Moskovskogo gosudarstvennogo istoriko-arkhivnogo instituta,* Vol. X (Moscow, 1957), 135-149. E. V. Chistiakova, "Volneniia sluzhilykh liudei v iuzhnykh raionakh Rossii v seredine XVII v." *Russko gosudarstvo v XVII veke.* (Moscow, 1961), 254-271. N. V. Ustiugov, "Volneniia krestian Simonova monastyria v sele Ilinskom Cheremozhskoi volosti Iaroslavskogo uezda v 1682-1683 gg." *Russkoe gosudarstvo v XVII veke.* (Moscow, 1961), 284-294. G. N. Obraztsov, "Ulozhenie 1649 g. i krestiane votchiny Antonievo-Siiskogo monastyria." *Istoricheskie zapiski,* No. 63 (1958), 269-282.

[52]A. G. Mankov, "Borba posada s feodalami vo vtoroi polovine XVII v." *Istoricheskie zapiski,* No. 64 (1959), 217-232.

[53]L. E. Ankundinova, "Sotsialnyi sostav pervykh raskolnikov." *Vestnik Leningradskog universiteta,* No. XIV. *Seriia istorii, iazyka i literatury.* Issue 3 (1956), 51-68. L. E. Ankundinova, "Obshchestvenno-politicheskie vzgliady pervykh raskolnikov i narodnye massy." *Uchenye zapiski Leningradskogo gosudarstvennogo universiteta,* No 270, *Seriia istoricheskikh nauk,* Issue 32 (1959), 60-82.

they have shown, included many members of the local military units as well as townsmen; it was against arbitrary rule of local administrators, against compulsory service, and against the landowning class. Being of an exceedingly complex socio-economic nature, the revolt also involved opponents to the reforms of Peter I.[54]

Though much has been written and published on the subject of the Pugachev rebellion during 1773-1775, time and again archival material turns up to add new detail to a generally well-explored field.[55] Recent publications on the Pugachev-led uprising have touched upon such subjects as the part played by the Ural peasants, by the Volga communities, and by the natives of Bashkiria. Another theme has been a study of the role played by some of Pugachev's close assistants, such as Ataman I. Beloborodov, who led the rebellion in the central Ural region. M. N. Martynov has studied particularly the role of peasants employed in or attached to industrial enterprises, while I. Ushakov has produced a similar study concerning a different locale.[56]

Historians have concentrated most of their attention on the participation of the serfs in the rebellion, which is only natural since by force of circumstances serfdom became the focal issue of that social upheaval. A number of Soviet writers, E. I. Glazatova, N. I. Sergeeva, V. N. Stepanov, and M. D. Kurmacheva, have enlarged the entire theme beyond the scope of pre-revolutionary study. The first two writers carefully examined the role of the serfs, while the latter two dealt with peasant partisans who operated along the right bank of the Volga during the late summer of 1774. The investigation by A. A. Kondrashenkov of the peasant revolts in the Ural areas is equally interesting. In addition, there are a number of special studies that deal with the type of weaponry used by Pugachev, such as the artillery, rifles, and other military equipment.[57]

[54]A. V. Chernov, "Astrakhanskoe vosstanie 1707-1708 gg." *Istoricheskie zapiski,* No. 64 (1959), 186-216. N. B. Golikova, *Politicheskie protsessy v tsarstvovanie Petra I (Po materialam Preobrazhenskogo prikaza).* (Moscow, 1957). M. D. Rabinovich, "Streltsy v pervoi chetverti XVIII v." *Istoricheskie zapiski,* No. 58 (1956), 273-305.

[55]*Pugachevshchina.* [A collection of documents.] (Moscow, 1926-31). 3 vols.

[56]M. N. Martynov, *Pugachevskii ataman Ivan Beloborodov.* (Perm, 1958). M. N. Martynov, "Satkinskii zavod vo vremia vosstaniia Emeliana Pugacheva." *Istoricheskie zapiski,* No. 58 (1956), 208-245. I. F. Ushakov, "Rabotnye liudi Beloretskogo zavoda v krestianskoi voine." *Istoriia SSSR,* No. 6 (1960), 131-135.

[57]E. I. Glazatova, "Vosstanie krestian Kazanskogo kraia na pervom etape krestianskoi voiny (konets 1773—nachalo 1774 g.)." *Uchenye zapiski Chitinskogo pedagogicheskogo instituta,* Issue 1 (1957). N. I. Sergeeva, "Krestiane i rabotnye liudi zavodov Iuzhnogo Urala v krestianskoi voine 1773-1775 gg." *Uchenye zapiski Leningradskogo bibliotechnogo instituta im. N. K. Krupskoi.* Part II (Leningrad, 1957). M. D. Kurmacheva, "Deistviia otriada Marka Petrova." *Istoriia SSSR,* No. 6 (1960), 135-138. V. N. Stepanov, "Dvizhenie krestian v Arzamasskom uezde v period krestianskoi voiny pod predvoditelstvom E. I. Pugacheva." *Trudy Moskovskogo gosudar-*

While some historians dealt with the Pugachev rebellion itself, others stud
ied the events that led up to the revolt, particularly the social and political
developments along the Iaik River, where discontent had been brewing for
some time among the Cossacks. There were numerous issues, such as the
conduct of Cossack official appointees from the national capital who never
understood the local sentiments, that could easily provoke protests and
cause unrest. There were conflicts over fishery rights, over salt monopoly
claims, over compulsory services, and over taxation. These are well presented by writers such as A. I. Andrushenko and I. G. Rozner. The rebellion continued in various parts of the Urals even after the suppression of
the uprising and the arrest of the main leaders.[58]

V. A. Golobutskii utilizes important documents and other recently found
papers to deal with the relationship between the Pugachev revolt and the
plottings of the same date in the Ukraine. A collaborative work under the
editorship of V. V. Mavrodin attempts to examine the Pugachev rebellion as
a consequence of specific social and economic conditions in the areas of
rebellion, as compared with conditions elsewhere in Russia.[59]

stvennogo istoriko-arkhivnogo instituta, Vol. X (1957), 371-374. A. A. Kondrashenko
"Krestianskie vosstaniia v Isetskoi provintsii v 60-70kh godakh XVIII v." Iz istorii
Urala. Sbornik statei. (Sverdlovsk, 1960), 114-124. N. E. Grebeniuk, "Artil-
leriia v krestianskoi voine pod rukovodstvom Pugacheva." Sbornik issledovanii i materialov Artilleriiskogo istoricheskogo muzeia. Issue IV. (Leningrad, 1959). D.
Kashintsev, "Gorno-zavodskaia promyshlennost Urala i krestianskaia voina 1773-177
gg." Istorik-marksist, No. 1(53) (1936).

[58]A. I. Andrushenko, "Klassovaia borba iaitskikh kazakov nakanune krestianskoi voiny
1773-1775 gg." Istoriia SSSR, No. 1 (1960), 143-159. I. G. Rozner, "Iaitskoe
kazachestvo nakanune krestianskoi voiny 1773-1775 gg." Voprosy istorii, No. 10
(1958), 97-112. I. G. Rozner, "Sotsialno-ekonomicheskie otnosheniia na Iaike nakanune krestianskoi voiny pod rukovodstvom E. Pugacheva." Nauchnye zapiski Kievskogo finansovo-ekonomicheskgo instituta. Vol. VII (1959), 238-260. P. A. Vaghina,
"Volneniia na Avziano-Petrovskikh zavodakh posle krestianskoi voiny pod rukovodstvom Pugacheva (1775-1781)." Iz istorii Urala. Sbornik statei. (Sverdlovsk, 1960),
125-135. P. A. Vaghina, "K istorii krestianskikh volneniia na Kyshtymskikh zavodak
v 70-90kh godakh XVIII v." Iz istorii zavodov i fabrik Urala. Issue 1. (Sverdlovsk,
1960). P. A. Vaghina, "K voprosu o sostoianii rabochei sily na zavodakh luzhnogo
Urala posle krestianskoi voiny 1773-1775 gg." Voprosy istorii Urala. Sbornik statei.
Issue 39. (Sverdlovsk, 1961), 45-64. A. V. Prussak, "Zavody rabotavshie na Pugacheva." Istoricheskie zapiski, No. 8 (1940), 174-207.

[59]V. A. Golobutskii, "Gaidamatskoe dvizhenie na Zaporozhie vo vremia 'Koliivshchin
i krestianskoe vosstanie pod predvoditelstvom E. I. Pugacheva." Istoricheskie zapiski,
No. 55 (1956), 310-343. V. V. Mavrodin, I. Z. Kadson, N. I. Sergeeva, and T. P.
Rzhanikova, "Ob osobennostiakh krestianskikh voin v Rossii." Voprosy istorii, No. ?
(1956), 69-79. V. I. Lebedev, "K voprosu o kharaktere krestianskikh dvizhenii v
Rossii XVII-XVIII vv." Voprosy istorii, No. 6 (1954), 90-98. V. V. Mavrodin,
"Sovetskaia istoricheskaia literatura o krestianskikh voinakh v Rossii XVII-XVIII vv."
Voprosy istorii, No. 5 (1961), 24-47. Also an editorial in Voprosy istorii, No. 5
(1961), 102-120, entitled "O krestianskoi voine v Russkom gosudarstve v nachale
XVII v."

From time to time, fragmentary new records emerge that further enrich the picture of the Pugachev rebellion. Only lately has there appeared a better account of the support rendered to Pugachev by the Don Cossacks. There is the case of the punitive expeditions composed of Cossacks dispatched against Pugachev that proved sympathetic with the cause of the rebels and resulted in a number of defections from the Cossack ranks.[60] The impact of the Pugachev revolt was felt particularly throughout the Altai region and Bashkiria. Documents on this subject were carefully compiled by V. G. Filov and N. F. Demidova.[61]

Finally, we must mention the contribution recently made in the field of cartography as an aid to the study of the peasant revolts. Many maps or plans gathered and printed by historians such as L. A. Goldenberg and R. V. Ovchinnikov serve as additional sources of evidence in the field of rebel military planning, tactics and strategic schemes, or deployment of rebel troops in the Ural region where the revolt originated.

It has been pointed out, not without sound reasoning, that the volume of recently published documents now demands a new effort to synthesize the materials so that they may be fully utilized. There is a great need for a new account of general national conditions at the outbreak of the revolt, a reassessment of the basic causes of the violence, and up-to-date biographical accounts of such rebel leaders as I. I. Bolotnikov, S. T. Razin, K. A. Bulavin, E. I. Pugachev, and their corresponding assistants, of whom little is known despite the fact that they contributed much to the spread of the conflict as well as to its prolongation.[62]

[60]V. V. Mavrodin, *Krestianskaia voina v Rossii v 1773-1775 gg. Vosstanie Pugacheva.* Vol. I (Leningrad, 1961); Vol. II (1966). The first volume contains a most useful historiography of the Pugachev rebellion, including a discussion of primary and secondary sources (pp. 5-282; 571-585). See review of Vol. II in *Istoriia SSSR,* No. 4 (1968), 145-148. V. V. Mavrodin, "Sovetskaia istoricheskaia literatura o krestianskikh voinakh v Rossii XVII-XVIII vv." *Voprosy istorii,* No. 5 (1961), 24-47. R. V. Ovchinnikov and L. N. Slobodskikh, "Novye dokumenty ob uchastii donskikh kazakov v krestianskoi voine pod predvoditelstvom Emeliana Pugacheva." *Izvestiia Rostovskogo muzeia kraevedeniia,* No. I (3), 84-94. (Rostov-na-Donu, 1959). A. P. Pronshtein, "K istorii krestianskogo dvizheniia v Rossii v 1775 g." *Istoricheskii arkhiv,* No. 1 (1960), 143-153. R. V. Ovchinnikov, "O pobede otriadov E. I. Pugacheva pod Orenburgom." *Istoricheskii arkhiv,* No. 1 (1960), 154-167. R. V. Ovchinnikov, "Avtografy E. I. Pugacheva." *Voprosy arkhivovedeniia,* No. IV (16), (1959). *Don i Nizhnee Povolzhie v period kresitanskoi voiny 1773-1775 gg. Sbornik dokumentov.* A. P. Pronshtein, ed. (Rostov-na-Donu, 1961).

[61]V. G. Filov, "Otkliki pugachevskogo dvizheniia na Altae (po dokumentam Altaiskogo kraevogo gosudarstvennogo arkhiva)." *Kraevedcheskie zapiski,* Issue I (Barnaul, 1956), 92-143. N. F. Demidova, "Vedomosti ob uchastii nerusskogo naseleniia Bashkirii v krestianskoi voine 1773-1775 gg." *Materialy po istorii SSSR,* Vol. V, 566-606.

[62]L. A. Goldenberg and R. V. Ovchinnikov, "Kartograficheskie materialy 70kh godov XVIII v. kak novyi istochnik po istorii krestianskoi voiny pod rukovodstvom E. I. Pugacheva." *Voprosy istorii,* No. 4 (1958), 193-197. L. A. Goldenberg and R. V. Ovchinnikov, "Gornozavodskie karty i plany 70-kh godov XVIII veka kak istochnik po istorii krestianskoi voiny pod rukovodstvom E. I. Pugacheva." *Problemy istochnikovedeniia,* No. 8 (1959), 239-266.

The subject of the peasantry during the second quarter of the eighteenth century has been dealt with more extensively since the late 1950's. Two recent studies by Pelageia K. Alefirenko and S. I. Volkov filled gaps in the field. The one by Alefirenko noted the rising output of agricultural commodities and the accompanying social stratification of the peasantry. Volkov, on the other hand, in studying a segment of the peasantry of the Moscow region, brought out the growth of the money economy. An additional work, by E. S. Kogan, stressed the profound changes that took place in the life of the peasantry and in the manorial economy under the influence of the commodity-money relationship.[63]

Several studies of the same period deal with the feudal serf system during the eighteenth century as a factor contributing to the widespread social unrest. These cover a vast range of issues involved: patrimonial estates and conditions of the peasants residing on them; hired labor on monastic estates; the nature of enterprises operated by landlords; growth of a landless peasantry and the decay of serfdom; the slow transformation of the feudalistic economy into a capitalistic one.[64] Most of the writers seem to agree upon the great changes that took place during the seventeenth and eighteenth centuries in the Russian agrarian economy. These were largely caused by the socio-economic changes that relentlessly kept forcing vital issues to the foreground of national life. Some writers discuss other factors that compelled Russia to yield to changes, such as the expanded area under cultivation, particularly by the end of the eighteenth century, the adoption of new grain cultures, the slow but inexorable progress in agricultural techniques, particularly in methods of soil cultivation. Another factor was the rise of prices of agricultural commodities, caused mainly by an increased demand for foodstuffs. Other changing conditions, such as the spread of land ownership by the merchant class, or the rising demand for land to rent or purchase by the peasantry, were all bound to have a deep impact upon the country at large.

[63]P. K. Alefirenko, *Krestianskoe dvizhenie i krestianskii vopros v 30-50kh godakh XVIII v.* (Moscow, 1958). S. I. Volkov, *Krestiane dvortsovykh vladenii Podmoskovia v seredine XVIII v. (30-70e gody).* (Moscow, 1959). E. S. Kogan, *Ocherki istorii krepostnogo khoziaistva po materialam votchin Kurakinykh vtoroi poloviny XVIII v.* (Moscow, 1960).

[64]*K voprosu o pervonachalnom nakoplenii v Rossii (XVII-XVIII vv). Sbornik.* (Moscow, 1958). See particularly the articles by I. V. Zasykina, I. A. Bulygin and others. P. K. Alefirenko, *Krupnoe votchinnoe khoziaistvo grafa M. G. Golovkina v Rossii pervoi poloviny XVIII v. Ezhegodnik za 1959 god.* (Moscow, 1961). Note especially pp. 137-152. L. V. Milov, "Ob izuchenii rosta obroka v Rossii vo vtoroi polovine XVIII veka." *Nauchnye doklady vysshei shkoly. Istoricheskie nauki.* No. 1 (1961), 95-114. K. N. Shchepetov, "Pomeshchiche predprinimatelstvo v XVII v. (Po materialam kniazei Cherkasskikh)." *Russkoe gosudarstvo v XVII v. Sbornik statei.* (Moscow, 1961), 17-37. E. I. Zaozerskaia, "Iz istorii feodalnoi votchiny i polozheniia krestian v pervoi polovine XVII veka. *Materialy po istorii selskogo khoziaistva i krestianstva SSSR. Sbornik IV.* (Moscow, 1960), 39-66. E. N. Oshanina, "Kho-

Other the other hand, a shift by the landlords to enterprises for additional income, such as distilleries, mills, or mines, was a development bound to cause both social and economic changes and produce resentment among the middle class at what they considered an encroachment of their exclusive economic sphere. Equally noticeable was the rise of the kulak, the hard-fisted ambitious peasant whose main goal was expansion of privately owned land and the creeping money economy. In part this was brought about by a dearth of desirable land, and partly it was due to the migration of a portion of the peasants from the villages to towns where they hoped to earn extra cash to meet pressing economic problems. Cumulatively, these developments signalled significant social and economic changes, particularly during the nineteenth century.

The symposia on agrarian history and allied subjects show beyond doubt how important coordination of research had become. This collaborative effort has accomplished much, though further systematization is still called for. Soviet agricultural historians often debate social stratification in the rural areas during the seventeenth and eighteenth centuries. Historians like V. K. Iatsunskii or A. L. Shapiro justly pointed out the complex nature of the peasantry as a class with its multiple problems. These writers maintain that no full grasp of the entire issue can be attained unless agriculture is studied in its relation to commercial and industrial activities of the peasants during the late feudal period; unless the rising departure of the peasantry from the countryside is fully appreciated; unless the impoverishment of the majority of the peasantry and the emergence of the kulak element are

ziaistvo pomeshchikov Pazukhinykh v XVII-XVIII vv." *Voprosy istorii*, No. 7 (1956), 84-92. E. N. Oshanina, "K istorii zaseleniia Srednego Povolzhia v XVII veke." *Russkoe gosudarstvo v XVII veke*. (Moscow, 1961). 49-73. L. S. Proko-fieva, *Votchinnoe khoziaistvo v XVII veke. (Po materialam Spaso-Prilutskogo mona-styria)*. (Moscow, 1960). G. N. Lokhteva, "Razvitie tovarno-denezhnykh otnoshenii v votchinnom khoziaistve XVII veka." *Uchenye zapiski Moskovskogo oblastnogo peda-gogicheskogo instituta*. Vol. XXIV (Moscow, 1958), 71-129. G. N. Lokhteva, "Na-iomnyi trud v monastyrskom khoziaistve XVII v. (Po materialam Troitskogo Gle-denskogo monastyria)." *Russkoe gosudarstvo v XVII veke. Sbornik statei*. (Moscow, 1961), 207-209. Z. A. Ogrizko, "Izmeneniia v ekonomicheskom polozhenii monastyrskikh polovnikov russkogo severa v XVII-XVIII vv." *K voprosu o pervo-nachalnom nakoplenii v Rossii (XVII-XVIII vv.). Sbornik*. (Moscow, 1958), 97-116. Z. A. Ogrizko, "Promyslovoe monastyrskoe selo v kontse XVII veka." *Ezhe-godnik za 1959 g*. (Moscow, 1961), 124-131. A. A. Novoselskii, "Raspad zemle-vladeniia sluzhilogo goroda v XVII veke." *Russkoe gosudarstvo v XVII veke*. Mos-cow, 1961), 230-252. A. L. Shapiro, "Evoliutsiia bobylstva v Rossii v XVII v." *Ezhegodnik za 1959 g*. (Tallin, 1959), 91-104. A. L. Shapiro, "Bobylstvo v Rossii XVI-XVII vv." *Istoriia SSSR*, No. 3 (1960), 49-66. V. N. Kolechenkova, "K voprosu o sosediakh kak sotsialnoi kategorii." *Russkoe gosudarstvo v XVII v*. (Moscow, 1961), 200-206. N. L. Rubinshtein, *Selskoe khoziaistvo Rossii vo vtoroi polovine XVIII v*. (Moscow, 1957). *Krestianskoe dvizhenie v Rossii v 1826-1849 gg. (Sbornik dokumentov. Krestianskoe dvizhenie v Rossii v 19-20 vv.)*. (Moscow, 1961). I. Kovalchenko, *Russkoe krepostnoe krestianstvo v pervoi polovine XIX veka*. (Moscow, 1967).

121

properly interpreted. In the opinion of Soviet historians, all these changes emanated from the social stratification that kept altering the nature of the Russian countryside and society.[65]

Carrying the subject from the eighteenth century into the following one, I. A. Gurzhii dealt with the peasant movement during the period from 1780 to 1861. The writer fully utilized many recently opened archival depositories, and included not only the unrest brewing and the occasional virulent uprisings of the peasantry, but the daily problems of managing their miserable lots, eking out a livelihood against heavy odds, attempts by serfs to escape from estates to which they were attached, and the problems of peasants theoretically free, yet unable to be affected by the general conditions created by the institution of serfdom.[66]

On the peasant movement in the Ukraine during the second half of the nineteenth century, M. N. Leshchenko and D. P. Poida have done considerable research. Leshchenko's monograph covers the period of enforcement of the 1861 legislation, including the peasant unrest that followed throughout the Ukrainian countryside during the sixties. The monograph of D. P. Poida is in fact a continuation of the same subject, though it covers a more extensive period, 1866-1900. The study reveals particularly the fact that social discontent, contrary to all former belief, did not subside after the abolition of serfdom. The author asserts that the country witnessed continuous unrest during the rest of the nineteenth century.[67]

A number of historians have taken up the same subject in other localities, such as the Baltic region, White Russia, and central Russia. All these regional developments were brought into a general national pattern by N. M. Druzhinin, in his work mentioned elsewhere, producing a fully synthesized account of the general national situation.[68]

[65]V. K. Iatsunskii, "Genezis kapitalizma v selskom khoziaistve Rossii." *Ezhegodnik za 1959 god.* (Moscow, 1961), 30-51. A. L. Shapiro, "Ob opasnosti modernizatsii ekonomicheskoi istorii russkogo krestianstva XVII—pervoi poloviny XVIII v." *Ezhegodnik za 1959 god.* (Moscow, 1961), 347-365. G. Favstov, "III Mezhrespublikanskii simpozium po agrarnoi istorii Vostochnoi Evropy." *Voprosy istorii*, No. 3 (1961), 135-144. I. V. Ledovskaia, "Tretii Mezhrespublikanskii simpozium po agrarnoi istorii Vostochnoi Evropy." *Istoriia SSSR*, No. 2 (1961), 115-127. B. B. Kafengauz, "Nekotorye voprosy genezisa kapitalizma v Rossii." *Voprosy genezisa kapitalizma v Rossii. Sbornik statei.* (Leningrad, 1960).

[66]I. A. Gurzhii, *Borba krestian i rabochikh Ukrainy protiv feodalno-krepostnicheskogo gneta (s 80kh godov XVIII v. do 1861 goda).* (Kiev, 1958).

[67]M. N. Leshchenko, *Krestianskoe dvizhenie na Ukraine v sviazi s provedeniem reformy 1861 g. (60e gody).* (Kiev, 1959). D. P. Poida, *Krestianskoe dvizhenie na Pravoberezhnoi Ukraine v poreformennyi period (1866-1900 gg.).* (Dnepropetrovsk, 1960).

[68]Iu. Iu. Kakhk, "Krestianskie volneniia 1858 g. v Estonii." *Istoriia SSSR*, No. 3 (1958), 129-144. N. N. Ulashchik, "O krestianskikh volneniiakh v Litve v pervoi polovine XIX v." *Istoriia SSSR*, No. 1 (1959), 155-168. *Krestianskoe dvizhenie v Belorussii posle otmeny krepostnogo prava. Dokumenty i materialy.* (Minsk,

The period following the reforms, though extensively explored, is far from being fully studied. Recent publications have traced the background of the sixties and seventies of the last century. A special collaborative volume dedicated to the revolutionary situation in Russia on the eve of the reforms appeared in 1960. Two essays in this volume are of special interest: one by S. A. Tokarev on the number of peasant uprisings; the other by V. A. Federov on the peasant demands prior to the announcement of the Emancipation Proclamation. These are complemented by the series of documentary publications that began to appear under the title of "The Peasant Movement in Russia in the XIX-XX Centuries," under the editorship of Professor N. M. Druzhinin.[69]

What Grekov has done for the history of the peasantry of earlier period, N. M. Druzhinin has achieved for the nineteenth century. His most distinguished work is his two-volume study of the socio-economic history of the state peasants. In this work Druzhinin includes a thorough analysis of other peasant groups, those attached to private, state, and court estates. It is an imposing contribution to modern Russian history. The focal theme is P. D. Kiselev's reforms of the 1840's and the influence these had upon the emancipation of the entire peasantry in 1861. Druzhinin also contributed considerable portions to the six-volume history of the city of Moscow, as well as to the multi-volume documentary collection on the peasant movement in Russia.[70]

1959). E. N. Sedova, "Borba pomeshchichikh krestian tsentralno-chernozemnykh gubernii za zemliu v 1861-1865 godakh." *Voprosy istorii*, No. 4 (1956), 115-124.

[69] S. A. Tokarev, "O chislennosti krestianskikh vystuplenii v Rossii v gody pervoi revoliutsionnoi situatsii." V. A. Fedorov, "Trebovaniia krestianskogo dvizheniia v nachale revoliutsionnoi situatsii do 19 fevralia 1861 g." Both essays appeared in *Revoliutsionnaia situatsiia v Rossii v 1856-1861 gg.* (Moscow, 1960). The series of documents were published under the title of *Krestianskoe dvizhenie v Rossii v XIX-XX v.* N. M. Druzhinin, ed. (Moscow, 1954).

[70] N. M. Druzhinin, *Gosudarstvennye krestiane i reforma P. D. Kiseleva.* (Moscow, 1946-1958). 2 vols. *Sbornik statei k 75-letiiu Akademika N. M. Druzhinina.* (Moscow 1961). P. G. Ryndziunskii, "Akademik Nikolai Mikhailovich Druzhinin." *Voprosy istorii*, No. 7 (1966), 164-172. N. M. Druzhinin, "Vospominaniia i mysli istorika." *Istoriia SSSR*, No. 6 (1961), 133-165.

CHAPTER VI

Socio-Economic Developments, XIX Century

A. SOCIO-ECONOMIC HISTORY

Two themes dominate nineteenth-century Soviet historiography: the decline and fall of the feudal system (serfdom), and the rise and development of capitalism. Much has been accomplished in both fields, though there is an ever-present desire to find new evidence or reexamine formerly utilized sources with the hope of offering a more suitable interpretation of socio-economic development. Soviet historians like to refer to this period as "the crisis of the feudal order," or sometimes as "the economy of serfdom," pointing out its necessity to disappear. The period presents a complex, multi-faceted historical process. Yet, as it is hammered out at the Marxist forge it inevitably becomes a tale of the decline and fall of the old order.

Every so often the question arises as to what social force or economic change became decisive in bringing down "the economy of serfdom." Until the 1930's, most of the Soviet historians who concentrated upon nineteenth-century agricultural history stressed the social transformation within the landowning aristocracy. They also referred to rationalization of agriculture, the role of grain contracting for foreign markets, and forms of rural production as contributory factors to the decline of the social structure of feudal Russia. Later, the study of economic changes within the peasant communities came in vogue, the class stratification (*rassloenie*) in rural areas leading, as it was interpreted, to capitalistic changes. But Soviet writers soon discovered that the practice of studying smaller facets of the general situation only deprived them of an all-embracing comprehension of national developments. It tended to exaggerate the importance of isolated phenomena and obscured the total record of nineteenth-century Russian history. ·

By the end of the forties and fifties a general attempt was made to abandon the one-sided, localized form of research and see history with all its implications. For illustration, the tendency now was to include the evolution of landlordism along with that of serfdom in the study of economic history. Both were indispensable to the explanation of a general historical phenomenon of the nineteenth century. This approach placed the entire complex problem in a different light. As an example, in 1958 there appeared the second volume of N. M. Druzhinin's study of state peasants and the Kiselev reform. This monumental study was the result of many years of labor; it covers exhaustively the status of the peasantry that dwelled on state-owned land, the reforms that affected these peasants, and the consequences of these reforms.[1]

In a broader sense, however, Druzhinin's work is a study in nineteenth-century Russian socio-economic development. The first volume analyzes conditions on the eve of the reforms (the end of 1850's) and the nature of the reforms themselves, as introduced by P. D. Kiselev. Druzhinin includes a minute analysis of both the general and the specific social problems which the state peasants presented at this time. The second volume deals with the enforcement and the consequences of the reforms. It adds a description of the economic and administrative situation of the state peasants to the historico-juridical status already dealt with in the preceding volume. The first chapter of the second volume gives a full account of the additional legislation that was required to carry out the Kiselev reform.

Aided by abundant archival material, N. M. Druzhinin handles the bulky sources masterfully, and lucidly describes the legal status of the peasantry during the 1840's and 1850's in the villages. Accounts of the economic development of the peasant communties and causes of the frequent revolts follow. Emphasis is also given to such economic factors as the rapid and wide expansion of trade, the rise of agricultural production, and the increased practice of engaging in trade.

The author further shows that the village communities, having enjoyed a greater degree of freedom than the privately owned serfs, also witnessed speedier economic and social development. This also led to a rapidly developed process of social stratification. Symptoms of capitalism in such forms as private initiative or early capital accumulation (*nakoplenie*) were accompanied simultaneously by pauperization and "proletarianization." This process had already been detected earlier. Inequality in property ownership was already a characteristic of pre-capitalistic formation, as was the decadence of the peasantry as a class which was to follow later. In his last chapters Druzhinin deals with the general peasant movement which became the chief factor in the development of the country.

N. M. Druzhinin's interpretation of the state peasants as an inseparable part of the entire feudal system is commonly accepted in historical literature. The state claimed portions of the peasantry—a legitimate claim under the feudal system. In principle, however, their lot did not differ much from from that of the serfs elsewhere. There was only one case where Druzhinin was challenged by another writer: in his book *Pervonachalnoe nakoplenie kapitala v Rossii*, F. Ia. Polianskii maintained that there could never have been any productive feudal relationship between state and privately owned serfs.[2] Polianskii's thesis did not meet with popular support among historians. Druzhinin had effectively proven that legal status and actual

[1]N. M. Druzhinin, *Gosudarstvennye krestiane i reforma P. D. Kiseleva.* Vol. I, *Predposylki i sushchnost reformy.* (Moscow, 1946). Vol. II, *Realizatsiia i posledstviia reform.* (Moscow, 1958).

[2]F. Ia. Polianskii, *Pervonachalnoe nakoplenie kapitala v Rossii.* (Moscow, 1958).

conditions were two different things: formally free peasants were in reality feudally dependent upon the established order as much as any attached peasant serfs. The number of such pseudo-free peasants increased particularly in areas which were recently annexed by the government.

It has long been pointed out that historians have not sufficiently studied that large portion of the serf population known as court peasants (*udelnye*). This oversight has recently been remedied by the monographic study of N. P. Gritsenko. The author made a special study of court peasants of the Central Volga region during 1797-1863, that is, from the time this class was formed to its emancipation.[3] Within this region dwelled nearly half of the court-owned peasants, and it was for this reason that the author had chosen to concentrate his research here. Historians who dealt with the subject before usually presented the court peasantry as far better off than those who were attached to private estates. Gritsenko corrected the erroneous view by showing that conditions did not differ substantially between the two classes; the court and the private serf-owner handled their respective serfs very much alike and the lot of either one or the other was not very different.

Works in the field of agrarian history and on the abolition of serfdom, along with general studies of economic conditions that led to the decline and collapse of the entire feudal order, brought about intensive study of prominent estates. There are voluminous materials on this subject in the various patrimonial archives, which I. D. Kovalchenko utilized superbly.[4] In one of his earlier studies Kovalchenko had concentrated on the peasantry and serfdom in the Tambov and Riazan guberniias during the last few decades prior to the Emancipation Act of 1861. The work is noted for its penetrating depth and clarity as well as for the amassed resources which the author put to good use. These came mostly from the patrimonial archives of such prominent estates as the Gagarins'. The author carefully examined the economy of both the peasantry and the landlords, the reasons for successful development as well as the retarding factors that hindered economic advancement.

The central theme of Kovalchenko's thesis is the concrete analysis of the feudal-serf system within the period concerned. His interpretation is that the crisis of the 1830's emanated largely from the curtailment of land allotments and the raising of feudal dues. This the peasantry refused to accept without open resistance, since the economic slump that started in the 1820's had already tested their patience. Behind the entire crisis was the paradoxical fact that prices on farm produce were rising and benefited the gentry considerably. This in turn stimulated the gentry not only to hold on to their land, but to expand their possessions further. This urge for land possession during the last decades before the Emancipation was perhaps the best proof

[3]N. P. Gritsenko, *Udelnye krestiane Srednego Povolzhia. Ocherki.* (Groznyi, 1959).

[4]I. D. Kovalchenko, *Krestiane i krepostnoe khoziaistvo v Tambovskoi gubernii v pervoi polovine XIX veka. (K istorii krizisa feodalno-krepostnicheskoi sistemy khoziaistva).* (Moscow, 1959). I. D. Kovalchenko, *Russkoe krepostnoe krestianstvo v pervoi polovine XIX veka.* (Moscow, 1967).

that a clash of interests between the gentry and the peasantry was imminent. The conflict of interests threatened an impasse which only civil strife might solve, unless timely reforms were granted.

Thus far there was not much in the thesis to be challenged. But there were some aspects that were met with less than unanimity. For example, when Kovalchenko stated that prior to the critical years under serfdom "any peasant had the possibility not only to remain static, but to expand production," he truly contradicted himself. Otherwise, his opponents contended, how could the crisis have come about? The true picture was really this: it was not the absence of a peasant drive toward increased production, but the absence of opportunity to gain more land with which to increase production, that accelerated the crisis and rapidly brought the issue of serfdom to its critical point. Still, regardless of minor points which might be challenged, the general thesis is sound and the material used is not only original, but well organized and basically correct.

Other authors followed patterns of study similar to that of Kovalchenko, basing their works on examination of archives of individual manors. In this connection we may mention the study of K. M. Moiseeva and the excellent paper on the subject by V. A. Fedorov.[5] Both Moiseeva and Fedorov based their research upon the archives of the Golitsyn family. These documents are kept in the State Historical Museum, Division of Written Records. The work of Fedorov is of special interest, demonstrating clearly and convincingly the early development of peasant trade enterprises, and signs of capitalistic tendencies amidst serfdom on patrimonial estates. This theme was touched upon by I. D. Kovalchenko, who traced in great detail the infiltration of capitalistic elements in the rural communities during the last two or three decades prior to the abolition of serfdom.

There has been much justifiable criticism of the general tendency in Soviet historiography to overemphasize the stratification of the peasantry after the reforms, tracing it back to the first half of the nineteenth century. This has been proven incorrect, and yet many authors have not freed themselves entirely from this thesis. An illustration is the admirable work of A. Ia. Pantskhava, who wrote on the history of the Georgian peasantry. His main theme is the stratification of the peasantry. To be sure, the author states at the start that the differentiation in the countryside before 1861 was mainly because of property ownership, which differed from the situation that followed the reforms. But as Pantskhava proceeds to develop the thesis he gets carried away from his correct position. By the end, Pantskhava discusses mainly social, not property, stratification. Nonetheless the author's valuable contribution lies in his superb documentation, and utilization of sources never used by previous writers. The work is ac-

---

[5]K. M. Moiseeva, "O tormoziashchem vliianii krespostnogo prava na rassloenie krestian (po materialam arkhiva Golitsynykh)." *Nauchnye doklady vysshei shkoly. Istoricheskie nauki.* (Moscow, 1958). V. A. Fedorov, "Krestiane podmoskovnoi votchiny v pervoi polovine XIX veka. (Po materialam Bogorodskoi votchiny Golitsynykh)." *Nauchnye doklady vysshei shkoly. Istoricheskie nauki.* No. 4 (1960), 106-124.

companied by an informative bibliographical essay—a rare phenomenon in Soviet historical literature.[6]

B. REGIONAL AGRARIAN HISTORY

Soviet historiography has an impressive record of accomplishment in the field of regional agrarian history, as well as the history of the peasantry in the various national republics. Areas and constituent republics such as the Ukraine, White Russia, Georgia, Armenia, the Baltic countries, Moldavia, and Siberia have been objects of special research. Many of the publications are in the local languages, which in some cases, regrettably, limits the usefulness of their writings. Recent studies stress less the juridical aspects of feudal society and emphasize more the social conflicts or class antagonism caused by privileges granted to few and deprivations imposed upon most. This trend imposes a certain "ideological parochialism," but it is frequently accompanied by more orthodox historical information of much broader scope.

Equally important research has been conducted in the field of nineteenth-century institutions. A. Ia Pantskhava, while dealing with eastern Georgia, incorporated much information on other ethnic and feudal groups in the rural areas.[7] There is a similar handling of various ethnic groups in other writings, such as the study by M. A. Adonts on Armenia and that by I. M. Gasanov on Azerbaidzhan. An extensive analytical work was produced by Ia. Grosul on the peasantry of Bessarabia. The author made a careful investigation of each of the feudal groups within the peasant communities of the first half of the nineteenth century. Similarly, V. P. Nevskaia de- scribes the social pattern of the Caucasian village communities, while G. P. Basharin discusses Iakut rural society at considerable length.[8]

Much time has been spent on discussions of the social development of the nomadic peoples of Kazakhstan and other parts of Central Asia. The work of S. Z. Zimanov stands out prominently in this field, particularly his monograph on the social life of the Kazakhs. The author presents detailed accounts of the economic structure of Kazakh society, of the class formations and the private ownership of land and cattle, which mainly determined the means of

[6]A. Ia. Pantskhava, *K voprosu o razvitii agrarnykh otnoshenii v doreformennoi Vostochnoi Gruzii.* (Moscow, Institut ekonomiki Akademii nauk SSSR, 1957).

[7]*Ibid.*

[8]Ia. Grosul, *Krestiane Bessarabii (1812-1861 gg.).* (Kishenev, 1956). M. A. Adonts, *Ekonomicheskoe razvitie Vostochnoi Armenii v XIX v.* (Erevan, 1957). I. M. Gasanov, *Chastno-vladelcheskie krestiane v Azerbaidzhane v pervoi polovine XIX v.* (Baku, 1957). V. P. Nevskaia, *Sotsialno-ekonomicheskoe razvitie Karachaia v XIX v. (doreformennyi period).* Karachaevo-Cherkesskii nauchno-issledovatelskii institut istorii iazyka i literatury. (Cherkessk, 1960). G. P. Basharin, *Istoriia agrarnykh otnoshenii v Iakutii.* (Moscow, 1956).

production. Feudal lords owned the pasture land so vital to the peasantry, thereby cementing the dependent status of the peasants.[9] While studying the regional areas, the different ethnic and national groups, the various authors came to a common view concerning the economic and cultural impact of Russia upon these incorporated parts of the Empire. Ia. Grosul argued that the incorporation of Bessarabia into Russia and, what is far more important, its simultaneous incorporation into the Russian market, had a significant salutary economic effect upon the country. Other historians argued similarly that despite some of the well-recognized negative aspects, the gains by far overshadowed the losses. Even in the case of Georgia, where the incorporation of the country brought serfdom with it, the arbitrary rule of the local feudal lords was simultaneously restrained.

I. D. Kovalchenko has published a series of articles on eighteenth-century agricultural productivity which are important for at least two reasons. One is that they represent a truly pioneering effort, and the second is that they are based on original first-hand sources, such as the annual reports of governors to the central administration.[10]

Most of the research in agricultural economy and the peasantry has dealt predominantly with the first half of the nineteenth century. The second half has been far less explored; it is only lately that more attention has been given to this period. There is one phase, however, of the second half of the last century about which extensive study has been made, and that is the abolition of serfdom and associated reforms, as well as the means of enforcement. Most prominent is the study of P. A. Zaionchkovskii, who in 1958 published a superbly synthesized monograph on the realization of the peasant reform of 1861. This work is in fact a continuation of his preceding study which came out in revised and enlarged form in 1960.[11]

Zaionchkovskii's works represent a most detailed analytical investigation of the application of the great legislative act of emancipation. If formerly the subject was dealt with mainly from a juridical standpoint, the present work is based exclusively on the statutory charters, of which there are more than seven thousand. Of these, the author and his assistants examined four thousand. Assisted by his students, Zaionchkovskii also made a painstaking

[9]S. Z. Zimanov, *Obshchestvennyi stroi kazakhov pervoi poloviny XIX veka.* (Alma-Ata, 1958).

[10]I. D. Kovalchenko, "K voprosu ob urovne selskokhoziaistvennogo proizvodstva v Riazanskoi i Tambovskoi guberniiakh v kontse XVIII—pervoi polovine XIX v." *Istoriia zemledelia. Sbornik III.* (Moscow, 1958), 241-279. I. D. Kovalchenko, "Dinamika urovnia zemledelcheskogo proizvodstva Rossii v pervoi polovine XIX v." *Istoriia SSSR,* No. 1 (1959), 53-86.

[11]P. A. Zaionchkovskii, *Provedenie v zhizn krestianskoi reformy 1861 g.* (Moscow, 1958). P. A. Zaionchkovskii, *Otmena krepostnogo prava v Rossii.* 2nd ed. revised and enlarged. (Moscow, 1960). See also his study of the critical period of the 1870's and early 1880's: *Krizis samoderzhaviia na rubezhe 1870-1880kh godov.* (Moscow, 1964).

study of some thirty-five hundred redemption acts. Both studies are noted for the organization of the immense amount of sources the author gathered and examined. The material is based on an economic and geographic principle which illustrates regional peculiarities and different conditions of the peasant economy in the various parts of European Russia. The entire subject of the 1861 reform has also been investigated along regional lines, the result of which is an indispensable source of information to future students of history who will delve further into the field.[12]

Among other scholars who dealt with the peasantry should be mentioned N. M. Druzhinin. We have already referred to his two-volume work on the state peasants and the Kiselev reforms. Here we may refer only to his authoritative writings on the first two decades following the Emanicipation Proclamation, a most significant period in the history of the Russian peasantry.[13]

Another outstanding contribution is a monographic study by V. D. Mochalov of the Transcaucasian peasant economy at the end of the nineteenth century. The author explains the peculiar conditions of Georgia, Armenia, and Azerbaidzhan, and the evolutionary process in agriculture at the time when capitalism was developing throughout the Russian Empire. Mochalov is presently engaged in a study of the rapid decay of feudal remnants in Transcaucasia.[14]

Finally, the research of N. A. Egiazarova analyzes the agrarian crisis of Russia at the end of the nineteenth century, revising the entire question of the reasons for Russia's involvement in the world crisis. Egiazarova believes that there were adequate national reasons for the crisis, chief among them being the interaction between remnants of serfdom and incoming capitalism. Combined, these had an adverse effect upon the peasantry.[15]

C. GROWTH OF RUSSIAN TOWNS AND CITIES, EARLY PERIOD

Intensive study has been applied to the growth of towns and cities during the later period of feudalism. There are a number of imposing collaborative works on the history of various cities, such as Ekaterinburg (Sverdlovsk), Kursk, Irkutsk, and many others. The reasons for city locations, growth of

[12]A critical survey of Soviet literature on the reform of 1861 may be found in: P. A. Zaionchkovskii, "Sovetskaia istoriografiia reformy 1861." *Voprosy istorii*, No. 2 (1961), 85-104. See also B. G. Litvak, "Sovetskaia istoriografiia reformy 19 fevralia 1861 g." *Istoriia SSSR*, No. 6 (1960), 99-120.

[13]N. M. Druzhinin, *Russkaia derevnia na perelome (60-70e gody XIX veka).* See the tribute paid to Druzhinin by P. G. Ryndziunskii, "Tvorcheskii otchet akademika N. M. Druzhinina." *Voprosy istorii*, No. 9 (1960), 114-117. See also *Istoricheskie zapiski*, No. 54 (1955), 5-18.

[14]V. D. Mochalov, *Krestianskoe khoziaistvo v Zakavkazie k kontsu XIX veka.* (Moscow, 1958).

[15]N. A. Egiazarova, *Agrarnyi krizis kontsa XIX veka v Rossii.* (Moscow, 1959).

population, development of trade and commerce, the granting of charters, and allied themes have been pursued. Special studies, such as those on the early period of St. Petersburg, Nizhnii Tagil, and several of the Siberian towns, have often been linked with research on the eighteenth-century economic development of Russia. A notable example is the informative survey by V. I. Sergeev of early Siberian cities, their military, economic, and cultural importance.[16]

In recent years, extensive studies have been made of the history of such cities as Kiev, Moscow, Novgorod, Smolensk, Iaroslavl, Leningrad, Minsk, and cities of Georgia, Azerbaidzhan, and Armenia. Their origins, cultural development, artistic and architectural peculiarities, early encounters with the feudal system, and in some cases their role in the struggle against invaders from the south, southeast, or east are all covered.[17]

In the various histories of cities, a good deal of space is devoted to the part the early urban communities played in the feudal economy or in the development of trade. Examples are the works of A. V. Artsikhovskii, B. A. Rybakov, M. N. Tikhomirov, B. A. Kolchin, I. I. Smirnov, P. P. Smirnov, and K. V. Bazilevich. In most cases, these analytical studies on the origins of early Slavic cities and their part in the general economy include comparisons between the eastern and western European cities. Some studies incorporate materials on the growth of Russian markets, citing data not only to show the volume of trade, but also to demonstrate the productive capacity of early society or its relationship to early feudal developments.[18]

[16]M. A. Gorlovskii, "Sotsialnyi sostav naseleniia Ekaterinburga vo vtoroi polovine XVIII v." *Iz istorii rabochego klassa i revoliutsionnogo dvizheniia.* (Moscow, 1958), 114-121. A. S. Cherkasova, "Sostav naseleniia Nizhnego Tagila v seredine XVIII v." *Voprosy istorii Urala. Sbornik statei.* Issue 39. Part 1. (Sverdlovsk, 1961), 31-44. S. P. Luppov, *Istoriia stroitelstva Peterburga v pervoi chetverti XVIII v.* (Moscow, 1937). V. Sergeev, "Pervye Sibirskie goroda, ikh voennoe, ekonomicheskoe i kulturnoe znachenie." *Vestnik istorii mirovoi kultury,* No. 3 (21), (1960), 113-124.

[17]N. M. Shelikhova, *Istoriia Kieva.* (Kiev, 1958-59). 2 vols. *Istoriia Kieva.* Published by the Ukrainian Academy of Sciences, Institute of History. (Kiev, 1963-64). 2 vols. Iu. Aseev, *Drevnii Kiev (X-XVII vv.).* (Moscow, 1956). M. K. Karger, *Drevnii Kiev. Ocherki po istorii materialov kultury drevnerusskogo goroda.* (Leningrad, 1958-61). 2 vols. M. K. Karger, *Zodchestvo drevnego Smolenska (XII-XIII vv.).* (Leningrad, 1962). M. K. Karger, *Novgorod Velikii.* (Leningrad, 1961). *Istoriia Moskvy.* (Moscow, 1952-59). 6 vols. *Ocherki istorii Leningrada.* (Moscow, 1955-67). 5 vols. A. I. Suslov, and S. S. Churakov, *Iaroslavl (Goroda Sovetskogo Soiuza).* (Moscow, 1960). Sh. A. Meskhia, *Goroda i gorodskoi stroi feodalnoi Gruzii XVII-XVIII vv.* (Tbilisi, 1959). V. I. Larina, *Ocherki istorii gorodov Severnoi Osetii (XVIII-XIX vv.).* (Ordzhonikidze, 1960). F. M. Aliev, *Goroda severnogo Azerbaidzhana vo vtoroi polovine XVIII v.* (Baku, 1960). A. P. Novoseltsev, "Goroda Azerbaidzhana i vostochnoi Armenii v XVII-XVIII vv." *Istoriia SSSR,* No. 1 (1959), 87-108.

[18]B. A. Kolchin, *Chernaia metallurgiia i metalloobrabotka v drevnei Rusi.* (Moscow, 1953). See also *Materialy i issledovaniia po arkheologii SSSR,* Nos. 12, 55, 65, 117, 123. M. N. Tikhomirov, *Pskovskoe vosstanie 1650 g.* (Moscow, 1935). M. N. Ti-

A subject closely related to the development of towns and cities which has also received much attention has been the growth of trade and commerce. B. B. Kafengauz and N. I. Pavlenko traced the development of the metallurgical industry, while E. I. Zaozerskaia made a similar study of the textile industry. The difference between earlier "bourgeois" historians and Soviet scholars may be described thus: whereas the former would attribute the origin of early industries mainly to state initiative, the latter would interpret their appearance as early signs of a natural capitalistic phenomenon rising amidst a decaying feudal economy.

While many economic historians have concentrated on the earlier periods of industrial and trade development in Russia, others have chosen the nineteenth century, with its problems brought about by the rise of manufacturing industries or of new social groups such as the industrial entrepreneurs and proletariat, both harbingers of modern capitalism. While V. K. Iatsunskii and S. G. Strumilin dealt with economic changes resulting from national manufacturing developments, others, like P. I. Liashchenko and A. L. Sidorov, took up the new economic development in its relation to Russian imperialism in the last century, basing their studies on the latest archival materials.[19]

khomirov, *Drevnerusskie goroda.* (Moscow, 1946; 2nd ed., Moscow, 1956). M. N. Tikhomirov, *Drevniaia Moskva XII-XV vv.* (Moscow, 1947). See also his article on the subject in the *Soviet Encyclopedia,* Vol. XXXXII, 499. I. I. Smirnov, *Vosstanie Bolotnikova, 1606-1607.* 2nd ed. (Moscow, 1951). I. I. Smirnov, "Sudebnik 1550 goda." *Istoricheskie zapiski,* No. 24 (1947), 262-352. P. P. Smirnov, *Goroda Moskovskogo gosudarstva v pervoi polovine XVIII veka.* Thesis. *Posadskie liudi i ikh klassovaia borba do serediny XVII veka.* (Moscow, 1947-1948). 2 vols. K. V. Bazilevich, *Gorodskie vosstaniia v Moskovskom gosudarstve v 17 veke.* (Moscow, 1936). K. V. Bazilevich, "Torgovlia Velikogo Ustiuga v seredine XVIII v." *Uchenye zapiski Instituta istorii RANION,* Vol. IV (Moscow, 1929). K. V. Bazilevich, "Kollektivnye chelobitiia torgovykh liudei i borba za russkii rynok v pervoi polovine XVII veka." *Izvestiia Akademii nauk,* Series 7, No. 2 (Leningrad, 1932). K. V. Bazilevich, "Elementy merkantilizma v ekonomicheskoi politike Alekseia Mikhailovicha." *Uchenye zapiski Moskovskogo gosudarstvennogo universiteta (MGU),* Issue 4 (Moscow, 1940). K. V. Bazilevich, "Novyi torgovyi ustav." *Izvestiia Akademii nauk,* Series 7, No. 2 (Leningrad, 1932).

[19] A complete list of B. B. Kafengauz's publications may be found in N. Ia. Kraineva and P. V. Pronina, "Spisok trudov B. B. Kafengauza i retsenzii na nikh." *Absolutizm v Rossii (XVII-XVIII vv.). Sbornik statei k semidesiatiletiiu so dnia rozhdeniia i soroka piatiletiiu nauchnoi i pedagogicheskoi deiatelnosti B. B. Kafengauza.* (Moscow, 1964), 508-518. B. B. Kafengauz and A. A. Preobrazhenskii, "Problemy istorii Rossii XVII-XVIII vv. v trudakh sovetskikh uchenykh." *Sovetskaia istoricheskaia nauka XX k XXII sezdu KPSS. Istoriia SSSR. Sbornik statei.* (Moscow, 1962), 137-186. B. B. Kafengauz, *Istoriia khoziaistva Demidovykh v XVIII-XIX vv. Opyt issledovaniia po istorii uralskoi metallurgii.* Vol. I. (Moscow, 1949). B. B. Kafengauz, *I. T. Pososhkov. Zhizn i deiatelnost.* 2nd ed. (Moscow, 1951).

A complete bibliographical list of V. K. Iatsunskii's works is cited in N. Ia. Kraineva and P. V. Pronina, "Spisok nauchnykh trudov V. K. Iatsunskogo." *Materialy po*

D. INDUSTRIAL DEVELOPMENT

The field of industrial development is unquestionably next to agricultural history in importance. Studies have covered mainly the forms of industrial production, trade, and manufacturing during the seventeenth and eighteenth centuries. In the late 1950's Soviet writers dealt mainly with the rise of capitalistic forms in industry, the relationship between large manufacturing and small commodity production, or the part free hired labor began to play in the national economy.

The main questions that interested writers were these: How widely had trade developed during these two centuries and to what degree had it developed into commodity production? How far had division of labor advanced, especially in industrial enterprises, and to what extent could it be regarded as the prelude to the rise of a national manufacturing industry? Could one trace through these developments the actual formation of a modern urbanized class of industrial society? Some writers took individual regions as typical areas of economic development; others examined larger portions of the country, analyzing the hiring methods, the nature of labor groups, the expanded production, the forms of labor exploitation, or the gradual change of small trade production into a large-scale manufacturing system.[20]

istorii selskogo khoziaistva i krestianstva SSSR. Sbornik V, K semidesiatiletiiu doktora istoricheskikh nauk V. K. Iatsunskogo. (Moscow, 1962), 492-499.

S. G. Strumilin, *Problemy ekonomiki truda.* (Moscow, 1925; 1957). *Ocherki Sovetskoi ekonomiki; resursy i perspektivy.* (Moscow, 1928; 1930). *Istoriia chernoi metallurgii v SSSR.* (Moscow, 1954).

P. I. Liashchenko, *Ocherki agrarnoi revoliutsii Rossii.* (Leningrad, 1925). *Istoriia narodnogo khoziaistva SSSR.* 4th ed. (Moscow, 1956). 3 vols. A bibliographical guide to Liashchenko's works may be found in P. P. Kiktenko and E. I. Skokan, *Petr Ivanovich Liashchenko (1876-1955). Bibliograficheskii ukazatel.* Preface by D. F. Virnyk. Kiev, Academy of Sciences of Ukrainian Republic. (Moscow, 1961).

A. L. Sidorov, *Finansovoe polozhenie Rossii v gody pervoi mirovoi voiny, 1914-1917. (Moscow, 1960).*

[20]L. V. Danilova, "Melkaia promyshlennost i promysly v russkom gorode vo vtoroi polovine XVII v. (Po materialam g. Iaroslavlaia)." *Istoriia SSSR,* No. 3 (1957), 87-111. P. A. Kolesnikov, "Sotsialno-ekonomicheskie otnosheniia na Totemskom posade v XVII v." *Istoriia SSSR,* No. 2 (1958), 131-143. K. N. Shchepetov, "Torgovo-promyshlennaia deiatelnost i rassloenie krestianstva v votchinakh Cherkasskikh v XVII v." *K voprosu o pervonachalnom nakoplenii v Rossii (XVII-XVIII vv.). Sbornik statei.* (Moscow, 1958), 53-72. A. M. Orekhov, "Tovarnoe proizvodstvo i naëmnyi trud v promyshlennosti po pererabotke zhivotnogo syria Novgoroda v XVII v." *Russkoe gosudarstvo v XVII v.* (Moscow, 1961), 74-108. A. M. Karpachev, "Goroda severo-zapadnoi okrainy Russkogo gosudarstva kak torgovo-promyshlennye tsentry i uchastie v torgovle i promyslakh razlichnykh razriadov ikh naseleniia v pervoi polovine XVII v. (Istoriko-statisticheskii ocherk)." *Trudy Instituta istorii Akademii nauk B[elorusskoi] SSR.* Issue III (Minsk, 1958), 66-90. G. T. Riabkov, "K voprosu razvitiia promyshlennosti Smolenskogo kraia vo vtoroi polovine XVIII v."

An outstanding monograph by N. V. Ustiugov, on salt mining during the seventeenth and eighteenth centuries, analyzes the transformation of a small industrial enterprise, such as the salt industry of the early seventeenth century, into a large manufacturing industry. The author traces the gradual concentration of manufacturing industries in the hands of a few families such as the Stroganovs. The salt mining industry being one of the earliest to become a large manufacturing process, it employed considerable numbers of workers with a variety of skills. Many of these were free hired laborers who came from among the impoverished peasantry, from among migratory workers, or from nearby suburbs (*posadskie*) in which they resided.[21]

Another study, by V. Ia. Krivonogov, deals with the growth of the metallurgical industry in the Urals and the system of hiring free labor during the eighteenth century.[22] The author concludes that hired labor at the beginning of the eighteenth century came mostly from among those who escaped to industrial plants and who by the 1730's had become permanently attached to industrial plants. It developed that manpower was supplied in part by peasants attached to plants (*possessionnye*), but the major portion were free hired laborers. The former often found substitutes to fulfill their obligatory service. N. I. Pavlenko discusses these practices and dwells on the difficulties, emanating largely from the institution of serfdom, which the metallurgical industry had to face.[23]

Materialy po izucheniiu Smolenskoi oblasti. Issue III. (Smolensk, 1959), 223-241. M. Ia. Volkov, "Rynok rabochei sily Iaroslavlia 20kh godov XVIII v." *Nauchnye doklady vysshei shkoly. Istoricheskie nauki.* No. 1 (1959), 72-84. A. M. Razgon, "Melkotovarnoe proizvodstvo vo vtoroi polovine XVIII v. Genezis kapitalisticheskoi manufaktury (po materialam Ivanovskogo promyshlennogo raiona)." *Istoriia SSSR,* No. 6 (1959), 63-82. A. P. Doroshenko, "Rabochaia sila v ukaznoi legkoi promyshlennosti Moskvy v 1730-1760 gg." *Istoriia SSSR,* No. 1 (1958), 160-176. Iu. R. Klokman, *Ocherki sotsialno-ekonomicheskoi istorii gorodov Severo-Zapada Rossii v seredine XVIII v.* (Moscow, 1960). A. V. Muraviev, "Posadskoe naselenie Moskvy v pervoi chetverti XVIII v." *"Nauchnye doklady vysshei shkoly. Istoricheskie nauki.* No. IV (1959). Kh. D. Sorina, "Sotsialno-ekonomicheskaia istoriia g. Tveri v nachale XVIII v." *Uchenye zapiski Kalininskogo gosudarstvennogo pedagogicheskogo instituta,* Vol. XIX, Issue 1. (Kalinin, 1956), 101-123. M. A. Il'in, "Gorod Tver v XVIII stoletii." *Iz istorii Kalininskoi oblasti. Stati i dokumenty.* (Kalinin, 1960), 41-77.

[21] N. V. Ustiugov, *Solevarennaia promyshlennost Soli-Kamskoi v XVII v. K voprosu o genezise kapitalisticheskikh otnoshenii v russkoi promyshlennosti.* (Moscow, 1957). D. Valueva, "Imushchestvennoe rassloenie i razvitie otkhodnichestva v Komi derevne v seredine XVIII v." *K voprosu o pervonachalnom nakoplenii v Rossii (XVII-XVIII vv.). Sbornik statei.* (Moscow, 1958), 222-242. A. A. Preobrazhenskii, "Sysk beglykh na Urale v 1671 g." *Iz istorii Urala. Sbornik statei.* (Sverdlovsk, 1960).

[22] V. Ia. Krivonogov, *Naëmnyi trud v gornozavodskoi promyshlennosti Urala v XVIII v.* (Sverdlovsk, 1959).

[23] N. I. Pavlenko, "Naëmnyi trud v metallurgicheskoi promyshlennosti Rossii vo vtoroi polovine XVIII v." *Voprosy istorii,* No. 6 (1958), 41-58. N. I. Pavlenko, "Prinuditelnyi i naëmnyi trud v metallurgii Rossii vtoroi poloviny XVIII v. (Po materialam

Manufacturing plants belonging to eminent families such as the Golitsyns, in the Perm region, are the subject of a monographic study by I. S. Kuritsyn. His investigation of the area revealed serfs employed in plants as well as free peasants being forced to seek extra money as shop workers. Some of the more enterprising peasants managed to engage in profitable trade.[24] The problem of hired labor and the labor market in the Ural metallurgical industry has been a subject frequently discussed and studied by various students of history. Much research has also been done concerning the extent to which the Ural region, during the eighteenth century, contributed to the formation of an industrial working class.[25]

The subject of the growth of the metallurgical industry in the Soviet Union, beginning with its origins in the Urals, was soon extended to include other areas. A number of writers launched extensive surveys of the growth and development of metallurgical and allied industries, such as the Olonetsk plants of the eighteenth century. A. P. Glagoleva and Ia. A. Balagurov examined the sharp struggle between the large and small industrial enterprises, and the utilization of local resources through small entrepreneurs. K. K. Demikhovskii extended the area of study to the Oka region. Iu. Ia. Kogan explored the Voronezh area, V. I. Nedosekin covered the region of Lipetsk, while Z. G. Karpenko and M. M. Odintsov surveyed all of Siberia. The Ukrainian mining industry during the seventeenth and eighteenth centuries was studied by P. K. Fedorenko.[26]

The textile industry has attracted an equal amount of attention of students in economic history. Prominent among these is the work of E. I. Zaozerskaia, who concentrated on the formation of the labor force in the Russian textile industry during the eighteenth century. She includes an extensive discussion on the changing relationships within the textile industry, the for-

vedomostei Berg-kollegii)." *Iz istorii rabochego klassa i revoliutsionnogo dvizheniia. Sbornik statei pamiati akademika Anny Mikhailovny Pankratovoi.* (Moscow, 1958), 101-112. N. I. Pavlenko, "K istorii iuzhno-uralskoi metallurgii v XVIII v." *Materialy nauchnoi sessii, posviashchennoi 400 letiiu prisoedineniia Bashkirii k Russkomu gosudarstvu.* (Ufa, 1958), 178-234.

[24]I. S. Kuritsyn, "Rabochaia sila na metallurgicheskikh zavodakh kniazei Golitsynykh vo vtoroi polovine XVIII v." *Istoricheskie zapiski,* No. 66 (1960), 206-238.

[25]A. P. Bazhova and V. G. Cheremnykh, "Izuchenie istorii rabochego klassa." *Istoriia SSSR,* No. 3 (1961), 326-329. "Nauchnaia konferentsiia po istorii rabochego klassa Urala." *Voprosy istorii,* No. 6 (1961), 150-153.

[26]A. P. Glagoleva, *Olonetskie zavody v XVIII v.* (Moscow, 1959). A. Ia. Balagurov, *Olonetskie gornye zavody v doreformennyi period.* (Petrozavodsk, 1958). K. K. Demikhovskii, "Istochniki i puti komplektovaniia rabochei sily na zavodakh Priokskogo gornogo okruga v XVIII v." *K voprosu o pervonachalnom nakoplenii v Rossii (XVII-XVIII vv.). Sbornik statei.* (Moscow, 1958), 465-496. V. I. Nedosekin, "Rabotnye liudi lipetskikh manufaktur v XVIII v." *Voprosy genezisa kapitalizma v Rossii. Sbornik statei.* (Leningrad, 1960), 135-156. P. K. Fedorenko, *Rudni Livoberezhnoi Ukrainy v XVII-XVIII vv.* (Moscow, 1960).

mation of both an industrial labor class and emerging bourgeois elements in Russian society.[27]

Several related fields still called for further research; there was a need for a fuller account of factory development in Russia in the time of serfdom. Equally necessary was a more satisfactory description of the individual factories and industrial plants that developed under the management of such leaders as the Morozovs or Ivanovs in the textile industry, or the industrial development under the leadership of the Stroganovs. Very early in the Soviet period, A. M. Gorky came to advocate the formation of a nation-wide research center that would embrace the study of all factories and plants of national or regional importance. The appeal found ready response and the gathering of sources soon began on a nation-wide scale. Individual republics as well as local administrations soon commenced to imitate the central government, establishing archival commissions and other appropriate bodies. Some of the regional organizations rendered valuable assistance in locating sources that pertained to the economy of the different parts of the country.[28]

In 1959 there appeared a monograph by A. A. Nesterenko on the history of industrial development in the Ukraine. The author observed that in the Ukraine, as elsewhere in Russia, industry began to make impressive headway during the last two decades of the nineteenth century. Other monographic works treated either special branches of industry or regional industrial growth In 1958, a volume appeared by K. A. Pazhitnov on the history of the Russian textile industry. This extensive study covers the feudal period and the subsequent "pre-monopoly and imperialistic periods of capitalism." Pazhitnov utilized an impressive amount of recently published sources, and also incorporated a mass of data that pertained to the Russian textile industry. A complementary essay by L. V. Filimonova deals with the Ivanov industry.[29]

[27] E. I. Zaozerskaia, *Rabochaia sila i klassovaia borba na tekstilnykh manufakturakh Rossii v 20-60kh godakh XVIII veka.* (Moscow, 1960). Other writers deal extensively with industrial labor problems. See Ch. G. Volodarskaia, "Naëmnyi trud na shelkovykh posessiakh v 60kh godakh XVIII v." *Voprosy genezisa kapitalizma.* (Leningrad, 1960). p. 120-134. Ch. G. Volodarskaia, "Sotsialnyi sostav rabotnykh liudei polotnianykh posessionykh manufaktur v 50-60kh godakh XVIII v." *Nauchnye doklady vysshei shkoly. Istoricheskie nauki,* No. 2 (1960), 116-145.

[28] A. M. Gorky, *Sobranie sochinenii.* (Moscow, 1953). Vol. XXVI. G. I. Tarlé, "Rannie opyty organizatsii sobiraniia materialov po istorii fabrik i zavodov." *Istoriia SSSR,* No. 2 (1959), 170-172.

[29] A. A. Nesterenko, *Razvitie promyshlennosti na Ukraine.* (Kiev, 1959). K. A. Pazhitnov, *Ocherki istorii tekstilnoi promyshlennosti dorevoliutsionnoi Rossii. Khlopchatobumazhnaia, l'no-pen'kovaia i shelkovaia promyshlennost.* (Moscow, 1958). L. V. Filimonova, "K istorii promyshlennogo perevorota v Rossii (Formirovanie kadrov rabochikh na khlopchatobumazhnykh fabrikakh sela Ivanova v 30kh-50kh godakh XIX v.)." *Istoriia SSSR,* No. 5 (1957), 86-111. P. G. Ryndziunskii, *Kresitanskaia promyshlennost v poreformennoi Rossii (60-80 gody XIX v.).* (Moscow, 1966).

136

Considerable advance has been witnessed in the study of the history of machine-tool, shipbuilding, chemical, sugar, and other important industrial enterprises in Russia.[30] The work of A. A. Nesterenko, referred to above, is a fundamental study of industrial development in the Ukraine that deserves further mention. The work includes a detailed discussion of trade and manufacturing, and is supplied with a mass of factual material and vital statistical data that strengthens the general thesis. It begins by describing the general industrial development in the country, and discusses small industrial enterprises, cooperative productive organizations, factories and mills. Individual chapters analyze industries in accordance with their method of production. Though an admirable approach, it tends to schematize the vast subject somewhat. Nesterenko adheres to the view that the industrial revolution in Russia had arrived rather late, while I. A. Gurzhii, on the other hand, in an equally extensive study, considers that the industrial revolution had taken place before the Great Reforms during the first half of the nineteenth century. As presented by Gurzhii, the assertion is plausible and well supported by extensive citations from reliable sources.[31]

The development of industry in Georgia is presented in a monographic study by G. K. Bakradze. This work is based not only on previously published sources, but on many documentary records the author claims to have found in formerly inaccessible central and local Georgian archives. Most of the book is devoted to the period prior to 1861. The author's conclusion is that Georgian capitalism developed slowly, and for some years was of a primitive character; it was largely because of unfavorable socio-political conditions in the country that capitalism was unable to expand more effectively or have a deeper impact upon the general economy of the country. Bakradze convincingly shows this by citing reports of various industrial enterprises that he discovered in the archives. Unfortunately, the author often fails to indicate the precise location or institution where the cited materials were found or are presently kept.[32]

On the industrial development elsewhere, there is an essay by V. Iu. Merkis, who states that early industrial enterprises began to appear in Lithuania only during the first half of the past century. An acceleration of industrial growth, the author states, began to appear in the countryside, notably on

---

[30]Ia. S. Rozenfeld and K. I. Klimenko, *Istoriia mashinostroeniia SSSR.* (Moscow, 1961). I. A. Baklanov, *Rabochie sudostroiteli v Rossii.* (Moscow, 1959). P. M. Lukianov, *Kratkaia istoriia khimicheskoi promyshlennosti SSSR.* (Moscow, 1959). B. V. Tikhonov, "Razvitie sveklosakharnoi promyshlennosti vo vtoroi polovine 40-50kh godov XIX v. (K istorii nachala promyshlennogo perevorota)." *Istoricheskie zapiski,* No. 62 (1958), 126-169.

[31]I. A. Gurzhii, *Zarozhdenie rabochego klassa Ukrainy. (Konets XVIII—pervaia polovina XIX veka).* (Kiev, 1958).

[32]G. K. Bakradze, *Vozniknovenie i razvitie kapitalisticheskoi promyshlennosti v Gruzii v XIX veke.* (Tbilisi, 1958).

137

the patrimonial estates. It was either introduced by landlords themselves or by peasants and merchants to whom landlords leased necessary facilities for industrial development. Merkis considers the 1850's as definitely the decade during which the industrial revolution made its full entry in Lithuania.[33]

One of the eminent students of Soviet economic history, V. K. Iatsunskii, has a general survey of Russian industrial development during the years 1790-1860. It is generally recognized as a distinguished scholarly accomplishment. Iatsunskii divides the history of Russian industrial development prior to 1861 as follows: (1) from the 1790's to the middle of the 1830's; (2) from the middle 1830's to 1860. Each period he divides in turn according to the nature of industrial production.[34]

Iatsunskii believes that the growth of manufacturing industry moved at a faster pace than the availability of free labor in Russia. For this reason factories had to employ "possessionary" labor, manpower that was transferred from the rapidly deteriorating feudal estates, relieving landlords of unwanted "souls." But the main point to note in the development of the second period, 1836-1860, was the fact that signs of industrial development were recognizable even prior to the emancipation of the serfs. Iatsunskii is fully aware of the uneven progress that is detected in the different spheres of industrial development. But, he states, some of the early factory-workshops in due course became leading industrial enterprises. Another development not to be overlooked is that free labor was bound to become predominant, gradually overshadowing all forms of forced labor. The capitalistic system, though winning unevenly, was surely making headway as the most effective form of production.

Markets, banking, and finance are not entirely heart-warming subjects to proletarian scholars, yet several Soviet historians have accomplished some admirable research in these fields. The development of trade and growth of markets have been dealt with by M. K. Rozhkova, while internal Russian trade is discussed by G. A. Dikhtiar. There is also a growing interest in financial problems, credits, and banking organizations and their relation to the general economic situation. Recently S. Ia. Borovoi made a thorough study of banks and credits in Russia to 1861, including the banking system, credit regulations, and other related subjects. A. I. Iukht has added a short study of Russian trade relations with Persia, which has some general bearing on the subject of markets.[35]

[33]V. Iu. Merkis, "K voprosu o razvitii promyshlennosti v Litve v 1795-1861 gg." *Trudy Akademii nauk Litovskoi SSR.* Series A, Vol. I (8),(1960).

[34]M. K. Rozhkova, ed., *Ocherki ekonomicheskoi istorii Rossii pervoi poloviny XIX veka. Sbornik statei.* (Moscow, 1958).

[35]M. K. Rozhkova, "Torgovlia." *Ocherki ekonomicheskoi istorii Rossii pervoi poloviny XIX veka. Sbornik statei.* M. K. Rozhkova, ed. (Moscow, 1958). G. A. Dikhtiar, *Vnutrenniaia torgovlia v dorevoliutsionnoi Rossii.* (Moscow, 1960). S. Ia. Borovoi, *Kredit i banki Rossii (seredina XVII v.−1861).* (Moscow, 1958). A. I. Iukht, "Torgovlia Rossii s Zakavkaziem i Persiei vo vtoroi chetverti XVIII veka." *Istoriia SSSR,* No. 1 (1961), 131-146.

A study subsequent to the one by Borovoi is the work of I. F. Gindin on the State Bank and the economic policy of Imperial Russia from 1861 to 1892. This covers a far wider range than the title perhaps suggests, for it incorporates a good deal of material and discussion on economic problems and methods of handling these during the important formative years of the 1880's and early 1890's. Gindin shows how the Russian gentry was forced to contribute to capitalistic development. In his research he fully utilized the State Bank archives as well as the records of the Ministry of Finance. The description clearly reflects the general characteristics of the tsarist economic policies and the government's participation or indirect interference in private economic activities. The government sought revenues from industries that it protected, or backed financially, or saved from bankruptcy in time of economic crisis.[36]

A work that supplements Gindin's monograph is the essay by V. K. Iatsunskii, on the basic stages of capitalism in Russia. The author believes that capitalism began to appear by the end of the eighteenth century. Prior to that time only symptoms and potential development could be detected, as the factories with serf labor became engaged in commodity production. Iatsunskii also states that until 1861 capitalism in the agrarian economy was extremely weak as compared with its position in industry. Finally, Iatsunskii points out, capitalism in Russia was not a nation-wide phenomenon, but rather was limited to certain areas.[37]

It was only reasonable to assume that the infiltration of capitalism would lead to a period of increased intensity in Russian economic theory. This is the subject of a collaborative work edited by A. I. Pashkov, entitled *Istoriia russkoi ekonomicheskoi mysli*.[38] The volume examines economic views of eminent thinkers and statesmen of the seventeenth century, such as A. L. Ordyn-Nashchokin; it takes up the development of Russian mercantilism as it expressed itself in the legislation of Peter I. The advanced economic theories of I. T. Pososhkov, the spokesman of the businessmen, and of V. N. Tatishchev and F. S. Saltykov, who represented the views of the nobility are analyzed here. The earlier representatives of the bourgeois economic philosophy of the eighteenth-century economists, men like M. D. Chulkov and I. A. Tretiakov, are included. In addition to this volume, individual writers like N. K. Karataev, I. S. Bak, and L. Mordukhovich have also published studies of eighteenth-century economic and philosophical thought.[39]

[36] I. F. Gindin, *Gosudarstvennyi bank i ekonomicheskaia politika tsarskogo pravitelstva (1861-1892 gg.)*. (Moscow, 1960).

[37] V. K. Iaksunskii, "Osnovnye etapy genezisa kapitalizma v Rossii." *Istoriia SSSR*, No. 5 (1958), 59-51.

[38] A. I. Pashkov, ed. *Istoriia russkoi ekonomicheskoi mysli*. (Moscow, 1955-56). 4 vols. A. I. Pashkov, ed. *Iz istorii ekonomicheskoi mysli narodov SSSR. Sbornik statei*. (Moscow, 1961).

[39] N. K. Karataev, *Ocherki po istorii ekonomicheskoi mysli v Rossii XVIII v.* (Moscow, 1960). I. S. Bak, *Antifeodalnye ekonomicheskie ucheniia vo vtoroi polovine*

The debate over the exact point at which capitalism could be said to exist would seem to be endless. S. G. Strumilin is representative of the scholars who believe that capitalism began to enter the Russian social and economic scene as early as the sixteenth century. As evidence, Strumilin cites the rise of towns, the increase in money circulation, the expansion of domestic and foreign trade, and the mercantile policy that Ivan IV had followed. These, Strumilin argues, serve as reasonable proof of the initial decline of feudalism. He declares that these developments were by no means accidental, for they are strikingly similar to those that developed in western Europe.[40] That many estates remained feudal, according to Strumilin, means little, since any form of manufacture is the result of bourgeois development. It makes little difference whether production is by serf or wage employed labor; what is important is not the form of employment, but the expansion of agricultural output for the market.

Many Soviet historians also believe that the transition of peasant duties from payment in kind to payment in money, as was the case during the middle of the sixteenth century, forced the peasant to trade more in farm products.[41] The transition to a money economy, these think, was bound to lead to social stratification between a moneyless peasantry and those who came to own money. Landowners, too, were forced to adapt themselves to a money economy for they soon recognized the economic advantages of commercial capitalism. Once they learned that commercial farming was profitable, they began to seek expansion of crop areas, which could only be done at the expense of the peasantry. In despair at these conditions, many peasants tried to find a solution by escaping either southward or eastward to regain their freedom and start life anew. S. G. Strumilin has figured that revenues derived from the peasant economy during the century between 1580 and 1680 decreased nearly two and a half times.[42]

The development as interpreted by Strumilin was bound to bear adverse effects upon serfdom, despite the fact that the institution lasted for another two centuries. Serfdom only delayed the complete collapse of the feudal order and impeded the development of capitalism, or, in Soviet terminology, had a tendency to "slow the development of commodity production" and hinder expansion of markets. During the sixteenth century, some writers show, the peasants were forced to sell nearly forty percent of their harvested crops to meet their obligations in taxes or quit-rent. Serf labor and corvée naturally reduced farm produce for the market, which in turn caused a reduc-

XVIII v. (Moscow, 1958). L. Mordukhovich, Ocherki istorii ekonomicheskikh uchenii. (Moscow, 1957).

[40]S. G. Strumilin, "K voprosu o genezise kapitalizma v Rossii." Voprosy istorii, No. 9 (1961), 56-69.

[41]D. P. Makovskii, Razvitie tovarno-denezhnykh otnoshenii v selskom khoziaistve Russkogo gosudarstva v XVI veke. (Smolensk, 1960).

[42]See S. D. Skazkin and A. N. Chistozvonov, "Zadachi izucheniia problemy genezisa kapitalizma." Voprosy istorii, No. 6 (1959), 38-46.

tion in town and country trade. This is best shown by the reduction in customs duties collected throughout the country.

What do these sixteenth-century developments prove? Wage labor came into use extensively, mostly in construction. The increase in money-commodity relations was bound to affect profoundly the very basis of the natural economy in agriculture. What added to this was a new factor: the gradual appearance of a hired labor element on the market. This was accompanied by a significant, though small, rise of capital accumulation in the handicraft industry and the occasional, though even more significant, appearance of factories. Together these developments indicate that capitalist forms had already commenced to appear in Russian society in the sixteenth century. Labor was already a commodity in the sixteenth century, even before serfdom came to be institutionalized. The small number of factory owners had to pay their hired labor, thereby forcing a capitalistic relationship upon the entire system--a total novelty in Russian society.

As late as the summer of 1967 several questions as to the time of Russia's transition from a feudal to a capitalistic economy still occupied Soviet historians. The use of the seventeenth century as the transitional period remained debatable. Some modified their views and argued that during that century it might be acceptable to speak of *agrarian capitalism*, and therefore they emphasized the study of agrarian changes that took place during that period. Some insisted that the dividing line and date could reasonably be established in the eighteenth century, during which capitalism began to emerge.[43]

The long and tedious polemics among Soviet historians on the genesis of capitalism went on. The interminable discussions led to another subject: the coexistence of feudalism and capitalism as means of production. Some writers argued that such conditions never could nor did exist.[44] Whatever the arguments were, both sides seemed to have agreed that the subject called for further study and clarification; that there was need for a more precise definition of the difference between early commodity production and "capitalistic production." The outside observer could learn his own lesson: as long as historians employed a misty Marxian terminology whose meaning they themselves were not certain of, lengthy fruitless polemics were bound

[43] A. M. Sakharov, *Russkaia derevnia XVII v. Po materialam patriarshego khoziaistva.* (Moscow, 1966). See review in *Voprosy istorii*, No. 7 (1967), 169-172.

[44] "K voprosu o dvukh stadiiakh razvitiia feodalnoi formatsii v Rossii." *Voprosy istorii*, No. 1 (1959), 98-107. F. Ia. Polianskii, *Pervonachalnoe nakoplenie kapitala v Rossii.* (Moscow, 1958). A. A. Preobrazhenskii and Iu. A. Tikhonov, "Itogi izucheniia nachalnogo etapa skladyvaniia vserossiiskogo rynka (XVII v.)." *Voprosy istorii*, No. 4 (1961), 80-109. Cf. S. G. Strumilin, "K voprosu o genezise kapitalizma v Rossii." *Voprosy istorii*, No. 9 (1961), 56-69. L. V. Cherepnin, "Aktovyi material kak istochnik po istorii russkogo krestianstva XV v. (iz istorii proizvodstvennykh i proizvoditelnykh otnoshenii)." *Problemy istochnikovedeniia*, Vol. IV (1955), 307-349. N. V. Ustiugov, "Remeslo i melkoe tovarnoe proizvodstvo v Russkom gosudarstve XVII veka." *Istoricheskie zapiski*, No. 34 (1950), 166-197.

to take place at any historical gathering. What is gratifying is that no penalty has been involved in whatever one believes about the exact stage at which capitalism appeared.

Amidst these misty definitions and rapidly incrustated party dogmas the path to a clear, acceptable answer was difficult indeed. According to Lenin himself, Russian capitalism moved along two dimensions—in depth and in width. It grew in areas long under control of Russian authority and expanded into more recently annexed territories. He put it graphically when he said that capitalism developed in Russia by way of "internal colonization" in some parts where no feudalism was known. This thesis A. V. Fadeev developed further when he reported to a session of the Academy of Sciences. He criticized some of the writers, such as P. I. Liashchenko, who regarded expansion of capitalism as colonialism. Fadeev considers such a view inapplicable, as the term "colonialism" itself is misplaced when one uses it in relation to Russian annexed areas. This is particularly true in regions which developed as rapidly as central Russia. Furthermore, while some annexed areas or "internal colonies" came through capitalistic expansion into areas already populated and developed before being "colonized," others were hardly settled or in any remote degree civilized. The course of economic development, argues Fadeev, was obviously in each case quite different. For his study Fadeev chose the northern Caucasus, where economic cross-currents formed the desirable social pattern. Among the elements that formed the community here were the colonizing free peasantry, the landlords, and the Cossacks.[45]

The social implications of industrial development during the seventeenth and eighteenth centuries were of utmost importance to many Soviet writers. The question frequently debated was whether it was justifiable to refer to these infant industries as "feudal" or "capitalistic." Another question was whether it was proper to regard early enterprises as truly "capitalistic." A goodly number of the industrial enterprises were owned and operated by merchants, even peasants, who utilized free hired labor but who could hardly be regarded as capitalistic entrepreneurs running capitalistic enterprises. There were other kinds of enterprises, the argument ran, state or privately owned plants and shops, where fully or partially free labor was employed, including recruited serfs. Though lately the theme has been less popular in historical literature, it is revived occasionally and even warmly debated.[46]

The discussions were largely reduced by the appearance of an increased number of monographs on industrial development. Research proved that dur-

[45]A. V. Fadeev, "Razvitie kapitalizma vshir' v poreformennoi Rossii." *Doklady i soobshcheniia Instituta istorii Akademii nauk SSSR,* Issue X (Moscow, 1956). See also, A. V. Fadeev, *Ocherki ekonomicheskogo razvitiia Stepnogo Predkavkazia v doreformennyi period.* (Moscow, 1957). Also his article "Vovlechenie Severnogo Kavkaza v ekonomicheskuiu sistemu poreformennoi Rossii (K probleme razvitiia kapitalizma vshir)." *Istoriia SSSR,* No. 6 (1959), 40-62.

[46]See, for instance, A. M. Karpachev, "O sotsialno-ekonomicheskoi soslovnosti votchinnoi manufaktury." *Voprosy istorii,* No. 8 (1957), 101-117.

ing the seventeenth and eighteenth centuries many industrial enterprises, as shown convincingly by S. G. Strumilin, operated on a semi-feudal basis. Strumilin proves that though Russia began to witness early capitalistic development it was only in its inchoate stage, often hovering between vanishing feudalism and rising capitalism.[47]

[47] S. G. Strumilin, *Istoriia chernoi metallurgii v SSSR*. (Moscow, 1954). Vol. I, 254 ff. Another writer, F. Ia. Polianskii, comes to the same conclusion, stating that the manufacturing process in the eighteenth century was still "feudal," though the social character of the industry was revealing tendencies of capitalistic development. See F. Ia. Polianskii, *Ekonomicheskii stroi manufaktury v Rossii XVIII v.* (Moscow, 1956). Another study by the same author: *Gorodskie remesla i manufaktura v Rossii XVIII v.* (Moscow, 1960).

CHAPTER VII

Penetration of Capitalism

A. EARLY CAPITAL ACCUMULATIONS
IN RUSSIA

It has been well established that Russian trade, during the seventeenth and eighteenth centuries, rendered Moscow considerable gain. Increased financial strength was instrumental in furthering trade and expanding manufactures, which utilized free labor wherever possible, or else used recruited labor; agriculture gained proportionately less from the expansion of trade and manufactures. It was this consideration that led Soviet scholars lately to examine the theme of original capital accumulations in Russia, an aspect of economic development historians had overlooked for some time. To answer this need N. A. Baklanova contributed an excellent monographic study of a leading merchant family, the Kalmykovs, of the eighteenth century. The Kalmykovs came from an old peasant line actively engaged in communal village life. Their wealth was originally derived from government contracts to supply various state agencies with fish and grain. Baklanova's study illustrates how privately accumulated capital was gradually reinvested in trade and commerce, and gradually expanded into industrial enterprises, a thesis well supported by N. V. Ustiugov.[1]

Widening the study of the earliest signs of bourgeois development in Russia or, as Soviet writers prefer to call it, "the genesis of capitalistic relations," additional works were published on various families whose private fortunes aided the expansion of national industry. V. A. Aleksandrov studied the Ushakov family, A. A. Preobrazhenskii carried out a similar investigation of the Tumashev family, while others analyzed more generally the Russian merchant class as the harbinger of capitalism during the eighteenth century. E. I. Indova wrote an absorbing essay which shows that the wealthy merchant and industrial classes of the first half of the eighteenth century were made up predominantly of former peasants who were successfully engaged in trade. N. I. Pavlenko traced the progress of a number of wealthy landowners who wisely invested their surplus capital in industrial enterprises. He cites many examples of how sound trade transactions, contracts, and the operation of distilleries and other businesses resulted in the accumulation of capital in the hands of either individuals or families. What is even more interesting, as the same author shows, is the way this *nouveau riche* class

[1]N. A. Baklanova, *Torgovo-promyshlennaia deiatelnost Kalmykovykh vo vtoroi polovine XVII v.* (Moscow, 1960). N. V. Ustiugov, *Solevarennaia promyshlennost Soli-Kamskoi v XVII v. K voprosu o genezise kapitalisticheskikh otnoshenii v russkoi promyshlennosti.* (Moscow, 1957).

144

managed to "coexist" with the feudal order, and even succeeded in gaining favors, winning titles, and being granted the right to utilize compulsory labor.[2] The subjects of "genesis of capitalism" and "earliest capitalist accumulation" in Russia were discussed at great length, in 1955, at a session especially organized by the Institute of History at the Academy of Sciences. The meeting only stimulated further research in the field. A series of additional studies by M. P. Rozhkov, E. S. Kozlovskii, A. A. Nesterenko, and others followed. The most impressive research in this field has been the monographic work of F. Ia. Polianskii, and a collaborative volume on the same subject, which includes some outstanding essays. Here, too, there remain many debatable questions. The chronology applied by some writers has been seriously questioned by others. The nature of "feudal-capitalistic coexistence" has been discussed without any agreement being reached. The dispute over when, precisely, capitalism began to assert itself in Russia remains undecided. N. L. Rubinshtein has offered a compromise solution to this problem by saying that the entire process should be considered one of continuous social stratification, going on even beyond the period of reforms during the 1860's and 1870's.[3]

[2]V. A. Aleksandrov, "Sibirskie torgovye liudi Ushakovy v XVII v." *Russkoe gosudarstvo v XVII v.* (Moscow, 1961). A. A. Preobrazhenskii, "Predprinimateli Tumashevy v XVII v." *Russkoe gosudarstvo v XVII v.* (Moscow, 1961). A. A. Preobrazhenskii, "Iz pervykh chastnykh zavodov na Urale v nachale XVII v." *Istoricheskie zapiski*, No. 63 (1958), 156-179. E. I. Indova, "Rol dvortsovoi derevni pervoi poloviny XVIII v. v formirovanii russkogo kupechestva." *Istoricheskie zapiski*, No. 68 (1961), 189-210. N. I. Pavlenko, "O proiskhozhdenii kapitalov, vlozhennykh v metallurgiiu Rossii XVIII v." *Istoricheskie zapiski*, No. 62 (1958), 170-197. N. I. Pavlenko, "Iz istorii sotsialno-ekonomicheskikh trebovanii russkoi burzhuazii vo vtoroi polovine XVIII v." *Istoricheskie zapiski*, No. 59 (1957), 328-344. N. I. Pavlenko, "Odvorianivanie russkoi burzhuazii v XVIII v." *Istoriia SSSR*, No. 2 (1961), 71-87.

[3]A full account of the discussion at the Institute of History is adequately presented by the following writers: M. D. Kurmacheva, "Obsuzhdenie voprosa o pervonachalnom nakoplenii v Rossii." *Voprosy istorii*, No. 11 (1955), 162-167. "Nauchno-teoreticheskaia konferentsiia o pervonachalnom nakoplenii v Rossii." *Istoricheskie zapiski*, No. 54 (1955), 420-429. Two of the papers read at this session have been published: N. I. Pavlenko, "O nekotorykh storonakh pervonachalnogo nakopleniia v Rossii (Po materialam XVII-XVIII vv.)." *Istoricheskie zapiski*, No. 54 (1955), 382-419. B. B. Kafengauz, "K voprosu o pervonachalnom nakoplenii v Rossii." *Voprosy ekonomiki, planirovaniia i statistiki. Sbornik statei, posviashchennyi 80-letiiu akademika S. G. Strumilina.* (Moscow, 1957), 219-234. M. P. Rozhkov, "Nekotorye osobennosti pervonachalnogo nakopleniia v Rossii." *Uchenye zapiski Velikolukskogo pedagogicheskogo instituta.* (Velikie Luki, 1958), Vol. III, 108-138. E. S. Kozlovskii, *Pervonachalnoe nakoplenie kapitala i ego osobennosti v Rossii.* (Moscow, 1956). A. A. Nesterenko, "Pervonachalnoe nakoplenie kapitala na Ukraine." *Voprosy istorii*, No. 11 (1958), 142-152. F. Ia. Polianskii, *Pervonachalnoe nakoplenie kapitala v Rossii.* (Moscow, 1958). *K voprosu o pervonachalnom nakoplenii v Rossii (XVII-XVIII vv.).* (Moscow, 1958). N. L. Rubinshtein, "O razlozhenii krestianstva i tak nazyvaemom pervonachalnom nakoplenii v Rossii." *Voprosy istorii*, No. 8 (1961), 61-85.

Finally, with reference to the subject of "capital accumulation" and "genesis of capitalism in Russia," several writers have attempted to bring the different views into some synthesized form. One of these is N. M. Druzhinin, who endeavored to apply some common denominator to the various opposing views and interpretations, defining the socio-economic conditions that favored the formation of a bourgeois society in Russia. A collaborative work on the genesis of capitalism in seventeenth-century Russia has been compiled by S. D. Skazkin. M. V. Nechkina re-introduced discussion of the so-called "ascending" and "descending" stages of feudal formation in Russia, a much debated theme during the 1950's, and it was later revived by A. L. Sidorov and S. G. Strumilin. Finally, an overall survey of the history of the national economy, including the feudal period, was published by P. A. Khromov.[4]

B. RISE OF A NATIONAL MARKET

The development of grain markets in Russia has attracted the interest of numerous scholars recently. Studies published during the 1950's clearly indicate how heavily the peasant economy came to depend upon market conditions. Regions such as the Urals and large sections of Siberia and of the Volga area, where agriculture began to make rapid progress, started to reveal typical capitalistic tendencies. A number of works already referred to, such as those of V. I. Shunkov, F. G. Safronov, A. A. Preobrazhenskii, A. Ts. Merzon, and Iu. A. Tikhonov, definitely show the newly developed market situation and its relation to the general agrarian economy. Attention should be called especially to the first-rate work of S. G. Strumilin, who pioneered a number of economic theories relating to the effects of the reforms of Peter I upon the growth of population, taxation, and general conditions of the peasantry.[5]

[4]N. M. Druzhinin, "Genezis kapitalizma v Rossii." *Desiatyi Mezhdunarodnyi kongress istorikov v Rime.* September 1955. Papers delivered by the Soviet delegation. (Moscow, 1956), 189-216. N. M. Druzhinin, "Sotsialno-ekonomicheskie usloviia obrazovaniia russkoi burzhuaznoi natsii." *Voprosy formirovaniia russkoi burzhuaznoi natsii. Sbornik statei.* (Moscow, 1958), 192-230. See also *Voprosy sovetskoi nauki. Genezis kapitalizma.* (Moscow, Academy of Sciences, 1958). M. V. Nechkina, "O 'voskhodiashchei' i 'snikhodiashchei' stadiiakh feodalnoi formatsii (K postanovke voprosa)." *Voprosy istorii,* No. 7 (1958), 86-108. Response to the article may be found in: *Voprosy istorii,* No. 1 (1959), 98-107; No. 9 (1959), 123-137; No. 11 (1959), 79-92. See also S. G. Strumilin, "K voprosu o genezise kapitalizma v Rossii." *Voprosy istorii,* No. 9 (1961), 56-69. A. L. Sidorov, "Nekotorye problemy razvitiia rossiiskogo kapitalizma v sovetskoi istoricheskoi nauke." *Voprosy istorii,* No. 12 (1961), 26-62. P. A. Khromov, *Ocherki ekonomiki feodalizma v Rossii.* (Moscow, 1957). Also P. A. Khromov, *Istoriia narodnogo khoziaistva SSSR. (Kurs lektsii).* (Moscow, 1960).

[5]A. Ts. Merzon and Iu. A. Tikhonov, *Rynok Ustiuga Velikogo v protsesse skladyvaniia vserossiiskogo rynka (XVII vek).* (Moscow, 1960). K. A. Gorbunova, "Rynok Il'inskogo pogosta Vilegotskoi volosti Solvychegodskogo uezda v XVII v." *Trudy MGIAI* [Moskovskii gosudarstvennyi istoriko-arkhivnyi institut], Vol. X (Moscow, 1957), 343-345. A. Zhuravleva, "Khoziaistvo chernososhnykh krestian poiuzhskikh volostei

Basing their work on the remarkably well-preserved and voluminous collection of custom house records of the seventeenth century, historians such as A. Ts. Merzon and Iu. A. Tikhonov have compiled an impressive amount of documentary evidence related to early economic development in Russia. A number of writers have ably utilized these materials, as in the case of L. G. Melnik, who wrote on Ustiug Velikii; S. M. Troitskii, who described in detail the city of Archangel as the center of the grain market in the north; and others who analyzed such regional Siberian markets as Tobolsk, Enisei, or Nerchinsk. An excellent account of Moscow as the national trade center, and its relation to the outlying frontier districts and towns, was compiled by D. I. Tverskaia.[6]

On a broader basis, the formation of a national market is described by B. B. Kafengauz. This study is based mainly on the custom house records of the first half of the eighteenth century. The author shows that throughout this period Moscow never lost the initiative, retained a leading role in the economic developments of the country, and managed to maintain ties with the peripheral markets within the state.[7] Later the construction of St. Petersburg contributed to the expansion of the national market because of the urgent demand for materials and commodities coming from all over the country. On the other hand, the new capital served as the terminal for all exports, thereby reducing the importance of outlying towns in the north such as Archangel. Trade with southern parts of Russia kept up at a brisk pace, as agricultural produce and cattle were shipped northward.

Much less has been written on the second half of the eighteenth century. This period requires further exploration with respect to territorial division of

Ustiuzheskogo uezda v XVII v." *Trudy MGIAI* [Moskovskii gosudarstvennyi istoriko-arkhivnyi institut], Vol. X (Moscow, 1957), 346-349. A. N. Kopylov, "Eniseiskii zemledelcheskii raion v seredine XVII v. i ego znachenie dlia snabzheniia Vostochnoi Sibiri khlebom." *Trudy MGIAI* [Moskovskii gosudarstvennyi istoriko-arkhivnyi institut], Vol. X (Moscow, 1957), 115-134. S. G. Strumilin, *Ocherki ekonomicheskoi istorii Rossii.* (Moscow, 1960), 313 ff. V. A. Aleksandrov, "Russko-kitaiskaia torgovlia i Nerchinskii torg v kontse XVIII v." *K voprosu o pervonachalnom nakoplenii v Rossii (XVII-XVIII vv.). Sbornik statei.* (Moscow, 1958).

[6]L. G. Melnik, "K voprosu ob imushchestvennom rassloenii torgovogo naseleniia posada Ustiuga Velikogo v XVII v." *Nauchnye doklady vysshei shkoly. Istoricheskie nauki.* No. 3 (1959), 81-100. A. A. Preobrazhenskii and Iu. A. Tikhonov, "Itogi izucheniia nachalnogo etapa skladyvaniia vserossiiskogo rynka (XVII v.)." *Voprosy istorii,* No. 4 (1961), 80-110. S. M. Troitskii, "Arkhangelskii khlebnyi rynok v pervoi chetverti XVIII v." *Trudy MGIAI* [Moskovskii gosudarstvennyi istoriko-arkhivnyi institut], Vol. X (Moscow, 1957), 177-193. D. I. Tverskaia, *Moskva vtoroi poloviny XVII stoletiia kak tsentr skladyvaiushchegosia vserossiiskogo rynka.* (Moscow, 1959). A. Ts. Merzon and Iu. A. Tikhonov, *Rynok Ustiuga Velikogo v protsesse skladyvaniia vserossiiskogo rynka (XVII vek).* (Moscow, 1960).

[7]B. B. Kafengauz, *Ocherki vnutrennego rynka Rossii pervoi poloviny XVIII v. (Po materialam vnutrennikh tamozhen).* (Moscow, 1958).

labor as a contributing factor to the development of a national market in Russia.[8]

A by-product of the investigations mentioned above was clarification of a formerly neglected subject, the economic relationship between Russia and her peripheral areas, such as Armenia, Azerbaidzhan, Kazakhstan, Uzbekistan, the Ukraine, or White Russia. The field has been greatly expanded in recent years, as shown by the selected bibliographical list cited below.[9]

C. INDUSTRIAL-FINANCIAL MONOPOLIES

There has been an increased interest lately in those industries of prerevolutionary Russia that came to wield monopolistic power. Studies have been made of the rise and development of the heavy metallurgical, coal, and oil industries in southern Russia; others detail the development of the ma-

[8]G. L. Vartanov, "Gorodskie iarmarki v Moskovskoi gubernii vo vtoroi polovine XVIII v." *Uchenye zapiski Leningradskogo pedagogicheskogo instituta im. A. I. Gertsena,* Vol. 194 (1958). N. L. Rubinshtein, "Territorialnoe razdelenie truda i razvitie vserossiiskogo rynka." *Iz istorii rabochego klassa i revoliutsionnogo dvizheniia.* (Moscow, 1958), 88-100.

[9]I. G. Shulga, "K voprosu o razvitii vserossiiskogo rynka vo vtoroi polovine XVIII v. (Po materialam Levoberezhnoi Ukrainy)." *Voprosy istorii,* No. 10 (1958), 35-45. I. G. Shulga, "Razvitie torgovli na Levoberezhnoi Ukraine vo vtoroi polovine XVIII v." *Voprosy genezisa kapitalizma v Rossii.* (Leningrad, 1960), 157-169. L. S. Abetsedarskii, "Torgovye sviazi Belorussii s Russkim gosudarstvom." *Uchenye zapiski Belorusskogo gosudarstvennogo universiteta.* Issue 36. (Minsk, 1957), 3-42. L. S. Abetsedarskii, *Belorusy v Moskve XVII v. Iz istorii russko-belorusskikh sviazei.* (Minsk, 1957). V. I. Meleshko, "O torgovle i torgovykh sviaziakh Mogileva v XVII v." *Trudy Instituta istorii Akademii nauk Belorusskoi SSSR.* Issue 3. (Minsk, 1958), 45-65. Sh. A. Meskhia and I. Z. Tsintsadze, *Iz istorii russko-gruzinskikh vzaimootnoshenii X-XVIII vv.* (Tbilisi, 1958). A. I. Iukht, "Vostochnaia torgovlia Rossii v 30-40kh godakh XVIII v. i rol v nei armianskikh kuptsov." *Izvestiia Akademii nauk Armianskoi SSR. Obshchestvennye nauki.* No. 8 (1956), 43-62. A. I. Iukht, "Sotsialnyi sostav naseleniia armianskoi kolonii v Astrakhani v pervoi polovine XVIII v." *Izvestiia Akademii nauk Armianskoi SSR. Obshchestvennye nauki.* No. 1 (1957), 47-60. G. B. Abdullaev, "Nekotorye voprosy russko-azerbaidzhanskoi torgovli." *Izvestiia Akademii nauk Azerbaidzhanskoi SSR. Seriia obshchestvennykh nauk.* No. 5 (1960), 17-33. N. G. Apollova, *Ekonomicheskie i politicheskie sviazi Kazakhstana s Rossiei vo vtoroi polovine XVIII—nachale XIX veka.* (Moscow, 1960). Kh. Ziiaev, "K istorii ekonomicheskikh sviazei Uzbekistana s Rossiei cherez Sibir v XVI-XVII vv." *Izvestiia Akademii nauk Uzbekskoi SSR. Seriia obshchestvennykh nauk.* No. 3 (1957). V. S. Batrakov, *Khoziaistvennye sviazi kochevykh narodov s Rossiei, Srednei Aziei i Kitaem (s XV do poloviny XVIII v.).* (Tashkent, 1958). P. S. Preobrazhenskaia, "K istorii russko-kalmytskikh otnoshenii v 50-60 godakh XVII veka." *Zapiski Kalmytskogo nauchno-issledovatelskogo instituta iazyka, literatury i istorii.* Issue 1. (Elista, 1960), 49-83.

chine, chemical, and light industries. Some of these studies extend into the twentieth century, and a few cover the history of regional developments.[10] Even more interesting studies have concerned the formation of monopolistic organizations in Russia. In addition to the general works of P. I. Liashchenko and of A. D. Breiterman, who examines the southern industrial monopolies, there are informative studies such as the one by D. I. Shpolianskii on the coal-metallurgical industry and that of Ia. I. Livshin, who surveys more fully the growth of monopolies throughout Russia. The subject was expanded further in the study of G. V. Tsyperovich on Russian syndicates and trusts.[11]

The history of one of the largest Russian syndicates, *Obshchestvo dlia prodazhi izdelii russkikh metallurgicheskikh zavodov (Prodamet)*, has been fully described by A. L. Tsukernik, after ten years of intensive research. A complementary essay on the same subject, by Z. Pustula, discusses the role of *Prodamet* in Poland. Regrettably, both studies end with 1914. There are others, by K. N. Tarnovskii and A. P. Pogrebinskii, that deal exclusively with the operation of *Prodamet* during the First World War years, and A. L. Tsukernik has contributed an exceedingly informative essay on the attempts to restore *Prodamet* in the Ukraine in 1918.[12]

[10]G. D. Bakulev, *Razvitie ugolnoi promyshlennosti Donbassa.* (Moscow, 1955). S. M. Lisichkin, *Ocherki po istorii razvitiia otechestvennoi neftianoi promyshlennosti. Dorevoliutsionnyi period.* (Moscow, 1954). A. A. Nesterenko, *Ocherki istorii promyshlennosti i polozheniia proletariata Ukrainy v kontse XIX i nachale XX v.* (Moscow, 1954). Ia. S. Rozenfeld and K. I. Klimenko, *Istoriia mashinostroeniia SSSR (s pervoi poloviny XIX v. do nashikh dnei).* (Moscow, 1961). P. M. Lukianov, *Kratkaia istoriia khimicheskoi promyshlennosti SSSR. Ot vozniknoveniia khimicheskoi promyshlennosti v Rossii do nashikh dnei.* (Moscow, 1959). K. A. Pazhitnov, *Ocherki istorii tekstilnoi promyshlennosti dorevoliutsionnoi Rossii. Sherstianaia promyshlennost.* (Moscow, 1955). G. I. Shigalin, *Voennaia ekonomika v pervuiu mirovuiu voinu (1914-1918 gg.).* I. V. Maevskii, *Ekonomika russkoi promyshlennosti v usloviiakh pervoi mirovoi voiny.* (Moscow, 1957). S. A. Zalesskii, "Chernaia metallurgiia Urala v gody pervoi mirovoi voiny." *Istoricheskie zapiski,* No. 55 (1956), 139-172. S. A. Zalesskii, "Mobilizatsiia gornozavodskoi promyshlennosti na Urale v gody pervoi mirovoi voiny." *Istoricheskie zapiski,* No. 65 (1959), 80-118. See also D. I. Shpolianskii, *Monopolii ugolno-metallurgicheskoi promyshlennosti Iuga Rossii v nachale XX veka.* (Moscow, 1953).

[11]D. I. Shpolianskii, *Monopolii ugolno-metallurgicheskoi promyshlennosti Iuga Rossii v nachale XX veka.* (Moscow, 1953). Ia. I. Livshin, *Monopolii v ekonomike Rossii. (Ekonomicheskie organizatsii i politika monopolisticheskogo kapitala).* (Moscow, 1961). G. V. Tsyperovich, *Sindikaty i tresty v Rossii i v SSSR.* (Moscow, 1927).

[12]A. L. Tsukernik, *Sindikat 'Prodamet'. Istoriko-ekonomicheskii ocherk. 1902—iiul 1914.* (Moscow, 1959). Zbignev Pustula, "Monopolii v metallurgicheskoi promyshlennosti Tsarstva Polskogo i ikh uchastie v 'Prodamete'." *Istoricheskie zapiski,* No. 62 (1958), 84-125. K. N. Tarnovskii, "Komitet po delam metallurgicheskoi promyshlennosti i monopolisticheskie organizatsii." *Istoricheskie zapiski,* No. 57 (1956), 80-143. A. P. Pogrebinskii, "Sindikat 'Prodamet' v gody pervoi mirovoi voiny (1914-1917 gg.)." *Voprosy istorii,* No. 10 (1958), 22-34. A. L. Tsukernik,

The fuel industry, including both coal and oil, has been thoroughly studied, particularly the prewar fuel monopolies (*Produgol*) of the Donets basin and the Caucasus. Finally, there are the important works of A. A. Fursenko, who made a study of Russia's place in the international oil monopolies.[13]

Extensive research has also been carried out on the metallurgical and ship-building industries, on the origin of industrial monopolies in the south and the Baltic areas, and on the military industries largely controlled by the Russian-Asiatic Bank, as well as on the development of industrial plants of Kolomna and Sormovo.[14]

Lately a series of studies were devoted to the subject of monopolies in rail and water transportation. Another series delved into textile and sugar interests of the Stakheevs and Riabushinskiis in the present century.[15] Far less progress is apparent in the study of stockholding commercial banks and

"Popytki restavratsii sindikata 'Prodamet' na Ukraine v 1918 g." *Istoricheskii arkhiv*, No. 3 (1958). P. I. Liashchenko, "Iz istorii monopolii v Rossii." *Istoricheskie zapiski*, No. 20 (1946), 150-158. M. Gefter, "Tsarizm i monopolishicheskii kapital v metallurgii Iuga Rossii do pervoi mirovoi voiny." *Istoricheskie zapiski*, No. 43 (1953), 70-130. A. P. Pogrebinskii, "Voenno-promyshlennye komitety." *Istoricheskie zapiski*, No. 11 (1941), 160-200.

[13]B. Iu. Akhundov, *Monopolisticheskii kapital v dorevoliutsionnoi bakinskoi neftianoi promyshlennosti.* (Moscow, 1959). P. V. Volobuev, "Iz istorii monopolizatsii neftianoi promyshlennosti dorevoliutsionnoi Rossii (1903-1914 gg.)." *Istoricheskie zapiski*, No. 52 (1955), 80-111. P. V. Volobuev, "Iz istorii sindikata 'Produgol'." *Istoricheskie zapiski*, No. 58 (1956), 107-144. T. D. Krupina, "K voprosu o vzaimoot-nosheniiakh tsarskogo pravitelstva s monopoliiami." *Istoricheskie zapiski*, No. 57 (1956), 144-176. A. A. Fursenko, "Iz istorii russko-amerikanskikh otnoshenii na ru-bezhe XIX-XX vv." *Sbornik iz istorii imperializma v Rossii. Trudy LOII Akademii nauk SSSR.* Issue I (Moscow, 1959). N. I. Mineeva, "Vliianie inostrannogo kapi-tala na razvitie neftianoi promyshlennosti dorevoliutsionnoi Rossii." *Nauchnye zapiski Moskovskogo finansovogo instituta*, Issue 8 (1957). A. Boikin, "Monopolnye tseny i monopolno-vysokie pribyli v neftianoi promyshlennosti tsarskoi Rossii." *Nauchnye doklady vysshei shkoly. Economicheskie nauki.* No. 1 (Moscow, 1959). See also D. I. Shpolianskii, *Monopolii ugolno-metallurgicheskoi promyshlennosti Iuga Rossii v nachale XX v. (K voprosu o sootnoshenii monopolii i konkurentsii).* (Moscow, 1953).

[14]V. I. Bovykin and K. N. Tarnovskii, "Kontsentratsiia proizvodstva i razvitie mono-polii v metalloobrabatyvaiushchei promyshlennosti Rossii." *Voprosy istorii*, No. 2 (1957), 19-31. V. I. Bovykin, "Banki i voennaia promyshlennost Rossii nakanune pervoi mirovoi voiny." *Istoricheskie zapiski*, No. 64 (1959), 82-135. A. P. Korelin, "Gruppa Russko-Aziatskogo banka v 1914-1915 gg." *Nauchnye doklady vysshei shkoly. Istoricheskie nauki*, No. 1 (1960).

[15]A. M. Solovieva, "K voprosu o roli finansovogo kapitala v zheleznodorozhnom stroi-telstve Rossii nakanune pervoi mirovoi voiny." *Istoricheskie zapiski*, No. 55 (1956), 173-209. V. P. Mozhin, "Monopolizatsiia vodnogo transporta Rossii (v nachale XX v.)." *Nauchnye doklady vysshei shkoly. Ekonomicheskie nauki*, No. 3 (1958). V. Ia. Laverychev, "K voprosu ob eksporte l'na iz Rossii v 1916-1917 gg." *Istoriia*

bank monopolies. There is hardly another study comparable to that of I. F. Gindin on the activities of the Moscow banks during the period 1900-1917. Gindin, in collaboration with L. E. Shepelev, has also contributed a short though highly informative essay on bank monopolies prior to October, 1917.[16]

During the late 1950's, the role of commercial banks, of government participation, and of foreign financial capital came under investigation by several scholars. Their studies extended to the activities of Russian banks, stockholding companies, and monopolies, as well as the general financial conditions of the country. Students who conducted research during the 1950's came to dismiss the earlier belief that Russian banks were completely dependent upon foreign capital; they came to the conclusion that Russian banks were far more independent than was formerly believed and that Russian capital was far more developed than had been assumed by earlier writers. The actual state of affairs was in reality quite complex. For instance, the Russian-Asiatic Bank cooperated closely with Austrian and German firms, while the German International Commercial Bank in turn cooperated with the well-known English Vickers firm and the French banks.[17]

A. L. Sidorov, on the other hand, in his monograph on the financial state of Russia during the First World War, having carefully investigated all archival materials related to Russia's foreign indebtedness, shows to what a large extent foreign loans had risen in the period between the Russo-Japanese War and October, 1917. Sidorov also shows the decisive role the tsarist government played in liquidating the foreign indebtedness of the Russian banks during 1914-1917. His information offers additional insight on the degree or character of Russia's dependence upon foreign capital. Many aspects of this complex question are left to be clarified by later scholars.[18]

Finally, there are several studies of limited scope in the field of distribution of financial capital within peripheral areas of the Russian Empire. Ts. L.

SSR, No. 1 (1958), 130-138. V. Ia. Laverychev, "Protsess monopolizatsii khlopchatobumazhnoi promyshlennosti Rossii (1900-1914 gody)." *Voprosy istorii,* No. 2 (1960), 137-151. P. V. Volobuev and I. F. Gindin, "K istorii kontserna I. Stakheeva." *Istoricheskii arkhiv,* No. 3 (1957), 160-173. T. M. Kitanina, "Iz istorii obrazovaniia kontserna Stakheeva." *Iz istorii imperializma Rossii. Trudy LOII Akademii nauk SSSR.* Issue I (Moscow, 1959). "K istorii kontserva br. Riabushinskikh." *Materialy po istorii SSSR.* Vol. VI (Moscow, 1959).

[16]I. F. Gindin, "Moskovskie banki v period imperializma (1900-1917 gg.)." *Istoricheskie zapiski,* Vol. 58 (1956), 38-106. See also I. F. Gindin and L. E. Shepelev, "Bankovskie monopolii v Rossii nakanune Velikoi Oktiabrskoi sotsialisticheskoi revoliutsii." *Istoricheskie zapiski,* No. 66 (1960), 20-95.

[17]K. F. Shatsillo, "Inostrannyi kapital i voenno-morskie programmy Rossii nakanune pervoi mirovoi voiny." *Istoricheskie zapiski,* No. 69 (1961), 73-100. See also Iu. Netesin, "Iz istorii proniknoveniia germanskogo kapitala v ekonomiku Rossii." *Izvestiia Akademii nauk Latviiskoi SSSR,* No. 4 (153), (1960).

[18]A. L. Sidorov, *Finansovoe polozhenie Rossii v gody pervoi mirovoi voiny (1914-1917).* (Moscow, 1960).

Friedman has written about the mining and metallurgical industries of Kazakh-stan, while D. E. Shemiakov and A. Ulmasov have studied Moldavia and Turkestan, respectively.[19] Cumulatively, the studies show several things quite clearly. First, that there is no relationship between the development of economic monopoly in Russia and the level of development of national productive forces. Second, that the syndicated industries in Russia were too diverse, and when P. I. Lia-shchenko regarded all of them as mere syndicated organizations he oversim-plified matters; there were actually syndicates, cartels, trusts, and other or-ganizational patterns. Finally, recent studies describe the various stages through which Russian monopolies passed: first the 1880's and 1890's, then the 1900-1908 period of sharp industrial crisis and the 1909-1913 period of prewar industrial recovery, and finally 1914-1917, the war years. The first period is noted for the initiation of cartel agreements in the metallurgical, mining, bridge construction, cable, coal, and oil industries. Between 1900 and 1908 the monopolies became basic in Russian economic life. Syndicates were formed in both light and heavy industries. In the final stages, 1909-1917, we find merely a continuation of the various monopolies. This process, though subject to question for a long time, has been confirmed by recent research.[20]

Economic historians have devoted considerable attention to the relation-ship between government and industrial monopolies in Russia, or to formu-late the issue more lucidly, the question of state-monopoly capitalism in Rus-sia. During the 1940's the general opinion was that monopoly capitalism in Russia was hardly detectable, or if it was present, was in a most inchoate stage of development. G. D. Bakulev, in his history of the metallurgical in-dustry in southern Russia, firmly denied the existence of monopoly capital-ism in Russia. Similar views were expressed by P. I. Liashchenko, I. V. Maevskii, G. I. Shigalin, A. P. Pogrebinskii, and others.[21]

[19]Ts. L. Friedman, *Inostrannyi kapital v dorevoliutsionnom Kazakhstane.* (Alma-Ata, 1960). D. E. Shemiakov, "Proniknovenie finansovogo kapitala v ekonomiku Mol-davii v epokhu imperializma (konets XIX v.–1917 g.)." *Uchenye zapiski Kishenev-skogo gosudarstvennogo universiteta. Mezhvuzovskii sbornik po istorii KPSS.* Issue I (Kishenev, 1960). A. Ulmasov, "K voprosu o pervykh monopoliiakh v Turkestane." *Izvestiia Akademii nauk Uzbekistanskoi SSR. Seriia obshchestvennykh nauk.* No. 1 (Tashkent, 1959).

[20]See M. Ia. Gefter, "Borba vokrug sozdaniia metallurgicheskogo tresta v Rossii v na-chale XX veka." *Istoricheskie zapiski,* No. 47 (1954), 124-148. P. V. Volobuev, "Iz istorii monopolizatsii neftianoi promyshlennosti dorevoliutsionnoi Rossii (1903-1914 gg.)." *Istoricheskie zapiski,* No. 52 (1955), 80-111. I. V. Foliushevskii, "Tresty i promyshlennosti dorevoliutsionnoi Ukrainy." *Nauchnye trudy kafedr ob-shchestvennykh nauk Kharkovskogo instituta inzhenerov zhelezno-dorozhnogo trans-porta.* Issue 37 (1960).

[21]G. D. Bakulev, *Chernaia metallurgiia Iuga Rossii.* (Moscow, 1953). P. I. Liashchenko, *Istoriia narodnogo khoziaistva SSSR.* 3rd ed. (Moscow, 1952), Vol. II, 598. A. P. Pogrebinskii, *Mobilizatsiia promyshlennosti tsarskoi Rossii v pervuiu mirovuiu voinu.*

Recent research has demolished the former belief in the weakness of Russian monpolies. One of the first scholars to reexamine the entire problem was M. Ia. Gefter. After minutely examining the sugar syndicate in Russia and undertaking similar studies of monopolies in the metallurgical, fuel, and other industries, he came to a completely different point of view. Others followed, to confirm his thesis.[22]

These studies led the economic historians to a closely related field—the development of state-monopoly capitalism in Russia during the First World War. Outstanding studies were produced by A. L. Sidorov, A. P. Pogrebinskii, and several others. Analytical studies were made of the metallurgical industries and of enterprises associated with war production, textiles, transportation, and mining, all of which combined to substantiate the belief that monopoly capitalism and government collaborated closely in Tsarist Russia.[23]

The latest studies of the development of state-monopoly capitalism in Russia during the short period of the Provisional Government are provided by a series of articles by P. V. Volobuev and a monographic work by I. F. Gindin. The latter emphasized particularly the economic policy of the tsarist government during the second half of the nineteenth century. This work broadened the field considerably, indicating not only the origins and early devel-

---

Ph.D. dissertation. (Moscow, 1948). I. V. Maevskii, *Ekonomika russkoi promyshlennosti v usloviiakh pervoi voiny.*(Moscow, 1957). G. I. Shigalin, *Voennaia ekonomika v pervuiu mirovuiu voinu (1914-1918 gg.).* (Moscow, 1956).

[22]M. Ia. Gefter, "Iz istorii monopolisticheskogo kapitalizma v Rossii (Sakharnyi sindikat)." *Istoricheskie zapiski,* No. 38 (1951), 104-153. M. Ia. Gefter, "Tsarism i monopolisticheskii kapital v metallurgii Iuga Rossii do pervoi mirovoi voiny (K voprosu o podchinenii gosudarstvennogo apparata tsarizma kapitalisticheskimi monopoliiami)." *Istoricheskie zapiski,* No. 43 (1953), 70-130. M. Ia. Gefter, "Tsarizm i zakonodatelnoe 'regulirovanie' deiatelnosti sindikatov i trestov v Rossii nakanune pervoi voiny." *Istoricheskie zapiski,* No. 54 (1955), 170-194. M. Ia. Gefter, "K istorii toplivno-metallurgicheskogo 'goloda' v Rossii nakanune pervoi mirovoi voiny (Publikatsiia dokumentov i vvodnaia statia)." *Sbornik. Istoricheskii arkhiv,* No. 6 (1951). See also *Materialy po istorii SSSR,* Vol. VI. Note documents, commentaries, and articles on "Monopolii v metalloobrabatyvaiushchei promyshlennosti i tsarizm v nachale XX veka," prepared by P. V. Volobuev and M. Ia. Gefter. T. D. Krupina, *Monopolisticheskii kapital v Rossii i tsarskoe samoderzhavie (1907-1914 gg.).* Dissertation. (Moscow, 1954). T. D. Krupina, "K voprosu o vzaimootnosheniiakh tsarskogo pravitelstva s monopoliiami." *Istoricheskie zapiski,* No. 57 (1956), 144-176.

[23]A. L. Sidorov, "Borba s krizisom vooruzheniia russkoi armii v 1915-1916 gg." *Istoricheskii zhurnal,* Nos. 10-11 (1944). A. L. Sidorov, "Otnosheniia Rossii s soiuznikami i inostrannye postavki vo vremia pervoi mirovoi voiny 1914-1917 gg." *Istoricheskie zapiski,* No. 15 (1945), 128-179. A. L. Sidorov, "Evakuatsiia russkoi promyshlennosti vo vremia pervoi mirovoi voiny." *Voprosy istorii,* No. 6 (1947), 3-25. A. L. Sidorov, "Zheleznodorozhnyi transport Rossii v pervoi mirovoi voine i obostrenie ekonomicheskogo krizisa v strane." *Istoricheskie zapiski,* No. 26 (1948), 3-64. A. L. Sidorov, "K voprosu o stroitelstve kazennykh voennykh zavodov v Rossii v gody pervoi mirovoi voiny." *Istoricheskie zapiski,* No. 54 (1955), 156-169. A. L. Sidorov, "K istorii toplivnogo krizisa v Rossii v gody pervoi mirovoi voiny

opment of Russian monopoly capitalism, but tracing it throughout its entire development, up to its logical finale, the October Revolution. These studies enabled other students to form a general synthesis, which was presented before a session of the Institute of History of the Academy of Sciences in December, 1958, and published a year later.[24]

P. I. Liashchenko is of the opinion that Russian economic imperialism should be placed in a special category which he prefers to call the "military-feudal type." This point of view met the approval of a number of writers who believe that Russian imperialism was of a distinctive character. Among them are P. A. Khromov, A. Ia. Grunt, V. I. Firtsova, and P. V. Volobuev.[25] Some of these writers define "military-feudal imperialism" merely as a natural superstructure characteristic of any economically backward country. I. Brover adopted this view after he studied Russian colonial policy, and F. A. Rotshtein derived his opinion from his research in Russian foreign policy. Others, like M. Ia. Gefter and V. I. Mantsev, accept the same view. On the other hand, A. L. Sidorov cautions his colleagues about the danger of stretching their interpretation of "military-feudal imperialism" too far, and urges

(1914-1917 gg.)." *Istoricheskie zapiski*, No. 59 (1957), 26-83. A. P. Pogrebinskii, "Voenno-promyshlennye komitety." *Istoricheskie zapiski*, No. 11 (1941), 160-200. A. P. Pogrebinskii, "K istorii soiuzov zemstv i gorodov v gody imperialisticheskoi voiny." *Istoricheskie zapiski*, No. 12 (1941), 39-61. K. N. Tarnovskii, *Formirovanie gosudarstvenno-monopolisticheskogo kapitalizma v Rossii v gody pervoi mirovoi voiny (na primere metallurgicheskoi promyshlennosti)*. (Moscow, 1958). *Istoricheskie zapiski*, No. 57 (1956), 80-143. K. F. Shatsillo, *Finansovyi kapital v morskoi sudostroitelnoi promyshlennosti Rossii (1910-1917)*. Dissertation. (Moscow, 1958). E. Uribes, "Koksobenzolnaia promyshlennost Rossii v gody pervoi mirovoi voiny." *Istoricheskie zapiski*, No. 69 (1961), 46-72.

[24]P. V. Volobuev, "O gosudarstvenno-monopolisticheskom kapitalizme v Rossii v 1917 g. (mart-oktiabr)." *Voprosy istorii*, No. 9 (1959), 44-63. P. V. Volobuev, "Monopolisticheskii kapital i ekonomicheskaia politika Vremennogo pravitelstva." *Istoriia SSSR*, No. 1 (1960), 34-58. P. V. Volobuev, "Ekonomicheskaia programma burzhuazii i Vremennogo pravitelstva." *Istoricheskie zapiski*, No. 67 (1960), 19-76. I. F. Gindin, *Gosudarstvennyi bank i ekonomicheskaia politika tsarskogo pravitelstva (1861-1892 gody)*. (Moscow, 1960). I. F. Gindin, "K voprosu ob ekonomicheskoi politike tsarskogo pravitelstva v 60-80 godakh XIX veka." *Voprosy istorii*, No. 5 (1959), 63-82. See also V. I. Bovykin, I. F. Gindin, and K.N. Tarnovskii, "Gosudarstvenno-monopolisticheskii kapitalizm v Rossii. K voprosu o predposylkakh sotsialisticheskoi revoliutsii." *Istoriia SSSR*, No. 3 (1959), 83-117.

[25]P. A. Khromov, *Ocherki ekonomiki Rossii perioda monopolisticheskogo kapitalizma*. (Moscow, 1960). A. Ia. Grunt and V. I. Firstova, *Rossiia v epokhu imperializma*. Issue I (1890-1907). (Moscow, 1959). Issue II (1907-1917). (Moscow, 1960). P. V. Volobuev, *Monopolisticheskii kapitalizm v Rossii i ego osobennosti*. (Moscow, 1956). P. V. Volobuev, "Ob osobennostiakh russkogo kapitalizma." *Prepodavanie istorii v shkole*, No. 4 (1957), 21-30. I. V. Foliushevskii, *Monopolisticheskii kapitalizm na Ukraine i ego osobennosti*. (Moscow, 1954).

that Russian expansionism be examined more closely in order to identify some of the distinctive circumstances peculiar to Russian history.[26]

Time and again debate has flared up concerning the degree to which "semi-colonial" Russia depended upon foreign capital. Such debates recurred in the 1950's, provoking a spirited exchange of views. Opposed to the opinion that Russia was even a "semi-colonial" country were those who maintained that though the country was backward, it was never in any sense "colonial." A correct description of her economic state, they assert, would be that of a country with an average or below average level of capitalistic development.[27]

D. NATURE OF THE PRE-REVOLUTIONARY ECONOMY

In the field of Russian economic history there was one especially disturbing question over which the party battled—the nature of the economy of Imperial Russia. Prominent economists such as P. I. Liashchenko dealt with the issue rather extensively, and his work, approved by the Ministry of Education, became the officially adopted university textbook. Since 1948, the two volumes have been revised on three occasions and have appeared in English translation. Liashchenko was one of the first Soviet economic historians to describe the Russian economy as a multi-national system of Russian capitalism. It developed unevenly, according to regional economic or peripheral conditions, he asserted. He also described extensively the economic conditions and policies of Tsarist Russia, and regarded government participation in economic activities prior to 1917 as a mere desire to accelerate the development of industrial capitalism.[28]

[26]I. Brover, "K voprosu ob osobennostiakh rossiiskogo imperializma." *Vestnik Akademii nauk Kazakhskoi SSR*, No. 7 (100), (1953). F. A. Rotshtein, *Mezhdunarodnye otnosheniia v kontse XIX veka.* (Moscow, 1960). M. Ia. Gefter, "Ekonomicheskie predposylki pervoi russkoi revoliutsii." *Doklady i soobshcheniia Instituta AN SSSR,* Issue 6 (1955). V. I. Mantsev, "V. I. Lenin o voenno-feodalnom 'imperializme' tsarskoi Rossii." *Voprosy politicheskoi ekonomii. Sbornik statei.* (Moscow, 1960). A. L. Sidorov, "Znachenie Velikoi Oktiabrskoi sotsialisticheskoi revoliutsii v ekonomicheskikh sudbakh nashei Rodiny." *Istoricheskie zapiski,* No. 25 (1948), 3-24. A. L. Sidorov, "Ekonomicheskie predposylki sotsialisticheskoi revoliutsii v Rossii." *Istoriia SSSR,* No. 4 (1957), 9-39. A. L. Sidorov, "V. I. Lenin o russkom voenno-feodalnom imperializme (O soderzhanii termina 'voenno-feodalnyi imperializm')." *Istoriia SSSR,* No. 3 (1961), 47-70.

[27]B. B. Gravé, "Byla li tsarskaia Rossiia polukoloniei?" *Voprosy istorii,* No. 6, (1956), 63-73. I. V. Maevskii, "K voprosu o zavisimosti Rossii v period pervoi mirovoi voiny." *Voprosy istorii,* No. 1 (1957), 69-76. A. E. Ioffe, "Ob usilenii zavisimosti Rossii ot stran Antanty v gody pervoi mirovoi voiny." *Voprosy istorii,* No. 3 (1957), 100-120.

[28]P. I. Liashchenko, *Istoriia narodnogo khoziaistva SSSR.* (Moscow, 1948; 3rd ed., 1952). 2 vols. English tr.: *History of the National Economy of Russia to the 1917 Revolution.* (New York, Macmillan, 1949). See also S. G. Strumilin, *Ocherki ekonomicheskoi istorii Rossii.* (Moscow, 1960).

N. I. Vanag was one of the economic historians whose attention concentrated on the formation of foreign financial capital in Russia prior to the Revolution. His opinion was that foreign capital was not only predominant in the financial realm but in industrial development as well. This was achieved, Vanag believed, by way of joint-stock commercial banks. In reality, he argued, the financial power was not Russian, but a combined Franco-German-British financial capital that ruled the Russian economy. In fact, financially, Russia was in the position of a semi-colonial nation depending upon the western European powers.[29]

Not all writers agreed with this interpretation of the capital coming into Russia. G. V. Tsyperovich, A. L. Sidorov, and others argued that the influx of foreign capital was a natural economic phenomenon derived from the general nature and development of capitalism, growth of industry and banking operations, or expansion of transportation. Foreign capital did not interfere; it aided the development of national monopolistic capitalism. The difference of opinion concerning the form and development of capitalism in pre-1917 Russia was no mere idle academic discussion during the 1920's and early 1930's. The conflict between the two views came to reflect the sharp ideological struggle that unfolded between Stalinists on one hand and opponents of Stalin on the other. It came to involve an important interpretation, and hence policy, concerning the level of development and maturity of pre-revolutionary capitalism, the nature of the October Revolution, the perspectives of "socialist construction" in the Soviet Union, and the Communist movement in the world. The issue was discussed extensively during the Sixth Congress of the Communist International.[30]

The official interpretation of the course of capitalistic development in relation to the revolutionary situation may be briefly summarized thus. There were three main types of countries: one, the countries with a highly developed capitalistic system; two, countries where capitalism was in process of growth; three, the colonial and semi-colonial countries. In the first two types of countries, Soviet economists argued, there were all the mate-

---

[29]N. I. Vanag, *Finansovyi kapital v Rossii nakanune mirovoi voiny. Opyt istoriko-ekonomicheskogo issledovaniia sistemy finansovogo kapitala v Rossii.* (Moscow, 1925). S. Ronin, *Inostrannyi kapital i russkie banki. K voprosu o finansovom kapitale v Rossii.* (Moscow, 1926). L. Gol'man, *Russkii imperializm.* (Leningrad, 1927).

[30]See G. V. Tsyperovich, *Sindikaty i tresty v dorevoliutsionnoi Rossii i v SSSR. Iz istorii organizatsionnykh form promyshlennosti za poslednie 50 let.* 4th ed. (Leningrad, 1927). I. F. Gindin, *Banki i promyshlennost v Rossii do 1917 g. K voprosu o finansovom kapitale v Rossii.* (Moscow, 1927). A. L. Sidorov, "Vliianie imperialisticheskoi voiny na ekonomiku Rossii." *Ocherki po istorii Oktiabrskoi revoliutsii.* Vol. I. (Moscow, 1927). E. L. Granovskii, *Monopolisticheskii kapitalizm v Rossii.* (Leningrad, 1929). See also the thesis of socialist development without need of passing through the phase of capitalism: A. M. Aminov, "Zakonomernost i osobennosti perekhoda otstalykh stran k sotsializmu, minuia kapitalisticheskuiu fazu razvitiia." *Nauchnye zapiski.* Tashkentskii institut narodnogo khoziaistva, Kafedra politicheskoi ekonomiki. Issue XXIII (Tashkent, 1965), 5-26.

rial prerequisites for a successful and independent construction of a socialist economy, while in the third category socialism was still premature. For this reason the establishment of a soviet system of government in colonial and semi-colonial countries, where medieval feudal conditions prevail, is possible only after a period of development that comes from the conversion of a bourgeois-democratic revolution into a socialist one. The last stage can be achieved in most cases only with the direct aid from the countries where the dictatorship of the proletariat has already been firmly established. [31]

The result amounted to this: the historians who regarded pre-revolutionary Russia as economically a semi-colonial or colonial type came unwittingly to accept what was officially labelled the Menshevik thesis or an anti-party line—namely, that Russia was not yet ready for advanced social construction. Some of these scholars continued to adhere tenaciously to their views and argued in favor of the theory of "denationalization of Russian capitalism"; they clung to their thesis of Russian dependence on western European capitalism. In the end they paid dearly for their firm stand. Others, such as N. I. Vanag, bowed to Stalinism and took the road to Canossa.[32]

During the mid-1930's a Soviet decree had ordered a change in the teaching of history that necessitated the training of an entirely new personnel. The granting of doctorate degrees was announced and topics for dissertations were expected to emphasize Soviet patriotism. However, in various fields, particularly in the field of economic history, the new assignment was complicated by Stalin's rigid dogmatism and the "cult of the individual" which began to dominate all writings. What is to be noted here particularly is the new interpretation demanded by Stalinism concerning the development of capitalism in pre-revolutionary Russia. All former evaluations, definitions, or interpretations of economic and historical literature were to be cast overboard, even if the author were no other than Stalin himself.

At the end of the 1920's, Stalin, basing his views on those of Lenin, or so he asserted, appeared at the Second Congress of the Communist International, and repeatedly expounded *differences* between the revolution in imperialist countries and the revolution in colonial countries. He referred to Tsarist Russia as one of the imperialist countries, while China he represented as the oppressed, semi-colonial country, forced to struggle against imperialist encroachment.[33] Stalin classified Tsarist Russia as the type of country in which capitalism was in the process of growth. Such was the Stalin thesis until the end of the 1920's. But in 1934, while writing his commentaries on the USSR history textbook and referring to N. I. Vanag as editor, Stalin, who had only recently condemned publicly the thesis of

[31]Bela Kun, ed., *Kommunisticheskii Internatsional v dokumentakh. Resheniia, tezisy i vozzvania kongressov Kominterna i plenumov IKKI, 1919-1932.* (Moscow, 1933), 29-30.

[32]See letter of N. I. Vanag to the editor of the magazine *Istorik-marksist,* Nos. 4-5 (1932), 355-359.

[33]I. V. Stalin, *Sochineniia,* X, 10-11, 12; VIII, 358; IX, 333.

colonial and semi-colonial dependence of Russia upon western European powers, now completely reversed his position. Now he criticized Vanag, saying that his editorial staff failed to take into account the dependent role tsarism and Russian capitalism had played in relation to the western European powers. Only the October Revolution, he asserted, freed Russia from her semi-colonial status. This, Stalin maintained, the textbook edited by N. I. Vanag failed to explain explicitly.[34]

A year later the thesis of Russia as a semi-colonial country dependent upon western European capitalism appeared in the first volume of the *Istoriia grazhdanskoi voiny v SSSR*. Then in 1938, in the *Istoriia Vsesoiuznoi kommunisticheskoi partii*, the same thesis was repeated even more emphatically. Citing the part played by foreign capital in the development of heavy industry in southern Russia, Stalin added: "All these circumstances, plus the billions in loans contracted between the tsarist regime and France and England, chained tsarism to Anglo-French imperialism, thereby turning Russia into a tributary of these countries, into a kind of a semi-colony."[35]

Thus the subject of the semi-colonial dependence of Russia upon western imperialism came once again under discussion. The subject which seemed to have been thoroughly settled in historical literature, as a result of research and long discussions in the past, emerged once more. This time, however, the Stalinist cult left no room for challenge. It stopped cold all further research in the field for fear that any change of viewpoint derived from further research might invoke party displeasure, with attendant consequences. Thus, according to Stalin's latest interpretation, the imperialism of Russia—a semi-colonial nation—could not be considered as purely military-feudal in character. This was a total departure from Lenin's view, though assertedly it was based on Leninism. This time N. I. Vanag came to the aid of Stalin by ascribing his belief to the original teaching of Lenin. Stalin's triumph in the economic interpretation of Russian history was as complete as his triumph in the political realm.[36]

In the 1950's the interest in Russian economic history during the era of imperialism was revived once more and, for good reasons, with new vigor. First, interest was aroused and motivated by the tremendous changes that resulted from the Second World War, such as the expansion of the Soviet Union and the extension of the Soviet system throughout eastern Europe. Arising almost of its own accord was the question regarding the "law-governed

---

[34]I. V. Stalin, *Sochineniia*, XI, 155. See also I. V. Stalin, A. Zhdanov, and S. Kirov, "Zamechaniia po povodu konspekta uchebnika po istorii SSSR." *Sbornik. K izucheniiu istorii.* (Moscow, 1938), 23.

[35]*Istoriia grazhdanskoi voiny v SSSR.* Vol. I (Moscow, 1936), 12. *Istoriia vsesoiuznoi kommunisticheskoi partii (bol'shevikov). Kratkii kurs.* (Moscow, 1946), 156. Cf. 3rd edition of 1969.

[36]*Istorik-marksist*, No. 1 (1934). A. L. Sidorov, "V. I. Lenin o russkom voenno-feodalnom imperializme. (O soderzhanii termina 'voenno-feodalnyi imperializm')." *Istoriia SSSR*, No. 3 (1961), 47-70.

process" initiated in October, 1917, when the Revolution began to transform capitalism into socialism. The October Revolution began to assume even more meaning or symbolic significance in history. It was from this point, mainly, that Soviet historians turned once more to economic history during the period of imperialism, seeking a new interpretation in the light of recent events.

Historians and economists turned their attention to the numerous archives throughout the Soviet Union. To their great satisfaction they discovered that their efforts were richly rewarded: there was much more documentary evidence than they had ever anticipated. This particularly concerned the history of monopolistic capitalism, a field which had been thought to be entirely explored. Formerly, most scholars based their research mainly on published statistical data and periodical literature. Later much of the new material came from government institutions such as the Council of Ministers, the Special Council on Defense and its committees, commercial banks, and joint-stock companies. Only a small portion of the new evidence was found in special magazines and other publications. And still, it is commonly believed that not all sources have yet been investigated, that there are more to come.[37]

[37]*Ekonomicheskoe polozhenie Rossii nakanune Velikoi Oktiabrskoi sotsialisticheskoi revoliutsii. Mart-oktiabra 1917 g. Dokumenty i materialy.* Parts 1-2. (Moscow, 1957). *Materialy po istorii SSSR.* Vol. VI. *Dokumenty po istorii monopolisticheskogo kapitalizma v Rossii.* (Moscow, 1959). *Monopolisticheskii kapital v neftianoi promyshlennosti Rossii, 1883-1914. Dokumenty i materialy.* (Moscow, 1961). Some of the documents cited here appeared in the magazine *Istoricheskii arkhiv.* See, for instance, the following: "K istorii toplivnogo 'goloda' v Rossii nakanune pervoi mirovoi voiny," No. 1 (1957). "K istorii kontserna Stakheeva," No. 3 (1957). "Iz istorii russko-amerikanskikh finansovo-ekonomicheskikh otnoshenii v 1916-1917 gg.," No. 4 (1957). "Popytki S. Iu. Vitte otkryt amerikanskii denezhnyi rynok dlia russkikh zaimov (1898-1902 gg.)," Nos. 1 and 2 (1959). "O politike sindikata 'Prodamet' nakanune i v gody pervoi mirovoi voiny (1914-1915 gg.)," No. 3 (1959). "K voprosu o nalichii v Rossii monopolisticheskikh organizatsii vysshego tipa," No. 3 (1960). There are several important surveys of archival collections. To mention a few: A. P. Pronshtein, "Dokumentalnye materialy Gosudarstvennogo arkhiva Rostovskoi oblasti po istorii dorevoliutsionnoi promyshlennosti Dona," No. 1 (1956). M. A. Pliukhina and L. E. Shepelev, "Ob ekonomicheskom polozhenii Rossii nakanune Velikoi Oktiabsrskoi sotsialisticheskoi revoliutsii. Obzor dokumentalnykh materialov TsGIAL," No. 1 (1957), 167-177. M. S. Semenova and G. S. Khomiakov, "Komplektovanie TsGIA SSSR v Leningrade dokumentalnymi materialami po istorii finansov, promyshlennosti i torgovli v XIX—nachale XX v. i ikh arkhivnye fondy." *Informatsionnyi biulleten GAU MVD SSSR,* No. 10 (1958). N. A. Maltseva, "Obzor dokumentalnykh materialov fondam ministerstva torgovli i promyshlennosti (za 1905-1917 gg.)." *Istoricheskii arkhiv,* No. 2 (1958). M. Ia. Stetskevich, *Materialy po sotsialno-ekonomicheskoi istorii Rossii v 1890-1917 gg.* Otdel rukopisei Gosudarstvennoi publichnoi biblioteki im. M. E. Saltykova-Shchedrina. "Iz istorii imperializma v Rossii." *Trudy LOII Akademii nauk SSSR,* Issue 1 (Moscow, 1959). L. E. Shepelev, "Vazhnyi istochnik izucheniia ekonomicheskikh predposylok Velikoi Oktiabrskoi sotsialisticheskoi revoliutsii." *Voprosy arkhivovedeniia,* No. 1 (1959). E. V. Bazhanova, "Publikatsii Vremennogo Pravitelstva i ego

E. FOREIGN TRADE

During the first five decades of Soviet rule, several important works appeared in the field of Russian foreign trade. G. Zhordaniia wrote on Franco-Russian relations during the end of the sixteenth and first half of the seventeenth century.[38] He describes the mutual economic interests the two countries established, and plausibly suggests, on the basis of some of the evidence, that an early Russian trade mission must have visited Paris during the period covered by this study. There is an even wider interest in and body of literature on Russian foreign trade with the east, which was an important factor at a time when the western borders were blocked by none too friendly relations with either Poland or Sweden. Sino-Russian trade carried on through Siberia during the seventeenth century has been dealt with by a number of writers, among them V. A. Aleksandrov and O. N. Vilkov, who describe Sino-Russian trade relations, and A. Chimitdorzhiev, who covers Russo-Mongolian relations. N. G. Kukanova and A. I. Iukhta have written on Russo-Iranian trade; and N. M. Goldberg and N. V. Baykova have produced studies on Russo-Indian trade relations. There is a conspicuous absence of studies of such subjects as Russian foreign trade in the eighteenth century, after the country came to control the Baltic shore and the northern shore of the Black Sea, and the impact the expansion of that trade must have produced, particularly upon northern Europe. There is further need of a combined study of the domestic market as it relates to the proportionate expansion of Russian foreign trade.[39]

There is an obvious relationship between the growth of towns and cities and the development of foreign trade. Among the publications on this subject is the monographic work of M. V. Flekhner, who utilized an immense

spetsialnykh ekonomicheskikh organov po voprosam narodnogo khoziaistva Rossii. (Obzor)." *Trudy Biblioteki Akademii nauk SSSR i Fundamentalnoi biblioteki obshchestvennykh nauk Akademii nauk SSSR*, Vol. V (Moscow, 1961).

[38]G. Zhordaniia, *Ocherki iz istorii franko-russkikh otnoshenii kontsa XVI i pervoi poloviny XVII v.* (Tbilisi, 1959). 2 parts.

[39]V. A. Aleksandrov, "Iz istorii russko-kitaiskikh ekonomicheskikh sviazei." *Istoriia SSSR*, No. 5 (1957), 203-208. V. A. Aleksandrov, "Russko-kitaiskaia torgovlia i Nerchinskii torg v kontse XVII v." *K voprosu o pervonachalnom nakoplenii v Rossii (XVII-XVIII vv.). Sbornik statei.* (Moscow, 1958), 422-464. O. N. Vilkov, "Kitaiskie tovary na tobolskom rynke v XVIII v." *Istoriia SSSR*, No. 1 (1958), 105-124. A. Chimitdorzhiev, "Russko-oirotskie (Zapadnomongolskie) sviazi v XVII v." *Vestnik Leningradskogo universiteta,* No. 20. *Seriia istorii, iazyka i literatury.* Issue 4 (Leningrad, 1958), 131-141. N. G. Kukanova, "Russko-iranskie torgovye otnosheniia v kontse XVII—nachale XVIII v." *Istoricheskie zapiski,* No. 57 (1956), 232-254. A. I. Iukht, "Torgovlia Rossii s Zakavkaziem i Persiei vo vtoroi chetverti XVIII v." *Istoriia SSSR,* No. 1 (1961), 131-146. A. I. Iukht, "Indiiskaia koloniia v Astrakhani." *Voprosy istorii,* No. 3 (1957), 135-143. N. B. Baykova, "K voprosu o russko-indiiskikh torgovykh otnosheniiakh v XVI-XVII vv." *Trudy Instituta vostokovedeniia Akademii nauk Uzbekistanskoi SSSR.* Issue IV (Tashkent, 1956), 75-94.

amount of source material related to early Russian trade with the East. The works of S. V. Bakhrushin, A. M. Sakharov, B. A. Rybakov and a number of others are of equal importance.[40] Flekhner's study describes the type of commodities the country exported, and clearly shows the important place export trade occupied in the economy of the time. The author believes that export to the east was economically far more important than export to the west, mainly because the former involved predominantly finished commodities, whereas the latter consisted mainly of raw materials.

Another work that merits mention is by M. M. Gromyko, whose interest centered upon Russo-Dutch trade in the Murmansk maritime area.[41] Gromyko lucidly describes, first, the economic development of Russia, and second, the infiltration of western capitalism into eastern peripheries. Gradually, early capitalistic methods reached out to the distant Russian coastal area of Murmansk, bringing the backward eastern trade within the western economic orbit.[42] The studies mentioned, though based on much newly uncovered material, still leave several aspects inadequately treated or hardly touched. One of these is the degree of economic unity within the Russian state during the sixteenth century. Thus far, the information one gathers from the accounts published confirms only the idea that sixteenth-century Russian conditions could hardly favor capitalistic development. Whatever

[40]S. V. Bakhrushin, *Ocherki po istorii remesla, torgovli i gorodov Russkogo tsentralizo-vannogo gosudarstva XVI–nachala XVIII vv.* (*K voprosu o predposylkakh vserossii-skogo rynka*). This is incorporated in his *Nauchnye trudy,* Vol. I. (Moscow, 1962). See particularly Parts III-IV on the origins and nature of Russian towns in the sixteenth century, pp. 107-156. A. M. Sakharov, "Remeslennoe proizvodstvo v gorod-akh Severo-Vostochnoi Rusi XIV-XV vekov." *Voprosy istorii,* No. 4 (1955), 59-71. B. A. Rybakov, *Remeslo drevnei Rusi.* (Moscow, 1948). M. N. Tikhomirov, *Drev-niaia Moskva.* (Moscow, 1943). M. N. Tikhomirov, *Srednevekovaia Moskva XIV-XV vv.* (Moscow, 1957). M. N. Tikhomirov, *Drevnerusskie goroda.* 2nd ed. (Moscow, 1956). M. P. Lesnikov, "Niderlandy i Vostochnaia Baltika v nachale XV veka. Iz istorii torgovykh snoshenii." *Izvestiia Akademii nauk SSSR. Seriia istorii i filosofii,* No. 5 (1951). M. P. Lesnikov, "Torgovye snosheniia Velikogo Novgoroda s Tevton-skim ordenom v kontse XIV i nachala XV v." *Istoricheskie zapiski,* No. 39 (1952), 259-278. N. A. Kazakova, "Iz istorii snosheniia Novgoroda s Ganzoi v XV veke." *Istoricheskie zapiski,* No. 28 (1949), 111-131. N. A. Kazakova, "Iz istorii torgovoi politiki Russkogo tsentralizovannogo gosudarstva XV veka." *Istoricheskie zapiski,* No. 47 (1954), 259-290. L. V. Danilova and V. T. Pashuto, "Tovarnoe proizvod-stvo na Rusi (do XVII v.)." *Voprosy istorii,* No. 1 (1954), 117-136. M. N. Tikho-mirov, "Spisok russkikh gorodov dalnikh i blizhnikh." *Istoricheskie zapiski,* No. 40 (1953), 214-259. M. V. Flakhner, *Torgovlia Russkogo gosudarstva so stranami Vos-toka v XVI v.* (Moscow, 1956). In the series *Trudy Gosudarstvennogo istorich-skogo muzeia,* Issue XXXI.

[41]M. M. Gromyko, "Russko-niderlandskaia torgovlia na Murmanskom beregu v XVI v." *Srednie veka,* No. 17 (Moscow, 1960).

[42]On this particular point see A. L. Khoroshkevich, "Vneshniaia torgovlia Rusi XIV-XVI vv. v osveshchenii sovremennoi burzhuaznoi istoriografii." *Voprosy istorii,* No. 2 (1960), 104-117.

commodity-money economy there was could hardly justify the assumption that the feudal order was in decay. On the contrary, the latter proved sufficiently viable to consolidate the institution of serfdom and survive for nearly three centuries. The feudal order within the state was successful in blocking bourgeois elements from gaining the upper hand in political life. Any territorial expansion only served to strengthen feudal tendencies, by enabling the landlord class to extend further claims to both land and the peasantry, with varying degrees of success, thereby retarding—or surely not stimulating—the growth of towns or cities, or the conditions that favor a bourgeois order.

F. SOCIAL AND POLITICAL IDEAS

Social and political movements in early Russian history have been studied extensively in Soviet historiography; an impressive amount of new source material has been published, utilized, newly interpreted, or reinterpreted. But the recent works have raised a goodly number of questions among historians, many of which have not been answered. Many of these queries are of a religious or social nature and for one reason or another are conveniently by-passed. Noteworthy writers on the political and social history of early Russia include I. U. Budovnits, A. I. Klibanov, N. A. Kazakova, Ia. S. Lurie, and A. A. Zimin.[43] Budovnits analyzed thoroughly most of the available materials recently uncovered, examined the Chronicles, the literary writings, and the folklore of the time. He concluded that, cumulatively, the new sources convincingly prove the indigenous nature of early cultural accomplishments, which were remarkably free of foreign influence. The writings indicate a close link with the political aspirations of the time and the social strife between the tilling masses and the domineering feudal class.

The literature of the same period sheds light on various heretical movements prevalent in Kievan Russia and elsewhere. Writers like Lurie and Kazakova have examined all possible evidence to detect any relationship between Russian heretical teachings and the reform movements and humanist ideas of western Europe. Soviet historians regard the Reformation as the early sign of capitalism; they detect in the religious upheaval socio-political developments leading to the downfall of the feudal order and the ascendancy ot a bourgeois capitalistic society. The Reformation also marks the revolt and decisive defeat of the peasantry, a defeat from which it was unable to recover for at least two centuries.

In his study of the Reformation movement A. I. Klibanov includes all Russian heretical teachings of the fourteenth through the sixteenth centuries.[44] According to Klibanov, these teachings, disguised as progressive reli-

[43]I. U. Budovnits, *Obshchestvenno-politicheskaia mysl' drevnei Rusi (XI-XIV vv.).* (Moscow, 1960). A. I. Klibanov, *Reformatsionnoe dvizhenie v Rossii v XIV—pervoi polovine XVI v.* (Moscow, 1960). N. A. Kazakova and Ia. S. Lurie, *Anti-feodalnye ereticheskie dvizheniia kontsa XV—nachala XVI v.* (Moscow, 1960). A. A. Zimin, *Peresvetov i ego sovremenniki.* (Moscow, 1958).

[44]A. I. Klibanov, *Reformatsionnoe dvizhenie v Rossii v XIV—pervoi polovine XVI v.* (Moscow, 1960).

gious ideas, were in fact directed against the feudal order. The mainspring of the movement came from the democratic middle-class townsmen. Though in an inchoate stage, the movement heralded the era of bourgeois capitalism that was to unfold later, particularly during the seventeenth century. Klibanov links the development of political and religious free thought in Russia with similar currents in the West. This has been challenged by some writers, although Klibanov clearly showed that the nearer the events occurred to western Europe the more violent they were in nature. Heresy spread largely in northwestern Russia, in Novgorod, Pskov, and in areas adjacent to the Baltic. Other heretical movements, such as in the northeastern regions, never proved to be of any lasting importance. In Moscow, heresy appeared only at the time of Ivan the Purser (1325-1340), though here its very existence remains hypothetical, says Klibanov. All writers agree upon one thing—that Russian heretical movements appeared to have been strongest by the end of the fifteenth century.

A. A. Zimin, on the other hand, adds that the heresy that emanated from the lower classes never succeeded in arousing popular peasant revolts against the feudal order; only when social and economic conditions combined their forces were heretical movements instrumental in bringing about violent uprisings. The reasons for this, Zimin believes, are of a dual nature: first, the absence of a strong middle class that would assume a leading role in the formation of a formidable opposition to the landed nobility; second, the absence of a stronger town population that might have served as a basis for an effective humanitarian reform movement.

There has been a noticeable increase of interest in social and cultural development in Russia during the seventeenth and eighteenth centuries. Studies on this subject have been carried out mainly at the Institute of Russian Literature. Since most of these works are closely related to the social and cultural history of Russia, there is every reason for including them in the present survey. Writers in these two fields generally agree on the nature of the seventeenth and eighteenth centuries: during this period there is witnessed a gradual decline in theological learning and an increase in secularized thought. There is also a rich folklore in rural communities, mostly satirical in nature, at the expense of the nobility or administrative authorities. A similar trend may be noted in the literature of the towns and cities where satire became popular. A notable contribution to the subject is a collaborative work on the history of Russian art, of which the fourth volume deals with architecture, sculpture, painting, and other arts of the seventeenth century. Along with the general work of D. S. Likhachev there have been several monographs on individual artists formerly overlooked or barely mentioned in historical literature. For example, M. A. Il'in published a monograph on the noted Russian architect Ia. G. Bukhvostov.[45]

[45]D. S. Likhachev, *Kultura russkogo naroda.* (Moscow, 1961). M. A. Il'in, *Zodchii Iakov Bukhvostov.* (Moscow, 1959). M. A. Il'in, *Riazan.* (Moscow, 1945). S. V. Bessonov, *Krepostnye arkhitektory.* (Moscow, 1938). V. N. Podkliuchnikov, *Tri pamiatnika XVII stoletiia.* (Moscow, 1945).

Among the seventeenth-century political thinkers should be included the name of Iurii Krizhanich. He has often been discussed in Soviet historical literature, and just as often misinterpreted, because of the failure to evaluate him in a proper perspective. Instead of placing Krizhanich in a correct historical setting, writers usually force him into a Procrustean bed of a Marxist type. Lately L. N. Pushkarev challenged the unjustified criticism of Krizhanich and called for a reevaluation of his role in Russian, as well as eastern European, history. Under the influence of a public discussion that followed, A. L. Goldberg and L. Mordukhovich published articles on Krizhanich: the former analyzed Krizhanich's views of seventeenth-century Russian society, while the latter presented Krizhanich's concept of feudalism. V. G. Mirzoev, on the other hand, presented Krizhanich's views as symptomatic of bourgeois interpretation![46]

An outstanding monographic work on the socio-political atmosphere among the peasantry during the first half of the eighteenth century was produced by P. K. Alefirenko. The subject assumed special importance in view of the fact that the theme was discussed in a proper historical perspective. Alefirenko examines the ideological developments within Russia during the eighteenth century and makes a special effort to analyze the views of M. V. Lomonosov, V. N. Tatishchev, A. D. Kantemir, and other prominent personalities of the time, particularly as they concern the peasantry. There is also a monograph by M. I. Radovskii on Kantemir and the Academy of Sciences at St. Petersburg, and another study of more general nature by Ia. D. Beliaev, concerning Russian socio-political and philosophical development during the first half of the eighteenth century, a complementary work to the others mentioned above.[47]

Finally, in connection with the awakened consciousness in Russian social thought and nationalism, should be added the name of M. V. Lomonosov. Soviet society recently marked the 250th anniversary of his birth, prompting much to be said and written about him. In the early 1960's there appeared a four-volume collaborative study of Lomonosov as a scholar, historian, and scientist. Several new points were brought out. For instance, it was learned that Lomonosov came under the influence of Professor Junker while he attended the University of Freiburg. One writer, I. D. Glazunov, came to

---

[46]L. N. Pushkarev, "Ob otsenke deiatelnosti Iuriia Krizhanicha." *Voprosy istorii,* No. 1 (1957), 77-86. "Obsuzhdenie voprosa o deiatelnosti Iu. Krizhanicha." *Voprosy istorii,* No. 2 (1957), 202-206. A. L. Goldberg, "Iurii Krizhanich o russkom obshchestve serediny XVII v." *Istoriia SSSR,* No. 6 (1960), 71-84. L. Mordukhovich, "Anti-feodalnaia kontseptsiia Iu. Krizhanicha." *Kratkie soobshcheniia Instituta slavianovedeniia,* No. 26 (1958), 25-49. L. Mordukhovich, *Ocherki istorii ekonomicheskikh uchenii.* (Moscow, 1957). V. G. Mirzoev, *Prisoedinenie i osvoenie Sibiri v istoricheskoi literature XVII v.* (Moscow, 1956), 165-186.

[47]P. K. Alefirenko, *Krestianskoe dvizhenie i krestianskii vopros v 30-50kh godakh XVIII v.* (Moscow, 1958). M. I. Radovskii, *Antiokh Kantemir i Peterburgskaia Akademiia nauk.* (Moscow, 1959). I. D. Beliaev, *Obshchestvenno-politicheskaia i filosofskaia mysl' v Rossii v pervoi polovine XVIII v.* (Saransk, 1959).

regard Lomonosov as the "founder of Russian materialistic philosophy";
others regarded him as the founder of modern Russian science and the
Benjamin Franklin of Russia.[48]

[48]M. V. Lomonosov, *Polnoe sobranie sochinenii*. (Moscow, 1950-1959). 10 vols. I. D.
Glazunov, M. V. *Lomonosov—osnovopolozhnik russkoi materialisticheskoi filosofii.*
(Moscow, 1961). M. V. Lomonosov, *Sochineniia.* Commentaries by A. A. Morozov.
(Leningrad, 1961). *Lomonosov. Sbornik statei i materialov.* (Moscow, 1960). 4
vols. M. V. Lomonosov, *Izbrannye filosofskie proizvedeniia.* (Moscow, 1950).

CHAPTER VIII

The Revolutionary Movement

A. SOCIAL AND REVOLUTIONARY THOUGHT
1800 - 1850

Historians whose field of study is the development of modern Russian libertarian ideas commonly agree that the pioneering figure of the movement is A. N. Radishchev, author of the well-known *Journey from Petersburg to Moscow*.[1] Liberal ideas in Russian thought have been largely inspired by events in France. M. M. Shtrangé has been preoccupied with the degree of influence the French Revolution had had upon Russian society at the end of the eighteenth century.[2] Others have focused on certain individuals who represent Russian society, such as Radishchev, citing his student experiences abroad, or his keen observations and deep concern with conditions at home. Among those who contributed to the study of Radishchev and the early ranks of the Russian intelligentsia, and who utilized fully the latest sources, are G. R. Makogonenko, A. Startsev, L. B. Svetlov, and many others.[3] These students of history have added a great deal of biographical detail which renders a full-length picture of Radishchev's life and his personality, as well as of his social philosophy. Despite all the recent literature, there are still some aspects that are not too clear. For illustration, Radishchev's view of the peasant problem, the constitutional concepts in which he was keenly interested—these are matters that have been frequently discussed and differently interpreted by many writers. Precisely what was the basic purpose of Radishchev's *Journey*? Was it purely a literary expression, a "social journey,"

[1]A. N. Radishchev, *Puteshestvie iz Peterburga v Moskvu.* (Moscow, 1935). Vol. I is a photolithographic reproduction of the original publication of 1790. Vol. II contains materials for the study of the *Journey* as well as two works on Radishchev by Ia. L. Barskov and M. V. Zhizhka.

[2]*A. N. Radishchev. Materialy i issledovaniia.* (Moscow, Academy of Sciences, 1936), (This volume contains most pertinent materials on Radishchev.) M. M. Shtrangé, *Russkoe obshchestvo i Frantsuzskaia revoliutsiia 1789-1794 gg.* (Moscow, 1956).

[3]G. P. Makogoneko, *Radishchev i ego vremia.* (Moscow, 1956). A. Startsev, *Universitetskie gody Radishcheva.* (Moscow, 1956). A. Startsev, *Radishchev v gody 'Puteshestviia'.* (Moscow, 1960). L. B. Svetlov, *A. N. Radishchev.* (Moscow, 1958). D. S. Babkina, *Biografiia A. N. Radishcheva, napisannaia ego synoviami.* (Moscow, 1959). See also studies of a more general nature: Iu. Ia. Kogan, *Prosvetitel XVIII veka P. Kozelskii.* (Moscow, 1958). M. T. Beliavskii, "Zarozhdenie prosvetitelstva v Rossii." *Nauchnye doklady vysshei shkoly. Istoricheskie nauki.* No. 3 (1958), 27-46. N. M. Usunova, "Iz istorii formirovaniia krepostnoi intelligentsii." *Ezhegodnik Gosudarstvennogo istoricheskogo muzeia.* (Moscow, 1960), 106-134.

or a disguised appeal to peasants to rebel against the unbearable conditions Radishchev graphically describes? Over these questions the journal *Voprosy filosofii* carried on a lively discussion for nearly three years (1955-1958). The general impression one is able to gather from the articles is that the revolutionary philosophy of Radishchev is tightly interwoven with the complex sociological and revolutionary conditions that prevailed at the time the *Journey* had been written. This in turn is an aid in understanding the political ideas Radishchev had endeavored to disseminate through his writings, and for which he paid in the end with exile, and eventually suicide.[4]

There are many other problems involved in any effort to interpret the personality and work of Radishchev. For example, to what extent had the Pugachev rebellion influenced Radishchev's thinking, or inspired him to write his *Journey*? How well was he familiar with conditions of the peasantry at home or in western Europe? Projecting events beyond the time of Radishchev, one is tempted to query further as to the degree of influence Radishchev and his tragic end had upon the following generations, particularly upon the Decembrists, or the generation of the 1840's.[5]

In recent years, new documentary evidence on Radishchev has been uncovered, but has not been fully utilized to date. There has appeared some information concerning his participation in student unrest while he attended the University of Leipzig. The episode suggests that there might still be revealed more evidence that will shed further light on his personality, his political views, and the purpose of his famous book.

Students of the liberal movement during the early part of the nineteenth century have spent much time debating periodization, at the same time that they have broadened interpretation of the entire subject. It has been commonly accepted that the first stage of the liberal movement was the period from the beginning of the last century to 1861. This would include the early "aristocratic" phase followed by the movement of the "intelligentsia" against autocracy. The first stage and the most investigated one was the Decembrist movement, which originated among the aristocratic army officers, who formed secret societies in the north and later in the south. The culmination of this period was the decisive defeat of the Decembrists on the Senate Square in 1825.

A full account of the Decembrist movement and revolt is best presented by M. V. Nechkina, in her two-volume work published in 1958. This work summarizes the labor of all the Soviet historians who investigated the subject for at least four decades. All the documentary evidence that was pub-

[4]Iu. F. Kariakin and E. G. Plimak, "O nekotorykh spornykh problemakh mirovozzreniia Radishcheva." *Istoricheskie zapiski,* No. 66 (1960), 137-205.

[5]P. N. Berkov, "Nekotorye spornye voprosy sovremennogo izucheniia zhizni i tvorchestva A. N. Radishcheva." *XVIII Vek.* Sbornik IV. (Moscow, 1959), 172-205. M. T. Beliavskii, "Iz istorii ideinoi borby A. N. Radishcheva." *Istoriia SSSR,* No. 6 (1960), 121-130. *Russkie prosvetiteli. Ot Radishcheva do dekabristov. Sobranie proizvedenii.* (Moscow, 1966). 2 vols.

lished prior to 1917, as well as the new material that had appeared since that date, was most carefully examined and utilized. What remains to be learned by those who still search for new evidence on this period is largely the episodic events, by-products of the main movement, and biographical sketches of less active participants.[6]

Among recent works on the Decembrists that are worthy of attention is that of S. S. Volk, entitled *Istoricheskie vzgliady dekabristov,* a study that has stimulated a good deal of discussion among Soviet historians. Volk's book is as original in interpretation as it is in breadth. The author points out first the deep interest all the Decembrists had demonstrated, without exception, in the field of history. He painstakingly points out the general concepts of history held by the Decembrists, and the interpretations they gave to world history. Being cosmopolitan as well as nationalist, they regarded Russia's past as an inseparable part of world history; for this reason they often drew heavily from ancient, medieval, and modern history as illustrative evidence. Fighting against serfdom and absolutism, they keenly appreciated the need of historical knowledge and lessons derived from the past of western Europe. And though some of them looked upon history as a form of belles lettres, their pursuit of historical study was strictly utilitarian. The reading and attention with which they followed historical literature of their time is sufficient evidence of their serious intentions. Volk compares some of the views held by the Decembrists with those currently held in Russia and in western Europe; he shows how advanced the leading Decembrists, these children of the Romantic Age, were. Some of their theories betray their romantic notions, such as their views of the *veche* or the popular assembly of Novgorod, which they idealized to the point of distortion. Nor were they realistic about or familiar with the theories of the origin of serfdom. But these fallacies should not be held against them, considering the social origin of most of the Decembrists and the fact that they were almost all military men. Unfortunately, the author fails to indicate clearly the actual link that tied the Decembrists to the liberals of the following decades—the 1830's and 1840's.[7]

The next logical period in the liberal movement is the second quarter of the nineteenth century, culminating with the events of 1848-1849. The effect

[6]M. V. Nechkina, *Dvizhenie dekabristov.* (Moscow, 1955). 2 vols. N. M. Chentsov, *Vosstanie dekabristov. Bibliografiia.* N. K. Piksanov, ed. (Moscow, 1929). R. G. Eimontova and A. A. Solennikova, *Dvizhenie dekabristov. Ukazatel literatury, 1928-1959.* M. V. Nechkina, ed. (Moscow, 1960). *Deiateli revoliutsionnogo dvizheniia v Rossii. Bio-bibliograficheskii slovar. Ot predshestvennikov dekabristov do padeniia tsarizma.* (Moscow, 1927-1934). Vols. I-III, V. (Vol. IV never appeared.)

[7]S. S. Volk, *Istoricheskie vzgliady dekabristov.* (Moscow, 1958). See also an article by the same author in *Voprosy istorii,* No. 12 (1950), 26-57. A. V. Predtechenskii, "Istoricheskie vzgliady dekabristov." *Ocherki istorii istoricheskoi nauki v SSSR.* (Moscow, 1955), Vol. I, 288-304. B. B. Kafengauz, "Ob istoricheskikh vzgliadakh dekabristov." *Doklady i soobshcheniia Instituta istorii Akademii nauk SSSR,* No. 10 (1956).

that the failure of the revolutions that took place throughout western Europe had upon Russia is best manifested by the sad fate of the Petrashevskii circle. The triumph of autocracy elsewhere forced a reexamination of many dearly cherished romantic ideas. Social changes led to corresponding ideological changes within the ranks of the liberals. The gentry kept contributing to the ranks of the intelligentsia or the *raznochinets* (rankless) elements; the vague liberal constitutional cravings of the aristocratic army officers yielded more to a bourgeois-democratic philosophy and a gradual crystallization of a modern revolutionary ideology.

Soviet writers have done extensive research on the liberal revolutionary ideas of the 1840's although most of them manifest a common weakness, forcing a standard interpretation into a narrow Marxist pattern. Some of the leading figures of the forties, such as Belinskii or Herzen, have been presented as veritable precursors of Soviet ideology—an artificial stretching of history, to say the least. Soviet historiography on this period also reveals a serious fallacy in underestimating the role of the discussion groups, the so-called salon literary circles and other "societies" which were engaged in camouflaged liberal activities during the second quarter of the nineteenth century.[8]

In 1958, I. A. Fedosov published a study which filled, in part, the need for new research in this area. Fedosov's monographic work is based on much new archival material. He authoritatively presents the story of revolutionary cricles such as the one led by the Kritskii brothers or by Sungurov during the 1820's and 1830's. Fedosov was the first to find evidence of formerly unknown societies such as the "Literary Evenings" in Novocherkassk, and of the secret circle that was formed in Orenburg in 1827. He deals with student societies in a number of universities during the late 1820's and the 1830's.

Fedosov's work, though admirable, cannot be regarded as definitive. There is need for further research in order to bring out the unity of purpose among the different circles or societies in which national figures like Belinskii, Herzen, Ogarev, and Petrashevskii had taken part. This would add to the history of the liberal movement a degree of continuity in place of the fragmentary, episodic form of narrative that we now have. The two schools of thought, the Slavophiles and the Westerners, should be fitted into a common pattern, constituting part of a larger national picture at a time of crisis. Only then could the role played by some of the leaders at this time be reexamined, and their place in the history of nineteenth-century Russian revolutionary thought be redefined. Such an attempt at a reexamination was made

[8]N. L. Brodskii, ed. *Literaturnye salony i kruzhki. Pervaia polovina XIX veka.* (Moscow, 1930).

[9]I. A. Fedosov, *Revoliutsionnoe dvizhenie v Rossii vo vtoroi chetverti XIX v. (Revoliutsionnye organizatsii i kruzhki).* (Moscow, 1958).

by I. Ia. Diakov, concerning the well-known literary critic of the past century, V. G. Belinskii.[10]

Many students who wrote on the mid-nineteenth century tended to oversimplify matters when they neatly explained that restless era in terms of a sharp rivalry between the two inimical camps—the "feudal-liberal" and the "revolutionary-democratic." Fedosov demolishes this interpretation by his argument that political thought during the middle of the past century was by no means as clearly crystallized into two camps as so many writers seem to have assumed. Herzen and, particularly, Belinskii already came to regard Slavophilism as the official ideology of the regime of Nicholas I, and nothing less. Fedosov leans toward the same view, though not as specifically or clearly as one would expect. Finally, in discussing the fateful year 1848, he devotes special attention to the Petrashevskii circle.

There seems to be a commonly accepted erroneous notion in Soviet historiography to overestimate the maturity and vigor of Russian revolutionary thought in the middle of the nineteenth century. Another error often repeated is the tendency to dissociate Russian ideological development from its fountainhead of revolutionary development in western Europe. The impression one gathers is that of a certain revolutionary parochialism, an intellectual movement that originated independently of developments in France, in the Germanic states, or anywhere else on the continent of Europe. Lately a few writers, Fedosov among them, have made an endeavor to broaden this view and stress more fully the Western impact upon Russian developments of the nineteenth century.[11]

The general weakness in the history of Russian social thought emanated mainly from the practice of measuring liberal movements of the first half of the past century by the writings of a few eminent figures, rather than the whole of their generation. Despite this error, many Soviet writers succeeded in contributing a good deal to nineteenth-century social history—for example, Iu. G. Oksman, who wrote on Belinskii, Herzen, and the Decembrists.

Oksman is a superb stylist and keen student of the social and literary history of the last century. His works represent the finest analytical interpretation of Pushkin and Belinskii. Having minutely examined all available sources, Oksman was able to pass sound judgment not only on what Belinskii professed or advocated, but on what he had failed to publish due to the severe

[10]I. Ia. Diakov, *Mirovozzrenie V. G. Belinskogo.* (Blagoveshchensk, Amurizdat, 1962). I. Ia. Diakov, "K voprosu o protivorechiiakh v mirovozzrenii Belinskogo 1830kh godov." *Uchenye zapiski Blagoveshchesnkogo pedagogicheskogo instituta.* Vol. IX (1958).

[11]G. S. Vasetskii, *Belinskii—velikii myslitel i revoliutsioner-demokrat.* (Moscow, 1948). V. G. Baskakov, *Sotsialisticheskie vozzreniia V. G. Belinskogo.* (Moscow, 1948). D. I. Chesnokov, *Mirovossrenie Gertsena.* (Moscow, 1948). I. A. Fedosov, *Revoliutsionnoe dvizhenie v Rossii vo vtoroi polovine XIX v.* (*Revoliutsionnye organizatsii i kruzhki.*). (Moscow, 1958).

censorship of the time. Oksman presents Belinskii as an astute thinker as well as a writer and literary critic, a keen political philosopher as well as a supreme polemicist and social observer. Oksman also made an excellent textual study of many of Belinskii's writings, and identified some parts long ascribed to him as having been inserted arbitrarily, either by the censor or by someone else, but never written by Belinskii.

Oksman also analyzes Belinskii's close associates during the 1830's and 1840's, and the topics they discussed during their meetings. The entire study is based on a huge amount of archival records and censored material that only lately became available, and have now been incorporated in the writings of Belinskii. Oksman also shows that Belinskii was entirely familiar with the Decembrist movement. He discusses the degree of "reconciliation with reality" he had made, his opinion of utopian socialism in western Europe, and even his possible acquaintance with the early writings of Marx. He also devotes a good deal of space to the famous "Letter of Belinskii to Gogol," which Oksman regards as a kind of manifesto of nineteenth-century Russian liberal thought, a document which superbly reflects the intellectual atmosphere of the second quarter of the century.[12]

Another writer on Belinskii as a libertarian and revolutionary critic, M. Ia. Poliakov, has complemented the interpretation of Oksman. While Oksman presents a bibliographical study of Belinskii, Poliakov, on the other hand, examines mainly his critical essays and considers their historical value.[13] The title itself is revealing: *Vissarion Belinskii. Personality—Ideas—The Epoch.* The author devotes most of his study to events of the 1830's, and only smaller portions deal with the following decade. There is an absorbing account of the Belinskii circle, its membership and their main interests, and Belinskii's place in this small but influential group of intellectuals. The author shows the intellectual originality, the independent thinking and high critical faculty Belinskii had already demonstrated at an early age. Even more interesting, and no less important, is the chapter on Belinskii during the 1840's, of which so little has previously been discussed in literature. Of particular interest to students of history are the parts pertaining to the relations between the Belinskii circle and the Petrashevskii group. According to Poliakov, the members of the latter circle held Belinskii in high esteem, and regarded him as a most influential teacher. Poliakov, like Oksman, mentions the probability of Belinskii's acquaintance with the writings of Marx and his philosophy at this time. One chapter deals in great detail with the letter he

[12]Iu. G. Oksman, *Letopis zhizni i tvorchestva V. G. Belinskogo.* (Moscow, 1958). A. S. Nifontov, *Rossiia v 1848 g.* (Moscow, 1949). V. R. Leikina-Svirskaia, "Revoliutsionnaia praktika petrashevtsev." *Istoricheskie zapiski,* No. 47 (1954), 181-223. V. R. Leikina-Svirskaia, "O kharatere kruzhkov petrashevtsev." *Voprosy istorii,* No. 4, (1956), 96-106. N. V. Minaeva, "Idei utopicheskogo sotsializma vo vzgliadakh petrashevtsev." *Uchenye zapiski Moskovskogo gorodskogo pedagogicheskogo instituta,* Vol. 78, Issue 5 (1957).

[13]M. Ia. Poliakov, *Vissarion Belinskii. Lichnost—idei—epokha.* (Moscow, 1960).

sent to Gogol that caused a public sensation. Finally, Poliakov cites original evidence showing the influence Belinskii had exercised on literary activities, as well as upon public opinion, in Russia during the 1840's.[14]

For a long time, historical literature lacked an authoritative study of N. P. Ogarev, the collaborator and close friend of A. Herzen throughout his life. This was most likely due to the fact that it was not until 1956 that Ogarev's writings were published for the first time, in a two-volume work entitled *Selected Socio-political and Philosophical Writings*. At about the same time, three volumes of *Literaturnoe nasledstvo* (Vols. 61-63) incorporated some of Ogarev's formerly unknown writings. The recent appearance of two works on Ogarev, one by M. V. Iakovlev and another by V. A. Putintsev, represent a most welcome contribution to historical literature. The most interesting parts to the student of history, in each of these works, are those concerning the formation of Ogarev's philosophy prior to his travels abroad, and his close friendship with Herzen, Belinskii, and other prominent figures of the time. Both authors also include original views on Ogarev's activities during the 1860's, while he was in western Europe.[15]

Another outstanding work is P. O. Zaionchkovskii's description of the secret Cyril-Methodius Society. It appeared originally in 1947, and was later revised and considerably expanded to become a classic piece of research. The subject had been dealt with before, but documentary evidence on this clandestine organization in the south was extremely scarce, as is clearly shown by the admirable bibliography that accompanies the study.[16]

The history of the Cyril-Methodius Society, as presented by Zaionchkovskii, includes a detailed discussion of the origin of the secret organization, its membership, its ideological basis, the tactics adopted, and, finally, the arrest and trial of its members. Using the latest sources, the author discusses the individual members, twelve of them, including the well-known Ukrainian poet Taras Shevchenko. The role of Shevchenko is somewhat problematic, since the evidence is quite contradictory to what has been asserted officially or personally by the poet himself. Earlier writers regarded Shevchenko as one of the leading members of the Cyril-Methodius Society, a view Zaionchkovskii insists is entirely fallacious. He analyzes minutely

---

[14] On the subject of Belinskii and Petrashevskii, see a most scholarly essay by A. M. Ardabatskaia, "Idei Belinskogo kak odin iz istochnikov formirovaniia revoliutsionnogo demokratizma petrashevtsev." *Uchenye zapiski Saratovskogo gosudarstvennogo universiteta*, Vol. 168 (1959). See also the review of Poliakov's monograph in *Voprosy istorii*, No. 8 (1961), by L. E. Iakobson. On the subject of the influence Belinskii enjoyed in Russia see the monograph of V. I. Kuleshov, *'Otechestvennye zapiski' i literatura 40kh godov XIX v.* (Moscow, 1958).

[15] M. V. Iakovlev, *Mirovozzrenie N. P. Ogareva*. (Moscow, 1957). See review of this work by V. A. Putintsev, in *Voprosy filosofii*, No. 7 (1958), 124-129. V. A. Putintsev, *N. P. Ogarev*. (Moscow, 1959). See review of Putintsev's work by N. Oś - makov in *Russkaia literatura*, No. 2 (1960).

[16] P. A. Zaionchkovskii, *Kirillo-Mefodievskoe obshchestvo*. (Moscow, 1959).

the program of the Society, including a document entitled "Divine Law" (*Zakon bozhii*), composed by, according to Zaionchkovskii, the well-known historian N. I. Kostomarov.

Zaionchkovskii holds that two intellectual trends of the time had a profound influence on the Cyril-Methodius Society: one was Christian socialism; the other was nationalism, best demonstrated by the strong aspiration the Society expressed in favor of liberation of the Ukraine "from oppression and ties to feudalism." The program was clearly anti-absolutism and anti-serfdom, and the Society hoped that its aims might be attained by peaceful means, through reforms, rather than by violence. However, other historians have assumed that the pacifist character of the Society was by no means unanimously accepted, and that some members considered violence entirely unavoidable. Zaionchkovskii fails to deal with the Slavophile influence upon the Cyril-Methodius Society, though it has been commonly agreed that the impact of Slavophilism is clearly apparent. A debatable subject is the role of Taras Shevchenko in the activities of the Society. Some historians consider his membership as rather passive, while others maintain that it was characterized by active support and unquestionable loyalty.[17]

B. REVOLUTIONARY DEVELOPMENTS DURING THE 1850's AND EARLY 1860's

Immediately after the Soviet Revolution, the study of serfdom, especially the final decline and fall of that institution, was dealt with almost exclusively under the influence of M. N. Pokrovskii. His general history, his special study *The Peasant Reforms,* his numerous articles, lectures, and symposiums, all had influenced the early cadres of history students. Pokrovskii viewed the "anti-feudal movement" as the earliest sign of the rise of Russian democratic opinion; it also served as a symptom of the decline of absolutism and a bourgeois trend in Russian society rather than a socio-economic crisis. He considered the peasant movement a condition which accelerated the reforms of the nineteenth century, but he continued to believe that the period from the ascendancy of Alexander II to the Emancipation Proclamation was a time of relatively "peaceful awaiting." The vacillation in official policies during this period Pokrovskii ascribed to dissent among the ruling elements as to a means of solving the problems that were rapidly reaching a climactic critical point, rather than the rise of a revolutionary crisis.

Thus for a long time Pokrovskii, while explaining the reform of 1861, viewed the situation quite differently from the official party line, namely, "the true concept of the revolutionary situation and the relationship between reform and revolution." This led, according to his critics, to his

[17]I. A. Fedosov, *Revoliutsionnoe dvizhenie v Rossii vo vtoroi chetverti XIX v.* (Moscow, 1968), 209. See also review of Zaionchkovskii's study in *Voprosy istorii,* No. 2 (1960), 190-194. V. N. Rozental, "Peterburgskii kruzhok K. D. Kavelina v kontse 40kh—nachale 50kh godov XIX v." *Uchenye zapiski Riazanskogo pedagogicheskogo instituta,* Vol. XVI (1957). V. N. Rozental, "Pervoe otkrytoe vystuplenie russkikh liberalov v 1855-1856 gg." *Istoriia SSSR,* No. 2 (1958), 113-130.

erroneous evaluation of the class basis underlying the revolutionary movement among the intelligentsia, whom Pokrovskii labelled as mere petty-
bourgeois intellectuals. For the same reason he came to regard political
groupings of the 1860's and 1870's as analogous with twentieth-century
political parties, and to regard Chernyshevskii as the forerunner of Menshe-
vism. Pokrovskii had also neglected the history of the "Land and Freedom"
movement of the 1860's and Chernyshevskii's long struggle for the unity of
all democratic forces in Russia.[18]

During his later years, Pokrovskii came to alter his interpretation, as witnessed in his articles on Chernyshevskii and the peasant movement on the
eve of the Emancipation Proclamation.[29] He came to link the reforms with
the massive struggle of the peasantry, while he labelled Chernyshevskii the
"speaking trumpet of peasant indignation." This has seldom been noted by
Soviet historians, who, during the late 1930's, led a most virulent anti-
Pokrovskii campaign. The Stalinist henchmen were deliberately silent on
Lenin's views, with which Pokrovskii was thoroughly familiar, as is clearly
shown by his references to Lenin on various occasions.[20]

Since 1934 many posthumous attacks have been made on Pokrovskii.
Yet despite the violent criticism to which the great mentor had been subjected, no definitive study on the subject for which he was so severely chas-
tised seems to have appeared as an acceptable substitute. In 1940, a college
textbook entitled *Russia in the XIX Century* was published. This volume
included a chapter by M. V. Nechkina on Chernyshevskii during the years
of the "revolutionary situation," 1858-1861. For the first time in Soviet
historiography, Nechkina, instead of polemicizing about Pokrovskii, undertook to analyze the general theme more seriously. Other studies soon followed, among which stands out the monographic work of Sh. M. Levin
published in 1958.[21] Levin makes a pioneering endeavor to analyze the
revolutionary atmosphere on the eve of the Reform and shortly after. He
includes a careful discussion of Chernyshevskii, Dobroliubov, and Herzen,
and of their contributions to the revolutionary movement; he also attempts to
explain the causes of unrest among the intelligentsia and their relationship
to the "Land and Freedom" movement. The monograph is based on hard

[18]M. V. Nechkina, "N. G. Chernyshevskii v borbe za splochenie sil russkogo demokraticheskogo dvizheniia v gody revoliutsionnoi situatsii (1859-1861)." *Voprosy
istorii*, No. 7 (1953), 56-73.

[19]*Istorik-marksist*, No. 10 (1928). M. N. Pokrovskii, "Po povodu Narodnoi Voli."
Istorik-marksist, No. 15 (1930), 74-86.

[20]Note particularly the unwarranted attack on Pokrovskii by S. Bushuev in the two-
volume collaborative publication entitled *Protiv antimarksistskoi kontseptsii Pokrovskogo*. (Moscow, 1940). Here the author accuses Pokrovskii of ignoring Lenin's
interpretation of the revolutionary situation on the eve of the Great Reforms.

[21]M. V. Nechkina, ed., *Istoriia SSSR*. (Moscow, 1940). Chapter 21 in Part II is by
Nechkina, "Rossiia v XIX v." See also Sh. M. Levin, *Obshchestvennoe dvizhenie
v Rossii v 60-70kh godakh XIX v.* (Moscow, 1958).

evidence derived from primary and secondary sources. It also pursues a discussion of the relationship between the revolutionary ideologies and the abolition of serfdom, as well as their impact upon the developments of the 1870's. Levin's thesis emphasizes chiefly the situation in Russia proper, and makes only occasional references to the Ukraine, White Russia, or Poland.

A group of scholars at the Institute of History of the Academy of Sciences, led by M. V. Nechkina, attempted to expand this field in 1958. As a result, the first volume of a collaborative work appeared in 1960, including a series of essays under the title "The Revolutionary Situation in Russia in 1859-1861." Most of these scholars have concentrated on the narrower aspects of the subject, with the exception of S. A. Tokarev, who made with considerable success a more general survey, encompassing the entire field under discussion.[22]

The term "revolutionary situation, 1859-1861" usually refers, in Soviet historical literature, to the general crisis in the feudal-serf system during this period. The inadequate supply of land for the peasantry, so runs the explanation, was bound to undermine the very economic basis upon which the entire system was supposed to have been built. It was intensified by the encroachment of the landlord class upon the communal lands claimed by the peasants, the reduction of allotments, and the continuous splintering of peasant households, which undermined the agrarian economic system further at an increasing rate. The net result was an increased antagonism between peasantry and gentry. The combined socio-economic contradictions formed the prerequisites of the general revolutionary situation.

A large number of historians were devoting their attention to this period in the 1930's, but there were even more in the 1950's. Some writers concentrated on the economic prerequisites of the revolutionary situation in various localities of Russia proper, in the Ukraine, Lithuania, or western White Russia.[23]

[22]See review of this volume in *Istoriia SSSR*, No. 4 (1961). S. A. Tokarev, *Revoliutsionnaia situatsiia v Rossii 1859-61 gg.* (Moscow, 1958). M. V. Nechkina, "N. G. Chernyshevskii i A. I. Gertsen v gody revoliutsionnoi situatsii (1859-1861)." *Izvestiia Akademii nauk SSSR. Otdel literatury i iazyka*, Vol. 13, Issue 1 (Moscow, 1954). M. V. Nechkina, "O vzaimo-otnosheniiakh peterburgskogo i londonskogo tsentrov russkogo osvoboditelnogo dvizheniia v gody revoliutsionnoi situatsii (1859-1861 gg.)." *Izvestiia Akademii nauk SSSR. Otdel literatury i iazyka*, Vol. 14, Issue 2 (Moscow, 1955). A. E. Koshovenko, "Gertsen i liberaly v period revoliutsionnoi situatsii (1859-1861)." *Uchenye zapiski Akademii obshchestvennykh nauk*, Issue 36. (Moscow, 1958). G. I. Ionova, "Voskresnye shkoly v gody pervoi revoliutsionnoi situatsii (1859-1861)." *Istoricheskie zapiski*, No. 57 (1956), 177-209. B. S. Ginzburg, " 'Kolokol' A. I. Gertsena i krestianskoe dvizhenie v Rossii v gody pervoi revoliutsionnoi situatsii (1859-1896 gg.)." *Istoriia SSSR*, No. 5 (1957), 173-187. Ia. I. Linkov, "O politicheskoi programme Chernyshevskogo v period revoliutsionnoi situatsii 1859-1861 gg." *Voprosy istorii*, No. 5 (1955), 110-116.

[23]I. D. Kovalchenko, *Krestiane i krepostnoe khoziaistvo Riazanskoi i Tambovskoi gubernii v pervoi polovine XIX veka (k istorii krizisa feodalno-krepostnicheskoi sistemy*

There appeared some noteworthy articles on the same theme by prominent Soviet historians, such as N. M. Druzhinin, V. K. Iatsunskii, and P. G.
Ryndziunskii.[24] Even more was written on the mass movement of the
peasantry. This was a field officially encouraged and made attractive by the
fact that a vast amount of archival material was opened for research.[25]
Some historians successfully digested the vast bulk of information available

khoziaistva). (Moscow, 1959). Iu. V. Kozhukhov, "Pomeshchich'e khoziaistvo
tsentralnogo zemledelcheskogo raiona Rossii v gody krizisa krepostnoi sistemy."Uchenye zapiski Leningradskogo pedagogicheskogo instituta (LGPI) im. A. I. Gertsena.
Istoricheskii fakultet, Vol. 102. (Leningrad, 1955). N. N. Ulashchik, "Obezzemelivanie krestian Litvy i Zapadnoi Belorussii nakanune otmeny krepostnogo prava."
Sbornik. Revoliutsionnaia situatsiia v Rossii v 1859-1861 gg. (Moscow, 1960). A. Z.
Baraboi, "Obezzemelivanie pomeshchikami krestian Kievskoi i Podolskoi gubernii nakanune i v period revoliutsionnoi situatsii 1859-1861 gg." Sbornik. Revoliutsionnaia
situatsiia v Rossii v 1859-1861 gg. (Moscow, 1960).

[24]N. M. Druzhinin, "Konflikt mezhdu proizvoditelnymi silami i feodalnymi otnosheni-
iami nakanune reformy 1861 goda." Voprosy istorii, No. 7 (1954), 56-76. V. K.
Iatsunskii, "Genezis kapitalizma v selskom khoziaistve Rossii." Ezhegodnik po
agrarnoi istorii Vostochnoi Evropy, 1959 g. (Moscow, 1961). P. G. Ryndziunskii,
"O melkotovarnom uklade v Rossii XIX veka." Istoriia SSSR, No. 2 (1961), 48-70.

[25]E. A. Morokhovets, ed., Krestianskoe dvizhenie 1827-1869 gg. Issues 1-2 (Moscow,
1931). Krestianskoe dvizhenie v 1861 godu posle otmeny krepostnogo prava. E. A.
Morokhovets and M. M. Druzhinin, eds. Parts I-II. Doneseniia svitskikh generalov i
fligel-adiutantov, gubernskikh prokurorov i uezdnykh striapchikh. (Moscow, 1949).
S. N. Valk, ed., Otmena krepostnogo prava. Doklady ministrov vnutrennikh del o
provedenii krestianskoi reformy, 1861-1862 gg. (Moscow, 1950). Bezdnenskoe
vosstanie 1861 g. Sbornik dokumentov. (Kazan, 1948). Krestianskoe dvizhenie v
Belorussii posle otmeny krepostnogo prava (1861-1862). Dokumenty i materialy.
(Minsk, 1959. O. Ia. Vares, Iu. Iu. Kakhk, Kh. A. Piirimiae, and V. M. Fainshtein,
eds. Krestianskoe dvizhenie v Estonii. Introduction by Iu. Iu. Kakhk. Istoricheskii
arkhiv, No. 4 (1958). "O pravitelstvennykh merakh dlia podavleniia narodnykh
volnenii v period otmeny krepostnogo prava. Publikatsiia dokumentov 1857-1861
gg." Introduction by P. A. Zaionchkovskii. Istoricheskii arkhiv, No. 1 (1957).
There are many published documents in the Krasnyi arkhiv, Istoricheskii arkhiv, and
other historical publications. On local developments see the following: V. P. Kri-
kunov, Sovmestnaia borba russkikh i kabardinskikh krestian protiv feodalnogo gneta
v 60-kh godakh XIX veka. (Nal'chik, 1956). E. N. Sedova, "Borba pomeshchichikh
krestian tsentralno-chernozemnykh gubernii za zemliu v 1861-1865 gg." Voprosy istorii, No. 4 (1956), 115-124. D. I. Budaev, "Krestianskoe dvizhenie v Smolenskoi
gubernii v 1861-1863 gg." Materialy po izucheniiu Smolenskoi oblasti, Issue 2
(Smolensk, 1957). M. B. Friedman, Otmena krepostnogo prava v Belorussii. (Minsk,
1958). G. T. Riabkov, "Massovoe dvizhenie v Smolenskoi gubernii v pervyi period
revoliutsionnoi situatsii." Revoliutsionnaia situatsiia v Rossii v 1859-1861 gg. (Moscow, 1960). L. N. Bakusova, "Krestianskoe dvizhenie nakanune reformy 1861 goda

and presented well-coordinated accounts of national conditions. Ia. I. Linkov, who wrote a history of the Russian peasant movement during the period 1828-1861, was able to do so.[26] Though it did not have the advantage of some of the sources published later, the work of Linkov is an impressive scholarly achievement, and deserves to be brought up to date by incorporating the latest sources. On the other hand, M. E. Naidenov dealt with a shorter period, with peasant uprisings on the eve of the reform of 1861. This serves as a supplement to Linkov's study, even though it fails to incorporate information about some of the unrest that preceded the Emancipation Proclamation.[27]

The general conditions in Russia during the early 1860's and the peasant movement are well handled by M. N. Leshchenko. The author attempts to present a more general picture of conditions in the Ukraine, perhaps the first of its kind in Ukrainian historiography. Having first analyzed local conditions, Leshchenko endeavors to stress the organic interrelationship between peasant unrest and the enforcement of the reform. His monograph is based on a mass of first-hand sources. He also raised a problem rarely dealt with in Soviet historiography, the influence of Polish national and social developments resulting from events of the early 1860's.[28]

Despite the numerous monographs on the mid-nineteenth century that appeared between 1940 and the middle of the 1960's, the subject is open to further research. It still calls for an overall treatment that will integrate all the events into some meaningful national pattern. Equally important is tracing the wider implications of the reforms, as they bear upon the peripheral areas, as well as upon the Empire at large. The administration of national archival institutions, in cooperation with the Institute of History of the Academy of Sciences, has been engaged in further examination of source materials related to peasant conditions during the significant years 1859-1861. Such work demands improved archival methodology, an overall plan or purpose as well as standardization of nomenclature used frequently and carelessly, such as "peasant struggle," "revolutionary situation," or "mass resistance." There should be further gathering of statistical data concerning local revolts, and the results should be integrated into a more meaningful description of national events. A modest endeavor along this

v tsentralno-chernozemnykh guberniiakh Rossii (1856-1860 gg.)." *Uchenye zapiski Pskovskogo pedagogicheskogo instituta*, Issue 6 (1958).

[26]Ia. I. Linkov, *Ocherki istorii krestianskogo dvizheniia v Rossii v 1828-1861 gg.* (Moscow, 1952).

[27]M. E. Naidenov, *Klassovaia borba v poreformennoi derevne (1861-1863 gg.).* (Moscow, 1955).

[28]M. N. Leshchenko, *Krestianskoe dvizhenie na Ukraine v sviazi s provedeniem reformy 1861 g. 60e gody XIX st.* (Kiev, 1959).

line was admirably initiated by S. A. Tokarev, but further spadework remains in bringing together the scattered source materials.[29]

Thus far, most of the research has dealt with unrest among peasants who belonged to individual landlords, but there is a conspicuous lack in the study of the emancipated state and apanage serfs. Nor is there to be found an entirely satisfactory description of the conditions in towns and cities. There is sufficient evidence of social unrest during 1860-1862 in Lithuania, in the Ukraine (particularly in the western part), and in White Russia.

An interesting peripheral study concerns the impact of general unrest upon the Russian army, about which V. A. Fedorov has written a fairly lucid account covering the period 1840-1860.[30]

C. REVOLUTIONARY DEVELOPMENTS
SINCE THE 1860's

One Soviet historians estimated in 1960 that since 1945 no less than 1,348 works have been devoted to the period 1859-1861.[31] Of these, the bulk have been interpretations of Chernyshevskii, Herzen, Dobroliubov, and a few others. Even Soviet scholars are inclined to believe that there is hardly any further need for additional works in this particular field.

Study of this revolutionary period began early. In 1897, the eminent Russian émigré Vladimir Burtsev published a volume in London under the title of *Za sto let* (One Hundred Years), describing social and political movements in Russia. Shortly afterwards there appeared the publication *Sources of the History of the Revolutionary Movement in Russia in the Sixties.* This was accompanied by a compilation, *State Crimes in Russia,* under the editorship of V. Bazilevskii (V. Bogucharskii). These publications touched briefly on various episodes of nineteenth-century revolutionary events, including the fall of serfdom. The same publications included extracts from A. I. Herzen's *Kolokol* (The Bell), extracts from underground publications in Russia, and proceedings of court trials of political criminals. But these were totally inadequate to give a full picture of the various revolutionary organizations, their activities, or their programs. They gave an impression of scattered, sporadic activities of various disorganized groups, isolated individuals, always struggling futilely against autocracy, squabbling among themselves over minor issues rather than for the common cause— the overthrow of autocracy.

[29]S. A. Tokarev, "O chislennosti krestianskikh vystuplenii v Rossii v gody pervoi revoliutsionnoi situatsii." *Sbornik. Revoliutsionnaia situatsii v Rossii v 1859-1861 gg.* (Moscow, 1960).

[30]V. A. Fedorov, *Obshchestvenno-politicheskoe dvizhenie v russkoi armii v 1840-1860 godakh.* (Moscow, 1958).

[31]N. I. Mukhina, "Izuchenie sovetskimi istorikami revoliutsionnoi situatsii 1859-1861 gg." *Sbornik. Revoliutsionniaia situatsiia v Rossii v 1859-1861 gg.* (Moscow, 1960).

During the brief period of political relaxation in Russia, 1905-1907, when some limited archival materials became available to the public, M. Lemke brought out a fuller account of the proceedings of famed political trials, involving such prominent figures as D. I. Pisarev, N. G. Chernyshevskii, and M. I. Mikhailov.[32] In addition, Lemke undertook the publication of the complete works and letters of A. I. Herzen, a pioneering enterprise of considerable value. It was of great assistance to writers who dealt with the liberal movement in Russia. Lemke also published a selection of archival sources and reminiscences of early revolutionaries such as A. A. Sleptsov. These describe, though briefly, the origin and activities of the underground organization "Land and Freedom." But the selection was often arbitrary or restricted because of limited availability of material, which from an historical point of view makes the collection inadequate and reduces its value for research purposes. Lemke, for instance, did not hesitate to publish the memoirs of A. A. Sleptsov and his own accounts of discussions with the author. The only problem is, which are the genuine memoirs and which the discussions? It is often difficult to distinguish between them, since Lemke incorporated both into a single piece and often cites both out of context. It was only after 1917 that many of these records were brought to light and became subject to more scholarly scrutiny.

Another case is that of the valuable memoirs of N. V. Shelgunov, on the revolutionary activities of the 1860's, originally published in 1891. In their original form, these were badly mutilated by the censor, and the unexpurgated edition was first published in 1923.[33] During the same year an attempt was made to publish a series of other documents related to the 1860's. For some inexplicable reason, only one volume appeared on the political trials of that decade, followed by no others.[34] Soon after, there were published a variety of documents on the revolutionary developments of the 1860's, in such irregular publications as *Byloe, Katorga i ssylka,* and *Krasnyi arkhiv,* all of them terminated at one time or another during the Stalinist regime. These documents, useful as they are to the student of history, were reduced in value by their sporadic rate of appearance, their fragmentary nature, casualness in selection, and lack of expert editing and of helpful glossaries. The numerous underground publications, pamphlets, appeals, manifestoes, and correspondence all call for a fully systematized, annotated, and properly indexed publication.

The fragmentary, scattered records, buried in numerous regular and irregular periodicals, are still of inestimable value since they shed abundant light

---

[32]M. Lemke, *Politicheskie protsessy M. I. Mikhailova, D. I. Pisareva, N. G. Chernyshevskogo.* (Moscow, 1907).

[33]N. V. Shelgunov, *Vospominaniia.* Ed. with introductory chapter and comments by A. A. Shilov. (Moscow, 1923).

[34]V. P. Alekseev, comp., B. P. Kozmin, ed., *Politicheskie protsessy shestidesiatykh godov.* (Moscow, 1923).

179

upon the underground political activities of the period. What have been successfully published to date are primarily the complete writings of N. G. Chernyshevskii and A. I. Herzen, and a reproduction of Herzen's émigré magazine *Kolokol,* which is not yet completed. All these constitute a mass of diaries, letters, novels, important articles, personal notations, and correspondence, which represent a treasury of significant events, and add much to the understanding of the times and lives of men involved in these formative decades of Russian history. In 1939, the complete proceedings of the trial of Chernyshevskii, appeared for the first time, adding many illuminating details concerning his personality as well as his era.[35]

Special reference should also be made to five volumes (Vols. 61-64 and Vol. 67) of the irregularly published journal *Literaturnoe nasledstvo.* These volumes incorporate archival materials of rare value on the social and political situation during the middle of the past century. The volumes include materials on Herzen and Ogarev, such as writings by them gathered from outside the Soviet Union, in various depositories in Prague and Sofia. The same volumes also incorporate formerly unknown documents on the revolutionary activities and social ideas of the 1860's. They include not only official documents of rare historical value, but articles and commentaries that are in themselves valuable, and based on profound, careful research. Cumulatively, these volumes represent a gold mine for students of the nineteenth-century political and social history of Russia and western Europe. Volume sixty-one contains new materials on the period of the reforms, found by M. V. Nechkina. The nature of these documents and an assessment of their historical value are discussed by Nechkina in a special report published in the *Izvestiia* of the Academy of Sciences.[36]

Voprosy istorii, the organ of Marxist historians, has on various occasions published articles and documentary materials on nineteenth-century secret organizations such as "Land and Freedom." It has also carried a variety of articles concerning A. I. Herzen, N. P. Ogarev, and the history of several clandestine societies and their internal tactical and ideological conflicts. Other publications, such as *Istoriia SSSR,* have from time to time published equally pertinent materials related to the same subject.[37]

[35]N. A. Alekseev, ed., *Protsess N. G. Chernyshevskogo. Arkhivnye dokumenty.* (Saratov, 1939).

[36]*Literaturnoe nasledstvo.* Vol. 61, *Gerzen i Ogarev,* Part 1 (Moscow, 1953). Vol. 62, Part 2 (Moscow, 1955). Vol. 63, Part 3 (Moscow, 1956). *Literaturnoe nasledstvo.* Vol. 64, *Gerzen v zagranichnykh kollektsiiakh.* (Moscow, 1958). *Literaturnoe nasledstvo.* Vol. 67, *Revoliutsionnye demokraty. Novye materialy.* (Moscow, 1959). "Ogarev v gody revoliutsionnoi situatsii." *Izvestiia Akademii nauk SSSR. Seriia istorii i filosofii,* Vol. II (Moscow, 1959).

[37]Ia. I. Linkov, "Ideinye i takticheskie raznoglasiia v riadakh revoliutsionnoi demokratii v epokhu padeniia krepostnogo prava." *Voprosy istorii,* No. 6 (1959), 47-68. Ia. I. Linkov, "Rol A. I. Gertsena i N. P. Ogareva v sozdanii i deiatelnosti obshchestva

It is reasonable to assume that Soviet historiography has extensively covered the early years of the Great Reforms and the revolutionary organizations of the same period. Much of this has been accomplished by the less-known local publishing enterprises which largely handle regional history. The source material contributed by regional institutions has considerably broadened the understanding of social and political conditions throughout Russia. In this connection, valuable historiographic studies by two Soviet scholars, B. G. Litvak and P. A. Zaionchkovskii, may be singled out.[38]

It is worthwhile mentioning a few other writings that bear indirectly upon the subject. One, by N. M. Druzhinin and T. G. Snytko, deals with the liberal circles in Moscow. Another study, by P. S. Tkachenko, concerns the role of the Moscow University students during the 1860's. An equally valuable monograph, by N. N. Ulashchik, is about the liberal and nationalistic movement in Lithuania. P. A. Zaionchkovskii has concentrated his attention on the application of the February (March n.s.), 1861, Manifesto emancipating the serfs. The liberal atmosphere that prevailed in student circles has been a subject of special research, producing several noteworthy studies.[39]

Since the Polish uprising of 1863 has been linked with the "revolutionary situation" of the same period, it has become a subject of considerable attention; one publication merits special mention—a collection of sources and interpretative materials on the uprising in Poland and on Russo-Polish relations during the 1860's.[40] That events in Russia connected with the advent of

'Zemlia i Volia'." *Voprosy istorii*, No. 3 (1954), 114-130. Ia. I. Linkov, "Problema revoliutsionnoi partii v Rossii v epokhu padeniia krepostnogo prava." *Voprosy istorii*, No. 9 (1957), 57-70. Ia. I. Linkov, "Osnovnye etapy istorii revoliutsionnogo obshchestva 'Zemlia i Volia' 1860kh godov." *Voprosy istorii*, No. 9 (1958), 33-57. M. V. Nechkina, "Voznikonovenie pervoi 'Zemli i Voli'." *Sbornik. Revoliutsionnaia situatsiia v Rossii v 1859-1861 gg.* (Moscow, 1960). M. V. Nechkina, "N. G. Chernyshevskii v borbe za splochenie sil russkogo demokraticheskogo dvizheniia v gody revoliutsionnoi situatsii (1859-1861)." *Voprosy istorii*, No. 7 (1953), 56-73. M. V. Nechkina, " 'Zemlia i Volia' 1860kh godov." *Istoriia SSSR*, No. 1 (1957), 105-134.

[38]P. A. Zaionchkovskii, "Sovetskaia istoriografiia reformy 1861 g." *Voprosy istorii*, No. 2 (1961), 85-104. B. G. Litvak, "Sovetskaia istoriografiia reformy 19 fevralia 1861 g." *Istoriia SSSR*, No. 6 (1960), 99-120.

[39]N. M. Druzhinin, "Moskva nakanune reformy 1861 goda." *Vestnik Moskovskogo gosudarstvennogo universiteta*, No. 9 (1947). T. G. Snytko, "Studencheskoe dvizhenie v russkikh universitetakh 60-kh godov i vosstanie 1863 g." *Sbornik. Vosstanie 1863 g. i russko-polskie revoliutsionnye sviazi 60-kh godov.* (Moscow, 1960). P. S. Tkachenko, *Moskovskoe studenchestvo v obshchestvenno-politicheskoi zhizni Rossii vtoroi poloviny XIX v.* (Moscow, 1958). N. N. Ulashchik, "Iz istorii reskripta 20 noiabria 1857 goda." *Istoricheskie zapiski*, No. 28 (1949), 164-181. N. N. Ulashchik, "Podgotovka krestianskoi reformy 1861 goda v Litve i Zapadnoi Belorussii." *Istoricheskie zapiski*, No. 33 (1950), 67-91. G. N. Vulfson and R. G. Bushkanets, *Obshchestvenno-politicheskaia borba v Kazanskom universitete v 1859-1861 gg.* (Moscow, 1958).

[40]*Vosstanie 1863 g. i russko-polskie revoliutsionnye sviazi 60kh godov.* (Moscow, 1960).

the reforms and the ensuing legislation had a profound impact upon developments in Poland, the Ukraine, Lithuania, and White Russia goes without saying. Chernyshevskii's publication, *Sovremennik*, and Herzen's *Kolokol* contributed a generous share to the radical philosophy, and were distributed mainly by way of Russian army officers stationed in those western parts of the Russian Empire.[41]

In summary, it can be said that Soviet historiography shows impressive accomplishments in the field that Soviet scholars call the first "revolutionary situation" in Russia—the period of the late 1850's and early 1860's. Much has been achieved in the study of mass movements, and considerable information uncovered and utilized in connection with underground circles of this period. Other organizations have been investigated and a fuller picture of the period has been contributed to historical literature, including a better understanding of the forces that accelerated the fall of serfdom in Russia.

And still more can be done. The peasant movement still calls for fuller investigation as to the deeper causes of unrest; equally important are further research in the causes of the social and political awakening among students and army officers, and additional interpretation of the rise and collapse of the "Land and Freedom" organization. All these will aid indirectly in effecting a fuller understanding of many of the leading figures. Lastly, there are still many unpublished archival materials to be brought out, while others that were published in the past need to be reissued, since they have become bibliographical rarities. A program of wider publication of original sources accompanied by adequate glossaries is urgently needed.

For a long while the populist movement had been woefully neglected, but since the middle 1950's there has been a revival of interest, the first indication of which was an article by P. S. Tkachenko in *Voprosy istorii.*[42] The author called for a reexamination of the entire subject, and urged the correction of some recent erroneous interpretations concerning the populist movement. A year later there appeared a study of the Russian Section of the First International by B. P. Kozmin. Among other things, the author examined in detail the evolution of Russian populism during the 1860's and 1870's.[43]

A detailed discussion of populism of the 1870's through the 1890's may be found in the second volume of *Ocherki istorii istoricheskoi nauki v SSSR*, by A. M. Stanislavskaia. Her chapter on populist historiography describes in detail the basic characteristics of the sociology of populism, and

[41]R. A. Taubin, "Revoliutsioner-demokrat S. S. Rymarenko." *Istoriia SSSR*, No. 1 (1959), 136-154. L. Khinkulov, *Taras Shevchenko.* (Moscow, 1960). V. Diakov, *Sigismund Serakovski.* (Moscow, 1959).

[42]P. S. Tkachenko, "O nekotorykh voprosakh istorii narodnichestva." *Voprosy istorii*, No. 5 (1956), 34-45.

[43]B. P. Kozmin, *Russkaia sektsiia pervogo Internatsionala.* (Moscow, 1957). B. P. Kozmin, *Izbrannye trudy. Iz istorii revoliutsionnoi mysli v Rossii.* (Moscow, 1961), 638-727.

discusses the difference between "revolutionary" and "liberal" populism.[44]

Sh. M. Levin examines the social struggle carried on during the 1860's and 1870's, though he obviously considers the first one far more important, since the latter decade receives only a cursory review. V. A. Tvardovskaia is the authoress of several articles on the same subject, though she stresses mainly the crisis period which the society "Land and Freedom" passed through by the end of the 1870's; Tvardovskaia also analyzes the tendencies to revolutionary populism that prevailed among the ranks of the "People's Will."[45]

Iu. Z. Polevoi contributed a study on the rise of Marxism in Russia which provoked considerable critical commentary in historical literature. One point that aroused special criticism was his assertion that, with the organization of the "People's Will," the highest state in the development of populism had been reached.

Other writers have contributed to related fields, such as the underground activities of the populists, or the relationship of the early revolutionary movement to Marxism. An article by E. S. Vilenskaia deals with utopian socialism and its associations in Russia during the 1860's.[46]

A closely related field is the history of the press of the second half of the nineteenth century, including "illegal" or underground publications. This subject, despite some recent research and published works, remains inadequately explored.

B. P. Verevkin examines in detail the contents of several underground publications issued in Russia and abroad during the 1870's and 1880's, and evaluates their effect on public opinion and whatever impact they might have had on the revolutionary movements. Equally important studies, though briefer, are by N. P. Emelianov, who analyzes the legal periodical *Otechestvennye zapiski* and its part in influencing social development in the country; by F. F. Kuznetsov, who analyzes the periodical *Russkoe slovo* and its impact upon populism; and by V. Serebrennikova, on the magazine *Delo*, a radical publication which championed the cause of the populist movement.[47]

[44]*Ocherki istorii istoricheskoi nauki v SSSR*. (Moscow, 1960). Vol. II, 171-218.

[45]Sh. M. Levin, *Obshchestvennoe dvizhenie v Rossii v 60-70e gody XIX veka*. (Moscow, 1958). V. A. Tvardovskaia, "Krizis 'Zemli i Voli' v kontse 70kh godov." *Istoriia SSSR*, No. 4 (1959), 61-75. V. A. Tvardovskaia, "Organizatsionnye osnovy Narodnoi Voli." *Istoricheskie zapiski*, No. 67 (1960), 103-144.

[46]Iu. Z. Polevoi, *Zarozhdenie marksizma v Rossii*. (Moscow, 1959). V. V. Shirokova, "K voprosu ob otsenke deiatelnosti 'Narodnoi Voli'." *Voprosy istorii*, No. 8 (1959), 47-62. B. S. Itenberg, "Nachalo massovogo 'khozhdeniia v narod'." *Istoricheskie zapiski*, No. 69 (1961), 142-177. E. S. Vilenskaia, "Proizvoditelnye assotsiatsii v Rossii v seredine 60kh godov XIX v. (Iz istorii ishutinskoi organizatsii)." *Istoricheskie zapiski*, No. 68 (1961), 51-80.

[47]B. P. Verevkin, *Russkaia nelegalnaia revoliutsionnaia pechat 70kh i 80kh godov XIX*

A whole series of popular biographical literature has appeared in recent years, including works on such well-known populists as I. Myshkin, Sophia Perovskaia, A. Zheliabov, Vera Figner, S. Khalturin, N. Kibalchich, G. Lopatin, and many others. Populism became a subject of study not only among historians, but among economists, philosophers, and sociologists; many of their studies, though they generally appear in popular journals, present historically informative accounts of the men and women who at one time or another played a decisive part in the revolutionary movement. It remains for the historian now to integrate all these writings into a more extensive general account, in order to cover the century-long struggle against autocracy in Russia. Together with a full history of such conspiratory organizations as "Land and Freedom," the "People's Will," or the "Black Partition," it would provide a more unified story of the nineteenth-century revolutionary movement in Russia.

There is also need for a general history of socialism in Russia. A work of this nature was published by K. A. Pazhitnov in 1912 and revised in 1924, but it is much outdated; badly needed is either further revision or a totally new study of the subject. Another lack is in the field of utopian socialism in Russia, its peculiarities, its ideological kinship to Western forms, its evolution and then its decline, yielding to Marxian and other socio-economic philosophies of later date.[48]

An even more important aspect of the populist movement is the question of its relation to and effect upon the peasantry. Populism was deeply rooted in peasant democratic idealism, and for this reason, populism and agrarianism became inseparable as subjects for investigation. Fortunately, a study of this nature can readily be carried out, using a series of archival sources on the history of the peasant movement recently issued by the Institute of History of the Academy of Sciences. These volumes suggest two main fields for research: one, the peasant movement during the 1870's and 1880's; the other, the agrarian problems as part of the populist-revolutionary ideology. This subject, which had been touched only on the surface during the 1920's, because of the political climate or inadequacy of source material, tended to be pictured as an idyllic populist movement.

veka. (Moscow, 1960). N. P. Emelianov, " 'Otechestvennye zapiski' borbe s perezhitkami krepostnichestva (1879-1880 gg.)." Uchenye zapiski Leningradskogo gosudarstvennogo universiteta, No. 218 (1957), Seriia filologicheskikh nauk, No. 33. N. P. Emelianov, "Zhurnal 'Otechestvennye zapiski' v gody revoliutsionnoi situatsii 1879-1880 gg." Vestnik Leningradskogo universiteta, No. 2 (1957), Seriia istorii, iazyka i literatury, Issue 1, 133-151. F. F. Kuznetsov, " 'Russkoe slovo' i narodnichestvo." Iz istorii russkoi zhurnalistiki. Stati i materialy. (Moscow, 1959), 84-119. V. G. Serebrennikova, "Demokraticheskii zhurnal 'Delo' v gody obshchestvennogo pod'ema (konets 80kh godov XIX veka)." Istoriia SSSR, No. 1 (1961), 118-130.

[48]K. A. Pazhitnov, Razvitie sotsialisticheskikh idei v Rossii. (Petrograd, 1924). Sh. M. Levin, "K voprosu ob osobennostiakh russkogo utopicheskogo sotsializma." Istoricheskie zapiski, No. 26 (1948), 217-257.

During the period of Stalinism, writers denied any historical importance whatever to populism. Evidently, neither the tendency to idealize it nor the tendency to obliterate it from history is right. A dispassionate evaluation of populism, as well as of such figures in the revolutionary ideology as M. A. Bakunin, P. L. Lavrov, and P. N. Tkachev, becomes necessary. Aside from these "ideologues," studies of figures such as Mark Natanson, Lev Deutsch, Vera Figner, Sergei Kravchinskii, Alexander Mikhailov, or Ippolit Myshkin are equally important. Their full biographies, as well as the story of their part in the demolition of the old order and their contribution to the social and political thought of the 1870's, are most vital. Finally, there remains a need for monographic studies of the ties that must have existed between the Russian revolutionaries and their counterparts in western Europe during the second half of the nineteenth century, and a full account of Russian political émigré life in the West.

Populism, though a significant factor in the revolutionary movement following the Great Reforms, was not the only revolutionary current. There were important concurrent movements in the general struggle against the absolutist regime. The field lends itself to approximately the following scheme, to cover satisfactorily and fully the second half of the past century: (1) a study of the social movements during the 1870's and 1880's, (2) revolutionary populism and the labor movement during the same period, (3) the liberation movement in the Balkans and Russian liberalism, (4) a comparative study of Russian populism and liberalism, (5) N. K. Mikhailovskii and social movements in post-reform Russia, (6) populism, Christian socialism, early Marxian socialism, and other related ideologies.

Can this be accomplished in Soviet historiography? At times, lingering doubts turn into negative convictions when one reads the following party advice to Soviet historians: "An appraisal of the populists in general, and the revolutionary populists in particular, demands a strict scientific Marxist approach. One must not lapse into an extreme preconceived scheme either to idealize the populists or to deny completely their historic merit. A sample of a correct attitude toward the populists are the numerous statements of V. I. Lenin concerning the question." The learned counsel sounds more like a chilling official party warning than a scholarly suggestion.[49]

Historians who came to deal with the development of revolutionary ideas in Russia came to face several serious problems. One of the delicate subjects involved was the role of the Bolshevik Party in history. Another was the role of the individual, which carried with it the problem of assessing the unique part of Lenin in the movement that led to the triumph of Bolshevism. Above all, if individuals like Lenin, and later Stalin, might be given such honors, what happens to the idea of historical materialism, which insists upon the inexorable course of history, with its own laws of development? During the 1920's these were already questions that troubled historians in

[49] *Sovetskaia istoricheskaia nauka ot XX k XXII sezdu KPSS. Istoriia SSSR. Sbornik statei.* (Moscow, 1962), 274.

the field of nineteenth-century revolutionary ideas, while in the 1930's they became grim realities that were to silence many of them. Among these were B. P. Kozmin, S. I. Mitskevich, N. N. Baturin, and B. I. Gorev.

Perhaps a most illustrative episode in this connection, involving conflicting ideas of party policy and historical interpretation, was the case of study of two nineteenth-century Blanquists and Jacobins, S. Nechaev and P. Tkachev. In 1923, S. I. Mitskevich wrote an essay which appeared in the magazine *Proletarskaia revoliutsiia*.[50] The essence of his article was that Jacobinism and Blanquism, as expressed in Tkachev's advocacy of revolution, can be regarded as the earliest contribution to the Bolshevik philosophy. Such ideas as the seizure of political power, the establishment of dictatorship by the working class, or the formation of a highly centralized government emanate from Tkachev, who advocated similar ideas of revolutionary action.

This interpretation soon caused serious ideological commotion. The author became the target of bitter criticism, particularly from N. N. Baturin, who maintained that Tkachev's ideas represented nothing but petty-bourgeois, thread-worn, inapplicable, and unsuitable Blanquist ideas that have nothing in common with either Marxism or Bolshevism. The analogy between Tkachev's *Pugachevshchina* and dialectical materialism was merely an effort to smuggle into Communist ideology Menshevik and Trotskyite hereseries. The false ideas of Mitskevich concerning continuity were nothing but dangerous infiltration of an alien ideology that would threaten pure Marxian historical interpretation.

What the debate might have led to is uncertain, but in 1931 Stalin entered the scene from the side wings, when he contributed a letter to *Proletarskaia revoliutsiia* in which he presented his own interpretation of "Certain Problems of the History of Bolshevism." The tempest in the teapot quickly terminated. What is more significant, B. P. Kozmin, who assumed the editorship of the complete works of Tkachev, was suddenly interrupted. By 1937 six volumes had appeared, but the seventh was never issued. The six volumes issued between 1932 and 1937 are not to be found on the shelves of Soviet libraries. At present, Tkachev's writings may be located only in a few libraries outside Russia.

That Soviet historical literature should devote a large share of its efforts to the history of the Russian proletariat is no surprise. Led by the Communist Academy of Sciences, together with the Society of Marxist Historians, a number of official commissions were assigned to study the history of the Russian working class. Between 1930 and 1935 a special periodical was published, *Istoriia proletariata*. A specially designated commission began to gather various memoirs of active union leaders. Some of these were published during the 1920's and have already become bibliographical rarities. Records of early attempts at organization of unions, formation of socialist groups and party "cells" within the unions, the setting up of an underground press, methods of propaganda, secret meetings, all were carefully

[50]S. I. Mitskevich, "Russkie iakobintsy." *Proletarskaia revoliutsiia*, Nos. 6-7 (18-19), (1923), 3-26.

186

gathered as valuable information and source material for the future historian. Soviet critics have repeatedly, though not always successfully, warned writers against certain pitfalls in their use of original sources. The terminology applied to these pitfalls is interesting if not unique and hardly submits to a liberal translation at times. There is, for instance, a warning against *nachetnichestvo*, which approximately means recitation or mechanical counting of rosary beads, or listing events without any general purpose. Another pitfall warned against is *tsitatnichestvo*, the falling into the habit of quoting long citations, to turn a study into some kind of an "anthology." A third offense is *golofaktizm*, literally "naked factism," endless listing of facts without interpreting them into any coordinated, meaningful narrative. Then there is the serious offense of *penkosnimatelstvo*, literally "cream skimming," a euphemism for plagiarism by slight paraphrasing. There is also *opisatelnost*, the tendency to over-embellish, incorporate dreamy descriptions of personalities or environment, unsubstantiated by facts. Lastly there is a warning against dogmatism and cultism, terms that hardly call for elaborate explanation. The historical narrative, Soviet critics insist, must have substance, must be "plethoric" (*polnokrovnyi*), backed by facts, synthesized into a well-coorindated narrative that conforms with "natural laws" (*zakonomernosti*).

This last request is the source of trouble. The student of history must never neglect the "ideological front," and always bear in mind that history must be studied "in close relation to the history of the [Communist] party." Historians are easily tempted into "naked factism" and other sins for fear of the many hazards to be encountered on the "ideological front."

It was in the spirit of this last counsel that a collection of "Documents and Materials" on the nineteenth-century labor movement was published in 1951-1952, and a new edition issued in 1955, under the editorship of the late A. M. Pankratova. The new four-volume edition covers the period 1800-1891. It is one of several similar editions. By 1960, more than sixty similar collections of documents and materials had appeared, including documents related to both labor and peasant movements. Obviously it is safer to "count rosary beads" than to engage in interpretative history. A goodly portion of these documents go as far back as the December, 1905, uprising, covering the number and nature of labor strikes, incorporating background material on unrest and revolts, and citing administrative measures to combat threats of violence. Some volumes extend to regions never before treated in history. Several of the volumes on the labor movement between 1907 and 1917 include events in the Ukraine, St. Petersburg, Kazakhstan, the Ural region, and other localities.

Considering the amount of source materials that is still left unpublished, the volumes mentioned may be considered valuable with some reservations. Partly, this is because we still do not know what other documentary sources may yet be revealed. It should also be stated that the volumes published to date display a tendency to repeat certain records, and lack adequate glossaries, helpful commentaries, or indexes. For these reasons if for no others, there is still a need for either a new and improved edition of the materials that have appeared or the publication of additional volumes in a way that would correct the omissions in those already in use.[51]

Some Soviet historians have endeavored to collect data on the history of the strike movement in Russia since the middle of the past century, and to judge the degree of class antagonism and intensity of struggle. In her introductory chapters to the volumes on the strike movement in Russia, A. M. Pankratova cites data to indicate the "ascending tempo of the revolution." V. V. Selchuk, who wrote on the press as the indicator of social developments in the country, cites much evidence in support of Pankratova's view, particularly with regard to the decade following the Emancipation, while A. S. Trofimov cites much data in support of a similar observation concerning the second half of the past century. Various other accounts describe the strikes during the turbulent years 1905 to 1907. Finally, I. I. Mints and others cover the two years, 1914-1916, preceding the February revolution. Together with the abundant, though not exhaustive, data available concerning regional conditions during the years 1912-1914, the figures gathered present some imposing evidence.[52] Finally, there is the brief but informative account of S. G. Strumilin, lucidly discussing the strike movement in Russia and its relation to the revolution.[53]

The peasant and labor movements during the early years of the present century, up to the revolution, occupy a special place in Soviet historiography.

[51]A. M. Pankratova, ed., *Rabochee dvizhenie v Rossii v XIX veke. Sbornik dokumentov i materialov.* (Moscow, 1951-1952). 3 vols. 2nd ed. (Moscow 1955-1961). 4 vols. *Pervaia russkaia revoliutsiia 1905-1907 gg. Ukazatel literatury, vyshedshei v 1954-1957 gg. v sviazi s 50-letiem revoliutsii.* (Moscow, 1957). *Revoliutsiia 1905-1907 gg. v Rossii. Dokumenty i materialy.* (Moscow, 1955-1960). Vol. I- . *Rabochee dvizhenie na Ukraine v gody novogo revoliutsionnogo pod'ema, 1910-1914 gg.* (Kiev, 1959). *Rabochee dvizhenie v Petrograde v 1912-1917 gg. Dokumenty i materialy.* (Leningrad, 1958). *Rabochee i agrarnoe dvizhenie v Kazakhstane v 1907-1914 gg. Sbornik dokumentov i materialov.* (Alma-Ata, 1957). *Rabochee dvizhenie vo Vladimirskoi gubernii 1910-1914 gg. Sbornik.* (Vladimir, 1957). *Polozhenie rabochikh Urala vo vtoroi polovine XIX—nachale XX v. 1861-1904 gg.* (Moscow, 1960).

[52]*Rabochee dvizhenie v Rossii v XIX v.* Introductory comments by A. M. Pankratova. See Vol. II, Part 1 (Moscow, 1950); Vol. III, Part 1. V. V. Selchuk, "Russkaia publitsistika kak istochnik dlia izucheniia rabochego dvizheniia v Rossii v 60e gody XIX v." *Trudy Gosudarstvennoi biblioteki SSSR im. V. I. Lenina,* Vol. I (1957). A. S. Trofimov, *Rabochee dvizhenie v Rossii, 1861-1894 gg.* (Moscow, 1957). E. E. Kruze, *Peterburgskie rabochie v 1912-1914 gg.* (Moscow, 1961). P. A. Lavrov, *Rabochee dvizhenie na Ukraine v 1913-1914 gg.* (Kiev, 1957). A. S. Amalrik, "K voprosu o chislennosti i geograficheskom razmeshchenii stachechnikov v Evropeiskoi Rossii v 1905 g." *Istoricheskie zapiski,* No. 52, (1955), 142-185. I. I. Mints, "Revoliutsionnaia borba proletariata Rossii v 1914-1916 godakh." *Voprosy istorii,* No. 11 (1959), 57-69; No. 12 (1959), 23-40. L. I. Leskova, "O statistike stachek rabochikh Urala v 1910-1914 gg." *Istoriia SSSR,* No. 4 (1960), 36-44.

[53]S. G. Strumilin, *Ocherki ekonomicheskoi istorii Rossii.* (Moscow, 1960), 524-544.

Much attention has been given to the circumstances which favored peasant-labor cooperation, unity of purpose in the multi-national Russian Empire, and international labor solidarity. These are the main themes historians have emphasized while either writing on this period or gathering source materials. A large number of monographs have appeared on the role of labor during the years 1905-1907 in the different national regions of Russia. On the other hand, there are a few obvious gaps in the field: there is not a single satisfactory study on the origin of the Russian trade union; there is a need for a history of the origin of the Soviet; and there is no

[54]*Pervaia russkaia revoliutsiia 1905-1907 gg. Ukazatel literatury, vyshedshei v 1954-1957 gg. v sviazi s 50-letiem revoliutsii.* (Moscow, 1957). L. M. Kresina, *Rabochee dvizhenie vo Vladimirskoi gubernii v kontse XIX—nachale XX v.* (Vladimir, 1959). N. V. Murovtsev, "Sotsial-demokraticheskoe podpolie i rabochee dvizhenie v Moskve vo vtoroi polovine 90kh godov." *Uchenye zapiski Moskovskogo gosudarstvennogo pedagogicheskogo instituta,* Vol. 135, Issue 5. (1959). V. Iu. Merkis, "Stachechnoe dvizhenie vilniusskikh rabochikh v 1895-1900 gg." *Trudy Akademii nauk Litovskoi SSR.* Series A, No. 1 (1959). A. Ushakov, "Moskovskii 'Soiuz borby za osvobozh-denie rabochego klassa' i stachka na fabrike Torntona v 1895 g." *Vestnik Lenin-gradskogo universiteta,* No. 20 (1958), *Seriia istorii, iazyka i literatury,* Issue 4. F. M. Suslova, "Leninskii 'Soiuz borby za osvobozhdenie rabochego klassa' vo glave peterburgskoi stachki tekstilshchikov 1896 g." *Uchenye zapiski Moskovskoi vysshei shkoly profdvizheniia,* Issue 1 (Moscow, 1957). Iu. Z. Polevoi, *Zarozhdenie mark-sizma v Rossii 1883-1894 gg.* (Moscow, 1959). N. N. Demochkin, "Borba tulskikh rabochikh za soiuz s krestianstvom nakanune i v gody pervoi revoliutsii (1901-1907 gg.)." *Uchenye zapiski Moskovskogo gosudarstvennogo pedagogicheskogo instituta,* Vol. 110. *Kafedra istorii SSSR,* Issue 4 (1957). P. I. Klimov, *Revoliutsionnaia de-iatelnost rabochikh v derevne v 1905-1907 gg.* (Moscow, 1960). *Sbornik. Pervaia russkaia revoliutsiia 1905-1907 gg. i mezhdunarodnoe revoliutsionnoe dvizhenie.* Parts I-II. (Moscow, 1955-1956). A. L. Sidorov, "K voprosu o peremeshchenii tsentra mezhdunarodnogo rabochego dvizheniia v Rossiiu." *Voprosy istorii,* No. 6 (1954), 3-18. L. S. Kuznetsova, *Stachechnaia borba peterburgskogo proletariata v 1905 g.* (Leningrad, 1955). A. S. Chebarin, *Moskva v revoliutsii 1905-1907 gg.* (Moscow, 1955). A. V. Piaskovskii, *Revoliutsiia 1905-1907 gg. v Turkestane.* (Moscow, 1958). Z. I. Ibragimov, *Revoliutsiia 1905-1907 gg. v Azerbaidzhane.* (Baku, 1955). *Revo-liutsiia 1905-1907 gg. v natsionalnykh raionakh Rossii. Sbornik statei.* (Moscow, 1955). N. M. Iakovlev, *Vooruzhennye vosstaniia v dekabre 1905 g.* (Moscow, 1957). L. V. Bogutskaia, *Ocherki po istorii vooruzhennykh vosstanii v revoliutsii 1905-1907 gg.* (Moscow, 1956). I. V. Spiridonov, *Vserossiiskaia politicheskaia stachka v oktia-bre 1905 g.* (Moscow, 1955). E. P. Kireev, *Proletariat Groznogo v revoliutsii 1905-1907 gg.* 2nd ed. (Groznyi, 1955). I. F. Muzhev, *Ocherki istorii revoliutsionnogo dvizheniia na Severnom Kavkaze v 1905-1907 gg.* (Nalchik, 1957). M. A. Kaziev, *Iz istorii revoliutsionnoi borby bakinskogo proletariata (1905-1910 gg.).* (Baku, 1956). Iu. N. Netesin, *Rabochee dvizhenie v Rige v gody stolypinskoi reaktsii.* (Riga, 1958). P. A. Lavrov, *Rabochee dvizhenie na Ukraine v 1913-1914 gg.* (Kiev, 1957). L. I. Leskova, *God pod'ema. Rabochii klass iuzhnogo Urala v period pod'ema rabochego dvizheniia (1910-1914 gg.).* (Cheliabinsk, 1958). G. F. Lukin, *Rabochee dvizhenie v Estonii v gody stolypinskoi reaktsii i novogo revoliutsionnogo pod'ema (1907-1914 gg.).* (Tallin, 1960). E. E. Kruze, *Peterburgskie rabochie v 1912-1914 gg.*

noteworthy monograph on the period between the revolution of 1905 and the one of March, 1917.[54]

(Moscow, 1961). M. V. Tsertsvadze, *Revoliutsionnoe dvizhenie v Gruzii v 1914-1917 gg.* Parts 1-2 (Moscow and Tbilisi, 1957-60). V. Ia. Laverychev, *Rabochee dvizhenie v Ivanovo-Voznesenske v gody pervoi mirovoi voiny (1914—fevral 1917 g.).* (Moscow, 1957). E. P. Tretiakova, "Fevralskie sobytiia 1917 g. v Moskve." *Voprosy istorii,* No. 3, (1957), 72-84. I. I. Mints, "Revoliutsionnaia borba proletariata Rossii v 1914-1916 gg." *Voprosy Istorii,* No. 11 (1959), 57-89; No. 12 (1959), 23-40. A. Ia. Avrekh, *Stolypin i Tretia Duma.* (Moscow, 1968). S. M. Dubrovskii, *Stolypinskaia zemelnaia reforma. Iz istorii selskogo khoziaistva i krestianstva Rossii v nachale 20 veka.* (Moscow, 1963).

CHAPTER IX

Intervention and Civil War

A. GENERAL OBSERVATIONS

The first writers on the Civil War were mostly political and military leaders who had taken an active part in the events which they later wrote about, firmly believing that their accounts would be vital to history. Among the military leaders who took up the writing of history were men like M. N. Tukhachevskii and B. M. Shaposhnikov, while A. S. Bubnov, S. I. Gusev, and R. I. Berzen were political leaders who also took part in military campaigns. Some of them, young men who only recently gained war experience, were now enthusiastically recording their freshly gained impressions. Among these two names stand out in particular, V. K. Triandafillov and G. D. Guy.[1]

Some of these men, aside from recording personal impressions, endeavored to interpret the entire war period. In 1919, a commission was appointed to make a preliminary study of the seven-year war period, including the First World War. As a result, a volume was published which dealt with the Civil War period of 1918-1919.[2] Two years later there appeared a general report of the military operations of the Red Army from July, 1919, to January, 1920, published by the Revolutionary Committee of the Red Army (RKKA). This report dwells entirely upon military developments during the period indicated. The documents try to cover the northern, western, southwestern, southern, Caucasian, Turkestan, and eastern fronts. During the same year there also appeared a number of jubilee editions and other publications that dealt extensively with the military aspects of the Civil War years, such as the special issue that marked the fifth anniversary of the Red Navy.[3] Several works described the problems of political indoctrination in the armed forces or the role the political commissars

---

[1] V. P. Naumov, *Sovetskaia istoriografiia grazhdanskoi voiny i imperialisticheskoi interventsii v Rossii do pervogo pokhoda Antanty.* (Moscow, 1958). A brief admirable historiographic survey of the Civil War period has been made by D. K. Shelestov. The author analyzes briefly some of the outstanding writings in the field and stresses some of the prominent accounts, though he gives preference mainly to what he calls "collective efforts" in the studies of the historiography of the Civil War. See D. K. Shelestov, "Ob izuchenii istoriografii grazhdanskoi voiny v SSSR." *Istoriia SSSR*, No. 6 (1968), 88-101. Also, *Voprosy istorii*, No. 11 (1968), 152-162.

[2] *Grazhdanskaia voina v Rossii v 1918-1919 gg. Trudy komissii po issledovaniiu i ispolzovaniiu opyta voiny 1914-1918 gg.* (Moscow, 1919).

[3] See *Piat let Krasnogo Flota.* (Moscow, 1921).

had played in the armed forces.[4] The main value of these publications is that, cumulatively, they represent the earliest attempt to analyze and synthesize the military operations on all fronts during the Civil War. Many of these later proved to be of considerable value, since they incorporate various documentary sources hardly available elsewhere, or record personal observations, some of which preserve rare material for historians.

During the 1920's, extensive works such as the general history of the Civil War by A. Anishev or the two-volume work by N. E. Kakurin[5] were published. The unique study by Anishev is of special interest as one of the earliest attempts to present the entire story of the Civil War from its outbreak to its final phase. Shortly thereafter a number of others appeared, particularly on the occasion of the tenth anniversary of the Revolution. Among these are many special monographic studies, memoirs, documentary compilations, and popular editions, and in particular Kakurin's two-volume monograph, which stands out as perhaps one of the earliest comprehensive research efforts for the entire war period.

N. E. Kakurin was among the first to utilize many archival collections to be found at home as well as abroad, though at times he used his sources uncritically. Most of his effort Kakurin devoted to military history and only from time to time did he include related topics. His work cannot be considered definitive, but Kakurin managed to embrace many aspects of the struggle which later were either deliberately neglected or distorted during the rule of Stalin. Kakurin's monograph became a fundamental one, from which authors of both more popularized and more serious versions drew much of their information.[6]

In 1928 there appeared the composite three-volume General History of the Civil War under the editorship of M. N. Tukhachevskii, A. S. Bubnov, S. S. Kamenev, and R. P. Eideman. For a while this series seemed to have been accepted as the definitive work in the field. The three volumes incorporated a wide range of factual and interpretive materials, and the entire work produced the impression of an earnest scholarly endeavor to fill the need in historical literature. The authors, as well as the editors, were all active war participants, and the three volumes still retain much that is of rare informative character, enhanced by valuable personal narratives. The first volume is devoted largely to the military operations, and gives full accounts of certain decisive battles. The second volume

[4]See, for example, *Kulturno-prosvetitelnaia rabota v Krasnoi Armii za 1918 g.* (Moscow, 1919). G. O. Lindov, *O politrabote i politicheskikh rabotnikakh na fronte.* (Moscow, 1918). Emelian Iaroslavskii, *Kulturno-prosvetitelnaia rabota v Krasnoi Armii.* (Moscow, 1919).

[5]A. Anishev, *Ocherki grazhdanskoi voiny 1917-1920 gg.* (Leningrad, 1925). N. E. Kakurin, *Kak srazhalas revoliutsiia.* Vol. I, *1917-1918 gg.* Vol. II, *1918-1920 gg.* (Moscow, 1925-1926).

[6]A. Korol, *Istoriia Krasnoi Armii i grazhdanskoi voiny.* (Moscow, 1925). A. Mavrogan, *Grazhdanskaia voina v Rossii.* (Moscow, 1927).

analyzes many of the important military problems faced during the three-year war. The third, finally, is a general survey of the strategy employed by both the Reds and the Whites.[7]

The Civil War is also dealt with by A. Golubev, who endeavored to integrate the events of the three eventful years into a single account. Incorporating the results of extensive research, and demonstrating interpretative skill, Golubev handled the period on a much broader scale than that of mere military developments. Golubev tried to include in a broader frame of reference the political, economic, social, cultural and ethnic aspects of the bitter three-year strife that extended throughout the vast Eurasian plain.[8]

During the 1920's most writers on the Civil War seemed not to have concerned themselves with defining the date when the conflict first broke out; each one assumed that the logical beginning was October, 1917, when the Bolsheviks seized power. Having accepted that, they came to regard the first phase of the Civil War, the period between October, 1917, and the spring of 1918, as the "echelon period," as they called it. During these first months, both sides fought mainly for control over the large cities and most important railroad junctions. Troops were moved prior to the outbreak of battle in echelons, hence the "echelon period."[9] Some writers, such as those who contributed material to the third volume of the *General History of the Civil War,* refer to it as the "October period," with the center of the struggle taking place in the south, the Russian Vendée. Some also stressed the struggle against German occupation of the Ukraine throughout the spring of 1918, shortly after the Treaty of Brest-Litovsk.

At the end of the 1920's there also appeared a few special works on the general history of the Red Army during the Civil War period, the methods of political indoctrination in the Red armed forces, and the role of the Military Commissars. While Soviet writers insisted on the need to retain the Commissars in the army, others, such as Trotsky and Smilga, advocated their removal in favor of restoration of the principle of single authority.[10]

Several periodicals came to assume considerable importance for the study of history, since they had systematically incorporated valuable materials on

[7]*Grazhdanskaia voina, 1918-1921 gg.* Vol. I, *Boevaia zhizn Krasnoi Armii.* Vol. II, *Voennoe iskusstvo Krasnoi Armii.* Vol. III, *Operativno-strategicheskii ocherk voennykh deistvii Krasnoi Armii.* (Moscow, 1928-1930). G. V. Kuzmin, *Grazhdanskaia voina i voennaia interventsiia v SSSR; voenno-politicheskii ocherk.* (Moscow, 1958). N. E. Kakurin, *Strategicheskii ocherk grazhdanskoi voiny.* (Moscow, 1926).

[8]A. Golubev, *Grazhdanskaia voina 1918-1920 gg.* (Moscow, 1932).

[9]S. Ventsov and S. Belitskii, *Krasnaia Gvardiia.* (Moscow, 1925).

[10]N. Savko, *Ocherki po istorii partiinykh organizatsii v Krasnoi Armii (1918-1923 gg.).* (Moscow, 1928). N. Mishchenko, *Partiino-politicheskaia rabota v Krasnoi Armii.* (Moscow, 1929). A. Geronimus, *Partiia i Krasnaia Armiia.* (Moscow, 1928).

the Civil War period. Among these are such magazines as *Voina i revoliutsiia, Voennyi vestnik, Voennoe znanie,* and *Krasnaia armiia.* From the start, these magazines recorded vital bibliographical material on military history. Thus, to cite only a few illustrations, an outstanding article on the war with Poland is that by S. S. Kamenev in *Voennyi vestnik,* No. 12, 1922; on the defense of Tsaritsyn, by L. L. Kliuev in *Krasnaia armiia,* No. 13, 1922; on the rout of the Fourth Corps of Bakich, in *Voina i revoliutsiia,* No. 23, 1923; on the cooperation of the western and southwestern fronts in the summer campaign against Poland in 1920, by V. K. Triandafillov, in *Voina i revoliutsiia,* No. 2, 1925. All these are basic readings for any historian in the field of the Russian Revolution.

A great deal of spadework was accomplished by the *Istpart* organizations. The *Istpart* was a commission formed for the collection and the study of materials pertaining to the history of the Russian Communist Party. It was founded in September, 1920, by a decision of the Soviet of People's Commissars (*Sovnarkom*). and originally was set up as a Division of the Commissariat of Education. What proved of particular benefit to history was the practice soon followed of setting up local *Istparts* all over Russia. These succeeded in amassing enormous quantities of resources materials of all kinds, and establishing local archives.

In 1923-1924 the archive for history and party study was established; here all documentary records were to be kept. Soon affiliates were organized in cities like Moscow, Leningrad, Kiev, Minsk, and Tbilisi to take charge of appropriate areas. In 1928, *Istpart* merged with the Lenin Institute, which three years later itself merged with the Marx-Engels Institute to form the Marx-Engels-Lenin Institute. This last institute (renamed the Institute of Marxism-Leninism in 1956) represented a central party institution aiming at the study of ideological history, the preservation of all documents concerning and the publication of works by Marx, Engels, Lenin, and Stalin, as well as the publication of research results. Other centers of similar studies are the Archives of the October Revolution and the Red Army Archives, set up during the middle of the 1920's with branches throughout the country. The organization of the Red Army Archives actually began in December, 1918, later to be taken over by the Central Archival Administration (*Glavarkhiv*).

Much of the writing on the Civil War was bound to be haphazard, highly partisan, and self-centered, since a good deal of it was personal reminiscing. One of the first to make a public appeal in favor of a more systematic recording of the eventful years 1918-1921 was the nationally known writer A. M. Gorky. In his appeal to all participants of the Civil War, Gorky stated that a knowledge of the history and of the experiences of the Russian people during the war years was of vital importance not only to the nation, but to the entire world, since the conflict was truly international in character. The history, as Gorky had envisioned it, was to include monographic works, essays, novels, poems, or any other literary form that had any bearing on the war years. Gorky's appeal was met with official approval and favorable response in the country. On July 30, 1931, the Central Committee of the Communist Party resolved "to approve the initiative of Comrade A. M. Gorky and begin to publish for the wide toiling masses a 'History of the Civil War'."[11]

Gorky did not live long enough to see his plan materialize, nor was the project carried out exactly in the spirit he had visualized at its initial stage. Head of the project, after Gorky died, was I. I. Mints. From the start an appeal was issued to all war participants to submit whatever materials they might possess or be able to gather, to help enrich the planned history. A special guide aimed at writers and editors was published, explaining the purpose of the project and methods of systematizing the amassed materials, with rough drafts of topical arrangements as envisioned by the editor-in-chief. Even from the initial stages serious signs of danger to the lofty endeavor were coming from the already entrenched cult of the individual. Thus, in outlining the course of events between the February and October revolutions or during the Civil War, the narrative was to be presented in such a manner that Lenin and Stalin would overshadow all other leading figures. Such simplification, if not outright falsification of history, extended little promise of the definitive work hoped for originally. And still, despite such signs, the cumulative process continued to move ahead rapidly, if not impressively.

The literature on the three years of civil strife kept growing rapidly and soon began to reach threatening proportions. The next logical step called for systematization of the accumulated materials, in order to apply some meaningful pattern to the fragmentary accounts, documentary reports, and personal narratives. Furthermore, the subject demanded analytical examination of all the factors that affected the period of years concerned. This implied a complex study of domestic, foreign, military, economic, social, and cultural events, and their impact upon developments within or outside Russia. Such a work, it was felt, was badly needed, and was bound to be so broad as to demand a multi-volume publication. For this reason a special editorial board was formed which started to gather, sift, classify all records, and put the voluminous materials into some topical and chronological order. In bringing the materials together, it soon became apparent that many accounts, such as those of Civil War veterans or labor union leaders, and reports dealing with the German occupation or the Allied intervention, became broad enough in themselves as to require special volumes.[12]

Already during the 1920's there were two distinct currents in Civil War history: one, the polemic, primarily military reminiscences, and the other, the *Istpart* publications. The latter gradually led to a broader

[11]*Pravda*, July 31, 1931.

[12]As an illustration see, for instance, such publications as *Dokumenty po istorii grazhdanskoi voiny v SSSR*. Vol. I. (Moscow, 1941). *Partizanskoe dvizhenie v Zapadnoi Sibiri v 1918-1919 gg. Sbornik dokumentov.* (Novosibirsk, 1936). *Profsoiuzy SSSR v sozdanii Krasnoi Armii, 1918-1920. Sbornik dokumentov.* (Moscow,

approach to historical interpretation. The earlier writings were still based on inadequate documentary evidence, often woefully parochial in scope as well as in interpretation.

As archival materials kept accumulating during the latter half of the 1920's there was a noticeable broadening in the subject matter treated, which included economic background, the role of the peasantry, the working classes in the cities, and the plight of the middle class and of the intelligentsia. In part, this wider interest is explained by the increase which had recently occurred in the ranks of trained students of history. Students who graduated from such Soviet-founded educational institutions as the RABFAK or RANION began to carry on research on their own and publish their findings. The tenth anniversary of the Revolution, in 1927, already saw an improvement in historical training.

An example of the attempt to approach the Civil War from a broad viewpoint is the article by S. I. Gusev on the "Lessons of the Civil War," in which the author analyzes the peculiarities of the war in Soviet Russia. He states that "the three-year Civil War within Soviet Russia offers the richest resources for conclusive study of the nature and peculiarities of civil war in an epoch of socialist revolution. From this experience our west European comrades can very likely derive more than from any other field of Soviet experience. The summary of the results of the three-year experience, the establishment of basic characteristics of modern civil warfare and the organization of a Red Army, has therefore not only a scientific historical importance, but a practical political one as well."[13]

Gusev's thesis is that the complex nature of the struggle derives from the fact that not only opposite classes are engaged in the conflict, but intermediate social groups that are noted for their vacillations between revolution and counterrevolution. He therefore foresees three groups eventually engaging in modern civil war: (1) the bourgeoisie and the large landowning elements, (2) the proletariat, and (3) the intermediate-passive, petty-bourgeois groups. The second group evidently includes the peasantry, the tradesmen, and various employed groups. The division is general, unreal, and often lacks clarity; it leads to erroneous interpretation or to distortion of the roles of the different classes in a modern society, particularly the role of the peasantry in time of civil war. According to Gusev, the intermediate groups shift loyalties from one camp to another and finally, having no choice, are forced to stand by the dictatorship of the proletariat. This may be true in individual cases, but Gusev fails to convince the reader of the general rule.

1940). *Krakh germanskoi okkupatsii na Pskovshchine.* (Leningrad, 1936). *Interventsiia na severe v dokumentakh.* (Moscow, 1933). *Dokumenty o geroicheskoi oborone Petrograda v 1919 godu.* (Moscow, 1941).

[13]S. I. Gusev, "Grazhdanskaia voina i Krasnaia Armiia." *Sbornik voenno-teoreticheskikh i voenno-politicheskikh statei (1918-1924).* The article subsequently appeared in book form entitled *Grazhdanskaia voina i Krasnaia Armiia.* (Moscow, 1925).

And yet, if we disregard this fallacy in Gusev's thesis his presentation has the merit of an able historical and methodological definition of some significant characteristics of the Civil War. One interesting feature he brings out, for instance, is the vital difference between conditions that favor the formation of an armed force of the masses to serve the proletarian cause and those that encourage the formation of a bourgeois state. The latter enjoys the loyalty of the higher-ranking officers and therefore is usually bound to remain a small, elite army. Militarily speaking, the bourgeois army is better qualified, but in due course is bound to lose that advantage since the opposing army sooner or later overcomes its inexperience while the opponent is bound to remain numerically a limited force.

The history of the armies of Kolchak, Denikin, or Vrangel, states Gusev, confirms this view, and he explains why they all had to act in haste, sacrifice long-range planning, witness a quick succession of victories, and lose vision of their distant goals. The stabilization of a political order demanded steady mastery over numerous situations with which the Whites were unable to cope. On the other hand, the proletariat was able to find wide support among the masses and to afford the time for building its armed force at a slower pace, overcoming errors committed during the early period of partisan warfare. For this reason the Red Army, at the end of the Civil War, though suffering from appalling losses and exhaustion of resources, was still in better shape than the White forces. The White defeat was virtually predetermined by its numerical inferiority and the war of swift movement, whereas the Red Army was able to overcome its shortage of command personnel and other original deficiencies.

A. N. Anishev[14] has made an important contribution to the field of modern Russian history with a book of superior analytical quality. The author had no intention of presenting a sequential, chronological history of the Revolution or of the Civil War. He chose a realistic and, at the time it was written, a theoretical generalization of the principal problems presented by the events of 1917-1920. Perhaps the most original aspect of this work is his methodological analysis of the historical process in the light of Marxist-Leninist interpretation. He examines the relationship between the peasantry and the proletariat throughout the revolutionary period, showing which aspect in particular was to be the determining factor in the outcome of the war.

Anishev was also among the first to outline the basic stages in the Civil War, which are briefly as follows: (1) The October Revolution, extending to March, 1918. He considers this the period during which the political opposition was beaten, disorganized, without support from the masses that might have decided the struggle at this time. The bourgeois class found itself in a state of complete disorganization, unable to put up any resistance.

(2) April-May, 1918, a breathing space during which the revolution consolidated its gains. During these weeks, with the assistance of German

[14]A. N. Anishev, *Ocherki istorii grazhdanskoi voiny, 1917-1920 gg.* (Leningrad, 1925).

197

imperialism, the counterrevolution managed to rear its head in the south, while the Entente powers managed counterrevolutionary plots in areas occupied by German armies. The petty-bourgeois elements bent every effort to resist Bolshevism.

(3) June-November, 1918, marked by the struggle of the proletariat and the poorer peasantry against what Anishev describes as the "democratic counterrevolution." This was a period of rivalry between two forms of imperialism, German and Entente, with the Czecholslovak mutiny supported by the kulak elements representing the latter. The July, 1918, crisis in the countryside is the period of the *Kombeds* (Committees of Poor Peasants), the rise of the White Volunteer Army (subsequently known as the Denikin Army), the formation of regular armies, and the complete collapse of attempts to revive the dissolved Constituent Assembly.

(4) The last period, from November, 1918, to the spring of 1920. This was the time during which the struggle between the proletariat and the peasantry against the bourgeois-landlord elements was fiercest, ending in victory for the former coalition. During the same period German imperialism was defeated by the Entente, the counterrevolutionary forces organized themselves for the forthcoming struggle, and the recently formed regular armies clashed, ending with the defeat of Kolchak, Denikin, and Iudenich.

Anishev, for some reason none too clear, brings the story of the Civil War to its end here. It is abruptly terminated at early 1920, leaving out both the Soviet-Polish war and the liquidation of the Vrangel army in the Crimea. Most likely Anishev believes that neither account belongs to the history of the Civil War. The periodization he offers has its merit, since it was the first to stress the importance of internal considerations such as the relationship between city and countryside. Another distinctive feature of his approach to this vast subject is the stress on what he calls the "democratic counterrevolution" led by the Social Revolutionary and Social Democratic parties. But the fact that he left out virtually a whole year of the war, the struggle with Poland and the final expulsion of the White Army from the Crimean Peninsula, or that he hardly discusses the foreign intervention and the blockade, seriously undermines his methodological scheme.

B. THE INTERVENTION

One of the earliest studies of the intervention and blockade appeared in 1922 and was the work of the well-known Soviet writer M. Pavlovich (M. P. Veltman). During the first half of the 1920's Pavlovich began a series of publications under the general title of "RSFSR Within Imperialistic Encirclement," some of which were reissued and expanded, including

198

new materials.[15] All of these books are schematically similar, consisting of three parts: (1) the relations between Russia and each of the countries discussed from the middle of the nineteenth century up to October, 1919, (2) the intervention by one of the Western powers, and (3) the relations between Soviet Russia and the country concerned since the end of the Civil War. The parts dealing with the intervention, in particular, are based on first-hand sources, though specific references are not cited. The style and tone are journalistic; objectivism is not the rule. Since these works were written shortly after the events had occurred, the reader frequently comes across some hasty conclusions that have since been disproved; at times one finds contradictory statements and, more often, assertions not substantiated by any evidence. The main value of Pavlovich's work is its pioneering synthesis of the entire subject of the foreign intervention and the blockade of Soviet Russia.

A few details of Pavlovich's general thesis may not be out of order. At the start he maintains that France was the implacable enemy of Soviet Russia and the leading organizer of the intervention. The main reason, Pavlovich explains, is that Russia was regarded in Paris as an indispensable source of manpower or "cannon fodder," some kind of a "gigantic Senegal." This was a somewhat oversimplified interpretation of Russia's place in the imperialist world prior to 1914. Pavlovich continues to state that the underlying cause of France's opposition to the Treaty of Brest-Litovsk, and the reason for French intervention, was her desire to bring Russia back into the war. As the world's predominant bourgeois state, according to Pavlovich, France was bound to be the most aggressive power, backing intervention in the west and even encouraging Japan to intervene in the Far East.

But Pavlovich points out another consideration: the drive for economic expansion and domination of the Russian market. Indirectly, according to Pavlovich, this explains France's support of Poland, as an attempt to turn this reborn national state into a buffer against both Russia and Germany, as well as against the newly formed Baltic states which were under British influence. Erroneously, Pavlovich maintained that the sole supporter of Vrangel in the Crimea was France.

It should be noted that Pavlovich did not consider Russia's repudiated debts to France as the main concern of French policy. He plausibly argues that regardless of the amount of the debt involved, about 25 billion francs, it could not have justified the intervention, but only served as a pretext.

In his revised edition, Pavlovich came to different conclusions. This time he believed that the leading anti-Soviet crusader was Great Britain. It was London that took the initial step toward military intervention, the

[15] M. Pavlovich (M. P. Veltman), *Sovetskaia Rossiia i kapitalisticheskaia Frantsiia.* (Moscow, 1922). *Sovetskaia Rossiia i kapitalisticheskaia Angliia.* (Moscow, 1922). *Sovetskaia Rossiia i kapitalisticheskaia Amerika.* (Moscow, 1922). New edition: *Sovetskaia Rossiia i kapitalisticheskaia Angliia.* (Moscow, 1925).

landing of English and Japanese troops in Vladivostok. Pavlovich adds a suggestion that hatred of Bolshevism was not, in fact, the determining factor in British conduct, since in London it was firmly believed that the Soviet regime was soon bound to collapse in any case, but he cites no authority for this interpretation.

One of the early general works dealing with the history of Soviet foreign policy, including the intervention and the blockade by the Entente powers, was by the well-known Soviet diplomat and later ambassador to London, Ivan Maiskii.[16] Maiskii's contention is that during the first few months of the Soviet regime the members of the Entente, though they did not conceal their anti-Soviet feelings, showed no active hostility. Partly, Maiskii believes, this is explained by their preoccupation with Germany, partly because of lack of armed forces needed to undertake a campaign against the Soviet regime. Furthermore, the Entente powers continued to cherish hopes that Russia might still reenter the war. During this period there were two distinct views in the Entente camp concerning the "Russian problem." There was a lack of agreement between France and Great Britain as to how far the powers could go in dealing with Russia. France lost more than any other power with the removal of Russia from the Entente: she lost the military support she was counting on and she lost money in the form of debts that were repudiated by the Soviet government. On the other hand, Great Britain, and for that matter the United States, felt less painfully the immediate impact of the October Revolution, and therefore they could afford to demonstrate less animosity and more patience toward the regime. London and Washington expressed readiness to render all possible aid to Russia should the latter reenter the war against Germany. This division of opinion prevailed, according to Maiskii, until the signing of the Treaty of Brest-Litovsk. After that the two views seemed to have been reconciled, both sides coming to agree that open war against Soviet Russia was a necessity.

The first incursions of Entente troops into Soviet territory in the spring of 1918 and the Czechoslovak mutiny formed what Maiskii calls the "small Entente intervention." While this early appearance of troops was still a relatively minor episode, being too far from the national center, the conduct of the Czechoslovak legion was a different matter—it portended far more serious consequences. It is quite clear that Maiskii regards the mutiny as the precursor of a nation-wide civil war and military intervention on a much wider scale. The "small intervention" served thus as a prelude to the far-flung conflict that was to unfold during 1919-1920. Maiskii traces the diplomatic relations between Soviet Russia and the members of the Entente and calls attention to the little-noted fact that complete severance of diplomatic relations took place only by the end of 1918, when the intervention and the blockade gained full force. Maiskii once

[16]I. M. Maiskii, *Vneshniaia politika RSFSR, 1917-1922 gg.* (Moscow, 1922). See footnote No. 4 to Preface.

more places the main burden of blame upon France for fanning the flames of hostility.

The "great intervention," as Maiskii would label it, begins with the all-out aid the Entente offered to Kolchak, Denikin, Iudenich, and other White Army leaders. Maiskii minimizes the role of nations other than France. Great Britain, according to Maiskii, was motivated mainly by her Near Eastern interests and Russian market potentialities. The hostility of the United States toward Soviet Russia, Maiskii believes, was of a passive nature. In the case of Japan, intervention stemmed exclusively from territorial aspiration and from the fact that Tokyo was apprehensive of both the Red and the White armies, fearing both Admiral Kolchak and Comrade Lenin.

In 1925, M. Levidov published a monograph concentrating on the diplomatic background of the Entente intervention.[17] Levidov bases his studies almost entirely on English press reports. He often incorporates contradictory statements that indicate conflicting interpretations of the roles the different nations played in the intervention. The United States, according to Levidov, had no major role in the intervention; France remained in the background, while Japan was an almost passive member under the command of Great Britain. The frequent and indiscriminate use of citations in the book tends to violate chronology and, what is worse, confuse facts. Nevertheless, Levidov's thesis is interesting: that the true object of the intervention from the very beginning was the overthrow of the Soviet regime.

Ia. Ioffe subsequently proposed the same thesis even more extensively in a book on the organization of the intervention and blockade. Only A. I. Gukovskii argued to the contrary, that the main purpose of France in adopting the militant policy of isolating the Soviet Union was to bring Russia back into the war against the central powers.[18]

In 1925 there appeared in the Ukraine the *Black Book,* which included many personal observations, reminiscences, and official documents, accompanied by an interpretative article written by F. Anulov. This was one of the first publications that concentrated upon France's role in the intervention. Later E. E. Iakushkin wrote on the same subject, identifying France as the leading anti-Soviet power. Iakushkin's work, however, lacks true analytical depth, and reveals inadequate familiarity with the sources that were available even at the time he wrote. A more successful attempt at presenting the same thesis was made by L. Poliarnyi and A. F. Speran-

[17]M. Levidov, *K istorii interventsii Rossii. Diplomaticheskaia podgotovka.* (Leningrad, 1925).

[18]Ia. Ioffe, *Organizatsiia interventsii i blokady Sovetskoi respubliki (1918-1920 gg.).* (Moscow, 1930). A. I. Gukovskii, *Frantsuzskaia interventsiia na Iuge Rossii.* (Moscow, 1928).

skii, in a collection of articles marking the tenth anniversary of the intervention.[19]

Other writers devoted their attention to the role of Great Britain, tracing the intervention in the north and arguing that she was the main organizer and leading force in carrying out the intervention and the blockade.[20] A second work by M. S. Kedrov was published in 1930, in which he deals with the English intervention in Murmansk and the treacherous conduct of some members of the local soviet. Finally, N. Kornatovskii and I. I. Mints made excellent use of a large quantity of documentary sources on the subject gathered from local and central archives. During the early 1930's other works were published that covered the British intervention in the Caucasus and in Central Asia, the German intervention in the west, and the Japanese penetration in the Far East.[21]

In addition, I. I. Mints has announced a projected three-volume history of the Revolution and the Civil War. Mints has travelled extensively, visited western European countries as well as the United States, is familiar with archival depositories abroad, and has a far broader grasp of historical developments than many of his colleagues. His lifework will be worth watching for.

The part played by the United States in the intervention is discussed far less in Soviet historiography. Occasional references to the participation of the United States demonstrate unusual restraint and moderation in judgment. "President Wilson emphasized many times," states I. M. Maiskii, "that he did not contemplate any intervention whatever in Russian affairs and that he wished the Russian people only freedom and prosperity." Maiskii further states that as one of the intervening powers,

[19] E. E. Iakushkin, *Angliiskaia interventsiia v 1918-1920 gg.* (Moscow, 1928). E. E. Iakushkin, *Frantsuzskaia interventsiia na iuge, 1918-1919.* (Moscow, 1929). L. Poliarnyi, "Interventy v Krymu." *Sbornik. K desiatiletiiu interventsii.* (Moscow, 1929). A. F. Speranskii, "Vmeshatelstvo inostrannykh derzhav vo vnutrennie dela Rossii." *Sbornik. K desiatiletiiu interventsii.* (Moscow, 1929).

[20] See N. N., "Angliiskaia interventsiia na Severe v 1919 g." *Murmanskii sbornik,* Nos. 7-8 (1923). M. Svechnikov, "Soiuznichskaia interventsiia na Severe Sovetskoi Rossii." *Kto dolzhnik? Sbornik.* (Moscow, 1926). M. K. Vetoshkin, *Revoliutsiia i grazhdanskaia voina na Severe.* (Moscow, 1927). M. S. Kedrov, *Za Sovetskii Sever.* (Moscow, 1927). E. E. Iakushkin, *Angliiskaia interventsiia v 1918-1920 gg.* (Moscow, 1928).

[21] M. S. Kedrov, *Bez bolshevistskogo rukovodstva. (Iz istorii interventsii na Murmane).* (Moscow, 1930). N. Kornatovskii, *Severnaia kontrrevoliutsiia.* (Moscow, 1931). I. I. Mints, *Angliiskaia interventsiia i severnaia kontrrevoliutsiia.* (Moscow, 1931). *Imperialicheskaia nemetskaia okkupatsiia.* (Moscow, 1929). A. Zimionko, *Okkupatsiia i interventsiia v Belorussii.* (Moscow, 1932). I. I. Mints, *Interventsiia na severe v dokumentakh.* (Moscow, 1933). Iu. N. Aleskerov, *Interventsiia i grazhdanskaia voina v Srednei Azii.* (Tashkent, 1959). A. B. Kadishev, *Interventsiia i grazhdanskaia voina v Zakavkaze.* (Moscow, 1960).

the United States was not as active as either Great Britain or France, but usually followed a conciliatory line.[22]

An article contributed by N. E. Kakurin to a book entitled *Kto dolzh-nik?* (Who's the Debtor?) deals with the part played by the Entente powers in the economy of the White governments during the Civil War.[23] Kakurin uses archival materials to show that without the economic aid of the intervening powers the White armies would not have been able to put up such a long and stubborn resistance. Kakurin points out further that the counterrevolutionary governments that emerged in the peripheral states had no economic basis for independent existence. The White governments had no opportunity to utilize to any extent the military stock left from the World War. The bases and arsenals where the revolution firmly established itself from the very start continued to be under Soviet control. The result was that only the imperialists were able to assure the White armies of sufficient supplies for any long struggle against the Soviet regime.

Kakurin divides the interventionist states into two groups, the active and the passive ones, defining each not so much by the material assistance rendered as by the goals toward which they aspired in the so-called "Russian solution." In the case of France, her goal was to preserve an undivided Russia, motivated largely by her need for a strong ally not only against Germany, but against an Anglo-Saxon coalition which favored German restoration. On the other hand, Great Britain and the United States were regarded as more serious potential foes of the Revolution since they were financially capable of supporting more effectively the cause of the White armies. Kakurin points out two forms of aid the Entente powers were able to render: one, direct equipment of the White governments with manpower, military supplies, and finance; the other, indirect aid, such as providing favorable conditions for procurement of military equipment and credits, and securing favorable communications with the outside world. Kakurin cites the case of Admiral Kolchak as illustration. Statistical data and charts indicate in detail the amount and form of aid the Entente members had given to the different White governments of Russia. Most of the figures are related to aid coming from the United States, yet the author emphasizes the special role France and Great Britain played in the intervention.

In 1928, on account of the tenth anniversary of the intervention, the Institute of World Economy and World Politics began to publish a series of books devoted to the relations of the Soviet Union with the outside

[22]I. M. Maiskii, *Vneshniaia politika RSFSR 1917-1922 gg.* (Moscow, 1922).

[23]N. E. Kakurin, "Rol derzhav Antanty v voennoi ekonomike belykh pravitelstv vo vremia grazhdanskoi voiny v Rossii." *Kto dolzhnik? Sbornik dokumentirovannykh statei po voprosu ot otnosheniiakh mezhdu Rossiei, Frantsiei i drugimi derzhavami Antanty do voiny 1914 g., vo vremia voiny i v period interventsii.* A. G. Shliapnikov, ed. (Moscow, 1926), 521-564.

world during the decade 1918-1928. The first book in this series was written by L. Ivanov and deals entirely with the foreign intervention.[24] The study is based on both Soviet and foreign sources. The author believes that the initial steps toward intervention took place early in 1918, when the Soviet government had publicly annulled all foreign debts.

Ivanov discusses at considerable length the reasons for and peculiarities of United States anti-Soviet policy. He explains that American animosity was not less than that of the Entente, the only difference being that its expression was more hesitant, less formulated or pronounced. American vacillations could be explained largely by fears that active intervention might be exploited by Japan, Great Britain, or France, in their own national interests, which accounts for the half-hearted participation of the United States in the Far East. However, insists the author, the American government looked with definite disfavor toward schemes of panicky, fearful allies who contemplated partitioning the eastern European colossus. In part, the author explains Washington's Soviet policy by the general inflexibility of the foreign policy pursued by the State Department, as well as by the leisurely, inefficient, or unwieldy American diplomatic machine at times when action was urgent.

Ivanov was one of the few Soviet historians during the 1920's who included France among those who at times supported a repartitioning of Russia. As proof he cited the Entente declaration made public on August 20, 1919, recognizing the independence of the Baltic States. The reason France joined this declaration, Ivanov believed, was her desire to use these peripheral states as anti-Soviet landing bases. Another proof, according to the same writer, were the offensives of Poland and Vrangel which were mainly instigated by France.

Ivanov concludes that the difference of opinion among the members of the Entente as to the Russian problem was largely instrumental in Soviet Russia's victory in 1920. The lack of unanimity led to the decision of France, Great Britain, and Italy to end the intervention while continuing the policy of blockade and isolation of Russia; it also led to the decision of the Supreme Economic Council of the Entente in January, 1920, favoring the resumption of trade relations with Russia. This, according to Ivanov, only contributed to widening the gulf between Great Britain and France in their effort to find a solution to the Russian question. These factors led Ivanov to the premature conclusion that the anti-Soviet united front had already collapsed in 1920 and that thereafter France was the only country that supported a policy of intervention.

The tenth anniversary of the intervention continued to be observed by articles appearing in the press and in periodical literature during 1929. B. E. Shtein reexamines the entire issue from a historico-juridical point of view,[25] suggesting that the semi-trade agreements concluded in

[24]L. Ivanov, *SSSR i imperialisticheskoe okruzhenie.* (Moscow, Komakademiia, 1928).

[25]B. E. Shtein, "Vooruzhennoe vmeshatelstvo—odin iz metodov interventsii." *Sbornik. K desiatiletiiu interventsii.* (Moscow, 1929). See footnote No. 4 to Preface.

1920-1921 between Soviet Russia and some of the capitalist countries
did not signify a complete end of the intervention. Shtein then proceeds
to differentiate between "intervention" and "armed intervention,"
arguing that with the end of the Civil War the latter was terminated, but
not the former. Intervention in a broad sense, as interference in affairs
of the Soviet Union on the part of the imperialist powers, was a common
phenomenon. It took different forms, such as military meddling, blockade
action, aid to counterrevolutionary armies, recognition of opposing governments, refusal to recognize the Soviet state, non-recognition of Soviet
laws, economic intervention, and other policies which tended to discrimi-
nate against the Soviet government.

I. I. Mints contributed a monograph on British participation and aid
to the counterrevolution in the north, which he originally presented
as a seminar paper in a class conducted by M. N. Pokrovskii.[26] Mints
tries to show, and with a degree of success, that direct interference by the
Entente countries in Russia's internal affairs might be detected as early
as 1916-1917, that is, at the time when there seemed imminent danger of
Russia's withdrawal from the war. The interference increased during the
months of the Provisional Government when prospects of a separate
peace seemed even greater. This, explains Mints, was partly the reason
why the British supported General Kornilov.

The defeat of Kornilov increased the fear in the west of the revolutionary advances and increased the reasons for intervention. With the
October Revolution the threat of direct intervention became a reality,
motivated by a multitude of new considerations. Mints challenges the
view that a major reason for the intervention was the annulment of foreign debts. He questions the belief that the Soviet government might, so
to speak, have paid off intervention. French insistence upon honoring
financial obligations began only in the fall of 1918. Besides, Foreign
Commissar B. Chicherin in January, 1919, and Lenin in March, 1919,
both informed the Entente through William Bullitt's secret mission that
the Soviet government was ready to recognize foreign debts in return
for diplomatic recognition and a peace settlement.

Mints was one of the first in Soviet historiography to examine carefully the question of foreign debts contracted prior to 1917. He cate-
gorized these and concluded that the real conflict was over the sums
that were loaned to Russia by private, mainly French, banks. These
loans, states Mints, though not of too great importance economically,
stimulated the inimical French petit bourgeoisie, and armed it with
slogans aimed against the Soviet regime. The issue was sharpened further when postwar economic difficulties in France, combined with
contractual obligations to pay French bond-holders the accumulated interests on Russian bonds, agitated public opinion in favor of intervention

[26] I. I. Mints, *Angliiskaia interventsiia i severnaia kontrrevoliutsiia.* (Moscow, 1931).
Part of this work originally appeared in *Proletarskaia revoliutsiia:* "Esery v Arkhangelske," No. 11 (58), (1926), 56-81.

as a means to force the Soviet government to meet its obligations. The conclusion Mints reaches is: it was primarily Soviet Russia's withdrawal from the war, and only secondly the annulment of foreign debts, that motivated the intervention. To obscure the true motive of the policy the Entente powers declared that the intervention was a means of self-defense against the threat of world revolution advocated by Bolshevism; that only by destroying Soviet armed power would the Western world rid itself of the imminent threat.

In a similar vein Mints tries to prove that the Treaty of Brest-Litovsk released an increased tide of anti-Soviet propaganda. It was during this very period that Great Britain urged Japan to intervene against Russia under the pretext of defending Siberia against possible German penetration into that area. Mints believed that the United States was not in favor of Japanese intervention; Japan and the United States, according to Mints, held conflicting views concerning Siberia, a fact which proved of indirect benefit to the Soviet government. It was under pressure from Washington that Britain, France, and the United States declared themselves to have no part in Japan's intervention, Mints asserts.

Finally, Mints observes that during the conferences of Versailles the enmity toward Soviet Russia increased, and the intervention was now motivated entirely by a desire to eradicate Bolshevism. But Mints holds the view of other Soviet historians, though his differs from that of Gukovskii, that France had no desire to break up the former Russian Empire or to establish spheres of influence in that country. He argues more convincingly than his colleagues that both British and American opinion favored the use of German occupation forces to destroy the Soviet regime; only France was adamantly against such a scheme. Mints was perhaps the first writer to analyze the abortive effort to summon the Prinkipo conference largely as a means to stall Bolshevist expansion and save the cause of the White armies. Mints' tendency to say much more about Great Britain than about the other Entente members is a result of his having utilized primarily English sources.

In summary, the historical literature that deals with the Civil War and foreign intervention handles successfully the following basic subjects: (1) the historic premises, peculiarities, and significance of the Civil War in Soviet Russia; (2) the national effort and the collaboration between the military and home fronts that contributed to victory; (3) the basic reasons for foreign intervention and the forms it assumed, as well as the conflicting interests among the intervening powers and the part each nation played; (4) the advantages Soviet military strategy enjoyed, and how these contributed to final victory; and (5) a clear periodization of the Civil War and foreign intervention, including the last phase, the Soviet-Polish conflict.

C. STALIN AND THE HISTORY OF
THE CIVIL WAR

Reference has already been made to the lengthening shadow of Stalin over historical writing, even during the late 1920's and early 1930's. Historical writing became increasingly uncritical, subservient, and obliging to the Stalinist line. From the lofty vantage point of national history—strident nationalism becoming extremely vociferous—the personality of Stalin entered the ranks of immortals. Stalin became a true incarnation of history. It would perhaps be neither out of order nor uninteresting to consider briefly this development.

Beginning with the late 1920's the entire story of the Civil War, nay, the entire account of the Revolution, began to revolve increasingly around the personality of Stalin. Historical facts were more crudely falsified, events were magnified where it was convenient, minimized when necessary, to fit them into the pattern of the "cult of the individual." Complex war problems were reduced to absurdly simplified and falsified accounts; many a prominent party leader was either reduced to insignificance or eliminated entirely from the records of history. On the other hand, the three-year Civil War with all its ramifications was confined within a narrow framework in order to magnify the figure of Stalin to proportions that would dominate the scene. The history of the Civil War, as the history of the Communist Party itself, became synonymous with the ubiquitous Stalin, whose word of wisdom in every field of human knowledge was authoritative and final. Any deviation detected was interpreted as deviation from the party line, a deadly heresy, sabotage against the Soviet state and Soviet society which Stalin was building with such success.

Henceforth, if an author hoped that any of his written works would be published, he had to pay tribute in most humble manner to Stalin, refer to his infinite wisdom, and represent him as the mastermind of the Revolution. Former publications that conflicted with the newly risen cult were either destroyed or banned from library shelves and placed under lock and key. Historians placed their livelihood in jeopardy, since the state controlled the publication of all books. Writers who were disinclined to betray their ideological faith were not only deprived of the right to publish, but came to face exile or even death.

The question was often asked, how one man could assume so much power without challenge. One episode might at least in part serve as an answer. In 1956, when N. S. Khrushchev denounced Stalin at the Twentieth Congress of the Communist Party, a written question handed to him asked where he was and what was he doing while Stalin was in power. Khrushchev read the note and then thrice asked the author to identify himself, but there was a dead silence. Whereupon Khrushchev concluded: "I did the same thing during the reign of Stalin."

Following the denunciation of Stalin some historians tried in all fairness to revise what they wrote during that period. More moderate writers seem willing to recognize Stalin's contribution to the Soviet war effort during the Civil War, though no more than that of any other prominent members of the party. Some point out that Stalin, like others, actually committed serious errors which his hagiographers failed to mention or refused to recognize. For instance, during the summer and fall of 1918 Stalin committed grave errors on the southern front, as well as in the spring of 1919 at Petrograd, and a year later on the southwestern front. Finding himself in the vicinity of Tsaritsyn during the early part of the Civil War, he contributed a good deal to the successful outcome of that battle by providing strategically vital materials and provisions, but surely it was an accomplishment no greater than that of many others on other fronts.

During the cult period, writers stressed that Stalin contributed both administratively and militarily to the war effort of the Red Army, but conveniently passed by in silence the various occasions when Stalin meddled in war affairs with harmful effects. It has been commonly recognized that the position of the Red Army on the southern front was worsened as a result of his insistence that effort be concentrated elsewhere. Stalin greatly overestimated the importance of the Tsaritsyn sector, and saw to it that the best forces and war supplies were sent there, thereby weakening other sectors of the front that were strategically more vital.

Stalin was skeptical and suspicious of all former tsarist army officers employed in the Red Army, despite the fact that they were desperately needed during the early stages of the Civil War. He badly underestimated the importance of the Don and Voronezh fronts. Both Stalin and Voroshilov at times demonstrated a high degree of insubordination in regard to the High Command, or even the southern command. They regarded some of the most capable high military officers, such as N. I. Podvoiskii, A. I. Okulov, and other loyal members of the party, with sheer contempt. In October, 1918, at the suggestion of Lenin, the Central Committee recalled Stalin and later Voroshilov from the southern front. Lenin correctly sensed that during the summer and fall months of 1918 the eastern front was bound to become the most important. It was here and not at Tsaritsyn that the first regularly organized and disciplined Red Army units were formed which later came to play a decisive part in the outcome of the Civil War.[27]

Many memoirs were published during the 1920's that concern the Civil War in the south, some of which deal wholly or in part with the defense of Tsaritsyn. Was the battle of Tsaritsyn strategically as significant as described by the Stalinist sycophants? Was it as decisive in every

---

[27] In 1967 there appeared a three-volume collection (in four parts) of valuable documents and materials on the history of the Civil War in the Ukraine, some of which were published for the first time. Altogether about 2,000 have been gathered in this collection. *Grazhdanskaia voina na Ukraine.* Arkhivnoe upravlenie pri Sovete Ministrov Uk. SSR. Tsentralnyi gosudarstvennyi arkhiv Oktiabrskoi revoliutsii i sotsialisticheskogo stroitelstva Uk. SSR. Institut istorii. (Kiev, 1967). 3 vols. in 4 parts.

other respect as they would make us believe? These issues became subjects of special strategic, as well as political, significance.[28] Two particularly distinguished accounts, one by A. Kamenskii, the other by D. Zhloba, were published in the *General History of the Civil War.*[29]

In the early 1920's there appeared a study by F. Anulov, the first extensive monographic work on the defense of Tsaritsyn. Here the author carefully examined the economic and strategic importance of Tsaritsyn. Located at the northeastern border of the Don region, the city became a strategic center; its possession signified control over most of the north-south transportation and over contacts with the Don region and the Caucasus. Possession of Tsaritsyn also meant a commanding position over the Lower Volga, the northern shores of the Caspian, and all traffic along the southeastern, Donets, and northern Caucasian railroad system. A combination of economic and geographic peculiarities, according to Anulov, determined the strategic importance of Tsaritsyn during the Civil War.[30]

Successful hold of Tsaritsyn meant a free hand in the northerly direction, and the unity of the defensive line between the Don and Volga regions, along which the Czechoslovak Legion had operated. Had General Krasnov been successful in seizing Tsaritsyn, he would have been able to link the front line with the rebellious Orenburg and Ural Cossacks. The capture of Tsaritsyn by the White armies of the south would have enabled them to move toward Turkestan, forming a united front that would have been able to join hands with the forces of Admiral Kolchak and coordinate a forceful offensive against Moscow. In short, as Anulov concludes, the fall of Tsaritsyn at this time might have made possible the political unification and formation of a common front of all the counterrevolutionary forces in the eastern and southeastern areas, presenting a formidable challenge to the Soviet regime.

These were all basically correct assumptions, though they displayed a degree of partiality. Anulov, for illustration, fails to point out that without the successful offensive carried out simultaneously by the Red Army on the eastern front during August and September of 1918, the successful

---

[28]A. A. Frenkel, *Orly revoliutsii. Russkaia Vandeia. Ocherki grazhdanskoi voiny na Donu.* (Moscow, 1920). Ia. Poluian, *Ocherki grazhdanskoi voiny na Kubani.* (Krasnodar, 1921). M. Dobrianitskii, "Zelenye partizany (1918-1920 gg.)." *Proletarskaia revoliutsiia,* Nos. 8-9 (1924). V. Favitskii, "Zelenaia armiia v Chernomorie." *Proletarskaia revoliutsiia,* Nos. 8-9 (1924). *Istoriia revoliutsionnogo dvizheniia na Tereke. Sbornik statei, vospominanii i materialov.* (Piatigorsk, 1924). Ia. Galov, comp., *1918 god na Severnom Kavkaze. Vospominanii uchastnikov.* (N.p., 1928). K. Butaev, *Borba gortsev za revoliutsiiu.* (Vladikavkaz, 1922). M. Pavlovich (M. P. Veltman), *Volonter. Na vysotakh krasnogo Dagestana.* (Moscow, 1921). G. I. Fedorov, *1918-1919 gg. v Chechne i Groznom.* (Groznyi, 1927).

[29]A. Kamenskii, "Ot Donbassa k Tsaritsynu," and D. Zhloba, "Ot Nevinnomyskoi do Tsaritsyna." *Grazhdanskaia voina, 1918-1921 gg.* (Moscow, 1928), Vol. I, 4-34.

[30]F. Anulov, "Krasnyi Verden (borba za Tsaritsyn v 1918-1919 gg.)." *Sbornik trudov voenno-nauchnogo obshchestva pri Voennoi akademii,* No. 3 (1922).

defense of Tsaritsyn would hardly have been possible. Moreover, it could be claimed that the main strategic problem was solved by the Red Army on the eastern front, and in the overall military plan the defense of Tsaritsyn played a secondary part. Furthermore, had Tsaritsyn fallen into the hands of the Whites in the summer of 1919 the event would have been far less decisive than in 1918, since by that time the army of Kolchak was pushed far eastward and a White victory at Tsaritsyn at this date would have been a triumph of limited local nature.

Another work on the Tsaritsyn front that should be cited is the one by L. L. Kliuev.[31] The author was one of the active participants in the defense of Tsaritsyn during the entire period of the Civil War. According to Kliuev, the successful establishment of the Soviet regime in the more industrially advanced areas of the country compelled the White Armies to seek firm bases in less advanced regions, such as the areas along the middle, and particularly the lower, Volga as well as in the Don Cossack country, with the exception of the Don basin. Here, it was believed, the counterrevolution could establish its main base in cooperation with the prosperous Cossack population, establish convenient contact with the Entente powers, and in due course launch a military offensive.

Kliuev correctly points out that from an economic as well as a strategic point of view Tsaritsyn was vital to both sides, the Whites and the Reds. But Kliuev errs seriously when he attaches the same importance to Tsaritsyn throughout the entire period of the Civil War. The city was far less important, strategically speaking, in the summer of 1919 than it was a year previously. Nor does Kliuev point out the role Tsaritsyn played in the summer of 1918 in the delivery of vital provisions to the Red Army, or the starving towns and cities. Still, all in all, taking into consideration that the work was published in 1928, Kliuev presents a fairly accurate, objective account of the defense of Tsaritsyn, free from the excessive praise and adulation of Stalin which later became so common.

Distorted accounts of the defense of Tsaritsyn began to appear during the 1920's. In 1930 a collection of essays was published under the title *Revoliutsionnyi Stalingrad* in which the first chapter, written by the then Marshal Voroshilov, was entitled "Stalin and the Red Army." The Voroshilov version set a pace and a pattern to the legend about Stalin that lasted throughout his lifetime. Writers cast aside all originality, objectivity, integrity, and bent every fact to a single purpose—to prove that Stalin alone was responsible for the triumph at Tsaritsyn; nay, that he was the only "distinguished organizer of the Civil War victories." Voroshilov presented his flattering thesis without citing any convincing evidence, profusely quoting carefully selected telegrams and other documents out of context. With the exception of the chapter by A. Urgapov, the entire volume is the earliest evidence of the inflated importance of the "Tsaritsyn front," at the expense of other fronts which

[31] L. L. Kliuev, *Borba za Tsaritsyn (1918-1919 gg.).* (Moscow, 1928).

in fact played a far more vital role during the same Civil War.[32] Not until the Twentieth Congress of the Communist Party was this fiction corrected in historical literature, were authors censured and publications given warning to cease falsifying history and glorifying individuals.[33]

The entire question of the role of Tsaritsyn in the overall strategy of the Civil War was gradually built up to become a subject of serious discussion. While Stalin was in power Tsaritsyn's military importance had been exaggerated beyond all proportions.[34] Other versions came from such writers as L. L. Kliuev, former Chief of Staff of the Tenth Army, and later of the First Cavalry Army. Another account is by S. Minin, former member of the Military Revolutionary Council (VRS). Though these writers were active participants in the events they describe, they do not rely only upon personal observations and experiences, but have used many of the archival records, official orders and decrees, and reports to substantiate their views. This is particularly notable in the case of Minin and the previously noted works of F. Anulov.[35]

While the defense of Tsaritsyn was magnified, the history of concurrent events suffered. The defense of Petrograd became a second-rate operation, since Stalin was not there. The southwestern front was given only casual mention, despite the fact that this theater of war, by the end of 1919, had become vitally important. The role of the Red Army was minimized, but the narrow strip of the front where Stalin happened to be became the hub of the Civil War. There is hardly a reference to the plans Lenin had recommended, which emphasized the grave danger of General Denikin's army. The Red cavalry units are given credit for their share in the defeat of Denikin's troops and for driving the invading Polish army out of the Ukraine, but the infantry is hardly cited. A. M. Gorky's original plan of presenting a full and true picture of the Civil War yielded to the construction of a pedestal for Stalin. The most flagrant illustration of this rising cult of the individual may be found in the article written by K. E. Voroshilov on the occasion of Stalin's fiftieth birthday,

[32] *Revoliutsionnyi Stalingrad. Sbornik.* (Moscow, 1930). See chapter by A. Urgapov, "God borby za Stalingrad, iiun 1918—iiun 1919 g."

[33] *Voprosy ideologicheskoi raboty. Sbornik vazhneishikh reshenii KPSS (1954-1961).* (Moscow, 1961). Note particularly the resolution of March 9, 1957, concerning the magazine *Voprosy istorii,* pp. 244-245.

[34] See, as an illustration, V. A. Melikov, *Geroicheskaia oborona Tsaritsyna (1918 g.).* (Moscow, 1938).

[35] L. L. Kliuev, *Borba za Tsaritsyn (1918-1919 gg.).* (Moscow, 1928). L. L. Kliuev, "Rol Krasnogo Tsaritsyna." *Krasnaia Armiia,* No. 13 (1923). L. L. Kliuev, *Kamyshinskaia operatsiia Desiatoi Krasnoi Armii, iiul 1919 g.* (Moscow, 1928). S. Minin, *Gorod-boets.* (Moscow, 1925).

and published in 1929 in the *General History of the Civil War,* referred to elsewhere.[36]

Voroshilov's essay on Stalin and the Red Army argues that it was Stalin's plan to make Tsaritsyn the focal battleground of the war, with priority over the defense of Petrograd and the war in the south. This legend, repeated in every history book on the Civil War as long as Stalin was at the helm of power, was often referred to as the "Stalin Plan."

The cult of the individual took a heavy toll in Russia, and left its deepest scars in the field of historical writing. The hosannas chanted for the leader failed occasionally to muffle the few scholarly efforts at presenting more objective accounts, but the fact remains that Stalinism ruled supreme. The rising fear of war with Germany encouraged an indigenous Soviet patriotism in which history was exploited almost brazenly. Episodes from the past, such as the futile German campaigns in eastern Europe, were revived "as a reminder." Some went so far back as to describe the defeat of the Teutonic Order by Alexander Nevskii, tracing history through the ages to the First World War and the "abominable Treaty of Brest-Litovsk," the occupation of the Ukraine, and the eventual expulsion of the occupying troops within less than a year.[37]

Stalin not only forced others to accept his political and military wisdom, but was himself convinced of his great acumen, to judge by his own version of his "Short Biography" that accompanies *The History of the Communist Party.* He says: "At various stages of the [civil] war, Stalin's genius found the correct solutions that took account of all the circumstances of the situation. . . . The battles in which Comrade Stalin directed the Soviet armies are brilliant examples of operational military skill."

From approximately 1930 until the middle of the 1950's, historians usually followed this pattern, tirelessly referring to Stalin as a military genius. A short history of the Civil War in Russia that appeared in 1933, by S. E. Rabinovich, was perhaps the first earnest attempt to present a general account of the war that reflected the new Stalinist version. Yet even this work was severely taken to task for not allowing greater prominence to Stalin's part in the war. Two years later, in a new "revised and enlarged" edition, the author eliminated some of the "errors"

[36]K. E. Voroshilov, *Stalin i Krasnaia Armiia.* (Moscow, 1929). *Stalin and the Red Army.* (Moscow, Foreign Languages Publishing House, 1942). K. E. Voroshilov, *Stalin i Vooruzhennye Sily SSSR.* (Moscow, 1950). *Stalin and the Armed Forces of the USSR.* (Moscow, Foreign Languages Publishing House, 1951). *Genialnyi polkovodets Velikoi Otechestvennoi Voiny.* (Moscow, 1950). *Stalin i Krasnaia Armiia. Stati i rechi.* (Moscow, 1934).

[37]A. Gukovskii, "Vtorzhenie nemtsev v Stranu Sovetov v 1918 godu." *Istoricheskie zapiski,* No. 13 (1942), 3-39.

detected by Voroshilov. The cringing style of historical writing began to establish itself firmly in Soviet historiography.[38]

The rewriting of history began to border on psychopathology, as reflected by the newly revised *Short Course of the History of the All-Union Communist Party (Bolsheviks)*. Even book titles and individual chapter headings came to tell a story. One of Melikov's books was called *Stalin's Plan to Rout Denikin*; another one, on the defense of Tsaritsyn, faithfully followed the Voroshilov version; a third was called *Cooperation Between the Western and Southwestern Fronts and the Battles in the Areas of Warsaw and Lvov in 1920*. The thesis of this last book was simply that the Red Army was defeated at the Vistula River mainly because of the blundering of the commanding officers.

The crowning example of all this is the new edition of the history of the Communist Party, and is best described by N. S. Khrushchev himself in his celebrated speech at the Twentieth Congress of the party. The passage deserves full citation. It reads:

> As is known, the *Short Course of the History of the All-Union Communist Party (Bolsheviks)* was written by a commission of the party Central Committee.
> This book, parenthetically, was also permeated with the cult of the individual and was written by a designated group of authors. This fact was reflected in the following formulation on the proof copy of the *Short Biography* of Stalin:
> "A commission of the Central Committee, All-Union Communist Party (Bolsheviks), under the direction of Comrade Stalin and with his most active personal participation, has prepared a *Short Course of the History of the All-Union Communist Party (Bolsheviks)*."
> But even this phrase did not satisfy Stalin. The following sentence replaced it in the final version of the *Short Biography*:
> "In 1938 appeared the book *History of the All-Union Communist Party (Bolsheviks), Short Course*, written by Comrade Stalin and approved by a commission of the Central Committee, All-Union Communist Party (Bolsheviks)."

The episode calls for no further comments! Stalinism was no mere paranoid fancy; to the last it remained brutal, oppressive, crushing. Veneration of Stalin came to reach trinitarian proportions.

From the early 1930's we find research expanding rapidly, mainly because of the impressive growth of archival collections. Regrettably, the period that followed coincided with the full exercise of power by Stalin. Many prominent party figures were either forced into the background or eliminated altogether from the stage of history, while Stalin kept looming ever larger. Even the Russian masses were assigned

[38]S. E. Rabinovich, *Istoriia grazhdanskoi voiny. Kratkii ocherk.* (Moscow, 1933). 2nd ed., revised and enlarged under the editorship of I. I. Mints. (Moscow, 1935). V. Voronov, *Oktiabrskii kontr-udar na iuzhnom fronte v 1919 g.* (Moscow, 1933). N. Evseev, *Flangovyi udar na Voronezh-Kastornaia.* (Moscow, 1936).

a minor role while the leader became the decisive figure at every turn in history. Historical writing became increasingly subjective, historical facts more mutilated for the sake of proving preconceived versions. Scholarly studies became more rare while works formerly published were placed under seven seals, available only to specially authorized persons.

As an illustration of a common practice, the following example may be cited. As late as 1955, a collection of 206 leaflets, originally issued in one form or another by the Caucasian Social-Democratic Party between 1903 and 1905, was gathered and published as a source-book. Of the 206 leaflets, eighty were republished for the first time. The collection is accompanied by a preface which explains the purpose of the reissue and reveals the general atmosphere of this time.[39]

According to the author of the preface, Stalin towered above all other members of the party. Furthermore, the author asserts, in 1901 and 1902 Stalin was responsible for organizing the Social-Democratic units in Tiflis (Tbilisi), Baku, and Batum; other party members who played an equally prominent part received only casual mention, or none at all. Names like Leonid Krasin, Mikhail Pleshakov, Stepan Shauman, Lado Ketskhoveli, or Viktor Kurnatovskii are not to be found.

The same preface also asserts that Stalin was the leader of the Caucasian Social-Democratic Party, when actually he was only one of the members of the Committee. One of the oldest members, Mikha Tskhakaia, is not mentioned at all. The same writer states that Stalin founded the illegal press in the autumn of 1903, the very period when Stalin happened to have been not in the Caucasus at all, but banished to Siberia, whence he escaped only in January, 1904. The preface states further that in December, 1904, Stalin led the Baku strike, whereas a more careful check reveals that the party committee in charge of the strike did not include Stalin but was made up of three other members, Dzhaparidze, Stopani, and Fioletov. This is the way history was written until the very end of the Stalin period!

In 1942, a collection of essays was published under the title *Twenty-five Years of Historical Science in the USSR*, in which I. I. Mints reported on the progress of the projected history of the Civil War. Of the sixteen volumes originally planned, the first one appeared in 1936, while the second did not make its appearance until six years later.[40] The war impeded further progress, though several related collections of documents were published on such subjects as the organization of the Red Army, the fiasco of the German occupation of the Ukraine (an

[39] *Listovki Kavkazskogo soiuza RSDRP 1903-1905 gg.* Published by the Institute of Party History at the Central Committee of Georgia. (Moscow, 1955). See review by G. A. Aratiunov in *Voprosy istorii*, No. 4 (1956), 158-160.

[40] *Istoriia grazhdanskoi voiny v SSSR.* Vol. I, *Podgotovka Velikoi proletarskoi revoliutsii.* (Moscow, 1936). Vol. II, *Velikaia proletarskaia revoliutsiia.* (Moscow, 1942).

earlier volume on the occupation of Georgia appeared in 1918), and the defense of Tsaritsyn during the Civil War. Undoubtedly war conditions provided the stimulus to publish these volumes, so as to re-emphasize the failure of former German aggression in Russia.[41]

At the end of World War II the Institute of Marxism-Leninism took charge of the long-delayed project and a special section of the Institute was designated to carry it out. Finally, in 1957 the third volume of the history of the Civil War appeared, covering the period of consolidation of the Soviet regime and the beginning of the foreign intervention and Civil War. The fourth came out in 1959, and in 1960 the final volume appeared.[42]

After 1956 there followed a rapid—possibly too rapid—reaction against the Stalinist cult, proceeding with a speed that makes one apprehensive. The standardized anathematization, in ritual cant, that condemns the cult of the individual seems at times mechanical and uniform. It becomes even more alarming when one finds among the ritualists many writers who only recently praised the genius of Stalin. There are only a few exceptions, as in the case of A. P. Nosov, who quite frankly admits his firm Stalinist views. His book on historiography has been banned, and references to it are frowned upon. Obviously it will take a long period of time to repair the damage Stalinism inflicted upon the historical science. It will also take some time to cleanse the stains from many of those who advanced their academic careers through "accommodation" during the rule of Stalin. A single sentence or two in a preface, condemning the cult of the individual, is scarcely adequate, and fails to conceal the indignity of scholars who quickly joined the chorus of critics formed shortly after the Twentieth Congress of the Communist Party.

In view of what has been said, it must be recognized that the completion of the five-volume *History of the Civil War in the USSR* was no minor achievement. The assigned task was complicated further by the location of evidence formerly withheld by the government. Only

[41]*Dokumenty o geroicheskoi oborone Tsaritsyna v 1918 g.* (Moscow, 1942). *Dokumenty o razgrome germanskikh okkupantov na Ukraine v 1918 g.* (Moscow, 1942). *Germanskie okkupanty v Gruzii v 1918 g.* (Tbilisi, 1918). *Razgrom nemetskikh zakhvatchikov v 1918 g.* (Moscow, 1943). *Organizatsiia Krasnoi Armii, 1917-1918.* (Moscow, 1943).

[42]*Istoriia grazhdanskoi voiny v SSSR.* Vol. III, *Uprochenie sovetskoi vlasti. Nachalo inostrannoi voennoi interventsii i grazhdanskoi voiny (noiabr 1917 g.—mart 1919 g.).* (Moscow, 1957). Vol. IV, *Reshaiushchie pobedy Krasnoi Armii nad obedinennymi silami Antanty i vnutrennei kontrrevoliutsii (mart 1919 g.—fevral 1920 g.).* (Moscow, 1959). Vol. V, *Konets voennoi interventsii i grazhdanskoi voiny v SSSR. Likvidatsiia poslednikh ochagov kontrrevoliutsii (fevral 1920 g.—oktiabr 1922 g.).* (Moscow, 1960). See reviews in *Voprosy istorii,* No. 6 (1958); No. 12 (1960). *Istoriia SSSR,* No. 4 (1958); No. 4 (1960). *Kommunist,* No. 11 (1958); No. 3 (1960); No. 3 (1961). *Voprosy istorii KPSS,* No. 12 (1958); No. 1 (1960); No. 1 (1961).

a year after the publication of the fifth volume, critics called the attention of the editors to newly uncovered records neglected during the revision. The fresh material cast new light on deliberate distortions in the former writing of history and the cultivation of the Stalinist myths.[43] S. S. Khesin, reviewing the fifth volume of the *History of the Civil War in the USSR*, wrote that while this volume, like the preceding ones, had incorporated much factual material related to the years concerned, the latest documentary evidence was obviously not utilized. This, Khesin states, was the main reason they were vulnerable to criticism. Another problem mentioned by critics, though more excusable, was the fact that the mountainous mass of resources that had accumulated over the years virtually defied any effort to explore the subject exhaustively.[44]

In 1962 there appeared a collective work on current historiography, to which D. K. Shelestov contributed a chapter on the need for a new history of the Civil War and foreign intervention.[45] This was followed by I. L. Sherman's historiography of the Civil War. Sherman believes that the war period, in order to be more meaningful in history and to achieve greater depth, should be considered to extend beyond the immediate termination of hostilities, and should include the subsequent stages of economic reconstruction. N. F. Vargin suggested, perhaps plausibly, a more extensive account of the Civil War and foreign intervention in Siberia, where, according to the author, decisive events of the war period had taken place.[46] Finally, a more recent historiography, published by Leningrad University under the editorship of V. A. Ovsiankin, handles graphically the fifty years of Soviet historical writing. Brief as this work is, it covers the salient points in the development of Soviet historical science quite well, and includes all the most important works on the Civil War period.[47]

It is perhaps premature to attempt assigning Soviet historiography its place in a true historical perspective. Yet the short though significant

[43]O. A. Vas'kovskii, "Novaia literatura po istorii grazhdanskoi voiny na Urale 1918-1919 gg." *Voprosy istorii Urala. Sbornik statei.* Issue 39, Part 2 (Sverdlovsk, 1961), 3-20.

[44]See S. S. Khesin, "Nekotorye voprosy istoriografii pervykh piati let sovetskoi vlasti. (K zaversheniiu izdaniia 'Istorii grazhdanskoi voiny v SSSR')." *Istoriia SSSR*, No. 3 (1961), 103-115.

[45]D. K. Shelestov, "Ob izuchenii istorii grazhdanskoi voiny i voennoi interventsii." *Sovetskaia istoricheskaia nauka ot XX k XXII sezdu KPSS. Istoriia SSSR.* (Moscow, 1962), 373-394.

[46]I. L. Sherman, *Sovetskaia istoriografiia grazhdanskoi voiny v SSSR (1920-1931).* (Kharkov, 1964). N. F. Vargin, "O literature po istorii grazhdanskoi voiny i inostrannoi voennoi interventsii v Sibiri." *Istoriia SSSR*, No. 4 (1964), 140-155.

[47]V. A. Ovsiankin, ed., *Sovetskaia istoriografiia klassovoi borby i revoliutsionnogo dvizheniia v Rossii.* (Leningrad, 1967). 2 parts.

period since the Russian Revolution is a vitally important era in modern history. Some critics argue that the brevity in time is bound to lead only to unfruitful debates. Still, there is a logical approach to periodization, not only of the war itself, but of the entire course of Soviet history. The few years from the outbreak of hostilities, in 1918, to 1930 are regarded as the first stage, during which Stalin's consolidation of power took place, with all the impact it was bound to have on historical writing. These years will have to be reassessed in Soviet history. Since the denunciation of the Stalinist cult in 1956, the atmosphere has been less tense, and scholars have come to enjoy greater freedom in handling their materials, though this freedom has not been absolute. With these preliminary comments, we may now make an effort to examine the foreign intervention and Civil War period in Soviet historiography in somewhat greater detail.

D. THE CIVIL WAR IN SIBERIA

The first striking impression one receives upon examining the literature on the Civil War in Siberia is the vastness of the area involved in the struggle, and the length of the frontiers along which tense fighting took place. One can scarcely visualize the extent of territory extending from the Volga to Vladivostok. The length of this land, the great variety of social, national, ethnic, and racial conditions, the political and geographic peculiarities—these combined to make the war in Siberia so different from the civil strife elsewhere.

Another peculiarity of the Civil War in the east is that all through Siberia and in the Far Eastern Maritime Province, from 1918 to 1922, the counterrevolutionary and interventionist forces on the one hand and the Red armies on the other fought bitterly to the end. The Civil War in Siberia is also noted for another reason: the Czechoslovak mutiny supported by the Social Revolutionary Party and members of the recently dissolved Constituent Assembly. Taking advantage of the weak directory recently formed, Admiral Kolchak, by a coup, seized power and assumed the supreme command of the White Army. In addition, the maneuverings of war lords like Semenov, Dutorov, and others, not to mention the foreign interventionists and particularly the Japanese, made the conflict a most virulent one. Finally, it should be pointed out, the party's extensive underground organizations added further complexity to the general setup. The underground network soon extended all the way from the Volga region, across the Urals, through the entire length of Siberia, and reached to Vladivostok in the Far East.

This vast struggle is recorded in the numerous memoirs of participants or eyewitnesses of the momentous events. Most of the memoirs of the early 1920's deal with the Czechoslovak mutiny, with the part the Social Revolutionary Party played during the early period of the revolution, and the circumstances under which they lost power to Admiral Kolchak.[48] Among the first accounts of the Czechoslovak mutiny and the role of the Social Revolutionary Party to appear during this period is the collection of essays published in Samara in 1919. Among these are several items which describe with great accuracy what took place in that city. There is much factual material on the counterrevolutionary regime formed here and the struggle carried on against the Soviet regime. The book concentrates mainly on two events: the Czechoslovak mutiny and the attempt of the Social Revolutionary Party to regain its lost power.[49]

I. M. Maiskii, in his *Democratic Counterrevolution,* includes a good deal of rare information on the activities of the Social Revolutionary Party. During the Revolution he served on the committee of deputies of the recently dissolved Constituent Assembly. This committee was short-lived, not being able to make progress even with the support of the Czechoslovak Legion; it was soon overthrown by a coup led by Admiral Kolchak. Without Kolchak's victory, neither General Denikin in the south, nor Iudenich in the west, nor General Miller in the north would have had a chance to form their respective White Armies. The Civil War would never have spread so far and been of such duration. For this reason, concludes Maiskii, the Czechoslovak mutiny must be regarded as a critical event, for it signalled a chain of tragic developments soon to follow in rapid succession. Maiskii stresses the role of the Entente in the Czechoslovak mutiny less than other writers. Critics have pointed out that Maiskii minimized the responsibility of the Allies for refusing, for instance, to provide means of transportation for the Czechoslovak Legion from Archangel to Europe as originally planned, forcing them to choose the long itinerary across Siberia. Maiskii believes that the French ambassador

[48]V. P. Naumov, *K istoriografii belocheshskogo miatezha v 1918 g. Sbornik statei po istorii rabochego klassa i sovetskoi istoriografii.* (Moscow, 1958). A. N. Turunov and V. D. Vegman, *Revoliutsiia i grazhdanskaia voina v Sibiri. Ukazatel knig i zhurnalnykh statei.* (Moscow, 1928). P. N. Kungurov, "Zapiski rabochego." *Proletarskaia revoliutsiia,* No. 4 (1922), 245-260. L. Reisner, "Kazan. (Leto i osen 1918 goda)." *Proletarskaia revoliutsiia,* No. 12 (1922), 180-196. A. Butsevich, "Pervye dni chekho-slovakov." *Proletarskaia revoliutsiia, No. 5* (1922), 262-274. A. Kuznetsov, "Kazan pod vlastiu chekhouchredilovtsev." *Proletarskaia revoliutsiia,* No. 8 (1922), 55-70. S. Moravskii, "Vosstanie chekhoslovakov v Sibiri." *Proletarskaia revoliutsiia,* No. 8 (1922), 225-228. Z. Kozlova, "K voprosu o dniakh Samarskoi uchredilki." *Proletarskaia revoliutsiia,* No. 9 (1922), 305-306. V. Vegman, "Kak i pochemu pala v 1918 g. Sovetskaia vlast v Tomske." *Sibirskie ogni,* Nos. 1-2 (1923), 127-147. "Borba za Kazan." *Sbornik materialov o chekho-uchredilovskoi interventsii v 1918 g.* (Kazan, 1924). S. Gruzdev, "Bolshevistskoe podpole v Samare v dni uchredilovshchiny." *Proletarskaia revoliutsiia,* No. 12 (35), (1924), 172-190. F. Shutskever, "Podpolnaia Samara." *Proletarskaia revoliutsiia,* No. 8 (43), (1925), 203-215.

[49]*Chetyre mesiatsa uchredilovshchiny. Istoriko-literaturnyi sbornik.* (Samara, 1926).

Noulens did intend to use the Legion for the overthrow of the Soviet regime.

According to Maiskii, Noulens took advantage of the absence of diplomatic relations and decided unilaterally to support the Czechoslovak Legion financially, thereby promoting and sanctioning the policies adopted by the Czechoslovak National Council in France. This was true, Maiskii's critics argued, but they believed that Maiskii had not sufficiently carried the thesis to its conclusion. Nor did the same critics accept his opinion that because the Legion included many socialists in its ranks, they favored cooperation with the Social Revolutionary and Social-Democratic parties against the Bolsheviks. Maiskii, they said, had underestimated the real aid the Czechoslovaks rendered Kolchak in seizing political power, even if they did betray him in the end to the Bolsheviks. It may be recalled that Maiskii himself was a former member of the Menshevik Party as well as a member of the Constituent Assembly, though he severed his relations in 1919 and joined the Bolsheviks.

In 1927 there appeared a monograph by V. Vladimirova, which contains an extraordinary account of the first period of the counterrevolutionary thrust in 1918, led by the Social-Democratic and Social Revolutionary parties. Her work is based on an impressive amount of collected materials, mostly from among the White papers, found both at home and abroad. Vladimirova also utilized some of the records that were used during the trial of the Social Revolutionary Party members in 1922, as well as press reports, magazine articles, and some archival documents. A goodly portion of her work deals with the Czechoslovak mutiny and the short-lived Social Revolutionary-led committee of the recently dissolved Constituent Assembly, as well as the foreign intervention and Entente aid from abroad. Despite her earnest effort, this is basically a chronological narrative devoid of penetrating interpretative analysis, and lacking political or ideological substance. All in all, a pedestrian presentation.[50]

A year after Vladimirova's book was published, there appeared a lengthy article by V. Alekseev, which traced the history of the Czechoslovak Legion from its beginnings. Alekseev tried to show that at the time of Kornilov's attempt to gain power the Legion already supported the cause of the military coup. The Czechoslovak mutiny, Alekseev believes, was the result of an agreement reached between the French government and Eduard Beneš; it was supported further by a verbal agreement between the Czechs and the Social Revolutionary Party and backed by the Entente powers.[51]

The war on the eastern front is described by many participants and students of history. One account of particular interest is by K. M. Molo-

[50]V. Vladimirova, *God sluzhby "sotsialistov" kapitalistam. Ocherki po istorii kontrrevoliutsii v 1918 g.* (Moscow, 1927).

[51]V. Alekseev, "Borba s chekhoslovatskim miatezhom v Povolzhi." *Proletarskaia revoliutsiia*, No. 4 (75), (1928), 45-88.

tov, who describes the underground activities in Siberia during the regime of Admiral Kolchak. Another work, by M. Golubykh, presents an absorbing description of the Ural partisans and their activities during the year 1919.[52] *Istpart* sections throughout Siberia have published documentary collections and reminiscences of party members who participated in the underground activities or took part in guerrilla activities.[53]

Accounts of the war in the east against Admiral Kolchak during the winter of 1918-1919 may be found in many works. One of these is by the commander of the Chapaev division, I. S. Kutiakov, who presents a full military picture of the events in Siberia, though the complex political and economic conditions of the time are dealt with rather superficially and not always reliably. This, as a general rule, is true of most of the writings by military men, who were completely absorbed in military matters. It is only natural that memoirs dwell heavily on military aspects of the Civil War.[54]

Those interested in specific military operations on the eastern front may find it profitable to consult the periodical and composite works to which various authors have contributed. For example, individual operations against General Bakich are discussed in detail by G. D. Guy; individual battles in the southern Ural region are adequately described by several authors, including P. Sanchuk and A. Smirnov. A number of articles deal with campaigns in which different Red Army units were engaged in decisive battles. Several composite works and collections of documents that pertain to specific localities in Siberia contribute to the history of the Civil War in the east in general. An overall history of the momentous events in Siberia between 1918 and 1921 may yet be achieved, with the aid of the ever-growing amount of source material.[55]

[52]A. Poliak, "Deistviia Piatoi armii ot reki Tobola do ozera Baikala." *Sbornik trudov voenno-nauchnogo obshchestva pri Voennoi akademii.* Vol. II (Moscow, 1922). D. Rybin, "Ufimskaia operatsiia 1919 g." *Sbornik trudov voenno-nauchnogo obshchestva pri Voennoi akademii.* Vol. IV. (Moscow, 1923). S. Belitskii, "Zlatoustovskaia operatsiia." *Sbornik trudov voenno-nauchnogo obshchestva pri Voennoi akademii.* Vol. IV. (Moscow, 1923). K. M. Molotov, *Kontrrevoliutsiia v Sibiri i borba za Sovetskuiu vlast.* (Moscow, 1924). M. Golubykh, *Uralskie partizany. Pokhod otriadov Bliukhera i Kashirina v 1919 g.* (Moscow, 1924).

[53]See *Revoliutsiia na Dalnem Vostoke.* (Moscow, 1923). See also *Sbornik istparta no. 1 Sibirskogo bureau TsK RKP (b).* (Moscow, 1923).

[54]I. S. Kutiakov, *S Chapaevym po uralskim stepiam. Borba s Uralskoi i Chekho-Slovatskoi kontrrevoliutsiei.* (Moscow, 1928). I. S. Kutiakov, *Razgrom Uralskoi beloi kazachei armii.* (Moscow, 1931).

[55]*Kratkii istoricheskii ocherk 26oi Zlatoustovskoi strelkovoi divizii.* (Moscow, 1925). G. D. Guy, *Pervyi udar po Kolchaku.* (Moscow, 1926). *Poslednie dni Kolchakovshchiny. Sbornik dokumentov.* (Moscow, 1926). P. S. Parfenov, *Grazhdanskaia voina v Sibiri i Severnoi Oblasti.* S. A. Alekseev, ed. (Moscow, 1927). P. Fedorov, *Pod krasnoi zvezdoi.* (Moscow, 1928). G. Kh. Eikhe, "Piataia armiia v borbe

Many writers who recorded their memoirs endeavored to turn their
personal experiences into monographic works; some of these authors
ably utilized their personal observations, and combined these with carefully researched information from national and local archives, to achieve
some impressive results.[56]

The war in the east passed through three main stages: first the struggle
with the Czechoslovak mutiny, then the contest with Kolchak, then the
struggle against Japanese intervention. The main problem was, naturally,
the struggle against Kolchak; the fight against the Czechs was of shorter
duration and less virulent in nature, while the hostilities with Japan were
limited to diplomatic maneuvering. The first military history of the
eastern front was undertaken by K. Podgoretskii, in an article describing
the battle for Kazan in August and September of 1918.[57] Podgoretskii's
view is that the loss of Kazan can largely be explained by the poor organizational work of the Revolutionary Military Committee, which failed to
transfer sufficient troops for the defense. Many of the units assigned to defend Kazan were held up along the lines between Moscow, Riazan, and
Sviazhsk, and their absence affected the outcome of the battle. The
early fighting in the Central Volga region and at Kazan during August
and September, 1918, was the first serious test for the leaders of the Red
Army, according to Podgoretskii. It demonstrated the interdependence
of military planning, tactical execution of plans, morale, and political
indoctrination—all elements that affect the fighting qualities of an army.
In the struggle for Kazan, Podgoretskii states further, the White Army
was still ahead of the Red Army in military technique, in organization,
in the art of war, but, as he aptly describes it, these advantages were all

za Zapadnuiu Sibir." *Grazhdanskaia voina 1918-1921 gg.* Vol. I. (Moscow, 1928).
V. Popovich and I. Gnusin, *Put borby. Kratkaia istoriia Piatoi Strelkovoi Divizii.*
(Moscow, 1929). P. Sanchuk, "Cheliabinskaia operatsiia letom 1919 g." *Voina i
revoliutsiia,* No. 11 (1930). A. Smirnov, "Zlatoustovskaia operatsiia." *Voina i
revoliutsiia,* Nos. 11-12 (1933). L. M. Papin, *Krakh Kolchakovshchiny i obrazovanie Dalnevostochnoi respubliki.* (Moscow, 1957). P. S. Luchevnikov, ed., *Grazhdanskaia voina na iuzhnom Urale, 1918-1919. Sbornik dokumentov i materialov.*
(Cheliabinsk, 1962). V. Shorin, "Borba za Ural. (Iz boevoi zhizni Vtoroi Armii)."
Grazhdanskaia voina 1918-1919 gg. Vol. I. (Moscow, 1928).

[56]N. I. Iliukhov and M. Titov, *Partizanskoe dvizhenie v Primore (1918-1920 gg.).*
(Moscow, 1928). G. Shpilev, "Iz istorii partiinoi raboty v Sibiri pri Kokchake."
Proletarskaia revoliutsiia, No. 1 (72), (1928), 67-84. P. E. Shchetinin, *Borba s
kolchakovshchinoi. Ocherk partizanskoi borby na Minusinskom fronte.* (Moscow,
1928). *Borba za Ural i Sibir.* (Moscow, 1926). S. Chukaev, comp., *Krasnogvardeitsy i krasnye partizany.* (Moscow, 1933). P. A. Kuznetsov, ed., *Grazhdanskaia
voina v Bashkirii; vospominaniia uchastnikov.* (Ufa, 1932). Z. Karpenko, *Grazhdanskaia voina na Dalnevostochnom krae (1918-1922).* (Khabarovsk, 1934). S. B.
Zhantuarov, *Grazhdanskaia voina v Kirgizii, 1918-1920 gg.* (Frunze, 1963).

[57]K. Podgoretskii, "Borba za Kazan." *Sbornik trudov voenno-nauchnogo obshchestva
pri Voennoi akademii.* Vol. III (1922).

"in historically dead hands." The recapture of Kazan strengthened the prestige of the Soviet regime and laid the firm basis for later victories.

A well-rounded account of the early engagements between the Reds and the Whites in the Urals, during the first year of the war, can be found in separate works by I. Podshivalov and by G. Rychkov. Both authors, in a somewhat popular vein, succeed in conveying a good deal of reliable information.[58]

The campaign that followed in the Urals, during 1918, is discussed in a series of articles by the military historian I. Kutiakov. The author describes the activities of the partisan units as well as those of the regular Red Army against the Ural Cossacks, the Czechs, and Kolchak. The articles are largely military accounts, based on reports of various commanders, reminiscences, and voluminous factual data.[59]

The story of the struggle against the Czechs and the army of Kolchak in 1918 and 1919 in the Urals is also told by V. Shorin, former commander of the Second Army. He describes the first encounters, the defeats and costly retreats the army suffered before it was to regain momentum for a renewal of the offensive and the successful drive eastward. These were the circumstances in which the Second Army was formed and battle-seasoned.[60]

The first effort to analyze historically the strategic breakthrough of Kolchak's army was made by the military writer S. Belitskii, who particularly praises M. V. Frunze. The appointment of Frunze to the post of commander of the southern army, Belitskii explains, was due to the superior organizational work he had performed while serving as Circuit Military Commissar and Commander of the Fourth Army. In his new post Frunze had the extremely difficult assignment, the author states, of taking this rebellious mass and turning it into an organization suited to wage war.[61]

The initial counterattack against Kolchak by the Soviet Army on the eastern front is described by G. D. Guy. The author used many military records which trace the build-up and eventual break through the Kolchak front during April and May, 1919. Describing the situation at the front during April of that year, Guy gives special credit to the First Army, which moved rapidly forward and invaded the upper Urals, placing itself in an extremely precarious position. The author then traces that operation in

[58] I. Podshivalov, *Grazhdanskaia voina na Urale, 1917-1918 gg.* (Moscow, 1925). G. Rychkov, *Krasnaia gvardiia na Urale.* (Moscow, 1933). *Grazhdanskaia voina na iuzhnom Urale, 1918-1919. Sbornik dokumentov i materialov.* (Cheliabinsk, 1962).

[59] I. Kutiakov, "Pervyi pokhod na Uralsk." *Grazhdanskaia voina 1918-1921.* Vol. I. (Moscow, 1928). "Osenniaia uralskaia operatsiia." *Voina revoliutsiia,* Nos. 2-3 (1930).

[60] V. Shorin, "Borba za Ural." *Grazhdanskaia voina 1918-1921 gg.* Vol. I. (Moscow, 1928).

[61] S. Belitskii, "M. V. Frunze—Komanduiushchii iuzhnoi gruppoi Vostochnogo fronta v 1919 g." *Voina i revoliutsiia,* Nos. 7-8 (1925).

great detail, leading up to the battle of April 22-26, and the capture of Orenburg.[62]

The history of the decisive breakthrough on the eastern front and the outstanding military talents of M. V. Frunze are discussed in an extensive article by F. Novitskii, based on personal reminiscences and records of the war. The author is a former tsarist general who joined the Red Army and later held important command posts. At the time of the events described Novitskii held the post of Chief of Staff of the Fourth Army, commanded by M. V. Frunze.[63]

A similar account of the battle against Kolchak's army is told by another well-known veteran of the same war, G. Kh. Eikhe. Eikhe's small book describes one of the stages of pursuit of Kolchak's defeated army by forces under the command of Frunze. He utilized the archives of the army he was with, and of other military units, to tell the reader about military activities during the May, 1919, campaign. Eikhe also published an article in which he describes the struggle of the Fifth Army for the liberation of western Siberia.[64]

One of the most valuable contributions in historical literature to the study of the Civil War is the collected volume published by the Central *Istpart* in 1926 under the title of *Borba za Ural i Sibir*. The entire volume is dedicated to the Fifth Army, led by the distinguished Commander M. Tukhachevskii. This army fought its way from the Volga to Vladivostok and played a most important part in the liberation of the Urals and Siberia from Kolchak.[65] Perhaps the most outstanding contributions are the articles and reminiscences of the Fifth Army leaders, M. N. Tukhachevskii, I. N. Smirnov, A. P. Rozengolts, V. K. Putna, and others. Putna gives an overall account of the continuous battles the Fifth Army underwent, from the reverses suffered during the earliest encounters with the Czechoslovak Legion in August, 1918, until the final defeat of Kolchak.

Among the memoirs by veterans of the war in the east, one by M. N. Tukhachevskii attracts special attention. The former warrior shows the strategic course taken by the Fifth Army at the front of Kurgan-Omsk after routing the White Army, and its retreat eastward. Tukhachevskii also describes his own disagreement with the higher strategists while pursuing the enemy in the Petropavlovsk area, when, due to battle fatigue and stiffened opposition from the Whites, the

[62]G. D. Guy, *Pervyi udar po Kolchaku. Voenno-istoricheskii ocherk*. (Moscow, 1927).

[63]F. Novitskii, "Protiv Kolchaka i na putiakh k Turkestanu (1918-1920 gg.)."*Grazhdanskaia voina 1918-1921 gg.* Vol. I (Moscow, 1928), 164-190.

[64]G. Kh. Eikhe, *Forsirovanie reki Beloi chastiami Vostochnogo fronta v iiune 1919 goda.* (Moscow, 1928). G. Kh. Eikhe, "V-ia Armiia i borba za Zapadnuiu Sibir." *Grazhdanskaia voina 1918-1921 gg.* Vol. I (Moscow, 1928), 190-205.

[65]*Borba za Ural i Sibir. Vospominaniia i stati uchastnikov borby s uchredilovskoi kolchakovskoi kontrrevoliutsiei.* (Moscow, 1926).

units under his command came to suffer temporary reverses near Tobolsk. Finally, he emphasizes the absolute need for close contact between the General Staff and the battle front during the Civil War. Its absence, says Tukhachevskii, was a recurrent problem during the war and often caused confusion, harm, and disunity in operations. Tukhachevskii ends with praise for the role played by the peasantry throughout the eastern campaign, and particularly the part the partisans played in the rear of the Kolchak armies. The combination of a military-strategic campaign supported by the "social campaign" of the peasant masses, concludes Tukhachevskii, delivered victory to the Red Army over the best-organized counterrevolutionary force in the country.[66]

Much less attention has been devoted to the war in the Far East during the last phase of the conflict, with the exception of the work of Ia. Pokus. The writer was military commander of the army of the Far Eastern Republic. Pokus describes the geographic and social peculiarities of the theater of war in the Maritime Province, and he also stresses the fact that when the war reached this area the Red Army was not only better seasoned but also better equipped in a military sense, though still poorly clothed and inadequately assured of provisions. At the end of his account, Pokus describes in detail the battle of Khabarovsk, which ended with the expulsion of the White armies from the Far Eastern Republic. There is also a description of the final battles with the remnants of the White armies and Japanese forces during the early part of April, 1922.[67]

To summarize the study of the eastern front during the period of the Civil War and foreign intervention, it can be said that Soviet historiography of the 1920's aimed largely at the following problems: (1) the causes of the Czechoslovak mutiny and the role of the Entente in provoking it; (2) the nature of the "democratic" and "monarchical" counterrevolution; (3) the partisan movement in Siberia and in the Far East; and (4) the general military strategy of the Red Army, and the role of the various military leaders during the campaign that led to the victory of the Soviet forces.

In searching for descriptions of the civil strife, with its multiple effects upon the Siberian people as well as upon political developments, one must never neglect the unbelievable wealth of materials to be found in the numerous periodicals and *sborniks* (collected works).[68] One of the historians

---

[66]M. N. Tukhachevskii, *Kurgan-Omsk. Borba za Ural i Sibir. Vospominaniia i stati uchastnikov borby s uchredilovskoi i kolchakovskoi kontrrevoliutsiei.* (Moscow, 1926).

[67]Ia. Pokus, *Shturm Volochaevki i Spasska; narodno-revoliutsionnaia armiia DVR v borbe za osvobozhdenie Dalnego Vostoka, 1921-1922 gody.* (Moscow, 1938).

[68]*Po tu storonu Urala (v tsarstve Kolchaka).* (Ufa, 1919). "Materialy po istorii kontrrevoliutsii." *Proletarskaia revoliutsiia,* No. 1 (1921), 114-149. "Omskie sobytiia pri Kolchake (dekabr 1918 g.)." Preface by M. M. Konstantinov. *Krasnyi*

whose writing encompasses the entire theater of war in the east, from the beginning until the total expulsion of the Whites, is P. S. Parfenov.[69] A participant himself in the struggle against the White armies in Siberia and in the Far East, he derived much of his information from personal experiences; a good deal of it he gathered from press reports or memoirs of his comrades in arms. Parfenov was overly preoccupied with military aspects of the war and for that reason he presents inadequately or neglects altogether the political developments of the Civil War years. This has one advantage from the history student's point of view—an absence of too personal a perspective, as is often found in histories of similar character. Parfenov simply observes that when the White Army leaders realized that their defeat was imminent, they commenced to sue for peace. Negotiations with the Far Eastern Republic started in April, 1920, in Nikolsk and on Chinese territory. Parfenov also relates how American diplomats negotiated with the Menshevik and Social Revolutionary leaders in the Far East for the creation of a buffer state, independent of both Moscow and Tokyo. In the midst of these negotiations the White Army, backed by the Japanese, organized a plot that caused the death of some of the most prominent Red leaders, such as Lazo, Lutskii, Utkin, and Sibirtsev.

arkhiv, No. 7 (1924), 204-246; No. 1 (1925), 176-192. *Dopros Kolchaka. Protokoly zasedanii Chrezvychainoi sledstvennoi komissii po delu Kolchaka (ianvar-fevral 1920 g.).* (Leningrad, 1925). *Poslednie dni Kolchakovshchiny. Sbornik materialov.* (Moscow, 1926). *Iz istorii Kolchakovschchiny na Urale (1918-1919 gg.). Sbornik dokumentov i materialov.* (Sverdlovsk, 1929). *Tri goda borby za diktaturu proletariata (1917-1920 gg.).* (Omsk, 1920). *Krasnaia Golgofa. Sbornik vospominanii.* (Blagoveshchensk, 1920). *Sbornik. Rabochaia revoliutsiia na Urale.* (Ekaterinburg, 1921). *Borba za Khabarovsk.* (Chita, 1922). *Sbornik materialov po istorii revoliutsionnogo dvizheniia na Dalnem Vostoke.* (Vladivostok, 1922). B. S. Gerasimov, *God v Kolchakovskom zastenke.* (Ekaterinburg, 1923). *Kolchakovshchina. Sbornik.* (Ekaterinburg, 1924). M. Golubykh, *Uralskie partizany.* (Ekaterinburg, 1924). T. Ragozin, *Partizany stepnogo Badsheia.* (Moscow, 1926). N. Iliukhov and M. Titov, *Partizanskoe dvizhenie v Primore, 1918-1920 gg.* (Moscow, 1928). P. Bykov, *Krasnaia Armiia v borbe za Ural.* (Sverdlovsk, 1928). P. Postyshev, *Grazhdanskaia voina na Vostoke Sibiri.* (Kharkov, 1928). S. Kurguzov, *Amurskie partizany.* Khabarovsk, 1929). V. D. Vilenskii (Sibiriakov), *Chernaia godina Sibirskoi reaktsii (interventsiia Sibiri).* (Moscow, 1919). A. Speranskii, *Materialy k istorii interventsii. Rol Iaponii v istorii Sibirskoi atamanshchiny po materialam arkhiva NKIDa. Sbornik NKIDa,* Nos. 1-3 (1922). P. Nikiforov, *Istoricheskie dokumenty o deistviiakh i zamyslakh mezhdunarodnykh khishchnikov na Dalnem Vostoke.* (Moscow, 1923). "K istorii interventsii v Sibiri." *Krasnyi arkhiv,* Vol. III (34), (1929), 126-165. G. E. Reikhberg, *Razgrom iaponskoi interventsii na Dalnem Vostoke.* (Moscow, 1940).

[69]P. S. Parfenov (Petr Altaiskii), *Uroki proshlogo. Grazhdanskaia voina v Sibiri 1918-1920 gg.* (Kharbin, 1921). P. S. Parfenov, "Peregovory s komandovaniem belykh Sibirskikh armii v 1920-1921 gg." *Proletarskaia revoliutsiia,* No. 11 (58), (1926), 143-195. P. S. Parfenov (Altaiskii). *Na soglashatelskikh frontakh.* (Moscow, 1927). P. S. Parfenov (Altaiskii). *Borba za Dalnii Vostok, 1920-1922 gg.* (Moscow, 1928). *Grazhdanskaia voina v Sibiri 1918-1920 gg.* (Moscow, 1924).

P. S. Parfenov's most extensive work, *Borba za Dalnii Vostok,* which is in fact a continuation of his earlier book on the Civil War in Siberia, appeared in 1928. This work concentrates largely on the climactic struggle during 1920-1922, from the rout and capture of Kolchak to the end of the Japanese adventure and intervention. It differs from Parfenov's previous publications in that it is based mainly on information found in archives and press reports, far more than on personal experience. There is much more discussion of foreign affairs, political shifts, party membership, and revolutionary committees, as well as the nature of the counter-revolutionary governments. Though weak from a scholarly point of view, Parfenov's book represented a real accomplishment for its time, since it introduced much new material, cast some new light on many aspects of the war and the intervention in Siberia never hitherto acknowledged, and above all, attempted the first overall picture of the entire war period in the east.

In the history of the struggle to establish the Soviet regime in Siberia the partisan movement played a most vital part. By 1919 the movement became a national phenomenon and Soviet historiography has devoted much attention to its development, in a number of outstanding works. In 1924 the Ural *Istpart* published a collective work, including essays and memoirs as well as materials concerning the second Siberian underground conference of the Bolshevik Party, which was held March 20-21, 1919. The minutes of the conference include a description of the underground organization throughout Siberia and the Far East, and of the preparation for the mass uprising. This composite work includes the memoirs of E. Shepaev and A. Popov, both describing the secret Bolshevik organization in the Urals and in the city of Ekaterinburg.[70]

Another volume devoted exclusively to the partisan movement in Siberia was published by the Central Archives in 1925. The collection of documents is accompanied by a preface written by V. V. Maksakov, who raises the question how Siberia, with its fairly prosperous peasantry, its multi-racial population, and its weak industrial development, could have witnessed a mass uprising and a well-organized partisan army. Maksakov points out that, to the surprise of the White government, the guerrillas fought effectively under difficult conditions; they opposed both the Whites and the foreign interventionists who hoped to turn Siberia into a center for anti-Soviet activities.[71]

Maksakov answers his own query as to why the Siberian peasantry rebelled against the intervention and the Kolchak regime. First, he says, the main Siberian railroad, by joining a series of large industrial plants with the major coal mines, provided a link for the Siberian proletarian class. Lingering memories of the revolutionary year 1905 had

[70]N. Raivid and V. Bykov, eds., *Kolchakovshchina. Sbornik.* (Ekaterinburg, 1924).

[71]*Partizanskoe dvizhenie v Sibiri. Sbornik.* V. V. Maksakov, ed. Vol. I, *Prieniseiskii krai.* Prepared by A. N. Turnov. (Moscow, 1925).

turned into a deep-seated revolutionary tradition; moreover, the population had changed radically since 1900, due to migration which was either officially encouraged or economically driven eastward from western Russia. The migrants tended to settle along the railroads as they arrived. The new arrivals came to change the character of the Siberian population, since the migrants, though they usually remained poor, became numerically superior. Politically, they were supported by the large contingents of railroad workers who favored and often actively supported the Revolution. The native Siberian peasantry, which had never experienced serfdom nor struggled with a landlord class like that of the western part of the Empire, at first looked upon the Soviet regime with a degree of suspicion. But as the Kolchak regime increased taxes, continued requisitions, expanded mobilization, and intensified repressions, the amount of discontent increased proportionately and finally ended with a general revolt.

Another outstanding study of the peasant revolt against the Kolchak regime was by V. Eltsin, published in 1926. This study too is based on widely gathered materials, memoirs, press reports, and archival records.[72] Eltsin's thesis is that the clash between the Siberian peasantry and the Kolchak regime was the result of deeply rooted conflicting economic interests. Eltsin stresses political or national factors far less, perhaps even underestimating their importance. Emphasizing economic considerations, Eltsin calls attention to the fact that peasant revolts took place mainly in the grain producing areas that depended upon external markets, such as Eniseisk or Altai, which became hotbeds of peasant revolts. The violence was especially ferocious where the effects of poor market conditions were intensified by irritating legislation of the Kolchak government, expanding mobilization, and increased taxes, which imposed economic and social burdens upon the peasantry.

Another cause of the partisan movement was found in regions such as Tobolsk or Tomsk, where there was a great number of poorer peasants. Here the reason for peasant revolts was, in addition to high taxes, land hunger. Class conflicts, causing strife between poorer peasants and kulak elements, or between both of these and the middle classes, at times assumed a violent character and added fuel to the partisan cause. In addition to the inadequate land allotment, private claims to large tracts of land, as in the Tobolsk region, were a cause of further social discontent. Where the forest was essential to the peasant economy, as in the taiga district of the Tarsk area, any attempt to restrain the use of forest resources easily provoked unrest.

In the Tomsk region, the suppression of the guerrilla movement by special punitive expeditions was most brutal, yet the guerrillas quickly managed to recuperate and revive their activities. Such persistence was less evident elsewhere, as is demonstrated in the regions of Altai and

[72]V. Eltsin, "Krestianskoe dvizhenie v Sibiri v period Kolchaka." *Proletarskaia revoliutsiia*, No. 2 (49), (1926), 5-48; No. 3 (50), (1926), 51-82.

Eniseisk. The reason for this, Eltsin explains, was the predominance in these areas of a middle class, which was less able than the peasantry to endure the hardships of guerrilla warfare, military maneuvering and ingenuity in the forest or fields, particularly after the shock of the first defeat. In Tomsk the guerrillas were recruited from among the poorer peasantry, sturdier and more determined. Eltsin's book represents a curious mixture of a wealth of superb information intermingled with oversimplifications; he tends to disregard such intangible factors in history as quality of individual leadership, organizing ingenuity, local political and social peculiarities, or geographic circumstances.

A genuine contribution to the history of the Civil War in Siberia and of the partisan movement was made by a collection of source materials related to the last phase of the Kolchak regime.[73] The documents were gathered and edited by the Central Archives, and deal exclusively with the critical period between December, 1919, and March, 1920. An article that stands out is by A. Shiriamov, former chairman of the Irkutsk Military Revolutionary Committee during the last days of Kolchak. The author vigorously denies the opinion that the partisan movement in Siberia was, as some assert, a spontaneous peasant phenomenon. On the contrary, argues Shiriamov, the entire movement was an organized struggle from beginning to end.

Another article, by G. Shpilev, a leading figure in the underground activities during the Kolchak regime, describes the party organizations in such widely scattered localities as Omsk, Tiumen, Irkutsk, Verkhneudinsk, Khabarovsk, and Vladivostok. He cites abundant statistical data, factual material, and other information regarding the type of underground activities carried out in the different factories, in trade unions, and among the peasants during 1918-1919.[74]

Historical literature has paid far less attention to the struggle against foreign intervention in the Far East. On this subject there are two articles that might be singled out, one by Ia. D. Ianson, the other by F. Chuchin. The former states that the foreign intervention was about the same everywhere; yet, he argues, in each locality where foreign troops were to be found the conduct of the intervening powers differed, according to local peculiarities, public reaction, economic conditions, and other factors. In Siberia, states Ianson, the intervention began earlier, spread more widely, and ended later than anywhere else in Russia. The common view that the Czechoslovaks were the first to act as interventionists was not entirely true, he argues. In fact there were two different directions in political intervention, one monarchist, represented by Japan, the other democratic, represented by the United States.[75]

[73] *Poslednie dni Kolchakovshchiny. Sbornik dokumentov.* (Moscow, 1926).

[74] G. Shpilev, "Iz istorii partiinoi raboty v Sibiri pri Kolchake." *Proletarskaia revoliutsiia*, No. 1 (1928), 67-84.

[75] Ia. Ianson, "Interventsiia v Sibiri." *Sbornik. K desiatiletiiu interventsii.* (Moscow, 1929).

Japan, according to Ianson, was bound, against its own logic, to support the monarchist counterrevolution. The United States, on the other hand, utilizing Japan's unpopularity, was backing the socialists and their democratic program. The interpretation is again, as in the case of Eltsin, somewhat oversimplified. For instance, the author does not take into consideration the all-out support Japan had rendered to Ataman Semenov, not because the latter was known for any monarchist proclivities, but because he proved a more subservient tool in the hands of the Japanese. Had they actually been in favor of a stable constitutional monarchy, as there is every reason to suppose, the Japanese would have supported Admiral Kolchak.

Ianson correctly points out that after the defeat of Kolchak the interventionists found themselves at an impasse. The Soviet regime won on all fronts, the masses were tired of war, the Czechs had departed, and the intervention could no longer be supported since the war had ended and the pretext of expelling German troops from Siberia had dissolved. Continuing the intervention meant one thing—open war against Soviet Russia, an act that would not have been supported by the nations involved. The only answer was to terminate the intervention and withdraw foreign troops from Russian soil.

Why, then, did Japan continue the intervention as late as 1922? Ianson's explanation is that the Allies at first supported Japan's presence in Russia, presumably to guarantee the safe departure of the Czechoslovaks from Vladivostok. After the embarkation of the Czechoslovak Legion, according to Ianson, the United States supported Japan's presence in Siberia, hoping eventually to take part in partitioning the Russian Far East. On the other hand, Japan aspired to seize the Maritime Province, to isolate Soviet Russia from Manchuria, China, and Mongolia. It was for this reason that Tokyo supported such adventurers as Semenov, Merkulov, and leaders of other bands.

The same theme is dealt with in an article by F. Chuchin, who is of the opinion that Admiral Kolchak was mainly the figurehead of the British.[76] Admiral Kolchak, the author writes, was enlisted by the British while he was in America, and then sent by way of Japan and China to Harbin, where he was to take charge of the counterrevolutionary activities and to that end assume, with the blessings of London, dictatorial power. Chuchin also stresses the role of the United States in planning the intervention, places the blame for the Czechoslovak mutiny largely upon Washington, and shows the subordinate roles of France and Great Britain in the creation of the complex Far Eastern situation that resulted from the Revolution and the Civil War.

[76]F. Chuchin, "Imperialisticheskaia interventsiia na Dalnem Vostoke i v Sibiri (1917-1918 gg.)." *Proletarskaia revoliutsiia*, No. 11 (1930), 21-51. See also V. M., "K istorii interventsii v Sibiri." Preface to documents. *Krasnyi arkhiv*, No. 3 (34), (1929), 126-165.

The entire Civil War, as can be seen, is closely related to the problem of foreign intervention. Formerly the two themes were regarded as inseparable parts of the 1918-1920 events. Lately there has been a new approach—a study of the intervention as an entirely separate subject, even though related to the general history of the revolutionary period. The intervention is treated on a much broader basis, partly as a study of international rivalry, partly as a consequence of the European war, partly as a policy of economic aggrandizement by the foreign powers, under the pretext of settling wartime and prewar debts. Combined, these resulted in the dispatch of troops to Russia, a gradual demoralization of these troops in occupied areas, and a rising hostility in various circles against France, Great Britain, and the United States, which led foreign forces to withdraw and to leave the White armies to their own fate.[77]

E. THE SOUTHERN FRONT

The southern front on the whole is adequately described in Soviet historiography, in documentary collections and in the form of reminiscences by individual participants, official reports of local operations against the army of General Denikin, and general reports to the Chief Headquarters

[77] A. E. Kunina, *Proval amerikanskikh planov zavoevaniia mirovogo gospodstva v 1918-1920 gg.* (Moscow, 1951). A. Berezkin, *Soedinennye Shtaty Ameriki—aktivnyi organizator i uchastnik voennoi interventsii protiv Sovetskoi Rossii.* (Moscow, 1952). F. D. Volkov, *Krakh angliiskoi politiki interventsii i diplomaticheskoi izoliatsii Sovetskogo gosudarstva.* (Moscow, 1954). G. G. Alakhverdov, "Falsifikatsiia burzhuaznymi istorikami Soedinennykh Shtatov Ameriki istorii amerikanskoi interventsii protiv Sovetskoi Rossii v 1917-1920 gg." *Voprosy istorii,* No. 11 (1958), 177-189. I. I. Mints, "Novaia vylazka falsifikatora istorii amerikanskoi interventsii v Rossii." *Istoriia SSSR,* No. 2 (1959), 239-243. R. E. Kantor, review of B. M. Unterberger's *America's Siberian Expedition, 1918-1920* (Durham, N.C., 1956), in *Istoriia SSSR,* No. 3 (1957), 217-221. See also a review of James W. Morley's *The Japanese Thrust into Siberia, 1918* (New York, 1957), in *Istoriia SSSR,* No. 3 (1959), 218-223. G. G. Alakhverdov, "Razlozhenie v voiskakh interventov i belogvardeitsev na Severe Rossii v 1918-1919 gg." *Voprosy istorii,* No. 7 (1960), 121-134. K. L. Seleznev, "Revoliutsionnaia rabota bolshevikov v voiskakh interventov (1918-1919 gg.)." *Istoriia SSSR,* No. 1 (1960), 127-136. V. G. Konovalov, *Geroi odesskogo podpolia.* (Moscow, 1954). S. Grigortsevich, *Amerikanskaia i iaponskaia interventsiia na Sovetskom Dalnem Vostoke i ee razgrom.* (Moscow, 1957). I. B. Gadzhiev, *Antisovetskaia interventsiia Anglii na Kavkaze.* (Makhachkala, 1958). A. Kh. Babakhodzhaev, *Proval angliiskoi antisovetskoi politiki v Srednei Azii i na Srednem Vostoke v period priznaniia Sovetskogo gosudarstva de-fakto i de-iure.* (Tashkent, 1959). V. Ia. Sipols, *Za kulisami inostrannoi interventsii v Latvii.* (Moscow, 1959). A. P. Baziiants, "K voprosu o zakhvatnicheskoi politike Soedinennykh Shtatov Ameriki v Azerbaidzhane." *Uchenye zapiski Instituta vostokovedeniia Akademii nauk SSSR,* Vol. XIX (1958).

on the course of the war.[78] A general survey of the southern front is contained in the third volume of the *General History of the Civil War.* The authors stress the point that after the initial fighting and rout of the White Army led by General Krasnov the southern front assumed special importance, since the center of military pressure shifted to the Donets Basin. Incidentally, it is in the same volume that K. E. Voroshilov first eulogized Stalin's role in the Red Army, giving a foretaste of the kowtowing that later infested Soviet historiography. Aside from Voroshilov's article, the volume in general was relatively free of distortion, as compared with the writings of later date.[79]

In 1931 A. I. Egorov published a book based on extensive documentary sources. The first half of the work is devoted to events in southern Russia from the end of 1918 to early 1919, dealing not only with military developments but with the impact of socio-economic and political circumstances in the vital Don and Kuban areas. According to the author, a striking change took place on the southern front during the winter of 1918-1919 when the forces of the "Volunteer Army," as they managed to extricate themselves from the northern Caucasus, were able to shift the weight of battle to the Donets Basin.[80]

A lucid description of the general course of events on the southern front is given by V. K. Triandafillov in an article entitled "Kratkii strategicheskii ocherk nastupatelnykh operatsii iuzhnogo fronta po likvidatsii

[78] I. Korolivskii et al., eds., *Grazhdanskaia voina na Ukraine 1918-1920. Sbornik dokumentov i materialov.* In 3 vols., 4 books. Vol. I, Book 1, *Osvoboditelnaia voina ukrainskogo naroda protiv nemetsko-avstriiskikh okkupantov. Razgrom burzhuazno-natsionalisticheskoi direktorii.* Vol. I, Book 2, *Borba rabochikh i krestian za osvobozhdenie Ukrainy ot interventov Antanty i denikintsev.* Vol. II, *Borba protiv denikinshchiny i petliurovshchiny na Ukraine. Mai 1919—fevral 1920 g.* Vol. III, *Krakh belopolskoi interventsii. Razgrom ukrainskoi natsionalisticheskoi kontrrevoliutsii i belogvardeiskikh voisk Vrangelia. Mart-noiabr 1920 g.* (Kiev, 1967). D. Kin, *Denikinshchina na Ukraine.* (Leningrad, 1927). B. Simonov, *Razgrom denikinshchiny.* (Moscow, 1928). A. Egorov, *Razgrom Denikina, 1919 g.* (Moscow, 1931). M. Rymshan, *Reid Mamontova.* (Moscow, 1926). B. V. Maistrakh, *Manych-Egorlykskaia-Novorossiisk.* (Moscow, 1929). L. L. Kliuev, *Kamyshinskaia operatsiia desiatoi Krasnoi Armii, iiul 1919 g.* (Moscow, 1928). A. A. Grechko, *Bitva za Kavkaz.* (Moscow, 1967). A. S. Zavialov and T. E. Kaliadin, *Bitva za Kavkaz.* (Moscow, 1957).

[79] At the celebrated Twentieth Congress of the Communist Party, during which the cult of Stalin was demolished, N. S. Khrushchev had this to say about the particular episode: "Let Klimentii Efremovich [Voroshilov], our dear friend, find the necessary courage and write the truth about Stalin; after all, he knows how Stalin had fought. It will be difficult for Comrade Voroshilov to undertake this, but it will be good if he does it. Everyone will approve of it, both the people and the party. Even his grandson will thank him."

[80] A. I. Egorov, *Razgrom Denikina, 1919 g.* (Moscow, 1931). K. V. Agureev, *Razgrom belogvardeiskikh voisk Denikina.* (Moscow, 1961).

denikinskoi armii." Triandafillov vividly describes the battles for such strategic points as Orel, Kroma, and Voronezh that eventually ended with a drive against the White Army to the very shores of the Black Sea. An excellent complementary article is that of V. I. Primakov, Commander of the Eighth Red Cossack Division.[81]

In the south, as in the east, the intervention entered into the picture of the civil conflict as an important factor, with many different interpretations as to the causes of the fiasco with which it ended. Some believe that the intervention failed because of the effective underground resistance that operated throughout the country. Others ascribe failure to the demoralization of the Entente troops in Russia. Still others viewed the end of the intervention as a victory of the Red Army over Western imperialism. A. I. Gukovskii severely criticizes those who maintained that the intervention ended because the Russian workers and the Red Army inflicted decisive defeat upon the interventionists. Historically, argues Gukovskii, such an explanation is incorrect and is contrary to all facts.[82]

Some writers, such as A. Sukhov, explained the defeat of the intervention by the absence of a strong White Army, and lack of agreement in the camp of the Whites.[83] Most of these explanations seem to be reasonable or conditionally acceptable, though the downfall of the intervention and the blockade is far more complicated than many Soviet writers seem to assume. M. N. Pokrovskii and others, such as P. Lisovskii, I. I. Mints, and V. Vladimirova, were of the opinion that the largest factor in the collapse of the intervention was the bourgeois parties themselves, but this thesis has not been pursued in detail and needs further discussion.[84]

For some years the opinion prevailed in Soviet historiography that the participation of the United States in the intervention was motivated mainly by a desire to check the rising power of Japan in the Pacific. Similar moderate views were expressed by A. F. Speranskii in a volume of collected essays, and by E. E. Iakushkin in his book entitled *Kolchakovshchina i interventsiia v Sibiri*, both published in 1928. Later writers rejected this point of view, labeling these authors as idealists who lightheartedly accepted American "pharisaical declarations."

[81] V. I. Primakov, "Reidy chervonnykh kazakov." *Sbornik trudov voenno-nauchnogo obshchestva pri Voennoi akademii*, Vol. II. (Moscow, 1932). A. Verkhoturskii, *Proryv Iuzhnoi gruppy*. (Moscow, 1924).

[82] A. I. Gukovskii, "Literatura o soiuznoi interventsii v Rossii v gody grazhdanskoi voiny." *Istorik-marksist*, No. 6 (1927), 242-253. Note review by A. Grek of D. Kin's "Denikinshchina" in *Istorik-marksist*, No. 6 (1927), 288-291.

[83] A. Sukhov, *Inostrannaia interventsiia na Odesshchine*. (Moscow, 1927).

[84] P. Lisovskii, *Na sluzhbe kapitala. Esero-Menshevistkaia kontrrevoliutsiia*. (Moscow, 1928. V. Vladimirova, *God sluzhby "sotsialistov" kapitalizam*. (Moscow, 1927). I. I. Mints, *Mensheviki v interventsii*. (Moscow, 1931).

Shortly after 1945, most likely because of the Cold War, Soviet historians began to revise their views. A number of works now published presented a different interpretation: the United States came to appear as an active organizer and aggressor in the intervention in Russia. This interpretation was obviously an ideological weapon used by Soviet writers prior to the thaw in the Cold War.[85]

Local *Istparts*, during the first decade following the Revolution, were active in gathering and publishing all kinds of materials related to the Civil War and the intervention. Books by M. K. Vetoshkin, M. Bunegin, A. Baranov, M. Ianchevskii, F. Emelianov, and F. Golovnichenko dealt with a multitude of subjects that in various degrees have a bearing on the Civil War years.[86]

During the 1920's Soviet historiography was enriched by a large number of memoirs and documentary sources dealing with German and later Entente intervention in southern Russia. The periodical of the Ukrainian *Istpart, Letopis revoliutsii*, played an important role, publishing the bulk of this literature. The published materials dwell heavily on the months that followed the Treaty of Brest-Litovsk, including the Entente policy of gradual withdrawal from the south and from the Crimean Peninsula during the spring of 1919. Other valuable documentary collections and memoirs were published by the *Istpart* of the Crimea in the periodical *Revoliutsiia v Krymu* and other journals.[87]

[85] A. V. Berezkin, *Soedinennye Shtaty Ameriki—aktivnyi organizator i uchastnik voennoi interventsii protiv Sovetskoi Rossii (1918-1920 gg.)*. (Moscow, 1949). P. N. Pospelov, *O XXVII godovshchine so dnia smerti V. I. Lenina*. (Moscow, 1951). A. Kunina, *Proval amerikanskikh planov zavoevaniia mirovogo gospodstva v 1917-1920 gg*. (Moscow, 1951). A. Gulyga and A. Geronimus, *Krakh antisovetskoi interventsii Soedinennykh Shtatov Ameriki v 1918-1919 gg*. (Moscow, 1952).

[86] V. Andreev and S. Kulaev, *Oktiabrskaia revoliutsiia i grazhdanskaia voina v Tambovskoi gubernii*. (Moscow, 1927). I. Kozhevnikov, *Voennye deistviia na territorii Samarskoi gubernii v 1918-1921 gg*. (Moscow, 1927). A. Konotkin, *Ocherki po istorii grazhdanskoi borby v Kostromskoi gubernii*. (Moscow, 1927). *Oktiabr i grazhdanskaia voina v Viatskoi gubernii*. (Moscow, 1927). M. K. Vetoshkin, *Revoliutsiia i grazhdanskaia voina na Severe; ocherki po istorii borby za vlast, organizatsiia sovetskoi vlasti i kommunisticheskoi partii na Severe*. (Vologda, 1927). M. F. Bunegin, *Revoliutsiia i grazhdanskaia voina v Krymu (1917-1920 gg.)*. ([Simferopol], 1927). A. Baranov, *Oktiabr i nachalo grazhdanskoi voiny na Urale*. (Moscow, 1928). N. Ianchevskii, *Grazhdanskaia voina na Kavkaze*. (Moscow, 1927).

[87] *Piataia godovshchina Oktiabrskoi revoliutsii. Sbornik statei i vospominanii*. (Ekaterinoslav, 1922). *Piat let. Sbornik statei i vospominanii*. (Kharkov, 1922). *Oktiabrskaia revoliutsiia. Pervoe piatiletie. Sbornik statei*. (Kharkov, 1922). *Stranitsy borby. Ocherki i materialy po istorii revoliutsionnogo dvizheniia v Nikolaeve*. (Nikolaev, 1923). *Desiat let borby i stroitelstva na Iziumshchine, 1917-1927 gg*. (Izium, 1927). *Krasnye partizany na Odesshchine, 1918-1919 gg*. (Odessa, 1927). *Ianvarskii raion v revoliutsionnom dvizhenii. Ocherki i vospominaniia o rabote partiinoi organizatsii bolshevikov i revoliutsionnom dvizhenii rabochikh Ianvarskogo raiona Kieva. Sbornik "Oktiabr na Odesshchine, 1917-1927 gg."* (Odessa, 1927). *1917 god v Kharkove. Sbornik statei i vospominanii*. (Kharkov, 1927).

One of the first to attempt a full history of the Entente intervention in the south was F. Anulov. The author, an active participant in the campaign against the foreign intervention, had much first-hand knowledge of the time. Anulov's work is in the form of a chronicle, recording personal experiences and observations; he utilizes the current press and from time to time incorporates documentary materials, though he fails to indicate the location of the sources to which he refers. The major portion of his writing describes the underground work of the Communist Party in Odessa.[88]

Material on Entente intervention in southern Russia may also be found in an article by F. Kostiaev, while the intervention in the Crimea is discussed by M. F. Bunegin. The latter compiles a considerable amount of archival material, press reports, statistical data, and citations from various memoirs. Much of it has been brought together and cited for the first time.[89] Bunegin begins with an analytical study of social problems and general conditions in the Crimea on the eve of the Revolution. Of the twenty-two different nationalities in the Crimea, Ukrainians and Russians were in the majority, comprising 61 per cent of the population in urban communities and 35 per cent in rural areas. Other nationality groups were Tartars, Jews, Germans, Greeks, and Bulgarians. The Revolution launched from the start a campaign against all petty-bourgeois elements, against the pan-Islamism of the Tartars and the pan-Turkic societies. Bunegin describes the initial establishment of the Soviet regime in the Crimea until its fall in April, 1918, followed at first by German, then by Entente intervention. Of particular interest are his descriptions of the activities of the Crimean Mohammedans, and their efforts to gain independence from Russia with the assistance of Turkey. Bunegin describes the struggle following the collapse of the Entente or French intervention, at first with Denikin, then with Vrangel, and finally ending with the total victory of the Red Army.

Some new information on the intervention in the Crimea was offered in an article by L. Poliarnyi which appeared in 1929. The author describes the counterrevolutionary government in the Crimea, headed by General Sulkevich supported by the Tartar nationalists, who hoped eventually to secede from Russia and ally themselves with Turkey. There is also much information on the French intervention and the regime of General Denikin. Poliarnyi covers particularly three areas under the rule of the White Army supported by the French interventionists: Odessa, Nikolaev, and the Crimean Peninsula.[90]

[88]F. Anulov, "Soiuznyi desant na Ukraine." *Letopis revoliutsii*, Nos. 5, 6, 7 (1925). This also appeared in the publication *Chernaia kniga* (Kharkov, 1925).

[89]F. Kostiaev, "Interventsiia na Iuge Rossii, Kavkaze i v Turkestane 1918-1920 gg." *Kto Dolzhnik? Sbornik.* (Moscow, 1925). M. F. Bunegin, *Revoliutsiia i grazhdanskaia voina v Krymu.* ([Simferopol], 1927).

[90]L. Poliarnyi, "Interventy v Krymu." *Sbornik. K desiatiletiiu interventsii.* (Moscow, 1929).

A. I. Gukovskii contributed to the same field an extensive monograph which appeared in part in the magazine *Proletarskaia revoliutsiia*, in 1926, and two years later as a separate publication. Gukovskii assembled for the first time an impressive amount of material that described in detail the French intervention in the south and the struggle against it. There is one serious fault in this work, namely, that a good deal of the archival sources have been only partially utilized. This leaves some obvious gaps in the history of the origin, the development, and the final outcome of the French intervention.[91]

Despite this failing in the work of Gukovskii, the author has brought together an enormous amount of material that is not to be found elsewhere. He believes that the defeat of Germany and her disappearance as a military factor in world affairs relieved the French and made them depend less upon Russian aid. After 1919, it seemed to Paris that a strong Poland would be adequate to replace Russia as a sentinel in eastern Europe. This explains the support rendered by France to Polish territorial claims in Lithuania and in the Ukraine. On this account relations between the French and General Denikin were not always cordial.

A revealing chapter deals with the relations between General Denikin and the Ukrainian nationalist leader Petliura. Gukovskii also includes a detailed discussion of the frictions between France and the White Army command over the question of Ukrainian nationalist aspirations and Polish territorial ambitions. As a result of French intrigues, the Ukrainian Directory began to shift its orientation in favor of the Entente, veering away from its former cooperation with Germany. Gukovskii was the first to describe the secret negotiations conducted by the Ukrainian Directory with the French interventionists, and the agreement they had reached on February 2, 1919. Two chapters describe the underground work and the partisan movement against the French intervention; however, the portion that deals with the underground activities has been severely criticized by some of the participants.[92] Finally, Gukovskii describes in considerable detail the failure of the intervention and analyzes the reasons for its total collapse and withdrawal from Russia.

During 1918-1920, the Ukraine became a caldron of political activity. The fiercest opponents of the Soviet regime were the Cossacks and the Ukrainian chauvinists, and both were regarded as potential allies, at first by Germany, and later by the Entente powers and Polish expansionists. Each of these came to test its strength, and assert its sound or fictitious claim to power and territory. And though the foreign intervention had collapsed rather soon, Ukrainian nationalism, Polish territorial aspirations, and the White cause lingered to challenge the Soviet state. Several factors contributed to the severity of the war in the south: the tense

[91]A. I. Gukovskii, *Frantsuzskaia interventsiia na Iuge Rossii, 1918-1919 gg.* (Moscow, 1928).

[92]*Proletarskaia revoliutsiia*, No. 1 (1927).

class struggle, the chauvinistic elements, and the geographic and historical peculiarities, particularly in areas such as the Don, the Kuban, the northern Caucasus, the Ukraine, and the Crimea. The protracted struggle in the south lends itself to the following periodization: (1) the struggle around Tsaritsyn, (2) the war in the northern Caucasus, (3) the war against the German invasion, followed by Entente intervention in the south, (4) the Civil War in the Ukraine, (5) the defeat of Denikin, and (6) the expulsion of the Whites from the Crimea.

Such writers as A. Takho-Godi, N. Samurskii, and G. D. Gotuev describe the Civil War in Dagestan. A rare work by Ia. N. Raenko-Turanskii describes the revolution in the little-known Caucasian region of Adygeia. I. I. Ulianov, whose works generally deal with the Don and Kuban Cossacks and their relation to the Soviet Republic, describes in great detail the long strife for the establishment of Soviet authority and effective control over the restless communities.[93]

The Denikin phase of the Civil War in the south has been extensively studied. An early study by I. Mal't was published in 1924 in a series of three articles, wherein the author stresses particularly the role of the peasantry in defeating the White Army of Denikin. According to Mal't, the most decisive factor in Denikin's defeat was the fear of the peasantry that the White Army was bound to bring back the former landlord class and restore to it the land the peasants were now claiming as their own.[94]

The White Army in the south is the subject of a study by D. Ia. Kin. Written originally as a seminar report under the guidance of M. N. Pokrovskii, the paper appeared in 1926 in the periodical *Letopis revoliutsii,* and in a much expanded form appeared as a book a year later.[95] The works of Mal't and of Kin represent perhaps the first extensive studies of the White Army in Soviet historical literature. Both works are based on wide research and archival materials and cover the entire period from the genesis of the White Army to its downfall. Kin examined the entire White movement with particular care, from the rise of General Kornilov to the fall of General Denikin.

D. Ia. Kin discusses at great length the international ties of the White Army, the Entente support, and other implications of its counterrevolu-

[93]A. Takho-Godi, *Revoliutsiia i kontrrevoliutsiia v Dagestane.* (Makhar-Kala, 1927). N. Samurskii, "Grazhdanskaia voina v Dagestane." *Novyi vostok,* No. 3 (1923), 230-240. G. D. Gotuev, "Imperiia Uzun-Khadzhi." *Revoliutsionnyi vostok,* No. 8 (1928). Ia. N. Raenko-Turanskii, *Adygheia do i posle Oktiabria.* (Rostov, 1927). I. I. Ulianov, *Kazaki i Sovetskaia respublika.* (Moscow, 1929).

[94]I. Mal't, "Denikinshchina i krestianstvo." *Proletarskaia revoliutsiia,* No. 1 (24), (1924), 140-157; No. 4 (27), (1924), 144-178. I Mal't, "Denikinshchina i rabochie." *Proletarskaia revoliutsiia,* No. 5 (28), (1924), 64-85.

[95]D. Ia. Kin, "Povstancheskoe dvizhenie protiv denikinshchiny na Ukraine." *Letopis revoliutsii,* No. 4 (1926). D. Ia. Kin, *Denikinshchina na Ukraine.* (Kharkov, 1927).

tionary schemes. He stresses the degree of interest and aid tendered by France and Great Britain to Denikin and the effect of the termination of the war in western Europe upon the Civil War in Russia. In one chapter Kin lucidly discusses the advantages geography rendered to the White Army in the south, where the Entente could either deliver aid or actually intervene in the Civil War by way of the Black and Azov seas. Kin stresses further the close interrelationship between the foreign intervention, the Cossack environment, the kulak and bourgeois reaction to the power of the Bolshevik Party, and, finally, the military elements endeavoring to launch the counterrevolutionary campaign—all these unfolded a national and international drama on an immense stage. The author maintains that without the aid given by the Entente the Denikin offensive would have never assumed the proportions it did by the end of 1918. The peasant revolts, or in some cases merely their hostile aloofness, contributed indirectly to the initial success of the counterrevolution against the Bolsheviks. It was the policy of wartime communism that alienated the peasant, who cast his lot with the White Army only to switch back later and in turn become instrumental in defeating the counterrevolution.

D. Ia. Kin examines with surprising detachment the problem of the peasantry during the crucial years of the Revolution. He recognizes that the cooperation between the regime and the peasantry was seriously damaged by the Soviet land policy in the Ukraine. It was a grave error, he believes, when despite peasant resentment, a large portion of land was given to the sugar industry for the cultivation of sugar beets. It was equally harmful when Soviet authorities were carried away in their enthusiasm for enforcing collectivization and communization of farming. Instigated largely by kulak elements, this policy spread violence throughout the countryside and caused widespread desertion in the Red Army. This is a rare admission in Soviet historical literature. Furthermore, Kin believes that it was not until the summer of 1919 that the Communist Party fully realized the serious threat Denikin presented in the south. At the end Kin presents a detailed description of the Bolshevik underground work throughout the Ukraine, particularly in Kharkov, Lugansk, Ekaterinoslav, Nikolaev, and a few other cities.

Having traced the origin of the White Army in the south under General Denikin, Kin then proceeds to examine the revolts it provoked throughout the Ukraine. At the same time the Red Army, utilizing conditions to its own advantage and slowly recovering from its initial defeats, began to renew its offensive. Peasant revolts spread throughout the Ukraine, even among the more prosperous peasantry, while in the western part of the Ukraine the nationalistic elements contributed their share to the defeat of the White Army, which they opposed because of its monarchist proclivities. In the Kuban region and Black Sea coastal areas the cause of unrest was largely war weariness and refusal to contribute further to the war effort as exacted by Denikin. The return, in many places, of the landlord class, with its claims to formerly owned estates, added fuel to smoldering discontent. In the northern Caucasus much of the rebelliousness was caused by an aroused nationalism, and by political indiscretion.

Kin divides the rapidly growing revolts against the White Army in the south into three groups: (1) the revolts led by Soviet activists, (2) those set off by the elemental partisan movement under Makhno, and (3) revolts by the Ukrainian national movement, led by Petliura and the Ukrainian Social Revolutionary Party. Among the individual leaders of the anti-Denikin movement Kin singles out several rarely referred to or even heard of by many writers. He introduces Kolosov, Lantukh, Pokus, Uspenskii, Zubenko, Svenitskii, and others who organized and led the revolt that eventually crushed the White movement. Kin also discusses the so-called red-green rebel movement in the Kuban and Black Sea regions, the detachments that operated between Novorossiisk and Tuapse, and in the area of Sochi-Adler. As in the Ukraine, the rebels were supported by the peasantry and later by the Red Army moving from the north, gradually forming a formidable challenge to Denikin. In Soviet historiography the last phase of the Civil War, the defeat of Denikin, is dealt with exhaustively. Many prominent participants, such as M. N. Tukhachevskii, R. P. Eideman, S. S. Kamenev, S. M. Budennyi, and A. I. Egorov, have written personal memoirs of the events during these decisive months.

V. K. Triandafillov[96] made an early effort to describe the military history of the last period of the Civil War in the south, shortly after the termination of hostilities in 1921. Though this early work contains a number of errors, most likely because of the speed with which it was published, nevertheless the author was first to bring the overall strategy into a single meaningful pattern, instead of dealing with the war in a fragmented manner, front-by-front and locality-by-locality.

A later study by B. Simonov concerning the liquidation of the Denikin front, though it lacks a logical sequential presentation, at least makes an earnest effort to analyze the strategy of both sides and to explain the reasons for the inevitable defeat of the White Army.[97] Simonov also offers a plan for periodization of the events thus: (1) early formation in 1918 of a military base and army force, (2) the campaign against Moscow in 1919, (3) main battles and reverses of the White Army during September-October, 1919, and (4) collapse and final rout of the White Army between November, 1919, and March, 1920. Of these four phases, according to Simonov, the most important one was the third, which

[96]V. K. Triandafillov, "Kratkii strategicheskii ocherk nastupatelnoi operatsii Iuzhnogo fronta po likvidatsii denikinskoi armii." *Sbornik trudov voenno-nauchnogo obshchestva pri Voennoi akademii.* Vol. I. (Moscow, 1921).

[97]B. Simonov, *Razgrom denikinshchiny. Pochemu my pobedili v oktiabre 1919 g.* (Moscow, 1928).

marked the height of Red success and the turning point in the war. The third phase already left Denikin a "living corpse." It was also during the third phase, Simonov believes, that the political situation changed to such a degree that it was bound to affect the military situation in favor of the Red Army. Lastly, Simonov correctly asserts, the actual situation during the last phase and the causes for the routing of the Denikin army will never be fully comprehended unless one examines the entire military situation, instead of merely singling out individual sectors of the front line.

S. M. Budennyi, the colorful Red cavalry leader, contributed his modest share to Soviet historiography on the subject of the formation of the Soviet cavalry within the Red Army. In a chapter Budennyi contributed to the *General History of the Civil War*, he describes the role the Red cavalry played during the entire period of conflict. He deals with the part of the First Cavalry Division in the defeat of the White cavalry units led by two generals well known at that time, Mamontov and Shkuro, in October, 1919. Until then these two had caused much damage by their raids on Bolshevik-occupied territories. After long preparations a face-to-face encounter took place between the White cavalry on the one side, led by professional military men armed with experience and theoretical knowledge acquired in military schooling, and the Red cavalry on the other, young, revolutionary, without tradition behind it, with little experience, led by men of low rank who had only recently passed their test on the battlefield instead of in military schools. Most of the Red cavalry officers were former privates or junior rank officers in the tsarist army.[98]

The military historian L. L. Kliuev describes the important operation of the Tenth Red Army at Kamyshinsk in June, 1919. Like so many others, Kliuev records his observations and experiences as an active and leading participant. He describes lucidly and in great detail the condition of the army at a time when it was baffled by conflicting views concerning strategy, and by adversities in battle. Though written in a lively style and describing clearly the important Kamyshinsk campaign, the narrative is too narrow, being entirely a military account that touches little on closely related matters of political or economic nature. Divorcing military strategy from other factors that affected it in the Civil War, the author leaves many gaps that badly need to be bridged.[99]

Still another work that describes the collapse of the White Army in the south is by B. V. Maistrakh. The author devotes the entire book to the late stage of the struggle with Denikin in 1920 in the northern Caucasus, where the Red Army headed by Tukhachevskii finished off the remnants of the White Army. Though poorly organized, describing

[98]S. M. Budennyi, "Iz istorii krasnoi konnitsy." *Grazhdanskaia voina 1918-1921 gg.* Vol. I (Moscow, 1928), 105-123.

[99]L. L. Kliuev, *Kamyshinskaia operatsiia desiatoi Krasnoi Armii. Iiun 1919 g.* (Moscow, 1928).

only certain episodes of the final conflict, Maistrakh's history contains interesting details of this complex campaign.[100]

A good part of the important third volume of the *General History of the Civil War* is devoted to the last months of Denikin.[101] Another large and impressive study that deals with the same events is by A. I. Egorov, the eminent military leader of the Red Army throughout the Civil War.[102] Egorov was in charge of the campaign that was assigned to liquidate the White Army in the south; after October 8, 1919, Egorov acted as Commander of the southern front. Much of the material in his book had been published prior to his monograph. It is regrettable that Egorov, who must have been only too familiar with the military campaign, had to publish his record at a time when the cult of Stalin was already weighing heavily on all writers. Egorov was compelled to suggest cautiously, as others have done more forcefully, that Stalin was the sole author of the strategy of 1919 that led to the triumph of the Red Army in the south. Egorov's work may be regarded as one of the earliest signs of surrender to the Stalin legend with all its consequences.

A considerable amount of material on the Civil War in the Ukraine was published in the magazine *Letopis revoliutsii.* This publication appeared regularly until 1928, first in the Russian and later in the Ukrainian language. The central and local *Istpart* organizations enriched documentary collections by publishing special jubilee editions which incorporated many indispensable records of this period. The memoirs of V. A. Antonov-Ovseenko, completed in 1932, appeared originally in *Letopis revoliutsii,* at first in Russian, and later in Ukrainian, and eventually in a four-volume set.[103]

These memoirs contain a chronological account of events from November, 1917, until June, 1919, with only a brief gap between May and November, 1918. Most parts deal with events in the Ukraine, while smaller sections are devoted to the war in the Don region and the Caucasus, though the author states that his intention is to describe the Civil War in the Ukraine. The memoirs cover the struggle against General Kaledin and against the nationalist Central Ukrainian Council or Rada, the German occupation, the Denikin army, and the partisan movement led by Grigorev.

Antonov-Ovseenko's memoirs represent an indispensable and original record of the Civil War; the author skillfully combines documentary evidence and personal observations. His frequent citations of docu-

[100]B. V. Maistrakh, *Manych Egorlykskaia—Novorossiisk.* (Moscow, 1929).

[101]*Grazhdanskaia voina 1918-1921 gg.* Vol. III. (Moscow, 1930). See particularly pp. 133-151; 226-256; 257-284; 285-305.

[102]A. I. Egorov, *Razgrom Denikina, 1919 g.* (Moscow, 1931).

[103]*Letopis revoliutsii,* No. 4 (1929); Nos. 1, 2 (1932). V. A. Antonov-Ovseenko, *Zapiski o grazhdanskoi voine.* (Moscow, 1924-1932). 4 vols.

ments alone present a contribution of inestimable value to the literature on the Civil War; occasional use of complete textual records supporting the author's thesis enriches the memoirs further. As a rule, the factual details and dates are correct, the chronological order in the narrative sound, but the interpretation is mainly from a military and strategic point of view, without reference to other phases of the Revolution.

In 1925-1926 there appeared a two-volume work by N. E. Kakurin, the well-known Soviet military historian of the 1920's.[104] Both volumes include a mass of factual and statistical data gathered in the military-scientific and Red Army archives. The author utilized most of the memoirs published to that date as well as information contained in the press. What is even more important is that the volumes contain a sound description of the economic situation, something rarely dealt with by military writers; they analyze problems of enforcing military communism; and finally, they discuss the class struggle throughout the country, particularly in areas held at one time or another by both the White and the Red armies. The volumes are extremely informative with respect to socio-economic developments during the decisive Civil War period. Furthermore, Kakurin was among the first to discuss the military and strategic aspects of the war as applied to the differing characteristics of the various fronts, which affected profoundly the tactics employed, the means of transportation and communications, and the contacts between civil and military authorities.

Kakurin also offers an original scheme of periodization for the Civil War. He regards the entire period as a projection of the October Revolution, including the events of late 1917 and early 1918, when the Ukrainian independent government and the counterrevolutionary uprising in the Don region sprang into action. The revolt of the Czechoslovak Legion in the summer of 1918, according to Kakurin, marked the formation of a military front and initiation of the Civil War by regular armies. The next phase, Kakurin suggests, was the armistice in the west, and the third stage was that during which Soviet Russia found herself isolated, surrounded, and faced with intervention by the Entente powers. This changed the entire course of Soviet foreign policy as well as the course of domestic affairs and military strategy. Kakurin traces the climax of the war to the early part of 1920, with the total defeat of the armies of Kolchak and Denikin.

It is interesting to note that Kakurin places the Soviet-Polish war outside the scope of the Civil War, as a regular conflict of historic and traditional nature between the two states. Along with it he seems to discard the final phase of the Civil War, the liquidation of the Vrangel army in the Crimea, treating it as episodic. One is left with the impression that the Crimean campaign had no relation either to the Soviet-Polish war or to the other events leading up to it.

[104]N. E. Kakurin, *Kak srazhalas revoliutsiia.* (Moscow, 1925-1926). 2 vols.

Kakurin carefully analyzes the military and governmental organizations involved in the conduct of the war in the south. He describes the peculiar local conditions that characterized the counterrevolutionary government on each front. This has its advantages, but it strips history of unity, of proper historical sequence, of any synthesized pattern, and tends to result in a somewhat superficial examination of bare facts without proper evaluation. The main reason for this tendency is the obvious fact that Kakurin was basically interested in military aspects of the Civil War. Even the chapters which seem to digress from military affairs are subordinated to the main theme. For example, parts that deal with local uprisings, desertion, banditry, and other problems of the home front naturally have their place in the general history of the Civil War, but they destroy the sequence, the continuity or thematic scheme of narrative. This often leads to repetition of the same episodes, facts, or statistical data.

Kakurin joined with R. P. Eideman to produce another historical record of the Ukrainian Civil War. In it, they point out the distinctive character of the struggle in the Ukraine and attempt to form an acceptable periodization, to provide a meaningful pattern for the series of events that seem at first glance like sheer chaos.[105]

The two authors describe peculiarities that characterized the Civil War in the Ukraine, such as the distinctive economic circumstances, the social patterns, the national loyalties—all adding a dynamic force to the struggle that was rarely witnessed elsewhere.

The authors assert that these peculiarities were often exploited by foreign interventionists against the Soviet regime. The same circumstances sharpened the struggle between the revolutionary forces on the one hand and Petliura and Denikin on the other. Eideman and Kakurin's original periodization of the war years in the Ukraine bases each period on the course and nature of the struggle. They divide the war era into five periods: (1) from October, 1917, to the beginning of the German intervention, March 14, 1918, called the October period of the Civil War; (2) the strategic retreat of the Revolution in the Ukraine along both military and diplomatic fronts—a period during which the opposing forces were crystallized; (3) the Entente intervention, November, 1918, to February, 1919, a time when entirely new factors entered into Ukrainian foreign relations; (4) the struggle with the White armies of Denikin and Vrangel, and the Polish aggression; and (5) the remainder of the time up to the end of 1921, marking the establishment of the Soviet regime. Though the book by Eideman and Kakurin is a compact one, the authors successfully managed to extract a meaningful pattern out of the confused and crowded events.

[105] R. P. Eideman and N. E. Kakurin, *Grazhdanskaia voina na Ukraine.* (Kharkov, 1928).

One of the minor works that merits mention is an article by A. S. Bubnov in *Proletarskaia revoliutsiia*. The author was a leading figure in the struggle against the German intervention and the German protégé Hetman Skoropadskii and later against the Ukrainian Directory. Bubnov deals particularly with the Bolshevik political and military strategy employed against counterrevolutionary opponents in the Ukraine.[106] A goodly portion of Bubnov's article deals with preparations for the armed uprising against the Directory for the restoration of the Soviet regime in Kiev. The author pays tribute to the leadership qualities of S. V. Kossior in the Ukrainian Bolshevik Party.[107]

An equally important contribution is the monograph of B. Kolesnikov, who describes the semi-clandestine struggle conducted by the trade unions in the Ukraine during the Civil War years. Kolesnikov includes valuable resource materials taken from the current press, from officials records, and from various memoirs. It is to be regretted that the author often failed to cite more specifically the reference sources he used.[108] The author's chief aim, to describe the trade union movement in the Ukraine under the counterrevolutionary government of Hetman Skoropadskii, the regime of the Directory, and the Denikin regime, is accomplished only partially. This may be explained partly because the work was published in 1923, when many of the pertinent source materials were still unavailable, being inadequately assembled or systematized, particularly the records that pertain to underground activities. The role of the trade unions in the organization of strikes and demands for economic improvement is closely related to the tense struggle against the so-called "independent" trade unions that were set up and supported by the counterrevolutionary governments. The largest portion of the work is devoted to the period of the Denikin regime, which includes the absorbing description of the counterrevolutionary efforts to infiltrate the unions.

Additional sidelights are cast on the same period by two articles by M. A. Rubach. The author describes particularly the last month of

[106] A. S. Bubnov, "Getmanshchina, Direktoriia, i nasha taktika." *Proletarskaia revoliutsiia*, No. 7 (66), (1927), 58-77.

[107] S. V. Kossior had been a member of the Communist Party since 1907, member of the Central Committee since 1924, member of the Politburo since 1930, and Secretary-General of the Ukrainian Communist Party. He was arrested in 1938 and perished along with many others the same year. His case was fabricated, according to Khrushchev, along with similar cases against other eminent party members. See the Special Report to the Twentieth Congress of the Communist Party of the Soviet Union by N. S. Khrushchev, at the closed session during February 24-25, 1956.

[108] B. Kolesnikov, *Professionalnoe dvizhenie i kontrrevoliutsiia. Ocherki istorii professionalnogo dvizheniia na Ukraine.* (Kharkov, 1923).

1918, during which underground activities began to show signs of effective opposition to the counterrevolutionary regimes.[109]

In the northern Caucasus the Civil War developed against a particularly complicated historical background. Here were involved such areas as the Don, Kuban, Terek, and Stavropol, each noted for its parochialism and distinctive national characteristics, each with deep-seated contempt for its "alien" neighbors and harboring antagonism nurtured for centuries.

These complex problems are illustrated by various memoirs of the war veterans, which add many illuminating details to the complex picture. These memoirs are to be found in various magazines, and in special editions of the north Caucasian *Istpart* publications, such as *Put' kommunizma* (Krasnodar), *Kommunisticheskii put'* (Piatigorsk), *Proletarskaia revoliutsiia na Donu, Istoriia proletarskoi borby v Taganroge,* and many others. A goodly number of the memoirs have appeared in special editions and in the frequently mentioned publication *Proletarskaia revoliutsiia.*

Two memoirs of the Civil War in the northern Caucasus stand out: the one by E. Kovtiukh and the other by G. Baturin. Both describe the campaign of the Taman armies during August and September, 1918, for the mastery of the shores of the Black and Azov seas. Both contain certain inaccuracies, noted by reviewers when they first appeared.[110] A general study of the civil conflict in the Kuban region by G. Ladokha, covering the years 1917-1919, is based on various archival records.[111] Ladokha emphasizes the fact that the population of the Kuban areas, as well as in the adjacent territories of the Black Sea, was noted for peculiar economic and social conditions prevalent only in the Cossack communities, with their distinctive land problems and class conflicts.

According to Ladokha, one of the reasons why the Soviet regime fell in the Kuban region in 1918 was the ill-advised economic policy which adversely affected the middle Cossack groups. This only aided the kulak Cossack elements to gain power and leadership and quickly to win support from the rest of the population. The most valuable parts of Ladokha's work are those in which he describes how the local leader, a certain Sorokin, managed to assume leadership of the anti-Soviet forces. The account is valuable since the episode is hardly mentioned by any other writer. Ladokha also describes developments in the Kuban region up

[109]M. A. Rubach, "K istorii grazhdanskoi voiny na Ukraine." *Letopis revoliutsii,* Nos. 3, 4 (1924).

[110]E. Kovtiukh, "Pokhody Krasnoi Tamanskoi armii." *Grazhdanskaia voina. Materialy po istorii Krasnoi Armii.* Vol. I. (Moscow, 1921). E. Kovtiukh, *Ot Kubani do Volgi i obratno.* (Moscow, 1926). G. I. Baturin, *Krasnaia Tamanskaia armiia.* (Moscow, 1923). See review of Baturin's work by I. Krechetov and D. Furmanov in *Proletarskaia revoliutsiia,* No. 4 (27), (1924), 284-287. See also *Voina i revoliutsiia,* No. 3 (1926).

[111]G. Ladokha, *Ocherki grazhdanskoi borby na Kubani.* (Krasnodar, 1923).

to 1919, that is, the establishment of the Denikin regime. At the end he summarizes the chief reasons for the collapse of Soviet power in the Kuban region. One reason, according to Ladokha, was the weakness of the proletariat and the lack of leadership that resulted, as the author states, from "bourgeois decadence." This in turn produced such leaders as Sorokin who favored the successfully claimed "autonomous privileges," formed guerrilla bands, and on occasion even demanded complete autonomy.

An even more impressive monographic work on the Civil War in the northern Caucasus is the one by N. L. Ianchevskii, published in 1927 and incorporating most valuable factual material gathered from various sources.[112] In the first volume Ianchevskii presents a history of the northern Caucasus, discusses the social conditions, national components, and basic stages in the revolutionary developments in the Caucasus prior to October, 1917. The second volume is devoted entirely to the Civil War. The main weaknesses of this volume are its poor organization of material, lack of logical sequence of developments, and frequently repetitive narrative. The poor organization is partly due to the absence of a satisfactory periodization of the Civil War in the northern Caucasus, a clear separation of the time of temporary revolutionary victory from the more important events that led to the Civil War. The narrative seems at times to fail to show the interrelationship among the numerous factors that resulted in the outbreak of hostilities. Ianchevskii colorfully describes the peculiar environmental conditions where the hostilities took place.

The literature concerning the struggle against General Denikin's White Army is as impressive as it is extensive. There exist some graphic narratives on the local theaters of war by such writers as E. Kovtiukh, G. I. Baturin, and others who describe developments in the Kuban area and in the northern Caucasus. Written mostly for the general reading public, the narratives often lack critical scrutiny. Still, the accounts contain illuminating details and add considerable data to the general picture of the war in the south.[113]

[112]N. L. Ianchevskii, *Grazhdanskaia borba na Severnom Kavkaze.* (Rostov, 1927). 2 vols.

[113]E. Kovtiukh, *Ot Kubani do Volgi i obratno.* (Moscow, 1926). A second edition appeared in 1931 under the title *Zheleznyi potok v voennom izlozhenii.* This edition includes editorial notes by V. Melikov which correct some glaring errors in the first edition. G. I. Baturin, *Krasnaia Tamanskaia armiia.* (Moscow, 1923; 2nd ed., 1940). M. Svechnikov, *Borba Krasnoi Armii na Severnom Kavkaze. Sentiabr 1918–aprel 1919.* (Moscow, 1926). F. Golovnichenko and F. Emelianov, *Grazhdanskaia voina v Stavropolskoi gubernii (1918-1920 gg.). Istoricheskii ocherk.* (Moscow, 1928). N. Ianchevskii, *Grazhdanskaia borba na Severnom Kavkaze.* (Moscow, 1927). 2 parts. A shorter version of this work appeared in 1931 under the title *Ot pobedy k pobede. Kratkii ocherk istorii grazhdanskoi voiny na Severnom Kavkaze.* M. D. Botoev, *Grazhdanskaia voina v Severnoi Osetii; po vospominaniiam uchastnikov.* (Ordzhonikidze, 1965).

F. GUERRILLA WARFARE IN THE SOUTH

Some of the guerrilla warfare conducted during the Civil War, particularly in the south, revealed a strong imprint of Russian anarchism. The deep-seated roots of this phenomenon were demonstrated particularly by the Makhno movement. Nestor Makhno and his close associates, such as F. Shchus', F. Kozhin, V. Kurilenko, and P. Arshinov, considered themselves anarchists, claimed to be disciples of M. Bakunin, W. Godwin, Max Stirner, J. Proudhon, or P. Kropotkin, and violently rejected Marxism.[114] Though an insignificant minority numerically, the anarchists were able to exploit the long-accumulated peasant grievances against historic inequities and the more recent discontent caused by Bolshevik agrarian policies. In this fashion they provoked widespread revolts against Soviet authorities or, for that matter, against any authority.

There is an extensive literature on the guerrilla warfare conducted by such well-known leaders as Nestor Makhno. The Makhno bands operated largely throughout the southern part of the Ukraine, in the regions of Ekaterinoslav, Kherson, Poltava, and adjacent areas. A number of publications on the Makhno movement appeared during the 1920's, of which the most extensive study is by M. Kubanin. Based largely on official and primary sources, Kubanin's research can be considered as the most authoritative study of this elemental, rebellious peasant spirit that swept through the Russian plains of the south, centering at Guliai Pole.[115]

[114] A. Borovoi, *Anarkhizm*. (Moscow, 1918). Ia. Iakovlev, *Russkii anarkhizm v velikoi russkoi revoliutsii*. (Petrograd, 1921). E. Iaroslavskii, *Anarkhizm v Rossii*. (Moscow, 1939). S. N. Kanev, "Sozdanie Vysshego Soveta Narodnogo Khoziaistva i borba Kommunisticheskoi partii protiv anarkhosindikalizma (noiabr 1917 g.–mai 1918 g.)." *Nekotorye voprosy istorii KPSS. Sbornik statei.* Issue III. (Leningrad, 1964). E. M. Kornoukhov, "Deiatelnost partii bolshevikov po razoblacheniiu melko-burzhuaznoi revoliutsionnosti anarkhistov v period podgotovki i pobedy Oktiabria." *Iz istorii borby leninskoi partii protiv opportunizma. Sbornik statei.* (Moscow, 1966). S. N. Kanev, "Krakh russkogo anarkhizma." *Voprosy istorii*, No. 9 (1968), 50-75. A. D. Kosichev, *Borba marksizma-leninizma s ideologiei anarkhizma i sovremennost.* (Moscow, 1964). L. A. Kuzina, "Iz istorii borby bolshevikov protiv anarkhistov v period podgotovki Oktiabrskoi revoliutsii." *Lenin, Partiia, Oktiabr. Sbornik statei.* (Leningrad, 1967). V. V. Sviatlovskii, *Anarkhizm. Ego sushchnost i uchenie.* (Petrograd, 1917). V. V. Sviatlovskii, *Ocherki po anarkhizmu.* (Petrograd, 1922). V. Zaleskii, *Anarkhisty v Rossii.* (Moscow, 1930). B. I. Gorev, *Anarkhisty v Rossii. Ot Bakunina do Makhno.* (Moscow, 1930).

[115] Two publications that appeared abroad are worth mentioning. Nestor Makhno's Memoirs were published in Paris in three parts: Part I, *Russkaia revoliutsiia na Ukraine (mart 1917–aprel 1918).* (Paris, 1929). Part II, *Pod udarami kontr-revoliutsii (aprel-iiun 1918).* (Paris, 1936). Part III, *Ukrainskaia revoliutsiia*

Kubanin makes a skillful analysis of the regional socio-economic conditions where Makhno had operated longest and derives the view that the phenomenon can be described in a term which is impossible to render in any other language—*makhnovshchina*. He states that the class differentiation among the peasantry of the southern Russian steppes on the eve of the Revolution had made deeper inroads than among the peasantry of the forested steppes. Among the former there was a much greater number of poor peasants than among the latter. But in the steppes the middle-class peasants, more prosperous than the middle-class peasants in the forested steppes, were the domineering group of the village. Kubanin's conclusion is that the poor peasantry, while numerically strong, in fact had no influence upon the village life at all. In most cases they departed for nearby towns or cities where they sought employment in industry, leaving behind them the middle-class peasantry and the kulaks who in turn employed seasonal laborers from the north. These were interested only in earning what they could and moving back to places whence they came.

Kubanin also observes that any government that wished to find wide support and attain stability in the south had to find means to appeal to both the peasantry and the urban working class. He notes further that the national problem in the steppes was not as acute as it was in the southwestern and western Ukraine. Nor was the peasant movement in the southern steppes as acute as it was in the southwestern and western Ukraine. The reason for this, explains Kubanin, is that the village of the steppes was not as coherent nationally and that agriculture was not exclusively a Ukrainian occupation; the land was tilled also by Bulgarians, Serbs, Jews, or Greeks. Finally, Kubanin believes that Makhno was the supporter of the middle-class peasantry in contrast to such a partisan leader as Grigorev, who represented exclusively the kulak elements. The sharp distinction between the two can only be partially supported by the evidence Kubanin himself cites.

The partisan movement was far more complex than Kubanin seems to believe; for one thing, it embraced a much greater variety of social

(*iiul-dekabr 1918*). (Paris, 1937). Parts II-III were prefaced and edited by B. M. Volin. The other publication is by P. Arshinov, *Istoriia makhnovskogo dvizheniia (1918-1921)* (Berlin, 1923). (Arshinov had been an anarchist since 1906, had participated in terroristic acts, was sentenced to death, escaped, and was later recaptured. His sentence was commuted to hard labor, which he served with Makhno. After 1917 he collaborated with Makhno, and in 1921 escaped abroad where he published his history of the Makhno movement.) Of the Soviet publications the following may be mentioned: R. Eideman, *Borba s kulatskim povstancheskim banditizmom.* (Kharkov, 1921). Ia. Iakovlev, *Sovetskaia vlast na Ukraine i makhnovshchina.* (Kharkov, 1920). M. Kubanin, *Makhnovshchina. Krestianskoe dvizhenie v stepnoi Ukraine v gody grazhdanskoi voiny.* (Leningrad, 1927). D. Lebed', *Itogi i uroki triokh let anarkho-makhnovshchiny.* (Kharkov, 1921). M. Ravich-Cherkasskii, *Makhno i makhnovshchina.* (Ekaterinoslav, 1920). S. N. Semanova, "Makhnovshchina i eë krakh." *Voprosy istorii*, No. 9 (1966), 37-60.

elements. The social groups involved in the Makhno movement demand minute scrutiny. The student of history who is removed from the events by more than a half a century can more properly project himself into the Makhno phenomenon than those who dealt with the subject in the 1920's. The romantic idealization of Makhno in which Kubanin at times indulges is understandable in view of the time when it was written, but it calls for a reappraisal half a century later.

The study of Makhno by V. V. Rudnev offers a somewhat more realistic interpretation. Rudnev seems to present a rather plausible argument, showing the Makhno movement in fact as a rebellious expression of the kulak aspirations. Originally, the author believes, Makhno attacked the landlord class and then turned against the proletarian regime. While there was reasonable fear that the temporarily dislodged landlord class might return, Makhno fought their supporters, the German interventionists and the Ukrainian nationalists, as well as the Bolsheviks. When the threat of the first two was largely removed, Makhno turned against both the White and the Red armies, as long as he suspected that either one or the other might consolidate itself in power.

As in the case of Kubanin's study, here too one must conclude that a final explanation of Makhno's campaign still remains to be proffered. The field requires less fascination with the romantic figure of Makhno and more attention to the environment in which *makhnovshchina* was able to thrive. The mass support given at times to Makhno is too complex to explain; the economic, sociological, psychological, and traditional aspects involved here are too deeply rooted in the past. The entire phenomenon calls for a more objective investigation by many social scientists.

In the field of guerrilla warfare, the study by S. Dubrovskii of Ataman Grigorev is of special interest. The study appeared in 1928 in the form of an extensive article, based on a wide use of archival records and other sources.[116] Dubrovskii discusses the relationship between Grigorev and Petliura and the nationalist Ukrainian goal as advocated by the former. Grigorev opened his campaign in May, 1919, at the time the Red Army was engaged in the bitterest and most decisive struggle with Denikin. Having followed the origin of the Grigorev revolt, Dubrovskii traces, step by step, the liquidation of *grigorevshchina* by the Red Army. His

[116]"Grigorevskaia avantiura (mai 1919 g.)." *Letopis revoliutsii,* No. 3 (1923). S. Dubrovskii, "Grigorevshchina." *Voina i revoliutsiia,* Nos. 4-5 (1928). M. Dobrianitskii, "Zelenye partizany (1918-1920 gg.)." *Proletarskaia revoliutsiia,* Nos. 8-9 (31-32), (1924), 72-98. V. Favitskii, "Zelenaia armiia v Chernomorie (1919-1920 gg.)." *Proletarskaia revoliutsiia,* Nos. 8-9 (31-32), (1924), 43-71. E. A. Shchadenko, "Grigorevshchina." *Grazhdanskaia voina 1918-1921.* Vol. I. (Moscow, 1928), 68-95. *Istoriia grazhdanskoi voiny v SSSR.* Vol. IV. (1959). See particularly pp. 176-178. See also *Antonovshchina. Sbornik statei, ocherkov, vospominanii i drugikh materialov k istorii esero-banditizma v Tambovskoi gubernii* (Tambov, 1923). I. Ia. Trifonov, *Klassy i klassovaia borba v SSSR v nachale NEPa (1921-1923 gg.).* (Leningrad, 1964).

conclusion is that Grigorev represented another link in the chain of the Ukrainian kulak class efforts to regain control in the economy of the countryside.

G. THE WAR IN THE NORTH

In the north, special conditions, such as backward economic development, an absence of a proletarian class, and social elements who favored intervention, all combined to form overwhelming obstacles to the new Soviet regime established shortly after the October Revolution.[117]

The intervention in the north from its start to its collapse was of a purely military nature. Assisted by absolute control over the sea lanes, Great Britain, France, and the United States came to use the ports of Murmansk and Archangel originally against Germany, and later against the Soviet regime. After October, 1919, when the intervention plans failed, the White Army of the north lasted no more than four months. On February 4, 1920, the Red Army took the offensive, and within two weeks routed the army of General Miller and occupied Archangel and Murmansk. The northern campaign was over.

The history of the foreign intervention in the north and the military campaign was told in a number of publications during the 1920's. Various documentary collections appeared in print; memoirs and historical works were sponsored by the *Istpart* of Archangel. The history of the Civil War in the north was also written up in other countries and some of the accounts suited the Soviet authorities so well that they were republished in the USSR. Among the memoirs of the 1920's, the most lengthy accounts are two works, one by A. Metelev and the other by M. S. Kedrov, which incorporate valuable material on the struggle against both the intervention and the counterrevolution in the north.[118]

M. Svechnikov has written lengthy articles on the Allied intervention in the north. Svechnikov begins with March 2, 1918, when the first landing of the Anglo-American-French troops took place. However,

[117] M. K. Vetoshkin, *Revoliutsiia i grazhdanskaia voina na Severe.* (Vologda, 1927). See review by M. Kedrov, *Proletarskaia revoliutsiia*, No. 2 (73), (1928), 172-178.

[118] A. Metelev, "Padenie Arkhangelska (1918-1919 gg.)." *Proletarskaia revoliutsiia*, No. 2 (1923), 62-90; No. 3 (1923), 83-108. M. S. Kedrov, *Za sovetskii Sever.* (Leningrad, 1927). I. Mints, "Esery v Arkhangelske." *Proletarskaia revoliutsiia*, No. 11 (58), (1926), 56-81. *Borba za Sovety na Severe. Sbornik Arkhangelskogo istparta.* (Archangel, 1927). E. Rabinovich, "V plenu u anglichan 1918 g." *Proletarskaia revoliutsiia*, No. 11 (34), (1924), 162-184. V. I. Kolosov, *Sluzhba v riadakh Krasnoi Armii i uzhasy belogvardeiskogo plena.* (Vologda, 1923). G. S. Iurchenkov, "Arkhangelskoe podpolie 1918-1919 gg." *Proletarskaia revoliu-*

the author's analytical ability falls short when he plunges into party politics and blames Trotsky for the intervention. The further he proceeds with the narrative, the deeper the author becomes involved in misinterpreting the entire development, and he ends up with complete distortion when he tries to discuss the formation of the anti-Bolshevik government headed by Chaikovskii in Archangel. The documents Svechnikov cites are selected to suit his thesis, and the author obviously becomes confused himself when he comes to face intricate local developments, turning into even more intricate international entanglements.[119]

A more challenging and less confused discussion of the Civil War in the north appeared in 1927, written by M. K. Vetoshkin. This monograph is based on documents and materials collected by the *istpart* of Vologda and Severo-Dvinsk, and supported further by the author's personal knowledge, since he was actively engaged in the Revolution and in the Civil War in the north.[120] Vetoshkin presents important sources as evidence of the conflict that developed around the Vologda area with regard to the White Army and foreign interventionists. The author points out that Vologda became a center of diplomatic intrigue when the diplomatic corps moved to this relatively obscure northern city, chosen because it was conveniently linked by railroad with Archangel, and through Viatka with the Urals and Siberia, main theaters of war against the Soviet regime.

But Vetoshkin errs when he regards Noulens, the French ambassador, as the only plotter of this campaign. Nor is he right in asserting that the intervention was motivated by a single and simple desire—to install in Russia a bourgeois regime that would favor Western capitalism. Still, Vetoshkin introduced some valuable evidence concerning the northern intervention, quoting from the proceedings of the trial of the Social Revolutionary members and other sources. Equally sound is his theory that the unsuccessful Iaroslavl uprising marked the begin-

tsiia, No. 8 (43), (1925), 164-202. *Vospominaniia o borbe za Sovety v grazhdanskoi voine v Emetskom (Kholmogorskom) uezde, 1917-1920 gg.* (Archangel, 1928). V. V. Marushevskii, *Belye v Arkhangelske.* (Moscow, 1930). A helpful bibliography on the history of the Civil War in the north has been compiled by A. I. Popov, including some 520 titles of memoirs, articles, and documents that appeared abroad, such as: S. Dobrovolskii, "Borba za vozrozhdenie Rossii v Severnoi oblasti." *Arkhiv russkoi revoliutsii.* Vol. III (Berlin, 1921), 5-147. V. I. Ignatev, *Nekotorye fakty i itogi chetyrekh let grazhdanskoi voiny.* (Moscow, 1932). B. Sokolov, "Padenie Severnoi oblasti." *Arkhiv russkoi revoliutsii.* Vol. IX (Berlin, 1923), 5-90. G. E. Chaplin, "Dva perevorota." *Beloe delo.* Vol. IV (Berlin, 1928), 12-32. N. Zelenov, *Tragediia Severnoi oblasti.* (Paris, 1922).

[119] M. Svechnikov, "Soiuznicheskaia interventsiia na Severe sovetskoi Rossii s 2 iiulia 1918 po 1 oktiabria 1919 g." *Kto dolzhnik? Sbornik.* (Moscow, 1926).

[120] M. K. Vetoshkin, *Revoliutsiia i grazhdanskaia voina na Severe.* (Vologda, 1927).

ning of failure of the entire counterrevolutionary scheme in the north. Vetoshkin cites documentary evidence that convincingly demonstrates the participation of the Mensheviks in the Iaroslavl revolt, whereas formerly the uprising was considered an exclusive adventure on the part of the Social Revolutionary Party.[121] In a special chapter, Vetoshkin also describes the situation in Archangel and suggests some of the reasons for failure of the intervention. Among these Vetoshkin lists such difficulties as severe climatic conditions which the foreign troops were unprepared to encounter, the absence of good roads, the taiga, the hostile peasantry and workers in towns, the long frontiers and lines of communication or transportation.[122]

Vetoshkin's views and interpretations of the intervention brought some sharp criticism, notably from M. S. Kedrov, who challenged particularly Vetoshkin's description of the conduct of the Vologodsk Bolshevik Party, and accused its local leaders of opportunism. But Vetoshkin would not yield to criticism and replied to Kedrov in an equally pointed critical article, after which an exchange of rebukes took place. Though neither side was willing to accept the views of the other, their opinions are of historical interest.

Another monograph, devoted mainly to the English intervention in the north with its foreign and domestic implications, is the work of I. I. Mints. Originally prepared by the author as a seminar report under Pokrovskii's guidance, part of it was published in 1926.[123] The study was gradually expanded into an extensive monograph and was published in 1931. The chief merit of Mints' monograph is that the author consulted and incorporated into it an enormous amount of documentary evidence. He gathered many foreign and Soviet archival materials, memoirs, press reports, statistical data, interviews, and other source materials. What is also notable is the fact that Mints successfully analyzes the opening of the northern front as an inseparable part of a nation-wide development, rather than an isolated local episode that came about through sheer chance at Archangel, Murmansk, or Vologda. He

[121]On the Iaroslavl revolt see the following: *Iz istorii Iaroslavskogo belogvardeiskogo miatezha (6-22 iiulia 1918 g.).* (Iaroslavl, 1922). S. Gurevich, "Iz vospominanii o Iaroslavskom vosstanii." *Proletarskaia revoliutsiia,* No. 8 (1922), 215-218. " 'Soiuz zashchity Rodiny i svobody,' i Iaroslavskii miatezh 1918 g. (dokumenty)." *Proletarskaia revoliutsiia,* No. 10 (1923). *Shestnadtsat dnei. Materialy po istorii Iaroslavskogo belogvardeiskogo miatezha (6-21 iiulia).* (Iaroslavl, 1924).

[122]M. O. Vetoshkin, "Kapitalisticheskaia interventsiia i belogvardeiskaia demokratiia na Severe." *Proletarskaia revoliutsiia,* No. 7 (66), (1927), 2-23. M. O. Vetoshkin, "O boshevistskoi taktike 'levoi' kritike i karikaturnoi istorii." *Proletarskaia revoliutsiia,* No. 9 (80), (1928), 88-105. M. S. Kedrov, "O neudachnoi zashchite nebolshevistskoi taktiki." *Proletarskaia revoliutsiia,* No. 9 (80), (1928), 106-120.

[123]I. I. Mints, "Esery v Arkhangelske." *Proletarskaia revoliutsiia,* No. 11 (58), (1926), 56-81.

stresses the thesis that intervention centers in the Far East, in the south, and in the north were not chosen at random, but carefully selected because western entry into Russia was still blocked by the belligerent nations of Germany and Austria-Hungary.[124]

Mints devotes much attention to the local economic, social, and political conditions of the area held by the interventionists and the White Army. The north never had any tradition of class struggle against landlordism. The peasantry was generally poor and for that reason cooperation with the poorer townsmen was marked by less friction than elsewhere. The interventionists had little to promise and less was expected from them, nor was the White Army able to present inspiring slogans except to use the area as a springboard for a national campaign against Moscow.

According to Mints, the intervention which assured the supremacy of the White Army found the Bolshevik Party in Archangel and its environs totally unprepared to handle the consequences. The slow comeback of the party to challenge the opponents is explained largely by the minor part the proletariat played in the north. All this explains why, with the arrival of the interventionists and the Whites, underground activities proved poorly organized and weak. Many party members, instead of going underground, evacuated with the Soviet apparatus, leaving behind an organization that was poorly led, lacked experience, and was confused as it faced the Whites, the English, the French, and the Americans.

The military aspects of the intervention and Civil War in the north are discussed by N. Kuzmin in another study.[125] The author states that rarely in history has there been a war conducted so far north as this one, fought along a frontier more than 1,000 kilometers long, intersected by only two railroads and by a few rivers navigable only during a short summer season, in an area covered by virgin forests and bogs, subject to brutal winters, and sparsely populated by a poor and suspicious people.

Kuzmin states that the superb organization, equipment, and discipline of the opposing army forced the Red Army to adopt similar conventional military organization and military tactics in addition to guerrilla strategy in order to cope more successfully with the enemy anywhere. With regard to the long front line that existed in September, 1918, Kuzmin says that this was in fact not a continuous line. The fighting was largely conducted along railroads and dirt roads, and along river banks. Fighting also occurred during long winter months in areas of frozen bogs and during short summer months in impenetrable forests. These encounters made this a strange war in an even stranger part of the world.

[124] I. I. Mints, *Angliiskaia interventsiia i severnaia kontrrevoliutsiia.* (Moscow, 1931). I. I. Mints, "Anglichane na Severe." *Krasnyi arkhiv*, Vol. VI (19), (1926), 39-52.

[125] N. Kuzmin, "Borba za Sever." *Grazhdanskaia voina 1918-1921 gg.* Vol. I. (Moscow, 1928).

One of the distinguishing features of the White onslaught against Petrograd in 1919 was the lack of a "home front" or rear guard on the part of General Rodzianko's and of General Iudenich's troops. Their only defense in the rear was the English fleet, which was not always completely reliable, while the loyalty of the recently formed Baltic states, Estonia, Latvia, and Finland, was perhaps even more doubtful. At the decisive moment, Estonia and Finland, despite pressure upon them from London, refused to aid General Iudenich. Precariously holding on to the national independence they had recently gained, these states feared to take sides and sought security in neutrality.

Publication of materials on the defense of Petrograd during the summer and fall of 1919 began within less than a year. These included official records, press reports, and memoirs of various participants in this memorable struggle. Following these early publications there appeared a second series, mainly in two periodicals, *Krasnyi flot* and *Krasnaia letopis*, as well as memoirs and military accounts. There has been a large accumulation of factual data on the role of the navy, which covers action along the sea and lake shores as well as river banks in the Petrograd area.[126]

The subject of defense of the former capital against the White Army of Rodzianko and Iudenich has been well and thoroughly investigated. Research has been based on archival materials as well as many other sources related to this phase of the Civil War. One of these is the outstanding work by N. A. Kornatovskii, published in 1929, parts of which appeared in *Krasnaia letopis*. In his preface Kornatovskii refers to the battle of Petrograd as a symbol of military significance. The account of the expulsion of the invading Whites led by Iudenich concentrates

[126]On the defense of Petrograd in 1919 see *Krasnaia letopis*, No. 3 (27), (1928); No. 5 (32), (1929), 5-156. M. Vilisov, "Na Putilovskom zavode v dni Iudenicha oseniu 1919 g. (Otchet zavodskogo komiteta)." *Krasnaia letopis*, No. 3 (27), (1928), 213-221. *Borba za Petrograd. Sbornik statei i materialov.* (Petrograd, 1920). P. Sivkov, "Pod Krasnoi Gorkoi." *Krasnyi flot*, No. 9 (1922). I. Khronov-Murmanskii, "Zhertva velikoi geroicheskoi borby. (Vospominaniia o Iustine Zhuk)." *Krasnaia letopis*, No. 9 (1923), 197-203. E. Bettyn', "Krasnogradskii miatezh." *Krasnyi flot*, No. 4 (1925). V. Sakharov (Krasnoborskii), "Vesnoi 1919 g. na stantsii 'Ostrov'." *Krasnaia letopis*, No. 3 (27), (1928). N. Kornatovskii, "Pervoe nastuplenie belogvardeitsev na Petrograd." *Krasnaia letopis*, No. 2 (26), (1928), 76-105; 3 (27), (1928), 91-140. K. V. Guy, "Kak byl sdan Pskov (mai 1919 g.)." *Krasnaia letopis*, No. 5 (32), (1932), 91-100. "Prichiny padeniia Pskova v 1919 g." *Krasnaia letopis*, No. 5 (32), (1929), 95-100. N. Podvoiskii, *Kommunary zashchishchaiut Petrograd.* (Moscow, 1927). *Borba za Petrograd. 15 oktiabria—6 noiabria, 1919 g.* (Moscow, 1923). *1919. Velikaia oborona krasnogo Petrograda. Vospominaniia rabochikh, krestian, krasnoarmeitsev, krasnoflottsev, kursantov.* (Leningrad, 1929). *Grazhdanskaia voina, boevye deistviia na moriakh, rechnykh i ozernykh sistemakh.* Vol. II, Part 1, *Baltiiskii flot 1918-1919 gg.* (Leningrad, 1926). Vol. II, Part 2, *Boevye deistviia Severo-Dvinskoi, Onezhskoi i Chudskoi flotilii.* (Leningrad, 1926).

mostly on the operation that took place in the fall of 1919, and ended with the successful stand against the onslaught upon the capital.[127]

Kornatovskii sees in the campaign against Petrograd not just an isolated military episode absent-mindedly conceived by General Iudenich, but rather a grandiose scheme which had its links to the overall plan of the war in the east and in the south. This was best illustrated, according to the author, by the appointment of Iudenich on June 14, 1919, as head of the campaign carried out by Kolchak and approved by Great Britain. Iudenich represented, according to Kornatovskii, the military element which hoped to bring Russia back into the fold of the Great Powers of pre-revolutionary days. Yet Iudenich had to maneuver between the Soviet Russia which he was to conquer and an uncooperative Estonia and Finland, whose territory would serve as the base from which he could operate and carry out his grandiose scheme.

Utilizing an impressive amount of documentary evidence, Kornatovskii found a good many conflicting problems which the White Army faced as it dealt with the hesitant Baltic governments, with British pressure and its own schemes on the northwestern fronts during the summer of 1919. There is some doubt about the assertion of Kornatovskii that Britain did not render any aid to the White Army until the fall of 1919, when it was too late to render any practical assistance. Kornatovskii is correct in asserting that British policy was not consistent, wavering between accepting the Soviet regime and extending all-out aid to the counterrevolution. There was a consistent dislike of the Soviet regime in evidence, accompanied by indecision that followed the fortunes of the White cause. The policy urged by Churchill, as he colorfully put it, to strangle the Bolshevist baby in its crib, was only a pious desire often accompanied by the fear of infanticide.

Kornatovskii offers interesting information concerning the German efforts to establish themselves in the Baltic by way of von der Goltz's presence there and his operations in Finland. The author also shows that as long as Iudenich was successful Great Britain was ready to aid his campaign, but as the campaign began to show signs of reverses the aid was rapidly curtailed. The indirect result of the defeat of Iudenich and Denikin, the author shows, was the signing of the peace treaty between Estonia and Soviet Russia.

Another historical account of the defense of Petrograd particularly in the fall of 1919 was published by A. A. Geronimus. This account was originally delivered as a lecture before an organization for the

[127] N. A. Kornatovskii, "Pervoe nastuplenie belogvardeitsev na Petrograd (1919)." *Krasnaia letopis,* No. 2 (26), (1928), 76-105; No. 3 (27), (1928), 91-140. N. A. Kornatovskii, *Borba za Krasnyi Petrograd (1919).* (Leningrad, 1928). N. A. Kornatovskii, *Borba za Krasnyi Piter.* (Moscow, 1929). N. A. Kornatovskii, *Severnaia kontrrevoliutsiia.* (Moscow, 1930). M. Podvoiskii, *Kommunary zashchishchaiut Krasnyi Piter.* (Moscow, 1920). V. Leikina, *Pokhod Iudenicha.* (Moscow, 1929).

study of military problems. In it Geronimus discusses some of the principles involved in the entire question and analyzes the sources and literature related to the issues involved.[128]

According to Geronimus, the defense of Petrograd stands out as a special case, different from any other military operation in the Civil War. It differs from the operation in the south against Denikin and from that in the east against Kolchak, for both men had found security in the rear guard. Iudenich, on the other hand, was forced to place his home front entirely on territories of the outlying Baltic states. Kolchak and Denikin depended upon both France and Great Britain, while Iudenich relied mostly upon British aid, since Britain dominated the Baltic area. Iudenich therefore found himself, according to Geronimus, in a most difficult position: on the one hand he championed "Russia one and indivisible," while on the other he was faced with the policy of a Great Britain that had strong reservations about restoring the Empire. Britain came in the end to accept the desire of the Baltic states to reach a peaceful settlement with Moscow, Geronimus believes, because these new states began to realize the futility of the war against the Soviet regime. The author also disagrees with the view of writers like Kakurin and Ventsov that the Iudenich campaign was a mere adventure. The campaign to seize Petrograd was no mere adventure, says Geronimus, but a campaign carefully planned and favored by Great Britain.[129]

Geronimus' interpretation aroused some criticism, notably from R. P. Eideman.[130] The main criticism came to this: Geronimus had overestimated the role of Great Britain, since Iudenich would most likely have attacked Petrograd even without being urged to do so by London. The strategy of Iudenich, according to Eideman, called for a "win or bust" policy and in this sense might be called adventurous. Eideman also seriously questioned whether the working class in the Baltic nations represented a sufficiently effective opposition that it could be regarded as instrumental in the defeat of Iudenich. The workers themselves suffered defeat in the Baltic countries and their leaders had to flee their homeland. As to the peasantry, according to Eideman, they opposed both von der Goltz and Iudenich since they feared mainly the return of the hated landlord class.

All in all, early historiography of the Civil War in the northwest was most adequate in the field of foreign and strategic affairs during

[128] *Krasnaia letopis*, No. 3 (27), (1928), 5-145. A. A. Geronimus, "Pokhod Iudenicha na Petrograd oseniu 1919 goda." *Zapiski sektsii po izucheniiu problem voin pri Komakademii*. Vol. II. (Moscow, 1931). "Oborona Krasnogo Petrograda v 1919 g." *Krasnaia letopis*, No. 3 (27), (1928), 91-146; No. 5 (32), (1929), 5-156 (includes an article by A. A. Geronimus, "Rabochii Petrograd i Iudenich," pp. 5-42.

[129] N. E. Kakurin, *Borba za Petrograd v 1919 g.* (Moscow, 1928). S. Ventsov, "Geroicheskii gorod." *Grazhdanskaia voina 1918-1921 gg.* Vol. I. (Moscow, 1928).

[130] *Zapiski sektsii po izucheniiu problem voin pri Komakademii*. Vol. II (Moscow, 1931), 98.

1918-1919, concerning the campaign against Petrograd and the part played by Great Britain. Other fields in which much was written were the defeat of the White Army and the intervention during the first and the second attack on Petrograd, the part played by the working class during the defense of Petrograd, and the cooperation of the war front and rear guard during the decisive part of the conflict.

H. EXPELLING THE WHITES FROM THE CRIMEA

The expulsion of General Vrangel's White Army from the Crimea marks the closing of the Civil War. This final phase of the three-year conflict has been dealt with in numerous books, articles, and memoirs, and in official records. It is impossible to discuss the bibliography fully and analyze each item that deals with the Crimean period of the war; suffice to state that by the end of 1920 more than 200 books, brochures, and articles had been published on the Vrangel fiasco.[131] From this mass there may be singled out a few works that have passed the test of time, such as those by M. Bunegin, A. Golubev, and V. K. Triandafillov. While some writers dealt exclusively with military aspects of the campaign against Vrangel in the Crimean Peninsula and in the Kuban area, others devoted their writings to such subjects as the partisan movement, the Bolshevik underground activities, the agrarian policies of Vrangel, and the political organization of the White government.[1]

[131]*Sbornik. Razgrom Vrangelia.* (Moscow, 1930). See particularly pp. 268-279.

[132]O. Shekun and R. M. Golubeva, comps., *Perekop. Sbornik vospominanii.* (Moscow, 1941). Ia. A. Slashchev, *Krym v 1920 godu.* Preface by D. Furmanov. (Moscow, 1924). N. F. Kuzmin, *Krushenie poslednego pokhoda Antanty.* (Moscow, 1958). M. Bunegin, *Revoliutsiia i grazhdanskaia voina v Krymu.* (Moscow, 1927). A. Golubev, *Vrangelevskie desanty na Kubani. Avgust-sentiabr 1920 g.* (Moscow, 1929). V. K. Triandafillov, "Perekopskaia operatsiia Krasnoi Armii." *Grazhdanskaia voina 1918-1921 gg.* Vol. I. (Moscow, 1928). E. Efimov, *Deistviia Vtoroi Konnoi armii v Krymu.* (Moscow, 1926). A. Buiskii, *Borba za Krym i razgrom Vrangelia.* (Moscow, 1928). Kulmakov and Lunin, *Perekopskaia v boiakh za Oktiabr.* (Moscow, 1927). I. Podshivalov, *Desantnaia ekspeditsiia Kovtiukha. Likvidatsiia vrangelevskogo desanta na Kubani v avguste 1920 g.* (Moscow, 1927). A. Golubev, *Vrangelevskie desanty na Kubani. Avgust-sentiabr 1920 g.* (Moscow, 1929). N. Babakhin, "Iz istorii Krymskogo podpolia." *Revoliutsiia v Krymu,* No. 3 (1924). L. Rempel, *Povstantsy v Krymu. K istorii krymskoi "zelenoi" sovetskoi povstancheskoi armii, 1920 g.* (Moscow, 1920). S. Sef, "Partiinye organizatsii Kryma v borbe s Denikinym i Vrangelem." *Proletarskaia revoliutsiia,* No. 10 (57), (1926), 114-155. A. Gukovskii, "K istorii agrarnoi politiki russkoi kontrrevoliutsii. (Agrarnaia politika pravitelstva Vrangelia)." *Na agrarnom fronte,* No. 6 (1927), 72-86; No. 7 (1927), 69-80. N. Kovalev, *Iuzhnaia kontrrevoliutsiia—Vrangel.* (Moscow, 1925). I. S. Korotkov, *Razgrom Vrangelia. Operativno-strategicheskii ocherk.* 2nd ed. (Moscow, 1948).

The end of the Polish conflict sealed the fate of the Whites in the Crimean Peninsula; from an anticipated prologue of a new drive against Moscow the campaign turned into an epilogue of the war. The Red offensive against the "Crimean Fortress" is described in many sources. Memoirs, essays, and collected documents were published in various magazines such as *Proletarskaia revoliutsiia* (Moscow) and *Letopis revoliutsii* (Kharkov), and in such collective publications as *Revoliutsiia v Krymu*, published by the Crimean *Istpart*. A goodly portion of the material pertaining to the liquidation of Vrangel may be found in military magazines such as *Voina i revoliutsiia, Armiia i revoliutsiia, Voennyi vestnik*, and *Krasnyi flot*; documentary sources appeared in *Krasnyi arkhiv*.

A book was already published by the end of 1920 which incorporated several accounts of the final campaign against Vrangel.[133] Others soon followed, covering the different military operations during the brief but decisive Red offensive that crossed the Perekop Isthmus and finally fanned out within the Crimean Peninsula. Most of these early writings are military accounts which hardly touch political or diplomatic implications of the last phase of the Civil War.[134]

Within a few years the writings were enriched by new sources. The first to utilize the newly published materials was V. Triandafillov, who on the fifth anniversary of the Crimean campaign reexamined and reinterpreted its significance. Looking back, Triandafillov states that in the summer of 1920 the threat of Vrangel was so serious that the Soviet military command was somewhat at a loss as to which front presented the graver problem, Poland encroaching upon Ukrainian territory or Vrangel moving out of the Crimea. For political and military reasons, it was thought, Vrangel had to be stopped before he reached the Donets Basin and was able to take over the southern Ukraine. This would have allowed Vrangel to open a new front where one had only recently been rolled back at such high cost.[135]

The increased volume of new sources forced new interpretations, best demonstrated in the work of K. Stutska and S. Belitskii, who published a reexamination of the campaign, stressing especially the aggressive motives of Vrangel. The authors maintain that the offensive launched by Vrangel

---

[133] *Razgrom Vrangelia.* (Kharkov, 1920).

[134] *15 Sivashskaia diviziia. Sbornik v pamiat piatiletiia divizii. 1918-1923 gg.* (Nikolaev, 1923). *Piatdesiat-pervaia Perekopskaia diviziia. Istoriia boevoi i mirnoi zhizni za piat let, 1919-1924 gg.* (Moscow, 1925). *Pod krasnym znamenem (1919-1925 gg.). Istoricheskii sbornik, 62 kavpolka Osoboi Kavbrigady.* (Moscow, 1925). *Boevoi put 57 Kharupanskogo Krasnoznamennogo kavaleriiskogo polka.* (Ostrogozhsk, 1928). I. Popov, "Shturm i vziatie Perekopskikh i Iushunskikh pozitsii." *Armiia i revoliutsiia,* Nos. 2 and 3 (1921). V. Triandafillov, "Perekopskaia operatsiia Krasnoi Armii." *Grazhdanskaia voina 1918-1921 gg.* Vol. I. (Moscow, 1928), 339-358.

[135] V. Triandafillov, "K piatiletiiu godovshchine likvidatsii Vrangelia." *Voina i revoliutsiia,* Nos. 7, 8 (1925). I. Grauzhis, "Kakhovskii platsdarm." *Armiia i revoliutsiia,* No. 2 (1922).

was promoted mainly by France, which was eager to aid Poland. Vrangel was also forced to undertake the campaign because of the shortage of provisions for his army as well as foodstuffs for export in exchange for arms.[136]

The White Crimean offensive was aimed in two directions: toward the right bank of the Dnieper, where Vrangel hoped to join the lingering and battered forces of Petliura; and toward the Donets Basin, where he might join the Don Cossacks, expecting to find support there. Unable to come to an agreement with Petliura, Vrangel had no choice but to take the latter course. In this connection the study of A. Golubev is worthy of attention even though it is predominantly a military investigation. In describing the military operation, which was actually of secondary importance, and the landing of the Vrangel troops in the Kuban area, Golubev incorporates some vital information about the last phase of the Civil War in the south.[137]

Another serious work which deals with the rout of Vrangel is the third volume of the *General History of the Civil War*, published in 1930, in which three chapters are devoted to the Crimean campaign. These chapters present some original sidelights on the Vrangel regime in the Crimea; for instance, while characterizing the administration of the Crimea the authors state that the Crimean authorities adopted the identical policy Denikin had followed previously. The best illustration, they say, was the agrarian policy, according to which Vrangel promised the peasants land that belonged to the landlord class, redeemable during a period of twenty-five years. Such a program alone was sufficient to doom the White cause from the very start.

As Vrangel enjoyed temporary success in his territorial aggrandizement, his general policy kept changing accordingly. At first Vrangel figured on establishing his regime firmly in the Crimea and then, with the aid of Great Britain, reaching an agreement with the Soviet government based on a modest program of mutual recognition. As Vrangel grew more successful he abandoned this plan, and began to envision himself as the liberator of all Russia. He hoped to rally the Cossacks of both the Don and the Kuban areas and to arouse a massive rebellion throughout the Ukrainian countryside.[138]

The third volume of the *General History of the Civil War* presents an excellent description of the peculiarities and specific difficulties which the Red Army had to overcome at this turn of events, before it could count on complete victory in the Crimea. The first formidable problem was crossing by way of the isthmuses or "bottlenecks" of Perekop and Chogarsk into the Crimean Peninsula. This was an especially complicated operation in view of the fact that the flotillas in the Azov and Black seas were entirely

[136] K. Stutska and S. Belitskii, "Kakhovka." *Grazhdanskaia voina 1918-1921 gg.* Vol. I (Moscow, 1928), 312-333.

[137] A. Golubev, *Vrangelevskie desanty na Kubani, avgust-sentiabr 1920 g.* (Leningrad, 1920).

[138] *Grazhdanskaia voina 1918-1921 gg.* Vol. III (Moscow, 1930), Chaps. 19-21.

in the hands of the Whites. In May, 1920, Vrangel's strategic plan provided
for a breakthrough northward and the establishment of a front line of
Rostov-Taganrog-Don Basin-Sinelnikovo. Had this been a successful operation it would have included the Don and Kuban regions upon which
Vrangel staked so much hope, anticipating the Cossacks rejoining his
cause. The British government was skeptical about such a scheme and
disclaimed any responsibility for undertaking such an operation, but
Vrangel paid no attention and moved ahead.

After a brief and successful campaign Vrangel began to encounter
stiffer resistance. First there came serious political failure when he was
unable to persuade the Don Cossacks to rebel. Vrangel then faced another disappointment when the troops he sent to land in the area of
Taganrog were driven back by the Red Army. He tried then to establish
contact with the partisans of Makhno, but this plan did not materialize
either. By August, 1920, the initial successes abruptly ended, largely due to
the lack of a firm base north of the Crimea which had been counted upon.
All efforts to establish some kind of a detente with Poland equally failed,
mainly because Vrangel, as General Denikin before him, firmly adhered to
a formula of "Russia one and indivisible." The idea of restoring the former
Empire had little appeal to Poland. On the other hand, the strength of the
Red Army was largely based on the control of the entire country north of
the Crimea. The initial gains of Vrangel, he soon realized, were in grave
danger should he be cut off from the peninsula and unable to escape across
the Perekop Isthmus.

In summary, the authors of the third volume of the *General History of
the Civil War* conclude that temporarily the desperate surge northward of
Vrangel weakened the Reds against Poland. In part, Vrangel is held responsible for the reverses Soviet Russia encountered in the west. When, however,
the Soviet-Polish war came to an end it was not reasonable to expect that
the entire Red force would turn against the Crimea. This was necessary
not only for military but for diplomatic reasons, so that Poland, while
negotiating peace at Riga, would not be able to exploit the military difficulties in the south for her own ends.

The total expulsion of Vrangel's army from the Crimea marked the end of
the Civil War. The only exception was a mopping operation here and there
in the Far East, where the Red Army finally occupied Vladivostok in 1922.
For all practical purposes the end of the Crimean campaign marked the end
of the three-year Civil War in Russia.

I. THE SOVIET-POLISH WAR

The campaign against Poland which ended with the Treaty of Riga has
been frequently discussed in print with regard to the causes of its failure,
and its political implications in both eastern and western European affairs.
In December, 1922, the former Commander-in-Chief of the Red Army,

S. S. Kamenev, contributed his views on the Soviet-Polish war and on the reason that the Red Army was stopped at the gates of Warsaw in 1920. Kamenev's central theme is that the aim of the Soviet offensive was to pass by the city of Warsaw from the north and drive a wedge between the Polish army and Danzig. This would have disrupted the line of communication used by the Entente powers to supply Poland with arms and ammunition. Kamenev dwells on the question of guilt for the outcome of the war. He does refer to serious administrative deficiencies and to sheer fatigue as a result of the long and rapid march from Kiev to Warsaw, which contributed in part to the outcome of the war. Beyond that, Kamenev says, there naturally followed an "elemental development of war" which in the end led to confusion and loss of combatant spirit.[139]

The first extensive reply to Kamenev concerning the Soviet-Polish war was published in 1923 by M. N. Tukhachevskii, former commander of the western front. The author discusses at great length some of the questions raised by S. S. Kamenev, and he comes to a somewhat different conclusion as to why the conflict ended unfavorably for the Red Army. Tukhachevskii regards the poor communication system that prevailed at that time, the inadequate technical facilities, combined with the fatal disagreements between the commands of the western and southwestern fronts, as the basic reason for the fiasco at Warsaw. At the most decisive moment, when the Red Army was at the very threshold of the Polish capital, the two fronts lacked unity both in motivation and in strategic planning.[140] Tukhachevskii also finds

[139] S. S. Kamenev, "Borba s beloi Polshei." *Voennyi vestnik,* No. 12 (1922), 7-15. Iu. Markhlevskii, *Voina i mir mezhdu burzhuaznoi Polshei i proletarskoi Rossiei.* (Moscow, 1921). M. Pavlovich (Veltman),\ *Voina s polskimi panami. (Polsko-shliakhetskaia avantiura).* (Moscow, 1920). S. S. Kislovskii, *Front i tyl v borbe s polskimi belogvardeitsami.* (Moscow, 1920). P. Stepanov, *S Krasnoi Armiei na panskuiu Polshu. Vpechatleniia i nabliudeniia.* (Moscow, 1920). Kh. Davydov, "Iz vospominanii o peremirii s poliakami." *Revoliutsionaia voennaia mysl,* No. 7 (1922). V. Kozervoskii, *V plenu u interventov.* (Moscow, 1925). B. Dunaev, *Dve evakuatsii.* (Moscow, 1926). I. Modenov, *Dvadtsataia diviziia na polskom fronte.* (Moscow, 1928). V. Kuznetsov, *Iz vospominanii politrabotnika.* (Moscow, 1930). S. Kotov, *Na Berezine (1920).* (Moscow, 1930). M. Pavlovich, *Ukraina kak obekt mezhdunarodnoi kontrrevoliutsii.* (Moscow, 1920). S. Mezheninov, *Nachalo borby s belopoliakami.* (Moscow, 1921). I. N. Sergeev, *Ot Dviny k Visle.* (Smolensk, 1923). K. Nevezhin, *Krasnaia Armiia na polskom fronte v 1920 g.* (Leningrad, 1925). N. Kakurin and V. Melikov, *Voina s belopoliakami 1920 g.* (Moscow, 1925). V. K. Putna, *K Visle i obratno.* (Moscow, 1927). V. Melikov, *Marna (1914), Visla (1920), Smyrna (1922).* (Moscow, 1928). E. Shilovskii, *Na Berezine.* (Moscow, 1928). G. Guy, *Na Varshavu! Deistviia konnogo korpusa na Zapadnom fronte.* (Moscow, 1928). N. Kakurin and K. Berends, *Kievskaia operatsiia poliakov.* (Moscow, 1928). N. Varfolomeev, *Mozyrskaia operatsiia.* (Moscow, 1930).

[140] M. N. Tukhachevskii, *Pokhod na Vislu.* (Moscow, 1923). M. N. Tukhachevskii, *Izbrannye proizvedeniia.* (Moscow, 1964). 2 vols. See Vol. I, 114-168. Lev Nikulin, *Tukhachevskii. Biograficheskii ocherk.* (Moscow, 1964). A. I. Todorskii, *Marshal Tukhachevskii.* (Moscow, 1964).

certain basic faults in the Soviet strategy and himself overestimates the revolutionary climate in Poland, as did Lenin in 1920. This he betrays when in a somewhat melancholy frame of mind he observes: "Capitalistic Europe was shaken to its foundation, and if it had not been for our strategic errors the Polish campaign would have served as the binding link between the October Revolution and the revolution in western Europe."

Tukhachevskii also has some critical things to say about the Fourth Army on the western front, which included the cavalry corps commanded by G. D. Guy. According to Tukhachevskii, the command of the entire Fourth Army was extremely unsatisfactory.

Many writers seem to believe that although Tukhachevskii listed some pertinent reasons for the reverses suffered by the Red Army at Warsaw, they were not the only ones that explained the Soviet failure to capture the Polish capital. In 1923 the former Commander of the Fourth Army, I. N. Sergeev, published his theory as to why the Soviet offensive met disaster.[141]

Another of the earliest published works on the history of the war with Poland appeared in 1922, written by the well-known Soviet military historian of the 1920's, N. E. Kakurin.[142] Kakurin divides the war with Poland into four main periods: (1) the time from the evacuation of Austro-German troops from the occupied territory to the emergence of the Soviet Republics of Lithuania and White Russia, (2) seizure of parts of these two republics, (3) pause and preparation for the forthcoming campaign against Soviet Russia, and (4) the war between Poland and Soviet Russia. From about the middle of July, 1920, the Soviet army began to break up into three directions, weakening its former unity and in the end contributing to its defeat at the gates of Warsaw.

On the other hand, Kakurin argues, the Polish army witnessed exactly the opposite development; instead of dispersing, it solidified its direction, shortened its lines, and retreated to its bases whence new and fresh reserves were efficiently supplied with arms and ammunition. Polish resistance increased proportionately as the army retreated deeper into Poland. Kakurin also states that Soviet troops, after a march of some 1,200 miles within a month, facing land devastated everywhere by the retreating army, lost contact with their own base. When the final encounter at Warsaw took place the Soviet army not only lost its momentum but its unified force, and faced the imminent danger of retreat or destruction.

In 1924, B. M. Shaposhnikov added his version of the episode, analyzing in considerable detail some of the outstanding operations carried out by the Soviet army; he also describes some of the glaring failures and the absence of coordination in administrative work.

[141] I. N. Sergeev, *Ot Dviny k Visle.* (Smolensk, 1923). Marshal Pilsudski refers to Sergeev's book as the "pearl of military literature." It has been translated into Polish: *Od Dźwiny ku Wiśle.* (Warsaw, 1925).

[142] N. E. Kakurin, *Russko-polskaia kampaniia 1918-1920 gg. Politiko-strategicheskii ocherk.* (Moscow, 1922). N. E. Kakurin and V. A. Melikov, *Voina s belopoliakami v 1920 g.* (Moscow, 1925).

However, the often-repeated view that the absence of coordinated action on the southwestern and western fronts proved fatal to the entire drive against Warsaw in 1920 has by no means been accepted universally.[143] Stalin and some of his adherents regarded the conduct of the southwestern command as correct, and whatever strategic errors had been committed were ascribed to western commanders. Closer to the truth, probably, was the fact that the war was lost largely because both commands erred in general strategy; both underestimated the strength of the enemy, and because of rapid initial success the command succumbed to overoptimism.

In this connection, the important account published by V. K. Putna, in 1928, should be mentioned. The author, a former commander of the Twenty-seventh Omsk Division, took an active part on the western front, which he described in considerable detail. Putna, it seems, correctly criticizes those who tend to cite single errors and present these as the main if not the single cause of the Polish fiasco. According to Putna, the fiasco at Warsaw was the result of a combination of circumstances, the sum of many errors. Involved in the general failure are political miscalculations such as minimizing the force of Polish chauvinism, overestimating the influence of the Polish working class, and failing to carry out agrarian reforms which might have won the support of the peasantry. All these fallacies the Polish government utilized to its own advantage, and it not only enjoyed the loyalty of the population throughout the conflict, but managed to win the war.[144]

B. M. Shaposhnikov, a well-known military figure during the Polish campaign, added his views to the general assessment of the campaign.[145] The author agrees with Tukhachevskii that once the counteroffensive went into operation to expel the invading Polish army from the Ukraine, the Soviet army could not possibly have stopped at the Russian-Polish border (wherever that border was!). The momentum gained and the entire international situation favored decisive action, compelling the offensive to surge westward. Shaposhnikov utilized an impressive amount of factual evidence concerning the course of the war, especially the drive toward the Vistula River and Warsaw. In the end he concluded that the advance of the army proved too rapid and the sudden successes resulted in underestimating the opponent's strength. The overall viewpoint of Shaposhnikov, it can be said, is against the search for single miscalculations and erring individuals in one or another campaign of the war. He is particularly resentful against those critics who describe the entire campaign against Warsaw as nothing more than a reckless adventure. This,

[143]V. K. Triandafillov, "Vzaimodeistvie mezhdu Zapadnym i Iugo-Zapadnym frontami vo vremia letnego nastupleniia Krasnoi Armii na Vislu v 1920 g." *Voina i revoliutsiia.* Book 2. (Moscow, 1925).

[144]B. M. Shaposhnikov, *Na Visle. K istorii kampanii 1920 g.* (Moscow, 1924). V. K. Putna, *K visle i obratno.* (Moscow, 1928).

[145]B. M. Shaposhnikov, *Na Visle. K istorii kampanii 1920 g.* (Moscow, 1924).

he believes, is unworthy of and humiliating to those valorous men who gave their lives for what they deeply believed in—a nobler social order.

In 1929 A. I. Egorov, the former commander of the southwestern front, published his story in a book entitled *Lvov-Warsaw*. Egorov's purpose was to determine to what degree, if any, the front at Lvov was responsible for the defeat at Warsaw. Using an immense amount of documentary evidence, the author carefully analyzed the strategic circumstances and plans of both sidès. In the end he denied all responsibility on the part of the southwestern theater for delaying aid. He cites the order to move an armed force from Lvov, which he had issued, and which Stalin failed to sign. In part Egorov seems to shift the blame to Stalin; in part he ascribes the failure to the general confusion that prevailed at the time.[146]

In his preface Egorov insists that despite the numerous discussions and strategic analyses published at home and abroad, there is still much evidence to be revealed before a full account of the war would be feasible. Meanwhile, he maintains, much blame for the military failure must rest upon the chief command for the absence of firm, consistent action and the lack of coordination among the regional commanders. The book, as might be expected, aroused as much hostility as praise and the magazine *Voina i revoliutsiia* opened its pages to some long and, at times, acrimonious disputes.[147]

In 1932 two more books were added, one by the Chief of Staff of the First Cavalry Army, L. L. Kliuev, another by the Commander of the Third Cavalry Corps, G. D. Guy. Both deal largely with the war on the northern and southern flanks of the Soviet-Polish front. The work by Kliuev is based on archival sources, on records in his own possession, and on materials he obtained from Poland. The book by Guy analyzes the participation of the Third Cavalry Corps and the Fourth Army in the Polish campaign and the reasons that both groups were forced in the end to be interned in Germany.[148] Kliuev's conclusion is that it was a serious error not to have the Red Cavalry under the exclusive command of the Commander-in-Chief, and left as a unit by itself. This permitted the cavalry to be shifted from one sector of the front to another in response to local interests instead of overall needs. Kliuev has reference to the famous Red Cavalry led by the later Marshal Budennyi during the Polish campaign.

The debates over the causes of the outcome of the war against Poland continued for many years. B. M. Shaposhnikov listed several contributing factors, such as maladministration and absence of coordinated action and cooperation, and later he pointed out the tardy arrival of provisions,

[146]A. I. Egorov, *Lvov-Varshava. 1920 god. Vzaimodeistvie frontov.* (Moscow, 1929).

[147]*Voina i revoliutsiia*, Nos. 5, 10 (1929); No. 2 (1930).

[148]L. L. Kliuev, *Pervaia konnaia Armiia na Polskom fronte v 1920 godu.* Preface by S. M. Budennyi. (Leningrad, 1925). G. D. Guy, *Na Varshavu!* (Moscow, 1932).

which gravely undermined the entire war effort. Shaposhnikov admitted that at the most decisive moments of the struggle at the gates of Warsaw, every commander tackled the problems he faced as he saw fit, without any concern for the overall plan. Furthermore, Shaposhnikov points out, the Red Command seriously underestimated Polish military potentialities and the strength of vigorous nationalism.

The opinions of N. E. Kakurin have been mentioned, and should be compared with the sharp rebuttal by V. K. Triandafillov.[149] According to Triandafillov, it was the absence of a synchronized strategy between the western and southwestern fronts that caused the overall plan to fail. He blamed especially the command of the southwestern front and the supreme command: the first failed to assess the actual assistance it might have rendered if the First Cavalry Army would have supported the attack on the western front instead of engaging in a battle of its own at Lvov; the latter, according to Triandafillov, faltered in carrying out the operation with all due firmness at the decisive moment.

Finally, P. V. Suslov discusses the entire subject not as a military man but as a party member, complementing the many analyses of the war from strictly strategic points of view.[150] After he examines the background of the Soviet-Polish conflict, and the origin of certain vital political issues between the two countries that led to the outbreak of hostilities, Suslov argues that the Soviet government was forced to defend the recently founded nation. The conflict with Pilsudski became not only a war to save the October Revolution but a war to defend the international revolution, since "White Poland" backed by the Entente powers was attempting to widen the barrier between Soviet Russia and the rising proletariat of western Europe.

Suslov maintains that the Soviet government had not aimed to annex Poland, nor was there any intention to force the Polish peasantry and proletariat to adopt a social revolutionary course. But Moscow could clearly see the link that tied Poland under the command of Pilsudski with Western imperialism, and the further complications that might well follow from such an alliance. This, more than anything else, forced Soviet Russia to accept the challenge and fight.

Suslov proceeds with other party problems involved in the war. He discusses the leftist deviations which in 1920 would not recognize any significance to or allow participation in the nationalist liberation movement or in war against imperialism; nor would they detect signs of an unfolding class struggle in such events as the Soviet-Polish war. Pilsudski only utilized former oppressive policies of the imperial government in Poland

[149]V. K. Triandafillov, "Vzaimodeistvie mezhdu Zapadnym i Iugo-Zapadnym frontami vo vremia letnego nastupleniia Krasnoi Armii na Vislu v 1920 g." *Voina i revoliutsiia.* Book 2. (Moscow, 1925).

[150]P. V. Suslov, *Politicheskoe obezpechenie sovetsko-polskoi kampanii 1920 g.* (Moscow, 1930).

and nationalistic sentiments against Soviet Russia and therefore deceived his own people.

The war with Poland, Suslov states further, though caused by deeply rooted traditional antagonisms, was bound to become counterrevolutionary and imperialistic in nature. All in all Moscow had no choice but to rise in defense of its recently established regime. It therefore stands to reason that political considerations were paramount during the Soviet-Polish conflict. Suslov then describes the role played by the party and the revolutionary committees in the occupational zone, and the formation of a Provisional Government of Poland made up of Polish members of the Communist Party, as aspects of the class struggle that were injected into the war. The military had committed strategic errors, but party leaders had done their share in committing ideological blunders during the war months.

According to Suslov, the most serious political mistake committed by the Polish Revolutionary Committee (*Revkom*), the failure to nationalize all Polish lands at once in favor of the peasantry, was bound to have fatal consequences. Had the land been distributed immediately, Suslov believes, it would have assured the support of the countryside and helped to form a solid revolutionary base.

The subject of the Soviet-Polish war kept recurring. In 1929, when V. A. Melikov endeavored to explain the failure of the war by the decision to drive needlessly against Warsaw instead of holding the line along the Bug River, he aroused a storm of criticism.[151] Melikov was challenged particularly by Tukhachevskii, who maintained that the revolutionary situation throughout Europe at the time of the outbreak of the war was favorable to an active Soviet policy, and that the defeat of the aggressor demanded an attack on the citadel of the enemy, Warsaw. It was, argued Tukhachevskii, undeniably a revolutionary act, but a necessary one, to overthrow the bourgeois, aggressive Polish state. Conditions in 1920 dictated the offensive as the only realistic act, despite the fact that economic circumstances in the Soviet Union did not favor the military operation undertaken.[152]

In an equally challenging essay S. R. Budkevich utilizes Polish documents in discussing the war.[153] After he analyzes the international situation in 1920, Budkevich concludes that there were serious disagreements between Poland and the Entente powers. Great Britain, says Budkevich, did not favor Polish intervention, for London believed that the economic blockade against Russia and the recovery of capitalism in western Europe

[151]V. A. Melikov, *Marna (1914), Visla (1920), Smyrna (1922)*. (Moscow, 1928).

[152]M. N. Tukhachevskii, "O kharaktere sovremennykh voin." *Zapiski sektsii po izucheniiu problem voin pri Komakademii*. Vol. I. (1930).

[153]S. R. Budkevich, "Operatsiia polskikh armii na Visle v 1920 godu. (V osveshchenii polskikh istochnikov)." *Zapiski sektsii po izucheniiu problem voin pri Komakademii*. Vol. II. (Moscow, 1931).

would bring about the collapse of the Soviet regime without the use of force. On the other hand, France supported Poland, and though she was inclined to favor a restored Russian national state, she rendered Poland enormous military aid in arms and ammunition. At the Spa Conference, on the other hand, Great Britain urged Poland to make peace with Moscow and restore Vilna to Lithuania.

Budkevich points out further that the proletariat throughout western Europe was against Poland and the latter was able to receive aid only by way of Danzig. As to the Polish Communist Party, he thinks that it overestimated bourgeois political strength or placed too much hope on the Red Army, instead of forcing agrarian reforms and labor legislation at home.

Both M. N. Tukhachevskii and R. P. Eideman criticized Budkevich, particularly for labeling the defeat at Warsaw a political fiasco. The Poles, argued Eideman, by September, 1920, feared another winter campaign, even though they had been victorious during the preceding months. For this reason the Treaty of Riga was accepted on far worse terms than Poland anticipated in January, 1920.

The Soviet-Polish war is also discussed in the third volume of the official Soviet history of the Civil War.[154] Here the main factors that hindered synchronized military action and contributed in the end to the failure of the war were enumerated as follows: (1) a belated realization of the need for cooperation and the belated decision to carry it out, (2) poor organization at the General Headquarters and an inadequate system of communication, and (3) failure of the southwestern front to carry out directives from the Commander-in-Chief to regroup the cavalry branch. Deriving from all these were also miscalculation in general strategy, delayed action, and lack of unified effort, which weakened the effort along the entire front.

J. HISTORICAL WRITING ON THE CIVIL WAR AFTER STALIN

In an effort to reassess historical development in the Soviet Union prior to 1953, one writer observed that the road traversed seemed like a "solid chain of pits and bumps, of flows and blunders, of unfulfilled assignments and mistaken decisions." The melancholy is understandable when one recalls the impact of the Stalinist years upon historical writing in the Soviet Union, and the recent tendency to sycophancy.

Khrushchev's attack on the cult of the individual at the Twentieth Congress of the Communist Party, in 1956, marked a change in Soviet historiography. The historian was now urged to rewrite the past, on

[154]*Grazhdanskaia voina 1918-1921 gg.* Vol. III, *Voenno-strategicheskii ocherk boevykh deistvii Krasnoi Armii.* A. S. Bubnov, S. S. Kamenev, M. N. Tukhachevskii, and R. P. Eideman, eds. (Moscow, 1930), Chaps. 13-18, pp. 305-470.

266

the basis of documentary evidence, and free his interpretations from fawning before Stalin—"the greatest genius of all lands and all times." The Soviet historian was also urged to turn once more to search for basic evidence. The writers of history were encouraged to stress the importance of "collective leadership" and present a balanced description of the role of the party or its leaders in the light of historical evidence, and not cringe before a single self-glorifying member of the party. The historian was also urged to present an objective account of the rise of the Red Army or Navy and its military record, and a similar history of the recent war accompanied by an analysis of the different phases which would explain the reasons for both reverses and successes that eventually led to final triumph. Simultaneously, a revision of the history of the Civil War was accompanied by a reexamination of all available resources upon which a truer interpretation might be based.

The Stalinist cult persisted to the last. As late as 1953 a short book published by I. F. Kondrashev presented a typical account designed to elevate Stalin to the highest pedestal of history. It is a mere compilatory work of secondary sources and repeatedly quotes material that would support the fading cult of Stalin. Nor were even more serious undertakings able immediately to rid themselves of the cult influence. A more pretentious monograph, published in 1954, by N. I. Shatagin, broader in design and based on selected sources, still displays the inability of the author to free himself entirely of the recent cult interpretation that led him to a number of serious errors concerning the course of the Civil War.[155] He repeats the former fashionable legend of the importance of the Tsaritsyn front, where Stalin was present, and allots him most of the credit as the strategist of the Civil War. At the same time there appeared another study on the Civil War in the Ukraine by A. V. Likholat. Though this study represents a superior handling of the subject, presenting the Civil War period in a truer historical perspective, nevertheless the author inadvertently makes occasional curtsies to the cult of Stalin, a habit that must have become deeply ingrained in many historians.[156]

On June 30, 1956, the Central Committee of the Communist Party adopted a resolution concerning the "Overcoming of the Cult of the Personality and Its Consequences." Shortly thereafter the magazine *Kommunist* (No. 12, 1956) published an article entitled "Some Problems Concerning the History of the Civil War," which served as an addendum to the resolution. It urged a reexamination of the role of the Communist Party and of the Central Committee in deciding military

[155]I. F. Kondrashev, *Lenin, Stalin—vdokhnoviteli i organizatory razgroma voennoi interventsii i vnutrennei kontrrevoliutsii v 1918-1920 gg.* (Moscow, 1953). N. I. Shatagin, *Organizatsiia i stroitelstvo Sovetskoi Armii v 1918-1920 godakh.* (Moscow, 1954).

[156]A. V. Likholat, *Razgrom natsionalisticheskoi kontrrevoliutsii na Ukraine v 1917-1922 gg.* (Moscow, 1954).

problems during the Civil War; it also urged clarification of the role played by each of the fronts during the summer and fall of 1918 and the strategy used against the army of Denikin. Judgment was to be based on a careful scrutiny of all available sources, old and new. The Central Committee was also to reexamine Stalin's participation during the defense of Petrograd in the spring of 1919 and in the southwest in 1920.

In 1956 the magazine *Voprosy istorii* carried an editorial and three articles on different problems concerning the rewriting of the history of the party and the Civil War. The editorial was a grave indictment of Stalinist historians. It appealed for a new way of writing history, rather than a simple dash from one extreme to another. Not in excluding citations and eliminating names alone can the cult of the individual be overcome, is the implication. Only in a genuine Marxist interpretation and clarification of historical processes and of the role of individuals can history be truthfully recorded. One of the three articles was by V. E. Belikov, on the campaign against Iudenich in the summer of 1919; another was by N. F. Kuzmin, on the campaign against Denikin; the third, by S. F. Naida and Iu. P. Petrov, reexamined the campaign in the east.[157]

The article by Belikov endeavored to correct the erroneous impression created by the *Short Course of the History of the All-Union Communist Party (Bolsheviks)*, namely, that Stalin played the decisive part in the defense of the city of Petrograd. Belikov's article was one of the first to question the validity of the interpretation presented in the *Short Course* and elsewhere that Stalin was the central figure in the war. The author was not discussing the general theme of the cult of the individual, but merely one aspect of the problem; nor did he even touch upon the erroneous views of Stalin concerning the defense of Petrograd. An article which appeared in the magazine *Kommunist* brought wider attention to the whole problem of historical falsification. The heads of the social sciences departments at a conference in June, 1957, as well as at subsequent conferences, took up the entire problem of the writing of history.[158]

They produced an astringent analysis of the histories written during the Stalinist decades, the eulogistic tales about various historical figures. The true tragedy of the former years, it was stated, was in the fact that moral ideological limits were no longer recognized. The more power Stalin came to enjoy, the more he seemed to have freed himself from moral restraints. The effect was unavoidable: historians who dared not

[157]"XX Sezd i zadachi issledovaniia istorii partii." *Voprosy istorii*, No. 3 (1956), 3-12. V. E. Belikov, "Partiinaia organizatsiia v borbe protiv Iudenicha letom 1919 goda." *Voprosy istorii*, No. 1 (1956), 31-44. N. F. Kuzmin, "K istorii razgroma belogvardeiskikh voisk Denikina." *Voprosy istorii*, No. 7 (1956), 18-32. S. F. Naida and Iu. P. Petrov, "Kommunisticheskaia partiia—organizator pobedy na Vostochnom fronte v 1918 godu." *Voprosy istorii*, No. 10 (1956), 3-15.

[158]See the report of S. F. Naida, *Ob osveshchenii nekotorykh voprosov KPSS v gody interventsii i grazhdanskoi voiny v kurse istorii partii dlia vuzov.* (Moscow, 1958).

challenge the cult resigned themselves to the absurdity of Stalin's infallability in whatever he did or thought he did in the past.

To combat the Stalinist cult in historical literature many new courses had to be organized; many works had to be rewritten and the training of young men in the field of history initiated all anew. Since the middle of the 1950's the number of documentary publications, and the training of young students of history have expanded considerably. Since 1957, the year that marked the fortieth anniversary of the October Revolution, additional documentary publications, memoirs, and monographs have been published that deal with the Civil War years of 1917-1920. Best evidence of this is seen in the two bibliographical guides published in 1959-1960.[159]

Many documentary sources on the period 1917-1923 appeared in the *Kommunist* in 1957 (Nos. 5 and 15), in *Voprosy istorii KPSS* in 1957 and 1958 (Nos. 1, 3; 1, 2, 4), in *Istoricheskii arkhiv* in 1958 (No. 4), and in many other journals. Lenin's fourth edition of his *Complete Works* (41 vols.) has been supplemented by a further volume. The latter contains material which first appeared in periodicals after 1956. The latest volumes also include his military correspondence, which had been unavailable since the middle 1930's. Also published in 1959 and 1960 were numerous documents related to the Civil War in the provinces and concerning the eighth and ninth party congresses.[160]

[159]*Velikaia Oktiabrskaia sotsialisticheskaia revoliutsiia. Borba za vlast Sovetov v period inostrannoi interventsii i grazhdanskoi voiny. Ukazatel literatury izdannoi v 1957-1958 gg. v sviazi s 40-letiem Velikoi Oktiabrskoi sotsialisticheskoi revoliutsii.* (Moscow, 1959). 4 parts. Two additional parts were published in 1960.

[160]*Protokoly VIII i IX sezdov RKP (b).* (Moscow, 1959 and 1960). *Iz istorii grazhdanskoi voiny v SSSR.* (Moscow, 1960-1961). 3 vols. *Sezdy Sovetov Soiuza SSR, Soiuznykh i Avtonomnykh Sotsialisticheskikh respublik.* Vol. I, *1917-1922 gg.* (Moscow, 1959). *Dokumenty vneshnei politiki SSSR.* (Moscow, 1958). 2 vols. Of the numerous accounts throughout the different parts of the Soviet Union the following may be cited: *Borba trudiashchikhsia za ustanovlenie Sovetskoi vlasti na Altae (1917-1920 gg.).* (Barnaul, 1957). *Borba za vlast Sovetov v Vologodskoi gubernii (1917-1919 gg.).* (Vologda, 1957). *Borba za vlast Sovetov na Donu, 1917-1920 gg.* (Rostov, 1957). *Borba za Sovetskuiu vlast na Kubani v 1917-1920 gg.* (Krasnodar, 1957). *V gody grazhdanskoi voiny.* (Ivanovo, 1957). *Za vlast Sovetov.* (Chita, 1957). *Grazhdanskaia voina v Orenburge.* (Orenburg, 1958). *Samarskaia guberniia v gody grazhdanskoi voiny.* (Kuibyshev, 1958). *Simbirskaia guberniia v gody grazhdanskoi voiny.* (Ulianovsk, 1958). *Borba za Sovetskuiu vlast v Severnoi Osetii.* (Ordzhonikidze, 1957). *Za vlast Sovetov v Kabarde i Balkarii.* (Nalchik, 1957). *Borba za Sovetskuiu vlast v Checheno-Ingushetii.* (Groznyi, 1958). *Borba za ustanovlenie i uprochenie Sovetskoi vlasti v Dagestane v 1917-1921 gg.* (Moscow, 1958). *Velikaia Oktiabrskaia sotsialisticheskaia revoliutsiia i grazhdanskaia voina v Kirgizii.* (Frunze, 1957). *Velikaia Oktiabrskaia sotsialisticheskaia revoliutsiia i pobeda Sovetskoi vlasti v Armenii.* (Erevan, 1957). *Borba za pobedu Sovetskoi vlasti v Gruzii.* (Tbilisi, 1958). *Turkmenistan v period inostrannoi voennoi interventsii i grazhdanskoi voiny.* (Ashkhabad, 1957).

To these publications must be added the increased list of memoirs which had virtually ceased to appear in print since the 1930's. Many memoirs of former years, totally unavailable for a long time, were reissued; others never before published were added to the lengthening list of current publications.161

The number of monographs on the Civil War published since 1956 is impressive. These deal mostly with the military campaigns of 1918, the defeat of the Kolchak army in the east, the collapse of the army commanded by Denikin in the south, the defense of Petrograd in 1919, and the campaign of the Entente powers against Bolshevism.162 Many of the studies deal with special localities such as the Volga or Ural regions, Siberia, or the Maritime Province in the east. Many publications discuss the struggle with the White Army supported by the Entente powers. Cumulatively these aid in gaining a fuller picture of the dimensional scope and variety of forms taken by the Civil War throughout the vast territory of Russia during those fateful years, 1918-1920.163

161V. V. Kuibyshev, *Epizody iz moei zhizni.* (Moscow, 1957). V. K. Putna, *Vostochnyi front (Shtrikhi).* (Moscow, 1959). P. P. Postyshev, *Grazhdanskaia voina na Vostoke Sibiri.* (Moscow, 1957). I. E. Iakir, *Vospominaniia o grazhdanskoi voine.* (Moscow, 1957). S. M. Budennyi, *Proidennyi put.* (Moscow, 1958). F. I. Golikov, *Krasnye orly.* (Moscow, 1959). O. I. Gorodovikov, *Vospominaniia.* (Moscow, 1957). M. D. Bonch-Bruevich, *Vsia vlast Sovetam.* (Moscow, 1958). A. Samoilo, *Dve zhizni.* (Moscow, 1958). Aside from these there appeared many collective reminiscences such as *Geroicheskaia oborona Petrograda v 1919 g.* (Leningrad, 1959). *Nezabyvaemye gody.* (Rostov, 1957). *Partizany Pribaikalia.* (Ulan-Ude, 1957).

162*Iz istorii borby sovetskogo naroda protiv inostrannoi voennoi interventsii i vnutrennei kontrrevoliutsii v 1918 g.* (Moscow, 1956). A. E. Antonov, *Boevoi vosemnadtsatyi god. (Voennye deistviia Krasnoi Armii v 1918—nachale 1919 gg.).* (Moscow, 1961). L. M. Spirin, *Razgrom armii Kolchaka.* (Moscow, 1957). G. Kh. Eikhe, *Ufimskaia avantiura Kolchaka.* (Moscow, 1960). *Reshaiushchie pobedy sovetskogo naroda nad interventami i belogvardeitsami v 1919 g.* (Moscow, 1960). M. V. Rybakov, *Iz istorii grazhdanskoi voiny na Severo-Zapade v 1919 g.* (Moscow, 1958). A. S. Pukhov, *Petrograd ne sdavat'!* (Moscow, 1960). N. F. Kuzmin, *Krushenie poslednego pokhoda Antanty.* (Moscow, 1958).

163A. I. Aksenov and A. I. Potylitsyn, *Pobeda Sovetskoi vlasti na Severe.* (Archangel, 1957). Iu. N. Aleskerov, *Interventsiia i grazhdanskaia voina v Srednei Azii.* (Tashkent, 1959). N. V. Berezniakov, *Borba trudiashchikhsia Bessarabii protiv interventov v 1917-1920 gg.* (Kishenev, 1957). A. M. Elchibekian, *Velikaia Oktiabrskaia revoliutsiia i pobeda Sovetskoi vlasti v Armenii.* (Erevan, 1957). M. A. Gudoshnikov, *Ocherki po istorii grazhdanskoi voiny v Sibiri.* (Irkutsk, 1959). R. Kh. Gugov and U. A. Uligov, *Borba trudiashchikhsia za vlast Sovetov v Kabarde i Balkarii.* (Nalchik, 1957). M. Irkaev, *Ocherk istorii Sovetskogo Tadzhikstana, 1917-1957.* (Stalinabad, 1957). M. Irkaev and Iu. Nikolaev, *V boiakh za Sovetskii Tadzhikstan.* (Moscow, 1957). V. A. Kadeikin, *Gody ognevye. Iz istorii grazhdanskoi voiny v Kuzbase.* (Kemerovo, 1959). A. B. Kadishev, *Interventsiia i grazhdanskaia voina v Zakavkaze.* (Moscow, 1960). G. V. Khachapuridze,

D. K. Shelestov, after having examined the general study of the Civil War in Soviet literature, made the following observation:
It is not a matter of large numbers of new works, but what is important in our opinion is the extent of the problems undertaken in research, the attention of scholars to questions and subjects that were formerly studied poorly if at all. Overcoming the trend of mere "citationism" [tsitatnichestov], of schematism, or of illustrative materials without textual contents or substance characteristic of so many preceding works, critically revising the ideological position taken under the influence of the cult of personality, historians of the Civil War period made an important step along the road toward a more advanced and deeper Marxist-Leninist analysis of the heroic events of 1918-1920.[164]

As long as Stalin was at the helm of the government the history of the Civil War had only a single aim—to show how Stalin won the war. After the middle of the 1950's many writers departed markedly from former patterns of interpretation. The stress was more on the role of Lenin and *the party* in the Civil War period, as in studies such as those made by D. M. Grinishin and I. I. Vlasov. The merit of these works is that they were among the first to break the ice—cutting Stalin to

Borba gruzinskogo naroda za ustanovlenie Sovetskoi vlasti. (Moscow, 1956). E. G. Koroleva and A. A. Popov, *Grazhdanskaia voina v Komi krae.* (Syktyvkar, 1957). I. M. Korzakov and M. I. Romanov, *Iz istorii Mordovii gody grazhdanskoi voiny.* (Saransk, 1958). S. Kovalskii, *Za vlast Sovetov.* (Alma-Ata, 1957). Ia. P. Krastyn', *Sovetskaia Latviia v 1919 g.* (Riga, 1959). P. S. Luchevnikov, *Grazhdanskaia voina na Iuzhnom Urale.* (Cheliabinsk, 1958). A. V. Makashov, *Utverzhdenie Sovetskoi vlasti v tsentralnom i iuzhnom Tadzhikstane.* (Stalinabad, 1957). K. Malyshev, *Borba za Sovety v Kirgizii i Turkestane.* (Frunze, 1958). E. I. Medvedev, *Grazhdanskaia voina i voennaia interventsiia na Srednei Volge v 1918 g.* (Kuibyshev, 1959). L. M. Papin, *Krakh kolchakovshchiny i obrazovanie Dalne-Vostochnoi Respubliki.* (Moscow, 1957). I. E. Petrov, *Chuvashiia v period inostrannoi interventsii i grazhdanskoi voiny.* (Cheboksary, 1959). P. Ia. Petrov, *Ustanovlenie Sovetskoi vlasti v Iakutii.* (Iakutsk, 1957). S. N. Pokrovskii, *Pobeda Sovetskoi vlasti v Semirechie.* (Alma-Ata, 1961). Kh. M. Seifulin, *K istorii inostrannoi voennoi interventsii i grazhdanskoi voiny v Tuve.* (Kyzyl, 1956). Iu. Ia. Taigro, *Borba trudiashchikhsia Estonii za Sovetskuiu vlast i za mir v gody grazhdanskoi voiny.* (Tallin, 1959).. V. V. Tarasov, *Borba s interventami na Severe Rossii.* (Moscow, 1958). M. S. Totoev, *Ocherk istorii revoliutsionnogo dvizheniia v Severnoi Osetii.* (Ordzhonikidze, 1957). E. A. Tokarzhevskii, *Iz istorii inostrannoi interventsiia i grazhdanskoi voiny v Azerbaidzhane.* (Baku, 1957). M. Iazykova, *Borba za ustanovlenie i uprochnenie Sovetskoi vlasti v Zapadnom Turkmenistane.* (Ashkhabad, 1957). A. I. Zevelev, *Iz istorii grazhdanskoi voiny v Uzbekistane.* (Tashkent, 1959). I. Kh. Keldiev, *Razgrom kontrrevoliutsii v Ferganskoi i Samarkandskoi oblastiakh Turkestanskoi ASSR.* (Tashkent, 1959).

[164]D. K. Shelestov, "Ob izuchenii istorii grazhdanskoi voiny i voennoi interventsii." *Sovetskaia istoricheskaia nauka ot XX k XXII sezdu KPSS.* (Moscow, 1962), 379.

size and putting him in his proper place. In communist parlance, historic developments were determined by collective rather than individual leadership. In support of this interpretation a new history of the Communist Party was published, in which revolutionary triumph was due to the valor of the organization and not to single heroes.[165]

Once again much attention has been devoted to the causes of the defeat of the White armies. During the 1930's and 1940's the oft-repeated thesis was that the Civil War was won because of Stalin's leadership; currently the subject has been explained differently. Thus, the defense of Tsaritsyn in 1918 was formerly interpreted as the strategic moment of the entire war; the eastern front and the southern, on the other hand, were minimized. More recent writings place the decisive date and location in the summer and fall of 1918 on the eastern front. Post-Stalin historiography presents a more acceptable picture of the eastern campaign, the defense of Petrograd in 1919, and the triumph in the south in 1919. It has been proven that the rout of Denikin's army was not, as formerly claimed, because of the Stalin plan, but the result of the plan adopted by the Council of Defense headed by Lenin. On the other hand, it was also shown that the failure of the Red Army on the western and southwestern fronts in the summer of 1920 was caused not by "Trotskyite treason," but by a combination of political and military circumstances.

Post-Stalin research in the Civil War period has contributed many illuminating details. These include the multitude of "fronts" against guerrillas in the Ukraine and elsewhere, the struggle against the uprising led by General Krasnov in the south, the part the navy played in the defense of Petrograd and in the north, and the Perekop operation and final defeat of Vrangel's army on the Crimean Peninsula. Much investigation has been devoted to the partisan movement, to which is attributed a good share of credit for the final victory over the entire White movement.[166]

[165] *Istoriia Kommunisticheskoi Partii Sovetskogo Soiuza.* (Moscow, 1959). See particularly *Istoriia Kommunisticheskoi partii Sovetskogo Soiuza* (Moscow, Institute of Marxism-Leninism, 1964-1967), 3 vols. Part 2 of Vol. III is forthcoming. Other samples of the "new interpretation" in historical literature are as follows: D. M. Grinishin, *Voennaia deiatelnost V. I. Lenina.* (Moscow, 1957). I. I. Vlasov, *V. I. Lenin i stroitelstvo Sovetskoi Armii.* (Moscow, 1958). N. F. Kuzmin, *Lenin vo glave oborony Sovetskoi strany (1918-1920 gg.).* (Moscow, 1958). V. S. Kirillov, "O nekotorykh storonakh voennoi deiatelnosti V. I. Lenina v gody grazhdanskoi voiny." *Voprosy istorii,* No. 4 (1957), 3-23. See also article by N. Lomov and N. Azovtsev, on Lenin and the Red Army, in *Voenno-istoricheskii zhurnal,* Nos. 3 and 4 (1960). *Kommunist,* No. 4 (1957). The publication of these articles was met with the approval of the party and greeted as a salutary sign in historical literature.

[166] A. P. Aleksashenko, "Partizanskoe dvizhenie v tylu Denikina v 1919 g." *Reshaiushchie pobedy sovetskogo naroda nad interventami i belogvardeitsami v 1919 g.* (Moscow, 1960). P. G. Doronin, *Izvailskie partizany.* (Syktyvkar, 1957). A. S.

272

In 1957, on the occasion of the fortieth anniversary of the Revolution and only four years after the death of Stalin, no less than 200 different publications were issued, containing much new source material. To these should be added the three-volume collection of documents prepared during 1960-1961 by the Institute of Marxism-Leninism and the various state archival institutions. This publication includes more than 2,000 documents, nearly a half of them appearing in print for the first time.[167]

After the Twentieth Congress of the Communist Party, many items formerly banned were published, such as the war correspondence of Lenin (1917-1920) and the thirty-sixth volume of his writings, which failed to be included in the fourth edition issued under Stalin. In 1958 some of the writings of A. S. Bubnov and S. I. Gusev, banned during the Stalin rule, were reissued.[168]

During the 1930's and 1940's the publication of memoirs by Civil War veterans virtually ceased. If a few managed to appear in print it was because they glorified Stalin. After the mid-1950's, publication of

Elagin, *Iz istorii geroicheskoi borby partizan Semirechia.* (Alma-Ata, 1957). N. Godnev, *Savinskie partizany.* (Archangel, 1959). S. L. Kovalskii, *Bolshevistskoe podpole Vostochnogo Kazakhstana v borbe s kolchakovshchinoi.* (Alma-Ata, 1957). K. K. Krasilnikov, *Partizanskoe dvizhenie na Kubani i Chernomore.* (Krasnodar, 1957). N. P. Lipatov, *1920 god na Chernom more. Voenno-morskie sily v razgrome Vrangelia.* (Moscow, 1958). V. G. Mirzoev, *Partizanskoe dvizhenie v Zapadnoi Sibiri.* (Kemerovo, 1957). N. V. Naumov, *Omskie bolsheviki v avangarde borby protiv belogvardeitsev i interventov.* (Omsk, 1960). *Polkovodtsy grazhdanskoi voiny.* (Moscow, 1960). A. S. Pukhov, *Baltiiskii flot na zashchite Petrograda.* (Moscow, 1958). M. Rekhachev, *V likhuiu godinu.* (Archangel, 1959). I. S. Shangin, *Moriaki v boiakh za Sovetskii Sever.* (Moscow, 1959). A. G. Solodiavkin, *Kommunisty Irkutska v borbe s kolchakovshchinoi.* (Irkutsk, 1960). S. Uzhgin and N. Frolov, *Partizanskoe dvizhenie protiv Kolchaka.* (Alma-Ata, 1957). D. G. Bazheev, *Kommunisticheskaia partiia—organizator i vdokhnovitel partizanskoi borby v Buriatii.* (Ulan-Ude, 1960).

[167] *Boevye podvigi chastei Krasnoi Armii 1918-1922 gg. Sbornik dokumentov.* (Moscow, 1957). *V gody grazhdanskoi voiny (Ivanovo-voznesenskie bolsheviki v period inostrannoi voennoi interventsii i grazhdanskoi voiny). Sbornik dokumentov i materialov.* (Moscow, 1957). *Borba rabochikh i krestian pod rukovodstvom bolshevistskoi partii za ustanovlenie i uprochenie sovetskoi vlasti v Tambovskoi gubernii (1917-1918 gg.). Sbornik dokumentov.* (Moscow, 1957). *Borba za Sovetskuiu vlast v Krymu. Dokumenty i materialy.* Vol. I. *Mart 1917—aprel 1918 g.* (Moscow, 1957). *Borba trudiashchikhsia Volyni za vlast Sovetov (mart 1917—dekabr 1920 g.) Sbornik dokumentov i materialov.* (Moscow, 1957). *Borba za vlast Sovetov v Moldavii (mart 1917—mart 1918 g.). Sbornik dokumentov i materialov.* (Moscow, 1957). *Bolsheviki Zapadnoi Sibiri v borbe za sotsialisticheskuiu revoliutsiiu (mart 1917-mai 1918 g.). Sbornik dokumentov i materialov.* (Moscow, 1957). *Borba za vlast Sovetov v Tomskoi gubernii (1917-1919 gg.). Sbornik dokumentalnykh materialov.* (Moscow, 1957).

[168] A. S. Bubnov, *O Krasnoi Armii.* (Moscow, 1958). S. I. Gusev, *Grazhdanskaia voina i Krasnaia Armiia.* (Moscow, 1958).

memoirs was revived and these once more became an important source of information for the student of history. In 1957 there appeared a whole series of memoirs by former partisans, members of the administration, and writers from every part of the Soviet Union—from Irkutsk, the Baikal region, or the Caucasus.[169]

An outstanding contribution during this period was made by the memoirs of the eminent general M. D. Bonch-Bruevich, the brother of the well-known veteran Communist and First Secretary of the Soviet of People's Commissars. His reminiscences cover only the very early period of the Civil War and the initial defense measures undertaken by the Soviet government. Another colorful figure, and later marshal, S. M. Budennyi, describes the formation of the Red Cavalry in 1918. His version of the war on the southern Tsaritsyn front in 1919 is of special interest. Budennyi's account adds considerably to the information on the war in the south during that year, but it suffers from serious defects: the author exaggerates somewhat the importance of the front at Tsaritsyn in 1918; his descriptions of some political leaders he seems to have had contact with are debatable, the author being no keen judge of human nature; nor was Budennyi able to appreciate fully the character of the overall war strategy and to fit into it the events of the front on which he operated.

In addition, shorter accounts by other war participants add considerably to the general picture. In this category should be included the important account of V. K. Bliukher (Bluecher) on the early formation of the partisan army which, under his command and that of N. D. Kashirin, fought all the way to the Far East to join the Third Eastern Army.[170]

The year 1962 saw many of the memoirs that were banned for some years reissued; among them were writings by such Red Army leaders as M. N. Tukhachevskii, I. E. Iakir, V. K. Bliukher, M. S. Kedrov, and S. S. Kamenev.[171] These memoirs had become bibliographic rarities since the late 1920's. Between 1956 and 1960 more than 500 titles were

[169]V. V. Riabikov, *Irkutsk—stolitsa revoliutsionnoi Sibiri.* (Moscow, 1957). *Za vlast Sovetov. Sbornik vospominanii byvshikh podpolnikov i partizan.* (Moscow, 1957). *Partizany Pribaikalia. Sbornik vospominanii uchastnikov grazhdanskoi voiny.* (Moscow, 1957). *Krasnogvardeitsy i partizany. Sbornik vospominanii uchastnikov grazhdanskoi voiny v Zabaikale.* (Moscow, 1957). *V borbe za vlast Sovetov. Sbornik vospominanii.* (Moscow, 1957). I. L. Khizhniak, *Gody boevye.* (Moscow, 1957). *Vospominaniia uchastnikov Oktiabrskoi revoliutsii i grazhdanskoi voiny v Kabardino-Balkarii.* (Moscow, 1957). *Pod pobednym znamenem Oktiabria.* (Moscow, 1957).

[170]M. D. Bonch-Bruevich, *Vsia vlast Sovetam.* (Moscow, 1958). S. M. Budennyi, *Proidennyi put.* Book 1. (Moscow, 1959). *Na Iuzhnom Urale. Sbornik vospominanii.* (Moscow, 1958). V. K. Bliukher, *Stati i rechi.* (Moscow, 1963), esp. pp. 181-220. S. F. Plotnikov, *Desiat tysiach geroev.* (Moscow, 1967). B. Verkhoven', *Legendarnyi reid.* (Moscow, 1959). N. D. Kondratev, *Marshal Bliukher.* (Moscow, 1965). V. V. Dushenkin, *Ot soldata do marshala.* (Moscow, 1961).

[171]*Etapy bolshogo puti. Vospominaniia o grazhdanskoi voine.* (Moscow, 1962).

added to the list of publications on the October Revolution and the Civil War.

In 1960 the fifth and final volume of the *History of the Civil War in the USSR* was finally issued, culminating the project originally sponsored by Maxim Gorky in the early 1930's. The fourth volume which appeared in 1959 dispels the legendary role of Stalin in the Civil War and contains fewer distortions than the preceding volumes.

The fifth volume covers the period from March to November, 1920, including the role of the United States in the foreign intervention. It places much responsibility for the intervention upon Washington. A good portion of the volume is devoted to the Soviet-Polish war and the liquidation of the Crimean front, as well as the struggles in the Caucasus, in Central Asia, and in the Far East. It ends with a summary of the entire five-volume publication, including a suggested periodization of the Civil War and foreign intervention which, for some reason, the preceding volumes did not follow. Still, all in all, the presentation of this volume is far superior to the early volumes and freer from "cultism," and may be recommended for the new source materials, the bibliographical suggestions, and the differences in interpretation offered by Stalinist and post-Stalin writers.[172]

Many other works published since 1958 merit mention. One of these is the popular work by G. V. Kuzmin, which is based on an impressive amount of reliable source materials; and another which takes up aspects of the same period is by S. F. Naida. However, unless some materials undiscovered to date are revealed, the subject now seems to be fairly well covered, and little remains that has not already been presented in historical literature. Below is cited a bibliographical list of the most representative writings of more recent date.[173]

[172]The following review articles evaluating the publication of the *History of the Civil War* may be suggested: *Voprosy istorii*, No. 4 (1958), 146-155; No. 6 (1958), 163-171; No. 12 (1960), 123-130. *Voprosy istorii KPSS*, No. 1 (1960), 196-201; No. 1 (1961), 180-187. See also S. S. Khesin, "Nekotorye voprosy istoriografii pervykh let Sovetskoi vlasti v SSSR (k zaversheniu izdaniia 'Istorii grazhdanskoi voiny v SSSR')." *Istoriia SSSR*, No. 3 (1961), 103-115; also No. 4 (1958), 146-155; No. 4 (1960), 159-166. V. T. Agalakov, "O nekotorykh netochnostiakh v IV tome 'Istoriia grazhdanskoi voiny v SSSR'." *Istoriia SSSR*, No. 4 (1961), 235. In addition to the five-volume *History of the Civil War* there appeared shorter accounts: G. V. Kuzmin, *Grazhdanskaia voina i voennaia interventsiia v SSSR*. (Moscow, 1958). G. G. Alakhverdov et al., *Kratkaia istoriia grazhdanskoi voiny v SSSR*. (Moscow, 1960). I. F. Kondrashev, *Ocherki istorii SSSR (1918-1920 gg.)*. (Moscow, 1960). See also *Sovetskaia Rossiia i kapitalisticheskii mir v 1917-1923 gg*. (Moscow, 1957). *Boevoi put Sovetskikh Vooruzhennykh Sil*. (Moscow, 1960). Also *Kommunist*, No. 3 (1960), 140-146; No. 3 (1961), 116-120. G. Kuzmin and S. Lipitskii, "Letopis geroicheskoi borby sovetskogo naroda." *Kommunist*, No. 11 (1958), 106-115.

[173]V. I. Adamiia, *Iz istorii angliiskoi interventsii v Gruzii*. (Moscow, 1961). A. E. Antonov, *Boevoi vosemnadtsatyi god (voennye deistviia Krasnoi Armii v 1918-*

275

Finally, it should be added that the first notable historiographic study of the Civil War period appeared during 1963-1964. It was in

nachale 1919 g.). (Moscow, 1961). A. Kh. Babakhodzhaev, *Proval angliiskoi politiki v Srednei Azii i na Blizhnem Vostoke.* (Moscow, 1962). Iu. A. Belan, *Otechestvennaia voina ukrainskogo naroda protiv germanskikh interventov v 1918 godu.* (Moscow, 1960). Ia. Dosumov, *Pobeda Velikoi Oktiabrskoi revoliutsii v Kara-Kalpakii.* (Moscow, 1958). G. Kh. Eikhe, *Ufimskaia avantiura Kolchaka.* (Moscow, 1960). G. A. Galoian, *Borba za Sovetskuiu vlast v Armenii.* (Moscow, 1957). V. P. Golionko, 'V *ogne borby (iz istorii grazhdanskoi voiny 1918-1922 gg. na Dalnem Vostoke).* (Moscow, 1958). S. Grigortsevich, *Amerikanskaia i iaponskaia interventsiia na Dalnem Vostoke i eë razgrom (1918-1922 gg.).* (Moscow, 1957). D. M. Grinishin, *Voennaia deiatelnost V. I. Lenina.* (Moscow, 1960). M. Irkaev and Iu. Nikolaev, *V boiakh za Sovetskii Tadzhikstan.* (Moscow, 1957). M. Iskanderov, *Iz istorii borby Kommunisticheskoi partii Azerbaidzhana za pobedu Sovetskoi vlasti.* (Moscow, 1958). *Iz istorii borby Sovetskogo naroda protiv inostrannoi interventsii i vnutrennei kontrrevoliutsii v 1918 g.* (Moscow, 1966). G. Keldiev, *Razgrom kontrrevoliutsii v Ferganskoi i Samarkandskoi oblastiakh Turkestanskoi ASSR.* (Tashkent, 1959). M. Kolesnik, *Vosstanovlenie i ukreplenie Sovetskoi vlasti na Ukraine v 1919-1920 gg.* (Moscow, 1958). A. I. Krushanov, *Borba za vlast Sovetov na Dalnem Vostoke i v Zabaikale.* (Moscow, 1962). G. V. Kuzmin, *Grazhdanskaia voina i voennaia interventsiia v SSSR.* (Moscow, 1958). N. F. Kuzmin, *Krushenie poslednego pokhoda Antanty.* (Moscow, 1958). N. F. Kuzmin, *V. I. Lenin vo glave oborony Sovetskoi strany.* (Moscow, 1958). N. P. Lipatov, *1920 god na Chernom more.* (Moscow, 1958). P. Makeev, *Na Denikina! Rol latyshskikh strelkov v razgrome denikinskih polchishch.* (Moscow, 1960). P. N. Nadinskii, *Ocherki po istorii Kryma.* Vol. II. (Moscow, 1957). S. F. Naida, *O nekotorykh voprosakh istorii grazhdanskoi voiny v SSSR.* (Moscow, 1958). *Pod znamenem Oktiabria. Sbornik vospominanii.* (Moscow, 1959). Iu. A. Poliakov and D. K. Shelestov, *Boevoi vosemnadtsatsyi god.* (Moscow, 1958). T. A. Pul'kov, *Borba za vlast Sovetov na Altae.* (Moscow, 1957). I. K. Rybalko, *Vosstanovlenie Sovetskoi vlasti na Ukraine, 1918-1919.* (Moscow, 1957). *Sbornik. Borba bolshevikov za uprochenie Sovetskoi vlasti, vosstanovlenie i razvitie narodnogo khoziaistva Kryma.* (Moscow, 1958). *Sbornik. Ustanovlenie Sovetskoi vlasti v oblastiakh Kazakhstana.* (Moscow, 1957). G. K. Seleznev, *Krakh zagovora.* (Moscow, 1963). G. K. Seleznev, *Ten' dollara nad Rossiei.* (Moscow, 1957). D. K. Shelestov, *Borba za vlast Sovetov na Altae v |1918-1919 gg.* (Moscow, 1959). I. S. Shangin, *Moriaki v boiakh za Sovetskii Sever, 1917-1920 gg.* (Moscow, 1957). G. M. Shevchuk, *Razgrom inozemnykh interventov na iuge Ukrainy i v Krymu.* (Moscow, 1959). R. Simonenko, *Imperialisticheskaia politika Soedinennykh Shtatov Ameriki na Ukraine v 1917-1918 gg.* (Moscow, 1957). S. N. Shishkin, *Grazhdanskaia voina na Dalnem Vostoke.* (Moscow, 1957). E. M. Skliarenko, *Borba trudiashchikhsia Ukrainy protiv nemetsko-avstriiskikh okkupantov i getmanshchiny v 1918 g.* (Moscow, 1960). M. I. Stishov, *Bolshevistskoe podpole i partizanskoe dvizhenie v Sibiri v gody grazhdanskoi voiny (1918-1920 gg.).* (Moscow, 1962). V. G. Sukhorukov, *XI Armiia v boiakh na Severnom Kavkaze i Nizhnei Volge v 1918-1920 gg.* (Moscow, 1961). Sh. Tashliev, *Ustanovlenie i uprochenie Sovetskoi vlasti v Turkestane.* (Ashkhabad, 1957). V. E. Tychina, *Borba protiv nemetskikh okkupantov na Chernigovshchine v 1918 godu.* (Moscow, 1959). V. Vartanian, *Pobeda Sovetskoi vlasti v Armenii.* (Moscow, 1959). V. S. Vladimirtsev,

this field especially that a careful reexamination was most necessary, since it was here that the damaging effects of the cult of the individual were felt most strongly.[174]

Kommunisticheskaia partiia—organizator razgroma vtorogo pokhoda Antanty. (Moscow, 1958). G. Zastavenko, *Razgrom nemetskikh interventov na Ukraine v 1918 g.* (Moscow, 1959). N. A. Zegzhda, *Kommunisticheskaia partiia—organizator razgroma tretego pokhoda Antanty.* (Moscow, 1959).

[174]D. K. Shelestov, "Sovetskaia istoriografiia grazhdanskoi voiny i voennoi interventsii v SSSR." *Voprosy istorii,* No. 2 (1964), 22-48. D. K. Shelestov, "Ob izuchenii istorii grazhdanskoi voiny i voennoi interventsii." *Sbornik. Sovetskaia istoricheskaia nauka ot XX k XXII sezdu KPSS. Istoriia SSSR.* (Moscow, 1962). A. I. Zevelev, "Grazhdanskaia voina v Turkestane v sovetskoi istoricheskoi literature." *Istoriia SSSR,* No. 3 (1963), 61-79. S. S. Khesin, "Nekotorye voprosy istoriografii pervykh let Sovetskoi vlasti (k zaversheniiu izdaniia 'Istoriia grazhdanskoi voiny v SSSR')." *Istoriia SSSR,* No. 3 (1961), 103-115. E. G. Gimpelson, "Literatura o Sovetakh pervykh let diktatury proletariata (noiabr 1917-1920 gg.)." *Istoriia SSSR,* No. 5 (1963), 152-163. I. L. Sherman, "Pervye issledovaniia po istorii grazhdanskoi voiny." *Voenno-istoricheskii zhurnal,* No. 2 (1964), 98-107. (In this article I. L. Sherman points out that most of the early writers stressed military experiences and hardly, if at all, mentioned anything else.)

CHAPTER X

Formation of the Soviet Apparatus

A. SETTING UP THE GOVERNMENT

During the last two decades of the "cult of the individual," studies of the October Revolution were drastically curtailed, and virtually ceased. The well-known periodical *Proletarskaia revoliutsiia,* published by *Istpart,* was discontinued in 1941, presumably because of war conditions, but it was never revived.[1] Many previously-published sources became almost impossible for students of history to locate. Many names of prominent figures of the early part of the Revolution vanished from the pages of history; many historical writings were removed from library shelves and turned into "underground literature." New writings and interpretations emerged; new names were often substituted by Stalinist henchmen as the makers of history. The story of the Revolution was turned into a narrative of tactical directives, of long lists of citations from officially recognized texts, dogmatically repeated. Not until after the death of Stalin was this situation altered; meanwhile, the damage to historical writing was incalculable.

Since 1956, the year the Twentieth Congress of the Communist Party demolished the cult of the individual, historiography has been granted a breathing spell. Archives and local depositories were once more opened to historians, and some important publications were once again at the disposal of scholars. Among such documents were, for illustration, the Proceedings of the Sixth and Seventh Congresses of the Bolshevik Party and the Protocols of the Central Committee of the party elected by the same congresses. Equally important was the correspondence between the secretariat of the Central Committee and the local party organizations. In addition, in 1957 the party undertook to publish a multi-volume history of the "Great October Socialist Revolution," accompanied by "Documents and Materials."[2]

[1] *Proletarskaia revoliutsiia,* a magazine aimed at the "gathering and study of materials related to the history of the October Revolution and of the Communist Party," was published from 1921 to 1941. Altogether 132 issues were published. In 1932 the magazine was taken over by the Marx-Engels-Lenin Institute.

[2] *Kommunisticheskaia partiia Sovetskogo Soiuza v borbe za pobedu sotsialisticheskoi revoliutsii v period dvoevlastiia. 27 fevralia—4 iiulia 1917 g. Sbornik dokumentov.* (Moscow, 1957). *Kommunisticheskaia partiia Sovetskogo Soiuza v borbe za pobedu Velikoi Oktiabrskoi sotsialisticheskoi revoliutsii. 5 iiulia—5 noiabria 1917 g.* (Moscow, 1957). *Perepiska Sekretariata TsK RSDRP (b) s mestnymi partiinymi organizatsiiami,* Parts I-II. (Moscow, 1957). *Ot fevralia k oktiabriu. (Iz anket uchastnikov Velikoi Oktiabrskoi sotsialisticheskoi revoliutsiia.) Sbornik.* (Moscow, 1957). *Doneseniia komissarov Petrogradskogo Voenno-revoliutsionnogo komiteta.* (Moscow, 1957). See also *Revoliutsionnoe dvizhenie v Rossii v aprele 1917 g. Aprelskii krizis.* (Moscow, 1958). *Revoliutsionnoe dvizhenie v Rossii posle sverzheniia samoderzhaviia.* (Moscow,

A series of documentary materials on the Revolution in the various parts of Russia was begun, and by the early 1960's some 140 volumes had been published, providing an impressive base from which broader studies of the historic events beginning in March, 1917, and leading up to the October Revolution, could be undertaken. Unfortunately, this series reveals a lack of coordination in content, most likely owing to the haste of publication. It suffers from lack of unity in purpose, in scheme and field of interest; the sources published have only a broad relationship to the fateful events that led up to those of October, 1917.[3]

The same problems exist with regard to the recent publication of memoirs. Some of these were published earlier and had been long out of print; others appeared for the first time. Many recent publications reveal inadequate editing and call for careful verification. On the other hand, one may speculate that in a more contemplative atmosphere many of them would never have seen the light at all, or would have lost much of their value by being "edited" by some official.

There is evident an effort to rewrite the history of the October Revolution in the light of the restored or newly uncovered evidence.[4] At the same time the focus of attention lately has shifted from the events preceding the Revolution, to post-Revolutionary developments, with emphasis on broader aspects of the period, such as the problems of the state during the dictatorship of the proletariat, social and cultural effects, application of economic policies, and the like.[5]

1957). *Revoliutsionnoe dvizhenie v mae-iiune 1917 g. Iiunskaia demonstratsiia.* (Moscow, 1959). *Revoliutsionnoe dvizhenie v Rossii v avguste 1917 g. Razgrom kornilovskogo miatezha.* (Moscow, 1959). *Revoliutsionnoe dvizhenie v Rossii v sentiabre 1917 g. Obshchenatsionalnyi krizis.* (Moscow, 1961). *Oktiabrskoe vooruzhennoe vosstanie v Petrograde.* (Moscow, 1957).

[3]E. A. Lutskii, "Mestnye publikatsii o pobede Velikoi Oktiabrskoi sotsialisticheskoi revoliutsii v Rossii." *Istoricheskii arkhiv,* No. 5 (1958), 184-194. M. A. Varshavchik, "Dokumenty po istorii Velikogo Oktiabria na Ukraine." *Istoricheskii arkhiv,* No. 5 (1958), 194-201. The following article in the same issue may be recommended: A. A. Voronetskaia, "Borba za pobedu Oktiabria na Urale." I. D. Anashkin, I. A. Rubin, and L. I. Gulchinskii, "Sborniki dokumentov po istorii Oktiabria v natsionalnykh raionakh RSFSR." *Istoricheskii arkhiv,* No. 6 (1958), 199-206. S. A. Sidorenko, "Sborniki dokumentov po istorii borby za vlast Sovetov v Sibiri." *Voprosy istorii,* No. 5 (1959), 176-187. M. I. Stishov and D. K. Shelestov, "O nekotorykh voprosakh izucheniia istorii borby za vlast Sovetov v Sibiri v 1917-1920 gg." *Voprosy istorii,* No. 6 (1959), 120-136.

[4]D. A. Chugaev, "K voprosu o publikatsiiakh dokumentov po istorii Oktiabrskoi revoliutsii." *Istoriia SSSR,* No. 3 (1959), 159-167. I. A. Bulygin, G. E. Reikhberg, and Iu. S. Tokarev, "Obzor dokumentalnykh istochnikov o podgotovke i provedenii Oktiabrskogo vooruzhennogo vosstaniia v Petrograde v 1917 g." *Arkheograficheskii ezhegodnik 1957 g.* (Moscow, 1957).

[5]M. E. Naidenov, "Velikaia Oktiabrskaia sotsialisticheskaia revoliutsiia v osveshchenii sovetskoi (russkoi) istoricheskoi literatury." *Sbornik. Iz istorii Velikoi Oktiabrskoi sotsia-*

279

As a result of the various efforts to produce a well-balanced account of the October Revolution and the events that followed communist victory, some positive results can already be seen. The new writings have been freed of Stalinist flavor and given at least a semblance of a more objective presentation, though some subjects, for party reasons, are still handled as "delicate" matters. References to the Civil War, for instance, still omit Leon Trotsky unless it is to remind the reader of his heresies. The formation of the Red Army is still regarded as the accomplishment of Lenin without even a hint of the names of members of the "diversionist" factions. War communism is still treated as the "triumph of the socialist state," despite the "retreat" through NEP to the "commanding heights." Many writings continue to repeat oversimplified explanations, treat complex historical events superficially, and accompany them with stereotyped phraseology. And yet there is a noticeable advance in at least one respect—the absence of obsequious praise of Stalin.[6]

Generally speaking, historical writing since the death of Stalin shows a distinct trend: interpretative works are based on broader bibliographical data than in previous years and supported by more convincing documentary evidence. There have appeared a number of general studies undertaken both collectively and individually, and on the whole carried through successfully. In cases of collective publications (sborniks) these sometimes suffer from lack of unity both in subject matter and in interpretation.

In the field of foreign affairs, which will receive special attention elsewhere, I. I. Mints has dealt with the international implications of the October Revolution. Mints also made an interesting effort to trace the origin of the Soviet as a political form of dictatorship of the proletariat. His conclu-

listicheskoi revoliutsii. (Moscow, 1957). V. G. Rusliakova, Borba s falsifikatsiei i vulgarizi-tsiei istorii Velikoi Oktiabrskoi sotsialisticheskoi revoliutsii. Sbornik statei po istorii rabo-chego klassa i sovetskoi istoriografii. (Moscow, 1958). V. G. Rusliakova, "Razrabotka istorii Oktiabrskoi revoliutsii posle XX sezda." Voprosy istorii, No. 5 (1960), 85-102. L. S. Gaponenko, "K voprosu ob osveshchenii istorii rabochego dvizheniia v Rossii v istoricheskoi literature." Istoriia SSSR, No. 1 (1959), 182-187. P. N. Sobolev, "Vopros o soiuze rabochego klassa i krestianstva v literature po istorii Oktiabrskoi revoliutsii." Voprosy istorii, No. 9 (1958), 107-119. V. Z. Drobizhev and T. A. Ignatenko, "Nekotorye itogi izucheniia istorii sovnarkhozov 1917-1932 gg." Voprosy istorii, No. 11 (1959), 93-108. L. S. Gamaiunov, "Izuchenie v Sovetskom Soiuze problemy 'Velikii Oktiabr i narody Vostoka'." Problemy vostokovedeniia, No. 5 (1959), 190-211. E. N. Gorodetskii, "K kharakteristike istoriografii Velikoi Oktiabrskoi sotsialisticheskoi revoliutsii (1917-1934)." Istoriia SSSR, No. 6 (1960), 85-98.

[6]Istoriia grazhdanskoi voiny v SSSR. Vol. III, Uprochenie Sovetskoi vlasti. Nachalo inostrannoi voennoi interventsii i grazhdanskoi voiny (noiabr 1917—mart 1919 g.). (Moscow, 1957). Pobeda Velikoi Oktiabrskoi sotsialisticheskoi revoliutsii. (Moscow, 1957). Oktiabrskoe vooruzhennoe vosstanie v Petrograde. (Moscow, 1957).

sion was that this idea was conceived by Lenin in 1906-1907, and developed further during the First World War.[7]

In dealing with the October Revolution many writers single out legal, economic, social, or political aspects. Few have attempted an overall study of the establishment of the Soviet system with all its implications. One of these is B. M. Morozov, who published a book in 1957 on the formation of the Soviet state apparatus, including economic, judicial, military, internal and external administrations, national minority questions, intelligence, and other problems involved in founding the "proletarian state."[8] However, the author, despite his originality of interpretation, demonstrated a too-liberal handling of what Soviet historians label "the problem of democratic centralism," a euphemism for arbitrary bureaucratic power. Morozov too frequently applies the early experiences of 1917-1918 to institutional development of later date, violating chronological order to produce the impression of a natural continuous evolutionary growth of the Soviet state. Many other historians turned during the late 1950's to research in the formation and development of the centralized Soviet state. Works have appeared by such competent writers as D. A. Chugaev, E. G. Gimpelson, and G. S. Kalinin.[9]

Soviet historiography in general has had a tendency to interpret the establishment of the Soviet regime with dogmatic rigidity. First, the narratives emphasized how the regime had been established in the industrial centers, then expanded more slowly into the peripheral parts of the country. These narratives usually ignored the many deviations from this general course. In various outlying parts of the Ukraine, in White Russia, in the Caucasus (Baku), and in Central Asia (Tashkent), Soviet power came on the scene almost simultaneously with its arrival in centers such as Petrograd or Moscow, according to the official version. There was little variation in this version between developments in the north or in the south, in the west or in the east. And

[7]I. I. Mints, *Mezhdunarodnoe znachenie Oktiabrskoi revoliutsii.* (Moscow, 1957). I. I. Mints, "Pobeda sotsialisticheskoi revoliutsii na mestakh." *Istoriia SSSR,* No. 4 (1957), 64-97. I. I. Mints, "Razvitie vzgliadov Lenina na Sovety (1905—April 1917 g.)." *Voprosy istorii KPSS,* No. 2 (1960), 61-80. I. I. Mints, "Ob osveshchenii nekotorykh voprosov istorii Velikoi Oktiabrskoi sotsialisticheskoi revoliutsii." *Voprosy istorii KPSS,* No. 2 (1957), 16-34.

[8]B. M. Morozov, *Sozdanie i ukreplenie sovetskogo gosudarstvennogo apparata (noiabr 1917—mart 1919 g.).* (Moscow, 1957).

[9]D. A. Chugaev, "Slom burzhuaznoi gosudarstvennoi mashiny i sozdanie sovetskogo gosudarstvennogo apparata." *Pobeda Velikoi Oktiabrskoi sotsialisticheskoi revoliutsii. Sbornik.* (Moscow, 1957). E. G. Gimpelson, *Iz istorii stroitelstva Sovetov (noiabr 1917—iiul 1918).* (Moscow, 1958). G. S. Kalinin, *Velikaia Oktiabrskaia sotsialisticheskaia revoliutsiia i sozdanie Sovetskogo gosudarstva.* (Moscow, 1959). K. G. Gedorov, *VTSIK v pervye gody Sovetskoi vlasti, 1917-1921 gg.* (Moscow, 1957). E. P. Podvigina, "Pervye dni raboty Soveta Narodnykh Komissarov (1917 g.)." *40 let Velikoi Oktiabrskoi sotsialisticheskoi revoliutsii.* (Moscow, 1958). E. N. Gorodetskii, "Iz istorii Petrogradskogo Voenno-revoliutsionnogo komiteta." *Iz istorii Velikoi Oktiabrskoi sotsialisticheskoi revoliutsii. Sbornik.* (Moscow, 1957).

the counterrevolution was treated as an equally spontaneous phenomenon, giving the impression that the White movement was merely a sporadic phenomenon doomed to early failure.[10]

An original attempt to interpret the breakdown of the pre-revolutionary government was made by Iu. E. Volkov. The author tried to show that the gradual collapse of the state mechanism began at the very start of the Revolution in February, 1917. Volkov shows how, step by step, the police department, the civil service, the military organization, all declined at an accelerating pace despite all measures taken to forestall the process of deterioration. This was particularly evident in the case of the armed forces where the so-called "democratization policy" had been initiated.[11]

The field of Soviet economic administration remained poorly explored until the middle of the 1950's when several historians took it up. A. A. Voronetskaia concentrated her research on the nationalization of industry and the creation of an administrative apparatus, and other studies were made by S. R. Gershberg, L. V. Strakhov, A. S. Barinov, and T. Kozlova.[12]

Several writers, such as T. Kozlova, seem to believe that the early development of the Soviet economic apparatus proceeded along exactly the same patterns as the banking organizations, the system of finance and credit, or the agencies to combat sabotage. This generalization, though a convenient

[10]Kh. Lukianov, *Krasnaia gvardiia Donbassa.* (Groznyi, 1958). E. P. Kireev, *Proletariat Groznogo v borbe za pobedu Velikoi Oktiabrskoi sotsialisticheskoi revoliutsii (mart 1917 g.—mai 1918 g.).* (Groznyi, 1957). E. I. Medvedev, *Ustanovlenie i uprochenie Sovetskoi vlasti na Srednei Volge.* Vol. I. (Kuibyshev, 1958). F. V. Chebaevskii, "O stroitelstve mestnykh sovetov v kontse 1917 i v pervoi polovine 1918 goda." *Istoricheskie zapiski,* No. 61 (1957), 224-261. S. Ivanov, *Bolsheviki Pskovskoi gubernii v borbe za pobedu Oktiabrskoi revoliutsii.* (Pskov, 1960). K. A. Tolstiakov, *Borba Kazanskoi organizatsii bolshevikov za uprochenie Sovetskoi vlasti (1917-1918 gg.).* (Kazan, 1960). V. I. Aratsev, *Borba bolshevitskikh organizatsii Vladimirskoi gubernii za uprochenie Sovetskoi vlasti (1917-1918 gg.).* (Vladimir, 1960). I. I. Glushchenko, *Bolshevitskie organizatsii primoria v period uprocheniia Sovetskoi vlasti.* (Vladivostok, 1960.)

[11]Iu. E. Volkov, "K istorii borby trudiashchikhsia Rossii za slom tsarsko-burzhuaznogo gosudarstvennogo apparata." *Uchenye zapiski Sverdlovskogo iuridicheskogo instituta.* Vol. VIII. (Sverdlovsk, 1959).

[12]A. A. Voronetskaia, "Organizatsiia Vysshego soveta narodnogo khoziaistva i ego rol v natsionalizatsii promyshlennosti." *Istoricheskie zapiski,* No. 43 (1953), 3-38. S. R. Gershberg, "V. I. Lenin i sozdanie VSNKh." *Voprosy istorii,* No. 7 (1958), 2-24. L. V. Strakhov, "Obrazovanie MSNKh." *Nauchnye doklady vysshei shkoly. Istoricheskie nauki,* No. 4 (Moscow, 1959). A. S. Barinov, "Iz istorii borby kommunisticheskoi partii i Sovetskogo gosudarstva za zavoevanie komandnykh vysot v narodnom khoziaistve i sozdanie VSNKh." *Uchenye zapiski Moskovskogo oblastnogo pedagogicheskogo instituta,* Vol. 53, Issue 5 (Moscow, 1957). T. Kozlova, "Znachenie pervogo Vserossiiskogo sezda sovnarkhozov." *Vestnik Moskovskogo gosudarstvennogo universiteta (MGU),* No. 4 (Moscow, 1957). A. V. Venediktov, *Organizatsiia gosudarstvennoi promyshlennosti v SSSR.* Vol. I. (Leningrad, 1957).

scheme that might lighten the task of tracing the development of different administrative branches of the Soviet state, does not in fact correspond to reality. A common pattern simply does not fit all agencies and organizations; the Soviet banking system, for instance, can hardly fit into the same pattern of compelling circumstances as the agency to combat "counterrevolution and sabotage."[13]

Economic historians studied the role of the working class in establishing the industrial administration. This involved the role of trade unions and other labor organizations and, above all, the struggle against the anti-Bolshevik elements among the workers. Particular problems were faced in the transportation industries where many members of the railway unions belonged to opposition parties.[14]

Modest attempts began to appear, belatedly, at studying such subjects as the earliest Soviet legislation in labor, social security, and insurance. Studies begun by Z. A. Astapovich, on labor legislation during the first eight months of the Soviet regime, were followed by those of M. N. Zimina. The field still remains poorly explored and calls for more intensive study.[15]

[13]B. Rivkin, *Finansovaia politika v period Velikoi Oktiabrskoi sotsialisticheskoi revoliutsii,* (Moscow, 1957). S. Mekhanik, *Finansovo-kreditnye problemy v period natsionalizatsii promyshlennosti v SSSR.* (Moscow, 1957). A. M. Gindin, *Kak bolsheviki ovladeli Gosudarstvennym bankom (fakty i dokumenty Oktiabrskikh dnei v Petrograde).* (Moscow, 1961).

[14]V. Ia. Laverychev, "Sozdanie tsentralnykh gosudarstvennykh organov upravleniia tekstilnoi promyshlennostiu v 1918 godu. (Iz istorii 'tsentrotekstilia')." *Iz istorii Velikoi Oktiabrskoi sotsialisticheskoi revoliutsii. Sbornik.* (Moscow, 1957). D. A. Baevskii, "Pervye sotsialisticheskie preobrazovaniia v ekonomike Rossii." *Pobeda Velikoi Oktiabrskoi sotsialisticheskoi revoliutsii. Sbornik.* (Moscow, 1957). V. Z. Drobizhev, "K istorii organov rabochego upravleniia na promyshlennykh predpriiatiiakh v 1917-1918 gg." *Istoriia SSSR,* No. 3 (1957), 38-56. V. Z. Drobizhev, "Obrazovanie Sovetov narodnogo khoziaistva v Moskovskom promyshlennom raione (1917-1918 gg.)." *Iz istorii Velikoi Oktiabrskoi sotsialisticheskoi revoliutsii. Sbornik.* (Moscow, 1957). V. Z. Drobizhev, "Uchastie profsoiuzov v sozdanii Sovetov narodnogo khoziaistva v 1917-1918 gody." *Uchenye zapiski Moskovskoi vysshei zaochnoi shkoly profdvizheniia.* Issue 2. (Moscow, 1960). A. V. Krasikova, "Kommunisticheskaia partiia v borbe za massy zheleznodorozhnikov v pervye mesiatsy Sovetskoi vlasti." *Iz istorii borby Kommunisticheskoi partii za razvitie sovetskogo zheleznodorozhnogo transporta.* (Leningrad, 1960). B. P. Orlov, "Zheleznodorozhnyi transport v pervyi god Sovetskoi vlasti." *Ocherki po istorii narodnogo khoziaistva SSSR.* (Moscow, 1959). D. S. Baburin, "Narkomprod v pervye gody Sovetskoi vlasti." *Istoricheskie zapiski,* No. 61 (1957), 333-369.

[15]Z. A. Astapovich, "Pervye meropriiatiia Sovetskogo gosudarstva v oblasti truda (1917-1918 gg.)." *Voprosy istorii,* No. 3 (1955), 11-23. Z. A. Astapovich, *Pervye meropriiatiia Sovetskoi vlasti v oblasti truda (1917-1918 gg.).* (Moscow, 1958). M. N. Zimina, "Politika Sovetskogo gosudarstva v oblasti truda i promyshlennosti (1917—pervaia polovina 1918 g.)." *Uchenye zapiski Kirovskogo gosudarstvennogo pedagogicheskogo instituta im. V. I. Lenina.* Issue 16 (Kirov, 1958).

B. THE SHORT-LIVED CONSTITUENT ASSEMBLY

The short-lived Constituent Assembly that gathered on January 18, 1918, and was forcibly dissolved by the Soviet authorities the following day, received virtually no attention whatever in Soviet historical literature. The fate of that Assembly was prejudged by Lenin, who frankly admitted that the dictatorship of the proletariat could not be accomplished by simply "tabulating votes."[16] A member of the Social Revolutionary Party, N. V. Sviatitskii, compiled some data on the Assembly which Lenin utilized for his own essay on the election, but little else was added during the next two decades. In 1938 there appeared a study of N. L. Rubinshtein on the Bolsheviks and the Constituent Assembly, but it added little that was new, nor did the various articles that occasionally appeared in the press. There was not even any serious attempt to check Sviatitskii's data.

In 1958, A. S. Dines of the University of Saratov made an earnest effort to verify the published data. He compared the suburban precincts of a number of large industrial cities, mostly populated by workers, with the precincts that were predominantly wealthy and middle class; he collected similar voting data in agrarian areas and arrived at some interesting conclusions as to the comparative strength of the right and left wings of the Social Revolutionary Party. Regrettably, the study was not pursued beyond the first effort, which was based on only two regions in Kazan and Kharkov. A continuation of such an intensive study might have revealed a much fuller picture of public opinion throughout the country at the crucial time when the Bolsheviks seized power and forcibly dissolved the Constituent Assembly.[17] The subject still awaits its historian.

C. THE RED ARMY

Until recently the history of the Soviet military forces has been dealt with rather generally. Then, in 1954, N. I. Shatagin published a monographic study of the formative years, 1918-1920, which was followed by several shorter works on related subjects by S. M. Kliatskin, I. Volkov, and V. Morozov. The essay by Volkov deals with the extreme difficulties the government encountered in organizing the armed forces at the crucial period of the Revolution, particularly with regard to the establishment of military com-

[16]See V. I. Lenin, *Polnoe sobranie sochinenii.* 5th ed. Vol. XXXV. (Moscow, 1962), 238-242.

[17]N. L. Rubinshtein, *Bolsheviki i Uchreditelnoe sobranie.* (Moscow, 1938). V. I. Lenin, "Vybory v Uchreditelnoe sobranie i diktatura proletariata." *Sochineniia.* 4th ed. Vol. XXX. (Moscow, 1950), 230-251. See also Lenin's speeches concerning the Constituent Assembly in Vol. XXVI and "About Constitutional Illusions" in Vol. XXV. A. S. Dines, "Nekotorye itogi vyborov v Uchreditelnoe sobranie." *Uchenye zapiski Saratovskogo gosudarstvennogo universiteta,* Vol. 59 (Saratov, 1958). T. Kozlova, "K voprosu o 'dniakh Samarskoi uchredilki'." *Proletarskaia revoliutsiia,* No. 9 (1922), 305-306. I. S. Malchevskii, *Vserossiiskoe Uchreditelnoe sobranie.* (Moscow, 1930).

missars. E. N. Gorodetskii has studied the demobilization of the army and its impact during 1917-1918.[18] Morozov's study deals with three main stages in the development of the Soviet armed forces: (1) the Red Guards, (2) the voluntary period of service in the Red Army, and (3) the introduction of compulsory military service. Several studies deal with Lenin and his early role in the organization of the Soviet armed forces.[19]

The Eighth and Ninth Congresses of the Communist Party, among their other resolutions, passed one that urged attention to the subject of military consolidation. The subsequent call upon historians for a history of the armed forces was answered by several writers, one of whom was N. Tsvetaev, whose research in the field soon inspired others to pursue the subject. Two other studies that merit mention are by Iu. P. Petrov, one tracing the role of military commissars during the Civil War, and the other analyzing the role of the Communist Party in the formation of the Red Army.[20]

One facet of the history of the armed forces in the Civil War that still awaits research is the extent of aid rendered by the international units to the

[18]I. Marevskii and S. Shishkin, "O nekotorykh voprosakh strategii v grazhdanskoi voine v SSSR (1917-1918 gg.)." *Voenno-istoricheskii zhurnal*, No. 11 (1960), 3-18. N. I. Shatagin, *Organizatsiia i stroitelstvo Sovetskoi Armii v period inostrannoi voennoi interventsii i grazhdanskoi voiny (1918-1920 gg.).* (Moscow, 1954). S. M. Kliatskin, "Iz istorii razrabotki i osushchestvleniia osnovnykh zakonopolozhenii o stroitelstve regulaiarnoi Krasnoi Armii v 1918-1920 gg." *Istoricheskie zapiski*, No. 58 (1956), 3-37. I. Volkov, "O nekotorykh voprosakh istorii nachalnogo perioda stroitelstva Sovetskikh Vooruzhennykh Sil." *Voenno-istoricheskii zhurnal*, No. 2 (1959). E. N. Gorodetskii, "Demobilizatsiia armii v 1917-1918 gg." *Istoriia SSSR*, No. 1 (1958), 3-31. V. Morozov, *Ot Krasnoi Gvardii k Krasnoi Armii. Borba Moskovskikh bolshevikov za sozdanie Vooruzhennykh sil Sovetskoi respubliki v 1917-1918 gg.* (Moscow, 1958). "Otchet Revoensoveta Respubliki 1917-1919 gg." Preface by S. M. Kliatskin. *Istoricheskii arkhiv*, No. 1 (1956), 132-156.

[19]D. M. Grinishin, *Voennaia deiatelnost V. I. Lenina.* 2nd ed. (Moscow, 1960). I. I. Vlasov, *Lenin i stroitelstvo Sovetskoi Armii.* (Moscow, 1958). N. F. Kuzmin, *V. I. Lenin vo glave oborony Sovetskoi strany (1918-1920 gg.).* (Moscow, 1958). Z. V. Grebelskii, "Deiatelnost Kommunisticheskoi partii i Sovetskogo pravitelstva po organizatsii Sovetskogo Voenno-Morskogo flota (1918-mart 1919 g.)." *Trudy Voenno-politicheskoi akademii im. V. I. Lenina.* Vol. XIX. (Moscow, 1958).

[20]N. Tsvetaev, *Voennye voprosy v resheniiakh VIII sezda RKP (b).* (Moscow, 1960). N. Tsvetaev, "Voennye voprosy na IX sezde RKP (b)." *Voenno-istoricheskii zhurnal*, No. 11 (1960). Iu. P. Petrov, *Voennye komissary v gody grazhdanskoi voiny.* (Moscow, 1956). Iu. P. Petrov, *KPSS—rukovoditel i vospitatel Krasnoi Armii (1918-1920 gg.).* (Moscow, 1961). N. I. Shatagin, "Kommunisticheskaia partiia—organizator Sovetskoi Armii." *Voprosy istorii KPSS*, No. 1 (1958), 10-28. I. Marevskii and S. Shishkin, "O nekotorykh voprosakh sovetskoi strategii v grazhdanskoi voine v SSSR." *Voenno-istoricheskii zhurnal*, No. 11 (1960). E. Putyrskii and E. Erykalov, *Petrogradskie rabochie v borbe za sozdanie Krasnoi Armii.* (Leningrad, 1958). E. Medvedev, *Organizatsiia vooruzhennykh sil na Srednei Volge v 1918 g.* (Kuibyshev, 1958).

Red Army and the Soviet government during the early years of the Revolution. There is only one superficial study of the participation of Chinese volunteers who played an important part in the Red armed forces during the first years of the Civil War. The Latvians, Czechs, Slovaks, Hungarians, and Poles, all in various degrees, formed units which rendered considerable assistance to the Red Army. Similarly lacking is research on the other sorts of aid from abroad, from labor unions and other workers' organizations. One form taken by this aid was political pressure upon their respective governments to terminate the intervention, cease aid to the White Army, and stop the blockade. Sympathetic workers in the port of Danzig refused to load or unload cargoes. Combined, these pressures served as a substantial moral weapon to undermine opposition to the Soviet cause and render it military advantage.[21]

By 1960 there appeared several works on the industrial mobilization during the Civil War. D. A. Kovalenko discusses in detail the subject rarely dealt with in literature of industrial evacuation during the first period of the Civil War, and though inadequately, the defense industry during 1918-1919. The

[21] I. Tipner, *O boevom puti estonskikh chastei Krasnoi Armii (1917-1920 gg.)*. (Tallin, 1957). P. V. Makeev, *Na Denikina. Rol latyshskikh strelkov v razgrome denikinskikh polchishch*. (Riga, 1960). P. Fradkina, "Litovskie bolsheviki v Rossii v borbe za Sovetskuiu vlast'." *Kommunist* (Vilnius), No. 9 (1957). Z. I. Siraev, "Bashkirskie natsionalnye chasti Krasnoi Armii v grazhdanskuiu voinu." *Oktiabrskaia revoliutsiia i rozhdenie Sovetskoi Bashkirii*. (Ufa, 1959). I. A. Elfond, "O deiatelnosti inostrannykh grupp RKP (b) v gody grazhdanskoi voiny i inostrannoi interventsii." *Uchenye zapiski Saratovskogo universiteta*, Vol. 59 (1958). N. D. Cherepnina, "Inostrannye kommunisticheskie gruppy v Sovetskoi Rossii i ikh deiatelnost." *Proletarskii internatsionalizm—boevoe znamia Kommunisticheskoi partii*. (Moscow, 1959). A. Kh. Klevanskii, "Nekotorye voprosy istorii chekhoslovatskikh revoliutsionnykh organizatsii v Rossii v sviazi s noveishimi rabotami chekhoslovatskikh istorikov." *Istoriia SSSR*, No. 5 (1958), 216-23. D. Lappo and A. Mel'chin, *Stranitsy velikoi druzhby*. (Moscow, 1959). N. A. Popov, *Oni s nami srazhalis za vlast Sovetov*. (Leningrad, 1959). G. Novogrudskii and A. Dunaevskii, *Tovarishchi kitaiskie boitsy*. (Moscow, 1959). I. I. Babichev, *Uchastie kitaiskikh i koreiskikh trudiashchikhsia v grazhdanskoi voine na Dalnem Vostoke*. (Tashkent, 1959). A. N. Kheifets, "Iz istorii sovmestnoi borby russkikh i kitaiskikh rabochikh KVZhD protiv interventov i belogvardeitsev (1918-1920 gody)." *Voprosy istorii*, No. 4 (1958), 127-145. N. Kolmogorov, *Vengerskie voennoplennye v borbe za vlast Sovetov v Omske*. (Omsk, 1958). P. A. Golub, "Polskie revoliutsionnye voiska v Rossii v 1917-1920 gg." *Voprosy istorii*, No. 3 (1958), 44-63. E. G. Shuliakovskii, "Iz istorii uchastiia trudiashchikhsia poliakov v borbe za vlast v Voronezhskoi gubernii." *Slavianskii sbornik*, Issue I (Voronezh, 1958). F. A. Komarova, *Internatsionalisty zarubezhnykh stran v borbe za vlast Sovetov v Rossii*. (Moscow, 1958). L. I. Zharov and V. M. Ustinov, *Internatsionalnye chasti Krasnoi Armii v boiakh za vlast Sovetov v gody inostrannoi voennoi interventsii i grazhdanskoi voiny v SSSR*. (Moscow, 1960). I. G. Matveev, *U istokov vechnoi druzhby. O bratskoi pomoshchi zarubezhnykh rabochikh v gody voennoi interventsii i grazhdanskoi voiny v Sibiri v 1918-1920 gg*. (Novosibirsk, 1959).

entire field is far from being exhausted and much remains to be written on this theme.[22]

D. THE CHEKA

The CHEKA (All-Russian Extraordinary Commission for the Combat of Counterrevolution and Sabotage) was formed at the initiative of Lenin and confirmed on December 7 (20), 1917, by the Soviet of People's Commissars. For understandable reasons, this organization and its activities remain shrouded in mystery. Though a good deal has been written that casts an indirect light on the subject, mostly memoirs and popular writings, the grim history of this institution has been hardly explored, particularly the early period of the "Red Terror" immediately following its establishment. The first documentary collection pertaining to the CHEKA that is of any value to the student of history appeared in 1958. It was followed two years later by the work of P. G. Sofinov, based on the most important available sources. Sofinov discusses the origin of the CHEKA and the methods it employed in combating counterrevolution, but neither the published documents nor Sofinov's study can be remotely regarded as definitive accomplishments in the field.

Research in this particular field is bound to face serious difficulties not only in locating sources, but in delineating, for instance, such delicate juridical or legal problems as the difference between "extraordinary" and "customary" law practices, or defining the "revolutionary justice" which justified the CHEKA's existence. Shortly after the October Revolution the responsibility for intelligence activities and vigilance against counterrevolution was first assigned to the existing Military-Revolutionary Committee. This organization, though a temporary one, rapidly gained power and was destined to play an important part in the successful overthrow of the Provisional Government.

After the Soviet government came into power the problem of counterrevolutionary activities assumed paramount importance. The issue became especially acute since by this time the old judicial apparatus had collapsed entirely. The function of political security passed quickly into the hands of the newly formed agency, the CHEKA. After its founding the agency passed

[22]M. M. Biziaeva, "Iz istorii organizatsii oboronnoi promyshlennosti v gody grazhdanskoi voiny." *Uchenye zapiski Akademii obshchestvennykh nauk,* No. 29 (1957). S. M. Kliatskin, "Iz istorii organizatsii proizvodstva vooruzheniia, boepripasov i boevogo snabzheniia Krasnoi Armii v 1918-1920 gg." *Doklady i soobshcheniia Instituta istorii Akademii nauk SSSR,* No. 11 (1957). A. P. Pogrebinskii, "K istorii mobilizatsii promyshlennosti Sovetskoi Rossii v 1918-1920 gg." *Nauchnye zapiski Moskovskogo finansovogo instituta,* No. 11 (1958). D. A. Kovalenko, "K istorii evakuatsii promyshlennosti v pervyi period grazhdanskoi voiny." *Nauchnye doklady vysshei shkoly. Istoricheskie nauki,* No. 2 (1958). D. A. Kovalenko, "Mobilizatsiia sovetskoi promyshlennosti na oboronu v 1918 g." *Iz istorii borby sovetskogo naroda protiv inostrannoi voennoi interventsii i vnutrennei kontr-revoliutsii v 1918 g.* (Moscow, 1958). D. A. Kovalenko, *Reshaiushchie pobedy sovetskogo naroda nad interventami i belogvardeitsami v 1919 g.* (Moscow, 1960).

through many changes, but the more it changed the more it remained the same dreaded "sword of the Revolution." No matter what new official name was attached to this institution, it remained basically what it was from the start, "The Terror of All Opposition," the agency that later operated forced labor camps, and vigilantly preserved external and internal security throughout the Soviet Union.[23]

E. MILITARY COMMUNISM

In the field of military communism during the Civil War period, 1918-1920, one may single out the work of I. A. Gladkov, published in 1956. Gladkov's book considers the basic characteristics of military communism, the conditions that led to its adoption, and the means by which it was enforced. Although P. I. Liashchenko, in his three-volume work on the economic development of the Soviet Union, had incorporated a large section on military communism, the monograph by Gladkov is of special interest since it is a concentrated piece of research and a minutely elaborated analysis of that particular phase of economic development. Two other fundamental monographs in the same field are those by D. A. Baevski and A. V. Venediktov, both of which dwell extensively on the same period of experimental, indecisive, and fateful decisions affecting the formation of the Soviet State.[24]

F. NATIONAL MINORITIES

The history of the formation of the Commissariat of National Minorities and its early policies is best presented by E. I. Pesikina. Until about the early 1950's the question was simply reduced to the policy of Stalin, while the cosmopolitan philosophy of the early years of the Revolution was forced

---

[23]*Krasnaia kniga VCHEKA.* (Moscow, 1920). M. Ia. Latsis, *Dva goda borby na vnutrennem fronte.* (Moscow, 1920). M. Ia. Latsis, *Chrezvychainye komissii po borbe s kontrrevoliutsiei.* (Moscow, 1921). M. Ia. Latsis, "Vozniknovenie narodnogo komissariata vnutrennikh del i organizatsiia vlasti na mestakh." *Proletarskaia revoliutsiia,* No. 2 (37), (1925), 136-159; No. 3 (37), (1925), 136-159; No. 3 (38), (1926), 142-166. M. Ia. Latsis, "Tov. Dzerzhinskii i VCHK." *Proletarskaia revoliutsiia,* No. 9 (56), (1926), 81-97. Ia. Peters, "Vospominaniia o rabote v VCHK v pervyi god revoliutsii." *Proletarskaia revoliutsiia,* No. 10 (33), (1924), 5-32. L. Bychkov, *VCHK v gody grazhdanskoi voiny.* (Moscow, 1940). *Iz istorii Vserossiiskoi Chrezvychainoi Komissii 1917-1921. Sbornik dokumentov.* (Moscow, 1958). V. Minaev, *Tainoe stanovitsia iavnym.* (Moscow, 1960). P. G. Sofinov, *Ocherki istorii Vserossiiskoi Chrezvychainoi Komissii (1917-1922 gg.).* (Moscow, 1960).

[24]I. A. Gladkov, *Ocherki sovetskoi ekonomiki, 1917-1920 gg.* (Moscow, 1956). P. I. Liashchenko, *Istoriia narodnogo khoziaistva SSSR.* Vol. III. (Moscow, 1956). D. A. Baevskii, *Ocherki po istorii khoziaistvennogo stroitelstva perioda grazhdanskoi voiny.* (Moscow, 1957). A. V. Venediktov, *Organizatsiia gosudarstvennoi promyshlennosti v SSSR, 1917-1920.* Vol. I. (Leningrad, 1957).

into the background or completely obliterated by the newly inflated "Soviet patriotism."[25]

Since Stalin's death a number of works have appeared which indicate a revival of interest in the national life of the Soviet Union; many of them deal with the impact of the October Revolution upon the various national republics. Studies of this nature have served to arouse interest in the history of the admission of different national republics to the Soviet Union.[26] Marxist critics seem to find one notable failure in current writings on this subject— the absence of a "general pattern of socialist development and the establishment of a proletarian dictatorship." With rare exceptions, critics say, Soviet historians fail to associate the socialist revolutions that took place in the Russian provinces between October, 1917, and February, 1918, with the significant national developments throughout the Soviet Union.[27]

[25]E. I. Pesikina, *Narodnyi komissariat po delam natsionalnostei i ego deiatelnost v 1917-1918 gg.* (Moscow, 1950).

[26]N. I. Suprunenko, *Pobeda Velikoi Oktiabrskoi sotsialisticheskoi revoliutsii na Ukraine.* (Kiev, 1957). B. M. Babii, *V. I. Lenin i stroitelstvo Ukrainskogo Sovetskogo gosudarstva.* (Kiev, 1957). E. I. Moshniaga, *Bolsheviki Kharkova v Oktiabrskoi revoliutsii.* (Kharkov, 1959). I. I. Saladkov, *Bolsheviki Belorussii v period podgotovki i provedeniia Velikoi Oktiabrskoi sotsialisticheskoi revoliutsii (mart 1917—fevral 1918).* (Minsk, 1957). N. B. Kamenskaia, *Pervye sotsialisticheskie preobrazovaniia v Belorussii (25 oktiabria 1917—iiul 1919 g.).* (Minsk, 1957). V. Ivashin, *Velikii Oktiabr v Minske.* (Minsk, 1957). I. E. Marchenko, *Agrarnye preobrazovaniia v Belorussii v 1917-1918 gg.* (Minsk, 1959). T. P. Guba, *Borba bolshevikov Kazakhstana za pobedu Oktiabrskoi sotsialisticheskoi revoliutsii v Turkestane.* (Alma-Ata, 1957). I. K. Dodonov, *Pobeda Oktiabrskoi revoliutsii v Turkestane.* (Tashkent, 1958). K. E. Zhitov, *Pobeda Velikoi Oktiabrskoi sotsialisticheskoi revoliutsii v Uzbekistane.* (Tashkent, 1957). Kh. Sh. Inoiatov, *Oktiabrskaia revoliutsiia v Uzbekistane.* (Moscow, 1958). T. Karimov, *Pobeda Velikoi Oktiabrskoi sotsialisticheskoi revoliutsii v Severnom Tadzhikstane (aprel 1917—1918 gg.).* (Stalinabad, 1957). S. N. Pokrovskii, *Pobeda Sovetskoi vlasti v Semirechie.* (Alma-Ata, 1961). Sh. Tashliev, *Ustanovlenie i uprochnenie Sovetskoi vlasti v Turkestane (1917-iiun 1918 g,).* (Ashkhabad, 1957). S. Kh. Karapetian, *Kommunisticheskaia partiia v borbe za pobedu Oktiabrskoi revoliutsii v Armenii.* (Erevan, 1959). M. V. Tsertsvadze, *Revoliutsionnoe dvizhenie v Gruzii v 1914-1917 gg.* Part II, *1917 god.* (Tbilisi, 1960). A. E. Ioffe, "Konferentsiia istorikov v Baku." *Voprosy istorii,* No. 6 (1959), 181-190. T. Draudin, *Bezzemelnoe krestianstvo Latvii v borbe za zemliu i vlast Sovetov v 1917-1919 gg.* (Riga, 1959). Ia. P. Kiastyn', "K voprosu ob agrarnoi politike Kommunisticheskoi partii Latvii (1917-1919 gg.)." *Voprosy istorii KPSS,* No. 4 (1959), 73-87. *Borba za pobedu sotsialisticheskoi revoliutsii v Moldavii.* (Kishenev, 1957). I. G. Dykov, "O nekotorykh voprosakh istorii ustanovleniia sovetskoi vlasti v Moldavii." *Voprosy istorii,* No. 7 (1959), 18-36. M. B. Itkis and I. I. Nemirov, *Borba krestian Bessarabii za zemliu v 1917 g.* (Kishenev, 1957). V. A. Sapegina, *Borba za sozdanie sovetskogo gosudarstvennogo apparata v Turkestane (fevral 1917—aprel 1918 g.).* (Tashkent, 1956).

[27]See as an example M. Suzikov, *Osobennosti Oktiabrskoi sotsialisticheskoi revoliutsii v Kazakhstane.* (Alma-Ata, 1959).

A. I. Lepeshkin investigated the related subject of local government during the period 1917-1920, in an outstanding work based on primary source materials found in local and central archives throughout the country. Other studies, such as those of P. P. Grishin or P. S. Stepanov, are concerned with governments of specific regions such as the province of Riazan or Smolensk. K. G. Fedorov devoted his entire work to the study of the All-Russian Central Executive Committee and its operations during 1917-1920, and P. G. Sofinov, mentioned previously, produced the rare study of the CHEKA with its local implications and operations during the particularly virulent phase of the Revolution, 1917-1922.[28]

The cultural impact of the Soviet Revolution upon Russian life is discussed in two main works. One is by M. P. Kim, who summarizes four decades of cultural achievements, including such policies as universal education, liquidation of illiteracy, new trends in literature and in the arts, and theatrical activities. A monographic work by I. S. Smirnov, the result of years of labor, emphasizes mainly Lenin's views on national and political education and on science and the arts, and evaluates some of the accomplishments during the forty years following the Revolution.[29]

[28]A. I. Lepeshkin, *Mestnye organy vlasti Sovetskogo gosudarstva.* (Moscow, 1957). P. P. Grishin, *Obrazovanie Sovetov v Riazanskoi gubernii i ikh deiatelnost v pervye gody proletarskoi diktatury.* (Riazan, 1957). P. S. Stepanov, *Borba za ukreplenie vlasti v Smolenskoi gubernii v 1917-1920 gg.* (Moscow, 1960). K. G. Fedorov, *VTSIK v pervye gody Sovetskoi vlasti (1917-1920 gg.).* (Moscow, 1960). P. G. Sofinov, *Ocherki istorii Vserossiiskoi Chrezvychainoi Komissii (1917-1922 gg.).* (Moscow, 1960).

[29]M. P. Kim, *40 let sovetskoi kultury.* (Moscow, 1957). I. S. Smirnov, *Lenin i sovetskaia kultura. Gosudarstvennaia deiatelnost V. I. Lenina v oblasti kulturnogo stroitelstva (oktiabr 1917 g.—leto 1918 g.).* (Moscow, 1960). As to others see: A. G. Slonimskii, *A. M. Gorky v borbe za sozdanie sovetskoi intelligentsii v gody inostrannoi interventsii i grazhdanskoi voiny.* (Moscow, 1956). F. F. Korolev, *Ocherki po istorii sovetskoi shkoly i pedagogiki, 1917-1920.* (Moscow, 1958). A. A. Maksimov, "Pervye sovetskie literaturno-khudozhestvennye zhurnaly." *Uchenye zapiski LGU,* Vol. 257, Issue 47 (Leningrad, 1959). *V pervye gody sovetskogo muzykalnogo stroitelstva. Sbornik.* (Leningrad, 1959). V. V. Gorbunov, "Borba V. I. Lenina s separatistskimi ustremleniiami Proletkulta." *Voprosy istorii KPSS,* No. 1 (1958), 29-39.

CHAPTER XI

Agriculture in the Soviet Union

A. THE PEASANTS AND THE LAND

One can hardly overestimate the importance of the land question, from the very start of the Russian Revolution; the fate of the government depended upon its successful solution. Several monographs, articles, and reviews illustrate the differences of opinion on the subject that prevailed in Soviet historiography, and still do.[1] Among the early writers who dealt with the initial Soviet land reforms, some took an openly critical stand, others steered a middle course (the "petit-bourgeois school"), while a third group outrightly favored the legislation. Among those who condemned the land reforms and utopian socialist ideas, and who ardently defended private ownership was, for example, L. Litoshenko, who wrote in 1918 on agrarian socialist legislation. He warned that land confiscation was not a solution of the agrarian problem; only private ownership and freedom from government interference could be the solution. He cited the chaos, the total anarchy that had reigned throughout the countryside since October, 1917, after private landownership was abolished. Litoshenko also pointed out to the remaining group of landless peasants their inability to earn a living by other means and the higher rate of taxation required to support the growing bureaucracy.[2]

---

[1] V. M. Selunskaia, "Rukovodiashchaia rol rabochego klassa v sotsialisticheskoi revoliutsii v derevne (1918 god)." *Voprosy istorii*, No. 3 (1958), 3-23. V. P. Danilov, "Izuchenie istorii Sovetskogo krestianstva." *Sovetskaia istoricheskaia nauka ot XX k XXII sezdu KPSS.* (Moscow, 1962). M. R. Naidenov and A. N. Lopatkin, "Iz istorii razrabotki agrarnoi programmy bolshevistskoi partii." *Sovetskaia kniga*, No. 4 (1953). V. R. Gerasimiuk, *Nachalo sotsialisticheskoi revoliutsii v derevne 1917-1918 gg.* (Moscow, 1958). See review by Iu. N. Amiantov in *Voprosy istorii KPSS*, No. 2 (1959), 206-208. *Agrarnaia politika Sovetskoi vlasti (1917-1918 gg.). Dokumenty i materialy.* See review by A. N. Lopatkin in *Voprosy istorii*, No. 2 (1955), 142-147. L. S. Zharikhin, *Bedneishee krestianstvo—soiuznik proletariata v Oktiabrskoi revoliutsii.* (Moscow, 1957). See review by P. N. Sobolev in *Voprosy istorii*, No. 3 (1959), 185-192. P. N. Sobolev, *"Soiuz rabochego klassa i bedneishego krestianstva v sotsialisticheskoi revoliutsii.* (Moscow, 1954). See review by V. Storozhev in *Voprosy istorii*, No. 10 (1955), 132-136. P. N. Sobolev, "Vopros o soiuze rabochego klassa i krestianstva v literature po istorii Oktiabrskoi revoliutsii." *Voprosy istorii,* No. 10 (1955), 132-136; No. 9 (1958), 107-118. V. P. Naumov and I. B. Cheliapov, "Kniga ob agrarnoi politike KPSS," a review of G. V. Sharapov's work entitled *Razreshenie agrarnogo voprosa v Rossii posle pobedy Oktiabrskoi revoliutsii (1917-1920 gg.)* (Moscow, 1961), in *Voprosy istorii*, No. 5 (1962), 201-205.

[2] L. Litoshenko, *Sotsialisticheskiia zemlia.* (Moscow, 1918).

The more moderate critics, such as A. Chaianov and S. Maslov, argued in favor of supporting a strong, healthy peasant household rather than a collective system as a basis for a sound agrarian economy. Chaianov defended private initiative as a most natural economic force. He gravely doubted that any agrarian collectivist group could ever successfully compete with an economy based on capitalistic principles. He strongly advocated peasant cooperatives which would be administered by "kulak elements." Such cooperatives could be economically sound, argued Chaianov, as long as they were in charge of marketing and procurement. Any attempt at collectivization of the agricultural economy, he believed, would be doomed to failure, for it would be contrary to the nature of the individualistic peasantry. S. Maslov maintained that only on a capitalistic basis could agriculture progress. Lenin read Maslov's thesis, labelled it a "trashy bourgeois 'scientific' lie," concluded that "only a fool or a malicious saboteur could have let such a book be printed," and requested authorities "to investigate and name *all* those responsible for its publication."[3]

The literature on Soviet land reforms indicates that the legislation must have been carried out in an atmosphere of sharp ideological conflicts and surprising freedom of expression during this early period of Soviet power. Among the historians who defended the Bolshevik reforms stood out the familiar figure of M. N. Pokrovskii, who attacked the critics with characteristic vehemence. Carried away by the battle, he argued, with dubious logic at times, that Russia was facing a double revolution: one, a socialist proletarian movement in the cities; the other an "indigenous" or "elemental" bourgeois-democratic peasant revolution in rural Russia. The thesis has been challenged by even communist writers, not to mention others.[4]

During the early part of the 1920's several writers examined extensively the socio-economic impact of the October Revolution upon the rural communities of Soviet Russia. Some of the numerous publications that appeared during the early years still retain their historical importance.[5] B. N. Knipo-

[3]A. Chaianov, *Osnovnye idei i formy organizatsii krestianskoi kooperatsii.* (Moscow, 1919). S. Maslov, *Chto takoe sotsializatsiia zemli.* (Viatka, 1918).

[4]M. N. Pokrovskii, *Kontrrevoliutsiia za 4 goda.* (Moscow, 1922).

[5]B. Knipovich, "Napravlenie i itogi agrarnoi politiki 1917-1920 gg." *O Zemle. Sbornik.* Issue I. (Moscow, 1921). B. Knipovich, *Ocherk deiatelnosti Narodnogo komissariata zemledeliia za tri goda (1918-1920).* (Moscow, 1920). P. N. Pershin, "Formy zemlepolzovaniia." *O Zemle. Sbornik.* Issue I. (Moscow, 1921). A. I. Khriashcheva, *Krestianstvo v voine i revoliutsii.* (Moscow, 1921). A. I. Khriascheva, *Gruppy i klassy v krestianstve.* (Moscow, 1926). A. I. Khriashcheva, "Evoliutsiia klassov v krestianstve." In *Evoliutsiia klassov v russkoi revoliutsii.* (Moscow, 1922). I. A. Kirillov, *Ocherki zemleustroistva za tri goda revoliutsii (1917-1920).* (Petrograd, 1922). S. M. Dubrovskii, *Ocherki russkoi revoliutsii.* Issue I, *Selskoe khoziaistvo.* (Moscow, 1923). V. Keller and I. Romanenko, *Pervye itogi agrarnoi reformy. Opyt issledovaniia rezultatov sovremennogo zemleustroistva na primere Zadonskogo uezda Voronezhskoi gubernii.* (Voronezh, 1922).

vich, as member of the Commissariat of Agriculture, was able to utilize official statistical data and other pertinent materials related to the conditions throughout Russia. A. I. Khriashcheva's numerous statistical tables and charts make her study particularly valuable. No less interesting is her observation of the socio-economic effects produced by land distribution in the rural communities throughout Russia.

Another outstanding monograph is by S. M. Dubrovskii, who discusses at considerable length the agrarian situation in Russia from 1861 to 1923. He describes the economically ruinous consequences of the land parcelling and first experiments with collective state farms. Dubrovskii, presently a senior member of the Institute of History and authority on the Stolypin period, observes that the Land Decree issued by the Soviet government, socializing all the land, constituted merely a recognition of an accomplished fact.[6] Land distribution was so elemental that no government could have regulated the mass action. The government had no choice but to legalize what had already become an accomplished fact. The peasants had simply taken the law into their own hands and achieved what their forefathers had dreamed of attaining centuries before them.

Another study of the agrarian reforms, concentrating mainly on the first three years (1917-1920) of the Revolution, is by I. A. Kirillov. He examines the forms of landownership in Russia prior to 1917, and makes a careful study of the consequences of land socialization. Kirillov depends heavily upon materials he uncovered in the central archives; he was unable to use local administrative materials and provincial archives—a single weakness of his otherwise scholarly accomplishment.

L. Kritsman argues with convincing logic that the Soviet agrarian policy did not correspond to the economic conditions in the country and for this reason he labels it an economically conservative policy. He criticizes particularly the Committees of Poor Peasants (Kombeds) which he regards as nothing less than a rural petit-bourgeois element whose general conduct was bound to have a negative effect on agrarian development. Kritsman's thesis was met with a chorus of severe criticism. [7]

The conditions that prevailed in the countryside at the time of the October Revolution have been dealt with by a legion of writers. A. V. Shestakov has analyzed the political realities of the agrarian revolution in two impressive works: one on the Bolsheviks and the peasantry during the Revolution in 1917; the other, on the class struggle in the countryside during the period of military communism.[8]

Shestakov suggests the reasons that the Bolsheviks agreed to cooperate with the left wing of the Social Revolutionary Party. With some logic, if

[6]S. M. Dubrovskii, *Krestianskoe dvizhenie 1905-1907 gg.* (Moscow, 1956).

[7]L. Kritsman, *Proletarskaia revoliutsiia v derevne.* (Moscow, 1929).

[8]A. V. Shestakov, *Bolsheviki i krestianstvo v revoliutsii 1917 goda.* (Moscow, 1929). A. V. Shestakov, *Klassovaia borba v derevne TsChO v epokhu voennogo kommunizma.* (Moscow, 1930). K. V. Gusev, *Borba bolshevikov za krestianstvo i krakh partii*

perhaps a degree of oversimplification, he believes that the formation of the *Kombeds*, their activities, and their accomplishments were largely due to this cooperation. Shestakov maintains, along with others such as S. M. Dubrovskii, that the liquidation of the landlord class was carried out by the peasantry independently, without the aid of either the Bolshevik Party or the city proletariat, a view that alienated some party officials. Shestakov also devised an original periodization for the history of the agrarian revolution: the "peaceful period," the months of March to July, 1917; and the "period of violence," beginning in August, 1917. According to Shestakov, the outbreak of violence came about when the peasantry concluded that only by direct action could the land be wrenched from the landlords.

The extensive publication of source materials related to the peasantry and the land problem has enabled many historians to deal with the subject more confidently, with the assurance that the period of document-gathering has virtually ended. Perhaps the most important documentary publication is the series that appeared during 1957-1958, on the occasion of the fortieth anniversary of the Revolution, including some volumes issued by the Academy of Sciences, and others by local party and government organs. Together, these form an impressive collection of materials for research in agrarian history.[9]

A number of monographs published after 1945 focused attention on agrarian questions and policies of the Soviet government shortly after coming to power. The studies of V. I. Ignatev, A. N. Lopatkin, and M. A. Kraev stand out particularly. Periodical literature in historical and other magazines treat smaller, though no less vital aspects of the general field of agrarian history.[10]

Much of the material on Soviet agrarian policy during 1917-1920 may also be found in some of the more general studies, such as the third volume

levykh eserov. Dissertation. (Moscow, 1959). I. V. Chernyshev, *Selskoe khoziaistvo dovoennoi Rossii i SSSR.* (Moscow, 1928). E. A. Morokhovets, *Agrarnye programmy rossikikh politicheskikh partii v 1917 godu.* (Moscow, 1929). P. N. Pershin, *Zemelnoe ustroistvo dorevoliutsionnoi derevni.* (Moscow, 1928). S. M. Dubrovskii, *Krestianstvo v 1917 g.* (Moscow, 1927).

[9]*Velikaia Oktiabrskaia sotsialisticheskaia revoliutsiia.* (Moscow, 1957-58). *Kommunisticheskaia partiia Sovetskogo Soiuza v borbe za pobedu sotsialisticheskoi revoliutsii.* (Moscow, 1957). *Protokoly TsK RSDRP (b).* (Moscow, 1958). *Perepiska Sekretariata TsK RSDRP (b) s mestnymi partiinymi organizatsiiami.* (Moscow, 1957).

[10]V. I. Ignatev, *O politike partii po otnosheniiu k krestianstvu v pervye gody Sovetskoi vlasti (noiabr 1917 g.—mart 1921 g.).* (Moscow, 1952). E. N. Kochetkovskaia, *Natsionalizatsiia zemli v SSSR.* (Moscow, 1952). A. N. Lopatkin, *Iz istorii razrabotki agrarnoi programmy bolshevistskoi partii.* (Moscow, 1952). I. A. Gladkov, *Ocherki stroitelstva sovetskogo planovogo khoziaistva v 1917-1920 gg.* (Moscow, 1956). N. G. Karotamm, *K istorii ucheniia o sotsialisticheskom selskom khoziaistve.* (Moscow, 1959). M. A. Kraev, *Pobeda kolkhoznogo stroia v SSSR.* (Moscow, 1954). S. P. Trapeznikov, *Istoricheskii opyt KPSS v sotsialisticheskom preobrazovanii selskogo khoziaistva.* (Moscow, 1959). S. P. Trapeznikov, *Agrarnyi vopros i*

of P. I. Liashchenko, the third volume of the *General History of the Civil War,* and in the different histories of the USSR. Finally, with some reservations, the *History of the Communist Party of the Soviet Union* might be mentioned. There is also a volume of excellent essays on the history of land tenure in Russia, written by a group of distinguished Soviet scholars. The authors examine the land reforms introduced during the first months after the October Revolution, and the measures that followed during the period 1918-1920.[11]

Of the many articles and several monographs written on the relationship between the Communist Party and the peasant problem, one by V. I. Ignatev merits particular attention. The author investigated the first crucial period, from November, 1917, to March, 1921, utilizing an enormous amount of source material to illuminate the overpowering difficulties faced by the Soviet government. Ignatev studied the confrontation between the government and the peasantry, and the almost desperate effort on the party of the former to have the peasants join in "the socialist reconstruction of the agrarian economy"—an effort that was totally futile. It is perhaps symbolic that Ignatev ends his study with March, 1921—the beginning of the New Economic Policy (NEP), which marks the government's admission of defeat, though temporary, in its attempt to socialize agriculture.[12]

Writing on the same subject, S. P. Trapeznikov discusses the agrarian question during the nineteenth and early twentieth centuries, the political programs advocated by the various parties, and Lenin's plans to solve the age-old problem.[13] A. N. Lopatkin, who covers the period between 1870 and the spring of 1919, stresses the struggle between the landless peasantry and

leninskie agrarnye programmy v trekh russkikh revoliutsiiakh. (Moscow, 1963). M. A. Rubach, *Ocherki po istorii revoliutsionnogo preobrazovaniia agrarnykh otnoshenii na Ukraine.* (Moscow, 1959). P. N. Pershin, *Ocherki agrarnoi revoliutsii v Rossii.* (Moscow, 1959). P. N. Pershin, *Agrarnye preobrazovaniia Velikoi Oktiabrskoi revoliutsii.* (Moscow, 1962). Of the numerous articles the following may be singled out: M. Snegirev, "Velikaia Oktiabrskaia sotsialisticheskaia revoliutsiia i raspredelenie zemel v 1917-1918 gg." *Voprosy istorii,* No. 11, (1947), 3-28. T. A. Remezova, "Organizuiushchaia rol' Sovetskogo gosudarstva v osuchchestvlenii agrarnykh preobrazovanii 1917-1918 gg." *Istoricheskie zapiski,* No. 42 (1953), 87-116. D. Baevskii, "Iz istorii sovetskogo krestianstva (1918-1920 gg.)." *Voprosy istorii,* Nos. 5-6 (1945), 3-22. V. P. Danilov, "Zemelnye otnosheniia v sovetskoi dokolkhoznoi derevne." *Istoriia SSSR,* No. 3 (1958), 90-128.

[11]P. I. Liashchenko, *Istoriia narodnogo khoziaistva SSSR.* (Moscow, 1956). N. V. Bochkov, P. N., Pershin, M. A. Snegirev, and V. F. Sharapov, *Istoriia zemelnykh otnoshenii i zemleustroistva.* (Moscow, 1957).

[12]V. I. Ignatev, *O politike partii po otnosheniiu k krestianstvu v pervye gody Sovetskoi vlasti (noiabr 1917 g.—mart 1921 g.).* (Moscow, 1952).

[13]S. P. Trapeznikov, *Agrarnyi vopros i leninskie agrarnye programmy v trekh russkikh revoliutsiiakh.* (Moscow, 1963).

the rural communities of Russia, and the program proposed by the Bolshevik Party as an answer to the problem. The weaknesses of this work are that the period after October, 1917, is dealt with rather summarily, the earliest attempts at collectivization are barely discussed, and the general effect of the land nationalization receives equally sketchy treatment.[14]

A more successful presentation of the Soviet government's earliest land reforms, shortly after October, 1917, is by A. A. Voronovich. The author analyzes the gradual formulation of the land program finally adopted by the Bolshevik Party, and its application during the early months after the October Revolution. In addition, Voronovich compares this program with the ones advocated by other political parties at the same time. Another study, devoted entirely to the Land Nationalization Decree, is by E. Kochetovskaia.[15] Though earnestly undertaken, this work is seriously weakened by the author's limited use of available resources.[16]

In his work on the same subject, P. N. Sobolev delves into an aspect rarely discussed, namely, the reasons for including members of the left-wing Social Revolutionary Party in the new Soviet government.[17] Sobolev attributes the discussion to the Soviet desire to undermine and eventually destroy the right wing of the party, as well as the Mensheviks. According to Sobolev the Bolsheviks later took advantage of the "petit-bourgeois vacillations of the left Social Revolutionary members" and utilized their ability to cooperate with the peasantry, then dropped them.

K. V. Gusev and M. V. Spiridonov explain the temporary political wedlock in somewhat less cynical terms.[18]

Once in a while there appears a "diversionary" view in Soviet historiography, and in 1962 I. M. Ignatenko offered an interpretation of these events that completely digressed from the usual party line. Shortly after the March Revolution, Ignatenko says, the peasantry supported the "bourgeois parties," and the Social Revolutionary Party enjoyed virtually unchallenged leadership in rural Russia. This fact explained the need for cooperation with this group

[14]A. N. Lopatkin, *Iz istorii razrabotki agrarnoi programmy bolshevistskoi partii.* (Moscow, 1952).

[15]E. N. Kochetovskaia, *Natsionalizatsiia zemli v SSSR.* (Moscow, 1947).

[16]V. M. Gubareva, *Razvertyvanie sotsialisticheskoi revoliutsii v derevne v 1918 godu.* (Moscow, 1957). V. R. Gerasimiuk, *Nachalo sotsialisticheskoi revoliutsii v derevne 1917-1918 gg.* (Moscow, 1958).

[17]P. N. Sobolev, *Bedneishee krestianstvo—soiuznik proletariata v Oktiabrskoi revoliutsii.* (Moscow, 1958).

[18]See K. V. Gusev, "Iz istorii soglasheniia bolshevikov s belymi eserami." *Istoriia SSSR*, No. 2 (1959), 73-94. K. V. Gusev, *Krakh partii levykh eserov.* (Moscow, 1963). See also review of this book by K. I. Sedov in *Voprosy istorii*, No. 10 (1964), 176-181. M. V. Spiridonov, "Borba kommunisticheskoi partii protiv levykh eserov v 1917-1918 gg." *Uchenye zapiski Karelskogo pedagogicheskogo instituta* (1960).

by the Bolsheviks. Needless to add that such an heretical opinion did not pass without some serious rebukes; indeed, it is surprising that such a story appeared in published form at all. The surprise is even greater when one finds in Ignatenko's book the statement that the peasantry supported the Provisional Government on the issue of the war, demanding its continuation until complete victory.[19]

For a more intensive study of the agrarian question, tracing the issue since 1861 and leading up to the October, 1917, Revolution, the monograph of P. N. Pershin may be recommended. Pershin begins with the legacy left by the institution of serfdom after its abolition, with all its ramifications and complex problems. Pershin made excellent use of all available materials and statistical information, taking into consideration social changes that had taken place since the 1860's throughout Russia. The author includes a good outline of land tenure in Russia, a description of methods of cultivation and individual allotments on the eve of the Revolution. The programs of different political parties, ranging from the right to the left in persuasion, as well as the policy followed by the Provisional Government during its short period in office, are accorded due importance.[20]

A. M. Anifimov, like Pershin, devoted much attention to the problems resulting from the conflicts between the remnants of feudalism and emerging capitalism, with their grave impact upon agrarian development. Anifimov covers a shorter period, only the war years of 1914-1917, but goes into the subject much more deeply. The study includes valuable statistical data, charts, and figures which illustrate the status of agriculture through the decisive war years. Perhaps one shortcoming of this book worth noting is the lack of an equally penetrating analysis of the development of capitalism, which, though mentioned, deserves more extensive analytical study.[21]

For a long time there has been a need for a study of the growth and development of the Peasant Councils, or Soviets, of the Russian rural areas. This need was partially met in 1959, when there was published a collection of articles on the early formation of local Soviets during 1917-1918, contributed by different authors and edited by D. A. Chugaev. This was followed a year later by two studies of P. N. Abramov. Abramov gathered materials in nineteen provinces, the majority of which confirm that most local Soviets were established during the months of January-February, 1918. This is confirmed by another writer, V. V. Grishaev. The research of both Abramov and Grishaev renders valuable information to anyone who might undertake a

[19] I. M. Ignatenko, *Bedneishee krestianstvo—soiuznik proletariata v borbe za pobedu Oktiabrskoi revoliutsii v Belorussii (1917-1918 gg.).* (Moscow, 1962).

[20] P. N. Pershin, *Uchastkovoe zemlepolzovanie v Rossii. Khutora i otruby, ikh rasprostranenie za desiatiletie 1907-1916 gg. i sudby vo vremia revoliutsii (1917-1920 gg.).* (Moscow, 1922). P. N. Pershin, *Narisi agrarnoi revoliutsii v Rossii.* (Kiev, 1959).

[21] A. M. Anifimov, *Rossiiskaia derevnia v gody pervoi mirovoi voiny.* (Moscow, 1962).

study of the same question on a national scale. Both studies fail to indicate specifically enough the social status of the majority of deputies elected to these early rural Soviets.[22]

And lastly, there is the admirable work of I. A. Kirillov, who traces land legislation and regulations during the vital three years following the Revolution. This short though significant period was marked by element action later recognized by the Soviet government as decisive.[23]

The significance of the October Revolution, as far as the land problem was concerned, is to be found in two basic acts—the Land Decree and the Fundamental Law that declared all lands nationalized. It was on the basis of these two decrees that landlordism was abolished, and whatever agrarian legislation followed emanated from these two acts. Many students of agrarian leglislation have traced the application of the laws promulgated and their effect upon the entire issue of land tenure, as well as the struggle that was to arise between the government and the peasantry. This subject was skillfully analyzed by P. N. Pershin in *Narisi agrarnoi revoliutsii v Rossii.*

Pershin was the first scholar to make an analytical study of the Land Decre He studied the personnel of the editorial committee in charge of the final text of the Fundamental Law, and noted that the text was approved by an editorial board consisting of four members, two Bolsheviks and two members of the left-wing Social Revolutionary Party. Pershin's most important contribution in this study is his analysis of the immediate effect of land socialization upon Russia. According to Pershin, the act in reality established only a fictitious equality in landholding, for there was no equality in capacity to cultivate the land recently acquired. Nor was there any assurance that the peasants might hold on to that land for any length of time, for the kulak elements, sooner or later, were ready to seize it and restore the pre-distribution balance.

There are a few writers who interpret the Fundamental Law, establishing universal land socialization, as contradictory to the spirit of Soviet agrarian policy. One of these is V. N. Sokolov, who labelled the law an act that potentially favored the kulak elements: a device of the left-wing Social Revolutionary Party to drive a wedge between the workers and the peasantry, weakening the Bolshevik power.[24]

[22]D. A. Chugaev, ed., *Ustanovlenie Sovetskoi vlasti na mestakh v 1917-1918 godakh. Sbornik statei.* 2nd issue. (Moscow, 1959). P. N. Abramov, *K voprosu o vremeni sozdaniia pervykh volostnykh Sovetov (po materialam tsentralnykh gubernii RSFSR).* (Moscow, 1960). P. N. Abramov, "Sovetskoe stroitelstvo na sele v dokombedovskii period (oktiabr 1917—iiul 1918 g.)." *Voprosy istorii KPSS,* No. 6 (1960), 59-74. V. V. Grishaev, "Sozdanie volostnykh Sovetov krestianskikh deputatov (noiabr 1917—mai 1918 g.)." *Vestnik MGU,* No. 4 (1957).

[23]I. A. Kirillov, *Ocherki zemleustroistva za tri goda revoliutsii (1917-1920).* (Petrograd, 1922).

[24]V. N. Sokolov, *Agrarnaia politika VKP(b).* (Moscow, 1938).

On the other hand, E. A. Lutskii believed that the Fundamental Law was a mere transitory step toward socialized agriculture; it simply corresponded with the Bolshevik program *at the time* of the October Revolution. The different views were subject to protracted discussions within the ranks of scholars and party members.[25] V. N. Iakovetskii, in a review of G. V. Sharapov's book on agrarian problems shortly after the Soviet regime came to power, attributes all shortcomings of the policy to the anti-Soviet Menshevik and Social Revolutionary elements who were still active in different administrations and charged with carrying out the agrarian reforms.[26]

A goodly number of Soviet scholars have devoted attention to the nationalization of the large estates, as provided by early Soviet legislation. The question has been discussed in several outstanding articles, based on primary sources located in provincial archives. Most of these authors seem to agree that Soviet agrarian policy was aimed at the preservation of these large estates in the hands of the government for the development at a later date of huge state farms.[27]

During the late 1950's and early 1960's there was a noticeable increase of interest in the history of the Committees of Poor Peasants *(Kombeds)*. This can be explained partially by the increased amount of archival materials and other sources now available for research. V. R. Gerasimiuk, using recently published sources, discovered that in thirty-three provinces of the RSFSR no less than 122,000 *Kombeds* were established to carry out Soviet legislation in their respective communities.[28]

[25] E. A. Lutskii, "O sushchnosti uravnitelnogo zemlepolzovaniia v Sovetskoi Rossii." *Voprosy istorii,* No. 9 (1956), 59-70. G. V. Sharapov, "K voprosu o sushchnosti uravnitelnogo zemlepolzovaniia v Sovetskoi Rossii." *Voprosy istorii,* No. 3 (1957), 113-120. A. N. Lopatkin, "Agrarnaia programma bolshevikov v Velikoi Oktiabrskoi sotsialisticheskoi revoliutsii." *Voprosy istorii,* No. 4 (1957), 43-58. V. M. Selunskaia, "Rukovodiashchaia rol rabochego klassa v sotsialisticheskoi derevne (1918 god)." *Voprosy istorii,* No. 3 (1958), 3-23. I. Shirinskii, "Kommunisticheskaia partiia v borbe za sozdanie i razvitie sotsialisticheskogo khoziaistva." *Voprosy ekonomiki,* No. 11 (1953), 18-32. N. S. Zhuravleva, "Konfiskatsiia pomeshchichikh imenii v Tverskoi gubernii v 1917-1918 gg." *Istoricheskie zapiski,* No. 29 (1949), 48-65.

[26] V. N. Iakovetskii, "Kniga o pervykh shagakh agrarnoi politiki Sovetskoi vlasti." *Istoriia SSSR,* No. 5 (1962), 174-177.

[27] See N. S. Zhuravleva, "Konfiskatsiia pomeshchichikh imenii v Tverskoi gubernii v 1917-1918 gg." *Istoricheskie zapiski,* No. 29 (1949), 48-65. L. A. Govorkov, "Voprosy konfiskatsii pomeshchichikh imenii v Kurskoi gubernii." *Uchenye zapiski Tambovskogo pedagogicheskogo instituta,* Vol. VIII (1949). V. R. Kopylov, "Konfiskatsiia pomeshchichikh imenii v Moskovskoi gubernii v 1917-1918 gg." *Trudy Moskovskogo istoriko-arkhivnogo instituta,* Vol. VI (1954). A. D. Maliavskii, "Konfiskatsiia pomeshchichikh imenii v Vladimirskoi gubernii v 1917-1918 gg." *Uchenye zapiski Kurskogo pedagogicheskogo instituta,* Issue 8 (1956).

[28] V. R. Gerasimiuk, "Kombedy Rossiiskoi federatsii v tsifrakh." *Istoriia SSSR,* No. 4 (1960), 120-126.

Several historical conferences were held during the early 1960's at which attempts were made to present a new evaluation of the agrarian revolution in Russia. These were followed by an exchange of views in the press, all of which indicated that there was no unanimity among Soviet historians as to the exact course of agrarian developments. A paper presented by Iu. A. Poliakov, on the history of the peasantry and the development of state farming, suggested that there was a formerly neglected "third stage in the agrarian revolution," which presumably took place between the spring of 1919 and 1921. During this period, Poliakov asserts, a levelling process took place among the peasantry which stabilized the new land tenure and weakened the position of the kulak elements in rural Russia.[29]

The thesis of Poliakov was challenged by a number of historians, notably by V. P. Danilov, who questioned it in a long article in *Voprosy istorii*. There were two stages only, maintained Danilov, and no others: one was the bourgeois-democratic stage which "passed by," with no effective pattern to events, since the peasantry took the law into its own hands, shaping events according to its own interests; the second was the introduction of a truly socialistic program of reforms by the Soviet government.[30]

A by-product of the increased research in the peasant question since 1917 was a simultaneous interest in the development of collective and state farming. A legion of students attacked the subject and some notable progress has been witnessed. Several monographs based on primary sources have shed light upon the early efforts to establish an agrarian economy based on two forms of management, collectivized and state-administered farms. Some studies indicate that the state-administered farms were usually created on estates that formerly belonged to the landlord class, to monastic orders, or, to a lesser degree, to prosperous individual kulaks. The contention is supported by vital statistical evidence gathered for the first time.[31]

[29]Iu. A. Poliakov, "Sotsialno-ekonomicheskie itogi agrarnykh preobrazovanii Oktiabrskoi revoliutsii (1917-1920 gg.)." Sbornik. *Istoriia sovetskogo krestianstva i kolkhoznogo stroitelstva v SSSR*. (Moscow, 1961).

[30]V. P. Danilov, "Nekotorye itogi nauchnoi sessii po istorii sovetskoi derevni." *Voprosy istorii*, No. 2 (1962), 20-43. V. P. Danilov, "Po povodu tak nazyvaemogo tretego etapa agrarnoi revoliutsii (otvet Ia. A. Poliakovu)." *Voprosy Istorii*, No. 9 (1962), 208-215. See also Iu. A. Poliakov, "K voprosu o soderzhanii i etapakh agrarnoi revoliutsii v SSSR." *Voprosy istorii*, No. 8 (1962), 204-210.

[31]I. A. Koniukov, *Ocherki o pervykh etapakh razvitiia kollektivnogo zemledeliia 1917-1925 gg.* (Moscow, 1949. N. P. Skrypnev, *Pervye shagi sotsialisticheskogo pereustroistva selskogo khoziaistva v 1918-1920 gg.* (Moscow, 1951). V. N. Lavrentev, *Stroitelstvo sovkhozov v pervye gody Sovetskoi vlasti.* (Moscow, 1957). V. A. Milovanov, *Pervye shagi kolkhoznogo dvizheniia v Belorussii.* (Moscow, 1958). G. V. Sharapov, *Nachalo sotsialisticheskikh preobrazovanii v derevne v pervye gody Sovetskoi vlasti.* (Moscow, 1960). B. N. Knipovich, "Napravlenie i itogi agrarnoi politiki 1917-1920 gg." *O Zemle. Sbornik.* Issue I. (Moscow, 1921). I. A. Kirillov, *Ocherki zemleustroistva za tri goda revoliutsii (1917-1920).* (Petrograd, 1922). A. V. Shestakov, *Klassovia borba v derevne TsChO v epokhu*

Though much has been written on the different forms of farm management there is a conspicuous absence of information about the success or, particularly, failure of the various types of farms. Nor is there any adequate description of the bitter opposition of the peasantry, upon whom Soviet farm management was foisted. This is barely touched upon by a single writer, who presents a jejune explanation for the subject's being evaded in current historical literature. To quote the writer:". . . because of an inadequate amount of factual material there was no possibility of showing the struggle for the creation of one or another collective form, its success and its failures. For this reason it was necessary to reduce the description to general processes of the origin of the collective economy, to one or another negative or positive aspect that was revealed during those years."[32] The treacherous semantics clearly suggest that for political reasons historians prefer to let the subject rest in obscurity.

In summary it can be said that though much has been written on agrarian reforms since the October Revolution, the field shows certain gaps. For political reasons there is a "conspiracy of silence" on certain subjects. The works published cover a rather limited period and for that reason lack a broad historical perspective. Too few dwell at proper length on the touchy decisive years of 1919-1920 or link these with the fateful period of the early 1930's. This robs the field of such vital material as the significant legislation adopted during the 1920's. Discussion of agrarian progress during the NEP years is avoided. Nor is there sufficient research on the socio-economic changes that came about as a result of the newly developed agrarian peasant cooperatives, or of consumer societies that emerged during the same time. There is sufficient archival material available to explore these subjects, vulnerable though they might be. Since 1956 particularly, much factual data in the fields mentioned has been accumulating, but most of it remains untouched, mainly because it is still regarded as politically sensitive material.

B. THE PERIOD OF THE KOMBEDS

Much of the early research into the nature of the agrarian revolution, the partition of the land, and its socio-economic impact upon rural Russia still retains its importance and originality.[33]

voennogo kommunizma. (Moscow, 1930). T. Zelenov, "K istorii vozniknoveniia selskokhoziaistvennykh kommun i artelei v SSSR (1918 g.)." Krasnyi arkhiv, No. 4 (101), (1940), 122-148. B. N. Knipovich, Ocherk deiatelnosti Narodnogo komissariata zemledeliia za tri goda (1917-1920). (Moscow, 1920). A. I. Sviderskii, Prodovolstvennaia politika. (Moscow, 1920).

[32]N. P. Skrynev, Pervye shagi sotsialisticheskogo pereustroistva selskogo khoziaistva v 1918-1920 gg. (Moscow, 1951).

[33]P. G. Arkhangelskii, Ocherki po istorii zemelnogo stroia Rossii. (Kazan, 1920). B. N. Knipovich, Ocherk deiatelnosti Narodnogo komissariata zemledeliia za tri goda (1917-1920). (Moscow, 1920). A. I. Khriashcheva, Gruppy i klassy v krestianstve. (Moscow, 1926). V. Keller and I. Romanenko, Pervye itogi agrarnoi reformy. Opty issledovania rezultatov sovremennogo zemleustroistva na primere Zadonskogo uezda

301

These pioneering publications, however, were not always able to deal adequately with the complex problems that were brought about by widespread land parcelling or slow technological improvement in agriculture, nor were they helpful in forecasting the disturbing developments that were yet to follow. There is perhaps one exception, the admirable study written in 1923 by S. M. Dubrovskii on the agrarian economy and its prospects.[34] M. N. Pokrovskii considered the agrarian situation a bourgeois-democratic revolution or, as he called it, "an indigenous revolution," which came about parallel with the proletarian socialist one in urban Russia. So did L. N. Kritsman, who wrote about the "dual character" of events in Russia since 1917: the anti-capitalist revolution in urban Russia and the anti-feudal movement throughout rural Russia. In broader terms, there were two simultaneous revolutions: one of bourgeois and the other of peasant nature.[35]

The situation, however, was not that simple and delimitations of this nature only obscured actual developments. Simultaneously with the liquidation of the remnants of "feudalism" there emerged the desire to solve the deeply entrenched legacy of feudal problems by social methods. A class struggle was bound to arise within rural areas as well as between rural and urban Russia. In Communist parlance, the effort to find a final solution aligned the poor peasantry with the city proletariat against the kulak class or the rural bourgeoisie. The question often asked was, why did this dual revolution come about in backward Russia and not in the advanced western nations? Historians like Pokrovskii or Kritsman attributed the events to historical coincidence, but Lenin interpreted it as an inevitable stage necessary for the October Revolution in the villages to be transformed from a bourgeois-democratic movement into a higher socialistic stage. For this reason many historians curtailed their studies of the agrarian revolution, ending with the act of land partition as the final stage. The *Kombeds* were barely mentioned, while collectivism was only a development in the distant future.

In the early 1930's, under the impact of termination of the New Economic Policy and the introduction of general economic planning, agricultural policy came under intensive reexamination. The drive against the kulak class and the campaign for collectivization led writers to reevaluate the agrarian situation in an entirely different light. Partitioning of land was regarded as

Voronezhskoi gubernii. (Voronezh, 1922). I. A. Kirillov, *Ocherki zemleustroistva za tri goda revoliutsii (1917-1920).* (Petrograd, 1922). P. N. Pershin, "Formy zemlepolzovaniia." *O Zemle. Sbornik.* Issue I. (Moscow, 1921).

[34]S. M. Dubrovskii, *Ocherki russkoi revoliutsii.* Issue I, *Selskoe khoziaistvo.* (Moscow, 1923).

[35]I. A. Kirillov, *Ocherki zemleustroistva za tri goda revoliutsii (1917-1920).* (Petrograd, 1922). V. Keller and I. Romanenko, *Pervye itogi agrarnoi reformy. Opyt issledovaniia rezultatov sovremennogo zemleustroistva na primere Zadonskogo uezda Voronezhskoi gubernii.* (Voronezh, 1922). M. N. Pokrovskii, *Kontrrevoliutsiia za 4 goda.* (Moscow, 1922). L. N. Kritsman, *Geroicheskii period velikoi russkoi revoliutsii.* (Moscow, 1926). E. N. Kochetovskaia, *Natsionalizatsiia zemli v SSSR.* (Moscow, 1947).

a completed phase, having given way to the socialist revolution. The *Kombeds* were now interpreted as an early phase which had served its purpose in facilitating the seizure and partition of the land; the new situation now required a further step—socialization and mechanization of agriculture which only collectivism could accomplish.[36]

Here, as elsewhere, the cult of the individual took a heavy toll: most of the writers usually had their eyes on the *History of the VKP (b)* and saw to it that they would not digress from the official interpretation of Soviet agrarian policy. Some writers, like M. I. Snegirev and E. A. Lutskii, managed to present fair accounts of agrarian developments, but most others found escape in compilatory work, publishing source materials, limiting explanatory remarks to the barest minimum, or resorting to a vacuous preface—a Soviet version of "publish or perish."[37]

It is of interest to note that histories of the *Kombeds* emphasize mainly the role these organizations played in meeting the national food crisis. The story of the socio-economic consequences of their activities, including their fight to obtain grain to supply the cities, has been deemphasized. This story was published in part during the late 1940's and the 1950's, when writers like I. A. Koniukov and N. Skrypnev undertook to record the earliest struggles for the establishment of the collective system. A closely related subject studied by others is the introduction of the huge state farms, the *sovkhozes*.[38]

Much research has been done in examining Lenin's so-called Land Nationalization Decree and the subsequent confiscation of landlord estates and organization of the *Kombeds*. Here too, the bulk of the written works have emphasized organizational and political aspects, while the socio-economic ramifications have barely been touched. Attempts to trace the social impact

[36] *Sovety v epokhu voennogo kommunizma (1918-1921 gg.). Sbornik dokumentov.* Part 1. (Moscow, 1928). *Komitety bednoty. Sbornik materialov.* Vols. I-II. (Moscow, 1933). *Kombedy RSFSR. Sbornik dekretov i dokumentov.* (Moscow, 1933). *Kombedy Voronezhskoi i Kurskoi oblastei. Materialy po istorii komitetov bednoty.* (Voronezh, 1935). See also A. V. Shestakov, *Klassovaia borba v derevne Tsentralno-Chernozemnoi Oblasti (TsChO) v epokhu voennogo kommunizma.* Issue 1. (Voronezh, 1930). I. T. Kizrin, *K istorii komitetov bednoty.* (Voronezh, 1932). E. A. Sokolova, *Komitety derevenskoi bednoty.* (Leningrad, 1940).

[37] E. N. Kochetovskaia, *Natsionalizatsiia zemli v SSSR.* (Moscow, 1947). M. I. Snegirev, "Velikaia Oktiabrskaia sotsialisticheskaia revoliutsiia i raspredelenie zemel v 1917-1918 godakh." *Voprosy istorii,* No. 11 (1947), 3-28. E. A. Lutskii, "K istorii konfiskatsii pomeshchichikh imenii v 1917-1918 gg." *Izvestiia Akademii nauk SSSR. Seriia istorii i filosofii,* Vol. V, No. 6 (1948), 503-515. E. A. Lutskii, "Peredely zemli vesnoi 1918 g." *Izvestiia Akademii nauk SSSR. Seriia istorii i filosofii,* No. 3 (1949), 227-245. N. S. Zhuravleva, "Konfiskatsiia pomeshchichikh imenii v Tverskoi gubernii v 1917-1918 gg." *Istoricheskie zapiski,* No. 29 (1949), 48-65. L. A. Govorkov, "Voprosy konfiskatsii pomeshchichikh imenii v Kurskoi gubernii." *Uchenye zapiski Tambovskogo pedagogicheskogo instituta,* Vol. VII (1949).

[38] I. A. Koniukov, *Ocherki o pervykh etapakh razvitiia kollektivnogo zemledeliia 1917-1925 gg.* (Moscow, 1949). N. Skrypnev, *Pervye shagi sotsialisticheskogo*

of the agrarian revolution have been undertaken most timidly by a few writers such as E. I. Medvedev, I. E. Marchenko, and E. A. Lutskii, but these still remain a minority.[39] These works are mostly in the form of brief articles or brochures, rather than solid monographic studies. Among the few monographs several works stand out: one, by M. A. Rubach, is a detailed investigation of the agrarian situation in the Ukraine from September, 1917, to the summer of 1918; another one, by G. V. Sharapov, is an analysis of the Soviet agrarian policy during 1917-1920; a third is a study in progress by P. N. Pershin, who promises an extensive investigation of the entire field of agrarian policy during the Revolution. At the moment Pershin's work is far from being completed, the first book covering only the period to the October, 1917, Revolution. Finally, reports of the discussions held by Soviet historians on the policy of equalization and landownership, as a transitory step toward socialism, are of interest. One historian regards the unlawful seizure of the land by the Soviet peasantry as merely a political maneuver, taken in order to solidify cordial relations between urban and rural parts of the country. The interpretations led to long and interesting expressions of opinion during the ensuing debates.[40]

Agrarian reforms in the different constituent and autonomous republics

pereustroistva selskogo khoziaistva v 1918-1920 gg. (Moscow, 1951). V. N. Lavrentev, *Stroitelstvo sovkhozov v pervye gody Sovetskoi vlasti (1917-1920).* (Moscow, 1957). V. A. Milovanov, *Pervye shagi kolkhoznogo dvizheniia v Belorussii.* (Minsk, 1958). G. V. Sharapov, *Nachalo sotsialisticheskikh preobrazovanii v derevne v pervye gody Sovetskoi vlasti.* (Moscow, 1960). I. Kh. Ganzha, *Pershi kollektyvni gospodarstva na Ukraini.* (Kiev, 1960). V. M. Selunskaia, "Kommunisticheskaia partiia—organizator i rukovoditel stroitelstva pervykh sovkhozov i kolkhozov (noiabr 1917-1920 gg.)." *Vestnik MGU. Istoriko-filologicheskaia seriia,* No. 4 (1957). A. G. Dolgopolov, S. I. Rodionov, and P. A. Butylkin, "Organizatsiia i deiatelnost kollektivnykh khoziaistv v pervye gody Sovetskoi vlasti." *Istoriia SSSR,* No. 5 (1959), 80-97.

[39] E. I. Medvedev, *Agrarnye preobrazovaniia v Samarskoi derevne v 1917-1918 gg.* (Kuibyshev, 1958). V. M. Gubareva, *Razvertyvanie sotsialisticheskoi revoliutsii v derevne v 1918 godu. Po materialam Petrogradskoi gubernii.* (Leningrad, 1957). I. E. Marchenko, *Agrarnye preobrazovaniia v Belorussii v 1917-1918 gg.* (Minsk, 1959). V. R. Gerasimiuk, *Nachalo sotsialisticheskoi revoliutsii v derevne 1917-1918 gg.* (Moscow, 1958). V. P. Kopylov, "Konfiskatsiia pomeshchichikh imenii v Moskovskoi gubernii v 1917-1918 gg." *Trudy Moskovskogo istoriko-arkhivnogo instituta,* Vol. VI (1954). E. A. Lutskii, "Razvitie sotsialisticheskoi revoliutsii v derevne letom i oseniu 1918 g." *Istoriia SSSR,* No. 5 (1957), 56-85.

[40] M. A. Rubach, *Ocherki po istorii revoliutsionnogo preobrazovaniia agrarnykh otnoshenii na Ukraine v period provedeniia Oktiabrskoi revoliutsii.* (Kiev, 1957). P. N. Pershin, *Narisi agrarnoi revoliutsii v Rossii.* (Kiev, 1959). G. V. Sharapov, "O sushchnosti uravnitelnogo zemlepolzovaniia v Sovetskoi Rossii." *Voprosy istorii,* No. 3 (1957), 113-120. A. N. Lopatkin, "Agrarnaia programma bolshevikov v Velikoi Oktiabrskoi sotsialisticheskoi revoliutsii." *Voprosy istorii,* No. 4 (1957), 43-58.

of the Soviet Union have also been widely discussed. These reforms, it is commonly acknowledged, played a major part in transforming backward societies into a more advanced economic state by skipping entirely the capitalistic stage in their development. This phase is of particular significance to the peripheral states of the Soviet Union, where backward economic conditions yielded to most advanced technological, social, and economic developments. Notable examples are Uzbekistan, Kazakhstan, Kirgizia, Tadzhikstan, Turkmenia, and some of the autonomous republics.[41]

A conference held in 1928 on class stratification of the peasantry illustrates the widespread interest during the 1920's in the socio-economic problems of rural Russia. It was only after the introduction of forced collectivization in 1930-1931 that the interest in events of the 1920's declined. Everyone became absorbed with the outcome of collectivization. Very few writers have devoted themselves to the later phase of the agrarian revolution, but a few who accomplished commendable research in this period are K. M. Shuvaev, K. V. Loseva, and O. B. Dzhamalov.[42]

C. AGRICULTURE SINCE THE 1930's

Since the mid-1930's emphasis in agrarian history has been predominantly upon collectivization and the "liquidation of the remnants of the kulak elements." Several attempts were made to evaluate the agrarian reforms to date and derive some constructive lessons from the accumulated experience. A number of publications appeared in 1949, to mark the twentieth anniversary of the introduction of collectivization. None of these publications are noted for any high standard of scholarship; nonetheless, they constitute a landmark in the field. The authors in most cases disregard socio-economic

[41]G. Rizaev, *Kratkii ocherk zemelno-vodnoi reformy v Uzbekistane.* (Tashkent, 1947). P. Iu. Babadzhanova, *Partiinomassovaia rabota Kommunisticheskoi partii Uzbekistana v kishlake v period zemelno-vodnoi reformy (1925-1926).* (Tashkent, 1959). A. P. Kuchkin, "Likvidatsiia kazakhskikh baev-polufeodalov v 1928 g." *Istoricheskie zapiski,* No. 35 (1950), 3-35. A. P. Kuchkin, "Zemelnaia reforma v Kazakhstane v 1925-1927 gg." *Voprosy istorii,* No. 9 (1954). 25-34. N. R. Mangutov, *Agrarnye preobrazovaniia v Sovetskoi Buriatii (1917-1933 gg.).* (Ulan-Ude, 1960).

[42]K. M. Shuvaev, *Staraia i novaia derevnia. (Materialy issledovaniia s. Novo-Zhivotinnogo i der. Mokhovatki Berezovskogo raiona Voronezhskoi oblasti za 1901, 1907, 1926 i 1937 gg.).* (Moscow, 1937). A. E. Arina, G. G. Kotov, and K. V. Loseva, *Sotsialno-ekonomicheskie izmeneniia v derevne. Melitopolskii raion (1885-1938).* (Moscow, 1939). O. B. Dzhamalov, *Sotsialno-ekonomicheskie predposylki sploshnoi kollektivizatsii selskogo khoziaistva v Uzbekistane.* (Tashkent, 1950). S. I. Iliasov, "Perezhitki patriarkhalno-rodovykh i feodalno-burzhuaznykh otnoshenii u kirgizov do provedeniia sploshnoi kollektivizatsii." *Trudy Instituta iazyka, literatury, istorii Kirgizskogo filiala Akademii nauk SSSR,* Issue 2 (1945). See also A. P. Loginov, "O perekhodnoi forme proizvodstvennykh otnoshenii." *Voprosy filosofii,* No. 3 (1948), 92-104. G. E. Glezerman, *Bazis i nadstroika v sovetskom obshchestve.* (Moscow, 1954).

aspects of the events; their writings are subjective and display lack of broad knowledge and of ability to utilize archival materials. Nor are the sources that were utilized handled critically, for they are interpreted at times with excessive liberality. On occasion the writers have not even bothered to interpret the material, but have merely incorporated lengthy citations, occasionally out of season. Still, some of these writers demonstrate an earnest interest and desire to reexamine the turbulent years, in order to gain some historical perspective of the events concerned.[43]

In September, 1953, the plenary session of the Central Committee of the Communist Party resolved that the history of collectivization in the Soviet Union be reexamined in order to interpret the past anew and render a more acceptable appraisal and understanding of the present conditions. The need for a reexamination was expounded in the magazine *Kommunist* by M. P. Kim and G. N. Golikov, who outlined for the first time the deficiencies in former studies of recent history, including the history of collectivization, and suggested means of overcoming them.[44]

Since then several studies of higher caliber have appeared. These have examined the preliminary preparations for collectivization as well as execution of the project. A goodly number of new sources have been utilized, enabling writers to expand their field and strengthen the foundation upon which they rested their interpretation. Qualitatively speaking, most of the writings of this time far outstrip the former studies, offering more solid research, deeper insight, and more successful defense of the various theses. Furthermore, two authors even dared to deal with the ideologically risky subject of shortcomings in carrying out the transformation from a socialist into a collectivized system.[45] A whole series of publications appeared simultaneously on the difficulties the government encountered in extracting foodstuffs from the peasants, and the sharp clash that resulted from the enforced action. It led to the "expropriation of the kulak class," to the forcible confiscation of the motorized farm equipment owned by the kulaks, to the confiscation of the excessive land claims of individual peasants or of tracts on which hired labor was employed. Each of these measures proved to be of such complexity

---

[43]G. M. Ovsianikov, *Moskovskie bolsheviki v borbe za kollektivizatsiiu selskogo khoziaistva (1930-1934).* (Moscow, 1949). S. P. Trapeznikov, *Borba partii bolshevikov za kollektivizatsiiu selskogo khoziaistva v gody pervoi piatiletki.* (Moscow, 1951). B. A. Abramov, *Partiia bolshevikov—organizator borby za likvidatsiiu kulachestva kak klassa.* (Moscow, 1952). E. V. Seminikhina, *Bolsheviki Kazakhstana v borbe za kollektivizatsiiu selskogo khoziaistva.* (Alma-Ata, 1952).

[44]M. P. Kim and G. N. Golikov, "Nekotorye voprosy razrabotki istorii sovetskogo obshchestva." *Kommunist,* No. 5 (1954), 46-59, See also V. P. Danilov and Juan Visens, "O nekotorykh nedostatkakh v rabotakh po istorii kolkhoznogo dvizheniia v SSSR." *Voprosy istorii,* No. 1 (1954), 137-145.

[45]S. P. Trapeznikov, *Istoricheskii opyt KPSS v sotsialisticheskom preobrazovanii selskogo khoziaistva.* (Moscow, 1959). V. M. Selunskaia, *Borba KPSS za sotsialisticheskoe preobrazovanie selskogo khoziaistva.* (Moscow, 1961).

that they required separate monographic studies.[46] Incidentally, with reference to collectivization and its aftermath, one comes across such euphemistic references as the "reduction of the considerable portion of former kulaks," or "the liquidation of the kulak elements." What grim events are obscured by this phraseology! Will the future student of history be able to detect the true character of this "economic experiment," or will he be able even in a footnote to history to record the price paid for the "advanced stage of socialization"?[47]

D. COLLECTIVIZATION AND THE AGRICULTURAL COOPERATIVES

One of the most complex subjects in the field of economic history is, without doubt, the process of transforming the system of individual landholding into a socialized and collectivized one. The execution of this enormous plan meant radical changes in the entire socio-economic order, affecting, above all, the peasantry. Attempts at describing the early stages in the development of collective agricultural economy were made by a few writers, notably I. A. Koniukov and O. B. Dzhamalov. The former dealt mainly with the period of 1917-1925, in a study published originally during the mid-1920's and reissued in 1949. In 1954, M. A. Kraev published a monograph utiliz-

[46]G. A. Koniukhov, KPSS v borbe s khlebnymi zatrudneniiami v strane (1928-1929 gg.). (Moscow, 1960). G. A. Limonov, "Borba partiinykh organizatsii Urala za preodolenie khlebozagotovitelnykh trudnostei v 1927-1928 gg." Trudy Uralskogo politekhnicheskogo instituta. Sbornik 86. (Sverdlovsk, 1957). P. S. Zagorskii and F. K. Stoian, Naris istorii komiteta nezamozhnikh selian Ukraini. (Kiev, 1960). N. A. Lysenko, Deiatelnost Kommunisticheskoi partii Ukrainy po podgotovke k vospitaniiu kolkhoznykh kadrov v period kollektivizatsii selskogo khoziaistva (1930-1932). (Odessa, 1959). Iu. V. Arutiunian, Mekhanizatory selskogo khoziaistva SSSR, 1929-1957. (Moscow, 1960). Iu. S. Borisov, Podgotovka proizvodstvennykh kadrov selskogo khoziaistva v rekonstruktivnyi period. (Moscow, 1960). E. I. Larkina, Podgotovka kolkhoznykh kadrov v period massovoi kollektivizatsii. (Moscow, 1960). A. F. Chmyga, Ocherki po istorii kolkhoznogo dvizheniia na Ukraine (1921-1925 gg.). (Moscow, 1959). I. P. Iarkov, "Pervye kolkhozy Sibiri (1918-1926 gg.)." Trudy Novosibirskogo instituta inzhenerov vodnogo transporta, Issue 8 (1960). I. L. Sherman, "Organizatsionno-khoziaistvennoe razvitie kolkhozov Ukrainy v 1927-1928 gg." Nauchnye zapiski Kharkovskogo pedagogicheskogo instituta, Vol. XIX (1957). I. E. Ustiuzhin, Kolkhoznoe stroitelstvo v Tatarii v nachalnyi period industrializatsii strany (1926-1929 gg.). (Kazan, 1959). S. I. Sdobnov, Vozniknovenie i razvitie kolkhoznoi sobstvennosti v SSSR. (Moscow, 1956). V. V. Bondarenko, Razvitie obshchestvennogo khoziaistva kolkhozov Ukrainy v gody dovoennykh piatiletok. (Kiev, 1957).

[47]Sovetskaia istoricheskaia nauka ot XX k XXII sezdu KPSS. Istoriia SSSR. Sbornik statei (Moscow, 1962), 477. See also P. V. Semernin, "O likvidatsii kulachestva kak klassa." Voprosy istorii KPSS, No. 4 (1958), 72-85. V. K. Medvedev, "Likvidatsiia kulachestva v Nizhne-Volzhskom krae." Istoriia SSSR, No. 6 (1958), 9-29. I. Ia. Trifonov, Ocherki istorii klassovoi borby v SSSR v gody Nepa. (Moscow, 1960).

ing an impressive amount of data to present a general survey of agrarian development during the first two decades of the Soviet regime.[48]

During the Stalin period the theme was hardly touched, for self-evident reasons, and even subjects indirectly related were better left alone, unless one gave the official version. It was only during the latter half of the 1950's that Soviet historiography witnessed a revival of interest and the publication of various studies in the neglected field. It began with the publication of documents on agricultural developments, followed soon by some monographic contributions dealing with collectivization throughout the Soviet Union. Simultaneously, a number of conferences were organized in various parts of the country, and sessions held by the Academy of Sciences were dedicated to a multitude of problems concerning Soviet agriculture. There were also published a number of critical essays, analyzing the mass collectivization during the early 1930's, reintegrating former studies of the methods of enforcement and the impact of the whole event upon the peasantry.[49]

Various Soviet historical conferences were the scenes of discussions on touchy problems. The most notable were the ones held in the spring of 1957 in Alma-Ata, and in April, 1961, in Moscow. There was seeming agreement on such points as the anti-feudal nature of all agrarian reforms to date, or the bourgeois-democratic character of the reforms. But there was no common agreement on other issues. For instance, some argued that the 1925-1928 reforms in Kazakhstan, in Central Asia, were far from representing the aims of the Soviet government, since the chief object was the establishment of a socialist order. In the process of reforms, anti-feudal policies and feudal traditions were intertwined to a degree where the two became inseparable. This, according to some historians, was the reason there arose a serious block to further socialist advancement.[50]

Many writers who studied the history of the socialist agrarian reforms considered the early cooperative plans the forerunners of later collectivism

[48]I. A. Koniukov, *Ocherki o pervykh etapakh razvitiia kollektivnogo zemledeliia 1917-1925 gg.* (Moscow, 1949). O. B. Dzhamalov, *Sotsialno-ekonomicheskie predposylki splochnoi kollektivizatsii selskogo khoziaistva v Uzbekistane.* (Tashkent, 1950). M. A. Kraev, *Pobeda kolkhoznogo stroia v SSSR.* (Moscow, 1954). S. P. Trapeznikov, *Borba partii bolshevikov za kollektivizatsiiu selskogo khoziaistva v gody Stalinskoi piatiletki.* (Moscow, 1951).

[49]V. P. Danilov and Juan Visens. "O nekotorykh nedostatkakh v rabotakh po istorii massovogo kolkhoznogo dvizheniia v SSSR." *Voprosy istorii,* No. 1 (1954), 137-145. V. I. Pogudin, "Nekotorye voprosy istoriografii kollektivizatsii v SSSR." *Voprosy istorii,* No. 9 (1958), 119-134. V. P. Danilov, "Izuchenie istorii sovetskogo krestianstva." *Sovetskaia istoricheskaia nauka ot XX k XXII sezdu KPSS. Istoriia SSSR. Sbornik statei.* (Moscow, 1962), 449-493.

[50]The discussions as well as the different views are well summarized in *Voprosy istorii,* No. 8 (1960). See editorials, pp. 3-18 and pp. 19-21, "O profile i strukture zhurnala 'Voprosy istorii'." See also *Materialy Obedinennoi nauchnoi sessii, posviashchennoi istorii Srednei Azii i Kazakhstana epokhi sotsializma.* (Alma-Ata, 1958).

on a national scale. Prominent works on this theme that have appeared since the middle of the 1950's are by S. P. Trapeznikov and V. M. Selunskaia.[51] Some of the other writers who contributed to the lively discussions on the subject used formerly neglected source materials to study the fate of the cooperatives after nation-wide collectivization was enforced. Still others scrutinized the various forms of cooperative organizations which managed to survive after mass collectivization went into effect. Despite the abundance of material published, there is still a conspicuous absence of a good overall survey of the subject; there is no study in depth or breadth, only a series of articles and books on specialized fields such as cooperatives for seed cultivation, credit operations, marketing, and allied functions. In addition, many of these fail to examine the social conditions among the peasants who formed these cooperatives or to indicate their predominant occupation; nor do they demonstrate the economic effects the cooperatives might have had upon their respective communities. Nor is there any clear picture of the role the cooperatives have played in the eventual transformation of these communities into collectivized farm organizations.[52]

In 1963, A. I. Kossoi published an essay in the periodical *Voprosy ekonomiki*, in which he challenged a thesis presented by Stalin in 1926 and widely accepted since in historical literature. Stalin's basic theme was that prior to 1923 Lenin had regarded cooperatives as one form of state capitalism, while he speculated on the possibility of making state capitalism the basic form of the agrarian economy. In 1923 Lenin modified his views to describe cooperatives as actually socialistic in nature. Capitalism, he said, had failed to adapt itself to the new economy while socialist industry kept

[51]S. P. Trapeznikov, *Istoricheskii opyt KPSS v sotsialisticheskom preobrazovanii selskogo khoziaistva.* (Moscow, 1959). S. P. Trapeznikov, *Istoricheskii opyt KPSS v osushchestvlenii leninskogo kooperativnogo plana.* (Moscow, 1965). V. M. Selunskaia, *Borba KPSS za sotsialisticheskoe preobrazovanie selskogo khoziaistva.* (Moscow, 1961). N. G. Karotamm, *K istorii ucheniia o sotsialisticheskom selskom khoziaistve.* (Moscow, 1959). I. I. Sergeev, "K voprosu o razrabotke V. I. Leninym kooperativnogo plana v pervye gody Sovetskoi vlasti (noiabr 1917-1920 gg.)." *Uchenye zapiski Saratovskogo gosudarstvennogo universiteta,* Vol. 73. (Saratov, 1959). V. M. Selunskaia, "Razrabotka V. I. Leninym kooperativnogo plana." *Voprosy istorii KPSS,* No. 2 (1960), 99-119. M. V. Gamaiunov, "Leninskoe uchenie o kooperatsii." *Doklady Selskokhoziaistvennoi akademii imeni K. A. Timiriazeva.* Issue 54. (Moscow, 1960). I. B. Berkhin, "Osnovnye etapy formirovaniia kooperativnogo plana V. I. Lenina." *Istoriia sovetskogo krestianstva i kolkhoznogo stroitelstva v SSSR. Materialy nauchnoi sessii sostoiavsheisia 18-21 aprelia 1961 goda v Moskve.* (Moscow, 1963).

[52]I. G. Bulatov, *Kooperatsiia i eё rol v podgotovke sploshnoi kollektivizatsii.* (Moscow, 1960). I. G. Bulatov, *Borba Kommunisticheskoi partii za razvitie kooperativnogo dvizheniia v SSSR (1921-1923 gg.).* (Moscow, 1961). V. A. Golikov, *Vazhneishie etapy razvitiia selskokhoziaistvennoi kooperatsii v SSSR (1921-1929 gg.).* (Moscow, 1963). A. Karevskii, "Razvitie selskokhoziaistvennoi kooperatsii v Srednem Povolzhe." *Uchenye zapiski Kuibyshevskogo pedagogicheskogo instituta.* Issue 18. (Kuibyshev, 1957). M. I. Ovchinnikova, "Iz istorii proizvodstvennogo

gaining ground. Kossoi challenged this interpretation, convincingly arguing that in 1921 as in 1923 Lenin believed that the cooperatives were only one form of state capitalism, and that socialism was not at all the issue. The actual question was, what was the function of the cooperatives? If the cooperatives appeared to be a form of state capitalism, then they also served as a means of state control over private capital. If this was true it was justifiable to regard the cooperatives as a force leading toward collectivism. In other words, there was a difference between the immediate and the prospective value of the cooperatives. This, according to Kossoi, must have been the viewpoint of Lenin, and not the one advanced by Stalin and unchallenged during his lifetime.[53]

The reasons for the mass collectivization begun in the early 1930's are still subject to debate by Soviet scholars. Most of the writings on the subject are filled with emotional fervor, ideological conviction, or pride of accomplishment, but they show hardly any objective effort to analyze the issues involved. Among those who believed in the urgent need for general farm collectivization the popular argument was that the land parcelled out among the peasantry after the October Revolution led to an intolerable situation. Agriculture became wasteful, unscientific, and unproductive. Reasonable as this argument sounds, it becomes less convincing upon closer scrutiny. For illustration, E. N. Kochetovskaia states that between 1917 and 1928 the number of farms increased from sixteen million to twenty-five million. Yet the 1916 census shows that during that year there were already twenty-one million farms. Furthermore, some writers have shown that the increase in small farm holdings was by no means as catastrophic as it might seem: the tendency toward increased land parcelling did not seriously interfere with the general production in the country. This did not mean a complete defense of land distribution and small farming, for the undesirable effects upon the agrarian economy are shown quite clearly by V. N. Iakovetskii.[54]

kooperirovaniia krestianstva na Severnom Kavkaze (1928-1929)." *Uchenye zapiski Rostovskogo gosudarstvennogo universiteta*, Vol. 63, Issue 3. (Rostov, 1958). M. P. Gubenko, "Selskokhoziaistvennaia kooperatsiia·v nachale massovoi kollektivizatsii (1929-1931 gg.)." *Istoricheskie zapiski*, No. 74 (1963), 3-37. V. P. Danilov, "O prosteishikh formakh proizvodstvennogo kooperirovaniia krestianstva." *Doklady i soobshcheniia Instituta istorii AN SSSR*. Issue 3 (1954). V. P. Danilov, "O kharaktere sotsialno-ekonomicheskikh otnoshenii sovetskogo krestianstva do kollektivizatsii selskogo khoziaistva." *Istoriia sovetskogo krestianstva i kolkhoznogo stroitelstva v SSSR. Materialy nauchnoi sessii, sostoiavsheisia 18-21 aprelia 1961 goda v Moskve. See also Doklady i soobshcheniia Instituta istorii AN SSSR*, Issue 3. *Ocherki po istorii kolletivizatsii selskogo khoziaistva v soiuznykh respublikakh.* (Moscow, 1963).

[53] A. I. Kossoi, "O prirode i roli kooperatsii v perekhodnyi period ot kapitalizma k sotsializmu." *Voprosy ekonomiki*, No. 2 (1963), 89-92. G. M. Krzhizhanovskii, *Tovaroobmen i planovaia rabota.* (Moscow, 1924).

[54] V. N. Iakovetskii, "Istoriia sovetskogo krestianstva i kolkhoznogo stroitelstva v SSSR." *Materialy nauchnoi sessii, sostoiavsheisia 18-21 aprelia 1961 goda v*

Another argument was that by the end of the 1920's the small farm system had virtually exhausted its potential for economic advancement, an argument repeatedly presented in Soviet historiography. Yet this thesis too has often been challenged, since neither statistical data nor any other evidence quite supports it. This point particularly was discussed at great length at the Sixteenth Party Conference in 1962.[55] Scholars have clearly shown that the level of the agricultural economy, including grain production, on the eve of collectivization was higher than before 1914. It was equally well established that the grain problem that came about at the end of the 1920's was not because of a drop in production, but the result of an enormous increase in demand for commodities resulting from the intensive industrialization program. The situation revealed the backwardness of the agricultural economy, and the alarming disproportion between the rising demand for agricultural produce on one hand and shortage of industrial commodities on the other.[56]

Most of the studies of mass collectivization cover the preliminary period; few go beyond 1930-1932, the two years when the enforcement took on truly brutal dimensions. The only aspect that has been fairly explored was the establishment of the Machine-Tractor Stations and their role in collectivization.[57] This discussion, however, was never carried beyond its narrow limits, to link, for instance, the establishment of the Stations with other related developments in the general process of collectivization. The absence of an adequate study in this area leaves a wide gap in Soviet historiography. Since the end of the 1950's, the formation of a skilled agricultural working class to man the MTS was studied by several historians. However, the field is still fraught with numerous difficulties as far as location of materials and publication are concerned.[58] Several works based on primary sources

Moskve." (Moscow, 1962). V. P. Danilov, "K itogam izucheniia istorii sovetskogo krestianstva i kolkhoznogo stroitelstva s SSSR." *Voprosy istorii*, No. 8 (1960), 34-64. V. P. Danilov, *Sozdanie materialno-tekhnicheskikh predposylok kollektivizatsii selskogo khoziaistva v SSSR*. (Moscow, 1957). E. N. Kochetovskaia, *Natsionalizatsiia zemli v SSSR*. (Moscow, 1952). E. N. Kochetovskaia, *Natsionalizatsiia zemli i kolkhozy v SSSR*. (Moscow, 1958).

[55]*XVI konferentsiia VKP (b). Stenograficheskii otchet*. (Moscow, 1962). N. I. Prokopenko, *KPPS v borbe za podgotovku massovogo kolkhoznogo dvizheniia*. (Moscow, 1961).

[56]V. P. Danilov, *Sozdanie materialno-tekhnicheskikh predposylok kollektivizatsii selskogo khoziaistva v SSSR*. (Moscow, 1957). Iu. A. Moshkov, "Zernovaia problema v gody kollektivizatsii selskogo khoziaistva." *Istoriia sovetskogo krestianstva i kolkhoznogo stroitelstva v SSSR. Materialy nauchnoi sessii, sostoiavsheisia 18-21 aprelia 1961 goda v Moskve*. (Moscow, 1963). *Postroenie fundamenta sotsialisticheskoi ekonomiki v SSSR 1926-1932*. (Moscow, 1960).

[57]P. I. Denisenko, "Iz istorii mashinno-traktornykh kolonn i pervykh mashinno-traktornykh stantsii." *Istoricheskie zapiski*, No. 48 (1954), 248-263.

[58]N. A. Lysenko, *Deiatelnost Kommunisticheskoi partii Ukrainy po podgotovke i vospitaniiu kolkhoznykh kadrov v period kollektivizatsii selskogo khoziaistva*

discuss the social conditions that prevailed at the time collectivization was enforced, or the influence of the kulak element upon the rural communities.[59] Friction between the kulaks and the authorities has already been dealt with and these studies reveal that state officials encountered considerable difficulty in gathering the grain they expected from the peasantry. The problem was discussed at length at the Fifteenth Party Congress, at which time the collectivization program was already envisaged as the only solution.[60]

The growth of collective farms prior to collectivization has been described by several authors, particularly with regard to the years 1926-1928.[61] The question as to when, precisely, mass collectivization actually began was often debated in Soviet historical literature. Several interesting studies

(1930-1932). (Moscow, 1959). Iu. V. Arutiunian, *Mekhanizatory selskogo khoziaistva SSSR 1929-1957 gg.* (Moscow, 1960). Iu. S. Borisov, *Podgotovka proizvodstvennykh kadrov selskogo khoziaistva v rekonstruktivnyi period.* (Moscow, 1960). E. I. Larkina, *Podgotovka kolkhoznykh kadrov v period massovoi kollektivizatsii.* (Moscow, 1960).

[59]V. P. Danilov, "Sotsialno-ekonomicheskie otnosheniia v sovetskoi derevne nakanune kollektivizatsii." *Istoricheskie zapiski,* No. 55 (1956), 89-138. V. P. Danilov, "Zemelnye otnosheniia v sovetskoi dokolkhoznoi derevne." *Istoriia SSSR,* No. 3 (1958), 90-128. I. Sh. Frenkel, "Sotsialno-ekonomicheskoe polozhenie krestianstva v Kurskoi gubernii nakanune kollektivizatsii." *Uchenye zapiski Kurskogo pedagogicheskogo instituta.* Issue 8 (1958).

[60]See *KPSS v rezoliutsiiakh i resheniiakh sezdov, konferentsii i plenumov TsK.* (Moscow, 1954). Part 2. (1924-1930). See particularly pp. 450-491. G. A. Koniukhov, *KPSS v borbe s zatrudneniiami v strane (1928-1929 gg.).* (Moscow, 1960). V. M. Rezvanov, "KPSS v borbe za preodolenie khlebnykh zatrudnenii v 1927-1928 gg." *Uchenye zapiski Rostovskogo gosudarstvennogo universiteta,* Vol. 31, Issue 1 (1955). P. S. Zagorskii and F. K. Stoian, *Naris istorii komitetiv nezamozhnikh selian Ukrainy.* (Kiev, 1960). I. S. Stepichev, *Borba Irkutskoi organizatsii KPSS za kollektivizatsiiu selskogo khoziaistva (1928-1930 gg.).* (Irkutsk, 1958). I. S. Stepichev, ed., *O nekotorykh voprosakh stroitelstva sotsializma v Vostochnoi Sibiri.* (Irkutsk, 1968). I. S. Stepichev, *Pobeda leninskogo kooperativnogo plana v vostochnosibirskoi derevne.* (Irkutsk, 1966). F. M. Podchafurov, *Tulskie kommunisty v period podgotovki massovogo kolkhoznogo dvizheniia (1924-1929 gg.).* (Moscow, 1959). B. A. Abramov, *Organizatorskaia rabota partii po osushchestvleniiu leninskogo kooperativnogo plana.* (Moscow, 1960). P. M. Diuvbanov, *Borba tatarskoi partiinoi organizatsii za podgotovku uslovii sploshnoi kollektivizatsii selskogo khoziaistva.* (Moscow, 1961).

[61]I. A. Koniukov, *Ocherki o pervykh etapakh razvitiia kollektivnogo zemledeliia 1917-1925 gg.* (Moscow, 1949). A. F. Chmyga, *Ocherki po istorii kolkhoznogo dvizheniia na Ukraine (1921-1925 gg.).* (Moscow, 1959). A. K. Kasian, "Pervye shagi kolkhoznogo stroitelstva v omskoi derevne v pervye gody Nepa (1921-1927 gg.)." *Uchenye zapiski Omskogo pedagogicheskogo instituta.* Issue 9 (Omsk, 1958). I. L. Sherman, "Organizatsionno-khoziaistvennoe razvitie kolkhozov Ukrainy v 1927-1928 gg." *Nauchnye zapiski Kharkovskogo pedagogicheskogo instituta,* Vol. XIX (Kharkov, 1957). A. S. Kuvshinskii, *Kolkhoznoe stroitelstvo v Mariiskoi ASSR v 1918-1929 gg.* (Kazan, 1959). I. E. Ustiuzhin, *Kolkhoznoe*

offer different dates.[62] During the early 1960's several analytical essays examined vital documentary collections published by the commission in charge of the collectivization and of the "liquidation of the kulak class."[63] Along with these have been also published accounts of the campaign conducted during the same period, urgently demanding collectivization. These records also describe the role played by local soviets during these critical years.[64]

Another subject well treated in Soviet historiography is the role the urban working class played in rural collectivization, or, in Soviet parlance, "hosting during the period of social transformation of the village."[65] During the campaign many errors in enforcement policy were committed which were euphemistically acknowledged much later as "dizziness from success," and for that reason the tempo of enforcement was slowed down. Among those who discussed the errors committed was S. P. Trapeznikov, who dealt with the arbitrary nature of policy enforcement, with the failure to summon the party conference to debate some of the vital issues, and the failure to send

stroitelstvo v Tatarii v nachalnyi period industrializatsii strany (1926-1929 gg.). (Kazan, 1959).

[62]G. A. Koniukhov, *KPSS v borbe s khlebnymi zatrudneniiami v strane (1928-1929 gg.).* (Moscow, 1960). S. P. Trapeznikov, *Istoricheskii opyt KPSS v sotsialisticheskom preobrazovanii selskogo khoziaistva.* (Moscow, 1959).

[63]N. A. Ivnitskii, "O nachalnom etape sploshnoi kollektivizatsii (osen 1929—vesna 1930 gg.)." *Voprosy istorii KPSS*, No. 4 (1962), 55-71. M. L. Bogdenko, "K istorii nachalnogo etapa sploshnoi kollektivizatsii selskogo khoziaistva SSSR." *Voprosy istorii*, No. 5 (1963), 19-35. N. V. Efremenkov, "Nachalo massovogo kolkhoznogo dvizheniia v uralskoi derevne." *Istoricheskie zapiski*, No. 74 (1963), 38-63.

[64]B. A. Abramov, *Organizatorskaia rabota partii po osushchestvleniiu leninskogo kooperativnogo plana.* (Moscow, 1956). G. L. Sanzhiev, *Kommunisticheskaia partiia—organizator pobedy kolkhoznogo stroia v Buriat-Mongolii.* (Moscow, 1957). S. D. Kakabaev, *Borba Kommunisticheskoi partii Turkmenistana za kollektivizatsiiu selskogo khoziaistva (1930-1934 gg.).* (Ashkhabad, 1959). E. P. Zagainov, *Selskie kommunisty v borbe za sozdanie kolkhoznogo stroia.* (Moscow, 1960). F. D. Pidzharyi, *Kommunistichna partiia Ukrainy v borothi za peremogu kolgosnogo ladu.* (Kiev, 1960). A. K. Tekuev, *Borba Kabardino-Balkarskoi partorganizatsii za sotsialisticheskoe preobrazovanie selskogo khoziaistva.* (Nalchik, 1961). K. K. Kamilov, *Rol selskikh Sovetov Uzbekistana v razvitii kolkhoznogo khoziaistva.* (Tashkent, 1960). Iu. S. Kukushkin, *Rol selskikh Sovetov v sotsialisticheskom pereustroistve derevni, 1929-1932 gg. po materialam RSFSR.* (Moscow, 1962). B. M. Mitupov and G. L. Sanzhiev, *Rukovodstvo Buriatskoi partiinoi organizatsii kulturnoi revoliutsiei v respublike, 1929-1937 gg.* (Ulan-Ude, 1962).

[65]N. P. Spektor, *Partiia—organizator shefstva rabochikh nad derevnei.* (Moscow, 1957). R. Ia. Rozenfelt, *Dvadtsatitysiachniki.* (Moscow, 1957). S. S. Ivashkin, *Rabochii klass v borbe za pobedu kolkhoznogo stroia v Mordovii.* (Alma-Ata, 1957). S. S. Ivashkin, *Rol sovetskogo rabochego klassa v sotsialisticheskom preobrazovanii khoziaistva Kazakhstana.* (Alma-Ata, 1962). L. V. Gentshke, *Shef-*

qualified men to rural communities to deal with the explosive situation created by the harsh administrative measures applied.[66] The acknowledgement of "dizziness from success" explained the errors only in part and ascribed the failures to causes other than the real ones. It was this "dizziness" that caused the departure of many peasants from the collective farms, an exodus lasting until the end of 1930. What percentage left the villages, and where these went, remain to be determined. Most of the available studies are based on sources published during 1929 and early 1930, which discuss the "great crisis," but fail to present a full picture of it.[67] The period that followed, from the autumn of 1930 to the end of 1932, is by no means entirely explored, and should be pursued further.[68]

E. AGRICULTURAL HISTORY SINCE 1953

Much of the new research accomplished since the mid-1950's covers developments in the eastern part of the Soviet Union. Collectivization in the economically backward republics raised peculiarly difficult problems, turning on the basic question whether the advanced stage of economic development could be successfully imposed in such areas and the capitalistic phase skipped altogether. Prior to 1953 most writers handled the complex issue rather casually, mentioning no specific localities or conditions, or names of responsible figures; whatever was mentioned fell within the party line. Later writers handled each republic as a separate unit, discussing peculiarities that affected the local socialist reforms, and the nature of opposition to them. It was acknowledged by now that the different developmental levels in each of the republics pre-

stvo rabochikh Uzbekistana nad kishlakom 1924-1930 gg. (Tashkent, 1966). L. V. Gentshke, Istoricheskii opyt uchastiia Uzbekistana v sotsialisticheskom stroitelstve, 1926-1932 gg. (Tashkent, 1966). K. K. German, Rol rabochego klassa v pobede kolkhoznogo stroia v Belorussii (1929-1934 gg.). (Minsk, 1963). P. M. Diuvbanov, Rol rabochego klassa v sotsialisticheskom pereustroistve selskoi Tatarii. (Kazan, 1963). M. I. Gioev, Borba bolshevikov Tereka za razreshenie agrarnogo voprosa v period pobedy sotsialisticheskoi revoliutsii i ustanovlenie sovetskoi vlasti, mart 1917—fevral 1919 gg. (Ordzhonikidze, 1966).

[66]S. P. Trapeznikov, Istoricheskii opyt KPSS v sotsialisticheskom preobrazovanii selskogo khoziaistva. (Moscow, 1959). N. A. Ivnitskii, "O nachalnom etape sploshnoi kollektivizatsii (osen 1929—vesna 1930 g.)." Voprosy istorii KPSS, No. 4 (1962), 55-71.

[67]M. Molchanov, Pobeda kolkhoznogo stroia na Donu i Kubani. (Rostov, 1960). V. K. Medvedev, Krutoi povorot. (Iz istorii kollektivizatsii selskogo khoziaistva Nizhnego Povolzhia). (Saratov, 1961). V. K. Medvedev, Povolzhskaia derevnia v period kombedov. (Saratov, 1966). V. K. Medvedev, Oktiabr v Povolzhie. (Saratov, 1967). P. N. Sharova, Kollektivizatsiia selskogo khoziaistva v Tsentralno-Chernozemnoi oblasti (1928-1932 gg.). (Moscow, 1963).

[68]I. E. Zelenin, "Kolkhoznoe stroitelstvo v SSSR v 1931-1932 gg. K itogam sploshnoi kollektivizatsii selskogo khoziaistva." Istoriia SSSR, No. 6 (1960), 19-39.

sented different problems, and only through a detailed investigation of all the factors could one arrive at a common denominator. Collectivization assumed entirely different forms, for example, in such areas as Central Asia, Buriatia, and Iakutia.[69]

Recent writings have defined more clearly the chronological framework into which the period of mass collectivization in the eastern part of the Soviet Union might be fitted. One encounters illuminating discussions on the peculiar difficulties faced by officials in the various regions where feudal institutions still survived, and cultural, political, or economic backwardness stubbornly resisted all changes. Still, collectivization was applied willy-nilly, beginning in 1930, affecting such wide areas as Kirgizia, Tadzhikstan, Turk-menia, Buriatia, and Iakutia. In these areas the struggle against collectivization lasted longer than anywhere else in the country. While mass collectivization was carried out in some of these places by the end of 1932, in most of them the process of enforcement continued throughout the second five-year plan.[70]

It is regrettable that one finds little in Soviet historiography dealing with the sociological or economic reverberations that took place when people who were still in a nomadic state were suddenly compelled to accept mechanized farming based on advanced collective principles. There is hardly any indica-tion of the impact the application of the collectivized economy had upon

[69]A. B. Tursunbaev, *Pobeda kolkhoznogo stroia v Kazakhstane.* (Moscow, 1957). *Ocherki po istorii Tadzhikstana.* Vol. I (Moscow, 1957). A. A. Uzbekova, *Po-beda kolkhoznogo stroia v Iakutskoi ASSR.* (Moscow, 1958). Ia. Sharipov, *Po-beda kolkhoznogo stroia v Bukharskoi oblasti.* (Moscow, 1958). M. S. Dzhunu-sov, *O nekapitalisticheskom puti razvitii kirgizskogo naroda k sotsializmu.* (Moscow, 1958). O. B. Dzhamalov, "Iz istorii kollektivizatsii selskogo khoziaistva v Uzbeki-stane." *Voprosy istorii,* No. 11 (1958), 45-61. P. K. Alpatskii, *K istorii osedaniia kochevykh i polukochevykh khoziaistv Kirgizii.* (Moscow, 1959). P. V. Vradii, "Tozy v Kirgizii." *Trudy Instituta istorii AN Kirgizskoi SSR.* Issue 4 (1958). G. L. Sanzhiev, "Nekotorye voprosy iz istorii kollektivizatsii selskogo khoziaistva Buriatii." *Zapiski Buriatskogo nauchno-issledovatelskogo instituta kultury.* Vol. XXV (1958). Kh. N. Drikker, *K istorii kollektivizatsii selskogo khoziaistva v Tadzhikistane v period pervoi i vtoroi piatiletki (1929-1937).* (Stalinabad, 1959). Sh. Iusupov, "Iz istorii perekhoda kochevogo kazakhskogo naseleniia k osedlosti." *Voprosy istorii,* No. 3 (1960), 34-49. N. R. Mangutov, *Agrarnye preobrazovaniia v Sovetskoi Buriatii (1917-1933 gg.).* (Ulan-Ude, 1960). S. E. Tolbybekov, L. A. Rakhlis, and M. G. Isaeva, "Perekhod Kazakhstana ot polufeodalnoi kolonialnoi ekonomiki k sotsialisticheskoi, minuia kapitalisticheskuiu stadiiu razvitiia." *Trudy Instituta ekonomiki AN Kazakhskoi SSR,* No. 5 (1960). *Minuia kapitalizm. (O perekhode k sotsializmu respublik Srednei Azii i Kazakhstana).* (Moscow, 1961). S. I. Iliasov, *Pobeda sotsialisticheskikh proizvodstvennykh otnoshenii v selskom khoziaistve Kirgizii.* (Frunze, 1961). See also *Sotsialisticheskoe narodnoe khoziai-stvo SSSR v 1933-1940 gg.* (Moscow, 1963), Chap. 11.

[70]*Istoriia Uzbekskoi SSSR.* Vol. II. (Moscow, 1957). *Istoriia Turkmenskoi SSR.* Vol. II. (1957). *Istoriia Kazakhskoi SSSR.* Vol. II. (1960). *Minuia kapitalizm. (O perekhode k sotsializmu respublik Srednei Azii i Kazakhstana).* (Moscow, 1961). *Trudy ekonomiki AN Kazakhskoi SSR,* No. 5 (1960).

this truly medieval society. To be sure, it has been admitted that a realistic assessment of conditions in the countries cited above was lacking at times. Forced collectivization, in official parlance, "was not in accordance with local economic peculiarities," and for that reason it was feared that serious unrest might develop.[71] These problems were usually attributed to the inefficiency of local officials or local party organizations. In describing the enforcement of mass collectivization, historians hardly mention errors in policy, in tempo of enforcement, or in administrative efficiency.[72]

The first writer to discuss the possible fallacies of forcible collectivization was A. B. Tursunbaev, who dealt with conditions in Kazakhstan. The author does not offer a full discussion of this politically touchy question, but he is one of the first to point out the high price that was exacted from the nomadic and semi-nomadic people by the application of socialism.[73] The subject has also been investigated by historians of other regions in Central Asia, though far less thoroughly than in Kazakhstan, but in general there has been no concentrated effort to explore the theme seriously or fully.[74]

Collectivization in other areas proceeded with noticeable differences. As an illustration, in the area of the Urals and of the Volga, where the population was often heterogeneous, the absence of a nationalistic feeling caused events to differ from those in Kazakhstan and other parts of Central Asia.[75]

In due course collectivization assumed common characteristics as tribal,

[71]See, for instance, *KPSS v rezoliutsiiakh i resheniiakh.* Part III (Moscow, 1954).

[72]See *Istoriia Kazakhskoi SSSR.* Vol. II. (Moscow, Alma-Ata, 1960). Sh. Iusupov, "Iz istorii perekhoda kochevogo kazakhskogo naseleniia k osedlosti." *Voprosy istorii,* No. 3 (1960), 34-49. P. K. Alpatskii, *K istorii osedaniia kochevykh i polukochevykh khoziaistv Kirgizii.* (Moscow, 1959). See also M. Irkaev, Iu. Nikolaev, and Ia. Sharipov, *Ocherki po istorii Tadzhikistana.* (Moscow, 1957). Also Ia. Sharipov, *Iz istorii postroeniia fundamenta sotsializma v Tadzhikistane (1929-1932).* (Stalinabad, 1960).

[73]A. B. Tursunbaev, *Pobeda kolkhoznogo stroia v Kazakhstane.* (Alma-Ata, 1957).

[74]Kh. Aliev and Kh. Alimirzoev, *Iz istorii kollektivizatsii selskogo khoziaistva Azerbaidzhana (1930-1934 gg.).* (Baku, 1957). A. Ia. Kikvidze, *Kolkhoznoe stroitelstvo v Gruzii.* (Tbilisi, 1961). See also Musa M. Aliev, ed., *Sovetskii Azerbaidzhan.* (Baku, 1958).

[75]M. A. Andreev, *Sotsialisticheskoe preobrazovanie selskogo khoziaistva Chuvashskoi ASSR.* (Cheboksary, 1956). T. G. Gusev and V. N. Liubimov, "Borba za kollektivizatsiiu selskogo khoziaistva Chuvashskoi ASSR." *Materialy po istorii Chuvashskoi ASSR.* Issue III (Cheboksary, 1957). M. V. Ageev, *Pobeda kolkhoznogo stroia v Mordovskoi ASSR.* (Saransk, 1960). K. I. Shibanov, *Sotsialisticheskoe preobrazovanie udmurtskoi derevni.* (Izhevsk, 1963). G. G. Osmanov, *Kollektivizatsiia selskogo khoziaistva v Dagestane.* (Makhachkala, 1961). G. G. Osmanov, *Sotsialno-ekonomicheskoe razvitie dagestanskogo dokolkhoznogo aula.* (Moscow, 1965). M. I. Gioev, *Pobeda kolkhoznogo stroia v Severnoi Osetii.* (Ordzhonikidze, 1967).

nomadic, and semi-nomadic peoples were forced to settle down and submit to collectivization, and as in some areas industrialization encroached upon communal life and left its own impact, problems came to assume a standard form. Local conditions lost their peculiarities, and economic and geographic distinctiveness faded away, fitting more and more into standard national patterns, forming in turn new issues of broader scope. In some parts of the country entire communities shifted to other localities; others grew to such an extent that the original character could hardly be detected, as witnessed in some of the western parts of the Soviet Union such as Belorussia.[76]

F. SUBJECTS TO BE EXPLORED

There has been much said about the kulak element and the drive against it, but there is hardly an objective study worthy of mention in Soviet historiography on either the kulak as a class, or on the liquidation of that class; there is also a conspicuous absence of an economic or sociological study of the bitter conflict that was witnessed during the early 1930's. Nor is there a reliable account to be found of the methods of so-called dekulakization (*raskulachivanie*) of the countryside, or the expropriation of the "peasant bourgeoisie." In 1958, P. V. Semernin and V. K. Medvedev each wrote on the battle against the kulak as a class. Each man produced an absorbing analytical study, based on party and state documents, that helped to illuminate the problem and define its broader ramifications. But the main issue remains to be explored, for both articles barely touch the surface of the real issues involved.[77] Perhaps the nearest to handling the question adequately was the monograph by B. A. Abramov, published in 1952, but even this admirable work needs a more extensive examination of newly available sources. Besides, there is still much confusion as to whether the kulak class was really as effectively "liquidated" as has been commonly assumed. According to one writer, M. A. Kraev, the kulaks were not thoroughly eliminated until the summer of 1934, with the completion of

[76]M. K. Ivasiuta, *Naris istorii kollektivizatsii na Ternopilshchini, 1939-1950 r.* (Kiev, 1958). M. K. Ivasiuta, *Ocherki istorii kolkhoznogo stroitelstva v zapadnykh oblastiakh Ukrainskoi SSR.* (Kiev, 1962). Iu. A. Moshkov, "Politika gosudarstvennykh zagotovok v gody sotsialisticheskoi rekonstruktsii selskogo khoziaistva (1930-1934 gg.)." *Istoriia SSSR*, No. 4 (1960), 101-111. V. P. Stoliarenko, *Sotsialisticheskoe preobrazovanie selskogo khoziaistva na Volyni (1944-1950).* (Kiev, 1958). P. Novitskii, *Po puti, ukazannomu Kommunisticheskoi partiei. (Kollektivizatsiia selskogo khoziaistva zapadnykh raionov Moldavskoi SSR).* (Kishenev, 1958). G. A. Borodach and I. Domorad, *Kollektivizatsiia selskogo khoziaistva v zapadnykh oblastiakh Belorusskoi SSR.* (Minsk, 1959). V. L. Varetskii, *Sotsialistichni peretvoreniia u zakhidnykh oblastiakh USSR, v dovoennii period.* (Kiev, 1960). [1] P. I. Olekas, "Borba Kommunisticheskoi partii Litvy za sotsialisticheskoe preobrazovanie selskogo khoziaistva." *Voprosy istorii*, No. 5 (1959), 44-62. *Ocherki istorii kollektivizatsii selskogo khoziaistva v soiuznykh respublikakh.* (Moscow, 1960).

[77]P. V. Semernin, "O likvidatsii kulachestva kak klassa." *Voprosy istorii KPSS*, No. 4 (1958). V. K. Medvedev, "Likvidatsiia kulachestva kak klassa v Nizhnevolzhskom krae." *Istoriia SSSR*, No. 6 (1958), 9-29.

mass collectivization. According to another, I. Ia. Trifonov, the kulaks had already disappeared by 1929-1930. There are still others, historians and economists, who hold the view that the liquidation was not completed until the end of the second five-year plan.[78]

For a full picture of the agrarian reforms that took place during the early 1930's it is of utmost importance to have a thorough organizational and economic study of the collective farms, as well as of their productive capacity. This question has attracted Soviet scholars particularly since the middle 1950's. Modest research projects have been carried out by several writers, but the field is still open for further research and promises to clarify much about Russia's economic revolution. Much that has been written to date is not entirely in accordance with factual conditions; descriptions of the prescribed norms, the setting up of efficient means of production, the degree of achievement—through all these runs a tendency to overestimate actualities. Some of the later publications touch upon these defects, though a bit coyly.[79]

Another subject that needs to be explored is the history of the Machine-Tractor Stations. Though there are numerous works on the subject, most of them were written during the early period of collectivization when many vital sources were entirely unavailable. Many of the accounts base their conclusions on statistical data that are no longer acceptable. Furthermore, there is hardly any reference to the purges and other oppressive acts from which the rank and file of the managerial and skilled labor classes suffered so much. Many agronomists, chemists, and others who were connected with the MTS were scattered to the far corners of the land, and the ranks of those left were dangerously thinned—in some areas entirely depleted. There is hardly a reliable solid work on the effects of these purges on the farm policy during the 1930's.[80]

Lastly, there should be further research in the field of Soviet purveyances during the years 1930-1934. Iu. A. Moshkov pioneered in 1960 with an

[78]M. A. Kraev, *Pobeda kolkhoznogo stroia v SSSR.* (Moscow, 1954). I. Ia. Trifonov, *Ocherki klassovoi borby v SSSR v nachale NEPa, 1921-1923 gg.* (Leningrad, 1964).

[79]See V. V. Bondarenko, *Razvitie obshchestvennogo khoziaistva kolkhozov Ukrainy v gody dovoennykh piatiletok.* (Moscow, 1957). S. P. Trapeznikov, *Istoricheskii opyt KPSS v sotsialisticheskom preobrazovanii selskogo khoziaistva.* (Moscow, 1959). Iu. A. Moshkov, "Politika gosudarstvennykh zagotovok v gody sotsialisti-cheskoi rekonstruktsii selskogo khoziaistva (1930-1936 gg.)." *Istoriia SSSR,* No. 5 (1960), 24-36.

[80]T. T. Tulebaev, *Politotdely MTS Kazakhstana v borbe za organizatsionno-kho-ziaistvennoe ukreplenie kolkhozov.* (Moscow, 1955). G. I. Volchenkov, "Politot-dely MTS Moskovskoi oblasti i ikh rol v organizatsionno-khoziaistvennom ukre-plenii kolkhozov v 1933-1934 gg." *Istoricheskie zapiski,* No. 58 (1956), 306-326.

article on the subject which only stressed the point that much is left to be done in this field.[81]

[81]Iu. A. Moshkov, "Politika gosudarstvennykh zagotovok v gody sotsialisticheskoi rekonstruktsii selskogo khoziaistva." *Istoriia SSSR*, No. 4 (1960). Iu. A. Moshkov, "Borba Kommunisticheskoi partii za razreshenie zernovoi problemy v gody sploshnoi kollektivizatsii sovetskoi derevni." *Vestnik MGU*, Series IX, Issue 4 (1962).

CHAPTER XII

Nationalization of Industry

A. PUBLICATION OF SOURCES

One of the first acts of the new Soviet regime concerned the nationalization of industry: shortly after assuming power in October, 1917, Lenin drafted a project entitled "Conditions of Labor Control," which, with some minor changes, went into effect on November 14, 1917. It provided for the formation of a Supreme Soviet of National Economy *(Sovnarkhoz)*.[1]

Yet, for reasons that are not too clear, the vital question of nationalization of industry was hardly dealt with in Soviet historical literature for many years. There is no substantial assemblage of documents or historical treatment to serve as evidence of an interest in the field until more recent times. The earliest collection of documentary evidence concerning formation of a socialized industry, which appeared in 1918-1919, was followed by a long period of neglect.[2] A few scattered documents dealing with the establishment of the workers' control over industry appeared much later in *Krasnyi arkhiv* and in *Istoricheskii arkhiv*. The collection of decrees issued by the Supreme Soviet of National Economy includes many rare documents which describe the central organization of the *Sovnarkhoz* as well as the local affiliates, their relation to the state, and policies concerning finance, transportation, agriculture, and labor. How these decrees were carried out or to what degree they proved successful is not mentioned.[3]

After the middle of the 1950's the field began to receive more attention. In 1954 I. A. Gladkov edited a collection of documents on the nationalization and organization of socialized industry during 1917-1920. The first of three parts deals with the establishment of labor control as the preliminary step toward industrial nationalization. It includes documents related to labor control in widely scattered areas such as Petrograd, the Moscow region, the Urals, and the Donets Basin. The second part is related to the progress of nationalization during the initial stages of 1917-1918, including the resistance exerted by private industrialists. The third part covers the

[1]S. R. Gershberg, "V. I. Lenin i sozdanie Vysshego Soveta Narodnogo Khoziaistva." *Voprosy istorii*, No. 7 (1958), 3-24.

[2]*Sbornik dekretov i postanovlenii po narodnomu khoziaistvu.* Issues I-III, published by VSNKh. (Moscow, 1918-1919).

[3]"Materialy k istorii rabochego kontrolia nad proizvodstvom (1917-1918 gg.)." *Krasnyi arkhiv*, No. 6 (103), (1940), 106-129. "Iz istorii rabochego kontrolia i promyshlennosti posle Velikoi Oktiabrskoi sotsialisticheskoi revoliutsii." *Istoricheskii arkhiv*, No. 4 (1949).

period from December, 1918, to January, 1919, in the Ukraine, in White Russia, and in the Baltic countries while the Soviets were in temporary control.[4] The collections fail to cite any records related to the nationalization of banks, an important factor that had considerable bearing upon the nationalization of industry. Still, the series stands out as a valuable record of a significant development during the trying experimental period of reorganization of the national economy.

Some of the publications that deal with nationalization of industry in the various component parts of the Soviet Union are equally important. A collection of documents edited by E. A. Voskoboinikov on labor control and nationalization of industry in Turkestan was published in 1955.[5] These records reveal some of the difficulties that had to be faced with the establishment first of labor control and then of nationalization of industry; most of these problems originated with the backward economic conditions throughout Central Asia. Suffice it to point out that many of the industrial workers, mainly in the textile industry, were dividing their time between farming and employment in industry. Another collection of documents, edited by A. A. Novoselskii, was issued in 1956. They concerned labor control and nationalization of industry in Ivanovo-Voznesensk, emphasizing the situation in the textile industry.[6]

In 1957, marking the fortieth anniversary of the Revolution, the Ukrainian Academy of Sciences published a selected and unique set of sources on industrial nationalization throughout the Ukrainian Republic.[7] The first of three parts traces the process of nationalization from the October Revolution to the German occupation of the Ukraine; the second part deals with the period immediately following the withdrawal of German troops from the Ukraine; the third covers the period from the end of the Civil War to the completion of nationalization.

Another publication of considerable aid to the student of Soviet economic history is the collection of documents concerning the mining industry in the Urals, gathered and published by the State Archives of Sverdlovsk in 1958.[8] Two other volumes of documents were published simultaneously

[4]*Natsionalizatsiia promyshlennosti v SSSR. Sbornik materialov.* (Moscow, 1954). See also *Rabochii kontrol v promyshlennosti Petrograda v 1917-1918 godakh. Sbornik materialov.* (Moscow, 1947).

[5]*Rabochii kontrol i natsionalizatsiia promyshlennosti v Turkestane. Sbornik dokumentov.* (Moscow, 1955).

[6]*Materialy po istorii SSSR.* Vol. III. *Rabochii kontrol i natsionalizatsiia krupnoi promshlennosti v Ivanovo-Voznesenskoi gubernii.* (Moscow, 1956).

[7]*Rabochii kontrol i natsionalizatsiia promyshlennosti na Ukraine. Sbornik dokumentov i materialov.* (Kiev, 1957).

[8]*Natsionalizatsiia promyshlennosti na Urale. Sbornik dokumentov.* (Sverdlovsk, 1958).

by the Academician A. V. Venediktov, covering the Petrograd area, including the initial administrative setup of the entire northern region.[9] The first volume contains materials related to the nationalization of industry in Petrograd and the formation of administrative apparatus (the National Economic Council of the Northern Region, later reorganized to become the Petrograd National Economic Council). The second volume covers the operation of the socialized industry of Petrograd, the establishment of planned production, and the use of the nationalized industry during the Civil War.

Another volume in a similar series published in 1960 concentrates its attention on the Kostroma region.[10]

One of the outstanding early monographic works on industrial socialization is that by A. M. Pankratova, published in 1923 under the editorship of M. N. Pokrovskii. She traces the early development of labor control and the gradual socialization of all industrial plants after November, 1917. This study, though of early date, has retained much of its original value mainly because of the number of rare sources utilized.[11] Pankratova considers the policy pursued between 1917 and the spring of 1918 the first period of industrial nationalization, which she characterizes as the period of "elemental 'punitive' nationalization." The reason for this is that the early plans for nationalization foresaw possible sabotage on the part of the plant owners, and therefore the early decrees included provisions for punishing such action. In a broader sense the description is not quite correct historically, since the Bolshevik Party advocated socialization of all industries long before it came to power.[12]

Other writings on the early history of labor control and of the nationalization of transport and banks have been published in periodical literature by writers such as B. G. Verkhoven' and A. I. Vasilkova.[13] Verkhoven' assembled valuable original sources on the nationalization of transport and certain other industries, particularly the metallurgical ones. He offers primarily a factual presentation of the subject, seldom becoming involved in

[9]Natsionalizatsiia promyshlennosti i organizatsiia sotsialisticheskogo proizvodstva v Petrograde (1917-1920 gg.). Vol. II. (Moscow, 1960).

[10]Rabochii kontrol i natsionalizatsiia promyshlennosti v Kostromskoi gubernii. (Moscow, 1960).

[11]A. M. Pankratova, Fabzavkomy Rossii v borbe za sotsialisticheskuiu fabriku. (Moscow, 1923).

[12]See, for instance, the resolutions adopted by the Sixth Congress of the Bolshevik Party. See also the various writings of Lenin prior to the Revolution.

[13]B. G. Verkhoven', "Leninskii plan pristupa k sotsialisticheskomu stroitelstvu (1918 g.)." Proletarskaia revoliutsiia, No. 1 (1940), 45-80. B. G. Verkhoven', "Sovetskii zakon o rabochem kontrole." Voprosy istorii, No. 10 (1948), 3-20. A. I. Vasilkova, "Rabochii kontrol nad proizvodstvom (fevral—oktiabr 1917 g.)." Voprosy istorii, No. 10 (1947), 40-64. A. I. Vasilkova, "Ekonomicheskaia platforma bolshevistskoi partii nakanune Velikoi Oktiabrskoi sotsialisticheskoi revoliutsii." Voprosy istorii, No. 12 (1953), 42-59.

ideological aspects of the success or failure of the enterprises.

Additional documentary sources dealing with labor control at the early stage of national socialization of industry were published during the later 1950's.[14]

B. NATIONALIZATION AND GROWTH OF THE ECONOMY

From the very start, the Communist Party associated a successful social order with successful industrialization of the USSR. Repeatedly, in party conferences and congressess, in public speeches and by way of the press, the idea was constantly and indefatigably hammered—"the formation of an industrial base for further advancement of socialism."[15]

V. I. Lenin quite clearly foresaw the enormous difficulties to be faced by the process of economic reconstruction in an agrarian society, but the complexity was to be doubled in a society predominantly based on small peasant landholding, hostile or indifferent to advanced capitalism. Yet, regardless of all difficulties, the industrialization program had to be carried out if the socialist citadel was to survive in the midst of the wreckage inherited from the Civil War within the country and hostile encirclement from outside.

Once the need for an accelerated industrialization program was recognized, the priority of heavy industry was accepted as most vital. Speaking before the Fourth Congress of the Third International in 1922, Lenin had already predicted that without the establishment of heavy industry there

[14]S. M. Babushkin, "Rabochii kontrol nad proizvodstvom na Urale (1918-1919 gg.)." *Uchenye zapiski Uralskogo gosudarstvennogo universiteta,* Issue 18 (1958). B. G. Verkhoven' and M. S. Seleznev, "Borba za rabochii kontrol nad proizvodstvom v Estonii (1917-1918 gg.)." *Istoriia SSSR,* No. 3 (1957), 134-141. V. S. Samigulin, "Tvorcheskaia aktivnost trudiashchikhsia mass Urala v borbe za rabochii kontrol (mart 1917—mai 1918 g.)." *Trudy Uralskogo politekhnicheskogo instituta.* Sbornik 88 (1958). V. D. Samsonov, "Iz istorii rabochego kontrola v tekstilnoi promyshlennosti Moskovskoi gubernii (1917-1918 gg.)." *Trudy Moskovskogo gosudarstvennogo istoriko-arkhivnogo instituta,* Vol. X (1957). P. I. Tugov, "Osushchestvlenie leninskogo dekreta o rabochem kontrole v promyshlennosti Kazakhstana (1917-1918 gg.)." *Vestnik Akademii nauk Kazakhskoi SSR,* No. 4 (1940). I. Sh. Chernomaz, *Borba rabochego klassa Ukrainy za rabochii kontrol nad proizvodstvom (mart 1917—mart 1918 g.).* (Moscow, 1958). A. B. Lazarev, "Iz istorii razrabotki leninskogo dekreta o rabochem kontrole." *Voprosy istorii KPSS,* No. 3 (1960), 131-140.

[15]*KPSS v rezoliutsiiakh i resheniiakh.* Part II. (Moscow, Gospolitizdat, 1954). See particularly pp. 193-202. A. A. Andreev, *Industrializatsiia strany, rezhim ekonomii i profsoiuzy.* (Moscow, 1926). F. E. Dzerzhinskii, *Ocherednye zadachi promyshlennoi politiki. Sbornik statei.* (Moscow, 1925). F. E. Dzerzhinskii, *Promyshlennoe stroitelstvo i khoziaistvennye zatrudneniia SSSR.* (Moscow, 1926). F. E. Dzerzhinskii, *Izbrannye proizvedeniia.* Vol. II. (Moscow, 1957). S. M. Kirov, *Zavershim postroenie fundamenta sotsialisticheskoi ekonomiki SSSR.* (Moscow, 1931). S. M. Kirov, *Delo chesti leningradskikh proletariev vypolnit' proizvodstvennuiu programmu.* (Moscow, 1933). V. V. Kuibyshev, *Industrializatsiia strany i rezhim ekonomii.*

could be no industry at all, and Soviet Russia could never be a great independent power. Lenin envisioned the division of the national economy into two groups, A and B. Within a decade or so it was expected that heavy industry (Group A) would increase production by as much, approximately, as 200 percent; while light industry (Group B), or production of consumer goods, would rise about 150 percent. If during the NEP years it was necessary to lean heavily in favor of agrarian development, it was not because of choice, but of the necessity to alleviate a critical situation that prevailed throughout the country during the early 1920's.

Literature on the subject of economic development during the 1920's and on the period immediately preceding the first five-year plan is rather sparse. Historians have yet to undertake an all-encompassing study of the national economy on the eve of the all-out planned economy, although there is ample material available, such as the stenographic reports of the conferences, the plenary sessions, the press reports, the discussions, and the acrimonious party debates over the policies to be applied for successful national industrialization.[16]

One of the most pressing problems of the time was the glaring inconsistency of a socialist government adhering to a Marxist philosophy and governing a country that was woefully backward economically. The answer to this dilemma was the rapid development of a heavy industry to assure necessary economic advancement, and in that case the question of priorities seemed virtually predetermined. Some party leaders held other views, however. Some argued that the aim of industrialization was not merely to seek higher rates of production as an end in themselves; increased production must be the means to assure a more abundant economic state which in turn must assure a socialist victory. The aim was not to extol statistical figures—capitalism can do this too—but to demonstrate what economic affluence can be accomplished under a dictatorship of the proletariat.[17]

(Moscow, 1926). V. V. Kuibyshev, *Promyshlennost SSSR.* (Moscow, 1927). V. V. Kuibyshev, *Piatiletnii plan razvitiia promyshlennosti.* (Moscow, 1929). V. V. Kuibyshev, *O vtoroi piatiletke.* (Moscow, 1932). A. I. Mikoian, *Disproportsiia i tovarnyi golod.* (Moscow, 1927). A. I. Mikoian, *Pishchevaia industriia Sovetskogo Souiza.* (Moscow, 1939). G. K. Ordzhonikidze, *Na rubezhe dvukh piatiletok.* (Moscow, 1933). G. K. Ordzhonikidze, *Zavershim rekonstruktsiiu vsego narodnogo khoziaistva.* (Moscow, 1934). G. K. Ordzhonikidze, *Zadachi tiazheloi promyshlennosti v sviazi s stakhanovskim dvizheniem.* (Moscow, 1936).

[16]A. A. Andreev, *Industriaizatsiia strany, rezhim ekonomiki i soiuzy.* (Moscow, 1926). V. V. Kuibyshev, *Industrializatsiia strany i rezhim ekonomiki.* (Moscow, 1926). V. V. Kuibyshev, *Promyshlennost SSSR.* (Moscow, 1927). V. V. Kuibyshev, *Piatiletnii plan razvitiia promyshlennosti.* (Moscow, 1929). V. V. Kuibyshev, *O vtoroi piatiletke.* (Moscow, 1932).

[17]G. I. Krumin, *Osnovnye voprosy khoziaistva i oppozitsiia.* (Moscow, 1927). G. I. Krumin, *Borba za industrializatsiiu i zadachi partii.* (Moscow, 1929). Ia. A. Iakovlev, *Selskoe khoziaistvo i industrializatsiia. Doklad v Komakademii.* 2nd ed. (Moscow, 1927).

Logical as this seemed, there were still others who urged incorporating into the Soviet economy a system of "universal division of labor," and eliminating the parochial "national" policy of building socialism in one country. Others, on the contrary, demanded a slower pace of industrialization for fear that an accelerated program might deliver untold hardships upon the nation, particularly with priorities to industries of long-range importance. Therefore, this group urged a program that would favor production of consumer goods. The entire question of industrial planning was fraught with ideological differences of opinion, left-wing "universalism," and right-wing fears of over-accelerated tempos in industrialization.[18]

Among the works which may be regarded as adequate studies of industrial achievements prior to the five-year planning, those of E. I. Kviring, V. P. Miliutin, M. A. Braun, and V. E. Motylev stand out.[19]

A general survey of economic progress made during the first decade after 1917 is well presented by V. E. Sarabianov.[20] The author shows how the industrialization program gradually reached a level far above that attained prior to 1914. Sarabianov also shows that heavy industry had made an appreciable gain, proportionate to the most favored position it occupied in the country. Light industry lagged for the simple reason that it was running an unfair contest. Sarabianov includes also a rare description of banking operations and credit practices under the Soviet system.

M. I. Leites and A. F. Khavin, in a work of similar character, discuss the earliest Soviet efforts at industrialization. The story goes back to March, 1920, when the Soviet of People's Commissars approved the formation of a State Commission for the Electrification of Russia (GOELRO). The plan

[18]A. Leontiev, V borbe za industrializatsiiu. (Moscow, 1929). G. M. Krzhizhanov-skii. Kak my stroili sotsializm. (Moscow, 1930). G. M. Krzhizhanovskii, Desiat let GOELRO. (Moscow, 1931). A. Shlikhter, V boiakh za sotsializm. (Moscow, 1930). K. Ia. Rozental, V zashchitu industrializatsii SSSR. (Moscow, 1928). A. Osipian and M. Lapidus, Industrializatsiia—osnova ekonomicheskoi nezavisimosti SSSR. (Moscow, 1928). A. K. Azizian, Dlia chego nuzhna krestianinu industrializatsiia strany. (Moscow, 1929). A. F. Gladun, Industrializatsiia SSSR i selkhozlesrabochie. (Moscow, 1929). A. Koldobskii, Vazhneishie zadachi promyshlennosti. (Moscow, 1930). M. I. Latsis, Kak stroitsia sotsializm v nashei strane. (Moscow, 1929). A. Leontiev, Osnovyne ustanovki piatiletki. (Moscow, 1930). T. Okhotnikov, Industrializatsiia strany i potrebitelskaia kooperatsiia. (Moscow, 1929). A. P. Serebrovskii, Industrializatsiia strany i krestianstvo. (Moscow, 1927). M. Orakhelashvili, Industrializatsiia i rezhim ekonomii. (Moscow, 1926).

[19]E. I. Kviring, Ocherki razvitiia promyshlennosti SSSR. 1917-1927. (Moscow, 1929). V. P. Miliutin, Istoriia ekonomicheskogo razvitiia SSSR (1917-1927). (Moscow, 1929). V. E. Motylev, Problema tempa razvitiia SSSR. (Moscow, 1929). M. A. Braun, Osnovnoi kapital promyshlennosti SSSR (ocherki ego sostoianiia, vosstanovleniia i rekonstruktsii). (Moscow, 1930). S. V. Minaev, ed., Osnovnye momenty rekonstruktsii promyshlennosti SSSR. (Ocherki). E. I. Kviring, Sbornik. Promyshlennost i narodnoe khoziaistvo. (Moscow, 1927).

[20]V. E. Sarabianov, Itogi vosstanovitelnogo perioda. (Moscow, 1927). V. E. Sarabianov, Industrializatsiia strany. (Moscow, 1928).

was formally adopted by the Eighth Congress of Soviets and went into effect in December, 1920. Analyzing the execution of this early plan, the authors concluded that 1925-1926 might be regarded as the decisive point, not only in the field of national electrification, but also in the general drive toward economic change. The same theme is handled by several other writers who discuss economic development prior to the adoption of the early five-year plans, such as A. Leontiev, E. I. Kviring, and G. Tochilnikov.[21]

Since the 1930's the rate of publication has increased, stimulated mainly by the new endeavor to reexamine the results of the first five-year plan.[22] Historians have studied such timely questions as the degree of interdependence between industry and agriculture in regard to national food supply. Some stressed the merits of mechanization of the light industries and food industries as a means of raising national production by releasing workers, particularly women, for other industries. Others analyzed the effect of industrialization upon the existing domestic industry, or plans for transforming the latter into a more mechanized system without seriously disturbing the general economy.[23] This question was of particular importance to some of the autonomous and constituent republics where handicraft industry constituted the economic basis of many communities. Some writers advised extreme caution, and warned against a uniform tempo of industrialization throughout the Soviet Union; this group urged consideration of local

[21] M. I. Leites and A. F. Khavin, *Novoe promyshlennoe stroitelstvo Sovetskogo Soiuza.* (Moscow, 1927). See also O. Kuperman, *Sotsialno-ekonomicheskie formy promyshlennosti SSSR.* (Moscow, 1929). A. Leontiev, *V borbe za industrializatsiiu.* (Moscow, 1929). E. S. Gorfinkel, *SSSR v sisteme mirovogo khoziaistva.* (Moscow, 1929). G. Tochilnikov, *Finansy i industrializatsiia.* (Moscow, 1929). E. I. Kviring, *Ocherki razvitiia promyshlennosti SSSR, 1917-1927.* (Moscow, 1929).

[22] E. Iu. Lokshin, *Promyshlennost SSSR za XV let.* (Moscow, 1932). E. Iu. Lokshin, *Promyshlennost SSSR v pervoi piatiletke.* (Moscow, 1934). B. Blinkov, *Khimicheskaia promyshlennost SSSR.* (Moscow, 1932). M. Tsaguriia, *15 let tiazheloi promyshlennosti SSSR.* (Moscow, 1932). M. Blank, M. Lapidus, A. Litvak, S. Nikolaev, B. Strizhevskii, and A. Filippov, *SSSR industrialnyi.* (Moscow, 1932). G. Streltsov, *Mashinostroenie v pervoi piatiletke.* (Moscow, 1933). A. I. Gurevich, *Pobeda partii. Chernaia metallurgiia k VII sezdu Sovetov SSSR.* (Moscow, 1934). G. Sakharov, N. Chernai, and O. Kobakov, *Ocherki organizatsii tiazheloi promyshlennosti SSSR.* (Moscow, 1934). N. F. Berezov, *Razmeshchenie chernoi metallurgii.* (Moscow, 1933). P. N. Ivanov, *Sovetskaia elektrotekhnicheskaia promyshlennost.* (Moscow, 1933).

[23] A. D. Kurskii, *Razmeshchenie promyshlennosti v pervoi piatiletke.* (Moscow, 1933). E. I. Pavchinskii, *Obshchestvennoe pitanie na sluzhbe industrializatsii.* (Moscow, 1931). F. Ia. Khrushchev, *Ot promysla k industrii (pishchevaia promyshlennost Kazakhstana).* (Moscow, 1935). P. I. Vasilevskii and E. I. Shlifshtein, *Ocherki kustarnoi promyshlennosti.* (Moscow, 1930).

peculiarities and maintained that industrialization must proceed in accordance with locally prevailing economic and social conditions.[24]

The tempo at which the planned industrialization was to take place became widely discussed. V. G. Myshkis wrote a painstakingly detailed study on industrialization in the Ukraine, in which he gave much space to the subject of priority problems related to heavy and light industries. Myshkis emphasized one point especially as the motivating one—the need for freedom from economic dependence upon foreign countries. The Soviet Union, he argued, must first of all be reasonably independent, whether in procurement of raw materials, machinery, or any other vital supplies.[25]

As the planned economy went into effect, discussions increased as to its proper application in accordance with existing conditions in various parts of the Soviet Union. Many writers displayed serious concern over the colossal undertaking, and expressed doubt whether the plan was feasible at all. An appeal was issued at the very start, calling Soviet local officials to study carefully their peculiar conditions and their ability to play their proper part in the national effort to industrialize. It was in this atmosphere that A. M. Gorky launched his campaign, urging that all related records be preserved in order to provide a complete history of Soviet economic development. Many local organizations responded to the call and proved instrumental in accumulating valuable source materials, covering the growth of factories and industrial plants, the rise of an industrial working class and of a managerial class, and the development of a national administrative apparatus.[26]

For a number of reasons the unusual productivity in Soviet historiography during the 1920's faded during the 1930's. To a large degree this was due to the impact of Stalinism. From the early 1930's to the end of the war the number of publications in economic history declined steadily, while monographic works virtually ceased to appear. There is a conspicuous absence of general studies on the achievements of the second and third five-year plans. Writing was limited to articles, to propaganda brochures, and to other forms suitable for mass consumption, in which general credit was

[24]*Kustarnaia promyshlennost i promyslovaia kooperatsiia natsionalnykh respublik i oblastei SSSR.* (Moscow, 1928). B. Segal, *Industrializatsiia okrain.* (Moscow, 1928).

[25]V. S. Myshkis, *Tempy industrializatsii i obobshchestvleniia na Ukraine.* (Kharkov, 1930).

[26]G. I. Tarlé, "Rannie opyty organizatsii sobiraniia materialov po istorii fabrik i zavodov." *Istoriia SSSR,* No. 2 (1959), 170-172. *A. M. Gorky i sozdanie istorii fabrik i zavodov. Sbornik dokumentov i materialov.* (Moscow, 1959). P. Paradizov, "O sozdanii nauchnoi istorii promyshlennosti i rabochego klassa SSSR." *Borba klassov,* No. 4 (1934). A. Pankratova, " 'Istoriia zavodov SSSR'. Zadachi i metody istoricheskogo issledovaniia v dele sozdaniia 'Istorii zavodov SSSR'. Doklad." *Borba klassov,* No. 10 (1933), 70-74.

given to Stalin and the party for every phase of development in the Soviet Union.[27]

Since 1945 there has been a decline in the popular type of literature and more serious effort at publication of monographic studies. Postwar studies are of a more general nature, more inclusive in their field of economic development, less boastful of record-breaking achievements, and more realistic in their evaluation of actual accomplishments. Postwar writings often dealt with the new geographic distribution of industrial centers and the growth of economic independence that resulted from war-related shifts and technological progress. It was commonly recognized that the Soviet Union had become an industrialized power to be seriously reckoned with. There is one glaring weakness in the writings of this period—a lack of originality, an absence of individuality in interpretation, a parallelism in themes and in utilization of source materials—observable as long as Stalin remained at the helm of both the party and the state.[28]

Another fault to be noted in many of the writings of this period is the tendency to minimize the industrial progress of pre-revolutionary Russia, and to emphasize the economic dependence of Imperial Russia upon Western capital, in the manner of a semi-colonial state. According to Soviet writers, it was only after the 1920's that Russia became recognized as an industrial power. Yet one achievement not minimized was the economic transformation that took place within some of the constituent republics of the Soviet Union, an impressive change from a primitive agrarian to a modern industrial state.[29]

[27] A. Moskalev, *Partiia bolshevikov v borbe za sotsialisticheskuiu industrializatsiiu strany.* (Moscow, 1939). E. N. Burdzhalov, *SSSR v borbe za sotsialisticheskuiu industrializatsiiu strany i kollektivizatsiiu selskogo khoziaistva.* (Moscow, 1944). A. F. Khavin, "Rozhdenie pervoi stalinskoi piatiletki." *Istoricheskii zhurnal,* No. 4 (1941). M. Iu. Galperin, *Sezd sotsialisticheskoi industrializatsii.* (Moscow, 1941). E. L. Granovskii, *Sotsialisticheskaia industrializatsiia—osnova voennoi moshchi SSSR.* (Moscow, 1942). E. Iu. Lokshin, *Sovetskii Soiuz—moguchaia industrialnaia derzhava.* (Moscow, 1942). G. M. Sorokin, *Znachenie industrializatsii dlia sudeb nashei strany.* (Moscow, 1945).

[28] P. Chesnokov, *Sotsialisticheskaia industrializatsiia—osnovy oborony SSSR.* (Moscow, 1943). L. M. Gatovskii, *Politika sotsialisticheskoi industrializatsii spasla nashu Rodinu.* (Moscow, 1946). E. Iu. Lokshin, "Sovetskii metod industrializatsii." *Planovoe khoziaistvo,* No. 4 (1946), 31-43. P. A. Belov, *Sotsialisticheskaia industrialization strany i kollektivizatsiia selskogo khoziaistva SSSR.* (Moscow, 1946). E. V. Kasimovskii, *Sotsialisticheskaia industrializatsiia spasla nashu Rodinu ot poraboshcheniia.* (Moscow, 1947). N. M. Mor, *SSSR—moguchaia industrialnaia derzhava.* (Moscow, 1947). M. M. Konstantinov, *Sotsialisticheskaia promyshlennost i eё vedushchaia rol v razvitii narodnogo khoziaistva SSSR.* (Moscow, 1950). E. N. Burdzhalov, *SSSR v period borby za sotsialisticheskuiu industrializatsiiu strany (1926-1929).* (Moscow, 1950).

[29] S. N. Malinin, *Razvitie promyshlennosti Belorusskoi SSR.* (Moscow, 1948). S. Ziiadullaev and I. Manokhin, *Sotsialisticheskaia promyshlennost Sovetskogo Uzbekistana.* (Moscow, 1949). S. B. Baishev, *Sotsialisticheskaia industrializatsiia*

A few studies from this period stand out for their high quality. One of these is the monograph of D. D. Mishustin, a study of Soviet foreign trade and industrialization. Though written as a textbook for a course in economics it is also a distinguished work in its field. The author used numerous Soviet and foreign source materials and minutely scrutinized Soviet exports and imports during the first two five-year-plans. His main object was to show by way of export and import figures the extent of economic dependence of the Soviet Union upon the West, and the impressive decrease of reliance upon foreign industries with the advance of the program of industrial expansion.[30] Equally important studies were made by such writers as L. I. Skvortsov and N. Riabov, who dealt largely with the subject of capital accumulation and its sources during the first two five-year plans. The work of Riabov in particular remains an authoritative study of Soviet financial policy during the early period of industrialization. Riabov's main theme is socialist accumulation and its sources during the first two five-year plans, while Skvortsov emphasizes mainly the crediting system and its contribution to Soviet industrialization.[31]

During the 1950's the areas of study in economic history expanded considerably. They began to include such subjects as the role of feminine labor in the industrialization program, or the impact of industrial expansion upon the various constituent parts of the Soviet Union, such as Armenia, Tadzhikstan, or Iakutia. I. Maslov, in an excellent monograph, discusses the impact of industrialization upon the Communist Party, upon the social origin of the newly enrolled party members, and the effects of these origins upon the organization. He concentrates upon a comparison between the party rank and file since 1950 and that of former years.[32]

Kazakhstana. (Moscow, 1949). A. Artykov, *Promyshlennost Turkmenskoi SSR za 25 let.* (Moscow, 1950). S. Sergeev, *Sotsialisticheskaia industrializatsiia Urala v gody predvoennykh stalinskikh piatiletok.* (Moscow, 1951). N. Kiikbaev, *Promyshlennost Kazakhstana v pervoi piatiletke.* (Moscow, 1951). G. N. Chulanov, *Promyshlennost Kazakhstana za gody Sovetskoi vlasti.* (Moscow, 1951). G. Dakhshleiger, *Turksib—pervenets sotsialisticheskoi industrializatsii.* (Moscow, 1953).

[30] D. D. Mishustin, *Vneshniaia torgovlia i industrializatsiia SSSR.* (Moscow, 1938).

[31] N. Riabov, *Sotsialisticheskoe nakoplenie i ego istochniki v pervoi i vtoroi piatiletkakh.* (Moscow, 1951). L. I. Skvortsov, *Rol kredita v industrializatsii SSSR.* (Moscow, 1951).

[32] N. A. Aralovets, *Zhenskii trud v promyshlennosti SSSR.* (Moscow, 1954). T. N. Belova, *Sovetskie profsoiuzy v period piatiletki.* (Moscow, 1953). A. I. Notkin, *Materialno-proizvodstvennaia baza sotsializma.* (Moscow, 1954). R. S. Livshits, *Ocherki po razmeshcheniiu promyshlennosti SSSR.* (Moscow, 1954). I. P. Semin, *God velikogo pereloma v promyshlennosti.* (Moscow, 1954). A. V. Mazaev, *Razvitie sotsialisticheskoi promyshlennosti Tadzhikskoi SSR za 25 let.* (Moscow, 1954). A. F. Khavin, *Karaganda—tretia ugolnaia baza SSSR.* (Moscow, 1954). V. Tiounov, *Promyshlennoe razvitie Zapadnogo Urala. Istoriko-ekonomicheskii ocherk.* (Moscow, 1954). K. N. Bedrintsev and B. A. Desiatchikov, *Promyshlennost Uzbekistana za 30 let.* (Moscow, 1955). I. Maslov, *Kommunisticheskaia*

In evaluating the economic achievements of the individual constituent republics of the Soviet Union, historians have lacked a broad synthesis. When a thorough description of the economic transformation that took place throughout the entire Soviet Union is available, it will undoubtedly reveal profound changes that took place in that vast Eurasian land.[33]

Outstanding works that complement those already listed are those of P. M. Alampiev, M. S. Dzhunusov, and M. M. Mitupov, who discuss particularly the industrialization of the eastern part of the Soviet Union. These authors have been able to show, for instance, how economic conditions in these formerly "underdeveloped areas," such as Kirgizia, Kazakhstan, and Buriatia, have been and still are affected by, or have in turn affected, the Soviet economy.[34]

Other aspects of early economic development that have been reexamined since 1953 are the history of the organization of the Council of National Economy (*Sovnarkhoz*) and the initial steps in economic organization of the entire Soviet Union.[35] A particularly solid work by P. I. Liashchenko

partiia Sovetskogo Soiuza v borbe za ukreplenie edinstva svoikh riadov i osushchestvlenie politiki sotsialisticheskoi industrializatsii strany (1925-1927 gg.). (Moscow, 1955).

[33] A. A. Annaklychev, *Razvitie promyshlennosti Turkmenistana za gody Sovetskoi vlasti (1921-1937 gg.).* (Moscow, 1938). I. K. Beliaev, *Sotsialisticheskaia industrializatsiia Zapadnoi Sibiri.* (Moscow, 1958). Sh. N. Ulmasbaev, *Promyshlennoe razvitie Sovetskogo Uzbekistana; istoriko-ekonomicheskii ocherk.* (Tashkent, 1958). N. G. Eroshkevich, *Razvitie promyshlennosti sovetskogo Altaia.* (Moscow, 1958). Kh. T. Medalev, *Sotsialisticheskaia industrializatsiia Kabardino-Balkarii (1928-1937 gg.).* (Moscow, 1959). A. V. Mazaev, *Razvitie sotsialisticheskoi promyshlennosti Tadzhikskoi SSR za 25 let.* (Moscow, 1954). R. D. Fedotova, *Ot ruchnogo truda k mashinnoi industrii (istoriko-ekonomicheskii ocherk razvitiia mashinnogo proizvodstva v promyshlennosti Molavskoi SSSR).* (Moscow, 1956). *Ocherki po razvitiiu promyshlennosti Komi ASSR.* (Moscow, 1956). N. S. Esipov, *Promyshlennost Kirgizii.* (Moscow, 1957). N. I. Shishkin, *Promyshlennost Komi ASSR.* (Moscow, 1957). K. N. Bedrintsev and B. A. Desiatchikov, *Promyshlennost Uzbekistana za 40 let.* (Moscow, 1957).

[34] P. M. Alampiev, *Likvidatsiia ekonomicheskogo neravenstva narodov Sovetskogo Vostoka i sotsialisticheskoe razmeshchenie promyshlennosti; istoricheskii opyt Kazakhskoi SSR.* (Moscow, 1958). B. M. Mitupov, *Razvitie promyshlennosti i formirovanie rabochego klassa v Buriatskoi ASSR (1923-1937 gg.).* (Moscow, 1958). M. S. Dzhunusov, *O nekapitalisticheskom puti razvitiia kirgizskogo naroda k sotsializmu.* (Moscow, 1958). Iu. F. Vorobev, "Vyravnivanie urovnei promyshlennosti razvitiia natsionalnykh respublik Sovetskogo Soiuza v period stroitelstva sotsializma." *Istoriia SSSR,* No. 4 (1962), 26-51. S. I. Iakubovskaia, "K voprosu o perekhode narodov Sovetskogo Severa k sotsializmu, minuia kapitalizm." *Voprosy istorii,* No. 8 (1951), 80-88. S. I. Iakubovskaia, "Likvidatsiia fakticheskogo neravenstva natsii (na primere istorii narodov Srednei Azii i Kazakhstana." *Istoricheskie zapiski,* No. 48 (1954), 156-201.

[35] V. Z. Drobizhev and I. T. Ignatenko, "Nekotorye itogi izucheniia istorii sovnar-

deals with a wide span of economic development in Russia, including an excellent chapter on the formative years of socialized industrial development; another general work covering a narrower range, but more detailed than Liashchenko's study, is by I. A. Gladkov.[36] Both authors regard the early labor control as the preliminary step toward complete nationalization of industry, as valuably gained experience in management of socialized industry. Gladkov covers only a four-year period from November, 1917, to the end of the Civil War. The author investigates the legislation fully, tracing it step by step, including labor control, nationalization, problems of labor discipline, methods of raising efficiency, and training of skilled labor. Two other monographic studies by Gladkov, closely related to the subject, deal with economic planning.[37]

Economic issues are also discussed in the history of the Civil War where industrial problems are presented in terms of broad national developments. Similarly these are also analyzed in the extensive history of the USSR in the volume on the "Epoch of Socialism." Party accounts of the same subject are given in the official history of the Communist Party, the rewritten version of 1962 that carries the stamp of party approval subsequent to the Twentieth Congress in 1956.[38] A monograph by V. A. Vinogradov, of 1954 vintage, covers only the first year of Soviet experiences. Vinogradov's study elaborates on many subjects formerly dealt with in more general terms, such as the training of skilled workers, the nationalization of banks, and the introduction of the foreign trade monopoly and its relation to the general program of industrialization throughout the Soviet Union.[39]

During the 1950's, A. V. Venediktov, member of the Academy of Sciences, began an extensive history of Soviet national industry in a multi-volume edition, the first of which appeared in 1957. Regrettably, the impressive project was abruptly ended by the premature death of the author.

khozov v 1917-1932 godakh." *Voprosy istorii*, No. 11 (1959), 93-108. A. A. Voronetskaia, "Organizatsiia Vysshego Soveta narodnogo khoziaistva i ego rol v natsionalizatsii promyshlennosti." *Istoricheskie zapiski*, No. 43 (1953), 3-38. S. R. Gershberg, "V. I. Lenin i sozdanie VSNKh." *Voprosy istorii*, No. 7 (1958), 3-24. N. V. Sviatitskii, *Organizatsiia promyshlennosti.* (Moscow, 1924).

[36]P. I. Liashchenko, *Istoriia narodnogo khoziaistva SSSR.* Vol. III. (Moscow, 1956), 15-39. I. A. Gladkov, *Ocherki sovetskoi ekonomiki 1917-1920 gg.* (Moscow, 1956), 44-101; 115-131.

[37]I. A. Gladkov, *Ocherki stroitelstva sovetskogo planovogo khoziaistva v 1917-1918 gg.* (Moscow, 1951). I. A. Gladkov, *Voprosy planirovaniia sovetskogo khoziaistva v 1918-1920 gg.* (Moscow, 1951).

[38]*Istoriia Kommunisticheskoi partii Sovetskogo Soiuza.* (Moscow, 1962). *Istoriia grazhdanskoi voiny v SSSR.* Vol. III. (Moscow, 1957), 121-132; 239-262. *Istoriia SSSR. Epokha sotsializma (1917-1957 gg.).* (Moscow, 1957).

[39]A. V. Vinogradov, *Sotsialisticheskoe obobshchestvlenie sredstv proizvodstva v*

The single volume covers the years 1917-1920, and deals mainly with the development of different forms of administration within the national industry.[40] Though stressing the formal aspects of the organization, Venediktov devotes much space to historical developments, growth of the administration and its increased complexity, and the impact the Civil War had upon the general evolution of the nation's economy. Though the work met with some criticism, even the critics admitted its merits, such as the author's extraordinary utilization of primary sources and his superb synthesis of an unusually broad subject.[41]

In 1957, on account of the fortieth anniversary of the Soviet Revolution, there appeared a number of articles devoted to the economic development of the USSR, two of which deserve special mention. To these, by P. V. Volobuev and V. Z. Drobizhev, should be added the monographic study of L. E. Ankundinova, who traced the history of nationalization of Russian industry.[42]

Though the field of economic history is slowly recovering from the stultifying effects of Stalinism, it has yet some wide gaps to be bridged. Certain industries, such as the oil, sugar beet, and mining industries, call for individual studies, as do the regional areas along the borders of the Soviet Union, particularly in the eastern part of the nation.

C. STUDIES IN SOVIET NATIONAL
ECONOMY AFTER STALIN

The subject of Soviet industrialization has been considered not only of national but of international importance. At a time when colonialism has been rapidly disappearing, when the so-called underdeveloped states that have recently gained independence lean toward social and economic legislation of one kind or another, the Soviet Union has come to be regarded as a huge laboratory, where experience has taught much that could be either imitated or avoided altogether.

The number of publications on the subject of Soviet industrialization is

promyshlennosti SSSR (1917-1918 gg.). (Moscow, 1954).

[40]A. V. Venediktov, *Organizatsiia gosudarstvennoi promyshlennosti v SSSR.* Vol. I. (Moscow, 1957). See also "Dokumenty V. I. Lenina ob organizatsii Gosplana i upravlenii narodnym khoziaistvom (aprel 1921 g.). Dokumenty Instituta marksizma-leninizma pri TsK KPSS." *Istoricheskii arkhiv,* No. 2 (1959), 3-11. A. Persov, "Materialy k istorii rabochego kontrolia nad proizvodstvom (1917-1918 gg.)." (Preface and documents.) *Krasnyi arkhiv,* No. 6 (103), (1940), 106-129.

[41]See *Voprosy istorii,* No. 11 (1959), 103-104.

[42]P. V. Volobuev and V. Z. Drobizhev, "Iz istorii goskapitalizma v nachalnyi period sotsialisticheskogo stroitelstva v SSSR." *Voprosy istorii,* No. 9 (1957), 107-122. V. Z. Drobizhev, "K istorii organov rabochego upravleniia na promyshlennykh predpriiatiiakh v 1917-1918 g." *Istoriia SSSR,* No. 3 (1957), 38-56. L. E. Anakundinova, *Natsionalizatsiia promyshlennosti v SSSR 1917-1920 gg.* (Moscow, 1963.

enormous and only a small portion of what has appeared, particularly in more recent years, may be cited. To begin with, one must cite the more general works, such as those by K. A. Petrosian, A. F. Khavin, and M. P. Kim. In addition there must be listed the numerous papers on the subject read at international and national historical congresses and conventions.[43]

From an international point of view the importance of Soviet industrialization can be summed up in an observation neatly made by a Hindu economist in the Soviet publication *Sovremennyi Vostok* (No. 12, 1958). Before the newly emerging nations, the writer states, there rise two alternatives: either to follow the road of the West and to industrialize "by a slow process that would last more than a century, a tempo that does not suit us, or to learn from the USSR." In this connection, G. E. Figurnov, in an excellent collection on Soviet industrialization, has contributed an essay on the general patterns of transition to socialism and their peculiarities in different countries.[44]

After nearly four decades of forced industrialization, historians have tried to trace the overall picture of Soviet industrial development. In analyzing the long and difficult road traversed thus far, they have isolated three stages in the economic development.

One covers the second half of the 1920's and early 1930's. Already in 1926 important aspects of the industrialization program were considered, data analyzed, and the final plans formed. Much has been written on the first stage, though most of the literature is not the work of historians, but of party members who actively participated in carrying out the adopted plans. Some of these writers left excellent accounts which no future historian can afford to overlook in his research. They deal with the first stumbling, agonizing steps toward industrialization, the overpowering human and material obstacles they had to encounter, and the successes as well as the fumblings and failures experienced during the early stages.[45]

[43] K. A. Petrosian, *Sovetskii metod industrializatsii.* (Moscow, 1951). A. F. Khavin, *Kratkii ocherk istorii industrializatsii SSSR.* (Moscow, 1962). M. P. Kim, *Sotsialisticheskaia industrializatsiia v SSSR.* (Moscow, 1955). (This was originally written as a paper to be delivered before the Eleventh International Congress of Historians.) Another paper of similar nature is that of L. V. Cherepnin and Iu. A. Poliakov, published in *Istoriia SSSR,* No. 1 (1961), 12-27.

[44] See *Obshchie zakonomernosti perekhoda k sotsializmu i osobennosti ikh proiavleniia v raznykh stranakh. Sbornik.* (Moscow, 1960).

[45] G. M. Krzhizhanovskii, *Desiat let khoziaisvennogo stroitelstva SSSR. 1917-1927.* (Moscow, 1927). E. I. Kviring, *Ocherki razvitiia promyshlennosti SSSR. 1917-1927.* (Moscow, 1929). V. P. Miliutin, *Istoriia ekonomicheskogo razvitiia SSSR (1917-1927).* 2nd ed. (Moscow, 1929). V. E. Motylev, *Problema tempa razvitiia SSSR.* 3rd ed. (Moscow, 1929). S. G. Strumilin, *Problemy planirovaniia v SSSR.* (Leningrad, 1932). S. G. Strumilin, *Ocherki sovetskoi ekonomiki.* 2nd ed. (Moscow, 1930). Many publications also include propaganda literature promoting industrialization and mechanization of agriculture. Among the latter may be mentioned the following: A. P. Serebrovskii, *Industrializatsiia strany i krestianstvo.* (Moscow, 1927). K. Ia. Rozental, *V zashchitu industrializatsii SSSR. Tovarnyi*

The second stage, from about 1933, lasted for some two decades. Neither the first nor particularly the second stage of industrial development has been dealt with satisfactorily in literature. With the exception of a few popular accounts and textbooks, the economic, political, and social implications seem scarcely to have been investigated.[46] What was written during the period was in essence what would coincide with the official version of the *History of the All-Union Communist Party.* Here one finds the familiar clichés about Stalin, about the grave urgency of industrialization, the need of an accelerated tempo to change the entire national economy of the USSR. Most writers were engaged in popular polemics to stimulate national production. Two monographs, one by N. Riabov and the other by L. I. Skvortsov, are exceptions.[47]

A fundamental work in the historical literature of economic development is the monograph already referred to, by K. A. Petrosian, published in 1951.[48] It was probably the first work in which the author made an effort to render a broad interpretation of Soviet industrial methods. The attempt, though commendable, was not entirely successful, mainly because of the prevailing political climate during which it was written: instead of making an objective evaluation within a true historical setting of the industrial revolution as well as the economic experiment, the author found himself caught in the common net of obsequies to Stalin. Factual material became subordinated to a desire to prove Stalin's economic and political acumen. At its best it is a rather worthy account of the development of Soviet heavy industry, which in itself is a common theme of most economic historians, who maintained the official line that national industrialization cannot be imagined without the establishment of a heavy industry. The theme was repeated by even the most prominent economists, like S. Baishev and S. Sergeev.[49]

golod i zadachi promyshlennosti. (Moscow, 1928). A. F. Gladun, *Industrializatsiia SSSR i selkhozlesrabochie.* (Moscow, 1929). T. Okhotnikov, *Industrializatsiia strany i potrebitelskaia kooperatsiia.* (Moscow, 1929). A. Osipian and M. Lapidus, *Industrializatsiia—osnova ekonomicheskoi nezavisimosti SSSR.* (Moscow, 1928). A. K. Azizian, *Dlia chego nuzhna krestianinu industrializatsiia strany.* (Moscow, 1929).

[46]D. D. Mishustin, *Vneshniaia torgovlia i industrializatsiia SSSR.* (Moscow, 1938). E. L. Granovskii, *Sotsialisticheskaia industrializatsiia—osnova voennoi moshchi SSSR.* (Alma-Ata, 1942). P. Chesnokov, *Sotsialisticheskaia industrializatsiia—osnova oborony SSSR.* (Moscow, 1943).

[47]N. Riabov, *Sotsialisticheskoe nakoplenie i ego istochniki v pervoi i vtoroi piatiletkakh.* (Moscow, 1951). L. I. Skvortsov, *Rol kredita v industrializatsii SSSR.* (Moscow, 1951).

[48]K. A. Petrosian, *Sovetskii metod industrializatsii.* (Moscow, 1951).

[49]S. Baishev, *Sotsialisticheskaia industrializatsiia Kazakhstana. Stenogramma publichnoi lektsii.* (Alma-Ata, 1949). S. Sergeev, *Sotsialisticheskaia industrializatsiia Urala v gody predvoennykh piatiletok.* (Sverdlovsk, 1961).

The third stage, finally, is the period that followed the death of Stalin in 1953. During 1954-1955 the magazine *Voprosy istorii* already managed to include a lively discussion about the periodization of Soviet history. Some writers like M. P. Kim and I. B. Berkhin chose the year 1926 to mark the economic recovery from the ravages of the Civil War, and the period immediately following was to be regarded as the initial period of Soviet industrialization. B. P. Orlov maintained that the recovery period ended at least by 1927, while A. M. Panfilova and A. M. Anifimov believed that the beginning of industrialization could logically be counted from the year 1925, when Russian industry reached the pre-1914 productive capacity, and henceforth industry had entered the stage of national economic growth along new modern lines.[50] Both views are inadequately reasoned out; neither uses convincing statistical data or takes into account the changes that took place in the economy during 1921-1925, which made possible the transition to industrialization at this early date. E. Iu. Lokshin, in his book on Soviet industry during the first fifteen years, states that already in 1926 the country was able to turn out diesel motors, electrical equipment, steam turbines, weaving looms, and other machinery that was not produced in Russia prior to 1914.[51]

Meanwhile, in 1957 there appeared a volume of collected articles on the industrialization of Azerbaidzhan (1926-1932), followed two years later by a collection of documents on the early industrialization of the Soviet Union in 1926-1927, edited by M. P. Kim. The appearance of these two books marks the beginning of publication of archival documents on the history of Soviet industrial development and more serious studies of economic conditions. These two were soon followed by other publications in Leningrad, Saratov, and elsewhere.[52]

The accelerated appearance of published documents pertaining to Soviet economic development stimulated additional research and writing in the field. Following 1956, the availability of improved data encouraged a long list of authors to publish the results of their research, among them such

---

[50] I. B. Berkhin and M. P. Kim, "O periodizatsii istorii sovetskogo obshchestva." *Voprosy istorii,* No. 10 (1954), 72-78. F. Ia. Polianskii, "Problema osnovnogo ekonomicheskogo zakona feodalizma." *Voprosy istorii,* No. 10 (1954), 79-84. P. V. Snesarevskii, "O deistvii osnovnogo ekonomicheskogo zakona feodalizma v Rossii." *Voprosy istorii,* No. 10 (1954), 85-89. A. P. Kuchkin, B. P. Orlov et al., "K voprosu o periodizatsii istorii sovetskogo obshchestva." *Voprosy istorii,* No. 3 (1955), 71-79.

[51] E. Iu. Lokshin, *Promyshlennost SSSR za 15 let.* (Moscow, 1932).

[52] *Sotsialisticheskaia industrializatsiia Azerbaidzhana (1926-1932 gg.). Dokumenty i materialy.* (Baku, 1957). M. P. Kim, ed., *Pervye shagi industrializatsii SSSR, 1926-1927.* (Moscow, 1959). *Kommunisty Leningrada v borbe za vypolnenie reshenii partii po industrializatsii strany (1926-1929 gg.). Sbornik dokumentov i materialov.* (Leningrad, 1960). *Saratovskaia Partiinaia organizatsiia v gody sotsialisticheskoi industrializatsii strany i sploshnoi kollektivizatsii selskogo khoziaistva. Dokumenty i materialy, 1926-1929 gg.* (Saratov, 1960).

economists as P. I. Liashchenko and E. M. Polianskaia. A noticeable feature in most of these writings is the stress upon the experimental atmosphere and daring, the plunge of an entire nation from a backward rural state in an effort to transform its economy into an advanced industrial one within a matter of a few years. The bitter toil and sweat, the hardships and deprivations with which the nation paid for the advancement, are nowhere to be noted.[53] During the 1960's Soviet citizens could scarcely visualize the national exertion required during "Russia's Iron Age," the frightful conditions in which the masses struggled to wrench themselves from the clutches of the primitive economy in order to shift themselves into the most advanced socialist technology. It took a Soviet journalist, not an historian, to revive vividly the memories of the 1930's when great tractor plants and industrial centers were constructed at Magnitogorsk, Cheliabinsk, Kuzbass, Karaganda, and Sverdlovsk, and dams such as the Dneprostroi were erected.[54]

D. HEAVY INDUSTRY IN THE PLAN OF SOCIALISM

Soviet historians maintain that their rapid technological development was due entirely to the socialized system. Such writers as P. N. Ivanov, E. Iu. Lokshin, and G. Sakharov argue that only under a Soviet system could industrialization have been carried out on such a scale and with such speed and effectiveness. This argument has been pursued with even greater conviction since the war by writers like P. A. Belov, L. M. Gatovskii, I, Bardin, and M. M. Konstantinov.[55] Besides the usual glowing description of socialistic

[53]P. I. Liashchenko, *Istoriia narodnogo khoziaistva SSSR.* Vol. III, *Sotsializm.* (Moscow, 1956). E. Iu. Lokshin, *Ocherk istorii promyshlennosti SSSR (1917-1940).* (Moscow, 1956). I. V. Maevskii, *Tiazhelaia promyshlennost SSSR v pervye gody sotsialisticheskoi industrializatsii (1926-1929).* (Moscow, 1959). I. M. Nekrasova, *Leninskii plan elektrifikatsii strany i ego osushchestvlenie v 1921-1931 gg.* (Moscow, 1960). E. M. Polianskaia, "Iz istorii sotsialisticheskoi industrializatsii Sibiri." *Voprosy istorii,* No. 8 (1956), 15-32. *Pervye shagi industrializatsii SSSR. Sbornik.* (Moscow, 1959). A. I. Notkin, "Sotsialisticheskaia industrializatsiia SSSR i novyi tekhnicheskii perevorot." *Vestnik Akademii nauk SSSR,* No. 1 (1958). *Postroenie fundamenta sotsialisticheskoi ekonomii v SSSR, 1926-1932 gg.* (Moscow, 1960).

[54]Iurii Zhukov, *Liudi 30kh godov.* (Moscow, "Sovetskaia Rossiia," 1967).

[55]P. N. Ivanov, *Sovetskaia elektrotekhnicheskaia promyshlennost. Ocherk razvitiia.* (Moscow, 1933). E. Iu. Lokshin, *Promyshlennost SSSR v pervoi piatiletke.* (Moscow, 1934). G. Sakharov, N. Chernai, and O. Kabakov, *Ocherki organizatsii tiazheloi promyshlennosti SSSR.* (Moscow, 1934). G. Streltsov, *Mashinostroenie v pervoi piatiletke.* (Moscow, 1933). B. Blinkov, *Khimicheskaia promyshlennost SSSR. Ekonomicheskii ocherk.* (Moscow, 1932). M. Tsaguria, *15 let tiazheloi promyshlennosti SSSR.* (Moscow, 1932). P. A. Belov, *Sotsialisticheskaia industrializatsiia strany i kollektivizatsiia selskogo khoziaistva SSSR.* (Moscow, 1946). E. Iu. Lokshin, *Partiia bolshevikov v borbe za industrializatsiiu SSSR.* (Moscow, 1946). L. M. Gatovskii, *Politika sotsialisticheskoi industrializatsii spasla nashu Rodinu.* (Moscow, 1946). N. M. Mor, *SSSR—moguchaia industrialnaia derzhava.*

methods and denigrating references to capitalism, there are genuine efforts
to write more realistically on the part of some writers. The best illustration of such an attempt is the work of I. M. Brover, which appeared in
1954. The author made a fairly successful effort to summarize numerous
resource works into a single basic study of the socialist economy.[56]

In 1955, the Soviet government decided to continue the consistent support and priorities assigned to heavy industry and declined the request to
favor similarly industries engaged in production of consumer goods. During the middle 1950's, E. Ia. Bagreev, A. G. Omarovskii, B. M. Levin, and
P. A. Gundyrin all wrote on this subject, emphasizing the long-standing
policy of the Communist Party that since heavy industry serves as a basis
of economic power it deserves the highest priority.[57]

The 1956 Plan is discussed by such eminent Soviet economists as P. I.
Liashchenko and E. Iu. Lokshin. Both of them analyze minutely the preceding five-year plans, the priority system followed, the growth of production, and the changes that ensued. It was the relentless drive and unswerv-
ing determination to favor heavy industry, argued the writers, that enabled
the Soviet Union successfully to withstand the impact of Nazi aggression,
that "saved the Fatherland."[58] It was not until the 1960's that a noticeable shift in opinion began to take place. There appeared an increased feeling among economists that an attempt must be made toward a fuller appreciation of Soviet economic conditions. There was a quest for an overall
reappraisal of national industrialization from the 1920's through the 1960's.
In addition, there was need for a reappraisal of priorities allotted to heavy
industries, the ferrous metals and other allied industrial plants. These
should be analyzed nationally as well as regionally, was the feeling, afford-
ing a rational appreciation of the impact industrialization had made upon
the country at large as well as upon outlying regions of the USSR.[59]

(Moscow, 1947). A. G. Omarovskii, *Sovetskoe stankostroenie i ego rol v industri-*
alizatsii SSSR i chernaia metallurgiia. (Moscow, 1950). M. M. Konstantinov, *So-*
tsialisticheskaia promyshlennost i eë vedushchaia rol v razvitii narodnogo khoziai-
stva SSSR. (Moscow, 1950). M. P. Kim, *SSSR v period industrializatsii. Lektsii.*
(Moscow, 1951).

[56]I. M. Brover, *Ocherki razvitiia tiazheloi promyshlennosti SSSR.* (Alma-Ata, 1954).

[57]E. Ia. Bagreev, *Tiazhelaia industriia—osnova mogushchestva SSSR.* (Sverdlovsk,
1955). A. G. Omarovskii, *Tiazhelaia industriia—osnova razvitiia narodnogo khoziai-*
stva SSSR. (Moscow, 1955). B. M. Levin, *Vsemirnoe razvitie tiazheloi industrii—*
generalnaia liniia KPSS. (Moscow, 1956). P. A. Gundyrin, *Tiazhelaia industriia—*
osnova razvitiia sovetskoi ekonomiki. (Moscow, 1956).

[58]L. M. Gatovskii, *Politika sotsialisticheskoi industrializatsii spasla nashu Rodinu.*
(Moscow, 1946).

[59]Several sound studies were produced as a result of this new demand: I. K. Beliaev,
Sotsialisticheskaia industrializatsiia Zapadnoi Sibiri. (Novosibirsk, 1958). N. G.
Eroshkevich, *Razvitie promyshlennosti Sovetskogo Altaia.* (Barnaul, 1958). A. F.
Khavin, "Iz istorii promyshlennogo stroitelstva na Vostoke SSSR." *Voprosy istorii,*
No. 5 (1960), 23-42. A. F. Khavin, "Razvitie tiazheloi promyshlennosti v tretei

Many industries that had not existed before 1914 were now important on the Russian scene, such as the apatite, automobile, truck, tractor, combine, synthetic fiber, and rubber industries. The foundations had been laid for gigantic industrial complexes such as the Magnitogorsk metallurgical, the Cheliabinsk and Stalingrad tractor, and the Ural and Novo-Kramatorsk machine-construction industries and the Gorky automobile plant. By the end of the first five-year plan in 1932, these industries were not only set up, but turned to production. This was brought out emphatically by writers like A. Kurskii and N. F. Berezov as early as 1933, and fully recognized many years later by other students of economics. The same writers, including such economists as R. S. Livshits and L. V. Opatskii, examined industrial development geographically, from the first five-year plan on. They show that in many localities industry had arisen where it had never existed before. There is general emphasis on heavy industry, while light industry or plants engaged in production of consumer goods received hardly any attention, reflecting the party position that only heavy industry was basic to Soviet power.[60]

When in 1957 *Voprosy istorii* reviewed E. Iu. Lokshin's *Voprosy ekonomiki materialnykh resursov v promyshlennosti SSSR* (Moscow, 1934), one of the criticisms was that he failed to incorporate a discussion of "Group B" industry, that is, industry classified as number two priority, light industry engaged in production of consumer goods. In his third volume of *Istoriia narodnogo khoziaistva SSSR*, P. I. Liashchenko devotes more attention to this area, though by no means allowing it adequate space. All the others who published during the 1940's and early 1950's bypassed the subject altogether. Even such a first-rate work as the one of K. A. Petrosian concentrates completely on the heavy industrial development. The light industry is referred to in very general terms and only in order to prove the wisdom of emphasis upon "Group A" industry. (In all fairness it should be added that "Group B" industry was deemphasized or given lower

piatiletke (1938—iiun 1941 g.)." *Istoriia SSSR*, No. 1 (1959), 10-35. P. M. Lukianov, *Kratkaia istoriia khimicheskoi promyshlennosti SSSR. Ot vozniknoveniia khimicheskoi promyshlennosti do nashikh dnei.* (Moscow, 1959). A. G. Ivanov, "Cheliabinskaia oblastnaia partiinaia organizatsiia v borbe za razvitie tiazheloi promyshlennosti v gody tretei piatiletki." *Sbornik statei po voprosam istorii KPSS.* (Cheliabinsk, 1960). Ia. S. Rozenfeld and K. I. Klimenko, *Istoriia mashinostroeniia SSSR (s pervoi poloviny XIX v. do nashikh dnei).* (Moscow, 1961).

[60]I. I. Kolomiichenko, "Sozdanie traktornoi promyshlennosti SSSR." *Istoriia SSSR*, No. 1 (1957), 74-104. A. Kurskii, *Razmeshchenie promyshlennosti v pervoi piatiletke.* (Moscow, 1933). N. F. Berezov, *Razmeshchenie chernoi metallurgii SSSR.* (Moscow, 1933). R. S. Livshits, *Ocherki po razmeshcheniiu promyshlennosti SSSR.* (Moscow, 1954). R. S. Livshits, *Razmeshchenie chernoi metallurgii SSSR.* (Moscow, 1958). L. V. Opatskii, *Razmeshchenie pishchevoi promyshlennosti SSSR.* (Moscow, 1958). P. V. Soloviev, "Osvoenie Khibin i sozdanie apatitovoi promyshlennosti v SSSR." *Voprosy istorii*, No. 2 (1958), 45-59. V. S. Lel'chuk, "Iz istorii sozdaniia promyshlennosti sinteticheskikh materialov v SSSR." *Voprosy istorii*, No. 1 (1960), 25-41.

338

priority during the second five-year plan, 1933-1937, mainly because of the acute awareness of the international situation.)

The monograph by I. K. Beliaev, *Sotsialisticheskaia industrializatsiia Zapadnoi Sibiri* (Novosibirsk, 1958), touches upon light industry while describing the early 1920's; in discussing later years the same industry is hardly considered.

After 1945 there was hardly a monograph or pamphlet published dealing with such industries as the textile, the food production, clothing, footwear, or any other within "Group B" industries. Nor do such extensive works as those by P. A. Khromov and L. V. Opatskii contain any material related to the problem, with the result that the general accounts of the economic situation of the USSR are limited in scope and unbalanced in content. There came a fixed conviction that only heavy industry will change Russian society into a modern one; that only heavy industry will gain for the USSR a respected place in world affairs. Light industry was forced into the background of economic planning and rarely discussed unless the "expectations" of a bright future were being dealt with.[61]

E. REGIONAL INDUSTRIAL DEVELOPMENT

Industrial development in the constituent republics of the Soviet Union was discussed in various popular Soviet publications during the early 1930's. Partly because writers waited to place events in a better historical perspective, partly because of the volume of source materials to be studied, scholarly studies appeared at later dates.[62] In an outstanding study, P. M. Alampiev deals with the republic of Kazakhstan and shows how industrialization

[61]P. A. Khromov, *Ocherki ekonomiki tekstilnoi promyshlennosti SSSR. (Moscow,* 1946). L. V. Opatskii, *Razmeshchenie pishchevoi promyshlennosti SSSR.* (Moscow, 1958).

[62]A short list of works on regional economic development may be offered here. V. Lavrentev, *Puti industrializatsii Srednei Azii.* (Samarkand, 1929). V. A. Khonin, *Problemy industrializatsii Srednego Povolzhia.* (Moscow, Samara, 1930). A. F. Khavin, *Sotsialisticheskaia industrializatsiia natsionalnykh respublik i oblastei.* (Moscow, 1933). Cf. with those published after 1945 and particularly since 1953. See S. N. Malinin, *Razvitie promyshlennosti Belorusskoi SSSR.* (Minsk, 1948). A. Artykov, *Promyshlennost Turkmenskoi SSR za 25 let.* (Ashkhabad, 1950). N. Kiikbaev, *Promyshlennost Kazakhstana v pervoi piatiletke.* (Alma-Ata, 1951). G. Chulanov, *Promyshlennost Kazakhstana za gody Sovetskoi vlasti.* (Alma-Ata, 1951). A. V. Mazaev, *Razvitie sotsialisticheskoi promyshlennosti Tadzhikskoi SSR za 25 let.* (Stalinabad, 1954). A. F. Khavin, *Karaganda—tretia ugolnaia baza SSSR.* (Alma-Ata, 1954). B. A. Desiatchikov, *Promyshlennost Uzbekistana za 30 let.* (Tashkent, 1955). G. O. Allakhverdian and S. I. Khrimlian, *Razvitie tiazheloi promyshlennosti Armianskoi SSR.* (Erevan, 1955). *Ocherki po razvitiiu promyshlennosti Komi ASSR.* (Syktyvkar, 1956). N. S. Esipov, *Promyshlennost Kirgizii.* (Frunze, 1957). Kh. T. Medalev, *Sotsialisticheskaia industrializatsiia Kabardino-Balkarii (1928-1937 gg.).* (Nalchik, 1959). Kh. Iuldashev, *Iz istorii razvitiia sotsialisticheskoi promyshlennosti Tashkenta.* (Tashkent, 1960). N. I. Shishkin,

affected the entire eastern part of the Soviet Union. Regional studies by other economic historians dealt with the developments in Uzbekistan, Armenia, Turkmenia, Bashkiria, and elsewhere.[63]

In general, however, few of the regional studies can be considered superior investigations. Some of the better ones are by B. M. Mitupov, A. A. Baishin, K. A. Akilov, and Kh. M. Musin. Mitupov's original and worthwhile study traces the history of industrial development and the formation of the laboring class in Buriatia. The main merit of this work is that the author, for the first time, discusses the national patterns in industrial growth and provides a keen analysis of regional developments. Buriatia is of special importance in this regard since the capitalistic phase never touched this region, which was transformed from a primitive agricultural state directly into a socialized industrial economy.[64] Soviet historiography still needs good monographic studies in the regional industrial developments of the Ukraine, Transcaucasia, and other constituent and autonomous republics.

F. SOVIET LABOR AND TECHNOLOGY

Recently there has been a renewed interest in the history of Russian labor and technology, indicated by the increased publication of documents, monographs, and articles since the middle of the 1950's.

The projected history of Russian labor, as part of a history of national industrial development originally suggested by A. M. Gorky and long in abeyance, came back to life. The Soviet Academy of Sciences, along with its sister institutions in the constituent republics, revived research on a national history of Soviet industry and of the labor class.

From a Soviet point of view this implied three things: the origin of the labor class; the role of the socialist revolutionary movement; and finally, the laboring class since 1917, engaged in building a socialist society. It was expected that such a history should also include topics like the growth of a

---

Promyshlennost Komi ASSR. (Moscow, 1957). Sh. N. Ulmasbaev, *Promyshlennoe razvitie Sovetskogo Uzbekistana. Istoriko-ekonomicheskii ocherk.* (Tashkent, 1958).

[63]P. M. Alampiev, *Likvidatsiia ekonomicheskogo neravenstva narodov Sovetskogo Vostoka i sotsialisticheskoe razmeshchenie promyshlennosti. Istoricheskii opyt Kazakhskoi SSR.* (Moscow, 1958). *Narodnoe khoziaistvo Uzbekskoi SSR. Statisticheskii sbornik.* (Tashkent, 1957). S. A. Tatybekov, *Ocherki sotsialisticheskogo preobrazovaniia ekonomiki Kirgizii, 1917-1940.* (Frunze, 1959). M. S. Dzhunusov, *Ob istoricheskom opyte stroitelstve sotsializma v ranee otstalykh stranakh.* (Moscow, 1958).

[64]B. M. Mitupov, *Razvitie promyshlennosti i formirovanie rabochego klassa v Buriatskoi ASSR (1923-1937 gg.).* (Ulan-Ude, 1958). A. A. Baishin, *Istoricheskie etapy formirovaniia rabochego klassa v Sovetskom Kazakhstane.* (Alma-Ata, 1958). K. A. Akilov, "Iz istorii formirovaniia rabochego klassa v Uzbekistane (1929-1932 gg.)." *Iz istorii Sovetskogo Uzbekistana. Sbornik statei.* (Tashkent, 1956). Kh. M. Musin, *Osnovnye etapy formirovaniia rabochego klassa v Kirgizskoi SSR. Sbornik statei Kirgizskogo gosudarstvennogo zaochnogo pedagogicheskogo instituta. Seriia istorii-geografii.* Issue III. (Frunze, 1957).

labor class since the adoption of the different five-year plans throughout the Soviet Union; the emergence of a new Soviet elite from the working class; the rise of technological and cultural levels; and improved living standards among the toiling masses. Only a history that incorporates these aspects will be acceptable for publication, Communist officials insist.[65]

At the same time there has been an increase of interest in the changing cultural and technological standards among Soviet workers. Two studies, one by O. V. Kozlova, the other by G. M. Okladnoi, utilize a considerable amount of statistical data and other source materials which convincingly show a rise in these aspects of life among the industrial workers. However, the emphasis is on the later years, while treatment of the earlier period is brief, matter-of-fact, and even superficial. The citation of statistical figures is often careless and occasionally misleading.[66]

V. I. Kasianenko has contributed an outstanding monograph, which, though it is a work neither entirely adequate nor complete, is entirely original in its interpretation of the technical and engineering achievements that resulted in a fair degree of economic independence for the Soviet Union. Kasianenko uses convincing evidence to make the point that the growth of new industries was mainly in the fields most dependent upon imports, and which were vital to the national economy.[67]

Finally, there are some excellent general works on economic development of the Soviet Union that include chapters on these subjects, such as those by P. I. Liashchenko, E. Iu. Lokshin, and V. F. Teeunov. In addition, historical periodicals contain numerous articles and data of vital importance.[68]

---

[65]Illustrative of such writings are the following: O. I. Shkaratan, "Izmeneniia v so-tsialnom sostave fabrichno-zavodskikh rabochikh Leningrada (1917-1928 gg.)." *Istoriia SSSR*, No. 5 (1959), 21-38. V. B. Telpukhovskii, "Izmeneniia v sostave pro-myshlennykh rabochikh SSSR v period Velikoi Otechestvennoi voiny." *Voprosy istorii*, No. 6 (1960), 27-42. A. G. Rashin, "O chislennosti i sostave rabochego klassa v 1928-1955." *Iz istorii rabochego klassa i revoliutsionnogo dvizheniia. Sbornik statei pamiati Anny Mikhailovny Pankratovoi.* (Moscow, 1958). B. M. Smekhov, "Rost i izmenenie sostava rabochego klassa SSSR." *Voprosy truda v SSSR. Sbornik statei.* (Moscow, 1958).

[66]O. V. Kozlova, *Podem kulturno-tekhnicheskogo urovnia rabochego klassa SSSR.* (Moscow, 1959). G. M. Okladnoi, *Podem kulturno-tekhnicheskogo urovnia rabochego klassa.* (Kharkov, 1957). Both works are reviewed, respectively, in *Kommunist*, No. 3 (1960), 149-153, and in *Vestnik statistiki*, No. 3 (1961), 72-75.

[67]V. I. Kasianenko, *Borba trudiashchikhsia SSSR za tekhnicheskuiu nezavisimost pro-myshlennosti (1926-1932 gg.).* (Moscow, 1960). See also E. A. Tokarzhevskii, *Ocherki istorii Sovetskogo Azerbaidzhana v period perekhoda na mirnuiu rabotu po vosstanovlenniiu narodnogo khoziaistva (1921-1925 gg.).* (Baku, 1956). K. Fazylkhodzhaev, *Profsoiuzy Uzbekistana v borbe za vypolnenie plana vtoroi piatiletki (1933-1937).* (Tashkent, 1960). I. D. Korzun, *Pervye shagi sotsialisticheskoi industrializatsii.* (Kalinin, 1960).

[68]P. I. Liashchenko, *Istoriia narodnogo khoziaistva SSSR.* Vol. III, *Sotsializm.*

Though the bibliography in the field of Soviet economic history is extensive, there are still noticeable gaps, one of which concerns the effects of industrialization upon regional socio-economic conditions. Most of the literature on this subject is of pamphlet nature, both in size and in depth, and written mainly for bolstering public spirits.[69]

The writings on such subjects as labor conditions or private industry during the period of the New Economic Policy (1921-1929), on the history of concessions to foreign capital, or on state capitalism in the Soviet Union during the transitionary period from capitalism to socialism are still too sparse. Treatment of the Soviet struggle for the establishment of technical independence in its industrialization program is equally inadequate.[70]

(Moscow, 1956). E. Iu. Lokshin, *Ocherk istorii promyshlennosti SSSR (1917-1940 gg.).* (Moscow, 1956). V. F. Teeunov, *Promyshlennoe razvitie Zapadnogo Urala. Istoriko-ekonomicheskii ocherk.* Books 2-3. (Perm, 1957-1958). I. M. Nekrasova, *Leninskii plan elektrifikatsii strany i ego osushchestvlenie v 1921-1931 gg.* (Moscow, 1960). G. Unpelev, *Rozhdenie Uralmasha (1928-1933 gg.).* (Moscow, 1960). N. P. Lipatov, *Chernaia metallurgiia Urala v gody Velikoi Otechestvennoi voiny (1941-1945 gg.). Ocherki stroitelstva.* (Moscow, 1960). A. F. Khavin, "Vosstanovlenie promyshlennosti Donbassa v period Velikoi Otechestvennoi voiny." *Voprosy istorii,* No. 5 (1956), 116-126. G. G. Morekhina, "Iz istorii perestroiki promyshlennosti Sovetskogo Soiuza v pervoi period Velikoi Otechestvennoi voiny (1941-1942 gg.)." *Voposy istorii,* No. 12 (1958), 27-49. E. B. Genkina, "Vozniknovenie proizvodstvennykh soveshchanii v gody vosstanovitelnogo perioda (1921-1925 gg.)." *Istoriia SSSR,* No. 3 (1958), 63-90. I. P. Ostapenko and Iu. P. Voskresenskii, "Iz istorii proizvodstvennykh soveshchanii po promyshlennosti SSSR (1926-1932 gg.)." *Voprosy istorii,* No. 6 (1958), 22-40.

[69]O. Kuperman, *Sotsialno-ekonomicheskie formy promyshlennosti SSSR.* (Moscow, 1929). Iu. Larin, *Chastnyi kapital v SSSR.* (Moscow, 1927). I. Mingulin, *Puti razvitiia chastnogo kapitala.* (Moscow, 1927). A. Fabrichnyi, *Chastnyi kapital na poroge piatiletki. Klassovaia borba v gorode i gosudarstvennyi apparat.* (Moscow, 1930). F. Ia. Khrushchev, *Ot promysla—k industrii. (Pishchevaia promyshlennost Kazakhstana).* (Alma-Ata, 1935). D. Shapiro, *Kustarnaia promyshlennost i narodnoe khoziaistvo SSSR.* (Moscow, 1928). P. I. Vasilevskii and E. I. Shlifshtein, *Ocherki kustarnoi promyshlennosti SSSR.* (Moscow, 1930).

[70]T. K. Rafailova, "Polozhenie rabochikh i klassovaia borba chastno-kapitalisticheskikh predpriiatiiakh v period nepa (1921-1929 gg.)." *Trudy Leningradskogo tekhnologicheskogo instituta im. Lensoveta.* Issue 47 (1958). V. I. Kasianenko, L. F. Morozov, and L. K. Shkarenkov, "Iz istorii kontsessionnoi politiki Sovetskogo gosudarstva." *Istoriia SSSR,* No. 4 (1959), 33-60. I. D. Brin, *Gosudarstvennyi kapitalizm v SSSR v perekhodnyi period ot kapitalizma k sotsializmu.* (Irkutsk, 1959). P. L. Bulat and S. L. Sverdlin, *Borba za tekhniko-ekonomicheskuiu nezavisimost SSSR.* (Leningrad, 1935). D. D. Mishustin, *Vneshniaia torgovlia i industrializatsiia SSSR.* (Moscow, 1938). K. P. Pavlov, *Rol gosudarstvennoi monopolii vneshnei torgovli v postroenii sotsializma v SSSR, 1918-1937.* (Moscow, 1960). (The work of Pavlov is especially recommended as an outstanding study in the field.)

A most glaring inadequacy in Soviet historiography is still the problem of light industry engaged in production of consumer goods. There is equal need for a better presentation of the impact of the planned economy upon the handicraft industry, and for a more penetrating examination of the second and third five-year plans.

CHAPTER XIII

Foreign Affairs

A. GENERAL SURVEY

Basic works which define the place of diplomacy in Soviet national affairs begin with the founder of the Soviet state, V. I. Lenin. Much has been written on such themes as Lenin and Soviet foreign policy, Lenin and the Orient, Lenin and world peace, and Lenin and his philosophy of foreign trade. Some writers, such as A. N. Kheifets and S. Iu. Vygodskii, present original ideas and little-known facts; for instance, they describe Lenin's earliest efforts to provide diplomatic aid to Oriental peoples. They also cite the first negotiations with foreign representatives from capitalist countries, and schemes elaborated for the Genoa and Hague conferences.[1]

Generally speaking, early Soviet diplomatic relations with Germany and with Czechoslovakia have been researched most thoroughly. In both cases sources at home and in the corresponding countries have been fully utilized.[2] Studies of Sino-Soviet relations of the 1950's shed light on the honeymoon period and show the extent of the "unselfish aid" Moscow extended to the Chinese people. Writers such as M. V. Meshcheriakov have

[1]M. Airapetian and P. Kabanov, *Leninskie printsipy vneshnei politiki Sovetskogo gosudarstva.* (Moscow, 1957). B. G. Gafurov, ed., *Lenin i Vostok. Sbornik statei.* (Moscow, 1960). A. N. Kheifets, *Lenin—velikii drug narodov Vostoka.* (Moscow, 1960). S. Iu. Vygodskii, *V. I. Lenin—rukovoditel vneshnei politiki Sovetskogo gosudarstva.* (Leningrad, 1960). V. M. Khvostov, "V. I. Lenin v borbe za mir." *Lenin i nauka.* (Moscow, 1960), 249-260. I. Ivashin, "Leninskii printsip mirnogo sosushchestvovaniia v deistvii." *Velikaia sila leninskikh idei. Sbornik statei.* (Moscow, 1960). A. Bogomolov, "V. I. Lenin i vneshniaia politika Sovetskogo gosudarstva." *Istoriia SSSR,* No. 2 (1960), 46-60. B. E. Shtein, "Lenin i Genuezskaia konferentsiia." *Vestnik Moskovskogo universiteta,* Series 9. *Istoricheskie nauki,* No. 2 (Moscow, 1960). N. N. Liubimov, "Deiatelnost V. I. Lenina v sviazi s Genuezskoi konferentsiei 1922 goda (po novym dokumentam XXXVI Leninskogo sbornika)." *Uchenye zapiski Instituta mezhdunarodnykh otnoshenii.* Issue 2. (Moscow, 1960). M. V. Misko, *Oktiabrskaia revoliutsiia i vosstanovlenie nezavisimosti Polshi.* (Moscow, 1957).

[2]I. K. Kobliakov, "Borba Sovetskogo gosudarstva za sokhranenie mira s Germaniei v period deistviia Brestskogo dogovora (mart—noiabr 1918 g.)." *Istoriia SSSR,* No. 4 (1958), 3-26. V. G. Briunin, "Sovetsko-germanskie otnosheniia nakanune noiabrskoi revoliutsii." *Noiabrskaia revoliutsiia v Germanii. Sbornik statei i materialov.* (Moscow, 1960). I. A. Rossenko, "Sovetsko-germanskie otnosheniia v period noiabrskoi revoliutsii v Germanii." *Noiabrskaia revoliutsiia v Germanii. Sbornik statei i materialov.* (Moscow, 1960). I. A. Rossenko, "Rappalskii dogovor—vazhnaia pobeda leninskoi politiki mira." *Vestnik Leningradskogo universiteta. Seriia istorii, iazyka i literatury.* Issue 2 (Moscow, 1960). A. A. Akhtamzian, "Antisovetskaia politika germanskogo imperializma posle zakliucheniia Brestskogo mira." *Iz istorii agressivnoi vneshnei politiki germanaskogo imperializma.* (Moscow, 1959). A. I. Stepanov, "Iz

dealt with Outer Mongolia and with the establishment of trade between the "East-West bloc" and the Soviet Union.[3] Many studies are devoted to relations with the non-communist countries, among which are those dealing with Anglo-Soviet, American-Soviet, French-Soviet and Japanese-Soviet relations.[4] Other excellent works deal with

istorii sovetsko-germanskogo ekonomicheskogo sotrudnichestva (1924-1926 gg.)." *Uchenye zapiski Instituta mezhdunarodnykh otnoshenii,* Issue 3 (Moscow, 1960). V. A. Shishkin, "Pozitsiia rabochego klassa i burzhuazii Chekhoslovakii v voprose ob okazanii pomoshchi Sovetskoi Rossii vo vremia goloda 1921-1922 gg." *Voprosy novoi i noveishei istorii. Sbornik statei.* (Moscow, 1959). The same publication also includes an article by the same author entitled: "Iz istorii chekhoslovatsko-sovetskikh ekonomicheskikh otnoshenii (1921-1925 gg.)." Ia. A. Peters, *Sodruzhestvo chekhoslovatskogo i sovetskogo narodov v borbe protiv fashizma v gody mirovoi voiny.* (Kiev, 1959).

[3]G. M. Slavin, "Iz istorii sovetsko-polskikh otnoshenii (ianvar—mai 1945 g.)." *Voprosy istorii,* No. 8 (1959), 79-95. M. S. Kapitsa, *Sovetsko-kitaiskie otnosheniia.* (Moscow, 1958). M. I. Sladkovskii, *Ocherki ekonomicheskikh otnoshenii SSSR s Kitaem.* (Moscow, 1957). V. I. Volkhovinskii, *Iz istorii sovetsko-kitaiskikh otnoshenii 1927-1929 gg.* (Kiev, 1960). M. V. Meshcheriakov, *Ocherk ekonomicheskogo sotrudnichestva Sovetskogo Soiuza i Mongolskoi Narodnoi Respubliki.* (Moscow, 1959). B. D. Zotov, *Vneshniaia torgovlia evropeiskikh stran narodnoi demokratii na sluzhbe stroitelstva sotsializma.* (Moscow, 1958). S. D. Sergeev, *Ekonomicheskoe sotrudnichestvo i vzaimopomoshch stran sotsialisticheskogo lageria.* 2nd ed. (Moscow, 1959).

[4]F. D. Volkov, *Anglo-sovetskie otnosheniia, 1924-1929 gg.* (Moscow, 1958). This is a continuation of a former study: *Krakh angliiskoi politiki interventsii i diplomaticheskoi izoliatsii Sovetskogo gosudarstva.* (Moscow, 1954). V. I. Popov, *Anglo-sovetskie otnosheniia (1927-1929).* (Moscow, 1958). A. N. Krasilnikov, *Politika Anglii v otnoshenii SSSR, 1929-1932 gg.* (Moscow, 1959). A. Kh. Babakhodzhaev, *Proval angliiskoi antisovetskoi politiki v Srednei Azii i na Srednem Vostoke v period priznaniia Sovetskogo gosudarstva de-fakto i de-iure (1921-1924 gg.).* (Tashkent, 1957). V. A. Loginov, *Vnutrenniaia politika vtorogo laboristskogo pravitelstva 1929-1931 gg. i vozobnovlenie diplomaticheskikh otnoshenii mezhdu Angliei i SSSR v 1929 g.* (Moscow, 1954). G. K. Seleznev, *Ten' dollara nad Rossiei. Iz istorii amerikano-russkikh otnoshenii.* (Moscow, 1957). R. G. Simonenko, *Imperialisticheskaia politika Soedinennykh Shtatov Ameriki po otnosheniiu k Ukraine v 1917-1918 g.* (Kiev, 1957). D. N. Stashevskii, *Ekspansiia Soedinennykh Shtatov Ameriki v Evrope pod vidom pomoshchi (1919-1923).* (Kiev, 1960). V. Ivanov and V. Leonian, *V interesakh narodov. K voprosu ob ustanovlenii diplomaticheskikh otnoshenii mezhdu SSSR i SShA v 1933.* (Moscow, 1957). R. G. Gorbunov, *Sovetsko-amerikanskie torgovye otnosheniia.* (Moscow, 1961). A. E. Ioffe, *Russko-frantsuzskie otnosheniia v 1917 godu.* (Moscow, 1958). Iu. V. Borisov, "Sovetskii Soiuz i Frantsiia v gody vtoroi mirovoi voiny (1941-1945)." *Novaia i noveishaia istoriia,* No. 3 (1960), 92-103. A. Z. Manfred, "Franko-sovetskie otnosheniia v mirovoi politike." *Mezhdunarodnaia zhizn,* No. 12 (1959), 24-35. *SSSR—Frantsiia. (Iz istorii politicheskikh, ekonomicheskikh i kulturnykh otnoshenii).* (Moscow, 1960). Iu. A. Boev and Iu. E. Egorov, *Traditsionnye sviazi mezhdu narodami SSSR i Frantsii.* (Kiev, 1960).

relations with smaller countries.[5]

A large number of books have appeared on such vital topics as disarmament and collective security since the First World War. A collection of articles edited by V. A. Zorin on the protracted disarmament during negotiations covering the years 1946-1960 contains individual chapters contributed by many Soviet diplomats.[6] Several other studies deal with the early period, covering the withdrawal of Russia from the war in 1917, and with foreign intervention.[7]

A general account of the years immediately following the Civil War and the intervention is contained in a publication edited by I. I. Mints and issued in 1957. In it the early foreign policy steps of the Soviet government are lucidly traced through 1923. I. L. Chikava investigated the case of Georgia and the foreign schemes to detach the Caucasus from the Soviet Union, while others described the origin of the policy of "peaceful coexistence," which is traced to 1921 by L. R. Kletskii.[8]

Far less has been written on foreign policy of the 1920's and 1930's. The first volume of the history of the Second World War covers generally

L. N. Kudashev, "Ustanovlenie diplomaticheskikh otnoshenii mezhdu SSSR i Iaponiei v 1925 godu." *Voprosy istorii*, No. 1 (1960), 124-138. L. N. Kudashev, "Iz istorii borby Sovetskogo gosudarstva za razvitie dobrososedskikh otnoshenii s Iaponiei (1925-1936 gg.)." *Istoriia SSSR*, No. 5 (1960), 24-36. E. M. Zhukov, ed., *Mezhdunarodnye otnosheniia na Dalnem Vostoke (1840-1949)*. 2nd ed. (Moscow, 1956).

[5]A. Efremov, *Sovetsko-avstriiskie otnosheniia posle vtoroi mirovoi voiny*. (Moscow, 1958). E. A. Ambartsumov, *Sovetsko-finliandskie otnosheniia*. (Moscow, 1956). P. Moiseev and Iu. Rozaliev, *K istorii sovetsko-turetskikh otnoshenii*. (Moscow, 1958). S. I. Kuznetsova, *Ustanovlenie sovetsko-turetskikh otnoshenii*. *(K 40-letiiu dogovora mezhdu RSFSR i Turtsiei)*. (Moscow, 1961).

[6]V. M. Khaitsman, *SSSR i problema razoruzheniia. (Mezhdu pervoi i vtoroi mirovymi voinami)*. (Moscow, 1959). A. S. Protopopov, *Sovetskii Soiuz v Organizatsii Obedinennykh Natsii. Iz istorii borby SSSR za mir i nezavisimost narodov (1945-1957 gg.)*. (Moscow, 1957). K. A. Baginian, *Borba Sovetskogo Soiuza protiv agressii*. (Moscow, 1959). G. I. Morozov, *Organizatsiia Obedinennykh Natsii (K 15-letiiu Ustava OON)*. (Moscow, 1960). O. V. Bogdanov, *Iadernoe razoruzhenie*. (Moscow, 1961). V. A. Zorin, ed., *Borba Sovetskogo Soiuza za razoruzhenie, 1946-1960. Sbornik*. (Moscow, 1961). S. Iu. Vygodskii, *Leninskii dekret o mire*. (Leningrad, 1958).

[7]S. M. Maiorov, *Borba Sovetskoi Rossii za vykhod iz imperialisticheskoi voiny*. (Moscow, 1959). A. O. Chubarian, *Brestskii mir i pozitsiia stran Antanty*. (Moscow, 1959). B. E. Shtein, *"Russkii vopros" v 1920-1921 gg*. (Moscow, 1958). This is a continuation of Shtein's other book entitled *"Russkii vopros" na Parizhskoi mirnoi konferentsii (1919-1920 gg.)*. (Moscow, 1949).

[8]I. I. Mints, ed., *Sovetskaia Rossiia i kapitalisticheskii mir v 1917-1923 gg*. (Moscow, 1957). I. L. Chikava, *Krakh antisovetskoi politiki zapadnykh gosudarstv na Genuezskoi i Gaagskoi konferentsiiakh*. (Tbilisi, 1960). L. R. Kletskii, *Leninskoe uchenie o*

the years 1933-1941. A general survey of Soviet foreign relations since 1945 is covered in a book by S. Vygodskii, which, together with some collaborative editions published in the 1950's, presents fairly objective and informative material. Several scholars have undertaken a history of Soviet foreign relations since 1870 under the direction of the prominent Soviet scholars V. M. Khvostov and I. F. Ivashin. Lastly, the work of E. A. Korovin deserves the attention of students of Soviet foreign affairs. Taken together, these studies cover a multitude of topics such as the issues involved in peaceful coexistence, the proletariat as a factor in world unity, the problem of neutrality, the problem of disarmament, and the role of the masses in international affairs. Needless to add, these are all presented with the ideological slant that is to be expected, but then one finds along with the chaff some healthy grain that is worth examining.[9]

B. INTERNATIONAL RELATIONS

A keen interest of Soviet historians in the field of international relations has been observable from the very start. Even before the October Revolution historians such as M. N. Pokrovskii, F. A. Rotshtein, and M. P. Pavlovich were known for their writings in the field of world diplomacy.

On October 26, 1917, shortly after the Soviet regime came to power, V. I. Lenin made the announcement before the All-Russian Congress of Soviets that the government would immediately initiate the complete publication of all secret treaties to which the overthrown Provisional Government was a party. The promise was soon fulfilled when a series of secret documents extracted from the archives of the former Ministry of Foreign Affairs was published.[10] The compilation of the first publication was by a former sailor and member of the Bolshevik Party, N. G. Markin. M. N. Pokrovskii later wrote that a more unusual editor of diplomatic publications could not

mirnom sosushchestvovanii dvukh sistem i ego realizatsiia v 1921-1925 godakh. (Leningrad, 1959). G. A. Deborin, *Vtoraia mirovaia voina.* (Moscow, 1958). L. N. Ivanov, *Ocherki mezhdunarodnykh otnoshenii v period vtoroi mirovoi voiny (1939-1945 gg.).* (Moscow, 1958). *Istoriia Velikoi Otechestvennoi voiny.* (Moscow, 1960-1963). 5 vols. A sixth volume is forthcoming.

[9]S. Vygodskii, *Vneshniaia politika SSSR—politika mira i mezhdunarodnogo sotrudnichestva.* (Moscow, 1958). G. A. Deborin, ed., *Mezhdunarodnye otnosheniia i vneshniaia politika Sovetskogo Soiuza, 1945-1949.* (Moscow, 1958). V. P. Nikhamin, ed., *Mezhdunarodnye otsnosheniia i vneshniaia politika SSSR, 1950-1959).* (Moscow, 1960). 2 parts. F. G. Zuev, ed., *Istoriia mezhdunarodnykh otnoshenii i vneshnei politiki SSSR, 1870-1957 gg.* (Moscow, 1958). V. M. Khvostov, *40 let borby za mir.* (Moscow, 1958). I. F. Ivashin, *Ocherki istorii vneshnei politiki SSSR.* (Moscow, 1958). V. G. Trukhanovskii, ed., *Istoriia mezhdunarodnykh otnoshenii i vneshnei politiki SSSR.* (Moscow, 1961-1964). Vol. I, 1917-1939; Vol. II, 1939-1945; Vol. III, 1945-1963.

[10]*Sbornik sekretnykh dokumentov iz arkhiva byvshego Ministerstva inostrannykh del.* Issues 1-7. (Petrograd, 1917).

have been found. Be that as it may, whatever material this unusual editor extracted from the archives was extraordinary and produced the sensation at which the Soviet government was obviously aiming.[11]

At the same time the Central Archives (headed by M. N. Pokrovskii) began to publish, with the cooperation of the Commissar of Foreign Affairs, a series of documentary collections related mainly to the First World War and to the diplomatic events preceding 1914. It is regrettable that some of these early publications were issued with unusual haste and evidently by men with little editorial experience, so that most of the documents lack adequate explanatory notes, glossaries, or indexes, and frequently fail to indicate the authors of documents cited.[12]

In 1922 the Central Archives began to publish a special irregular journal under the title of *Krasnyi arkhiv*. Some of the issues were devoted to a single general theme, such as the one dedicated to Russo-German relations during the period 1873-1914, but most of the issues included a variety of documents, a goodly portion of which are related to international affairs. *Krasnyi arkhiv* ceased publication in 1941, followed some years later by the appearance of an annotated index to all volumes issued which makes the entire set an indispensable documentary publication.[13] The preface to the first volume of *Krasnyi arkhiv* promised the reader an editorial policy that would prove the old adage, "There is no secret that does not eventually become manifest." The voluminous publication fully justified this promise.

A more systematic undertaking on a grand scale was the effort to prepare a multi-volume publication of diplomatic documents which, regrettably, was never completed, though the first volume appeared in 1931. A group of outstanding Soviet scholars were engaged in the publication of this collection: E. A. Adamov, A. L. Popov, E. D. Grimm, A. S. Ierusalimskii, F. O. Notovich, B. G. Veber, V. V. Altman, L. A. Telesheva, and B. Ia. Galina. The plan was first outlined in 1928, when the Soviet

---

[11]M. N. Pokrovskii, *Imperialisticheskaia voina. Sbornik statei.* (Moscow, 1934), 356. See Iu. K. Krasnov, "M. N. Pokrovskii o nekotorykh voprosakh vneshnei politiki Rossii kontsa XIX v.," and "Sovetskaia vneshniaia politika (1918-1920 gg.) v trudakh M. N. Pokrovskogo." *Voprosy istoriografii i istochnikovedeniia. Kazanskii gosudarstvennyi pedagogicheskii institut. Kafedra istorii SSSR. Sbornik 2.* (Kazan, 1967), 211-217; 218-226.

[12]*Evropeiskie derzhavy i Gretsiia v epokhu mirovoi voiny po sekretnym materialam Ministerstva inostrannykh del s prilozheniem knigi diplomaticheskikh dokumentov.* (Moscow, 1922). *Materialy po istorii franko-russkikh otnoshenii za 1910-1914 gg.* Vol. I. (Moscow, 1922). *Perepiska Vilgelma II s Nikolaem II, 1904-1914 gg.* (Moscow, 1923). *Tsarskaia Rossiia v mirovoi voine.* Vol. I. (Leningrad, 1925). *Konstantinopol i prolivy. Po sekretnym dokumentam Ministerstva inostrannykh del.* (Moscow, 1926). 2 vols. E. D. Grimm, *Sbornik dogovorov i drugikh dokumentov po istorii mezhdunarodnykh otnoshenii na Dalnem Vostoke (1842-1925).* (Moscow, 1927).

[13]*Krasnyi arkhiv, 1922-1941. Annotirovannyi ukazatel soderzhaniia.* (Moscow, 1960).

government formed a special commission in charge of publication of documents related to the epoch of imperialism. The chairman of this commission and editor of the series was the ubiquitous M. N. Pokrovskii, who edited altogether five volumes.[14]

In this whole undertaking M. N. Pokrovskii played a paramount part. Not only was he in charge of editing the documents, but he was busily interpreting the published sources in numerous articles either written by him personally or by his disciple, Ia. M. Zakher.[15]

The appearance of the Soviet diplomatic documents aroused considerable interest among historians. A number of articles were published, commenting on the value of the series and comparing these with similar documents published by other governments. The Soviet historians A. S. Ierusalimskii and V. M. Khvostov made a lengthy analysis of the different "color" books that the Western nations issued after 1914 and compared these with the contents of the more recently revealed Soviet documents.[16] The Soviet documents attracted particularly the attention of the Germans, and the eminent historian Otto Hoetzsch undertook their translation into German.[17]

In addition, Soviet published documents forced the governments of other countries, such as France, Great Britain, and Austria, to open their archives. It is quite understandable why German scholars more than any others were eager to translate and publish the Soviet diplomatic documents: their contents could support the assertion that the Entente in general and Russia in particular were eager to annex Constantinople and the Straits, a gain for which tsarism was ready to pay any price. Pokrovskii himself supported the thesis that the "Turkish inheritance" was the dream which led Imperial Russia to commit aggression. He regarded tsarist foreign policy throughout the late nineteenth and early twentieth centuries through the single prism of the Bosphorus and the Dardanelles problem; the Straits were the "keys to

[14]*Mezhdunarodnye otnosheniia v epokhu imperializma. Dokumenty iz arkhivov tsarskogo i Vremennogo pravitelstv, 1878-1917. Seriia III. 1914-1917.* (Moscow, 1931-1938). See also A. S. Ierusalimskii, "Vopros ob otvetstvennosti za voinu. (Dokumenty po istorii mirovoi voiny kak orudie politicheskoi borby)." *Istorik-marksist,* Vols. I-II (1932), 26-74. See also a review of the publication by V. M. Khvostov in *Problemy marksizma,* Nos. 8-9 (1931).

[15]M. N. Pokrovskii, *Imperialisticheskaia voina. Sbornik statei, 1915-1927 gg.* (Moscow, 1928). See particularly the articles: "Istoricheskie zadachi," "Vinovniki voiny," and "K vystupeniiu Turtsii." Ia. M. Zakher, "K istorii russkoi politiki po voprosu o prolivakh v period mezhdu russko-iaponskoi i tripolitanskoi voinami." *Iz dalekogo i blizkogo proshlogo.* (Petrograd, 1923). Ia. M. Zakher, "Russkaia politika po voprosu o Konstantinopole i prolivakh vo vremia tripolitanskoi voiny." *Izvestiia LGPI im. A. I. Gertsena.* (Leningrad, 1928).

[16]*Istorik-marksist,* Nos. 1-2 (1932), 26-74. *Problemy marksizma,* No. 8-9 (1931).

[17]*Die internationalen Beziehungen im Zeitalter des Imperialismus.* Otto Hoetzsch, ed. Eleven volumes of these documents were published in Germany between 1931 and 1944.

Russia's own house."[18] It was only later, as he familiarized himself more intimately with the documentary evidence, that he came to place a good share of the war guilt upon Germany. But to the end of his life he remained of the firm opinion that the Entente was responsible for a policy of preventive war.[19]

Another Soviet historian, N. P. Poletika, simplified somewhat the war-guilt thesis. Concentrating his study upon Austro-Serbian relations and Russia's Balkan policy during 1908-1914, Poletika came to the conclusion that Germany was provoked to war; that the Sarajevo assassination was the act of a Serbian state under Russian control.[20] Poletika utilized a vast amount of diplomatic source material related to the outbreak of the war, particularly pertaining to the July, 1914, crisis. The original manuscript Poletika published in 1935; some thirty years later he published a new edition in which he revised considerably some of his former conclusions. This, Poletika explained, was because he came across new documentary evidence which compelled him to lighten the burden of war guilt he originally placed on Russia.[21]

By the middle of the 1930's Soviet historiography could list a good number of outstanding monographs and articles in the field of international relations. A long series of articles was published by A. L. Popov, covering foreign policies of the belligerent countries during the period 1914-1918. These articles are based on the recently revealed diplomatic documents and discuss particularly the rivalry of the nations in the Near and Middle East. Popov also wrote on the entrance of the United States into the war and undertook to analyze some of Pokrovskii's erroneous views on the question of war guilt, and his interpretation of imperialism.[22] Some of Popov's other works were on the relations of the European belligerents with the

[18]M. N. Pokrovskii, *Imperialisticheskaia voina.* (Moscow, 1928), 112.

[19]M. N. Pokrovskii, *Imperialisticheskaia voina.* (Moscow, 1928), 360. M. N. Pokrovskii, "Amerika i voina 1914 goda." *Istorik-marksist,* No. 15 (1929).

[20]N. P. Poletika, *Saraevskoe ubiistvo. Issledovanie po istorii avstro-serbskikh otnoshenii i balkanskoi politiki Rossii v period 1908-1914 gg.* (Leningrad, 1930).

[21]N. P. Poletika, *Vozniknovenie mirovoi voiny.* (Moscow, 1935; rev. ed., Moscow, 1964).

[22]A. L. Popov, "Stranitsy iz istorii russkoi politiki v Persii." *Mezhdunarodnaia zhizn,* Nos. 4-5 (1924). A. L. Popov, "Anglo-russkoe sopernichestvo na Iranskikh putiakh." *Novyi vostok,* Book 12 (1926), 126-148. A. L. Popov, "Rossiia i Tibet." *Novyi vostok,* Book 18 (1927), 101-120. A. L. Popov, "Tsarskaia diplomatiia v epokhu Taipinskogo vosstaniia." *Krasnyi arkhiv,* II (21), (1927), 182-199. A. L. Popov, "Anglo-russkoe soglashenie o razdele Kitaia (1899)." *Krasnyi arkhiv,* VI (25), (1927), 111-134. A. L. Popov, "Pervye shagi russkogo imperializma na Dalnem Vostoke, 1888-1903 gg." *Krasnyi arkhiv,* III (52), (1932), 34-124. "Pervaia balkanskaia voina." Foreword by A. L. Popov. *Krasnyi arkhiv,* XV, (1926), 1-29. "Vokrug poezdki Viviani i Albera Toma." Reported by A. L. Popov. *Krasnyi arkhiv,*

United States, and on imperialism in Iran, Tibet, and China. Pokrovskii's views were critically reexamined by A. S. Ierusalimskii and B. Veber, particularly with regard to the new version of imperialism, with special emphasis on its application in the Near and Middle East and throughout Asia.[23]

In 1928 S. D. Skazkin published a superb monograph on the history of European international relations during the end of the nineteenth century. The work is concerned mainly with the Near Eastern question, with Austro-Russian and German-Russian relations. Another outstanding work is by B. A. Romanov, on Russia and Manchuria, a monograph based entirely on new archival materials. According to Romanov, Manchuria was the area that received the greatest attention in the formulation of foreign policies by the Russian Foreign Office between 1892 and 1906.[24] V. M. Khvostov studied Bismarck's foreign policy, showing that basically the Iron Chancellor followed an anti-Russian, anti-French policy. In addition, Khvostov made a special investigation of the intricate Near Eastern situation at the end of the nineteenth century, while A. S. Ierusalimskii dealt with the military panic of 1875 and with German-American relations during the same period.[25]

Contrary to the thesis of Pokrovskii, who placed much of the blame for the outbreak of the war in 1914 upon France and Russia, E. V. Tarlé endeavored to show the responsibility of Germany for the outbreak of the conflict. He considered the entry of the United States into the war as the best example of imperialism resulting from "democratization of capitalism." Tarlé was criticized for regarding Germany as the nation mainly responsible for the outbreak of the war, by the same critics who later came to accept

II (15), (1926), 223-229. A. L. Popov, "Vstuplenie Ameriki v voinu." *Istorik-marksist*, No. 7 (1928), 36-68. M. N. Pokrovskii, "Amerika i voina 1914 goda." *Istorik-marksist*, No. 13 (1929), 3-18; No. 15 (1930), 3-42. M. N. Pokrovskii, "Russkie dokumenty imperialisticheskoi voiny." *Istorik-marksist*, No. 17 (1930), 3-16.

[23]M. N. Pokrovskii, *Diplomatiia i voiny tsarskoi Rossii v XIX stoletii. Sbornik statei.* (Moscow, 1923; reissued, Moscow, 1934). See review by B. Veber entitled "Imperializm v otsenke M. N. Pokrovskogo." *Kniga i proletarskaia revoliutsiia*, No. 4 (1935), 43-52. A. S. Ierusalimskii, "Imperialisticheskie gruppirovki i diplomaticheskaia podgotovka mirovoi voiny 1914 g." *Mirovoe khoziaistvo i mirovaia politika*, No. 6 (1934).

[24]S. D. Skazkin, *Konets avstro-russko-germanskogo Soiuza, 1879-1884.* Vol. I. (Moscow, 1928). B. A. Romanov, *Rossiia v Manchzhurii (1892-1906). Ocherki po istorii vneshnei politiki samoderzhaviia v epokhu imperializma.* (Leningrad, 1928).

[25]V. M. Khvostov, "Krizis vneshnei politiki Bismarka." *Istorik-marksist*, No. 5 (39), (1934), 35-55. V. M. Khvostov, "Blizhne-vostochnyi krizis 1895-1897 gg." *Istorik-marksist*, No. 13 (1929), 19-54. V. M. Khvostov, "Problema zakhvata Bosfora v 90kh godakh XIX v." *Istorik-marksist*, No. 20 (1930), 100-130. A. S. Ierusalimskii, "Germano-amerikanskie otnosheniia v kontse XIX v." *Mirovoe khoziaistvo i mirovaia politika*, Nos. 10-11 (1926), 110-131. A. S. Ierusalimskii, "Voennaia trevoga 1875 goda." *Uchenye zapiski Instituta istorii RANION*, Vol. VI. (Moscow, 1928).

Tarlé's views themselves.[26] Another historian, A. N. Savin, undertook the subject of Nicholas I's foreign policy. Unfortunately the work was interrupted by his sudden death. The partially completed manuscript was published and covers only Franco-Prussian relations just prior to the year 1848. Later the study was completed by P. F. Preobrazhenskii, one of Savin's students.[27]

A number of Soviet historians wrote on earlier Russian foreign policy, among them such men as V. I. Veselovskii, V. I. Picheta, M. S. Balabanov, I. S. Zvavich, V. A. Butenko, E. V. Tarlé, and L. A. Feigina.[28] Another group concentrated on events of 1848, among them M. N. Pokrovskii, A. A. Shilov, and N. S. Platonova. A. S. Nifontov, who examined the original diplomatic sources, wrote on Russia and the revolutions of 1848, while R. A. Averbukh dealt at considerable length with the intervention of Russia in Hungary.[29]

The Paris Commune of 1871 was studied by a number of Soviet historians, among them M. I. Mebel, I. Ia. Braslavskii, M. S. Balabanov, and L. M. Dobrovolskii. Later writers profited considerably by the materials

[26] E. V. Tarlé, *Evropa v epokhu imperializma.* 2nd rev. ed. (Moscow, 1928). E. V. Tarlé, *Sochineniia.* (Moscow, 1958). Vol. V. M. N. Pokrovskii, " 'Novye' techeniia v russkoi istoricheskoi literature." *Istorik-marksist,* No. 7 (1928), 3-17. E. I. Chapkevich, "Zhizn i deiatelnost E. V. Tarlé v dorevoliutsionnyi period." *Nekotorye problemy klassovoi borby v period kapitalizma. Trudy kafedry istorii SSSR. Uchenye zapiski Moskovskogo gosudarstvennogo pedagogicheskogo instituta im. V. I. Lenina,* No. 249 (Moscow, 1966), 140-169.

[27] A. N. Savin, "Nikolai I i Fridrikh-Vilgelm IV (1840-1848)." *Rossiia i Zapad.* (Petrograd, 1923). S. D. Skazkin, "A. N. Savin kak uchitel." *Trudy Instituta istorii RANION,* Vol. I. *Pamiati Aleksandra Nikolaevicha Savina.* (Moscow, 1926). P. F. Preobrazhenskii, *Ocherk istorii sovremennogo imperializma.* (Moscow, 1926).

[28] V. I. Veselovskii, "Russko-datskii soiuz 1699-1700 gg." *Uchenye zapiski Instituta istorii RANION,* Vol. IV (1929). V. I. Picheta, "Frantsuzskie diplomaty o torgovle Rossii s Frantsiei v pervye gody tsarstvovaniia Ekateriny II." *Trudy Belorusskogo universiteta,* No. 20 (1928). M. S. Balabanov, *Rossiia i evropeiskie revoliutsii v proshlom.* Issue I, *Rossiia i Velikaia frantsuzskaia revoliutsiia.* (Kiev, 1924). I. S. Zvavich, "Vosstanie 14 dekabria i angliiskoe obshchestvennoe mnenie." *Pechat i revoliutsiia,* No. 8 (1925), 31-52. E. V. Tarlé, "Imperator Nikolai I i krestianskii vopros v Rossii po neizvestnym doneseniiam frantsuzskikh diplomatov 1842-1847 gg." *Zapad i Rossiia.* (Petrograd, 1918). V. Boutenko, "Un projet d'alliance franco-russe en 1856, d'après des documents inédits des archives russes." *Revue historique,* Vol. CLV (May-August, 1927). L. A. Feigina, "Iz istorii russko-frantsuzskikh otnoshenii (Sekretnyi dogovor 3 marta 1859 g.)." *Veka. Istoricheskii sbornik.* Vol. I. (Petrograd, 1924).

[29] M. N. Pokrovskii, "Lamartin, Kaveniak i Nikolai I." *K 75-letiiu revoliutsii 1848 goda.* (Moscow, 1923). A. A. Shilov, "Revoliutsiia 1848 g. i ozhidanie ee v Rossii. *Golos minuvshego,* Nos. 4-6 (1918). N. S. Platonova, "Nikolai I i revoliutsionnoe dvizhenie vo Frantsii." *Annaly,* No. 2 (1922). A. S. Nifontov, "Vliianie revoliutsii 1848 g. v Rossii." *Katorga i ssylka,* No. 10 (1930). A. S. Nifontov, *1848 god*

newly published since 1933. Historical resources were enriched especially by the documents published by the Central Archives after 1933 that covered the period from January 12 to November 21, 1871. These were found in the Archives of the Russian Foreign Office, among which the most valuable were compiled under the title "Tsarist Diplomacy and the Paris Commune of 1871." This collection contains letters, telegrams, dispatches, and reports of Russian diplomatic representatives from various capitals in Europe to Prince A. M. Gorchakov.[30]

In 1960 the Soviet government began to publish in seven series all documents related to Russian foreign policy, covering the years March 1801— March 1917.[31]

v Rossii. Ocherki po istorii 40kh godov. (Moscow, 1931). R. A. Averbukh, *Tsarskaia interventsiia v borbe s vengerskoi revoliutsiei 1848-1849 g.* (Moscow, 1935).

[30]M. S. Balabanov, *Rossiia i evropeiskie revoliutsii v proshlom.* Issue 3. *Parizhskaia kommuna.* (Kiev, 1925). M. I. Mebel, "Parizhskaia kommuna v otrazhenii sovremennoi ei russkoi pechati." *Sovremennik,* Book 1 (1922). I. Ia. Braslavskii, "Parizhskaia Kommuna pered sudom russkoi reaktskii." *Krasnaia nov,* No. 5 (1927), 164-183. L. M. Dobrovolskii, "Parizhskaia Kommuna v russkikh zapreshchennykh izdaniiakh 70kh godov." *Kniga o knige,* Vol. III. (Leningrad, 1932). *Tsarskaia diplomatiia i Parizhskaia Kommuna 1871 goda.* (Moscow, 1933). B. M. Volin, *Parizhskaia Kommuna po doneseniiam tsarskogo posla.* (Moscow, 1926). Ts. Fridliand, *Tsarskaia diplomatiia i Parizhskaia Kommuna. Sbornik statei.* (Moscow, 1932).

[31]*Vneshniaia politika Rossii XIX i nachala XX veka: Dokumenty Rossiiskogo Ministerstva inostrannykh del.* (Moscow, 1960-). Vol. I- .

CHAPTER XIV

World War II

The Second World War is too close an event to expect full historical evaluation as to its origins, the conduct of individual allies, the contributions made by each party toward final victory, or the impact upon Soviet society. Complex questions pertaining to the war period, to the armament race that followed the conflict, accusations of appeasement policies and who appeased whom—these remain debatable and harassing questions.

Yet, surprisingly, a good amount of literature that has already appeared seems to promise lasting historical value. Numerous accounts of the military and guerrilla campaigns, the role of labor and the peasantry during the crucial war years, the benefit derived from cooperation with the western allies, and the continuously increasing publication of memoirs of different military leaders have already proved to be of historical interest.

In December, 1941, a special commission was formed at the Academy of Sciences by I. I. Mints, the purpose of which was to gather all possible sources related to the Second World War. In addition to the gathering of written sources the Commission recorded interviews with prominent political and military leaders. The collected materials were deposited with the Division of Manuscripts of the Institute of History of the Academy of Sciences. The Presidium of the Academy also set up at the Institute of History, in December, 1943, a military-historical division composed of two sections devoted to the army and the navy. During the war literally thousands of pamphlets, leaflets, brochures, placards, all sorts of appeals, and underground literature designed for occupied areas were issued, which now provide invaluable material for the study of various aspects of the war period.

After 1945 came the true test, involving not only compilation of this mass of records, but putting it to use. The cardinal question was how to bring these thousands of documents into some general meaningful shape that might render constructive value to the history of the war years. At the start many factors hindered progress. First, while Stalin was still ruling the country the entire credit for the victory had to be assigned to him. Secondly, official documentary evidence was not available to any large extent, while the systematization of gathered records continued to be extremely slow. Nor were even all the records in the depositories available to students of history. Yet, despite some of these obvious difficulties, attempts made by authors like A. Krutikov and S. Golikov to present some general account of the war period were executed with a fair degree of success.[1]

[1]On the defense industry on the eve of the war see: B. I. Vannikov, "Oboronnaia promyshlennost SSSR nakanune voiny. (Iz zapisok narkoma.)" *Voprosy istorii,*

In 1953 there appeared a brief history of the Second World War by F. D. Vorobev and V. M. Kravtsov. This represented a more serious effort to present an accurate account of the military campaigns during 1941–1945, and the authors brought in much new material not previously consulted by other writers. This was followed by several more specialized studies, such as that of N. Voznesenskii, who traced the economic history of the war years. The fate of the author as well as his work is generally known, though not in detail: the book was soon condemned and withdrawn from circulation as "unscientific and anti-Marxist," while the author himself perished during the last years of Stalinism.[2]

On September 12, 1957, the Central Committee of the Communist Party voted to publish a six-volume history of the Second World War. The responsibility for carrying out the project was assigned to a group of historians who formed a special division at the Institute of Marxism-Leninism. Various experts in the fields of military sciences, economics, and social history were summoned to render aid to the editorial board headed by P. N. Pospelov. The first problem before the board was to adopt an acceptable periodization of the years under consideration. For instance, Soviet historians did not accept the notion popular in the west, that the temporary lulls during the war were caused by events in Africa or in western Europe. They asserted that a correct periodization of the war could

No. 10 (1968), 114-123; No. 1 (1969), 122-135. A. Krutikov, *Velikaia Otechestvennaia voina Sovetskogo Soiuza. (Populiarnyi ocherk).* (Moscow, 1947). S. Golikov, *Vydaiushchiesia pobedy Sovetskoi Armii v Velikoi Otechestvennoi voine.* (Moscow, 1952).

[2]F. D. Vorobev and V. M. Kravtsov, *Pobedy Sovetskikh vooruzhennykh Sil v Velikoi Otechestvennoi voine, 1941-1945.* (Moscow, 1953). I. V. Anisimov, *Velikaia Otechestvennaia voina Sovetskogo Soiuza.* (Moscow, 1947). I. V. Anisimov and G. V. Kuzmin, *Velikaia Otechestvennaia voina Sovetskogo Soiuza, 1941-1945 gg.* (Moscow, 1952). B. S. Telpukhovskii, *Velikaia Otechestvennaia Voina Sovetskogo Soiuza (1941-1945).* (Moscow, 1952). N. Voznesenskii, *Voennaia ekonomika SSSR v period Otechestvennoi voiny.* (Moscow, 1948). E. Soldatenko, *Trudovoi podvig sovetskogo naroda v Velikoi Otechestvennoi voine.* (Moscow, 1954). B. S. Telpukhovskii, *Velikaia pobeda Sovetskoi Armii pod Stalingradom.* (Moscow, 1953). V. A. Zakharov, *Ocherk nachalnogo perioda Velikoi Otechestvennoi voiny.* (Moscow, 1949). V. V. Voznenko and G. M. Utkin, *Osvobozhdenie Kieva (osen 1943 g.).* (Moscow, 1953). N. D. Stepanov and M. I. Golyshev, *V boiakh za Dnepr.* (Moscow, 1954). M. M. Minasian, *Pobeda v Belorussii.* (Moscow, 1952). N. M. Rumiantsev, *Pobeda Sovetskoi Armii v Zapoliare. Desiatyi udar (1944).* (Moscow, 1955). M. I. Traktuev, *Osvobozhdenie Zapadnoi Ukrainy. Shestoi udar Sovetskoi Armii (1944).* (Moscow, 1954). A. Vasiliev, *Velikaia pobeda pod Moskvoi.* (Moscow, 1952). A. Vasiliev, *Voennye budni (O patriotizme trudiashchikhsia goroda Ivanova v gody Velikoi Otechestvennoi voiny).* (Ivanovo, 1954). E. A. Voskoboinikov, *Uzbekskii narod v gody Velikoi Otechestvennoi voiny.* (Tashkent, 1947). A. Kazanskii, *Kirgizskii narod v Velikoi Otechestvennoi voine Sovetskogo Soiuza 1941-1945 gg.* (Frunze, 1954). K. K. Rokossovskii. "Na Stalingradskom napravlenii." *Novaia i noveishaia istoriia,* No. 2 (1968), 12-29.

only be determined by the entire course of the war against Nazi Germany, thus granting much credit for the final triumph over the common enemy—the Third Reich—to the Red Army.[3]

The editorial board also held the view that the period prior to the entry of the Soviet Union into the war, September, 1939, to June, 1941, was the *imperialist* phase of the world conflict, the so-called "unjust" war as far as the Soviet government was concerned. Only after the summer of 1941 did the imperialist war alter its character and turn into a war for emancipation from Nazism, Fascism, and colonialism. The forced entrance of the Soviet Union into the conflict marked the beginning of an entirely new phase of a truly global war.

In August, 1939, a Soviet magazine entitled *Voenno-istoricheskii zhurnal* began publication; suspended in July, 1941, it was revived in July, 1958. The magazine began to publish much of the research carried out by military experts and history students. Subjects such as the lessons to be derived from the Second World War, the distinctive nature of the different military campaigns, employment of up-to-date arms and deployment of troops, cooperation with the allied armies, the question of the second front, guerrilla warfare—all these are fully discussed by different writers. Contributors to the magazine formed a kind of a "collective" that enabled them to publish in book form the original articles and the results of their research. Such a book appeared in 1956, devoted primarily to the most vital military operations during the war.[4]

Two years later the military publishing house issued a history of the war written by a group of writers of the Military Historical Division of the General Staff, covering the entire war period. The volume includes various strategic schemes of the war years, basic chronological data, and an extensive and helpful bibliography. This publication was largely designed for military schools, for armed land and sea forces, as well as for members of the general staff. It represents perhaps the first serious attempt at a synthesized scientific study of military strategy as employed throughout the entire course of the war.[5]

Following these publications there appeared a considerable number of monographs, most of them based on a wide accumulation of evidence, by authors such as G. A. Deborin, A. M. Samsonov, and B. S. Telpukhovskii. Numerous memoirs have been published, such as those of A. I. Eremenko on Stalingrad, D. V. Pavlov on the defense of Leningrad, V. I. Achkasov and B. A. Vainer on the role of the Baltic fleet. Combined, these form a

---

[3]*Istoriia Velikoi Otechestvennoi voiny.* (Moscow, 1960-1963). 5 vols. A sixth volume is forthcoming. G. A. Deborin, *Vtoraia mirovaia voina.* (Moscow, 1958).

[4]*Vazhneishie operatsii Velikoi Otechestvennoi voiny 1941-1945 gg. Ocherki po istorii voiny.* (Moscow, 1956).

[5]*Vtoraia mirovaia voina 1939-1945 gg. Voenno-istoricheskii ocherk.* (Moscow, 1958).

valuable source of general information for the student of history.[6] One subject that deserves a more extensive study is the role of the partisan or guerrilla movement during the war. The few publications that exist are mostly collected essays, memoirs, or eye-witness accounts. The extent of the general organization, the degree of collaboration of partisan leaders with Soviet authorities and military leaders, either within the occupied areas or elsewhere, the degree of government support received by guerrilla units, and the degree of ingenuity employed by the guerrilla leaders when left to their own devices are still open to much study in the future.[7]

Scholars in search of material on the history of the Second World War must not overlook the periodical literature. In this respect the *Voenno-istoricheskii zhurnal,* which made its maiden appearance in 1959, is of special interest. The journal includes many accounts by eye-witnesses and leading participants in the war, such as those of Marshals G. Zhukov, I. Konev, and K. Rokossovskii, and of Admiral Kuznetsov.[8] The accounts are as fascinating as they are significant as historical records. The descriptions of the winter campaign of 1941, the heroic though distressingly costly battle of Moscow, the vexing interference in military operations, the tragic retreat of the Soviet armed forces from Tallinn (for a long time presented as the "Soviet Dunkirk"), the role of Stalin—these descriptions, along with many others, offer valuable details rarely found elsewhere.

[6]B. S. Telpukhovskii, *Ocherki istorii Velikoi Otechestvennoi voiny, 1941-1945.* (Moscow, 1955). G. A. Deborin, *Vtoraia mirovaia voina. Voenno-politicheskii ocherk.* (Moscow, 1958). V. L. Israelian, *Diplomaticheskaia istoriia Velikoi Otechestvennoi voiny 1941-1945 gg.* (Moscow, 1959). A. M. Samsonov, *Stalingradskaia bitva. Ot oborony i otstupleniia k velikoi pobede na Volge. Istoricheskii ocherk.* (Moscow, 1960). A. M. Samsonov, *Velikaia bitva pod Moskvoi.* (Moscow, 1958). A. I. Eremenko, *Stalingrad. Zapiski komanduiushchego frontom.* (Moscow, 1961). D. V. Pavlov, *Leningrad v blokade, 1941 g.* (Moscow, 1958). V. I. Achkasov and B. A. Vainer, *Krasnoznamennyi Baltiiskii flot v Velikoi Otechestvennoi voine.* (Moscow, 1957). A. N. Mushnikov, *Baltiitsy v boiakh za Leningrad (1941-1944).* (Moscow, 1955). N. D. Khudiakova, *Vsia strana s Leningradom. KPSS—organizator vsenarodnoi pomoshchi Leningradu v gody blokady.* (Leningrad, 1960). T. A. Zhdanova, *Krepost na Neve. Oborona Leningrada v Velikoi Otechestvennoi voine.* (Moscow, 1959). S. Beliaev and P. Kuznetsov, *Narodnoe opolchenie Leningrada.* (Leningrad, 1959). A. V. Karasev, *Leningradtsy v gody blokady 1949-1943 gg.* (Moscow, 1959).

[7]*Sovetskie partizany. Iz istorii partizanskogo dvizheniia v gody Velikoi Otechestvennoi voiny.* (Moscow, 1951). "Azerbaidzhanskaia sovetskaia istoriografiia Velikoi Otechestvennoi voiny (1941-1945 gg.)." *Voenno-istoricheskii zhurnal,* No. 11 (1966), 79-82.

[8]G. Zhukov, "V bitve za stolitsu." *Voenno-istoricheskii zhurnal,* No. 8 (1966), 53-63; No. 9 (1966), 55-66. G. Zhukov, "Kontrnastuplenie pod Moskvoi." *Voenno-istoricheskii zhurnal,* No. 10 (1966), 68-86. I. Konev, "Nachalo Moskovskoi bitvy." *Voenno-istoricheskii zhurnal,* No. 10 (1966), 56-67. V. Achkasov, "Operatsiia po proryvu Krasnoznamennogo Baltiiskogo flota." *Voenno-istoricheskii zhurnal,* No. 10 (1966), 19-32. K. K. Rokossovskii, *Soldatskii dolg.* (Moscow, 1968).

Marshal G. Zhukov, for instance, condemns Stalin for the pigheadedness which on occasion had to be paid for dearly by the nation. Sometimes Zhukov and Stalin had some grave differences of opinion over military policies and strategies. Yet Zhukov does not completely condemn Stalin and at times credits him with admirable tenacity and even gives him much credit for remaining in the capital to the last minute at the darkest hours of the war. Others have written in the same vein, presenting Stalin as erring in party affairs or his drive for power, but mitigating their judgment by admitting his successfully adamant war policy.

During 1968 a number of important books in the field of military history made their appearance. Collectively these offer rich material to the student of Soviet military and war-period history. Many of them may be tendentious (and what accounts of military men are not?). The fact remains that if one is in search of source material dealing with the eastern front during the last war it is no longer necessary to consult exclusively German accounts.[9]

Outstanding among the Russian accounts is Marshal Zhukov's *Reminiscences and Contemplations.* The author believes that Stalin's failure to mobilize earlier had an inadvertent beneficial effect. Had there been an earlier mobilization there would have been only a greater waste of manpower during the earlier months of the war. It may be recalled that very few of the generals were successful in extricating themselves from being trapped by the German invading forces; most of them, especially in the south, were unable to retreat and were captured by the surging enemy. Considering the early debacles, the battles of Moscow, Stalingrad, Kursk, Rostov, and other places, where the Germans were either stopped cold or never allowed to regain their initiative, are truly miraculous.

The memoirs of K. A. Meretskov, A. I. Eremenko, and others present a more balanced account of the war years than those of the 1950's. One gathers the impression that despite Stalin's appalling blunders at the beginning of the conflict, he soon recovered to make correct decisions. The writers discuss the decisive engagements of Moscow and Stalingrad, the grim "900 days" of besieged Leningrad, and many other episodes of the war. The outstanding fact remains that the command displayed unbelievable valor, iron discipline, and determination to win by remaining loyal to Stalin. In this connection the case of Marshal K. Rokossovskii is particularly noteworthy. Rokossovskii had little reason for admiration of Stalin: he miraculously escaped liquidation during the purges of the

[9] A. M. Samsonov, ed., *Stalingradskaia epopeia.* (Moscow, 1968). A. A. Grechko, *Bitva za Kavkaz.* (Moscow, 1968). S. M. Shtemenko, *Generalnyi shtab v gody voiny.* (Moscow, 1968). A. I. Eremenko, *Na zapadnom napravlenii. Vospominaniia.* (Moscow, 1969). G. K. Zhukov, *Vospominaniia i razmyshleniia.* (Moscow, 1969). K. A. Meretskov, *Na sluzhbe narodu.* (Moscow, 1969). S. I. Rudenko, ed., *Sovetskie voenno-vozdushnye sily v Velikoi Otechestvennoi voine 1941-1945 gg.* (Moscow, 1968).

thirties. As a matter of fact, Rokossovskii was freed from prison only because of the desperate need for military experts.

Prominent among the recently published wartime memoirs are the reminiscences of General S. M. Shtemenko, former Chief of Staff and more recently Chief of Staff of the Warsaw Pact Forces. Shtemenko has presented an objective account of the turbulent war years; and Stalin is given credit for competence and determination after having quickly recovered from the early jolting experiences of war. Shtemenko does not conceal the costly blunders Stalin made, such as the appointments of some glaring mediocrities and the shooting of capable commanders. He recalls some of Stalin's illogical demands from such military experts as Shapnoshnikov and Vasilevskii.

CHAPTER XV

Conclusion

Soviet historiography has travelled a rocky road. During the Civil War years, with the exception of documents which were published largely to compromise the old regime, very little historical writing was accomplished nor could it have been expected. The "Old Guard" historians were either forced to emigrate or were silenced at home. It was only during the late 1920's and early 1930's that Communist historiography began to come into its own.[1] Signs of cooperation between Soviet and Western historians emerged, as evidenced by the attendance of the Russians at the World Historical Congress at Brussels in 1928 and at Oslo in 1932.

The intensified struggle within party ranks and the rise of Stalin to absolute power checked further rapprochement between Soviet and Western historians. Attacks upon old-school writers for their "bourgeois interpretation" of history increased, while some were severely persecuted. Many of them were attacked because of Menshevik or Revisionist proclivities, because of Eurasian views, or because of their acceptance of the Normanist interpretation of the war-guilt question.

Historical writing came under stricter censorship against the infiltration of heresies. Historians were urged to concentrate more on current problems, on Menshevist and Trotskyite deviations, which came under increased vigilance and attack. It was not until after the death in 1932 of M. N. Pokrovskii, dean of Soviet historians, that the academic climate mellowed somewhat, mainly because of political expedience; but other harsh policies that followed offered little relief to students of history.

One of the oft-recurring issues was the problem of periodization in history. In Marxist-Leninist parlance periodization is based on socio-economic formation, which leads to a simple division of history into epochs such as primitive communism, slavery, feudalism, capitalism, socialism, and finally, communism. This schematism, largely employed by the Pokrovskii school, was supplanted later by dialectical materialism, and Pokrovskii was criticized for having neglected dialectical materialism, supplanting it with sociology and crude economic materialism. He was equally taken to task for concentrating attention on Great Russia while overlooking such component parts as the Ukraine or White Russia and their respective national sentiments. Such sociological schematism, critics argued, came about largely because Pokrovskii was preoccupied with economics and assumed that societies

---

[1] See L. V. Ivanova, *U istokov sovetskoi istoricheskoi nauki (podgotovka kadrov marksistov 1917-1929 gg.).* (Moscow, 1968). See review in *Istorik-marksist,* No. 1 (1970), 163-165.

developed automatically in accordance with economic laws without any relationship to the will of the individual.

The anti-Pokrovskii school attacked the former founder of Soviet historiography particularly for his economic materialism. The main fallacy was, these critics insisted, that Pokrovskii arrived at an ideological superstructure directly from its economic basis, and ignored the dialectical relationship between the superstructure and the base.

The economist in Pokrovskii gave rise to his oversimplified construction of history in terms of social and economic developments. The result was a sociological scheme which interpreted history in abstracts periods such as merchant capitalism, disregarding such observable phenomena as military and political developments or the role of individual figures in the past. Nor did Pokrovskii pay much attention to chronology or to sovereigns and their periods of reign, which he considered the preoccupation of bourgeois historians. It was truly a case of placing history on its head.

The middle of the 1930's witnessed not only severe criticism of Pokrovskii, but the rise of a Soviet patriotism which left deep scars on historiography. Historians came under violent attack for interpreting Russian history as distinct or remote from western European events. The same critics went farther, attacking writers for not stressing the continuity of socialism and communism throughout the entire continent including Russia, for failing to evaluate properly the growth of ideas in the western world, and for minimizing the role of illustrious individual leaders in history. History, they said, must cease to be dominated by sociology and socio-economic formations, or by economic factors in a narrow sense. Instead it should be enriched by the incorporation of factual history concerning class struggle and achievements, by socio-political developments and cultural progress. Names, dates, individual statesmen and distinguished figures in the various sciences must be also cited, otherwise the past becomes a sterile record that lacks moral strength and arms the German racists who regard Russia as a cultural and political vacuum. By the end of the 1930's we thus witness not only the fall of the Pokrovskii school, but the rise of Soviet nationalism in Soviet historiography, along with the notorious "cult of the individual." The latter delivered perhaps the most severe of all the blows to historical science. The Battle of Tsaritsyn, which is discussed in great detail, marks the beginning of the deliberate distortions and ravaging effects Stalinism was to have upon historical science.

The Second World War, quite naturally, stimulated interest in military history, in Soviet relations with the Allies, with the causes of conflict with Fascism, and Nazism, and with the ideological victory in eastern Europe. Histories of such recent developments, because of lack of sufficient perspective and an excess of ideological intoxication, were distinguished by more heat than light. With the exception of a few publications of general character and the memoirs of many participants, appearing generally in periodicals since 1953, most of these works are of dubious value. During the last years of Stalinism Soviet historians were vociferously demanding an effective campaign against "foreign falsifiers of history" and against the kowtowing to the West; they insisted upon a vigorous offensive against bourgeois objectivism, cosmopolitanism, Eurasianism, which denied native Russian culture, and Normanism, which was considered the invention of German nationalists.

"Objectivism" has been defined as an historical analysis which neglects class struggle. Thus the *Historiography* by N. L. Rubinshtein, aside from other sins, has been also labelled as "objectivist" since it failed to reflect the class orientation of the various scholars discussed and overemphasized the influence of foreign historians upon Russian historical science. Rubinshtein's case illustrates the overpowering difficulties the Soviet historian has often to overcome, either prior to the publication of his work or after; legions of critics are liable to attack and destroy a scholar's lifelong labor. If some historians were presented as "objectivists" or "cosmopolitans," others were pilloried for delving too far into the past while minimizing or neglecting Soviet history, or inadequately studying the revolutionary movement, or the Soviet working class, or industrialization, collectivization of agriculture, foreign affairs, or cultural history.

"Cosmopolitanism" was defined now as a "reactionary ideology" that preached reciprocal influence and did not credit sufficiently national traditions; it represented a nihilistic attitude toward one's own nation and toward Soviet patriotism, and minimized national traditional values. Cosmopolitanism was presented as nothing but a renunciation of national independence and state sovereignty in favor of world government advocated by American imperialism for the enslavement of smaller nations. It was a movement which was bound to impute foreign origins to Russian science and culture and deny national cultural legacy. Consequently Soviet historical research had to reemphasize and recover Russian primacy in scientific research and cultural accomplishment. In the same spirit the thread-worn debate over the origins of the Russian state reemerged. P. L. Liashchenko was taken to task for stating that the genesis of the Kievan state originated with the Varangians, which was wrong, for in fact, the recent version claimed, that state went back to the sixth century as proven by the Rus campaign against Byzantium. Even B. D. Grekov was criticized for stating that Russian society was inert and in a "fluid state" until virtually the reign of Peter I.

The same negative criticism was often expressed against "idealism." Marxian dialectical materialism recognized the positive relationship between productive force and social organization; it accepted progress of organized society through developmental stages and the dependence of political ideas upon concrete social events. But the Communists firmly negated the deduction of political or historical ideas from sets of ideas. True Marxists, they maintained, must consider the explanation of one ideological system as a source of another ideology as nothing but a Revisionist or Menshevik misinterpretation. Any historical interpretation which seeks to assign to historical developments causes other than actual social relations must be met with vigorous rebuff from the party.

How then could true Marxist-Leninist dialeticism be defined? In simplest terms it was an interpretation of historical phenomena derived from class struggle. It represented an endeavor to interpret historical phenomena in the light of their dependence upon socio-economic conditions or productive forces and class antagonism throughout the entire historical process. History should not become a mere bourgeois method of "objective listing of facts that emasculates class content and national form," argued the Marxist historians. It was not a superficial scheme of cultural borrowings and interrelationships of ideas that underlie historical processes. The only genuine methodology in historical science is dialectical materialism as explained above. As long as the Soviet historian was on this "dialectical track" he was safe; any deviation from the designated direction sooner or later was bound to lead him to grave trouble. The methodology and philosophy of history as designated by the party line was and still is a path which Soviet historians must tread cautiously; some may deviate, but subtly and barely perceptibly. The difficulty is intensified further by the fact that the line itself has never been clear or consistent: it varied from the days of Pokrovskii to the anti-Pokrovskii insurgency; it deteriorated during the "cult of the individual," and became misty with the "anti-cult" reaction. It has been an ill-defined line which has caused recurrent acrimonious debates, inconclusive resolutions, violent condemnations, and uncertain acceptances of a number of writings for publication.

In summary, several generalizations may be advanced. The "bourgeois historical legacy" left a profound imprint upon Soviet historiography in methodology and factual compilation, the utilization of which led at times to what was labelled deviationism or "falsification." During the first decade of the Soviet regime, historians of the "Old Guard" were tolerated at best; by the early 1930's they had to pay dearly for their views. Among those are some illustrious members of the craft; to mention only a few: M. K. Liubavskii, S. F. Platonov, N. P. Likhachev, D. N. Egorov, E. V. Tarlé, Iu. V. Gautier, S. V. Rozhdestvenskii, V. A. Butenko, M. P. Smirnov, and G. S. Gabaev. Many others were imprisoned or banished, while some were sent to concentration camps.

The party whiplashed writers for numerous "ideological errors," such as bourgeois objectivism, romanticism, reformism, idealism, cosmopolitanism, and other heresies. All of these narrowed considerably the path toward a generally acceptable version of the past. Whatever subject the Soviet historian dealt with, he had to interpret from the vantage point of class struggle and socio-economic formations as defined by the party. Any deviation from the pre-designated course invited confrontation with the party, which, in fact, meant the state.

During the half century of Soviet rule there occasionally occurred a thaw, but basically the official line remained the same—opposition to "bourgeois methodology," rejection of Western influence. Thus, N. L. Rubinshtein, who compared Soviet and Western historiography during the 1940's and found some common characteristics, discovered to his sorrow that he gravely erred, and his book vanished in no time.

The demolition of the Pokrovskii school shortly after the historian's death in 1932 did not radically alter the situation. It permitted a wider appliance of periodization; it lessened, to be sure, the rigidity of historical methodology; writers became once more cognizant of the role of personalities in history and rather timidly came to recognize certain contributing factors of a non-economic nature. In principle, whether during Pokrovskii's lifetime or after, the party resolutely stood upon a dialectical approach to history and tolerated no deviation from it. If during the first half of the Soviet period the official line attacked Menshevik idealism and Western revisionism, during the later years the index was extended to include new heresies derived from the Stalinist cult. It banned any advocacy of continuity or unity in world culture, insisting that Soviet historiography was unique in both ideological and practical leadership. If the anti-Pokrovskii school allowed a greater degree of flexibility in historical interpretation, it also brought with it a manifestation of socialist or "Soviet nationalism" in order to denigrate Western culture and extol national virtues.

The mellowing criticism of Pokrovskii during the 1960's only confirmed the uncertainty of direction in the party line. The same can be said with the removal of Stalin from the political scene, when it was no longer necessary to idealize those tsars who might have been "cruel by necessity but wise in decisions." Among such rulers, presumably, was Stalin himself. Needless to add that this theory has been adequately demolished since N. S. Khrushchev destroyed the image of Stalin. The important thing to observe here, however, is that whatever political changes took place in the past or will take place, they had and are bound to keep on having a profound effect upon historical writing. In view of all this, it is truly remarkable how much Soviet historiography has managed to accomplish.

Index

Abdullaev, G. B., 148
Abdushukurov, R. Kh., 107
Abetsedarskii, L. S., 148
Abramov, B. A., 306, 312, 313, 317
Abramov, P. N., 297, 298
Achkasov, V. I., 356, 357
Adamiia, V. I., 275
Adamov, E. A., 348
Adler, Friedrich W., 2
Adonts, M. A., 105, 128
Adrianova-Peretts, V. P., 69
Agalakov, V. T., 275
Ageev, M. V., 316
Agureev, K. V., 231
Airapetian, M., 344
Akhtamzian, A. A., 344
Akhundov, B. Iu., 150
Akilov, K. A., 340
Aksenov, A. I., 270
Alakhverdov, G. G., 230, 275
Alampiev, P. M., 330, 339, 340
Alefirenko, P. K., 109, 115, 120, 164
Aleksandrov, G. F., 27
Aleksandrov, V. A., 94, 116, 145, 147, 160
Aleksashenko, A. P., 272
Alekseev, N. A., 180
Alekseev, S. A., 220
Alekseev, V. P., 179, 219
Alekseeva, E. P., 87
Aleskerov, Iu. N., 106, 202, 270
Alexander II, 173
Alexander Nevskii, 212
Alexis, Tsar, 95, 132
Aliev, F. M., 131
Aliev, Kh., 316
Aliev, Musa M., 316
Alimirzoev, Kh., 316
Alkor, Ia. P., 106
Allakhverdian, G. O., 339
Alpatskii, P. K., 315, 316
Al'shits, D. N., 75
Altman, V. V., 348
Amalrik, A. S., 188
Ambarian, A. S., 105
Ambartsumov, E. A., 346
Amiantov, Iu. N., 291
Aminov, A. M., 156
Aminov, R. Kh., 107

Anarchism, 246
Anashkin, I. D., 279
Anchabadze, Z. V., 103
Andreev, A. A., 323, 324
Andreev, A. I., 33, 34, 49, 97, 98, 102
Andreev, M. A., 316
Andreev, V., 233
Andrushenko, A. I., 118
Anifimov, A. M., 297, 335
Anishev, A. N., 192, 197, 198
Anisimov, I. V., 355
Ankundinova, L. E., 116, 332
Annaklychev, A. A., 330
Anne, Empress, 28
Annenkov, I. P., 96
Anpilogov, G., 111
Antonov, A. E., 270, 275
Antonov-Ovseenko, V. A., 240
Antonova, K. A., 89
Anulov, F., 201, 209, 211, 234
Apollova, N. G., 43, 148
Aralovets, N. A., 329
Aratiunov, G. A., 214
Aratsev, V. I., 282
Archeographic Commission, 11, 34, 36
Archeological Commission, 5
Archeology and history, 46-54
Ardabatskaia, A. M., 172
Areshin, S. G., 105
Arina, A. E., 305
Arkhangelskii, P. G., 301
Arkhangelskii, S. I., 41
Arkheologiia (periodical), 47
Armenia, 103, 105
Arsh, G. A., 92
Arshinov, P., 246, 247
Artsikhovskii, A. V., 47, 131
Artykov, A., 329, 339
Arutiunian, Iu. V., 307
Arutiunian, P. T., 105
Astakhov, V. I., 30
Astapovich, Z. A., 283
Averbukh, R. A., 352, 353
Avrekh, A. Ia., 190
Avsharova, M. P., 107
Avvakum, Father, 99
Azarov, A. I., 108
Azbelev, S. N., 36, 99
Azerbaidzhan, 103

366

Gorskaia, N. A., 54
Gorskii, A. D., 54, 79
Gotuev, G. D., 236
Govorkov, L. A., 299, 303
Granovskii, E. L., 156, 328, 334
Grauzhis, I., 257
Gravé, B. B., 155
Grebelskii, Z. V., 285
Grebeniuk, N. E., 118
Grechko, A. A., 231
Gregorian, G. O., 103
Gregorian, Z. T., 105
Grek, A., 232
Grekov, B. D., 41, 54-57, 79, 85, 96,
    104, 106, 109, 362
Grekul, F. A., 43
Grekulov, N. A., 101
Grigorev, Ataman, 240, 247, 248, 249;
    Grigorevshchina, 248
Grigortsevich, S., 230, 276
Grimm, E. D., 348
Grinishin, D. M., 271, 272, 276, 285
Grishaev, V. V., 297, 298
Grishin, P. P., 290
Gritsenko, N. P., 126
Gromyko, M. M., 90, 161
Grossman, Iu. M., 42
Grosul, Ia., 128, 129
Grunt, A. Ia., 154
Gruzdev, S., 218
Guba, T. B., 289
Gubareva, V. M., 296, 304
Gubenko, M. P., 310
Gubnye gramoty, 45, 48
Gudoshnikov, M. A., 270
Gudzenko, P. P., 104
Gudzii, N. K., 99
Gudzinskaia, A. P., 113, 114
Guerrilla warfare, 246-249
Gugov, R. Kh., 270
Gukovskii, A. I., 12, 15, 201, 212, 232,
    235, 256
Gulchinskii, L. I., 279
Guliai Pole, see Makhno, Nestor
Guliev, A. N., 103
Gulyga, A., 233
Gundyrin, P. A., 337
Guoev, M. I., 314
Gurevich, A. Ia., xiii, 326
Gurevich, S., 251
Gurzhii, I. A. (Gurzhii, I. O), 104, 122,
    137
Guseinov, I. A., 103
Gusev, K. V., 296
Gusev, S. I., 191, 196, 273
Gusev, T. G., 316

Gusev, V. E., 41, 99
Gutnova, E. V., 59
Guy, G. D., 191, 220, 222, 223, 260,
    261, 263
Guy, K. V., 253

Hegel, G. W. F., 26, 27
Herzen, A. I., 2, 170, 172, 174, 178,
    179, 180; and Kolokol (The Bell),
    180, 182
Hilferding, R., 20
Hoetzsch, Otto, 349
Hrushevskii, M. S., 55

Iakir, I. E., 270, 274
Iakobson, L. E., 172
Iakovetskii, V. N., 299, 310
Iakovlev, A. I., 32, 108
Iakovlev, Ia. A., 246, 247, 324
Iakovlev, M. V., 172
Iakovlev, N. M., 189
Iakovlev, S. O., 104
Iakovleva, O. A., 35
Iakovleva, P. T., 87, 90, 91
Iakubovskaia, S. I., 330
Iakubovskii, A. Iu., 107
Iakushkin, E. E., 201, 202, 232
Iakutia, 105
Ianchevskii, M., 233
Ianchevskii, N. L., 245
Ianin, V. L., 53
Ianson, Ia. D., 228, 229
Iarkov, I. P., 307
Iaroslavskii, E. M., 5, 17, 246
Iatsunskii, V. K., 35, 83, 97, 108, 121,
    122, 132, 138, 139, 176
Iazykova, M., 271
Ibragimov, Z. I., 189
"Idealism," 362
Ierusalimskii, A. S., 7, 348, 351
Ignatenko, I. M., 296, 297
Ignatenko, I. T., 330
Ignatenko, T. A., 280
Ignatev, V. I., 250, 294, 295
Iliasov, S. I., 305, 315
Il'in, M. A., 134, 163
Il'in, N. I., 36
Iliukhov, N. I., 221, 225
Illeritskii, V. E., 30
Indova, E. I., 145
Inkin, V. F., 22
Inoiatov, Kh. Sh., 107, 289
Institute of History of Material Culture
    (IIMK), 5
Institute of Karl Marx and Friedrich
    Engels, see Marx-Engels Institute

Institute of Marxism-Leninism, 194, 215, 273, 355
Institute of Red Professorship, 2, 3, 5
Intervention, 198-206
Ioannisian, A. G., 103
Ioffe, A. E., 155, 289, 345
Ioffe, Ia., 201
Ionova, G. I., 175
Iosif, Abbot of Volokolamsk, 38
Irkaev, M., 270, 276, 316
Isaeva, M. G., 315
Iskandarov, R. G., 39-40
Iskenderov, M., 103, 276
Islamov, N. A., 106
Israelian, V. L., 357
Istpart, 3, 10, 194, 220, 233, 244, 249, 250, 257, 278
Itenberg, B. S., 183
Itkis, M. B., 289
Iudashev, M. Iu., 87
Iudenich, General N. N., 198, 201, 253, 254, 255, 268
Iukht, A. I., 138, 148, 160
Iuldashev, B. K., 105
Iuldashev, Kh., 339
Iurchenkov, G. S., 249
Iushkov, S. V., 48, 61
Iusupov, Sh., 315, 316
Ivan III, 63, 67
Ivan IV, 50, 63-75 *passim,* 85, 86, 110, 140
Ivanov, A. G., 338
Ivanov, L., 31, 204
Ivanov, P. N., 326, 336
Ivanov, S., 282
Ivanov, V., 345
Ivanova, L. V., 360
Ivashin, I. F., 344, 347
Ivashin, V., 289
Ivashkin, S. S., 313
Ivasiuta, M. K., 317
Ivin, L. I., 43
Ivnitskii, N. A., 313, 314
Izgoi, 78

Jordaniia, G., 88, 89

Kabakov, O., 336
Kabanov, A. S., 103
Kabuzan, V. M., 97, 98
Kachenovskii, M. T., 26
Kadeikin, V. A., 270
Kadishev, A. B., 202, 270
Kadson, I. Z., 111, 118
Kafengauz, B. B., 35, 40, 48, 99, 108, 109, 122, 132, 145, 147, 168

Kakabaev, S. F., 313
Kakhk, Iu. Iu., 122, 176
Kakurin, N. E., 192, 193, 203, 241, 242, 255, 260, 261, 264
Kaliadin, T. E., 231
Kalinin, G. S., 281
Kalinin, M. I., 36
Kamenev, S. S., 192, 194, 238, 260, 266, 274
Kamenskaia, N. B., 289
Kamenskii, A., 209
Kamilov, K. K., 313
Kanapin, A. K., 106
Kanev, S. N., 246
Kantemir, A. D., 164
Kantor, R. E., 230
Kapitsa, M. S., 87, 345
Kapustina, G. D., 108
Karamzin, N. M., 28
Karapetian, S. Kh., 289
Karasev, A. V., 357
Karataev, N. K., 139
Karevskii, A., 309
Karger, M. K., 53, 131
Kariakin, Iu. F., 167
Karimov, T., 289
Karotamm, N. G., 294, 309
Karpachev, A. M., 133, 142
Karpensko, Z. G., 135, 221
Karsavin, L. P., 4
Kary-Niiazov, T. N., 107
Karyev, A., 107
Kashik, O. I., 110
Kashintsev, A., 118
Kashirin, N. D., 274
Kashtanov, S. M., 35, 43, 44, 63, 65, 70, 72, 74, 75, 83
Kasian, A. K., 312
Kasianenko, V. I., 341, 342
Kasimovskii, E. V., 328
Katayama, Sen, 2
Kautsky, Karl, 2
Kavelin, K. D., 11
Kazakhstan, 106
Kazakova, N. A., 37, 101, 161, 162
Kazanskii, A., 355
Kaziev, M. A., 189
Kedrov, M. S., 202, 249, 251, 274
Keldier, G., 276
Keldiev, I. Kh., 271
Keller, V., 292, 301, 302
Ketskhoveli, Lado, 214
Khachapuridze, G. V., 270
Khaitsman, V. M., 346
Khalturin, S. N., 184